CW00666655

THE NEW TESTAMENT
with *Lectio Divina*

THE NEW TESTAMENT

with *Lectio Divina*

CHRISTIAN COMMUNITY BIBLE

Paulist Press
New York / Mahwah, NJ

THE NEW TESTAMENT WITH *LECTIO DIVINA*

2013 Revised Edition editors and copy editors:
Patricia Grogan, FCJ, Roger Butland, Adolph Dias, Robert and Bernardine Caminita, Paul Ginivan,
Ma. Susana C. Basmayor, Miriam Cruz, John Ledesma, SDB, Alberto Rossa, CMF

Imprimatur
Catholic Bishops' Conference of the Philippines

PAULIST PRESS
997 Macarthur Boulevard
Mahwah, New Jersey 07430
United States of America
www.paulistpress.com
ISBN 978-0-8091-0664-6 (hardcover)

World rights except Asia and Africa

PASTORAL BIBLE FOUNDATION
P.O. 1608
Macao, China
www.bibleclaret.org

Pastoral Bible Foundation is a part of

CLARET Bangalore | Barcelona | Buenos Aires | Chennai | Colombo
PUBLISHING GROUP Macau | Madrid | Manila | São Paulo | Yaounde

Printed and bound in China by Nanjing Amity Printing Company
APC–FT 1096301

TABLE OF CONTENTS

THE NEW TESTAMENT

"We urgently need to grow in our knowledge and love of the
Scriptures and of the risen Lord, who continues to speak his
word and to break bread in the community of believers. For this
reason, we need to develop a closer relationship with sacred
Scripture; otherwise, our hearts will remain cold and our eyes
shut, struck as we are by so many forms of blindness."

+Pope Francis

*L*ectio divina is a way of praying with Scripture that uniquely
opens our heart to the Lord. With this prayer we enter the Scriptures personally, allowing the original context to touch our everyday lives, lead us into prayer, and call us to action. Each chapter in the
New Testament is accompanied by a text that helps you read, reflect,
pray, and act inspired by the Word of God.

This special way of praying the Scriptures will introduce you to parts
of the New Testament with which you may not be familiar, making them
easier to understand and apply to your life. Here the Holy Spirit will
surprise you and motivate you to make the Bible an intimate, everyday
experience.

God is truly present to us in the Bible. The more we read it, the closer we are to God, and the more God will be reflected in our lives. May the Holy Spirit who inspired the writing of the Scriptures, invite you to that intimate dialogue between God, who speaks, and you who listen.

MATTHEW

Who was Matthew, known also as Levi? We read in the Gospel that he was a tax collector and that Jesus called him to be one of his apostles (Mt 9:9 and Mk 2:13). The earliest witnesses (Papias around the year 130 A.D.; Irenaeus around the year 180 A.D.; Origen around the year 200 A.D.) attribute to him a Gospel written in Hebrew that was still known at the time of St. Jerome (fourth century). We only know the Greek version of this Gospel that must have been written during the same years by Matthew or by one of his collaborators.

In all probability, this Gospel was written in a Christian community both Jews and Greek origin, perhaps in Antioch (see Acts 12:1, 19:1, and 13:1). This was the time when the high priest, Ananias, had James, the Bishop of Jerusalem, stoned to death. At that time, Christians were excluded from the synagogues and were no longer protected by Roman laws that had allowed the Jews not to offer sacrifices to Roman gods. Within a short time, they would be persecuted by Nero (the years 64-65 A.D.).

This Gospel attempts to show that Christians should not be concerned if their own people are rejecting them now. The official community that refused to believe was left outside of the kingdom to which those who acknowledged the Messiah had access. This minority received the "good things of the Covenant" that had been promised by the prophets. From then on, they will have to share them with all believers who will seek to join the Church whatever their origin may be.

From this perspective the whole history of Jesus is presented as a conflict, ending in a separation. The turning point corresponds with the end of Chapter 13 where Jesus no longer speaks to the crowd, but to his disciples.

Matthew had singled out the figure of Jesus as a preacher and as a teacher of Scripture. Matthew is especially interested in the words of Jesus and in his Gospel: Jesus' words are more numerous than in the other Gospels. On the other hand, his gestures and miracles are presented in the most schematic way possible.

Therefore, we should not be surprised that Matthew built up his Gospel around five "discourses," in which he gathered the words that Jesus had said on different occasions. These discourses are:

– The Sermon on the Mount: Matthew 5–7. This "Magna Carta" of the children of God is completed by ten signs of power that announce our liberation from sin (Chaps. 8 and 9).
– Instructions to Missionaries: Matthew 10. These instructions are completed by the controversies that oppose Jesus and his adversaries (Chaps. 11-12).
– Parables of the Kingdom: Matthew 13. Then comes the blinding of the Pharisees, while the faith of the Twelve and of Peter enables Jesus to establish his Church.
– Warnings to the Christian community: Matthew 18. The fundamental law of fraternal forgiveness is completed by various instructions. The guides of the Jewish people are closed, showing by contrast what the guides of the Christian people will have to be.
– How to live while waiting for the end of the world: Matthew 24 and 25.

Matthew put the first two chapters on the infancy of Jesus to serve as an introduction. First, he recalls how Joseph adopted the child born of the Virgin Mary as the son of David. Then we have accounts of a special type, in which Matthew shows little concern for the historicity of the facts, since he intends to present a theological teaching by way of images. These two chapters form a whole (1:1—4:16) with the activity of John the Baptist who introduces the Son of God.

MATTHEW

The family background of Jesus

1 ¹This is the account of the genealogy of Jesus Christ, son of David, son of Abraham.

²Abraham was the father of Isaac, Isaac the father of Jacob, Jacob the father of Judah and his brothers.

³Judah was the father of Perez and Zerah (their mother was Tamar), Perez was the father of Hezron, and Hezron of Aram. ⁴Aram was the father of Aminadab, Aminadab of Nahshon, Nahshon of Salmon.

⁵Salmon was the father of Boaz. His mother was Rahab. Boaz was the father of Obed. His mother was Ruth. Obed was the father of Jesse.

⁶Jesse was the father of David, the king. David was the father of Solomon. His mother had been Uriah's wife.

⁷Solomon was the father of Rehoboam. Then came the kings: Abijah, Asaph, ⁸Jehoshaphat, Joram, Uzziah, ⁹Jotham, Ahaz, Hezekiah, ¹⁰Manasseh, Amon, Josiah.

¹¹Josiah was the father of Jechoniah and his brothers at the time of the deportation to Babylon.

¹²After the deportation to Babylon, Jechoniah was the father of Salathiel and Salathiel of Zerubbabel.

¹³Zerubbabel was the father of Abiud, Abiud of Eliakim, and Eliakim of Azor. ¹⁴Azor was the father of Zadok, Zadok the father of Akim, and Akim the father of Eliud. ¹⁵Eliud was the father of Eleazar, Eleazar of Matthan, and Matthan of Jacob.

¹⁶Jacob was the father of Joseph, the husband of Mary, and from her came Jesus who is called the Christ—the Messiah.

¹⁷There were then fourteen generations from Abraham to David, and fourteen generations from David to the deportation to Babylon, and fourteen generations from the deportation to Babylon to the birth of Christ.

MATTHEW 1:1-17

Read: Notice the first verse: Jesus is relevant to the Jews ("son of David"), and the non-Jews, the Gentiles ("son of Abraham"). According to the divine promises, all peoples would be blessed in Abraham (cf. Gen 12:3; 22:18). Also note the mention of women in the passage.

Reflect: The community of Matthew was made up of Jews and Gentiles. All are welcomed into the family of God: men and women, saints and sinners, Jews and Gentiles. In Jesus, the promises of the Old Testament are made. What do the women mentioned have in common?

Pray: Pray for the unity of all peoples, that all will feel as members of God's people. Pray also that the dignity and role of women in society and in the Church will be duly respected and valued.

Act: What should I do to feel and make those around me feel like they are members of God's people?

Jesus born of a virgin mother
(Lk 1:27)

¹⁸ This is how Jesus Christ was born: Mary his mother had been given to Joseph in marriage, but before they lived together, she was found to be pregnant through the Holy Spirit.

¹⁹ Then Joseph, her husband, made plans to divorce her in all secrecy. He was an upright man, and in no way did he want to disgrace her.

²⁰ While he was pondering over this, an angel of the Lord appeared to him in a dream and said, "Joseph, descendant of David, do not be afraid to take Mary as your wife. She has conceived by the Holy Spirit, ²¹ and now she will bear a son. You shall call him 'Jesus' for he will save his people from their sins."

²² All this happened in order to fulfill what the Lord had said through the prophet: ²³ *The virgin will conceive and bear a son, and he will be called Emmanuel*, which means: God-with-us. ²⁴ When Joseph awoke, he did what the angel of the Lord had told him to do, and he took his wife to his home. ²⁵ He did not have any marital relations with her. When she gave birth to a son, Joseph gave him the name Jesus.

> **MATTHEW 1:18-25**
>
> **Read:** Matthew recounts the birth of Jesus, and highlights the role of Joseph. Everything happens as a fulfillment of the Scriptures.
>
> **Reflect:** Joseph was "just" (he fulfilled the Law), but before Mary, his intuition was more than duty because he considered her innocent of any sin. Reflect on this situation. How does it affect your understanding of the Law?
>
> **Pray:** Pray that the Holy Spirit will help you with important decisions in your relationship with God, with others, and with yourself.
>
> **Act:** At peace with yourself, act according to what the Holy Spirit inspires you.

Wise men from the east

2 ¹When Jesus was born in Bethlehem, in Judea, during the days of King Herod, wise men from the East arrived in Jerusalem. ²They asked, "Where is the newborn king of the Jews? We saw the rising of his star in the East and have come to honor him."

³When Herod heard this he was greatly disturbed and with him all Jerusalem. ⁴He immediately called a meeting of all high-ranking priests and teachers of the law and asked them where the Messiah was to be born.

⁵"In the town of Bethlehem in Judea," they told him, "for this is what the prophet wrote: ⁶ *And you, Bethlehem, in the land of Judah, you are by no means the least among the clans of Judah, for from you will come a leader, one who is to shepherd my people Israel.*"

⁷Then Herod secretly called the wise men and asked them the precise time the star appeared. ⁸He sent them to Bethlehem with these instructions, "Go and get accurate information about the child. As soon as you have found him, report to me, so that I, too, may go and honor him."

⁹After the meeting with the king, they set out. The star that they had seen in the East went ahead of them and stopped over the place where the child was. ¹⁰The wise men were overjoyed on seeing the star again.

¹¹ They went into the house, and when they saw the child with Mary his mother, they knelt and worshiped him. They opened their bags and offered him their gifts of gold, incense, and myrrh.

¹² In a dream they were warned not to go back to Herod, so they returned to their home country by another way.

Escape to Egypt

¹³ After the wise men had left, an angel of the Lord appeared in a dream to Joseph, and said, "Get up, take the child and his mother, and flee to Egypt and stay there until I tell you, for Herod will soon be looking for the child in order to kill him."

¹⁴ Joseph got up, took the child and his mother and left that night for Egypt, ¹⁵ where he stayed until the death of Herod. In this way, what the Lord had said through the prophet was fulfilled: *I called my son out of Egypt.*

¹⁶ When Herod found out that he had been tricked by the wise men, he was furious. He gave orders to kill all the boys in Bethlehem and its neighborhood who were two years old or under. This was done, according to what he had learned from the wise men about the time when the star appeared.

¹⁷ In this way, what the prophet Jeremiah had said was fulfilled: ¹⁸ *A cry is heard in Ramah, wailing and loud lamentation: Rachel weeps for her children. She refuses to be comforted, for they are no more.*

Joseph and Mary return to Nazareth

¹⁹ After Herod's death, an angel of the Lord appeared in a dream to Joseph and said, ²⁰ "Get up, take the child and his mother and go back to the land of Israel, because those who tried to kill the child are dead." ²¹ So Joseph got up, took the child and his mother and went to the land of Israel.

²² But when Joseph heard that Archelaus had succeeded his father Herod as king of Judea, he was afraid to go there. Joseph was given further instructions in a dream and went to the region of Galilee.

²³ There he settled, in a town called Nazareth. In this way, what was said by the prophets was fulfilled: *He shall be called a Nazarene.*

> **MATTHEW 2:1-23**
>
> **Read:** The Magi, Gentiles, recognize Jesus as the Messiah, not the Jewish authorities.
>
> **Reflect:** Herod and the high priests and scribes reject the Magi's recognition of Jesus as the Messiah.
>
> **Pray:** Believing in Jesus as the Messiah is not easy. Faith needs to be accredited by the testimony. Ask God to help you in this.
>
> **Act:** How do I express my faith in Jesus today?

John the Baptist prepares the way
(Mk 1:1; Lk 3:1; Jn 1:19)

3 [1] In the course of time, John the Baptist appeared in the desert of Judea and began to proclaim his message: [2] "Change your ways; the kingdom of heaven is at hand!" [3] It was about him that the prophet Isaiah had spoken when he said: *A voice is shouting in the desert, 'Prepare a way for the Lord; make his paths straight!'*

[4] John had a leather garment around his waist and wore a cloak of camel's hair; his food was locusts and wild honey. [5] People came to him from Jerusalem, from all Judea, and from the whole Jordan valley [6] and they were baptized by him in the Jordan as they confessed their sins.

[7] When he saw several Pharisees and Sadducees coming to where he baptized, he said to them, "Brood of vipers! Who told you that you could escape the punishment that is to come? [8] Let it be seen that you are serious in your conversion; [9] and do not think: We have Abraham for our father. I tell you that God can raise children for Abraham from these stones! [10] The ax is already laid to the roots of the trees; any tree that does not produce good fruit will be cut down and thrown in the fire.

[11] I baptize you in water for a change of heart, but the one who is coming after me is more powerful than I am; indeed, I am not worthy to carry his sandals. He will baptize you with the Holy Spirit and fire. [12] He has the winnowing fan in his hand, and he will clear out his threshing floor. He will gather his wheat into the barn, but the chaff he will burn with inextinguishable fire."

Jesus baptized by John
(Mk 1:9; Lk 3:2; Jn 1:29)

¹³At that time, Jesus arrived from Galilee and came to John at the Jordan to be baptized by him. ¹⁴But John tried to prevent him and said, "How is it you come to me? I should be baptized by you!"

¹⁵But Jesus answered him, "Let it be like that for now; so that we may fulfill the right order." John agreed.

¹⁶As soon as he was baptized Jesus came up out of the water. All at once the heavens opened and he saw the Spirit of God come down like a dove and rest upon him. ¹⁷At the same time, a voice from heaven was heard, "This is my Son, the Beloved; he is my Chosen One."

MATTHEW 3:1-17

Read: John the Baptist preaches repentance, for the kingdom of heaven is near. He recognizes the divinity of Jesus and baptizes him.

Reflect: Repent means "rethink." In baptism, Jesus is declared Son of God, and we by our baptism share this condition. Do we constantly "rethink" our way of following Jesus?

Pray: We must always rethink the way we live our faith. Pray to God to help you in this.

Act: Every day is a great opportunity to live our faith, rejecting evil and sin and living with the freedom proper to the children of God. Take advantage of it.

Jesus tempted in the wilderness
(Lk 4:1; Mk 1:12)

4 ¹Then the Spirit led Jesus into the desert that he might be put to the test by the devil. ²After Jesus fasted forty days and nights he was famished.

³Then the tempter came to him and said, "If you are the Son of God, order these stones to turn into bread." ⁴But Jesus answered, "Scripture says: *One does not live on bread alone, but on every word that comes from the mouth of God.*"

⁵Then the devil took Jesus to the Holy City, set him on the highest

wall of the temple, and said to him, [6]"If you are the Son of God, throw yourself down, for scripture says: *God has given orders to his angels concerning you. Their hands will hold you up, lest you hurt your foot against a stone.*" [7]Jesus answered, "But scripture also says: *You shall not put the Lord your God to the test.*"

[8]Then the devil took Jesus to a very high mountain and showed him all the nations of the world in all their greatness and splendor. And he said, [9]"All this I will give you if you kneel down and worship me." [10]Then Jesus answered, "Be off, Satan! Scripture says: *Worship the Lord your God and serve him alone!*"

[11]Then the devil left him, and angels came to serve him.

MATTHEW 4:1-11

Read: In life, temptations always arise. Look at what Jesus faces: pleasure (bread), manipulation of the divine (to jump from the top of the temple) and absolute power.

Reflect: What temptations do you face and how do you solve them?

Pray: Ask the Holy Spirit to help you face them.

Act: Identify the temptation that causes you the most problems and take the necessary steps to overcome it.

(Mk 1:14; Lk 4:14)

[12]When Jesus heard that John had been arrested, he withdrew into Galilee. [13]He left Nazareth and went to live in Capernaum, a town by the lake of Galilee, at the border of Zebulun and Naphtali.

[14]In this way the word of the prophet Isaiah was fulfilled: [15]*Land of Zebulun and the land of Naphtali, crossed by the Road of the Sea; and you, who live beyond the Jordan, Galilee, a land of pagans:*

[16]*The people who lived in darkness have seen a great light; on those who live in the land of the shadow of death, a light has shone.*

[17]From that time on, Jesus began to proclaim his message, "Change your ways: the kingdom of heaven is near."

[18]As Jesus walked by the lake of Galilee, he saw two brothers, Simon called Peter, and Andrew his brother, casting a net into the lake for they

were fishermen. ¹⁹He said to them, "Come, follow me; and I will make you fish for people."

²⁰At once they left their nets and followed him.

²¹He went on from there and saw two other brothers, James, the son of Zebedee, and his brother John, in a boat with their father Zebedee, mending their nets. Jesus called them.

²²At once they left the boat and their father and followed him.

²³Jesus went around all Galilee, teaching in their synagogues proclaiming the good news of the kingdom and curing all kinds of sickness and disease among the people.

²⁴The news about him spread through the whole of Syria; and the people brought all their sick to him and all those who suffered: the possessed, the deranged, the paralyzed; and he healed them all. ²⁵Large crowds followed him from Galilee and the Ten Cities, from Jerusalem, Judea, and from across the Jordan.

MATTHEW 4:12-25

Read: Jesus begins his ministry in his own region: Galilee, a region despised by other Jews. There he calls his first followers and they follow him.

Reflect: Jesus calls his followers to do the same things he does: teach, heal and expel the forces of evil.

Pray: Pray to the Lord to help you continue the mission of Jesus. Teaching and serving others is the sign of all Christians.

Act: May your life be an example to others, and be committed to the fight against injustice.

The Beatitudes
(Lk 6:17)

5 ¹When Jesus saw the crowds, he went up the mountain. He sat down and his disciples gathered around him. ²Then he spoke and began to teach them:

³Fortunate are those who are poor in spirit, for theirs is the kingdom of heaven.

⁴Fortunate are those who mourn; they shall be comforted.

⁵Fortunate are the gentle; they shall possess the land.

⁶Fortunate are those who hunger and thirst for justice, for they shall be satisfied.

⁷Fortunate are the merciful, for they shall find mercy.

⁸Fortunate are those with pure hearts, for they shall see God.

⁹Fortunate are those who work for peace; they shall be called children of God.

¹⁰Fortunate are those who are persecuted for the cause of righteousness, for theirs is the kingdom of heaven.

¹¹Fortunate are you when people insult you and persecute you and speak all kinds of evil against you because you are my followers. ¹²Be glad and joyful for a great reward is kept for you in God. For that is how they persecuted the prophets who lived before you.

MATTHEW 5:1-12

Read: The Sermon on the Mount begins. The first great discourse of Jesus in the Gospel of Matthew. The beatitudes make reference to that which makes possible the presence of the kingdom, which makes us happy.

Reflect: In the first four verses (3-6), there are situations in which the kingdom breaks out; while in the last four (7-11), attitudes that the disciples must promote are proposed to reveal the irruption of the kingdom.

Pray: Identify a beatitude you need to promote in your life. Ask the Holy Spirit to help you in this.

Act: Promote that beatitude you have identified as important for your life.

Salt and light
(Mk 4:21; Lk 14:34; 8:16; 11:33)

¹³You are the salt of the earth. But if salt has lost its saltiness, how can it be made salty again? It has become useless. It can only be thrown away and people will trample on it.

¹⁴You are the light of the world. A city built on a mountain cannot be hidden. ¹⁵No one lights a lamp and covers it; instead, it is put on a lampstand where it gives light to everyone in the house. ¹⁶In the same way,

your light must shine before others so that they may see the good you do and praise your Father in heaven.

More perfect law

¹⁷Do not think that I have come to annul the law and the prophets. I have not come to annul them, but to fulfill them. ¹⁸I tell you this: as long as heaven and earth last, not the smallest letter or dot in the law will change until all is fulfilled.

¹⁹So then, whoever breaks the least important of these commandments and teaches others to do the same, will be the least in the kingdom of heaven. On the other hand, whoever obeys them and teaches others to do the same, will be great in the kingdom of heaven.

²⁰I tell you, if your sense of right and wrong is not keener than that of the Lawyers and the Pharisees, you will not enter the kingdom of heaven.

MATTHEW 5:13-20

Read: In his teaching, Jesus uses parables of ordinary life. We must be consistent with what we profess and preach.

Reflect: Think of the images that Jesus uses: salt, light, the city on the mountain, the lamp. What do they suggest?

Pray: Pray that the Church and her members may be like a city on the mountain, reflecting the glory of God for all.

Act: Act in such a way that others can give glory to God for His good works.

---

²¹You have heard that it was said to our people in the past: *Do not commit murder; anyone who murders will have to face trial.* ²²Now I tell you: whoever gets angry with a brother or sister will have to face trial. Whoever insults a brother or sister is liable to be brought before the council. Whoever calls a brother or sister "Fool!" is liable for being thrown into the fire of hell. ²³So, if you are about to offer your gift at the altar, and you remember that your brother has something against you, ²⁴leave your gift there in front of the altar; go at once and make peace with your brother and then come back and offer your gift to God.

²⁵Don't forget this: be reconciled with your opponent quickly when

you are together on the way to court. Otherwise, he will turn you over to the judge who will hand you over to the police who will put you in jail. ²⁶There you will stay until you have paid the last penny.

²⁷You have heard that it was said: *Do not commit adultery.* ²⁸Now I tell you this: anyone who looks at a woman with lustful intent has already committed adultery with her in his heart.

²⁹So, if your right eye causes you to sin, pluck it out and throw it away! It is much better for you to lose a part of your body than to have your whole body thrown into hell. ³⁰If your right hand causes you to sin, cut it off and throw it away! It is better for you to lose a part of your body than to have your whole body thrown into hell.

³¹It was also said: *Anyone who divorces his wife must give her a written notice of divorce.* ³²Now I tell you is this: if a man divorces his wife, except in the case of unlawful union, he causes her to commit adultery. And the man who marries a divorced woman commits adultery.

Oaths

³³You have also heard that people were told in the past: *Do not break your oath; an oath sworn to the Lord must be kept.* ³⁴Now I tell you this: do not take oaths. Do not swear by the heavens, for they are God's throne; ³⁵nor by the earth, because it is his footstool; nor by Jerusalem, because it is the city of the great king. ³⁶Do not even swear by your head, because you cannot make a single hair white or black. ³⁷Let your *'Yes'* mean *'Yes'* and your *'No'* mean *'No.'* Anything else you say comes from the evil one.

Love of enemies
(Lk 6:29)

³⁸You have heard, that it was said: *An eye for an eye and a tooth for a tooth.* ³⁹Now I tell you this: do not oppose evil with evil; if someone slaps you on your right cheek, turn and offer the other. ⁴⁰If someone sues you in court for your shirt, give him your coat as well. ⁴¹If someone forces you to go one mile, go two miles with him. ⁴²Give when asked and do not turn your back on anyone who wants to borrow from you.

⁴³You have heard, that it was said: *Love your neighbor and do not do good to your enemy.* ⁴⁴Now I tell you this: love your enemies; and pray for those who persecute you, ⁴⁵so that you may be children of your

Father in Heaven. For he makes his sun rise on both the wicked and the good, and he gives rain to both the just and the unjust.

46 If you love those who love you, what is special about that? Do not even tax collectors do as much? 47 And if you are friendly only to your friends, what is so exceptional about that? Do not even the pagans do as much? 48 As for you, be perfect as your heavenly Father is perfect.

MATTHEW 5:21-48

Read: Throughout the Sermon on the Mount, Jesus talks about concrete things. His proposals, which exceed the laws of the Old Testament, invite the people to rethink their way of life.

Reflect: Jesus expects his followers to overcome the fulfillment of the Law as well. The generous love of the Father must be our model.

Pray: Ask the Lord to help you overcome the mere fulfillment of the law, that your life be modeled by the generous love of the Father.

Act: Anger is the cause of many problems. Think of a situation that ordinarily angers you, and practice the virtue of patience. Remember that our actions must be the result of the beliefs and values we profess.

Doing good for God alone

6 1 Be careful not to make a show of your good deeds before people. If you do so, you do not gain anything from your Father in heaven. 2 When you give something to the poor, do not have it trumpeted before you, as do those who want to be noticed in the synagogues and in the streets in order to be praised by people. I assure you they have their reward.

3 If you give something to the poor, do not let your left hand know what your right hand is doing, 4 so that your gift remains really secret. Your Father, who sees what is kept secret, will reward you.

5 When you pray, do not be like those who want to be noticed. They love to stand and pray in the synagogues or on street corners in order to be seen by everyone. I assure you they have their reward. 6 When you

pray, go into your room, close the door and pray to your Father who is with you in secret; and your Father who sees what is kept secret will reward you.

Our Father...
(Lk 11:1; Mk 11:25)

[7] When you pray, do not use a lot of words as the pagans do; for they believe that the more they say, the more chance they have of being heard. [8] Do not be like them. Your Father knows what you need even before you ask him.

[9] This, then, is how you should pray:

Our Father in heaven,
holy be your name,
[10] your kingdom, come,
your will be done
on earth as in heaven.
[11] Give us today our daily bread.
[12] Forgive us our debts
as we forgive those who are in debt to us.
[13] Do not bring us to the test,
but deliver us from the evil one.

[14] If you forgive others their wrongdoings, your Father in heaven will also forgive yours. [15] If you do not forgive others, then your Father will not forgive you.

[16] When you fast, do not put on a miserable face, as do the hypocrites. They put on a gloomy face so that people can see they are fasting. I tell you this: they have been paid in full already. [17] When you fast, wash your face and make yourself look cheerful, [18] because you are not fasting for appearances or for people but for your Father who sees beyond appearances. And your Father, who sees what is kept secret, will reward you.

MATTHEW 6:1-18

Read: Jesus continues to talk about matters of the ordinary life of his people, this time about religious piety (charity, prayer, and fasting). In this context, he teaches his disciples the prayer of the Our Father.

> **Reflect:** Is the practice of charity, prayer and fasting part of your ordinary life? Notice how in the Our Father, we first praise God, then ask for bread, forgiveness (to the extent that we also forgive), and to never see ourselves in a situation that we cannot overcome.
>
> **Pray:** Pray the Our Father slowly, meditating each part of the prayer.
>
> **Act:** When you pray the Our Father, especially at Mass, remember that your prayer unites you, as in one voice, with that of all the Christians of the world.

(Lk 11:34; 12:13)

¹⁹ Do not store up treasures for yourself here on earth, where moth and rust destroy it, and where thieves can steal it. ²⁰ Store up treasures for yourself with God, where no moth or rust can destroy it, nor thief comes and steals it.

²¹ For where your treasure is, there also, will your heart be.

²² The lamp of the body is the eye; if your eyes are sound, your whole body will be full of light. ²³ If your eyes are diseased, your whole body will be full of darkness. If, then, the light in you is darkness, how great is that darkness!

Set your heart on the kingdom
(Lk 12:23; 16:13)

²⁴ No one can serve two masters; for he will either hate one and love the other; or he will be loyal to the first and look down on the second. You cannot, at the same time, serve God and money.

²⁵ Therefore, I tell you not to be worried about food and drink for yourself, or about clothes for your body. Is not life more important than food; and is not the body more important than clothes? ²⁶ Look at the birds of the air; they do not sow, they do not harvest, and do not store food in barns, and yet your heavenly Father feeds them. Are not you more important than they?

²⁷ Can any of you add a day to your life by worrying about it? ²⁸ Why are you so worried about your clothes? Look at how the flowers in the fields grow. They do not toil or spin. ²⁹ But I tell you that not even

Solomon in all his glory was clothed like one of these. ³⁰If God so clothes the grass in the field which blooms today and is to be burned in an oven tomorrow, how much more will he clothe you? What little faith you have!

³¹Do not worry and say: What are we going to eat? What are we going to drink? or: What shall we wear? ³²The pagans busy themselves with such things, but your heavenly Father knows that you need them all. ³³Set your heart first on the kingdom and righteousness of God, and all these things will also be given to you. ³⁴Do not worry about tomorrow, for tomorrow will worry about itself. Each day has enough trouble of its own.

Don't be a judge
(Lk 6:37; 11:9; 6:31; 13:23)

7 ¹Do not judge, and you will not be judged. ²In the same way, you judge others, you will be judged; and the measure you use for others will be used for you. ³Why do you look at the speck in your brother's eye and not see the plank in your own eye? ⁴How can you say to your brother, 'Come, let me take the speck from your eye,' as long as that plank is in your own? ⁵Hypocrite, remove the plank out of your own eye, then you will see clearly to remove the speck out of your brother's eye.

⁶Do not give what is holy to the dogs, or throw your pearls before pigs. They might trample on them and then turn on you and tear you to pieces.

⁷Ask, and you will receive; seek and you will find; knock and the door will be opened. ⁸For everyone who asks receives; whoever seeks finds; and to him who knocks the door will be opened. ⁹Would any of you give a stone to your son when he asks for bread? ¹⁰Or give him a snake when he asks for a fish? ¹¹However bad you may be, you know how to give good things to your children. How much more, then, will your Father in heaven give good things to those who ask him!

¹²So, do to others whatever you would that others do to you: there you have the law and the prophets.

¹³Enter through the narrow gate: for wide is the gate and broad is the road that leads to destruction, and many go that way. ¹⁴How narrow is the gate that leads to life; and how rough the road; few there are who find it.

MATTHEW 6:19—7:12

Read: Observe the different sayings presented in this section. All refer to specific aspects of daily life.

Reflect: Can one live without worrying about the necessities of life? How and how much should one correct another?

Pray: Ask for understanding and patience to accept the complexity of life and of people, especially those that are close to you and that can cause you problems.

Act: Practice the golden rule.

The tree is known by its fruits
(Lk 6:43)

¹⁵ Beware of false prophets: they come to you in sheep's clothing, but inside they are voracious wolves. ¹⁶ You will recognize them by their fruits. Do you ever pick grapes from thorn bushes; or figs from thistles?

¹⁷ A good tree always produces good fruit. A rotten tree produces bad fruit. ¹⁸ A good tree cannot produce bad fruit, and a rotten tree cannot bear good fruit. ¹⁹ Any tree that does not bear good fruit is cut down and thrown into the fire. ²⁰ So then, you will know them by their fruit.

Wise and foolish builders
(Lk 6:46; 13:26; Mk 1:22)

²¹ Not everyone who says to me, 'Lord! Lord!' will enter the kingdom of heaven, but the one who does the will of my heavenly Father. ²² Many will say to me on that day, 'Lord, Lord, did we not speak in your name? Did we not cast out devils and perform many miracles in your name?' ²³ Then I will tell them openly, 'I have never known you; *away from me, you evil people!*'

²⁴ "Therefore, anyone who hears these words of mine and acts according to them is like a wise man who built his house on rock. ²⁵ The rain poured down, the rivers flooded and the wind blew and struck that house. But it did not collapse, because it was built on rock. ²⁶ But anyone who hears these words of mine and does not act accordingly is like a fool who built his house on sand. ²⁷ The rain poured, the rivers flooded,

and the wind blew and struck that house; it collapsed and what a terrible collapse that was!"

28 When Jesus had finished this discourse, the crowds were struck by the way he taught, 29 because he taught with authority, unlike their teachers of the law.

MATTHEW 7:13-29

Read: This section ends the Sermon on the Mount. Jesus invites his disciples to base their lives on solid realities: in listening and practicing his Word.

Reflect: Prayer and good works walk together. Our actions must manifest the values and beliefs we profess. Being coherent is not easy, it always demands sacrifice.

Pray: Pray to the Lord to help you live in coherence with the values and faith you professes.

Act: Try to put into practice that teaching of the Sermon on the Mount that you consider essential in your life.

Cure of a leper
(Mk 1:40; Lk 5:12)

8 1 When Jesus came down from the mountain, large crowds followed him.

2 Then a leper came forward. He knelt before him and said, "Sir, if you want to, you can make me clean." 3 Jesus stretched out his hand, touched him and said, "I want to, be clean again." At that very moment, the man was cleansed from his leprosy. 4 Then Jesus said to him, "See that you do not tell anyone; but go to the priest, have yourself declared clean, and offer the gift that Moses commanded as evidence for them."

The faith of the centurion
(Lk 7:1; Jn 4:46)

5 When Jesus entered Capernaum, an army captain approached him to ask his help, 6 "Sir, my servant lies sick at home. He is paralyzed and suffers terribly." 7 Jesus said to him, "I will come and heal him."

8 The captain answered, "I am not worthy to have you under my roof. Just give an order and my boy will be healed. 9 For I myself, a junior

officer, give orders to my soldiers. And if I say to one, 'Go!' he goes; and if I say to another, 'Come!' he comes; and if I say to my servant, 'Do this!' he does it."

¹⁰When Jesus heard this, he was astonished; and said to those who were following him, "I tell you, I have not found such faith in Israel. ¹¹I say to you, many will come from east and west and sit down with Abraham, Isaac, and Jacob at the feast in the kingdom of heaven; ¹²but the heirs of the kingdom will be thrown out into the extreme darkness; there they will wail and grind their teeth."

¹³Then Jesus said to the captain, "Go home now. As you believed, so let it be." And at that moment, his servant was healed.

¹⁴Jesus went to Peter's house and found Peter's mother-in-law in bed with a fever. ¹⁵He took her by the hand and the fever left her; she got up and began to wait on him.

¹⁶Toward evening, they brought to Jesus many people possessed by evil spirits; and with a word, he drove out the spirits. He also healed all who were sick. ¹⁷In this way, what was said by the prophet Isaiah was fulfilled: *He bore our infirmities and took on himself our diseases.*

MATTHEW 8:1-17

Read: Jesus expresses his compassion and solidarity toward those who suffer, reveals his authority not only with words but also with his healing power. Observe the courteous treatment of the centurion.

Reflect: Jesus admires the faith of the centurion. Sometimes the people we think as least are closer to God than ourselves. All religions tend to be exclusive. How would Jesus react to the exclusionary tendencies of our religion?

Pray: The healing performed by Jesus is not only a physical healing but an integral one. Ask the Lord for such healing.

Act: Become aware of the people who need your presence to heal, especially those closest to you.

¹⁸When Jesus saw the crowd pressing around him, he gave orders to cross to the other side of the lake. ¹⁹A teacher of the law approached him; and said, "Master, I will follow you wherever you go." ²⁰Jesus said

to him, "Foxes have holes and birds have nests, but the Son of Man has nowhere to lay his head."

²¹ Another disciple said to him, "Lord, let me go and bury my father first." ²² But Jesus said to him, "Follow me and let the dead bury their dead."

Jesus calms the storm
(Mk 4:35; Lk 8:22)

²³ Jesus got into the boat and his disciples followed him. ²⁴ Without warning, a fierce storm burst upon the lake with waves sweeping the boat. But Jesus was asleep.

²⁵ The disciples woke him up and cried, "Lord save us! We are lost!" ²⁶ But Jesus answered, "Why are you so afraid, you of little faith?" Then he stood up and rebuked the wind and sea, and it became completely calm.

²⁷ The disciples were astonished. They said, "What kind of man is he? Even the winds and the sea obey him."

MATTHEW 8:18-27

Read: The boat in the middle of the storm is the image of the Church in the midst of tribulations. Like the disciples, the Church must also say: Lord, save us!

Reflect: We all experience storms in life. In this passage, Jesus asks his disciples to be men of faith.

Pray: Pray to the Lord to increase your faith.

Act: Is it easy for you to pray in the midst of difficulties? If it is not, pray the Our Father, paying special attention to the last two petitions: "lead us not into temptation" and "deliver us from evil."

The demoniacs and the pigs
(Mk 5:1; Lk 8:26)

²⁸ When Jesus reached Gadara on the other side, he was met by two men possessed by devils, who came out of the tombs. They were so fierce that no one dared to pass that way. ²⁹ They cried out, "Son of God, leave us alone! Have you come here to torment us before the time?"

³⁰ Some distance away there was a large herd of pigs feeding. ³¹ So the

demons begged him, "If you drive us out, send us into that herd of pigs." [32] Jesus ordered them, "Go!" So the demons left the men and went into the pigs. The whole herd rushed down the cliff into the lake and was drowned.

[33] The men in charge of the pigs ran off to the town, where they told the whole story; and also what had happened to the men possessed with the demons. [34] The whole town went out to meet Jesus; and when they saw him, they begged him to leave their region.

Jesus cures a paralytic
(Mk 2:1; Lk 5:17)

9 [1] Jesus got back into the boat, crossed the lake again and came to his hometown. [2] Here, they brought to him a paralyzed man lying on a bed. Jesus saw their faith and said to the paralytic, "Courage, my son! Your sins are forgiven."

[3] Some teachers of the law said within themselves, "This man insults God." [4] Jesus was aware of what they were thinking; and said, "Why have you such evil thoughts? [5] Which is easier to say: 'Your sins are forgiven' or 'Stand up and walk'? [6] But that you may know that the Son of Man has power on earth to forgive sins," he said to the paralyzed man, "Stand up! Take your stretcher and go home!" [7] The man got up and went home.

[8] When the crowds saw this, they were filled with awe and praised God for giving such power to human beings.

MATTHEW 8:28–9:8

Read: Jesus has power over all kinds of evil, be it spiritual, psychological, moral or physical.

Reflect: The expression "Son of Man" is of Aramaic origin and means "man/human." "Can every person" forgive sins? Remember the Our Father: "Forgive our trespasses as we forgive those who trespass against us."

Pray: Pray the Our Father slowly, meditating especially on the request for forgiveness.

Act: Think of someone who has offended you and forgive that person from the heart. Think of someone you have offended and seek forgiveness.

Jesus calls Matthew
(Mk 2:13; Lk 5:27)

⁹ As Jesus moved on from there, he saw a man named Matthew at his seat in the customhouse; and he said to him, "Follow me!" And Matthew got up and followed him. ¹⁰ Now it happened while Jesus was at table in Matthew's house, many tax collectors and sinners joined Jesus and his disciples. ¹¹ When the Pharisees saw this, they said to his disciples, "Why is it, that your master eats with sinners and tax collectors?"

¹² When Jesus heard this, he said, "Healthy people do not need a doctor, but sick people do. ¹³ Go, and find out what this means: *What I want is mercy, not sacrifice.* I did not come to call the righteous, but sinners."

¹⁴ Then the disciples of John came to him with the question, "How is it that we and the Pharisees fast on many occasions but not your disciples?"

¹⁵ Jesus answered them, "How can you expect wedding guests to mourn as long as the bridegroom is with them? The time will come when the bridegroom will be taken away from them and then they will fast.

¹⁶ No one patches an old coat with a piece of unshrunk cloth, for the patch will shrink and tear an even bigger hole in the coat. ¹⁷ In the same way, you don't put new wine into old wineskins. If you do, the wineskins will burst and the wine will be spilt. No, you put new wine into fresh skins; then both are preserved."

MATTHEW 9:9-17

Read: Jesus calls sinners and eats with them. He also says that there is a time to fast and another time to celebrate.

Reflect: What does "I want mercy and not sacrifices" mean for your personal life? What does that say about "new wine in new wineskins"?

Pray: Ask in prayer for humility to welcome everyone and not to exclude anyone.

Act: Be attentive to those who need to experience forgiveness and welcome.

A woman healed, a child raised to life
(Mk 5:21; Lk 8:40)

[18] While Jesus was speaking to them, an official of the synagogue came up to him, bowed before him and said, "My daughter has just died, but come and place your hands on her and she will live." [19] Jesus stood up and followed him with his disciples.

[20] Then a woman, who had suffered from severe bleeding for twelve years, came up from behind and touched the edge of his cloak; [21] for she thought, "If I only touch his cloak, I will be healed." [22] Jesus turned, saw her, and said, "Courage, my daughter, your faith has saved you." And from that moment the woman was cured.

[23] When Jesus arrived at the official's house and saw the flute players and the excited crowd, he said, [24] "Get out of here! The girl is not dead. She is only sleeping!" And they laughed at him. [25] But once the crowd had been turned out, Jesus went in and took the girl by the hand and she stood up. [26] The news of this spread throughout the whole area.

[27] As Jesus moved on from there, two blind men followed him shouting, "Son of David, help us!" [28] When he was about to enter the house, the blind men caught up with him; and Jesus said to them, "Do you believe that I am able to do what you want?" They answered, "Yes, sir!"

[29] Then Jesus touched their eyes and said, "As you have believed, so let it be." [30] And their eyes were opened. Then Jesus gave them a stern warning, "Be careful that no one knows about this." [31] But as soon as they went away, they spread the news about him through the whole area.

[32] As they were going away, some people brought to Jesus a man who was dumb because he was possessed by a demon. [33] When the demon was driven out, the dumb man began to speak. The crowds were astonished and said, "Nothing like this has ever been seen in Israel." [34] But the Pharisees said, "He drives away demons with the help of the prince of demons."

[35] Jesus went around all the towns and villages, teaching in their synagogues and proclaiming the good news of the kingdom; and he cured every sickness and disease. [36] When he saw the crowds, he was moved with pity; for they were harassed and helpless, like sheep without a shepherd. [37] Then he said to his disciples, "The harvest is abundant, but the workers are only few. [38] Ask the master of the harvest to send workers to gather his harvest."

MATTHEW 9:18-38

Read: Jesus continues to manifest his power over evil, even over death. As a good shepherd, he is compassionate to everyone.

Reflect: What does this sentence suggest to you: "the harvest is plentiful, but the workers are few"?

Pray: Pray to the Lord so that through your life the compassion and kindness of Jesus in the world may continue to be present.

Act: Become aware of how God has generously blessed you, your loved ones, and the world around you.

The Twelve apostles
(Mk 3:13; Lk 6:12)

10 [1] Jesus called his Twelve disciples to him and gave them authority over unclean spirits, to drive them out and to heal every disease and sickness.

[2] These are the names of the Twelve apostles: first, Simon, called Peter, and his brother Andrew; [3] James, the son of Zebedee, and his brother John; Philip and Bartholomew; Thomas and Matthew, the tax collector; James, the son of Alphaeus, and Thaddaeus; [4] Simon, the Canaanite, and Judas Iscariot, the man who would betray him.

Jesus sends out the first missionaries
(Lk 9:1; 10:1; Mk 6:7)

[5] Jesus sent these Twelve on a mission with the instructions: "Do not visit pagan territory and do not enter a Samaritan town. [6] Go, instead, to the lost sheep of the people of Israel.

[7] Go and proclaim this message: The kingdom of heaven is near. [8] Heal the sick, bring the dead back to life, cleanse the lepers and drive out demons. Freely have you received, freely give. [9] Do not carry any gold or silver or money in your purses. [10] Do not take a traveling bag, or an extra shirt, or sandals, or a walking stick: workers deserve to be compensated.

[11] When you come to a town or a village, look for a worthy person, and stay there until you leave.

¹²When you enter the house, wish it peace. ¹³If the people are worthy people, your peace will rest on them; if they are not worthy people, your blessing will come back to you.

¹⁴And if you are not welcomed, and your words are not listened to, leave that house or that town, and shake the dust off your feet. ¹⁵I assure you, it will go easier for the people of Sodom and Gomorrah on the day of judgment than it will for the people of that town.

MATTHEW 10:1-15

Read: Jesus calls his disciples to collaborate in his mission. Observe how he entrusts them to perform it.

Reflect: How does the mission of Jesus continue in your life? What meaning does peace have in your life?

Pray: Pray that those you meet will be filled with the blessing of God.

Act: Pay attention to the gesture of peace in the mass. That be not an empty rite, but an expression of your decision to work for peace.

You will be persecuted
(Lk 12:11; Mk 13:9; 8:38)

¹⁶Look, I send you out like sheep among wolves. You must be as clever as snakes and as innocent as doves. ¹⁷Be on your guard with people, for they will hand you over to their courts and they will flog you in their synagogues. ¹⁸You will be brought to trial before rulers and kings because of me, so that you may witness to them and the pagans.

¹⁹But when you are arrested, do not worry about what you are to say, or how you are to say it; when the hour comes, you will be given what you are to say. ²⁰For it will not be you who speak, but the Spirit of your Father speaking through you.

²¹Brother will hand over his brother to death, and a father his child; children will turn against their parents and have them put to death. ²²Everyone will hate you because of me, but whoever stands firm to the end will be saved.

²³ When they persecute you in one town, flee to the next. I tell you the truth, you will not have passed through all the towns of Israel before the Son of Man comes.

²⁴ A student is not above his teacher, nor a slave above his master. ²⁵ A student should be content to become like his teacher and the slave like his master. If the head of the household has been called Beelzebul, how much more those of his household! So, do not be afraid of them!

²⁶ There is nothing covered that will not be uncovered. There is nothing hidden that will not be made known. ²⁷ What I am telling you in the dark, you must speak in the light. What you hear in private, proclaim from the housetops.

²⁸ Do not be afraid of those who kill the body, but have no power to kill the soul. Rather, be afraid of him who can destroy both body and soul in hell. ²⁹ For a few cents you can buy two sparrows. Yet not one sparrow falls to the ground without your Father knowing. ³⁰ As for you, every hair of your head has been counted. ³¹ Do not be afraid: you are worth more than many sparrows!

³² Whoever acknowledges me before others, I will acknowledge before my Father in heaven. ³³ Whoever rejects me before others, I will reject before my Father in heaven.

³⁴ Do not think that I have come to establish peace on earth. I have not come to bring peace, but a sword. ³⁵ For I have come to set a man against his father, and a daughter against her mother, a daughter-in-law against her mother-in-law. ³⁶ Each one will have as enemies those of one's own family.

³⁷ Whoever loves father or mother more than me, is not worthy of me. And whoever loves son or daughter more than me, is not worthy of me. ³⁸ And whoever does not take up his cross and follow me, is not worthy of me. ³⁹ Whoever finds his life will lose it; but whoever loses his life, for my sake, will find it.

⁴⁰ Whoever welcomes you, welcomes me; and whoever welcomes me, welcomes him who sent me. ⁴¹ The one who welcomes a prophet, as a prophet will receive the reward of a prophet; the one who welcomes a just man, because he is a just man, will receive the reward of a just man. ⁴² And if anyone gives even a cup of cold water to one of these little ones, because he is my disciple, I assure you, he will not go unrewarded."

MATTHEW 10:16-42

Read: The second great discourse of Jesus in the Gospel of Matthew: the Mission. Look at the specific instructions given to the Twelve. Pay attention to the images he uses: sheep, snake, and pigeon.

Reflect: What conflicts does the reception of the Gospel generate in your life?

Pray: Abandon yourself trustingly in the hands of God, let Him be your strength and encouragement.

Act: Express your faith in compassionate treatment of others, especially toward the weakest members of your community.

Jesus and John the Baptist
(Lk 7:18; 16:16; 10:13)

11 ¹When Jesus had finished giving his twelve disciples these instructions, he went on from there to teach and to proclaim his message in their towns. ²When John the Baptist heard in prison about the deeds of Christ, he sent a message by his disciples ³asking him, "Are you the one who is to come, or should we expect someone else?"

⁴Jesus answered them, "Go back and report to John what you hear and see: ⁵the blind see, the lame walk, the lepers are made clean, the deaf hear, the dead are brought back to life, and the poor hear the good news; ⁶and how fortunate is the one who does not take offense at me!"

⁷As the messengers left, Jesus began to speak to the crowds about John: "When you went out to the desert, what did you expect to see? A reed swept by the wind? ⁸What did you go out to see? A man dressed in fine clothes? People who wear fine clothes live in palaces. ⁹What did you really go out to see? A prophet? Yes, indeed, and even more than a prophet. ¹⁰He is the man of whom Scripture says: *I send my messenger ahead of you to prepare the way before you.*

¹¹I tell you this: no one greater than John the Baptist has arisen from among the sons of women and yet the least in the kingdom of heaven is greater than he. ¹²From the days of John the Baptist until now the kingdom of heaven is something to be conquered and violent men seize it.

[13] Up to the time of John there was only prophesy: all the prophets and the law. [14] And if you believe me, John is indeed that Elijah, whose coming was predicted. [15] Let anyone with ears listen!

[16] Now, to what can I compare the people of this day? They are like children sitting in the marketplace about whom their companions complain: [17] 'We played the flute for you, but you would not dance. We sang a funeral song, but you would not cry!'

[18] For John came fasting and people said, 'He is possessed by a demon!' [19] Then the Son of Man came. He ate and drank; and people said, 'Look at this man: a glutton and drunkard, a friend of tax collectors and sinners!' Yet, wisdom is vindicated by her works."

MATTHEW 11:1-19

Read: The question of the Baptist seems not to take into account what is related in 3:13-15. However, Matthew reveals that Jesus is the true Messiah, God's anointed (some thought the Baptist was).

Reflect: What kind of Messiah did the people of Israel expect? What kind of Messiah do you expect? Does the Jesus of the Gospel satisfy your hopes?

Pray: Ask God to help you recognize Jesus as the Messiah. And may such recognition push you to work for his kingdom.

Act: May your life be a testimony of Jesus to others.

---

[20] Then Jesus began to denounce the cities in which he had performed most of his miracles because the people there did not change their ways. [21] "Alas for you Chorazin and Bethsaida! If the miracles worked in you had taken place in Tyre and Sidon, the people there would have repented long ago in sackcloth and ashes. [22] But I assure you, for Tyre and Sidon; it will be more bearable for Tyre and Sidon on the day of judgment than for you. [23] And you, Capernaum, will you be lifted up to heaven? You will be thrown down to the place of the dead! For if the miracles which were performed in you had been performed in Sodom, it would still be there today! [24] But I tell you, it will be more bearable for Sodom on the day of judgment than for you."

Take my yoke upon you
(Lk 10:21)

25 On that occasion, Jesus said, "Father, Lord of heaven and earth, I praise you; because you have hidden these things from the wise and learned, and revealed them to simple people. 26 Yes, Father, this was your gracious will.

27 Everything has been entrusted to me by my Father. No one knows the Son except the Father and no one knows the Father except the Son and those to whom the Son chooses to reveal him.

28 Come to me all you who are weary and burdened, and I will give you rest. 29 Take my yoke upon you and learn from me, for I am gentle and humble of heart; and you will find rest. 30 For my yoke is easy and my burden is light."

MATTHEW 11:20-30

Read: Jesus reproaches the cities where he has most manifested his power. To whom much is given, much is also demanded. Observe Jesus' invitation to those who are tired and burdened: in him, they will find comfort (28).

Reflect: How is the salvation of God manifested in your life? What does the expression: "Come to me, those who are weary and burdened, and I will give you rest" tells you?

Pray: Pray to God who is Father, Son, and Holy Spirit. Ask for the grace so that you can recognize the saving action of God in your life.

Act: Be kind to everyone, so that your presence inspires confidence and relief and witnesses to God's love for others.

Jesus, Lord of the Sabbath
(Mk 2:23; 3:1; Lk 6:1; 14:1)

12 1 It happened that Jesus was walking through the wheat fields on a Sabbath. His disciples were hungry, and they began to pick some heads of wheat to crush and to eat the grain. 2 When the Pharisees noticed this, they said to Jesus, "Look at your disciples! They are doing what is prohibited on the Sabbath!"

3 Jesus answered, "Have you not read what David did when he and his

men were hungry? ⁴He went into the House of God and they ate the bread offered to God, though neither he nor his men had the right to eat it but only the priests. ⁵And have you not read in the law how, on the Sabbath, the priests in the temple desecrate the Sabbath, yet they are not guilty?

⁶I tell you there is greater than the temple here. ⁷If you really knew the meaning of the words: *It is mercy I want, not sacrifice*, you would not have condemned the innocent.

⁸Besides, the Son of Man is Lord of the Sabbath."

⁹Jesus then left that place and went into one of their synagogues. ¹⁰A man was there with a paralyzed hand, and the people who wanted to bring a charge against Jesus asked him, "Is it permitted to heal on the Sabbath?"

¹¹But he said to them, "What if one of you has a sheep and it falls into a pit on the Sabbath? Will you not take hold of your sheep and lift it out? ¹²Is a human being less worthy of help than a sheep? Therefore, it is permitted to do good on the Sabbath." ¹³Then Jesus said to the man, "Stretch out your arm." He stretched it out and it was completely restored as sound as the other one.

¹⁴Then the Pharisees went out and made plans to get rid of Jesus. ¹⁵As Jesus was aware of their plans, he left that place. Many people followed him and he cured all who were sick. ¹⁶But he gave them strict orders not to make him known.

¹⁷In this way, Isaiah's prophecy was fulfilled:

¹⁸*Here is my servant whom I have chosen; the one I love and with whom I am pleased. I will put my spirit upon him, and he will announce my judgment to the nations.*

¹⁹*He will not argue or shout, nor will his voice be heard in the streets.* ²⁰*The bruised reed he will not crush, nor snuff out the smoldering wick until he brings justice to victory,* ²¹*and in him, all the nations will put their hope.*

MATTHEW 12:1-21

Read: Jesus puts the practice of good before the observance of the Sabbath. This generates conflicts with the religious authorities, who decide to kill him.

Reflect: Does the exercise of mercy precede any religious, moral or legal precept? There are those who think that this way of proceeding generates many problems, what is your opinion?

Pray: Pray to the Holy Spirit to help you choose life when conflicts arise between the fulfillment of a certain law and the practice of good.

Act: That your observance of the law be always based on the love of God and neighbor.

The unforgivable sin
(Mk 3:22; Lk 11:15)

²² Then some people brought to him a possessed man who was blind and mute. Jesus healed the man; who was then able to speak and see. ²³ All in the crowd were amazed and said, "Could he be the Son of David?" ²⁴ When the Pharisees heard this, they said, "It is by Beelzebul, prince of the devils, that this man drives out devils."

²⁵ Jesus, knowing their thoughts, said to them, "Every kingdom that is divided against itself is destroyed; and every city, or family, that is divided against itself will not last long. ²⁶ So if Satan drives out Satan, he is divided: how then can his reign endure? ²⁷ And if it is by Beelzebul that I drive out devils, by whom do your own people drive them out? For this reason, they will be your judges.

²⁸ But if it is by the Spirit of God that I drive out devils, then the kingdom of God has already come upon you. ²⁹ How can anyone break into the strong man's house and make off with his belongings, unless he first ties him up? Only then can he plunder his house.

³⁰ The one who is not with me is against me, and the one who does not gather with me scatters.

³¹ And so I tell you this: people can be forgiven any sin and any evil thing they say against God, but blasphemy against the Spirit will not be forgiven. ³² The one who speaks against the Son of Man will be forgiven; but the one who speaks against the Holy Spirit will not be forgiven, either in this age or in the age to come.

³³ If you have a healthy tree, its fruit will be healthy; if you have a rotten tree, its fruit will be rotten. You can know a tree by its fruit. ³⁴ You brood

of vipers, how can you say anything good when you are so evil? For the mouth speaks what fills the heart. [35] A good person produces good things from his good store and an evil person produces evil things from his evil store.

[36] I tell you this: on the day of judgment people will have to give an account of any careless word they have spoken. [37] Your own words will declare you either innocent or guilty."

Jesus criticizes his own generation
(Mk 8:11; Lk 11:16)

[38] Then, some teachers of the law and some Pharisees spoke up, "Teacher, we want to see a sign from you." [39] Jesus answered them, "An evil and unfaithful people want a sign; but no sign will be given them except the sign of the prophet Jonah. [40] In the same way, as Jonah spent three days and three nights in the belly of the whale, so will the Son of Man spend three days and three nights in the heart of the earth.

[41] At the judgment, the people of Nineveh will rise with this generation and condemn it; because they reformed their lives at the preaching of Jonah and here there is greater than Jonah. [42] At the judgment, the Queen of the South will stand up and condemn you. She came from the ends of the earth to hear the wisdom of Solomon and here there is greater than Solomon.

[43] When an evil spirit goes out of a person, it wanders over arid wastelands looking for a place to rest, but it cannot find any. [44] Then it says: 'I will go back to my house which I had to leave.' So it goes back and finds the house empty, clean, and in order. [45] Off it goes again, to bring back with itself this time, seven spirits, more evil than itself. They move in and settle there; so that this person is, finally, in a worse state at the end than he was at the beginning. This is what will happen to this evil generation."

[46] While Jesus was talking to the people, his mother and his brothers wanted to speak to him and they waited outside. [47] So someone said to him, "Your mother and your brothers are standing outside; they want to speak with you."

[48] Jesus answered, "Who is my mother? Who are my brothers?" [49] Then he pointed to his disciples and said, "Look! Here are my mother and my brothers. [50] Whoever does the will of my Father in heaven is my brother and sister and mother."

> **MATTHEW 12:22-50**
>
> **Read:** Observe how Jesus' conflict with religious authorities becomes acute. They do not recognize the saving action of Jesus, on the contrary, they reject it by identifying it with the Devil's own actions.
>
> **Reflect:** What do the following expressions suggest to you: "Any sin or blasphemy can be forgiven to men, but blasphemy against the Spirit has no forgiveness"; "God who created you without you will not save you without you"?
>
> **Pray:** Ask God to help you have a heart always open to the manifestations of His goodness and love.
>
> **Act:** Identify the prejudices you have with that person who does not like you. And make a concrete gesture of friendship with her or him.

The parable of the sower
(Mk 4:1; Lk 8:4; 10:23; 13:20)

13 ¹That same day, Jesus left the house and sat down by the lakeside. ²Many people gathered around him. So he got into a boat and sat down, while the crowds stood on the shore; ³and he spoke to them in parables about many things.

⁴Jesus said, "The sower went out to sow; and as he sowed, some seeds fell along the path; and the birds came and ate them up. ⁵Other seeds fell on rocky ground where there was little soil and the seeds sprouted quickly because the soil was not deep. ⁶But as soon as the sun rose, the plants were scorched; and they withered, because they had no roots. ⁷Again, other seeds fell among the thistles; and the thistles grew and choked the plants. ⁸Still, other seeds fell on good soil and produced a crop: some a hundredfold, others sixty, and others thirty. ⁹If you have ears, then hear!"

¹⁰Then his disciples came to him and said, "Why do you speak to them in parables?"

¹¹Jesus answered, "To you, it has been given to know the secrets of the kingdom of heaven, but not to these people. ¹²For the one who has will be given more, and he will have in abundance. But the one who does

not have will be deprived of even what he has. [13] That is why I speak to them in parables; because they look and do not see; they hear, but they do not listen or understand.

[14] In them, the words of the prophet Isaiah are fulfilled: *However much you hear, you do not understand; however much you see, you do not perceive.*

[15] *For the heart of this people has grown dull. Their ears hardly hear and their eyes dare not see. If they were to see with their eyes, hear with their ears and understand with their heart, they would turn back, and I would heal them.*

[16] But blessed are your eyes because they see; and your ears, because they hear.

[17] For I tell you, many prophets and righteous people have longed to see the things you see, but they did not see them; and to hear the things you hear, but they did not hear them.

[18] Now listen to the parable of the sower.

[19] When a person hears the message of the kingdom but does not take it seriously, the devil comes and snatches away what was sown in his heart. This is the seed that fell along the footpath.

[20] The seed that fell on rocky ground stands for the one who hears the word and accepts it at once with joy. [21] But such a person has no roots and endures only for a while. No sooner is he harassed or persecuted because of the word, than he gives up.

[22] The seed that fell among the thistles is the one who hears the word but then the worries of this life and the love of money choke the word; and it does not bear fruit.

[23] As for the seed that fell on good soil, it is the one who hears the word and understands it; this seed bears fruit and produces a hundred, or sixty, or thirty times more."

MATTHEW 13:1-23

Read: The third great discourse of Jesus in the Gospel of Matthew. Jesus teaches in parables, with them he encourages his followers to embrace the Gospel in their lives.

Reflect: What implications in your daily life does the parable of the sower suggest?

> **Pray:** To accept the word of God and live according to it is not easy. Pray to the Lord to help you in this.
>
> **Act:** Listen carefully to the Word of God at Mass, and put it into practice.

The parable of the weeds

24 Jesus told the people another parable, "The kingdom of heaven can be compared to a man who sowed good seed in his field. 25 While everyone was asleep, his enemy came and sowed weeds among the wheat and went away.

26 When the plants sprouted and produced grain, the weeds also appeared. 27 Then the servants of the owner came and said to him, 'Sir, was it not good seed that you sowed in your field? Where did the weeds come from?'

28 He answered them, 'This is the work of an enemy.' They asked him, 'Do you want us to go and pull up the weeds?' 29 He told them, 'No, when you pull up the weeds, you might uproot the wheat with them. 30 Let them grow together until harvest; and, at harvest time, I will say to the workers: Pull up the weeds first, tie them in bundles and burn them; then gather the wheat into my barn.'"

The mustard seed and the yeast
(Mk 4:30; Lk 13:18)

31 Jesus offered them another parable: "The kingdom of heaven is like a mustard seed that a man took and sowed in his field.

32 It is smaller than all other seeds, but once it is fully grown it is bigger than any garden plant; like *a tree, the birds come and rest in its branches.*"

33 He told them another parable, "The kingdom of heaven is like the yeast that a woman took and hid in three measures of flour until the whole mass of dough began to rise."

34 Jesus taught all these things to the crowds by means of parables; he did not say anything to them without using a parable. 35 This fulfilled what was spoken by the Prophet: *I will speak in parables. I will proclaim things kept secret since the beginning of the world.*

36 Then he sent the crowds away and went into the house. And his disciples came to him, saying, "Explain to us the parable of the weeds

in the field." [37] Jesus answered them, "The one who sows the good seed is the Son of Man. [38] The field is the world; the good seed are the people of the kingdom; the weeds are those who follow the evil one. [39] The enemy who sows the weeds is the devil; the harvest is the end of time and the workers are the angels.

[40] Just as the weeds are pulled up and burned in the fire, so will it be at the end of time. [41] The Son of Man will send his angels, and they will weed out of his kingdom all that is scandalous and all who do evil. [42] And these will be thrown into the blazing furnace, where there will be weeping and gnashing of teeth. [43] Then the just will shine like the sun in the kingdom of their Father. If you have ears, then hear.

The treasure, the pearl, and the net

[44] The kingdom of heaven is like a treasure hidden in a field. The one who finds it buries it again; and so happy is he that he goes and sells everything he has in order to buy that field.

[45] Again, the kingdom of heaven is like a trader who is looking for fine pearls. [46] Once he has found a pearl of exceptional quality, he goes away, sells everything he has and buys it.

[47] Again, the kingdom of heaven is like a big fishing net let down into the sea, in which every kind of fish has been caught. [48] When the net is full, it is dragged ashore. Then they sit down and gather the good fish into buckets, but throw the bad away. [49] That is how it will be at the end of time; the angels will go out to separate the wicked from the just [50] and to throw the wicked into the blazing furnace where they will weep and gnash their teeth."

[51] Jesus asked, "Have you understood all these things?" "Yes," they answered. [52] So he said to them, "Therefore, every teacher of the law who becomes a disciple of the kingdom of heaven is like a householder who can produce from his store things both new and old."

[53] When Jesus had finished these parables, he left that place. [54] He went to his hometown and taught the people in their synagogue. They were amazed and said, "Where did he get this wisdom and these special powers? [55] Isn't he the carpenter's son? Isn't Mary his mother and aren't James, Joseph, Simon, and Judas his brothers? [56] Aren't all his sisters living here? Where did he get all these things?" [57] And so they took offense at him.

Jesus said to them, "The only place where a prophet is not welcome is his hometown and in his own family." [58] And he did not perform many miracles there because of their lack of faith.

MATTHEW 13:24-58

Read: Jesus continues speaking in parables; with them, he highlights two realities: the constant presence of evil (the darnel), and the irruption of the kingdom in history through small things.

Reflect: What things does the parable of the darnel suggests to you? Do you perceive the presence of the kingdom of God in the daily and small events of reconciliation, justice, love, that happens in your day to day?

Pray: Pray the Our Father and pay special attention to the request: "May your kingdom come."

Act: Promote in your daily life those gestures and actions that, in your consideration, manifest the presence of the kingdom of God in your life.

John the Baptist beheaded
(Mk 6:14; Lk 9:7)

14 [1] At that time, the reports about Jesus reached King Herod. [2] And he said to his servants, "This man is John the Baptist. John has risen from the dead, and that is why miraculous powers are at work in John."

[3] Herod had, in fact, ordered that John be arrested, bound in chains and put in prison because of Herodias, the wife of his brother Philip. [4] For John had said to Herod, "It is not right for you to have her as your wife." [5] Herod wanted to kill him but he did not dare, because he feared the people, who regarded John as a prophet.

[6] On Herod's birthday the daughter of Herodias danced among the guests; she so delighted Herod [7] that he promised under oath to give her anything she asked for. [8] The girl, following the advice of her mother, said, "Give me the head of John the Baptist, here, on a dish."

[9] The king was very displeased, but because he had made his promise under oath, in the presence of his guests, he ordered it to be given to

her. ¹⁰So he had John beheaded in prison ¹¹and his head brought on a dish and given to the girl. The girl then took it to her mother.

¹²Then John's disciples came, took his body and buried it. Then they went and told Jesus.

> **MATTHEW 14:1-12**
>
> **Read:** Observe the action of Herod (political power). His ulti-mate motivation is not justice, but public approval.
>
> **Reflect:** Look at your own actions. To what extent do your ac-tions depend on "what people will say"?
>
> **Pray:** Ask the Lord to give you strength to work for justice more than for "what others will say about you."
>
> **Act:** Perform the action that should be done by justice, but not by "what people will say."

The first miracle of the loaves
(Mk 6:32; Jn 6)

¹³When Jesus heard of it, he set out by boat for a secluded place to be alone. But the people heard of it and they followed him on foot from their towns. ¹⁴When Jesus went ashore, he saw the crowd gathered there and he had compassion on them. And he healed their sick.

¹⁵Late in the afternoon, his disciples came to him and said, "We are in a lonely place and it is now late. You should send these people away so that they can go to the villages and buy something for themselves to eat."

¹⁶But Jesus replied, "They do not need to go away; you give them something to eat." ¹⁷They answered, "We have nothing here but five loaves and two fishes." ¹⁸Jesus said to them, "Bring them here to me."

¹⁹Then he made everyone sit down on the grass. He took the five loaves and the two fishes, raised his eyes to heaven, pronounced the blessing, broke the loaves and handed them to the disciples to distribute to the people. ²⁰And they all ate, and everyone had enough; then the disciples gathered up the leftovers, filling twelve baskets. ²¹About five thousand men had eaten there, besides women and children.

Jesus walks on the water
(Mk 6:45; Jn 6:16)

22 Immediately, Jesus obliged his disciples to get into the boat and go ahead of him to the other side, while he sent the crowd away.

23 And having sent the people away, he went up to the mountain by himself, to pray. At nightfall, he was there alone. 24 Meanwhile, the boat was very far from land, dangerously rocked by the waves, for the wind was against it.

25 At daybreak, Jesus came to them walking on the sea. 26 When they saw him walking on the sea, they were terrified, thinking that it was a ghost. And they cried out in fear. 27 But at once, Jesus said to them, "Courage! Don't be afraid. It's me!" 28 Peter answered, "Lord, if it is you, command me to come to you on the water."

29 Jesus said to him, "Come!" And Peter got out of the boat and walked on the water to go to Jesus. 30 But seeing the strong wind, he was afraid, and began to sink; and he cried out, "Lord, save me!" 31 Jesus immediately stretched out his hand and took hold of him, saying, "Man of little faith, why did you doubt?"

32 As they got into the boat, the wind dropped. 33 Then those in the boat bowed down before Jesus, saying, "Truly, you are the Son of God!"

34 They came ashore at Gennesaret. 35 The local people recognized Jesus and spread the news throughout the region. So they brought to him all the sick people, 36 begging him to let them touch just the hem of his cloak. All who touched it became perfectly well.

MATTHEW 14:13-36

Read: Jesus feels sorry for the crowd who follows him, he does not abandon them, but he heals, teaches and feeds them. This story is a prefiguration of the Eucharist.

Reflect: What is the miracle: the multiplication of some loaves and fishes or in the fulfillment of the teachings of Jesus: solidarity? Can there be Eucharist outside of the celebration of the Mass?

Pray: Pray to God so that you may fulfill your commitment to live the Eucharist outside of the Mass, in your day to day, with your family, your friends, and colleagues at work.

> **Act:** May your life be Eucharist, a "thanksgiving," bread shared with others.

God's command and human tradition
(Mk 7:1)

15 ¹ Then, some Pharisees and teachers of the law who had come from Jerusalem, gathered around Jesus. And they said to him, ² "Why don't your disciples follow the tradition of the elders? For they don't wash their hands before eating."

³ Jesus answered, "And you, why do you break God's command for the sake of your traditions? ⁴ For God commanded: *Do your duty to your father and your mother, and: Whoever curses his father or his mother is to be put to death.* ⁵ But you say that anyone may say to his father or mother, 'What you could have expected from me is given to God.' ⁶ In this case, according to you, a person is freed from his duty to his father and mother. And so, you have nullified the command of God for the sake of your traditions.

⁷ Hypocrites! Isaiah rightly prophesied of you when he said: ⁸ *This people honors me with their lips, but their heart is far from me.* ⁹ *The worship they offer me is worthless, for they only teach human rules.*"

Washing hands and cleanness of heart
(Mk 7:14; Lk 6:39)

¹⁰ Jesus then called the people to him and said to them, "Listen and understand: ¹¹ What enters into the mouth does not make a person unclean. What defiles a person is what comes out of his mouth."

¹² After a while, the disciples gathered around Jesus and said, "Do you know that the Pharisees were offended by what you said?" ¹³ Jesus answered, "Every plant, which my heavenly Father has not planted shall be uprooted. ¹⁴ Pay no attention to them! They are blind leading the blind. When a blind person leads another the two will fall into a pit."

¹⁵ Peter said to him, "Explain this parable to us." ¹⁶ Jesus replied, "So even you, too, are dull? ¹⁷ Do you not see that whatever enters the mouth goes into the stomach and then out of the body? ¹⁸ But what comes out of the mouth comes from the heart and that is what makes a person unclean.

¹⁹ Indeed, it is from the heart that evil desires come: murder, adultery, immorality, theft, lies, slander. ²⁰ These are the things that make a person unclean, but eating without washing the hands does not make a person unclean."

MATTHEW 15:1-20

Read: Jesus points out that the practice of good and justice comes before the fulfillment of religious traditions.

Reflect: What does this expression suggest to you: "What comes out of the mouth comes from the heart, and that makes a person unclean"?

Pray: Pray to the Lord to help you choose good and justice, and to expel from your heart all the bad feelings that contaminate you.

Act: Look at the religious traditions you practice. Promote those that agree with the teachings of Jesus.

The faith of the Canaanite woman
(Mk 7:24)

²¹ Leaving that place, Jesus withdrew to the region of Tyre and Sidon. ²² A Canaanite woman from the area came and cried out, "Lord, Son of David, have pity on me! My daughter is tormented by a demon." ²³ But Jesus did not answer her, not even a word. So his disciples approached him and said, "Send her away! See how she is shouting after us."

²⁴ Then Jesus said to her, "I was sent only to the lost sheep of the nation of Israel."

²⁵ But the woman was already kneeling before Jesus and said, "Sir, help me!" ²⁶ Jesus answered, "It is not right to take the bread from the children and throw it to puppies." ²⁷ The woman replied, "That is true, sir, but even puppies eat the crumbs which fall from their master's table." ²⁸ Then Jesus said, "Woman, how great is your faith! Let it be as you wish." And her daughter was healed at that moment.

The second miracle of the loaves
(Mk 7:31)

²⁹ From there, Jesus went to the shore of Lake Galilee and then went

up into the hills where he sat down. [30] Great crowds came to him bringing the dumb, the blind, the lame, the crippled, and many with other infirmities. People carried them to the feet of Jesus, and he healed them. [31] All were astonished when they saw the dumb speaking, the lame walking, the crippled healed, and the blind able to see; and they glorified the God of Israel.

[32] Jesus called his disciples and said to them, "I am filled with compassion for these people; they have already followed me for three days and now have nothing to eat. I do not want to send them away fasting, or they may faint on the way." [33] His disciples said to him, "And where shall we find enough bread in this wilderness to feed such a crowd?" [34] Jesus said to them, "How many loaves do you have?" They answered, "Seven, and a few small fish."

[35] Jesus ordered the people to sit on the ground. [36] Then, he took the seven loaves and the small fish and gave thanks to God. He broke them and gave them to his disciples who distributed them to the people.

[37] They all ate and were satisfied, and the leftover pieces filled seven wicker baskets. [38] Four thousand men had eaten, besides women and children. [39] Then Jesus sent the crowd away, got into the boat and went to Magdala.

MATTHEW 15:21-39

Read: Jesus puts his previous teaching into practice: he opts for the practice of good and justice rather than for tradition. He welcomes the excluded (foreigners, lame, disabled, blind, mute and many other sick), heals and feeds them: shares the bread with them.

Reflect: Who are the current excluded from our society? Do we welcome them and break bread with them as Jesus taught us?

Pray: Ask the Lord for the courage to share your life and your bread with everyone, especially with those excluded from society.

Act: Collaborate in an initiative of your parish or diocese in which solidarity with the excluded is promoted.

The Pharisees ask for a sign
(Mk 8:11; Lk 11:16; 12:54)

16¹ The Pharisees and Sadducees appeared. They wanted to put Jesus to the test and asked him for some heavenly sign.

² Jesus answered, "(When evening comes, you say, 'It will be a good day, for the sky is red.' ³ And in the morning you say, 'Stormy weather today, for the sky in the east is red.' If you know how to interpret the appearance of the sky, why can't you interpret the signs of the times?) ⁴ An evil and unbelieving people want a sign, but no sign will be given them except the sign of Jonah."

And Jesus left them and went away.

⁵ When the disciples went to the other side, they forgot to take bread. ⁶ Jesus said to them, "Pay attention and beware of the yeast of the Pharisees and Sadducees." ⁷ But the disciples said to one another, "He means the bread we did not bring."

⁸ Aware of this, Jesus said to them, "You of little faith! Why are you arguing among yourselves about having no bread? ⁹ Do you still not understand? Do you not remember the five loaves for the five thousand; and how many baskets you took up? ¹⁰ Or the seven loaves for the four thousand, and how many wicker baskets you took up?

¹¹ How can you not understand that I was not talking about bread when I said to you: Beware of the yeast of the Pharisees and Sadducees?" ¹² Then they understood that he was not talking about yeast for bread, but about the teaching of the Pharisees and Sadducees.

Peter's faith; Jesus' promises
(Mk 8:27; Lk 9:18; Jn 6:69)

¹³ After that, Jesus came to Caesarea Philippi. He asked his disciples, "Who do people say the Son of Man is?" ¹⁴ They said, "For some of them you are John the Baptist; for others Elijah, or Jeremiah, or one of the prophets."

¹⁵ Jesus asked them, "But you, who do you say I am?" ¹⁶ Peter answered, "You are the Messiah, the Son of the living God." ¹⁷ Jesus replied, "It is well for you, Simon Barjona, for it is not flesh or blood that has revealed this to you, but my Father in heaven.

¹⁸ And now I say to you: You are Peter, and on this Rock, I will build my Church; and never will the powers of death overcome it.

¹⁹I will give you the keys of the kingdom of heaven: whatever you bind on earth shall be bound in heaven, and whatever you unbind on earth shall be unbound in heaven."

²⁰Then he ordered his disciples not to tell anyone that he was the Christ.

Jesus predicts his death
(Mk 8:31; Lk 9:22; 12:9; 14:27)

²¹From that day, Jesus began to make it clear to his disciples that he must go to Jerusalem; that he would suffer many things from the Jewish authorities, the chief priests and the teachers of the law; and that he would be killed and be raised on the third day.

²²Then Peter took him aside and began to reproach him, "Never, Lord! No, this must never happen to you!" ²³But he turned and said to Peter, "Get behind me, Satan! You are an obstacle in my path. You are thinking not as God does, but as people do."

²⁴Then Jesus said to his disciples, "If you want to follow me, deny yourself. Take up your cross and follow me. ²⁵For whoever chooses to save his life will lose it, but the one who loses his life for my sake will find it. ²⁶What will one gain by winning the whole world, if he destroys his soul? Or what can a person give in exchange for his life?

²⁷Know that the Son of Man will come in the glory of his Father with the holy angels and he will reward each one according to his deeds. ²⁸Truly, I tell you, there are some standing here who will not taste death before they see the Son of Man coming in his kingdom."

MATTHEW 16:1-28

Read: Peter confesses Jesus as Messiah, but rejects the cross: self-giving, service, and donation for others.

Reflect: What does the expression suggest to you: "Whoever wants to follow me should deny himself, carry his cross and follow me"?

Pray: Ask for the grace to become a faithful disciple of Jesus.

Act: Take on the difficulties of your daily life as a call from the Lord to "carry your own cross and follow Him."

The transfiguration of Jesus
(Mk 9:2; Lk 9:28)

17 ¹Six days later, Jesus took with him Peter and James, and his brother John, and led them up a high mountain where they were alone. ²Jesus' appearance was changed before them: his face shone like the sun and his clothes became white as snow. ³Then suddenly, Moses and Elijah appeared to them, talking with Jesus.

⁴Peter spoke up and said to Jesus, "Master, it is good for us to be here. If you wish, I will make three tents: one for you, one for Moses and one for Elijah."

⁵Peter was still speaking, when a bright cloud covered them with its shadow; and a voice from the cloud said, "This is my Son, the Beloved, my Chosen One. Listen to him."

⁶On hearing the voice, the disciples fell to the ground full of fear. ⁷But Jesus came, touched them and said, "Stand up, do not be afraid!" ⁸When they raised their eyes, they no longer saw anyone except Jesus. ⁹And as they came down the mountain, Jesus commanded them not to tell anyone what they had seen, until the Son of Man be raised from the dead.

¹⁰The disciples asked him, "Why do the teachers of the law say that Elijah must come first?" ¹¹Jesus answered, "So it is: first comes Elijah; and he will restore all things. ¹²But I tell you, Elijah has already come and they did not recognize him; and they treated him as they pleased. And they will also make the Son of Man suffer."

¹³Then the disciples understood that Jesus was referring to John the Baptist.

Jesus heals an epileptic boy
(Mk 9:14; Lk 9:37)

¹⁴When they came to the crowd, a man approached Jesus, knelt before him and said, ¹⁵"Sir, have pity on my son who is an epileptic and suffers terribly. He has often fallen into the fire and at other times into the water. ¹⁶I brought him to your disciples, but they could not heal him."

¹⁷Jesus replied, "O you people, faithless and misled! How long must I be with you? How long must I put up with you? Bring him here to me." ¹⁸And Jesus commanded the evil spirit to leave the boy, and the boy was immediately healed.

¹⁹Later, the disciples approached Jesus and asked him privately, "Why

couldn't we drive out the spirit?" 20 Jesus said to them, "Because you have little faith. I say to you: if only you had faith the size of a mustard seed, you could tell that mountain to move from here to there and the mountain would obey. Nothing would be impossible for you. 21 (Only prayer and fasting can drive out this kind of spirit.)"

> **MATTHEW 17:1-21**
>
> **Read:** The transfiguration is a story of encouragement to the disciples who fear the way of the cross. It is an experience of encounter with the divine.
>
> **Reflect:** Religious experiences occur frequently in life. They cannot be described. Remember yours.
>
> **Pray:** Feel the presence of the divine at this time.
>
> **Act:** Contemplate the presence of God in everything that surrounds you.

22 While Jesus was in Galilee with the Twelve, he said to them, "The Son of Man will be delivered into the hands of men 23 and they will kill him. But he will rise on the third day." The Twelve were deeply grieved.

The temple tax

24 When they returned to Capernaum, the temple tax collectors came to Peter and asked him, "Does your master pay the temple tax?" 25 He answered, "Yes."

Peter then entered the house; and immediately, Jesus asked him, "What do you think, Simon? Who pays taxes or tribute to the kings of the earth: their sons or strangers and aliens?" 26 Peter replied, "Strangers and aliens." And Jesus told him, "The sons, then, are tax-free. 27 But, so as not to offend these people, go to the sea, throw in a hook and open the mouth of the first fish you catch. You will find a coin in it. Take the coin and give it to them for you and for me."

Who is the greatest? Scandals

18 1 At that time, the disciples came to Jesus and asked him, "Who is the greatest in the kingdom of heaven?"

2 Then Jesus called a little child, set the child in the midst of the disciples 3 and said, "I assure you that unless you change and become like

little children, you cannot enter the kingdom of heaven. [4]Whoever becomes humble like this child, is the greatest in the kingdom of heaven, [5]and whoever receives such a child in my name, receives me.

[6]If any of you should cause one of these little ones, who believe in me, to stumble and fall, it would be better for him to be thrown into the depths of the sea with a great millstone around his neck.

[7]Woe to the world, because of so many scandals! Scandals necessarily come, but woe to the one who causes a scandal.

[8]If your hand or foot causes you to sin, cut it off and throw it away. It is better for you to enter life without a hand or a foot than to be thrown into the eternal fire with two hands and two feet. [9]And if your eye causes you to sin, tear it out and throw it away. It is better for you to enter life with one eye than to be thrown into the fire of hell with two eyes.

[10]See that you do not despise any of these little ones; for I tell you, their angels in heaven continually see the face of my heavenly Father.

[11](The Son of Man has come to save the lost.)

[12]What do you think of this? If someone has a hundred sheep and one of them strays, won't he leave the ninety-nine on the hillside and go to look for the stray one? [13]And I tell you, when he finally finds it, he is more pleased about it than about the ninety-nine that did not go astray. [14]It is the same with your Father in heaven. Your Father in heaven doesn't want even one of these little ones to perish.

Living together in the Church
(Lk 17:3)

[15]If your brother has sinned against you, go and point out the fault to him when the two of you are alone; and if he listens to you, you have won back your brother. [16]If he doesn't listen to you, take with you one or two others, so that *the case may be decided by the evidence of two or three witnesses.* [17]And if he refuses to listen to them, tell it to the assembled Church. But if he does not listen to the Church, then regard him as a pagan or a tax collector.

[18]I say to you: whatever you bind on earth, heaven will keep bound; and whatever you unbind on earth, heaven will keep unbound.

[19]In like manner, I say to you, if on earth two of you agree in asking for anything, it will be granted to you by my heavenly Father; [20]for where two or three are gathered in my name, I am there among them."

²¹ Then Peter asked him, "Lord, how many times must I forgive the offenses of my brother or sister? Seven times?" ²² Jesus answered, "No, not seven times, but seventy-seven times.

The unmerciful servant

²³ This story throws light on the kingdom of Heaven: A king decided to settle accounts with his servants. ²⁴ Among the first of them was one who owed him ten thousand pieces of gold. ²⁵ As the man could not repay the debt, the king commanded that he be sold as a slave with his wife, his children, and all his goods, as repayment.

²⁶ The servant threw himself at the feet of the king and said, 'Give me time and I will pay you back everything.' ²⁷ The king took pity on him and not only set him free but even canceled his debt.

MATTHEW 17:22—18:27

Read: Matthew presents Jesus as the Son of God: he has no obligation to pay the Temple tax. However, he does it to avoid scandal.

Reflect: What does Jesus' attitude to the Law suggest to you?

Pray: Pray to the Lord so that at all times you may act with justice.

Act: Work according to what the Holy Spirit has inspired you in your prayer.

---

²⁸ When this servant left the king's presence, he met one of his fellow servants who owed him a hundred pieces of silver. He grabbed him by the throat and almost choked him, shouting, 'Pay me what you owe!' ²⁹ His fellow servant threw himself at his feet and begged him, 'Give me time and I will pay everything.' ³⁰ But the other did not agree and sent him to prison until he had paid all his debt.

³¹ Now the servants of the king saw what had happened. They were extremely upset and so they went and reported everything to their lord. ³² Then the lord summoned his servant and said, 'Wicked servant, I forgave you all that you owed me when you begged me to do so. ³³ Weren't you bound to have pity on your fellow servant, as I had pity on you?' ³⁴ The lord was now angry. He handed the wicked servant over to be punished until he had paid the whole debt."

³⁵ Jesus added, "So will my heavenly Father do with you unless you sincerely forgive your brothers and sisters."

MATTHEW 18:28-35

Read: The fourth great discourse of Jesus in the Gospel of Matthew. Jesus warns his disciples of the danger of arrogance and resentment, asks them to be humble and willing to forgive. Notice how the authority that Jesus gave to Peter in 16:19 now extends to all the disciples (18:18).

Reflect: What does the expression suggest to you: "Unless you change and become like little children, you cannot enter the kingdom of heaven"? How many times should we forgive?

Pray: Pray to God to give you a humble and willing heart to forgive forever. Pray the Our Father meditating in a special way the supplication: "forgive us our trespasses as we forgive those who trespass against us."

Act: Seek the forgiveness of someone you have offended.

Jesus speaks about divorce
(Mk 10:2; Mt 5:31; Lk 16:18)

19 ¹ When Jesus had finished these sayings, he left Galilee and arrived at the border of Judea, on the other side of the Jordan River. ² Large crowds followed him; and there, too, he healed their sick.

³ Some Pharisees approached him. They wanted to test him and asked, "Is a man allowed to divorce his wife for any reason he wants?"

⁴ Jesus replied, "Have you not read, that in the beginning, the Creator *made them male and female?* ⁵ And the Creator said: *Therefore, a man shall leave father and mother and be joined to his wife and the two shall become one body.* ⁶ So, they are no longer two, but one body. Let no one separate what God has joined."

⁷ They asked him, "Then why did Moses command us to write a bill of dismissal in order to divorce?" ⁸ Jesus replied, "Moses knew the hardness of your hearts, so he allowed you to divorce your wives, but it was not so in the beginning. ⁹ Therefore, I say to you: whoever divorces his wife, unless it be for immorality, and marries another, commits adultery."

[10] The disciples said, "If that is the condition of a married man, it is better not to marry." [11] Jesus said to them, "Not everybody can accept what you have just said, but only those who have received this gift. [12] There are eunuchs born so from their mother's womb. Some have been made that way by others. But there are some who have given up the possibility of marriage, for the sake of the kingdom of heaven. Let the one who can accept it, accept it."

Jesus and the children
(Mk 10:13; Lk 18:15)

[13] Then little children were brought to Jesus that he might lay his hands on them and pray for them. But the disciples scolded those who brought them. [14] Jesus then said, "Let the children be! Don't hinder them from coming to me; for the kingdom of heaven belongs to those who are humble like these children." [15] Jesus laid his hands on them and went away.

The rich young man
(Mk 10:17-22; Lk 18:18-23)

[16] It was then that a young man approached him and asked, "Master, what good work must I do to receive eternal life?" [17] Jesus answered, "Why do you ask me about what is good? One only is good. If you want to enter eternal life, keep the commandments." [18] The young man said, "Which commandments?" Jesus replied, "*Do not kill; do not commit adultery; do not steal; do not bear false witness*; [19] *honor your father and mother. And love your neighbor as yourself.*"

[20] The young man said to him, "I have kept all these commandments. What do I still lack?" [21] Jesus answered, "If you wish to be perfect, go, sell all that you possess and give the money to the poor; and you will have treasure in heaven. Then come back and follow me."

[22] On hearing this, the young man went away sad, for he was a man of great wealth.

[23] Jesus said to his disciples, "Truly I say to you: it will be hard for one who is rich to enter the kingdom of heaven. [24] Yes, believe me: it is easier for a camel to go through the eye of the needle than for the one who is rich to enter the kingdom of heaven."

[25] On hearing this, the disciples were astonished and said, "Who then can be saved?" [26] Jesus looked at them and answered, "For human beings it is impossible, but for God all things are possible."

²⁷ Then Peter spoke up and said, "You see, we have given up everything to follow you. What then will there be for us?"

²⁸ Jesus answered, "You who have followed me, listen to my words: on the Day of Renewal when the Son of Man sits on his throne in glory, you also will sit on twelve thrones to judge the twelve tribes of Israel. ²⁹ As for those who have left houses, brothers, sisters, father, mother, children or property, for my Name's sake, they will receive a hundredfold and be given eternal life. ³⁰ Many who are now first, will be last, and many who are now last, will be first.

MATTHEW 19:1-30

Read: Jesus reveals the depth of conjugal commitment and commitment to the kingdom (wealth can be an obstacle).

Reflect: What value does he give to marital commitment? What implications does celibacy have for the kingdom? Is wealth an obstacle to follow Jesus?

Pray: Ask the Lord for all the vocations of the Church, so that in their diversity they may manifest the richness of the kingdom.

Act: Live your vocation in constant thanksgiving. Do not cling to your goods, be charitable.

The workers in the vineyard

20 ¹ This story throws light on the kingdom of heaven: A landowner went out early in the morning to hire workers for his vineyard. ² He agreed to pay each worker the usual daily wage and sent them to his vineyard.

³ He went out again at about nine in the morning and, seeing others idle in the town square, ⁴ he said to them, 'You also go to my vineyard and I will pay you what is just.' ⁵ So they went.

The owner went out at midday, and again at three in the afternoon, and he made the same offer. ⁶ Again he went out at the last working hour—the eleventh—and he saw others standing around. So he said to them, 'Why do you stand idle the whole day?' ⁷ They answered, 'Because no one has hired us.' The master said, 'Go and work in my vineyard.'

⁸ When evening came, the owner of the vineyard said to his manager,

'Call the workers and pay them their wages, beginning with the last and ending with the first.' ⁹Those who had gone to work at the eleventh hour came up and were each given a silver coin. ¹⁰When it was the turn of the first, they thought they would receive more. ¹¹But they, too, received one silver coin. On receiving it, they began to grumble against the landowner.

¹²They said, 'These last, hardly worked an hour; yet you have treated them the same as us who have endured the heavy work of the day and the heat.' ¹³The owner said to one of them, 'Friend, I have not been unjust to you. Did we not agree on one silver coin per day? ¹⁴So, take what is yours and go. I want to give to the last the same as I give to you. ¹⁵Don't I have the right to do as I please with what is mine? Why are you envious when I am kind?'

¹⁶So will it be: the last will be first, the first will be last."

MATTHEW 20:1-16

Read: This parable is disconcerting, but it illustrates well the generous love of God that goes beyond the agreed upon. Like the landowner, God gives us His grace without taking into account our merits, but the acceptance of His call.

Reflect: What things does this parable suggest? Does your generosity remain in what is "just," or does the Spirit encourage you to go beyond the agreed upon?

Pray: Pray for God to help you have a generous, supportive heart, and free from any envy.

Act: Celebrate the accomplishments of someone close to you and see in it the generous presence of God.

Third prophecy of the passion
(Mk 10:32; Lk 18:31)

¹⁷When Jesus was going to Jerusalem, he took the twelve disciples aside and said to them, ¹⁸"See, we are going to Jerusalem. There, the Son of Man will be betrayed to the chief priests and the teachers of the law; and they will condemn him to death. ¹⁹They will hand him over to the foreigners, who will mock him, scourge him and crucify him. But he will be raised to life on the third day."

The mother of James and John asks for the first seats
(Mk 10:35)

²⁰ Then the mother of James and John came to Jesus with her sons, and she knelt down to ask a favor. ²¹ Jesus said to her, "What do you want?" And she answered, "Here you have my two sons. Grant that they may sit, one at your right hand and one at your left in your kingdom."

²² Jesus said to the brothers, "You do not know what you are asking. Can you drink the cup that I am about to drink?" They answered, "We can." ²³ Jesus replied, "You will indeed drink my cup, but to sit at my right or at my left is not for me to grant. That will be for those for whom my Father has prepared it."

²⁴ The other ten heard all this and were angry with the two brothers. ²⁵ Then Jesus called them to him and said, "You know that the rulers of nations behave like tyrants and the powerful oppress them. ²⁶ It shall not be so among you: whoever wants to be great in your community, let him minister to the community. ²⁷ And if you want to be the first of all, make yourself the servant of all. ²⁸ Be like the Son of Man who came not to be served, but to serve, and to give his life to redeem many."

²⁹ As they left Jericho, a great crowd followed them on the way. ³⁰ Two blind men were sitting by the roadside; and when they heard that Jesus was passing by, they began to call out, "Son of David, have mercy on us!" ³¹ The people told them to keep quiet. But they shouted even louder, "Lord, Son of David, have mercy on us!" ³² Jesus stopped, called out to them, and asked, "What do you want me to do for you?" ³³ They said, "Lord, open our eyes."

³⁴ Jesus was moved with compassion and touched their eyes. Immediately, they recovered their sight, and they began to follow Jesus.

MATTHEW 20:17-34

Read: Jesus predicts his passion for the third time. The disciples still do not understand that the kingdom that Jesus announces is love, solidarity, service, and dedication to others.

Reflect: What is Christian glory? For Mother Teresa of Calcutta, it consisted in sharing her life with the less fortunate ones. And for you?

> **Pray:** Ask the Lord Jesus for the grace of being able to follow his path of service and dedication to others.
>
> **Act:** Collaborate actively and discreetly (without bragging) in a charity action toward the poorest promoted by your parish or diocese.

Jesus enters Jerusalem
(Mk 11:1; Lk 19:28; Jn 12:12)

21 [1] When they drew near Jerusalem and arrived at Bethphage on the Mount of Olives, Jesus sent two of his disciples, [2] saying, "Go to the village ahead and there you will find a donkey tied up with its colt by her. Untie them and bring them to me. [3] If anyone says something to you, say that the Lord needs them and that he will send them back immediately."

[4] This happened in fulfillment of what the prophet said: [5] *Say to the daughter of Zion: See, your king comes to you in all simplicity riding on a donkey, a beast of burden, with its colt.*

[6] The disciples went, as Jesus had instructed them [7] and they brought the donkey with its colt. Then they threw their cloaks on its back, and Jesus sat on them.

[8] Many people also spread their cloaks on the road, while others cut leafy branches from the trees and spread them on the road. [9] The people who walked ahead of Jesus and those who followed him began to shout, "*Hosanna to the Son of David! Blessed is he who comes in the name of the Lord! Hosanna in the highest!*"

[10] When Jesus entered Jerusalem, the whole city was disturbed. The people asked, "Who is this man?" [11] And the crowd answered, "This is the Prophet Jesus from Nazareth of Galilee."

Jesus expels the dealers
(Mk 11:11; Lk 13:35; Jn 2:14)

[12] Jesus went into the temple and drove out all who were buying and selling in the temple area. He overturned the tables of the moneychangers and the stools of those who sold pigeons. [13] And he said to them, "*It is written: My house shall be called a house of prayer.* But you have turned it *into a den of thieves.*"

¹⁴ The blind and the lame came to him in the temple and Jesus healed them.

¹⁵ The chief priests and the teachers of the law saw the wonderful things that Jesus did and the children shouting in the temple area, "Hosanna to the Son of David!" ¹⁶ They became angry and said to Jesus, "Do you hear what they say?" Jesus answered them, "Yes. But have you never read this text: *From the mouths of children and infants you have perfect praise?*"

¹⁷ So leaving them, he went out of the city and came to Bethany, where he spent the night.

MATTHEW 21:1-17

Read: Messianic entrance of Jesus in Jerusalem. People acclaim him. Jesus expels the sellers from the Temple.

Reflect: Recognizing and confessing Jesus as Messiah demands the gift of faith. What would it imply in your daily life to recognize Jesus as Messiah?

Pray: Confess Jesus as Messiah, as Christ, and ask him to help you live as a Christian.

Act: Do what the Spirit inspired you in your prayer.

Jesus curses the fig tree
(Mk 11:12; Lk 13:6)

¹⁸ While returning to the city early in the morning, Jesus felt hungry. ¹⁹ He noticed a fig tree by the road, went up to it and found nothing on it but leaves. So he said to the tree, "Never again bear fruit!" And immediately, the fig tree withered.

²⁰ When the disciples saw this, they were astonished and said, "How did the fig tree suddenly dry up?" ²¹ Jesus said, "Truly, I say to you: if you had faith and did not doubt, not only could you do what I did to the fig tree, but you could even say to that mountain, 'Go and throw yourself into the sea!' and it would be done. ²² Whatever you ask for in prayer full of faith, you will receive."

Jesus' response to the authorities
(Mk 11:27; Lk 20:1)

23 Jesus had entered the temple and was teaching, when the chief priests, the teachers of the law and the Jewish authorities came to him and asked, "What authority have you to act like this? Who gave you the authority to do all this?"

24 Jesus answered them, "I will also ask you one question. If you answer me, then I will also tell you by what authority I do these things." 25 Where did John's baptism come from? From heaven or from people?"

They discussed this among themselves saying, "If we say, 'From heaven,' he will say, 'Then why did you not believe him?' 26 And if we say, 'The baptism of John was merely something human,' we've got to beware of the people, for all consider John to be a prophet." 27 So they answered Jesus, "We do not know."

And Jesus said to them, "Neither will I tell you by what authority I do these things."

MATTHEW 21:18-27

Read: The story about "the dry fig tree" is strange: Jesus acts so capriciously. It was probably a parable that alluded to the people of Israel who rejected the message of Jesus, and that was why it was sterile.

Reflect: Even though this story may have referred to the people of Israel, its message also affects us. Christians must make the fruits of Jesus' message manifest in the world.

Pray: In prayer, ask the Lord to help you discern if your actions correspond to what Jesus expects from his followers.

Act: Examine your conscience, give thanks to the Lord if your actions have manifested the presence of his kingdom, or ask that be manifested the next day.

The parable of the two sons

28 Jesus went on to say, "What do you think of this? A man had two sons. He went to the first and said to him, 'Son, go and work today in my vineyard.' 29 And the son answered, 'I don't want to.' But later he thought better of it and went. 30 Then the father went to his other son and

said the same thing to him. This son replied, 'I will go, sir,' but he did not go.

³¹ Which of the two did what the father wanted?" They answered, "The first." And Jesus said to them, "Truly, I say to you: the publicans and the prostitutes are ahead of you on the way to the kingdom of heaven. ³² For John came to show you the way of goodness and you did not believe him, but the publicans and the prostitutes did. You were witnesses of this, but you neither repented nor believed him.

The parable of the tenants
(Mk 12:1; Lk 20:9)

³³ Listen to another example: There was a landowner who planted a vineyard. He put a fence around it, dug a hole for the winepress, built a watchtower, leased the vineyard to tenants and then, went to a distant country. ³⁴ When harvest time came, the landowner sent his servants to the tenants to collect his share of the harvest. ³⁵ But the tenants seized his servants, beat one, killed another, and stoned a third.

³⁶ Again, the owner sent more servants; but they were treated in the same way.

³⁷ Finally, he sent his son, thinking, 'They will respect my son.' ³⁸ But when the tenants saw the son, they thought, 'This is the one who is to inherit the vineyard. Let us kill him and his inheritance will be ours.' ³⁹ So they seized him, threw him out of the vineyard and killed him.

⁴⁰ Now, what will the owner of the vineyard do with the tenants when he comes?" ⁴¹ They said to him, "He will bring those evil men to an evil end and lease the vineyard to others, who will pay him in due time."

⁴² And Jesus replied, "Have you never read what the Scriptures say? *The stone, which the builders rejected, has become the cornerstone. This was the Lord's doing and we marvel at it.* ⁴³ Therefore I say to you: the kingdom of heaven will be taken from you and given to a people who will produce its fruit.

⁴⁴ (Whoever falls on this stone, he will be broken to pieces; on whomsoever this stone falls, he will be ground to dust.)"

⁴⁵ When the chief priests and the Pharisees heard these parables, they realized that Jesus was referring to them. ⁴⁶ They would have arrested him, but they were afraid of the crowd who regarded him as a prophet.

The wedding feast
(Lk 14:15)

22 [1] Jesus continued speaking to them in parables:

[2] "This story throws light on the kingdom of heaven: A king gave a wedding banquet for his son. [3] He sent his servants to call the invited guests to the banquet, but the guests refused to come.

[4] Again, he sent other servants, instructing them to say to the invited guests, 'I have prepared a banquet, slaughtered my fattened calves and other animals, and now, everything is ready. Come to the wedding!' [5] But they paid no attention and went away, some to their farms and some to their work. [6] Others seized the servants of the king, insulted them and killed them.

[7] The king was furious. He sent his troops to destroy those murderers and burn their city. [8] Then he said to his servants, 'The wedding banquet is prepared, but the invited guests were not worthy. [9] Go instead to the main streets and invite everyone you find to the wedding feast.'

[10] The servants went out into the streets and gathered all they found, good and bad alike, so that the hall was filled with guests.

[11] The king came in to see the wedding guests, and he noticed a man not wearing a wedding garment. [12] So he said to him, 'Friend, how did you get in without the wedding clothes?' But the man remained silent. [13] So the king said to his servants, 'Bind his hands and feet and throw him into the outer darkness, where there will be weeping and gnashing of teeth.'

[14] For many are called, but few are chosen."

MATTHEW 21:28–22:14

Read: Jesus questions the actions of the religious leaders of his time: instead of preparing the people to receive the Messiah, they do the opposite. That is why his vineyard (his people) will be given to those who are ready to welcome it and make it produce fruit.

Reflect: Can you see yourself reflected in any of the parables? How do these parables affect your life?

Pray: Pray to the Lord for the leaders of the Church. May they be able to prepare the people to accept the message of Jesus and to produce in the world the fruits that he expects.

Act: Pray this week for the leaders of the Church.

Paying taxes to Caesar
(Mk 12:13; Lk 20:20)

¹⁵ The Pharisees went away, considering how they could trap Jesus by his own words. ¹⁶ They sent to him their disciples, along with members of Herod's party, saying, "Master, we know that you are an honest man and truly teach God's way. You are not influenced by others, nor are you afraid of anyone. ¹⁷ So tell us what you think: is it against the law to pay taxes to Caesar or not?"

¹⁸ But Jesus understood their evil intentions and said to them, "Hypocrites, why are you trying to trap me? ¹⁹ Show me the coin with which you pay taxes."

They showed him a silver coin ²⁰ and Jesus said to them, "Whose head is this and whose name?" ²¹ They answered, "Caesar's." Then Jesus replied, "So give to Caesar what is Caesar's, and give to God what is God's."

²² Astonished by his answer, they left him and went away.

The resurrection of the dead
(Mk 12:18; Lk 20:27)

²³ That same day, some of the Sadducees came to Jesus. Since they claim that there is no resurrection, they questioned him in this way: ²⁴ "Master, Moses said that if a man dies without any children, his brother must take the wife and have a child, who will be considered the child of the deceased man. ²⁵ Now, there were seven brothers. The first married a woman, but he died; since he had no children, he left his wife to his brother. ²⁶ The same thing happened to the second brother, and to the third, until the seventh. ²⁷ Then, last of all, the woman died. ²⁸ Now, in the resurrection of the dead, to which of the seven will she be wife, for they all had her as a wife?"

²⁹ Jesus answered, "You are totally wrong because you understand neither the Scriptures nor the power of God. ³⁰ First of all, in the resurrection of the dead, neither men nor women will marry, but they will be like the

angels in heaven. [31] As for the resurrection of the dead, have you never reflected on what God said to you: [32] *I am the God of Abraham, the God of Isaac, and the God of Jacob?* He is God, not of the dead but of the living."

[33] The people who heard him were astonished at his teaching.

[34] When the Pharisees heard how Jesus had silenced the Sadducees, they assembled together. [35] One of them, a lawyer, questioned him to test him, [36] "Teacher, which commandment of the law is the greatest?"

[37] Jesus answered, "*You shall love the Lord your God with all your heart, with all your soul, and with all your mind.* [38] This is the first and the most important of the commandments. [39] The second is like it: *You shall love your neighbor as yourself.* [40] The whole law and the prophets are founded on these two commandments."

The Messiah, Son of God
(Mk 12:35; Lk 20:41)

[41] While the Pharisees were assembled, Jesus asked them, [42] "What do you think of the Messiah? Whose son is he?" They answered, "David's."

[43] Jesus then asked them, "Why did David, inspired by God, call the Messiah Lord? For David says in a psalm: [44] *The Lord said to my Lord: Sit at my right hand until I put your enemies under your feet.* [45] If David calls him Lord, how can he be his son?"

[46] No one could answer him, not even a word. From that day on, no one dared question him anymore.

MATTHEW 22:15-46

Read: Matthew develops here four controversies that the Jewish people lived at that time: Is it appropriate to pay tribute to the Romans? Can we wait for the resurrection of the dead? What is the most important precept of the Law? And what does it mean that the Messiah will be David's son?

Reflect: Do such controversies make sense today? Should the Church not interfere in matters of the State? In your daily life, are you aware that life is fragile, but does your faith wait for the resurrection of the dead and eternal life? What does it imply in your day-to-day life that "love" is the most important precept? Describe the messianism you expect from Jesus.

Pray: Pray to the Lord to help you manifest in your daily life that love of God and neighbor is the most important value of your faith. Also, give thanks for the gift of resurrection and eternal life.

Act: Be aware of all the important actions of your daily life and assess whether you are moved by love for God and your neighbor.

Do not imitate the teachers of the law
(Lk 20:45; Mk 12:38)

23 [1] Then Jesus said to the crowds and to his disciples,

[2] "The teachers of the law and the Pharisees have sat down on the chair of Moses. [3] So you shall do and observe all they say; but do not do as they do, [4] for they do not do what they say. They tie up heavy burdens and load them on the shoulders of the people, but they do not even lift a finger to move them. [5] They do everything in order to be seen by people: they wear very wide bands of the law around their foreheads and robes with large tassels. [6] They enjoy the first places at feasts and the best seats in the synagogues, [7] and they like being greeted in the marketplace and being called 'Master' by the people.

[8] But you, do not let yourselves be called Master, because you have only one Master, and all of you are brothers and sisters. [9] Neither should you call anyone on earth Father because you have only one Father, he who is in heaven. [10] Nor should you be called Leader, because Christ is the only Leader for you. [11] Let the greatest among you be the servant of all. [12] For whoever makes himself great shall be humbled, and whoever humbles himself shall be made great.

Seven woes for the Pharisees
(Lk 11:39)

[13] But woe to you, teachers of the law and Pharisees, you hypocrites! You shut the door to the kingdom of heaven in people's faces. You, yourselves, do not enter it, nor do you allow others to do so.

[14] Woe to you, scribes and Pharisees, you hypocrites! You devour

widows' property; and as a show, you pray long prayers! Therefore, you shall receive greater condemnation. [15] Woe to you, teachers of the law and Pharisees, you hypocrites! You travel by sea and land to make a single convert; yet, once he is converted, you make him twice as fit for hell as yourselves!

[16] Woe to you, blind guides! You say: To swear by the temple is not binding, but to swear by the gold of the temple is binding. [17] Foolish men! Blind men! Which is of more worth: the gold in the temple, or the temple, which makes the gold a sacred treasure? You say: [18] To swear by the altar is not binding, but to swear by the offering on the altar is binding. [19] How blind you are! Which is of more value: the offering on the altar, or the altar, which makes the offering sacred? [20] Whoever swears by the altar, is swearing by the altar and by everything on it. [21] Whoever swears by the temple, is swearing by the temple and by God, who dwells in the temple. [22] Whoever swears by heaven, is swearing by the throne of God and by him, who is seated on it.

[23] Woe to you, teachers of the law and Pharisees, you hypocrites! You do not forget the mint, anise and cumin seeds when you demand the tenth of everything; but then, you forget what is most fundamental in the law: justice, mercy, and faith! You should have done these things without neglecting the others. [24] Blind guides! You strain out a mosquito but swallow a camel.

[25] Woe to you, teachers of the law and Pharisees, you hypocrites! You fill the plate and the cup with theft and violence and then pronounce a blessing over them. [26] Blind Pharisee! Purify the inside first then the outside, too, will be purified.

[27] Woe to you, teachers of the law and Pharisees, you hypocrites! You are like whitewashed tombs, beautiful in appearance; but inside there are only dead bones and uncleanness. [28] In the same way, you appear religious to others, but you are full of hypocrisy and wickedness within.

[29] Woe to you, teachers of the law and Pharisees, you hypocrites! You build tombs for the prophets and decorate the monuments of the righteous. [30] You say: Had we lived in the time of our ancestors, we would not have joined them in shedding the blood of the prophets. [31] So, you, yourselves, confess to be the descendants of those who murdered the prophets. [32] And now, finish off what your ancestors began!

[33] Serpents, race of vipers! How can you escape condemnation to hell?

34 Therefore, indeed, I send prophets, wise men and teachers to you; but some you will murder and crucify; some you will flog in your synagogues; some you will drive from one city to the next.

35 Because of this, you will be accountable for all the innocent blood that has been shed on the earth, from the blood of upright Abel to the blood of Zechariah, son of Barachiah, whom you murdered between the altar and the Sanctuary. 36 Truly I say to you: the present generation will pay for all this.

37 Jerusalem, Jerusalem! You murder the prophets and stone those sent to you by God. How often would I have gathered your children together, just as a hen gathers her chicks under her wings; but you refused! 38 Look! Your house shall be left to you, deserted! 39 I tell you, that you will no longer see me until you say: *Blessed is he who comes in the name of the Lord!*

MATTHEW 23:1-39

Read: Jesus makes a harsh criticism of the Pharisees and lawyers who claim to be "teachers of the Law" and yet live as if they did not know it. Jesus wants his disciples to be coherent with what they preach.

Reflect: What things does the following expression suggest: "You do and do what they (the Pharisees and the lawyers) say, but do not imitate them; because they say and do not"?

Pray: Pray to the Lord to give us the grace of a coherent life, without masks or hypocrisy.

Act: Write down the concrete things you do as an act of faith. Check if they manifest the centrality of Jesus' message or if they only remain in appearances.

The ruin of Jerusalem and the end of the world
(Mk 13; Lk 21; 17:23; 12:36)

24 1 Jesus left the temple and as he was walking away, his disciples came to him and pointed out to him the imposing temple buildings. 2 But he said, "You see all this? Truly I say to you: not one stone will be left upon another here. All will be torn down."

3 Later, when Jesus was sitting on the Mount of Olives, the disciples

approached him privately and asked, "Tell us when this will take place. What sign will be given us of your coming, and the end of the world?"

⁴Jesus answered, "Be on your guard; and let no one mislead you. ⁵Many will come in my name, saying: 'I am the Messiah,' and they will mislead many people. ⁶You will hear about wars and rumors of wars; but do not be troubled, for these things must happen; but the end is still to come. ⁷Nations will fight one another and kingdoms oppose one another. There will be famine and earthquakes in different places; ⁸but all this is only the beginning, the first pains of childbirth.

⁹Then, they will arrest you; they will torture and kill you. All nations will hate you, for you bear my name. ¹⁰In those days, many will be led into sin; they will betray and hate one another. ¹¹False prophets will appear and mislead many; ¹²and because of such great wickedness, love in many people will grow cold. ¹³But the one who holds out to the end will be saved. ¹⁴The Good News of the kingdom will be proclaimed throughout the world, to all the nations, a Testament to all peoples. Then will the end come.

MATTHEW 24:1-14

Read: Beginning of the last great discourse of Jesus in the Gospel of Matthew: the eschatological discourse (about the last days). Jesus leaves behind the temple area (predicts its destruction) and on the Mount of Olives answers the question of his disciples about the end of the world.

Reflect: Do you understand the answers of Jesus to his disciples? How do you think the end of the world will be? What do you think about the end of your time in the world?

Pray: Pray that the Good News of Jesus may manifest itself more and more in your life, in your family, and in your society. The important thing is not to know the date of the end of the world, but to be prepared for it at all times.

Act: Make a list of the most important actions you would like to take on the last day of your life. Try to make them this day.

---

¹⁵When you see what the prophet Daniel spoke about, *the idol of the invader set up in the temple* (let the reader understand!), ¹⁶then let those in Judea flee to the mountains.

¹⁷ If you are on the housetop, do not come down to take anything with you. ¹⁸ If you are in the field, do not turn back to fetch your coat. ¹⁹ How hard it will be for pregnant women and for mothers with babies at the breast! ²⁰ Pray that you don't have to flee in winter, or on a Sabbath; ²¹ for there will be great tribulation, such as was never known from the beginning of the world until now and is never to be known again. ²² And if that time were not to be shortened, no one would survive. But God will shorten those days for the sake of his chosen ones. ²³ Then, if anyone says to you, 'Look! The Messiah is here! He is there!', do not believe it. ²⁴ For false Messiahs and false prophets will appear and perform signs and wonders so great that they would deceive even God's chosen people if that were possible. ²⁵ See, I have told you everything ahead of time.

²⁶ So, if anyone tells you, 'He is in the desert,' do not go. If they say, 'He is in the inner rooms,' do not believe it. ²⁷ For the coming of the Son of Man will be like lightning, which flashes from the east even to the west. ²⁸ Wherever the body is, the vultures will gather.

The coming of the Son of Man
(Mk 13:28; Lk 17:20)

²⁹ And later, after that distress, the sun will grow dark, the moon will not give its light, the stars will fall from the skies, and the whole universe will be shaken. ³⁰ Then the sign of the Son of Man will appear in heaven. As all the nations of the earth beat their breasts, *they will see the Son of Man coming in the clouds of heaven* with divine power and great glory. ³¹ He will send his angels to sound the trumpet; and they will gather his chosen ones from the four winds, from one end of the earth to the other.

MATTHEW 24:15-31

Read: Jesus' discourse on the last days continues. Matthew combines events of his time with the teachings of Jesus. The cosmic commotions with bleak images indicate that the final judgment may come suddenly and unexpectedly to everyone, so we must be prepared.

Reflect: Do you think we live in apocalyptic times? Are things worse than before? Remember that there have always been great tragedies in the world. Should we interpret this text to the letter? What does all this suggest?

> **Pray:** Ask the Lord to comfort those who suffer due to natural catastrophes or human unreason like wars or genocides. Also, ask for the grace of having words and gestures that are appropriate for such circumstances.
>
> **Act:** Find out about the work done by institutions that are dedicated to alleviating the suffering caused by natural disasters, wars or genocides. Collaborate, to the extent of your possibilities, with any of them.

³²Learn a lesson from the fig tree: when its branches grow tender and its leaves begin to sprout, you know that summer is near. ³³In the same way, when you see all these things, know that the time is near, even at the door. ³⁴Truly I say to you, this generation will not pass away until all these things have happened. ³⁵Heaven and earth will pass away, but my words will not pass away.

³⁶But, as for that Day and that Hour, no one knows when it will come, not even the angels of God, nor the Son, but only the Father.

³⁷At the coming of the Son of Man, it will be just as it was in the time of Noah. ³⁸In those days before the Flood, people were eating and drinking and marrying, until that day when Noah went into the ark. ³⁹Yet, they did not know what would happen, until the flood came and swept them away. So will it be at the coming of the Son of Man: ⁴⁰of two men in the field, one will be taken and the other left; ⁴¹of two women grinding wheat together at the mill, one will be taken and the other left.

Be on the alert

⁴²Stay awake then, for you do not know on what day your Lord will come. ⁴³Obviously, if the owner of the house knew at what time the thief was coming, he would certainly stay up and not allow his house to be broken into. ⁴⁴So be alert, for the Son of Man will come at the hour you least expect.

⁴⁵Imagine a faithful and prudent servant, whom his master has put in charge of his household, to give them food at the proper time. ⁴⁶Fortunate, indeed, is that servant, whom his master will find at work when he comes. ⁴⁷Truly, I say to you, his lord will entrust him with everything he has.

⁴⁸Not so with the bad servant who thinks, 'My master is delayed.'

⁴⁹ And he begins to ill-treat his fellow servants while eating and drinking with drunkards. ⁵⁰ But his master will come on the day he does not know and at the hour he least expects. ⁵¹ He will punish that servant severely and place him with the hypocrites. There will be weeping and gnashing of teeth.

The ten bridesmaids
(Mk 13:35; Lk 13:25)

25 ¹ This story throws light on what will happen in the kingdom of heaven: Ten bridesmaids went out with their lamps to meet the bridegroom. ² Five of them were foolish, and five were sensible.

³ The careless bridesmaids took their lamps as they were and did not take extra oil. ⁴ But those who were sensible took flasks of oil with their lamps. ⁵ As the bridegroom delayed, they all grew drowsy and fell asleep.

⁶ But at midnight, a cry rang out, 'The bridegroom is here, come out and meet him!' ⁷ All the maidens woke up at once and trimmed their lamps. ⁸ Then the foolish ones said to the sensible ones, 'Give us some oil for our lamps are going out.' ⁹ The sensible ones answered, 'There may not be enough for us and for you. You had better go to those who sell and buy some for yourselves.'

¹⁰ When the bridegroom came, the foolish maidens were out buying oil, but those who were ready went with him into the wedding feast and the doors were shut.

¹¹ Later the other bridesmaids arrived and called out, 'Lord, Lord, open to us!' ¹² But he answered, 'Truly I do not know you.'

¹³ So stay awake, for you do not know the day nor the hour.

The parable of the talents
(Lk 19:12; Mk 4:25; 13:34)

¹⁴ Imagine someone who, before going abroad, summoned his servants to entrust his property to them. ¹⁵ He gave five talents of silver to one servant, two talents, to another servant and one talent to a third, to each, according to his ability; and he went away. ¹⁶ He who received five talents went at once to do business with the talents and gained another five. ¹⁷ The one who received two talents did the same and gained another two. ¹⁸ But the one who received one talent dug a hole in the ground and hid his master's money.

¹⁹ After a long time, the master of those servants returned and asked for a reckoning. ²⁰ The one who had received five talents came with another five talents, saying, 'Lord, you entrusted me with five talents, but see, I have gained five more.' ²¹ The master answered, 'Well done, good and faithful servant since you have been faithful in a few things, I will entrust you in charge of many things. Come and share the joy of your master.'

²² Then the one who had received two talents came and said, 'Lord, you entrusted me with two talents; with them, I have gained two more.' ²³ The master said, 'Well done, good and faithful servant since you have been faithful in little things, I will entrust you in charge of many things. Come and share the joy of your master.'

²⁴ Finally, the one who had received one talent came and said, 'Master, I know that you are a hard man. You reap what you have not sown and gather what you have not scattered. ²⁵ I was afraid, so I hid your money in the ground. Here, take what is yours!' ²⁶ But his master replied, 'Wicked and worthless servant, you know that I reap where I have not sown and gather where I have not scattered. ²⁷ You should have deposited my money in the bank and given it back to me with interest on my return.

²⁸ Therefore, take the talent from him and give it to the one who has ten. ²⁹ For to all those who have, more will be given, and they will have an abundance; but from those who are unproductive, even what they have will be taken from them. ³⁰ As for that useless servant, throw him out into outer darkness where there will be weeping and gnashing of teeth.'

MATTHEW 24:32—25:30

Read: Jesus' discourse on the last days continues. Through parables, Jesus exhorts his followers to be attentive, vigilant, prepared for his second coming.

Reflect: What things do these parables suggest for your daily life? Do you consider yourself ready for the coming of the Lord? Do you invest well the gifts you have (your talents) to make of this a better world?

Pray: In prayer, examine your actions, especially those you consider most important. Are you prepared for the final encounter with the Lord? Or, on the contrary, do they numb you and take you away from him?

Act: Invest your time and your talents in those things that will help you in your final encounter with the Lord.

The last judgment
(Lk 9:26)

[31] When the Son of Man comes in his glory with all his angels, he will sit on the throne of his glory. [32] All the nations will be brought before him; and as a shepherd separates the sheep from the goats, [33] so will he do with them, placing the sheep on his right hand and the goats on his left.

[34] The king will say to those on his right, 'Come, blessed of my Father! Take possession of the kingdom prepared for you from the beginning of the world. [35] For I was hungry and you fed me. I was thirsty and you gave me something to drink. [36] I was a stranger and you welcomed me into your home. I was naked and you clothed me. I was sick and you visited me. I was in prison and you came to see me.'

[37] Then the righteous will ask him, 'Lord, when did we see you hungry and give you food; thirsty and give you something to drink; [38] or a stranger and welcome you; or naked and clothe you? [39] When did we see you sick, or in prison, and go to see you?' [40] The king will answer, 'Truly, I say to you: just as you did it for one of the least of these brothers or sisters of mine, you did it to me.'

[41] Then he will say to those on his left, 'Go, cursed people, out of my sight into the eternal fire, which has been prepared for the devil and his angels! [42] For I was hungry and you did not give me anything to eat; I was thirsty and you gave me nothing to drink; [43] I was a stranger and you did not welcome me into your house; I was naked and you did not clothe me; I was sick, and in prison, and you did not visit me.'

[44] They, too, will ask, 'Lord, when did we see you hungry, thirsty, naked or a stranger, sick or in prison, and did not help you?' [45] The king will answer them, 'Truly I say to you: just as you did not do it for one of the least of these, you did not do it for me.'

[46] And these will go into eternal punishment; but the just, to eternal life."

> **MATTHEW 25:31-46**
>
> **Read:** End of Jesus' discourse on the last days. Jesus offers the ultimate criterion of Christian salvation: love, solidarity toward the fallen and abandoned brother and sister.
>
> **Reflect:** What does this criterion suggest? Is it not too mundane, that it erodes religious obligations? If the important thing is to do good, why believe in Jesus? Why be Christians?
>
> **Pray:** Ask the Lord so that, with the strength of the Holy Spirit, you may recognize the face of God in the face of the needy, and can worship Him by raising the fallen dignity of those brothers and sisters.
>
> **Act:** Visit a relative or neighbor in need and offer your support for free.

26 ¹When Jesus had finished all he wanted to say, he told his disciples, ²"You know that in two days' time it will be the Passover, and the Son of Man will be handed over to be crucified."

³Then the chief priests and the elders of the people gathered together at the palace of the High Priest, whose name was Caiaphas, ⁴and they agreed to arrest Jesus and to kill him. ⁵But they said, "Not during the feast, lest there be an uprising among the people."

The anointing at Bethany
(Jn 12; Mk 14:9)

⁶While Jesus was in Bethany, in the house of Simon the leper, ⁷a woman came up to him, carrying an alabaster jar of expensive perfume. She poured it on Jesus' head as he was at table. ⁸Seeing this, the disciples became indignant and said, "What a useless waste! ⁹The perfume could have been sold for a large sum and the money given to the poor."

¹⁰Jesus was aware of this, and said to them, "Why are you troubling this woman? What she has done for me is indeed a good work. ¹¹You have the poor with you always; but me, you will not have always. ¹²When she anointed my body with perfume, she was preparing me for my burial. ¹³Truly I say to you: wherever the gospel is proclaimed, all over the world, what she has done will be told in memory of her."

¹⁴ Then one of the Twelve, who was called Judas Iscariot, went to the chief priests and said, ¹⁵ "How much will you give me if I hand him over to you?" They promised to give him thirty pieces of silver; ¹⁶ and from then on, he kept looking for the best way to hand Jesus over to them.

MATTHEW 26:1-16

Read: Beginning of Jesus' passion. The religious authorities of Jerusalem decide to kill him. Jesus is aware that his death is near. Judas betrays the Master.

Reflect: What is bothering you the most about Jesus' message? If Jesus foresees his death near, why do you think he does not run away from it?

Pray: Pray to the Lord so that in your daily life you may not abandon your commitments for a better world facing the problems and difficulties of life.

Act: Leave yourself in the hands of God. Whenever you remember the problem that bothers you and that you do not know how to overcome it, close your eyes and say inwardly: "In your hands, Lord, I commend my spirit."

The last supper
(Mk 14:12; Lk 22:7; Jn 13:1)

¹⁷ On the first day of the Festival of Unleavened Bread, the disciples came to Jesus and said to him, "Where do you want us to prepare the Passover meal for you?" ¹⁸ Jesus answered, "Go into the city, to the house of a certain man, and tell him, 'The Master says: My hour is near and I will celebrate the Passover with my disciples in your house.'"

¹⁹ The disciples did as Jesus had ordered and prepared the Passover meal.

²⁰ When it was evening, Jesus sat at table with the Twelve. ²¹ While they were eating, Jesus said, "Truly, I say to you: one of you will betray me." ²² They were deeply distressed, and they asked him, one after the other, "You do not mean me, do you, Lord?"

²³ He answered, *The one who dips his bread with me will betray me.* ²⁴ The Son of Man is going as the Scriptures say he will. But alas for that one who betrays the Son of Man: better for him not to have been born."

²⁵ Judas, the one who would betray him, also asked, "You do not mean me, Master, do you?" Jesus replied, "You have said it."

²⁶ While they were eating, Jesus took bread, said a blessing and broke it, and gave it to his disciples, saying, "Take and eat: this is my body." ²⁷ Then he took a cup, and gave thanks, and passed it to them, saying, "Drink this, all of you, ²⁸ for this is my blood, the blood of the Covenant, which is poured out for many for the forgiveness of sins. ²⁹ Yes, I say to you: From now on I will not taste the fruit of the vine, until that day when I drink new wine with you in my Father's kingdom."

³⁰ After singing psalms of praise, they went out to the Mount of Olives. ³¹ Then Jesus said to them, "You will falter tonight because of me and all of you will fall. For Scripture says: *I will strike the shepherd and the sheep will be scattered.* ³² But after my resurrection, I will go before you to Galilee."

³³ Peter responded, "Even though all stumble and fall, I will never fall away!" ³⁴ Jesus replied, "Truly I say to you: this very night, before the cock crows, you will deny me three times." ³⁵ Peter said, "Even if I must die with you, I will never deny you!" And all the disciples said the same thing.

MATTHEW 26:17-35

Read: Jesus celebrates his last supper with his family (his disciples) and institutes the Eucharist. Discover Judas as a traitor and announces the abandonment of all of them.

Reflect: What does the celebration of the Eucharist mean to you? Are you willing to share your life, to be Eucharist, with others for the construction of a better world, the kingdom of God?

Pray: As a family, pray that Christians will be the leaven of a better world, in words, but above all, with our way of living.

Act: Manifest today your faith in Jesus Christ not with words (forbidden to make speeches), but with concrete actions and gestures.

Gethsemane
(Mk 14:32; Lk 22:39)

36 Jesus came with them to a place called Gethsemane and he said to his disciples, "Sit here while I go over there to pray."

37 He took Peter and the two sons of Zebedee with him and he began to be overwhelmed by anguish and distress. 38 And he said to them, "My soul is full of sorrow, even to death. Remain here and stay awake with me."

39 He went a little farther and fell to the ground, with his face touching the earth, and prayed, "Father, if it is possible, take this cup away from me. Yet, not what I will, but what you will." 40 He went back to his disciples and found them asleep; and he said to Peter, "Could you not stay awake with me for one hour? 41 Stay awake and pray, so that you may not fall into temptation. The spirit indeed is willing, but the flesh is weak."

42 He went away again and prayed, "Father, if this cup cannot be taken away from me without my drinking it, your will must be done." 43 When he came back to his disciples, he again found them asleep, for they could not keep their eyes open. 44 So leaving them again, Jesus went to pray for the third time, saying the same words.

45 Then he came back to his disciples and said to them, "You can sleep on now and take your rest! The hour has come, and the Son of Man will be handed over to sinners. 46 Get up, let us go! See, the betrayer is here!"

Jesus arrested

47 Jesus was still speaking when Judas, one of the Twelve, arrived. With him was a crowd armed with swords and clubs who had been sent by the chief priests and the elders of the people. 48 The traitor had given them a sign: "The one I kiss, he is the man; arrest him!" 49 Judas went directly to Jesus and said, "Greetings, Rabbi!" and he kissed him. 50 Jesus said to him, "Friend, do what you came to do." Then they laid hands on Jesus and arrested him.

51 One of those who was with Jesus drew his sword and struck at the servant of the High Priest cutting off his ear. 52 Then, Jesus said to him, "Put your sword back in its place! For all who take hold of the sword will die by the sword. 53 Do you not know that I could call on my Father, and he would at once send me more than twelve legions of angels? 54 If Scripture says that these things must be, should Scripture not be fulfilled?"

⁵⁵ At that hour, Jesus said to the crowd, "Why do you come to arrest me with swords and clubs, as if I were a robber? Day after day I sat among you, teaching in the temple, yet you did not arrest me. ⁵⁶ But all this has happened in fulfillment of what the Prophets said." Then all his disciples deserted Jesus and fled.

Jesus before the Sanhedrin
(Mk 14:53; Lk 22:54)

⁵⁷ Those who had arrested Jesus took him to the house of the High Priest Caiaphas, where the teachers of the law and the elders were assembled.

⁵⁸ Peter followed Jesus at a distance, as far as the courtyard of the High Priest; he entered and sat with the guards, waiting to see the end.

⁵⁹ The chief priests and the whole Supreme Council needed some false evidence against Jesus so that they might put him to death. ⁶⁰ But they were unable to find any, even though false witnesses came forward. ⁶¹ At last, two men came forward and declared, "This man said, 'I am able to destroy the Temple of God and rebuild it in three days.'"

⁶² The High Priest stood up and asked Jesus, "What is the evidence against you? Have you no answer to the things they testify against you?" ⁶³ But Jesus remained silent.

So the High Priest said to him, "In the name of the living God, I command you to tell us: Are you the Messiah, the Son of God?" ⁶⁴ Jesus answered, "You have said it yourself. But I tell you: from now on, you will see *the Son of Man, seated at the right hand of God most powerful, and coming on the clouds of heaven.*"

⁶⁵ Then the High Priest tore his clothes, saying, "He has blasphemed. What more evidence do we need? You have heard the blasphemy! ⁶⁶ What is your decision?" They answered, "He must die!" ⁶⁷ Then they spat in his face and slapped him, while others hit him with their fists, ⁶⁸ saying, "Messiah, prophesy! Who hit you?"

Peter disowns Jesus
(Mk 14:66; Lk 22:56)

⁶⁹ Meanwhile, as Peter sat outside in the courtyard, a young servant-girl said to him, "You also were with Jesus of Galilee." ⁷⁰ But he denied it before everyone, saying, "I do not know what you are talking about."

⁷¹ Later, as Peter was going out through the gateway, another servant-

girl saw him and said to the bystanders, "This man was with Jesus of Nazareth."

⁷²Peter again denied it with an oath, saying, "I do not know the man."

⁷³After a little while, those who were standing there approached Peter and said to him, "Surely you are one of the Galileans: your accent gives you away." ⁷⁴Peter began to justify himself with curses and oaths, protesting that he did not know Jesus. Just then, a cock crowed.

⁷⁵And Peter remembered the words of Jesus, "Before the cock crows, you will deny me three times." And going out, he wept bitterly.

MATTHEW 26:57-75

Read: Religious authorities bring Jesus to trial. They try to condemn him to death with false witnesses, but Jesus declares himself Son of God, and for that reason, he is condemned. Peter rejects any relationship with the Master.

Reflect: Do you consider Jesus guilty of blasphemy? What would it be to blaspheme today? What do you think about Peter? Is your attitude worse than Judas'? Why?

Pray: Ask God so that Christians can confess Jesus as "the Son of God," and not only with words, but above all, with our way of life.

Act: Manifest today your faith in Jesus Christ not with words (forbidden to make speeches), but with concrete actions and gestures.

---

27 ¹Early in the morning, all the chief priests and the elders of the people met together to look for ways of putting Jesus to death. ²They had him bound and delivered him to Pilate, the governor.

The death of Judas

³When Judas, the traitor, realized that Jesus had been condemned, he was filled with remorse, and returned the thirty pieces of silver to the chief priests and the elders, ⁴saying, "I have sinned by betraying an innocent man to death." They answered, "What does it matter to us? That is your concern." ⁵So, throwing down the money in the temple, he went away and hanged himself.

⁶ The chief priests picked up the money and said, "This money cannot be put into the temple treasury, for it is the price of blood." ⁷ So they conferred together and decided to buy the potter's field with the money and to make it a cemetery for foreigners. ⁸ That is why, to this day, that place has been called the *Field of Blood*.

⁹ What the prophet Jeremiah said was fulfilled: *They took the thirty pieces of silver, the price which the Sons of Israel estimated as his value*, ¹⁰ *and they gave them for the potter's field, as the Lord commanded me.*

Jesus before Pilate
(Mk 15:1; Lk 23:2; Jn 18:28)

¹¹ Jesus stood before the governor. Pilate asked him, "Are you the king of the Jews?" Jesus answered, "You say so."

¹² The chief priests and the elders of the people accused him, but he made no answer. ¹³ Pilate said to him, "Do you hear all the charges they bring against you?" ¹⁴ But he did not answer even one question so that the governor wondered greatly.

¹⁵ At Passover, it was customary for the governor to release any prisoner the people asked for. ¹⁶ Now, there was a well-known prisoner called Barabbas. ¹⁷ When the people had gathered, Pilate asked them, "Whom do you want me to set free: Barabbas or Jesus called the Messiah?" ¹⁸ for he knew that Jesus had been handed over to him out of envy.

¹⁹ While Pilate was sitting in court, his wife sent him this message, "Have nothing to do with that holy man. Because of him, I had a dream last night that disturbed me greatly."

²⁰ But the chief priests and the elders of the people stirred up the crowds to ask for the release of Barabbas and the death of Jesus. ²¹ When the governor asked them again, "Which of the two do you want me to set free?" they answered, "Barabbas!" ²² Pilate said to them, "And what shall I do with Jesus called the Messiah?" All answered, "Crucify him!" ²³ Pilate asked, "Why? What evil has he done?" But they shouted louder, "Crucify him!"

²⁴ Pilate saw that he was getting nowhere and that there could be a riot. He asked for water, washed his hands before the people, and said, "I am innocent of this man's blood. Do what you want!" ²⁵ And all the people answered, "His blood be on us and on our children!"

²⁶ Then Pilate set Barabbas free but had Jesus scourged, and handed over to be crucified.

MATTHEW 27:1-26

Read: Judas regrets his action and commits suicide. Pilate sees no reason to condemn Jesus, but yields to the pressure of the crowd that asks for his crucifixion.

Reflect: What do you think of the action of Judas: wait on the mercy of God or despair before the gravity of his sin? What do you think of Pilate's action? In circumstances like Judas or Pilate, how should a follower of Jesus act?

Pray: Pray for God to grant you the grace to trust more in His mercy than in the gravity of sin, and that in the moments of decision making you always decide for the right thing.

Act: Always trust in the mercy of God, and have the courage to stand up for what you think is right.

The way of the cross
(Mk 15:16; Lk 23:11)

²⁷ The Roman soldiers took Jesus into the palace of the governor and the whole troop gathered around him. ²⁸ They stripped him and dressed him in a purple cloak. ²⁹ Then, weaving a crown of thorns, they forced it onto his head and placed a reed in his right hand. They knelt before Jesus and mocked him, saying, "Hail, king of the Jews!" ³⁰ They spat on him, took the reed from his hand and struck him on the head with it.

³¹ When they had finished mocking him, they pulled off the purple cloak and dressed him in his own clothes, and led him out to be crucified.

³² On the way, they met a man from Cyrene called Simon and forced him to carry the cross of Jesus. ³³ When they reached the place called Golgotha, which means the Skull, ³⁴ they offered him wine mixed with gall. He tasted it, but would not drink it.

³⁵ There they crucified him, and divided his clothes among themselves, casting lots to decide what each one should take. ³⁶ Then they sat down to guard him. ³⁷ The statement of his offense was displayed above his head, and it read, "This is Jesus, the King of the Jews." ³⁸ They

also crucified two thieves with him, one on his right hand and one on his left.

³⁹ The people passing by shook their heads and insulted him, ⁴⁰ saying, "Aha! You, who destroy the temple and in three days rebuild it, save yourself—if you are God's Son—and come down from the cross!"

⁴¹ In the same way, the chief priests, the elders and the teachers of the law mocked him. ⁴² They said, "The man who saved others cannot save himself. Let the king of Israel come down from his cross and we will believe in him. ⁴³ He trusted in God; let God rescue him if God wants to, for he himself said, 'I am the Son of God.'"

⁴⁴ Even the thieves who were crucified with him insulted him.

MATTHEW 27:27-44

Read: The soldiers make fun of Jesus and then take him to Calvary, where they crucify him with two malefactors.

Reflect: What do you think about teasing? Do you promote them or suffer them? Why do you think Jesus did not get off the cross?

Pray: Pray that Christians will be consistent with our faith, and promote respect for human dignity.

Act: Avoid making fun of others, and promote dignified treatment for everyone in your family.

---

⁴⁵ From midday, darkness fell over all the land until mid-afternoon. ⁴⁶ At about three o'clock, Jesus cried out in a loud voice, "Eloi, Eloi, lamma sabbacthani?" which means: My God, my God, why have you forsaken me? ⁴⁷ As soon as they heard this, some of the bystanders said, "He is calling for Elijah." ⁴⁸ And one of them ran, took a sponge and soaked it in vinegar and, putting it on a reed, gave it to him to drink. ⁴⁹ Others said, "Leave him alone; let us see whether Elijah will come to save him."

⁵⁰ Then Jesus cried out again in a loud voice and gave up his spirit.

After the death of Jesus

⁵¹ At that very moment, the curtain of the temple Sanctuary was torn in two from top to bottom, the earth quaked, rocks were split, ⁵² tombs

were opened, and many holy people who had died were raised to life. [53] They came out of the tombs after the Resurrection of Jesus, entered the Holy City, and appeared to many.

[54] The captain and the soldiers who were guarding Jesus, having seen the earthquake and everything else that had happened were terribly afraid and said, "Truly, this was God's Son."

[55] There were also many women there, who watched from a distance; they had followed Jesus from Galilee and had seen to his needs. [56] Among them were Mary Magdalene, Mary the mother of James and Joseph, and the mother of Zebedee's sons.

The burial
(Mk 15:42; Lk 23:50; Jn 19:38)

[57] When it was evening, there came a wealthy man from Arimathea named Joseph, who was also a disciple of Jesus. [58] He went to Pilate and asked for the body of Jesus, and the governor ordered that the body be given to him. [59] So Joseph took the body of Jesus, wrapped it in a clean linen sheet, [60] and laid it in his own new tomb that he had cut in the rock. Then he rolled a huge stone across the entrance to the tomb and left. [61] Mary Magdalene and the other Mary remained, sitting there in front of the tomb.

The guards at the tomb

[62] On the following day, which is after the day of preparation, the chief priests and the Pharisees went to Pilate [63] and said to him, "Sir, we remember that when that impostor was still alive, he said, 'After three days I will rise again.' [64] Therefore, have his tomb secured until the third day, lest his disciples come and steal the body and say to the people: He is risen from the dead. That would be a deception worse than the first." [65] Pilate answered them, "You have soldiers, go and take all the necessary precautions." [66] So they went to the tomb and secured it, sealing the stone, placing the tomb under guard.

MATTHEW 27:45-66

Read: Darkness covers the earth. Jesus dies as a malefactor. The veil of the temple is torn and the most sacred place of the Jews is exposed. The women remain faithful to the Master and

Joseph of Arimathea buries his corpse. Religious authorities, even after the death of Jesus, fear his words.

Reflect: How do you explain the expression of Jesus: "My God, my God, why have you forsaken me?" Do you consider that the ripping of the veil of the temple symbolizes the breaking of the access barriers with the divine? What does all this mean for your life of faith?

Pray: Pray for all the people who have lost loved ones because of the injustice of the world. Ask the Lord not to feel abandoned, and for Christians to work for the justice that announces the Gospel.

Act: Get close to an acquaintance who has lost a loved one and comfort this person with your presence.

Jesus appears to the women
(Mk 16:1; Lk 24:1; Jn 20:1)

28 [1] After the Sabbath, at dawn on the first day of the week, Mary Magdalene and the other Mary went to visit the tomb. [2] Suddenly, there was a violent earthquake: an angel of the Lord descending from heaven, came to the stone, rolled it from the entrance of the tomb and sat on it. [3] His appearance was like lightning, and his garment white as snow. [4] When they saw the angel, the guards were struck with terror.

[5] The angel said to the women, "Do not be afraid, for I know that you are looking for Jesus who was crucified. [6] He is not here, for he is risen, as he said. Come, see the place where they laid him; [7] then go at once and tell his disciples that he is risen from the dead and is going before you to Galilee. You will see him there. This is my message for you."

[8] In fear, yet with great joy, the women left the tomb and ran to tell the news to his disciples.

[9] Suddenly, Jesus met them on the way and said, "Rejoice!" The women approached him, embraced his feet and worshiped him. [10] But Jesus said to them, "Do not be afraid! Go and tell my brothers to set out for Galilee; there, they will see me."

[11] As the women proceeded on their way, some of the guards went into the city and reported to the chief priests all that had happened. [12] The chief priests met with the elders and decided to give the soldiers a large

sum of money [13] with this order, "Say that his disciples came by night while you were asleep and stole the body of Jesus. [14] If Pilate comes to know of this, we will explain the situation and keep you out of trouble." [15] The soldiers accepted the money and did as they were told. This story has circulated among the Jews until this day.

MATTHEW 28:1-15

Read: An angel announces to women the resurrection of Jesus. They run to break the news to the disciples. On their way, Jesus himself comes out to meet them. The tomb guards tell what happened to the religious authorities, who distort the truth of what happened.

Reflect: Do you need pieces of evidence to believe in the resurrection of Jesus? Is an empty grave enough? On what is your faith in Jesus based? Do you need empty graves?

Pray: Ask the Lord for the grace of being able to feel his resurrected presence in daily events, and that he may announce it with his own life. Hallelujah.

Act: Celebrate the resurrection of Jesus by collaborating with some community activity that takes place in your parish.

Jesus sends the apostles

[16] As for the eleven disciples, they went to Galilee, to the mountain where Jesus had told them to go. [17] When they saw Jesus, they bowed before him, although some doubted.

[18] "All authority has been given to me in heaven and on earth. [19] Go, therefore, and make disciples of all nations. Baptize them in the Name of the Father and of the Son and of the Holy Spirit, [20] and teach them to observe all that I have commanded you. I am with you always, even to the end of the world."

MATTHEW 28:16-20

Read: End of the Gospel: Jesus sends his disciples to announce the Good News to all nations.

Reflect: Today, is it necessary to announce the Good News of Jesus to the whole world? Why? How should we do it?

Pray: Pray to God so that Christians may be salt and light for the world, and so that the Good News of Jesus may be present in all of humanity.

Act: May your life always be an announcement of the Good News of Jesus. Hallelujah!

MARK

Since the end of the first century or at the beginning of the second century after Christ, there were texts stating that the second Gospel was the work of Mark. He had accompanied Peter to Rome where he also met Paul and he faithfully put Peter's teaching into writing.

Any reader comparing this Gospel with those of Matthew and Luke will see immediately Mark does not say anything about the birth of Jesus and the years he spent in Nazareth. If we look carefully at the last paragraph of the Gospel (Mk 16:9-20), we will be surprised to see that Mark's early text concluded with the discovery of the empty tomb and it did not mention the appearances of the risen Jesus. In other words, Mark's Gospel seems to be stripped of its beginning and normal end.

However, this is not the case. Mark gave his work the same perimeters that the apostles had assigned to the first documents that determined the catechesis of the Church. Believers were not told all that they would have liked to know but they were given the essence of what Jesus had said and done (Acts 1:21-22).

The Gospel of Mark consists of two parts. Each one of them starts with a divine manifestation: in the first one, it is the word of God at Jesus' baptism by John and in the second one, it is the Transfiguration. The first part of the Gospel unfolds in Galilee, the province of Jesus and the second one takes us to Judea and Jerusalem, the heart of the Jewish nation. These two parts are like the two sides of the same adventure. The first part shows us the power and the newness of Jesus: the impact of his teachings on the crowds. Then disillusionment sets in and we have the second part. The crowds are no longer following as Jesus refuses to be what they wanted him to be. Finally, we have his death on the cross that seems to cancel his entire mission.

When Jesus died on the cross, the Roman officer admitted that the crucified one was truly the Son of God (Mk 15:39). And this is all that Mark says. It is now up to the evangelizer to give witness to the resurrection and proclaim Jesus Christ as savior, beginning with the scandal of the cross.

MARK

1 ¹This is the beginning of the Good News of Jesus Christ, the Son of God. ²It is written in the book of Isaiah, the prophet, "*I am sending my messenger ahead of you, to prepare your way.* ³*Let the people hear the voice calling in the desert: Prepare the way of the Lord, level his paths.*"

⁴So John began to baptize in the desert; he preached a baptism of repentance for the forgiveness of sins. ⁵All Judea and all the people from the city of Jerusalem went out to John to confess their sins, and to be baptized by him in the river Jordan.

⁶John was clothed in camel's hair and wore a leather belt around his waist. His food was locusts and honey. ⁷He preached to the people, saying, "After me comes one who is more powerful than I am; ⁸I have baptized you with water, but he will baptize you in the Holy Spirit."

⁹At that time, Jesus came from Nazareth, a town of Galilee, and was baptized by John in the Jordan. ¹⁰And the moment he came up out of the water, heaven opened before him, and he saw the Spirit coming down on him like a dove. ¹¹And these words were heard from heaven, "You are my Son, the Beloved, the One I have chosen."

¹²Then the Spirit drove him into the desert. ¹³Jesus stayed in the desert forty days and was tempted by Satan. He was with the wild animals, but angels ministered to him.

Jesus calls his first disciples
(Mt 4:12; Lk 4:14)

¹⁴After John was arrested, Jesus went into Galilee and began preaching the Good News of God. ¹⁵He said, "The time has come; the kingdom of God is at hand. Change your ways and believe the Good News."

MARK 1:1-15

Read: Mark introduces Jesus Christ as Son of God and points out the purpose of his work: writing about the Good News. Remember the ministry and teaching of John the Baptist, as well as baptism and the subsequent withdrawal of Jesus into the desert. Jesus, like John, preaches conversion.

Reflect: The Good News is the victory over evil, sin and death. Let's think about the meaning of baptism and conversion in our own life. Does the temptation come directly from Satan (from the Adversary) or through the everyday situations of life?

Pray: Pray for a deeper awareness of the meaning of baptism and ask God not to leave aside our responsibilities to our community and to ourselves.

Act: Live this day with confidence, knowing that Jesus overcomes evil, sin and death.

16 As Jesus was walking along the shore of Lake Galilee, he saw Simon and his brother Andrew casting a net into the lake, for they were fishermen. 17 And Jesus said to them, "Follow me and I will make you fish for people." 18 At once, they abandoned their nets and followed him. 19 Jesus went a little farther on and saw James and John, the sons of Zebedee; they were in their boat mending their nets. 20 Immediately, Jesus called them and they followed him, leaving their father Zebedee in the boat with the hired men.

Jesus teaches and drives out an evil spirit
(Mt 7:28; Lk 4:31)

21 They went into the town of Capernaum and Jesus taught in the synagogue on the Sabbath day. 22 The people were astonished at the way he taught, for he spoke as one having authority, and not like the teachers of the law.

23 It happened that, a man with an evil spirit was in their synagogue 24 and he shouted, "What do you want with us, Jesus of Nazareth? Have you come to destroy us? I know who you are: you are the Holy One of God." 25 Then Jesus faced him and said with authority, "Be silent and

come out of this man!" [26] The evil spirit shook the man violently and, with a loud shriek, came out of him.

[27] All the people were astonished, and they wondered, "What is this? With what authority he preaches! He even gives orders to evil spirits and they obey him!" [28] And Jesus' fame spread throughout all the country of Galilee.

Jesus heals many
(Mt 8:14; Lk 4:38)

[29] On leaving the synagogue, Jesus went to the home of Simon and Andrew, with James and John. [30] As Simon's mother-in-law was sick in bed with a fever, they immediately told him about her. [31] Jesus went to her and, taking her by the hand, raised her up. The fever left her and she began to wait on them. [32] That evening, at sundown, people brought to Jesus all the sick and those who had evil spirits: [33] the whole town was pressing around the door. [34] Jesus healed many who had various diseases and drove out many demons; but he did not let them speak, for they knew who he was.

Jesus' prayer at night
(Lk 4:42)

[35] Very early in the morning, before daylight, Jesus went off to a lonely place where he prayed. [36] Simon and the others went out also, searching for him; [37] and when they found him, they said, "Everyone is looking for you." [38] Then Jesus answered, "Let us go to the nearby villages so that I may preach there too; for that is why I came."

[39] So Jesus set out to preach in all the synagogues throughout Galilee; he also cast out demons.

Jesus cures a leper
(Mt 8:2; Lk 5:12)

[40] A leper came to Jesus and begged him, "If you want to, you can make me clean." [41] Moved with pity, Jesus stretched out his hand and touched him, saying, "I do want to; be clean." [42] The leprosy left the man at once and he was made clean. [43] As Jesus sent the man away, he sternly warned him, [44] "Don't tell anyone about this, but go and show yourself to the priest; and for the cleansing, bring the offering ordered by Moses; in this way, you will give to them your testimony."

⁴⁵ However, as soon as the man went out, he began spreading the news everywhere, so that Jesus could no longer openly enter any town. But even though he stayed in the rural areas, people came to him from everywhere.

MARK 1:16-45

Read: Jesus calls his first disciples. They respond without hesitation. Jesus begins his healing ministry. He has power over all evil: unclean spirits, fever, leprosy.

Reflect: If Jesus has power over all evil, why do we suffer so much? Is it good to ask for physical healing? And what happens if it does not happen? Are the physical pain and suffering related to sin?

Pray: The disciples of Jesus can ask for anything they wish. Pray for the physical healing of someone you know.

Act: Visit a sick person in a hospital.

Jesus forgives and cures a paralytic
(Mt 9:1; Lk 5:17)

2 ¹ After some days, Jesus returned to Capernaum. As the news spread that he was in the house, ² so many people gathered that there was no longer room even outside the door. While Jesus was preaching the word to them, ³ some people brought to him a paralyzed man.

⁴ The four men who carried him couldn't get near Jesus because of the crowd, so they opened the roof above the room where Jesus was and, through the hole, lowered the man on his mat. ⁵ When Jesus saw the faith of these people, he said to the paralytic, "My son, your sins are forgiven."

⁶ Now, some teachers of the law, who were sitting there, wondered within themselves, ⁷ "How can he speak like this, insulting God? Who can forgive sins but God?"

⁸ At once, Jesus knew in his spirit what they were thinking and asked, "Why do you wonder? ⁹ Is it easier to say to this paralyzed man, 'Your sins are forgiven,' or to say, 'Rise, take up your mat and walk?' ¹⁰ But now you shall know that the Son of Man has authority on earth to forgive sins."

And he said to the paralytic, [11]"Stand up, take up your mat and go home." [12]The man rose and, in the sight of all those people, he took up his mat and went out. All of them were astonished and praised God, saying, "Never have we seen anything like this!"

The call of Levi
(Mt 9:9; Lk 5:27)

[13]When Jesus went out again, beside the lake, a crowd came to him, and he taught them. [14]As he walked along, he saw a tax collector sitting in his office. This was Levi, the son of Alpheus. Jesus said to him, "Follow me!" And Levi got up and followed him.

[15]And it so happened that, when Jesus was eating in Levi's house, tax collectors and sinners sat with him and his disciples; there were a lot of them and they used to follow Jesus.

[16]But Pharisees, men educated in the law, when they saw Jesus eating with sinners and tax collectors, said to his disciples, "Why does your master eat and drink with tax collectors and sinners?"

[17]Jesus heard them and answered, "Healthy people don't need a doctor, but sick people do. I did not come to call the righteous, but sinners."

New wine, new skin
(Mt 9:14; Lk 5:33)

[18]One day, when the Pharisees and the disciples of John the Baptist were fasting, some people asked Jesus, "Why is it, that both the Pharisees and the disciples of John fast, but yours do not?" [19]Jesus answered, "How can the wedding guests fast while the bridegroom is with them? As long as they have the bridegroom with them, they cannot fast. [20]But the day will come when the bridegroom will be taken from them, and on that day they will fast.

[21]No one sews a piece of new cloth on an old coat, because the new patch will shrink and tear away from the old cloth, making a worse tear. [22]And no one puts new wine into old wineskins, for the wine would burst the skins and then both the wine and the skins would be lost. But new wine, new skins!"

(Mt 12:1; Lk 6:1)

[23]One Sabbath he was walking through grain fields. As his disciples walked along with him, they began to pick the heads of grain and crush

them in their hands. ²⁴ Then the Pharisees said to Jesus, "Look! They are doing what is forbidden on the Sabbath!"

²⁵ And he said to them, "Have you never read what David did in his time of need; when he and his men were very hungry? ²⁶ He went into the House of God, when Abiathar was High Priest, and ate the bread of offering, which only the priests are allowed to eat and he also gave some to the men who were with him." ²⁷ Then Jesus said to them, "The Sabbath was made for man, not man for the Sabbath. ²⁸ So the Son of Man is master even of the Sabbath."

MARK 2:1-28

Read: Jesus heals a paralytic, forgives his sins. The controversy is generated by Jewish leaders. Jesus allows his disciples to break a particular interpretation of the law of the Sabbath.

Reflect: The paralytic does not ask for anything. However, Jesus heals him. Do the actions of the friends of the paralytic suggest something to him? What do you consider to be new and what is old in the parable of wineskins?

Pray: Pray that the leaders of the Church and all Christians in general will always opt for the good, not resorting to only fulfilling norms.

Act: The paralytic's friends took great pains for him because they loved him. Let us make our actions express our love for those who are closest to us.

Cure of the man with a withered hand
(Lk 6:6; Mt 12:9; Lk 14:1)

3 ¹ Again, Jesus entered the synagogue. A man who had a paralyzed hand was there; ² and some people watched Jesus: would he heal the man on the Sabbath? If he did, they could accuse him.

³ Jesus said to the man with the paralyzed hand, "Stand here, in the center." ⁴ Then he asked them, "What does the law allow us to do on the Sabbath, to do good or to do harm? To save life or to kill?" But they were silent.

⁵ Then Jesus looked around at them with anger and deep sadness at their hardness of heart. And he said to the man, "Stretch out your hand."

He stretched it out, and his hand was healed. [6]As soon as the Pharisees left, they met with Herod's supporters, looking for a way to destroy Jesus.

(Mt 12:15; Lk 6:17)

[7]Jesus and his disciples withdrew to the lakeside and a large crowd from Galilee followed him. A great number of people also came from Judea, [8]Jerusalem, Idumea, Transjordan, and from the region of Tyre and Sidon for they had heard of all that he was doing.

[9]Because of the crowd, Jesus told his disciples to have a boat ready for him to prevent the people from crushing him. [10]He healed so many that all who had diseases kept pressing toward him to touch him. [11]Even the people who had evil spirits, whenever they saw him, they would fall down before him and cry out, "You are the Son of God." [12]But he warned them sternly not to tell anyone who he was.

The Twelve apostles
(Mt 10:1; Lk 6:12)

[13]Then Jesus went up into the hill country and called those he wanted and they came to him. [14]He appointed Twelve to be with him and he called them 'apostles.' He wanted to send them out to preach; [15]and he gave them authority to drive out demons.

[16]These are the Twelve: Simon, to whom he gave the name Peter; [17]James, son of Zebedee, and John his brother, to whom he gave the name Boanerges, which means 'men of thunder'; [18]Andrew, Philip, Bartholomew, Matthew, Thomas, James son of Alpheus, Thaddeus, Simon the Cananean, [19]and Judas Iscariot, the one who betrayed him.

The sin against the Spirit
(Mt 12:24; Lk 11:15)

[20]They went home. The crowd began to gather again and they couldn't even have a meal. [21]Knowing what was happening, his relatives came to take charge of him. "He is out of his mind," they said. [22]Meanwhile, the teachers of the law who had come from Jerusalem said, "He is in the power of Beelzebul: the chief of the demons helps him to drive out demons."

[23]Jesus called them to him and began teaching them by means of stories or parables. "How can Satan drive out Satan? [24]If a nation is divided

by civil war, that nation cannot stand. ²⁵If a family divides itself into groups, that family will not survive. ²⁶In the same way, if Satan has risen against himself and is divided, he will not stand; he is finished. ²⁷No one can break into the house of a strong man in order to plunder his goods unless he first ties up the strong man. Then indeed, he can plunder his house.

²⁸Truly, I say to you, all sins and all blasphemies that people utter will be forgiven them. ²⁹But whoever slanders the Holy Spirit will never be forgiven. He carries the guilt of his sin forever."

³⁰This was their sin when they said, "He has an unclean spirit in him."

Jesus' true family
(Mt 12:46; Lk 8:19)

³¹Then his mother and his brothers came. As they stood outside, they sent someone to call him. ³²The crowd sitting around Jesus told him, "Your mother and your brothers are outside asking for you." ³³He replied, "Who are my mother and my brothers?"

³⁴And looking around at those who sat there, he said, "Here are my mother and my brothers. ³⁵Whoever does the will of God is brother and sister and mother to me."

MARK 3:1-35

Read: Jesus again breaks the law of the Sabbath. He teaches, heals and calls the Twelve. His family thinks he has gone crazy. The Pharisees accuse him of being possessed by Satan. Jesus extends his family ties: everyone who does the will of his Father.

Reflect: Why do you believe that Jesus generates so much conflict? Do you consider that everyone who does God's will is a family member? How do you understand that the sin against the Holy Spirit will not be forgiven?

Pray: The Christian prays as a member of the family of Jesus. Ask God to grant you the grace to do his will at every moment of your life.

Act: Do not be afraid to express your faith in everyday life. Talk to others about what you really believe.

The sower
(Mt 13:1; Lk 8:4)

4 [1] Again, Jesus began to teach by the lake; but such a large crowd gathered about him, that he got into a boat and sat in it on the lake, while the crowd stood on the shore. [2] He taught them many things through parables. In his teaching he said,

[3] "Listen! The sower went out to sow. [4] As he sowed, some of the seed fell along a path; and the birds came and ate it up. [5] Some of the seed fell on rocky ground where it had little soil; it sprang up immediately because it had no depth; [6] but when the sun rose and burned it, it withered, because it had no roots. [7] Other seed fell among thorn bushes, and the thorns grew and choked it; so it didn't produce any grain. [8] But some seed fell on good soil, grew and increased and yielded grain; some seed produced thirty times as much, some sixty, and some one hundred times as much." [9] And Jesus added, "Listen then, if you have ears."

[10] When the crowd went away, some who were present along with the Twelve asked about the parables.

[11] He answered them, "The mystery of the kingdom of God has been given to you. But for those outside, everything comes in parables, [12] so, that, *the more they see, they don't perceive; the more they hear, they don't understand; otherwise they would be converted and pardoned.*"

[13] Jesus said to them, "Don't you understand this parable? How, then, will you understand any of the parables?

[14] What the sower is sowing is the word. [15] Those along the path where the seed fell are people who hear the word, but as soon as they hear it, Satan comes and takes away the word that was sown in them.

[16] Other people receive the word like rocky ground. As soon as they hear the word, they accept it with joy. [17] But they have no roots, so it lasts only a little while. No sooner does trouble or persecution come because of the word than they fall.

[18] Others receive the seed as seed among thorns. After they hear the word, [19] they are caught up in the worries of this life, false hopes of riches and other desires. All these come in and choke the word so that finally it produces nothing.

[20] And there are others who receive the word as good soil. They hear the word, take it to heart and produce: some thirty, some sixty, and some one hundred times as much."

Parable of the lamp
(Mt 10:26; Lk 8:16)

21 Jesus also said to them, "When the light comes, is it put under a basket or a bed? Surely it is put on a lampstand. 22 Whatever is hidden will be disclosed and whatever is kept secret will be brought to light. 23 Listen then, if you have ears!"

24 And he also said to them, "Pay attention to what you hear. In the measure you give, so shall you receive, and still more will be given to you. 25 For to the one who produces something, more will be given; and from him who does not produce anything, even what he has will be taken away from him."

The seed growing by itself

26 Jesus also said, "In the kingdom of God, it is like this: a man scatters seed upon the soil. 27 Whether he is asleep or awake, be it day or night, the seed sprouts and grows; he knows not how. 28 The soil produces of itself; first the blade; then the ear; then the full grain in the ear. 29 And when it is ripe for harvesting, they take the sickle for the cutting: the time for the harvest has come."

The mustard seed
(Mt 13:31; Lk 13:18)

30 Jesus also said, "What is the kingdom of God like? To what shall we compare it? 31 It is like a mustard seed, which, when sown, is the smallest of all the seeds scattered upon the soil. 32 But once sown, it grows up and becomes the largest of the plants in the garden; and even grows branches so big that the birds of the air can take shelter in its shade."

33 Jesus used many such stories, in order to proclaim the word to them in a way that they would be able to understand. 34 He would not teach them without parables; but privately, to his disciples, he explained everything.

MARK 4:1-34

Read: Jesus preaches in parables. In the proclamation of the Gospel there will always be a good harvest, even when many seeds do not bear fruit. The kingdom of God grows in silence, but with great force.

> **Reflect:** What does the parable of the sower and its interpretation suggests to you? Think about what you believe and how you live it in your day to day.
>
> **Pray:** If on this day you have shared many fruits of love, give thanks to God. If not, ask for forgiveness and may the Holy Spirit help you in this.
>
> **Act:** Perform a brief examination of conscience every night about the events that occurred during the day.

Jesus calms the storm
(Mt 8:18; Lk 8:22)

³⁵On that same day, when evening had come, Jesus said to them, "Let's go across to the other side of the lake." ³⁶So they left the crowd and took him along in the boat he had been sitting in, and other boats set out with him. ³⁷Then a storm gathered and it began to blow a gale. The waves spilled over into the boat so that it was soon filled with water. ³⁸Jesus was in the stern, sleeping on a cushion.

They woke him up and said, "Master, don't you care if we drown?" ³⁹And rising up, Jesus rebuked the wind and ordered the sea, "Quiet now! Be still!" The wind dropped, and there was a great calm. ⁴⁰Then Jesus said to them, "Why are you so frightened? Do you still have no faith?"

⁴¹But they were terrified and they said to one another, "Who can this be? Even the wind and the sea obey him!"

The Gerasene demoniac
(Mt 8:28; Lk 8:26)

5 ¹They arrived at the other side of the lake, in the region of the Gerasenes. ²No sooner did Jesus leave the boat than he was met by a man with evil spirits who had come from the tombs. ³The man lived among the tombs, and no one could restrain him even with a chain. ⁴He had often been bound with fetters and chains, but he would pull the chains apart and smash the fetters, and no one had the strength to control him. ⁵Night and day he stayed among the tombs on the hillsides and was continually screaming and beating himself with stones.

⁶When he saw Jesus from afar, he ran and fell at his feet ⁷and cried

with a loud voice, "What do you want with me, Jesus, Son of the Most High God? For God's sake, I beg you, do not torment me!" [8] He said this because Jesus had commanded, "Evil spirit, come out of the man!" [9] When Jesus asked the evil spirit, "What is your name?" it replied, "Legion is my name, for we are many." [10] And it kept begging Jesus not to send them out of that region.

[11] Now a great herd of pigs was feeding on the hillside, [12] and the evil spirits begged him, "Send us to the pigs, and let us go into them." [13] So Jesus let them go. The evil spirits came out of the man and went into the pigs, and immediately the herd rushed down the cliff, and all were drowned in the lake. [14] The herdsmen fled, and reported this in the town and in the countryside. So all the people came to see what had happened.

[15] They came to Jesus and saw the man freed of the evil spirits, sitting there clothed and in his right mind; the same man who had been possessed by the legion. They were afraid. [16] And when those who had seen it told what had happened to the man and to the pigs, [17] the people begged Jesus to leave their neighborhood.

[18] When Jesus was getting into the boat, the man, who had been possessed, begged to stay with him. [19] Jesus would not let him and said, "Go home to your people and tell them how much the Lord has done for you and how he has had mercy on you." [20] So he went throughout the country of Decapolis telling everyone how much Jesus had done for him, and all the people were astonished.

Jesus raises the daughter of Jairus
(Mt 9:18; Lk 8:40)

[21] Jesus then crossed to the other side of the lake; and while he was still on the shore, a large crowd gathered around him. [22] Jairus, an official of the synagogue, came up and, seeing Jesus, threw himself at his feet; [23] and begged him earnestly, "My little daughter is at the point of death. Come and lay your hands on her, so that she may get well and live."

[24] Jesus went with him and many people followed, pressing around him. [25] Among the crowd was a woman who had suffered from bleeding for twelve years. [26] She had suffered a lot at the hands of many doctors and had spent everything she had, but instead of getting better, she was worse. [27] Because she had heard about Jesus, this woman came up

behind him and touched his cloak, [28] thinking, "If I just touch his clothing, I shall get well." [29] Her flow of blood dried up at once, and she felt in her body that she was healed of her complaint.

[30] But Jesus was conscious that healing power had gone out from him, so he turned around in the crowd and asked, "Who touched my clothes?" [31] His disciples answered, "You see how the people are crowding around you. Why do you ask who touched you?" [32] But he kept looking around to see who had done it. [33] Then the woman, aware of what had happened, came forward trembling and afraid. She knelt before him and told him the whole truth.

[34] Then Jesus said to her, "Daughter, your faith has saved you. Go in peace and be free of this illness."

[35] While Jesus was still speaking, some people arrived from the official's house to inform him, "Your daughter is dead. Why trouble the Master any further?" [36] But Jesus ignored what they said and told the official, "Do not fear, just believe." [37] And he allowed no one to follow him except Peter, James, and John, the brother of James.

[38] When they arrived at the house, Jesus saw a great commotion, with people weeping and wailing loudly. [39] Jesus entered and said to them, "Why all this commotion and weeping? The child is not dead, but asleep."

[40] They laughed at him. So Jesus sent them outside and went with the child's father and mother and his companions into the room, where the child lay. [41] Taking her by the hand, he said to her, "Talitha kumi!" which means, "Little girl, get up!"

[42] The girl got up at once and began to walk around. (She was twelve years old.) The parents were amazed, greatly amazed. [43] Jesus strictly ordered them not to let anyone know about it, and he told them to give her something to eat.

MARK 4:35—5:43

Read: Jesus calms the storm, exorcises and heals the sick. He reveals his power over evil; the kingdom of God manifests itself. Two miracles intermingle: the healing of a woman with hemorrhage and the resurrection of a young girl.

Reflect: Today, can you contemplate the manifestation of

> Jesus' power? How? In the present circumstances, what would it mean for the followers of Jesus to fight against wrong?
>
> **Pray:** Pray to God so that we can continue with the mission of Jesus to fight against evil and manifest the power of his reign in the world.
>
> **Act:** Continue Jesus' mission to fight against evil by promoting respect, justice, solidarity, and love among all in his family.

Is he not the carpenter?
(Mt 13:53; Lk 4:16)

6 ¹Leaving that place, Jesus returned to his own country and his disciples followed him. ²When the Sabbath came, he began to teach in the synagogue and most of those who heard him were astonished. But they said, "How did this come to him? What kind of wisdom has been given to him, that he also performs such miracles? ³Who is he but the carpenter, the Son of Mary and the brother of James and Joses and Judas and Simon? His sisters, too, are they not here among us?" So they took offense at him.

⁴And Jesus said to them, "Prophets are despised only in their own country, among their relatives and in their own family." ⁵And he could work no miracles there, but only healed a few sick people, by laying his hands on them. ⁶Jesus himself was astounded at their unbelief.

Jesus sends out the Twelve
(Mt 10:1; Lk 9:1; 10:1)

Jesus then went around the villages, teaching. ⁷He called the Twelve to him and began to send them out two by two, giving them authority over evil spirits. ⁸And he ordered them to take nothing for the journey, except a staff: no food, no bag, no money in their belts. ⁹They were to wear sandals and were not to take an extra tunic.

¹⁰And he added, "In whatever house you are welcomed, stay there until you leave the place. ¹¹If any place doesn't receive you, and the people refuse to listen to you, leave after shaking the dust off your feet. It will be a testimony against them."

¹²So they set out to proclaim that this was the time to repent. ¹³They drove out many demons and healed many sick people by anointing them.

John the Baptist beheaded
(Mt 14:1; Lk 9:7)

¹⁴King Herod also heard about Jesus, because his name had become well-known. Some people said, "John the Baptist has been raised from the dead and that is why miraculous powers are at work in him." ¹⁵Others thought, "He is Elijah," and others, "He is a prophet like the prophets of times past." ¹⁶When Herod was told of this, he thought, "I had John beheaded; yet, he has risen from the dead!"

¹⁷For this is what had happened: Herod had ordered John to be arrested; and had had him bound and put in prison because of Herodias, the wife of his brother Philip. Herod had married her; ¹⁸and John had told him, "It is not right for you to live with your brother's wife." ¹⁹So Herodias held a grudge against John and wanted to kill him; but she could not, ²⁰because Herod respected John. He knew John to be an upright and holy man and kept him safe. And he liked listening to him although he became very disturbed whenever he heard him.

²¹Herodias had her chance on Herod's birthday when he gave a dinner for all the senior government officials, military chiefs and the leaders of Galilee. ²²On that occasion, the daughter of Herodias came in and danced; and she delighted Herod and his guests. The king said to the girl, "Ask me for anything you want and I will give it to you." ²³And he went so far as to say with many oaths, "I will give you anything you ask, even half my kingdom." ²⁴She went out and said to her mother, "What shall I ask for?" The mother replied, "The head of John the Baptist." ²⁵The girl hurried to the king and made her request, "I want you to give me the head of John the Baptist here and now, on a dish."

²⁶The king was very displeased, but he would not refuse in front of his guests because of his oaths. ²⁷So he sent one of the bodyguards with orders to bring John's head. He went and beheaded John in prison; ²⁸then he brought the head on a dish and gave it to the girl. And the girl gave it to her mother. ²⁹When John's disciples heard of this, they came and took his body and buried it.

MARK 6:1-29

Read: Jesus teaches in his hometown and his own people reject him. He sends the Twelve to continue his mission. Herod kills John the Baptist. The disciples return and, together with Jesus, withdraw from the crowds to rest.

Reflect: Can you recognize the voice of God in that person who corrects you of some error? Would he assume the role of a prophet in his community?

Pray: Pray that our leaders and governors will be moved by the right thing and not by public acceptance or personal gain.

Act: Try to act always moved by the right thing rather than by peer pressure.

Jesus, shepherd, and prophet

³⁰ The apostles returned and reported to Jesus all they had done and taught. ³¹ Then he said to them, "Let us go off by ourselves into a remote place and have some rest." For there were so many people coming and going that the apostles had no time even to eat. ³² And they went away in the boat to a secluded area by themselves.

³³ But people saw them leaving, and many could guess where they were going. So, from all the towns they hurried there on foot, arriving ahead of them.

³⁴ As Jesus went ashore, he saw a large crowd, and he had compassion on them for they were like sheep without a shepherd. And he began to teach them many things.

The first miracle of the loaves
(Mt 14:13; Lk 9:10; Jn 6:1)

³⁵ It was now getting late, so his disciples came to him and said, "This is a lonely place and it is now late. ³⁶ You should send the people away and let them go to the farms and villages around here, to buy themselves something to eat."

³⁷ Jesus replied, "You, yourselves, give them something to eat." They answered, "If we are to feed them, we need two hundred silver coins to go and buy enough bread." ³⁸ But Jesus said, "You have some loaves; how many? Go and see." The disciples found out and said, "There are five loaves and two fish."

³⁹ Then he told them to have the people sit down, together in groups, on the green grass. ⁴⁰ This they did, in groups of hundreds and fifties.

⁴¹ And Jesus took the five loaves and the two fish and, raising his eyes to heaven, he pronounced a blessing, broke the loaves and handed them to his disciples to distribute to the people. He also divided the two fish among them.

⁴² They all ate and everyone had enough. ⁴³ The disciples gathered up what was left, and filled twelve baskets with broken pieces of bread and fish. ⁴⁴ Five thousand men had eaten there.

Jesus walks on the water
(Mt 14:22; Jn 6:16)

⁴⁵ Immediately, Jesus obliged his disciples to get into the boat and go ahead of him to the other side, toward Bethsaida, while he himself sent the crowd away. ⁴⁶ And having sent the people off, he went by himself to the hillside to pray.

⁴⁷ When evening came, the boat was far out on the lake while he was alone on the land. ⁴⁸ Jesus saw his disciples straining at the oars for the wind was against them, and before daybreak, he came to them walking on the lake, and he was going to pass them by.

⁴⁹ When they saw him walking on the lake, they thought it was a ghost and cried out; ⁵⁰ for they all saw him and were terrified. But, at once, he called to them, "Courage! It is I; don't be afraid!" ⁵¹ Then Jesus got into the boat with them and the wind died down. They were completely astonished, ⁵² for they had not really grasped the fact of the loaves; their minds were dull.

⁵³ Having crossed the lake, they came ashore at Gennesaret where they tied up the boat. ⁵⁴ As soon as they landed, people recognized Jesus ⁵⁵ and ran to spread the news throughout the countryside. Wherever he was, they brought to him the sick lying on their mats; ⁵⁶ and wherever he went, to villages, towns or farms, they laid the sick in the marketplace and begged him to let them touch just the fringe of his cloak. And all who touched him were cured.

True cleanness
(Mt 15:10; Lk 6:39)

7 ¹ One day, the Pharisees gathered around Jesus, and with them were some teachers of the law who had just come from Jerusalem.

² They noticed that some of his disciples were eating their meal with unclean hands, that is, without washing them. ³ Now the Pharisees, and

in fact, all the Jews, never eat without washing their hands, for they follow the tradition received from their ancestors. [4]Nor do they eat anything when they come from the market without first sprinkling themselves. And there are many other traditions they observe; for example, the ritual washing of cups, pots, and plates.

[5]So the Pharisees and the teachers of the law asked him, "Why do your disciples not follow the tradition of the elders, but eat with unclean hands?"

[6]Jesus answered, "You shallow people! How well Isaiah prophesied of you when he wrote: *This people honors me with their lips, but their heart is far from me.* [7] *The worship they offer me is worthless, for what they teach are only human rules.* [8]You even put aside the commandment of God to hold fast to human tradition."

[9]And Jesus commented, "You have a fine way of disregarding the commandments of God in order to enforce your own traditions! [10]For example, Moses said: *Do your duty to your father and your mother, and: Whoever curses his father or his mother is to be put to death.* [11]But according to you, someone could say to his father or mother, 'I already declared Corban (which means "offered to God") what you could have expected from me.' [12]In this case, you no longer require him to do anything for his father or mother; [13]and so you nullify the word of God through the tradition you have handed on. And you do many other things like that."

[14]Jesus then called the people to him again and said to them, "Listen to me, all of you, and try to understand. [15]Nothing that enters a person from the outside can make that person unclean. It is what comes from within that makes a person unclean. [16]Let everyone who has ears listen."

[17]When Jesus got home and was away from the crowd, his disciples asked him about this saying [18]and he replied, "So even you are dull? Do you not see that whatever comes from outside cannot make a person unclean, [19]since it enters not the heart but the stomach and is finally passed out?"

Thus Jesus declared that all foods are clean.

[20]And he went on, "What comes out of a person is what defiles him, [21]for evil designs come out of the heart: theft, murder, [22]adultery, jealousy, greed, maliciousness, deceit, indecency, slander, pride, and folly. [23]All these evil things come from within and make a person unclean."

MARK 6:30—7:23

Read: Jesus feeds five thousand people, walks on water and continues to reveal his power over evil. New controversy with the Pharisees and lawyers, this time about the observance of tradition and the true purity.

Reflect: For our current circumstances, what does all this suggest? Is it possible to repeat the multiplication of the loaves again? Are we able to trust Jesus, even in the midst of doubts? Do our acts of faith spring from the heart, or are they limited to mere compliance with standards?

Pray: Pray that no human being will lack food and that world leaders and other leaders will seriously commit themselves to it. Pray also that your faith in Jesus will increase each day and be manifested in a coherent way in your daily life.

Act: As far as possible, commit yourself to some social justice action that takes place in your parish.

The faith of the Syrophoenician
(Mt 15:21)

²⁴When Jesus left that place, he went to the border of the Tyrian country. There, he entered a house, and did not want anyone to know he was there; but he could not remain hidden. ²⁵A woman, whose small daughter had an evil spirit, heard of him, and came and fell at his feet. ²⁶Now this woman was a pagan, a Syrophoenician by birth, and she begged him to drive the demon out of her daughter.

²⁷Jesus told her, "Let the children be fed first, for it is not right to take the children's bread and throw it to the puppies." ²⁸But she replied, "Sir, even the puppies under the table eat the crumbs from the children's bread." ²⁹Then Jesus said to her, "You may go your way; because of such a response, the demon has gone out of your daughter." ³⁰And when the woman went home, she found her child lying in bed, and the demon gone.

Healing a deaf and dumb man

³¹Again, Jesus set out; from the country of Tyre he passed through Sidon and, skirting the sea of Galilee, he came to the territory of

Decapolis. [32] There, a deaf man, who also had difficulty in speaking, was brought to him. They asked Jesus to lay his hand upon him.

[33] Jesus took him apart from the crowd, put his fingers into the man's ears and touched his tongue with spittle. [34] Then, looking up to heaven, he said with a deep sigh, "Ephphata!" that is, "Be opened!"

[35] And immediately, his ears were opened, his tongue was loosened, and he began to speak clearly. [36] Jesus ordered them not to tell anyone about it; but the more he insisted, the more they proclaimed it. [37] The people were completely astonished and said, "He has done all things well; he makes the deaf hear and the dumb speak."

The second miracle of the loaves
(Mt 15:32)

8 [1] Soon afterward, Jesus was in the midst of another large crowd that obviously had nothing to eat. So he called his disciples and said to them, [2] "I feel sorry for these people because they have been with me for three days and now have nothing to eat. [3] If I send them to their homes hungry, they will faint on the way; some of them have come a long way."

[4] His disciples replied, "Where, in a deserted place like this, could we get enough bread to feed these people?" [5] He asked them, "How many loaves have you?" And they answered, "Seven."

[6] Then he ordered the crowd to sit down on the ground. Taking the seven loaves and giving thanks, he broke them and handed them to his disciples to distribute. And they distributed them among the people. [7] They also had some small fish. So Jesus said a blessing and asked that these be shared as well.

[8] The people ate and were satisfied, and they picked up the broken pieces left over, seven baskets full. [9] Now those who had eaten were about four thousand in number. Jesus sent them away [10] and immediately got into the boat with his disciples and went to the region of Dalmanutha.

Why do they demand a sign?
(Mt 16:1; Lk 12:54)

[11] The Pharisees came and started to argue with Jesus. Hoping to embarrass him, they asked for some heavenly sign. [12] Then his spirit was moved. He gave a deep sigh and said, "Why do the people of this present

time ask for a sign? Truly, I say to you, no sign shall be given to this people." ¹³Then he left them, got into the boat again and went to the other side of the lake.

¹⁴The disciples had forgotten to bring more bread and had only one loaf with them in the boat. ¹⁵Then Jesus warned them, "Keep your eyes open and beware of the yeast of the Pharisees and the yeast of Herod." ¹⁶And they said to one another, "He saw that we have no bread."

¹⁷Aware of this, Jesus asked them, "Why are you talking about the loaves you are short of? Do you not see or understand? Are your minds closed? ¹⁸Have you eyes that don't see and ears that don't hear? And do you not remember ¹⁹when I broke the five loaves among five thousand? How many baskets full of leftovers did you collect?" They answered, "Twelve." ²⁰"And having distributed seven loaves to the four thousand, how many wicker baskets of leftovers did you collect?" They answered, "Seven." ²¹Then Jesus said to them, "Do you still not understand?"

MARK 7:24—8:21

Read: Jesus exorcises the daughter of a Siro-Phoenician woman. He heals a deaf mute. Gives food to four thousand people. The Pharisees ask him for a sign from heaven, but he refuses to give it. He rebukes his disciples because they do not understand his actions.

Reflect: There are still those who ask for signs from heaven to believe, are you one of them? Why do you think healing and sharing bread are so prominent in this Gospel? Does the Church continue with this ministry? And you?

Pray: Ask God for the grace of being able to recognize Him in all that surrounds you, and to continue the saving work of Jesus.

Act: Share your bread, your food, invite someone who is hungry or who eats alone to eat with you. May our good works be signs of the presence of God.

Cure of the blind man at Bethsaida

²²When they came to Bethsaida, Jesus was asked to touch a blind man who was brought to him. ²³He took the blind man by the hand and

led him outside the village. When he had put spittle on his eyes and laid his hands upon him, he asked, "Can you see anything?" 24 The man, who was beginning to see, replied, "I see people! They look like trees, but they move around." 25 Then Jesus laid his hands on his eyes again and the man could see perfectly. His sight was restored and he could see everything clearly.

26 Then Jesus sent him home, saying, "Do not return to the village."

Peter's profession of faith
(Mt 16:13; Lk 9:18; Jn 6:69)

27 Jesus set out with his disciples for the villages around Caesarea Philippi; and on the way, he asked them, "Who do people say I am?" 28 And they told him, "Some say, you are John the Baptist; others say, you are Elijah or one of the prophets."

Then Jesus asked them, 29 "But you, who do you say I am?" Peter answered, "You are the Messiah." 30 And he ordered them not to tell anyone about him.

31 Jesus then began to teach them that the Son of Man had to suffer many things and be rejected by the elders, the chief priests and the teachers of the law. He would be killed, and after three days rise again. 32 Jesus said all this quite openly so that Peter took him aside and began to protest strongly. 33 But Jesus, turning around, and looking at his disciples, rebuked Peter, saying, "Get behind me, Satan! You are thinking not as God does, but as people do."

Take up your cross
(Mt 16:24; Lk 9:23)

34 Then Jesus called the people and his disciples and said, "If you want to follow me, deny yourself; take up your cross and follow me. 35 For if you choose to save your life, you will lose it; and if you lose your life for my sake, and for the sake of the gospel, you will save it.

36 What good is it to gain the whole world while destroying your soul? 37 There is nothing more precious than your soul. 38 I tell you, if anyone is ashamed of me and of my words, among this adulterous and sinful people, the Son of Man will also be ashamed of him when he comes in the glory of his Father with the holy angels."

The transfiguration of Jesus
(Mt 17:1; Lk 9:28)

9 ¹ And he went on to say, "Truly I tell you, there are some here who will not die before they see the kingdom of God coming with power."

MARK 8:22—9:1

Read: Jesus heals a blind man. Peter confesses him as Messiah, but does not understand what the passion is. Jesus, then, talks about the demands of following him.

Reflect: And you, who do you say Jesus is? Are you willing to follow him with all his demands?

Pray: Ask for the grace to confess Jesus as the Messiah and to accept his demands even when they seem difficult.

Act: See the difficulties and problems of daily life as an invitation to "carry the cross of Jesus" and proclaim in your midst that he is the Messiah.

---

² Six days later, Jesus took with him Peter and James and John and led them up a high mountain. There, his appearance was changed before their eyes. ³ Even his clothes shone, becoming as white as no bleach of this world could make them. ⁴ Elijah and Moses appeared to them; the two were talking with Jesus.

⁵ Then Peter spoke and said to Jesus, "Master, it is good that we are here; let us make three tents, one for you, one for Moses and one for Elijah." ⁶ For he did not know what to say: they were overcome with awe. ⁷ But a cloud formed, covering them in a shadow and from the cloud came a voice, "This is my Son, the Beloved: listen to him!" ⁸ And suddenly, as they looked around, they no longer saw anyone except Jesus with them.

⁹ As they came down the mountain, he ordered them to tell no one what they had seen until the Son of Man had risen from the dead. ¹⁰ So they kept this to themselves, although they discussed with one another what 'to rise from the dead' could mean.

The question about Elijah
¹¹ Finally, they asked him, "Why, then, do the teachers of the law say

that Elijah must come first?" [12] Jesus answered them, "Of course, Elijah will come first so that everything may be as it should be. But why do the Scriptures say that the Son of Man must suffer many things and be despised? [13] I tell you that Elijah has already come; and they have treated him as they pleased, as the Scriptures say of him."

The boy with an evil spirit

[14] When they came to the place where they had left the disciples, they saw many people around them and some teachers of the law arguing with them. [15] When the people saw Jesus, they were astonished and ran to greet him.

[16] He asked, "What are you arguing about with them?" [17] A man answered him from the crowd, "Master, I brought my son to you, for he has a spirit, deaf and mute. [18] Whenever the spirit seizes him, it throws him down and he foams at the mouth, grinds his teeth and becomes stiff all over. I asked your disciples to drive the spirit out, but they could not."

[19] Jesus replied, "You faithless people! How long must I be with you? How long must I put up with you? Bring him to me." [20] And they brought the boy to him.

As soon as the spirit saw Jesus, it shook and convulsed the boy, who fell on the ground and began rolling about, foaming at the mouth. [21] Then Jesus asked the father, "How long has this been happening to him?" He replied, "From childhood. [22] And it has often thrown him into the fire and into the water to destroy him. If you can do anything, have pity on us and help us."

[23] Jesus said to him, "Why do you say, 'If you can?' All things are possible for one who believes." [24] Immediately, the father of the boy cried out, "I do believe, but help the little faith I have."

[25] Jesus saw that the crowd was increasing rapidly, so he ordered the evil spirit, "Dumb and deaf spirit, I command you: Leave the boy and never enter him again." [26] The evil spirit shook and convulsed the boy and with a terrible shriek came out. The boy lay like a corpse and people said, "He is dead." [27] But Jesus took him by the hand and raised him, and the boy stood up.

[28] After Jesus had gone indoors, his disciples asked him privately, "Why couldn't we drive out the spirit?" [29] And he answered, "Only prayer can drive out this kind, nothing else."

Jesus again speaks of his passion
(Mt 17:22; Lk 9:43)

³⁰ After leaving that place, they made their way through Galilee; but Jesus did not want people to know where he was ³¹ because he was teaching his disciples. And he told them, "The Son of Man will be delivered into the hands of men. They will kill him, but three days after he has been killed, he will rise." ³² The disciples, however, did not understand these words and they were afraid to ask him what he meant.

Who is the greatest?
(Mt 18:1; Lk 9:46; 18:17; 22:24)

³³ They came to Capernaum and, once inside the house, Jesus asked them, "What were you discussing on the way?" ³⁴ But they did not answer, because they had been arguing about who was the greatest.

³⁵ Then he sat down, called the Twelve and said to them, "If someone wants to be first, let him be last of all and servant of all." ³⁶ Then he took a little child, placed him in their midst, and putting his arms around him, he said to them, ³⁷ "Whoever welcomes a child such as this in my name, welcomes me; and whoever welcomes me, welcomes not me, but the One who sent me."

³⁸ John said to him, "Master, we saw someone who drove out demons by calling upon your name, and we tried to forbid him because he does not belong to our group." ³⁹ Jesus answered, "Do not forbid him, for no one who works a miracle in my name can soon after speak evil of me. ⁴⁰ For whoever is not against us is for us.

⁴¹ If anyone gives you a drink of water because you belong to Christ and bear his name, truly, I say to you, he will not go without reward.

If your eye causes you to sin
(5:13; Mt 18:6; Lk 17:1)

⁴² If anyone should cause one of these little ones who believe in me to stumble and sin, it would be better for him to be thrown into the sea with a great millstone around his neck.

⁴³ If your hand makes you fall into sin, cut it off! It is better for you to enter life without a hand than with two hands to go to hell, to the fire that never goes out. ⁴⁵ And if your foot makes you fall into sin, cut it off! It is better for you to enter life without a foot than with both feet to be thrown

into hell. ⁴⁷ And if your eye makes you fall into sin, tear it out! It is better for you to enter the kingdom of God with one eye, than, keeping both eyes, to be thrown into hell, ⁴⁸ where the *worms that eat them never die and the fire never goes out.* ⁴⁹ The fire itself will preserve them.

⁵⁰ Salt is a good thing; but if it loses its saltiness, how can you make it salty again? Have salt in yourselves and be at peace with one another."

MARK 9:2-50

Read: The transfiguration of Jesus: the spiritual shines through the material. Jesus explains to his disciples the need for prayer in the exercise of ministry. He announces again his passion, but the disciples still do not understand, so again he talks about the demands of discipleship.

Reflect: Are you aware of the presence of the spiritual in your daily life? What are you inspired to do? Why do you believe that Jesus must suffer and die? Should a disciple of Jesus always aspire to be the first? What does the image of a child suggest?

Pray: Pray so that you can contemplate God at all times, so that your trust in Him is like that of a child who absolutely trusts his or her parents. Pray also that as disciples of Jesus we aspire always to serve others.

Act: Try this day to contemplate the presence of God in all things, and give thanks by offering your service to others.

Divorce
(5:31; Mt 19:1; Lk 16:18)

10 ¹ Jesus then left that place and went to the province of Judea, beyond the Jordan River. Once more, crowds gathered around him and, once more, he taught them as he always did. ² Some (Pharisees came and) put him to the test with this question: "Is it right for a husband to divorce his wife?" ³ He replied, "What law did Moses give you?" ⁴ They answered, "Moses allowed us to write a certificate of dismissal in order to divorce."

⁵ Then Jesus said to them, "Moses wrote this law for you, because you have hearts of stone. ⁶ But from the beginning of creation, *God made them male and female;* ⁷ *and because of this, man has to leave father*

and mother and be joined to his wife; [8] *and the two shall become one body.* So, they are no longer two, but one body. [9] Therefore, let no one separate what God has joined."

[10] When they were indoors at home, the disciples again asked him about this [11] and he told them, "Whoever divorces his wife and marries another, commits adultery against his wife; [12] and the woman who divorces her husband and marries another, also commits adultery."

Let the children come to me
(Mt 19:13; Lk 18:15)

[13] People were bringing their little children to him to have him touch them, and the disciples rebuked them for this.

[14] When Jesus noticed it, he was very angry and said, "Let the children come to me and don't stop them, for the kingdom of God belongs to such as these. [15] Truly, I say to you, whoever does not receive the kingdom of God like a child will not enter it." [16] Then he took the children in his arms and, laying his hands on them, blessed them.

Jesus and the rich man
(Mt 19:16; Lk 18:18)

[17] Just as Jesus was setting out on his journey again, a man ran up, knelt before him and asked, "Good Master, what must I do to have eternal life?"

[18] Jesus answered, "Why do you call me good? No one is good but God alone. [19] You know the commandments: Do not kill; do not commit adultery; do not steal; do not bear false witness; do not cheat; honor your father and mother." [20] The man replied, "I have obeyed all these commandments since my childhood."

[21] Then Jesus looked steadily at him and loved him; and he said, "For you, one thing is lacking. Go, sell what you have and give the money to the poor; and you will have riches in heaven. Then, come, and follow me." [22] On hearing these words, his face fell and he went away sorrowful, for he was a man of great wealth.

How hard for the rich to discover the kingdom!

[23] Jesus looked around and said to his disciples, "How hard it is for those who have riches to enter the kingdom of God!" [24] The disciples were shocked at these words, but Jesus insisted, "Children, how hard it

is to enter the kingdom of God! ²⁵ It is easier for a camel to go through the eye of the needle than for one who is rich to enter the kingdom of God."

²⁶ They were more astonished than ever and wondered, "Who, then, can be saved?" ²⁷ Jesus looked steadily at them and said, "For human beings, it is impossible, but not for God; all things are possible with God."

The reward for those who follow Jesus
(Mt 19:27; Lk 18:28)

²⁸ Peter spoke up and said, "We have given up everything to follow you." ²⁹ Jesus answered, "Truly, there is no one who has left house, or brothers or sisters, or father or mother, or children, or lands, for my sake and for the gospel, ³⁰ who will not receive his reward. I say to you: even in the midst of persecution, he will receive a hundred times as many houses, brothers, sisters, mothers, children, and lands in the present time; and, in the world to come, eternal life. ³¹ Do pay attention: many who now are the first will be last, and the last, first."

MARK 10:1-31

Read: Jesus takes a position on the divorce practices of his day. He blesses some children. He is saddened by the choice of the man who desists to follow him by clinging to his riches, and talks about the reward that awaits his followers.

Reflect: What is your position on divorce? Have you left anything to follow Jesus? What do you think is the greatest reward that awaits you to follow him?

Pray: Pray to God for the matrimonial vocation, that married people reveal in their daily life the teaching of the Gospel. Pray also so that Christians always aspire to the kingdom and its justice rather than material goods.

Act: Live your vocation with generosity and detachment from material things.

---

³² They were on the road going up to Jerusalem, and Jesus was walking ahead. The Twelve were anxious, and those who followed were afraid. Once more Jesus took the Twelve aside to tell them what was to

happen to him. ³³ "You see we are going up to Jerusalem, and the Son of Man will be given over to the chief priests and the teachers of the law. They will condemn him to death and hand him over to the foreigners ³⁴ who will make fun of him, spit on him, scourge him, and kill him; but three days later he will rise."

James and John ask for the first places
(Mt 20:20; Lk 22:24)

³⁵ James and John, the sons of Zebedee, came to Jesus and said to him, "Master, we want you to grant us what we are going to ask of you." ³⁶ And he said, "What do you want me to do for you?" ³⁷ They answered, "Grant us to sit, one at your right hand and one at your left when you come in your glory."

³⁸ But Jesus said to them, "You don't know what you are asking. Can you drink the cup that I drink, or be baptized in the way I am baptized?" ³⁹ They answered, "We can." And Jesus told them, "The cup that I drink, you will drink; and you will be baptized in the way that I am baptized; ⁴⁰ but to sit at my right hand or at my left is not mine to grant. It has been prepared for others."

⁴¹ On hearing this, the other ten were angry with James and John. ⁴² Jesus then called them to him and said, "As you know, the so-called rulers of the nations behave like tyrants and those in authority oppress the people. ⁴³ But it shall not be so among you; whoever would be great among you must be your servant, ⁴⁴ and whoever would be first among you shall make himself slave of all. ⁴⁵ Think of the Son of Man who has not come to be served, but to serve, and to give his life to redeem many."

The blind man of Jericho
(Mt 20:29; Lk 18:35)

⁴⁶ They came to Jericho. As Jesus was leaving Jericho with his disciples and a large crowd, a blind beggar, Bartimaeus, the son of Timaeus, was sitting by the roadside. ⁴⁷ On hearing that it was Jesus of Nazareth passing by, he began to call out, "Son of David, Jesus, have mercy on me!" ⁴⁸ Many people scolded him and told him to keep quiet, but he shouted all the louder, "Son of David, have mercy on me!"

⁴⁹ Jesus, stopped and said, "Call him." So they called the blind man, saying, "Take heart! Get up, he is calling you!" ⁵⁰ He immediately threw aside his cloak, jumped up and went to Jesus.

⁵¹Then Jesus asked him, "What do you want me to do for you?" The blind man said, "Master, let me see again!" ⁵²And Jesus said to him, "Go your way, your faith has made you well." And, immediately, he could see, and he followed Jesus along the road.

> **MARK 10:32-52**
>
> **Read:** For the third time Jesus predicts his passion. The disciples still do not understand his teaching, and James and John ask for the first place. Jesus emphasizes that discipleship is about service to others. Finally, Jesus returns the sight to Bartimaeus.
>
> **Reflect:** Why do you think the disciples do not understand the teachings of Jesus? What does the following expression suggest to you: "The Son of Man did not come to be served, but to serve and to give his life as a ransom for many"?
>
> **Pray:** Ask God for the necessary strength to live the teachings of the Gospel with an attitude of service and dedication to others.
>
> **Act:** Make a special gesture of service to each of your own. Do it as if it were the last thing you could do for them.

The triumphant entry into Jerusalem
(Mt 21:1; Lk 19:28; Jn 12:12)

11 ¹When they drew near to Jerusalem and arrived at Bethphage and Bethany, at the Mount of Olives, Jesus sent two of his disciples with these instructions, ²"Go to the village ahead of you and, as you enter it, you will find there a colt tied up that no one has ridden. Untie it and bring it here. ³If anyone says to you, 'What are you doing?' give this answer, 'The Lord needs it, but he will send it back immediately.'"

⁴They went off and found the colt, out in the street, tied at the door. ⁵As they were untying it, some of the bystanders asked, "Why are you untying that colt?" ⁶They answered as Jesus had told them, and the people allowed them to continue.

⁷They brought the colt to Jesus, threw their cloaks on its back, and Jesus sat upon it. ⁸Many people also spread their cloaks on the road, while others spread leafy branches from the fields. ⁹Then the people

who walked ahead, and those who followed behind Jesus, began to shout, "Hosannah! *Blessed is he who comes in the name of the Lord!* [10] Blessed is the kingdom of our father David, which comes! Hosannah in the highest!"

[11] So Jesus entered Jerusalem and went into the temple. And after he had looked all around, as it was already late, he went out to Bethany with the Twelve.

Jesus curses the barren fig tree
(Mt 21:18; Lk 13:6)

[12] The next day, when they were leaving Bethany, he felt hungry. [13] In the distance, he noticed a fig tree covered with leaves; so he went to see if he could find anything on it. When he reached it, he found nothing but leaves, for it was not the season for figs. [14] Then Jesus said to the fig tree, "May no one ever eat your fruit!" And his disciples heard these words.

Jesus clears the temple
(Mt 21:10; Lk 19:45; Jn 2:14)

[15] When they reached Jerusalem, Jesus went to the temple and began to drive away all the people he saw buying and selling there. He overturned the tables of the moneychangers and the stools of those who sold pigeons. [16] And he would not let anyone carry anything through the temple area.

[17] Jesus then taught the people, "Does not God say in the Scriptures: *My house will be called a House of Prayer for all the nations?* But you have turned it into a den of thieves."

[18] The chief priests and the teachers of the law heard of this, and they tried to find a way to destroy him. They were afraid of him because all the people were astonished by his teaching.

[19] When evening came, Jesus left the city.

The power of faith
(Mt 21:20)

[20] Early the next morning, as they walked along the road, the disciples saw the fig tree withered to its roots. [21] Peter then said to him, "Master, look! The fig tree you cursed has withered."

[22] And Jesus replied, "Have faith in God. [23] Truly, I say to you, if you say to this mountain, 'Be taken up and cast into the sea,' and have no

doubt in your heart, but believe that what you say will happen, it will be done for you. 24 Therefore, I tell you, whatever you ask in prayer, believe that you have received it and it shall be done for you. 25 And when you stand to pray, if you have anything against anyone, forgive, 26 so that your heavenly Father may also forgive your sins."

By what authority do you act?
(Mt 21:23; Lk 20:1)

27 They were once again in Jerusalem. As Jesus was walking in the temple, the chief priests, the teachers of the law and the elders came to him 28 and asked, "What authority do you have to act like this? Who gave you the authority to do the things you do?"

29 Jesus said to them, "I will ask you a question, only one, and if you give me an answer, then I will tell you what authority I have to act like this. 30 Was John's baptism of heavenly or human origin? Answer me."

31 And they kept arguing among themselves, "If we answer that it was a work of God, he will say, 'Why then did you not believe him?'" 32 But neither could they answer before the people that the baptism of John was merely something human, for everyone regarded John as a prophet. 33 So they answered Jesus, "We don't know," and Jesus said to them, "Neither will I tell you what authority I have to act as I do."

MARK 11:1-33

Read: Jesus enters triumphantly into Jerusalem. He curses a fig tree and it dies. He expels merchants from the temple. And the religious leaders of Jerusalem complain about the authority of his actions.

Reflect: What does the event of the fig tree suggest? Is not it out of place? Are our temples houses of prayer? If they were not, what would you do?

Pray: Pray that you may contemplate and venerate the presence of God everywhere, especially in those who suffer and are marginalized.

Act: Treat those around you as if they were living temples of God, with respect, dignity and veneration.

Parable of the tenants
(Mt 21:33; Lk 20:9)

12 [1] Using parables, Jesus went on to say, "A man planted a vineyard, put a fence around it, dug a hole for the winepress and built a watchtower. Then he leased the vineyard to tenants and went abroad.

[2] In due time, he sent a servant to receive from the tenants the fruit of the vineyard. [3] But they seized the servant, struck him and sent him back empty-handed. [4] Again, the man sent another servant. They also struck him on the head and treated him shamefully. [5] He sent another and they killed him. In the same way, they treated many others: some they beat up and others they killed. [6] One was still left, his beloved son. And so, last of all, he sent him to the tenants, for he said, 'They will respect my son.'

[7] But those tenants said to one another, 'This is the one who is to inherit the vineyard. Let's kill him and the property will be ours.' [8] So they seized him and killed him and threw him out of the vineyard. [9] Now, what will the owner of the vineyard do? He will come and destroy those tenants and give the vineyard to others."

[10] And Jesus added, "Have you not read this text of the Scriptures: *The stone which the builders rejected has become the keystone;* [11] *this is the Lord's doing, and we marvel at it?*"

[12] They wanted to arrest him, for they realized that Jesus meant this parable for them, but they were afraid of the crowd; so they left him and went away.

Paying taxes to Caesar
(Mt 22:15; Lk 20:20)

[13] They sent to Jesus some Pharisees with members of Herod's party, with the purpose of trapping him by his own words. [14] They came and said to Jesus, "Master, we know that you are truthful; you are not influenced by anyone, and your answers do not vary according to who is listening to you, but you truly teach God's way. Tell us, is it against the law to pay taxes to Caesar? Should we pay them or not?"

[15] But Jesus saw through their trick and answered, "Why are you testing me? Bring me a silver coin and let me see it." [16] They brought him one and Jesus asked, "Whose image is this and whose name?" They

answered, "Caesar's." [17] Then Jesus said, "Give back to Caesar what is Caesar's and to God what is God's."

And they were greatly astonished.

The resurrection
(Mt 22:23; Lk 20:27)

[18] The Sadducees also came to Jesus. Since they claim that there is no resurrection, they questioned him in this way, [19] "Master, in the Scriptures, Moses gave us this law: If anyone dies and leaves a wife but no children, his brother must take the woman and, with her, have a baby who will be considered the child of his deceased brother. [20] Now, there were seven brothers. The first married a wife, but he died without leaving any children. [21] The second took the wife, and he also died, leaving no children. The same thing happened to the third. [22] In fact, all seven brothers died, leaving no children. Last of all, the woman died. [23] Now, in the resurrection, to which of them will she be wife? For all seven brothers had her as wife."

[24] Jesus replied, "Is this not the reason you are mistaken, that you do not understand the Scriptures or the power of God? [25] When they rise from the dead, men and women do not marry, but are like the angels in heaven.

[26] Now, about the resurrection of the dead, have you never had thoughts about the burning bush in the book of Moses? God said to Moses: *I am the God of Abraham, the God of Isaac and the God of Jacob.* [27] He is the God, not of the dead, but of the living. You are totally wrong."

MARK 12:1-27

Read: With the parable of the evil vinedressers, Jesus summarizes the activity of the religious leaders. The Pharisees and the Herodians set a trap by raising the issue of the tribute to the empire, but Jesus eludes it. The Sadducees, on the other hand, raise the theme of the resurrection of the dead, and Jesus clarifies that God is a God of the living, not of the dead.

Reflect: What do you think about the activity of our religious leaders? Should the Church interfere in matters of the State? Do you really expect the resurrection of the dead?

Pray: Pray for the leaders of the Church and for those who govern the country, so that they may be faithful to the mission they have received. Pray also that your faith will grow day by day and always wait in hope for the resurrection of the dead.

Act: Find out about the activities your local diocese is carrying out to promote life, peace, respect and justice in society.

The greatest commandment
(Mt 22:34; Lk 10:25; 20:40)

²⁸ A teacher of the law had been listening to this discussion and admired how Jesus answered them. So he came up and asked him, "Which commandment is the first of all?"

²⁹ Jesus answered, "The first is: *Hear, Israel! The Lord, our God, is One Lord*; ³⁰ *and you shall love the Lord, your God, with all your heart, with all your soul, with all your mind, and with all your strength.* ³¹ And after this comes a second commandment: *You shall love your neighbor as yourself.* There is no commandment greater than these two."

³² The teacher of the law said to him, "Well spoken, Master; you are right when you say that he is one and there is no other besides him. ³³ To love him with all our heart, with all our understanding and with all our strength and to love our neighbor as ourselves is more important than any burnt offering or sacrifice."

³⁴ Jesus approved this answer and said, "You are not far from the kingdom of God." And after that, no one dared to ask him any more questions.

Whose Son is the Christ?
(Mt 22:41; Lk 20:41; Mt 23:6)

³⁵ As Jesus was teaching in the temple, he said, "The teachers of the law say that the Messiah is the Son of David. How can that be? ³⁶ For David himself, inspired by the Holy Spirit, declared: The Lord said to my Lord, '*Sit at my right hand until I put your enemies under your feet!*' ³⁷ If David himself calls him Lord, in what way can he be his Son?"

Many people came to Jesus and listened to him gladly.

³⁸ As he was teaching, he also said to them, "Beware of those teachers of the law who enjoy walking around in long robes and being greeted in

the marketplace; 39 and who like to occupy reserved seats in the syna-gogues; and the first places at feasts. 40 They even devour the widow's and the orphan's goods while making a show of long prayers. How severe a sentence they will receive!"

The widow's offering
(Lk 21:1)

41 Jesus sat down opposite the temple treasury and watched the people dropping money into the treasury box and many rich people put in large offerings. 42 But a poor widow also came and dropped in two small coins.

43 Then Jesus called his disciples and said to them, "Truly, I say to you, this poor widow put in more than all those who gave offerings. 44 For all of them gave from their plenty; but she gave from her poverty and put in everything she had, her very living."

MARK 12:28-44

Read: Jesus defines the main point of the Law: love of God and neighbor. He questions the interpretation of the Scripture that deals with the Messiah and David. He warns about those who use religion for their own purpose and praises the generosity of a widow.

Reflect: Do you consider that there is a close relationship between love for God and neighbor? Why? Do you confess that Jesus is the Messiah? Why? Do you know people who use religion for their own benefit? Are you generous as the poor widow?

Pray: Ask God for the grace of being able to love him by loving others, and of confessing Jesus as Messiah by doing what he did.

Act: Share what you consider valuable (money, time, friendship, etc.) with someone in need.

Jesus speaks of the end
(Mt 24:1; Lk 21:5; 19:41; 17:23)

13 1 As Jesus left the temple, one of his disciples said, "Look, Master, at the enormous stones and wonderful buildings here!" 2 And Jesus answered, "You see these great buildings? Not one stone will be left upon another, but all will be torn down."

³After a while, when Jesus was sitting on the Mount of Olives facing the temple, Peter, James, John, and Andrew approached him privately and asked, ⁴"Tell us when this will be. What sign will be given us before all this happens?"

⁵Then Jesus began to tell them, "Don't let anyone mislead you. ⁶Many will come in my name saying, 'I am he,' and they will deceive many people.

⁷When you hear of wars and threats of war, don't be troubled; this must occur, but the end is not yet. ⁸Nation will fight nation and kingdom will oppose kingdom. There will be earthquakes everywhere and famines, too. And these will be like the first pains of childbirth. ⁹Be on your guard, for you will be arrested and taken to court. You will be beaten in synagogues; and you will stand before governors and kings for my sake, to bear witness before them. ¹⁰For the preaching of the gospel to all nations has to come first.

¹¹So, when you are arrested and brought to trial, don't worry about what you are to say; for you shall say what will be given to you in that hour. It is not you who speak, but the Holy Spirit.

¹²Brother will betray brother even to death, and the father his child. Children will turn against their parents and have them put to death. ¹³You will be hated by all for my name's sake, but whoever holds out to the end will be saved.

Last days of Jerusalem

¹⁴So, when you see the desolating abomination set in the place where it should not be (may the reader understand!), then let those in Judea flee to the mountains. ¹⁵If you are on the housetop, don't come down to take anything with you. ¹⁶If you are in the field, don't turn back to fetch your cloak. ¹⁷How hard it will be then for pregnant women and mothers with babies at the breast! ¹⁸Pray that it may not happen in winter. ¹⁹For this will be a time of distress, such as was never known from the beginning, when God created the world, until now; and is never to be known again. ²⁰So that, if the Lord had not shortened that time, no one would survive; but he decided to shorten it for the sake of those whom he has chosen.

²¹And if anyone says to you at that time, 'Look, here is the Messiah! Look, he is there!'—do not believe it. ²²For false messiahs and false

prophets will arise and perform signs and wonders in order to deceive even God's chosen people, if that were possible. 23 Be on your guard then; I have told you everything ahead of time.

The coming of the Son of Man
(Mt 24:29; Lk 21:25)

24 Later on in those days, after that disastrous time, *the sun will grow dark, the moon will not give its light,* 25 *the stars will fall out of the sky, and the whole universe will be shaken.* 26 Then people *will see the Son of Man coming in the clouds* with great power and glory. 27 And he will send the angels to gather his chosen people from the four winds, from the ends of the earth to the ends of the sky.

28 Learn a lesson from the fig tree: as soon as its branches become tender and it begins to sprout leaves, you know that summer is near. 29 In the same way, when you see these things happening, know that the time is near, even at the door. 30 Truly, I say to you, this generation will not pass away until all this has happened. 31 Heaven and earth will pass away, but my words will not pass away.

32 But, regarding that day and that hour, no one knows when it will come, not even the angels, not even the Son, but only the Father.

33 Be alert and watch, for you don't know when the time will come. 34 When a man goes abroad and leaves his home, he puts his servants in charge, giving to each one some responsibility; and he orders the doorkeeper to stay awake. 35 So stay awake for you don't know when the Lord of the house will come, in the evening, or at midnight, when the cock crows or before dawn. 36 If he comes suddenly do not let him catch you asleep.

37 And what I say to you, I say to all: Stay awake!"

MARK 13:1-37

Read: Chapter thirteen develops the eschatological discourse (about the last days) of Jesus. With apocalyptic language he invites the disciples to be prepared, attentive, at the arrival of the Messiah.

Reflect: Do you consider that we are living in times worse than before? How should we prepare for the coming of the Lord?

> **Pray:** Ask the Lord for perseverance and strength to live the Gospel message, work for the kingdom and its justice, and always be ready to meet the Lord.
>
> **Act:** Make a list of those things you think you should do before your final encounter with the Lord. Try to make them this day.

Conspiracy against Jesus
(Mt 26:2; Lk 22:1; Jn 11:47)

14 ¹It was now two days before the feast of the Passover and Unleavened Bread. The chief priests and the teachers of the law were looking for a way to arrest Jesus on a false charge and put him to death; ²but they said, "Not during the Festival, for there might be trouble among the people."

Jesus anointed at Bethany
(Mt 26:6; Jn 12:1)

³Jesus was in Bethany in the house of Simon the leper. As he was reclining at dinner, a woman entered carrying an alabaster jar of expensive perfume made of pure nard. She broke the jar and poured the perfumed oil on Jesus' head. ⁴Then some of them became angry and said, "What a useless waste of perfume. ⁵It could have been sold for more than three hundred silver coins and the money given to the poor." And they criticized her.

⁶But Jesus said, "Let her alone; why are you troubling her? What she has just done for me is a very charitable work. ⁷At any time you can help the poor, for you always have them with you; but you will not have me forever. ⁸This woman did what she had to do: she anointed my body for burial before I die. ⁹Truly, I say to you, wherever the Good News is proclaimed, and this will be throughout the world, what she has done will be told in praise of her."

¹⁰Then Judas Iscariot, one of the Twelve, went off to the chief priests in order to betray Jesus to them. ¹¹On hearing him, they were excited and promised to give him money. So Judas started planning the best way to hand Jesus over to them.

The Lord's Supper
(Mt 26:17; Lk 22:7; 1 Cor 11:23; Jn 13)

[12] On the first day of the Festival of Unleavened Bread, the day when the Passover Lamb was killed, the disciples asked him, "Where would you have us go to prepare the Passover meal for you?"

[13] So Jesus sent two of his disciples with these instructions, "Go into the city, and there, a man will come to you carrying a jar of water. Follow him to the house he enters and say to the owner, [14] 'The Master says, "Where is the room where I may eat the Passover meal with my disciples?"' [15] Then he will show you a large room upstairs, already arranged and furnished. There, you will prepare for us." [16] The disciples went off. When they reached the city they found everything just as Jesus had told them and they prepared the Passover meal.

[17] When it was evening, Jesus arrived with the Twelve. [18] While they were at table eating, Jesus said, "Truly, I tell you, one of you will betray me, *one who shares my meal.*" [19] They were deeply distressed at hearing this and asked him, one after the other, "You don't mean me, do you?" [20] And Jesus answered, "It is one of you Twelve, one who dips his bread in the dish with me. [21] The Son of Man is going as the Scriptures say he will. But alas for that man by whom the Son of Man is betrayed; better for him if he had never been born."

[22] While they were eating, Jesus took bread, blessed it and broke it, and gave it to them. And he said, "Take this. It is my body." [23] Then he took a cup; and after he had given thanks, he passed it to them and they all drank from it. [24] And he said, "This is my blood, the blood of the Covenant poured out for many. [25] Truly, I say to you, I will not taste the fruit of the vine again, until that day when I drink the new wine in the kingdom of God."

Peter's denial foretold
(Mt 26:30; Lk 22:34; Jn 13:37)

[26] After singing psalms of praise, they went out to the Mount of Olives. [27] And Jesus said to them, "All of you will be dismayed and fall away; for the Scripture says: *I will strike the shepherd and the sheep will be scattered.* [28] But after I am raised, I will go to Galilee ahead of you."

[29] Then Peter said to him, "Even though all the others fall away, I will not." [30] And Jesus replied, "Truly I say to you, today, this very night,

before the cock crows twice, you will deny me three times." [31] But Peter insisted, "Though I have to die with you, I will never deny you." And all of them said the same.

MARK 14:1-31

Read: Jesus' adversaries seek him out to kill him. Jesus is aware of the proximity of his death, he lets himself be anointed with oil, he celebrates his last supper: he institutes the Eucharist, announces the betrayal of one of their own and the abandonment of all.

Reflect: Are you willing to be Eucharist for others as Jesus was? Do you consider yourself prepared to follow Jesus to the ultimate consequences?

Pray: Pray that the Christian life will always be Eucharist for others: donation, self-giving, service. Pray also that we will not be tempted to trust more in our strength than in the presence of our Lord.

Act: Visit Jesus in the sacrament of the altar; offer your wishes, concerns and fears there.

Gethsemane
(Lk 22:40; Jn 18:1)

[32] They came to a place, which is called Gethsemane; and Jesus said to his disciples, "Sit here while I pray."

[33] But he took Peter, James, and John along with him, and, becoming filled with fear and distress, [34] he said to them, "My soul is full of sorrow, even to death. Remain here and stay awake."

[35] Then he went a little further on and fell to the ground, praying that, if possible, this hour might pass him by. Jesus said, [36] "Abba, Father, all things are possible for you. Take this cup away from me. Yet, not what I want, but what you want."

[37] Then he came and found them asleep; and he said to Peter, "Simon, are you sleeping? Couldn't you stay awake for one hour? [38] Stay awake and pray, all of you, so that you may not slip into temptation. The spirit indeed is willing, but the body is weak." [39] And, going away, he prayed saying the same words. [40] When he came back to the disciples, he found

them asleep again. They could not keep their eyes open and they did not know what to say to him.

⁴¹ When he came back the third time, he said to them, "Are you still sleeping and resting? It is all over, the time has come: the Son of Man is now given into the hands of sinners. ⁴² Get up, let us go! Look: the one who betrays me is approaching."

The arrest
(Mt 26:47; Lk 22:47; Jn 18:2)

⁴³ While Jesus was still speaking, Judas, one of the Twelve, came up. With him was a crowd armed with swords and clubs, who had been sent by the chief priests, the teachers of the law and the elders. ⁴⁴ The traitor had arranged a signal for them, "The one I kiss, he is the man. Arrest him and take him away under guard."

⁴⁵ So, when he came, he went directly to Jesus, and said, "Master! Master!" and kissed him. ⁴⁶ Then they seized Jesus and arrested him. ⁴ One of the bystanders drew his sword and struck out at the High Priest's servant, cutting off his ear.

⁴⁸ Jesus turned to them and said, "So, you have set out against a robber! Did you need swords and clubs to arrest me? ⁴⁹ Day after day, I was among you, teaching in the temple, and you did not arrest me. But let the Scriptures be fulfilled." ⁵⁰ Then they all deserted him and fled.

⁵¹ A young man, covered by nothing but a linen cloth, followed Jesus. When they took hold of him, ⁵² he left the cloth in their hands and fled away naked.

⁵³ They led Jesus to the High Priest, and all the chief priests assembled with the elders and the teachers of the law. ⁵⁴ Peter had followed him at a distance; and went right into the courtyard of the High Priest, where he sat with the guards, warming himself at the fire.

⁵⁵ Now the chief priests and the whole Council tried to find some evidence against Jesus so that they might put him to death, but they were unable to find anything. ⁵⁶ Even though many came up to speak falsely against him, their evidence did not agree. ⁵⁷ At last, some stood up and gave this false witness: ⁵⁸ "We heard him say, 'I will destroy this temple made by human hands, and in three days I will build another not made by human hands.'" ⁵⁹ But even so, their evidence did not agree.

⁶⁰ The High Priest then stood up in the midst of them and asked Jesus, "Have you no answer at all? What about this evidence against you?" ⁶¹ But Jesus was silent and made no reply.

The High Priest put a second question to him, "Are you the Christ, the Son of the Blessed One?" ⁶² Then Jesus answered, "I am, and you will see *the Son of Man seated at the right hand of the Most Powerful, and coming with the clouds of heaven around him.*" ⁶³ Then the High Priest, tearing his garments to show his horror, said, "What more evidence do we need? ⁶⁴ You have just heard his blasphemous words. What is your decision?" They all condemned Jesus, saying, "He must die."

⁶⁵ Some of them began to spit on Jesus; and, blindfolding him, they struck him and said, "Play the prophet!" And the guards set upon him with blows.

Peter disowns Jesus
(Mt 26:69; Jn 18:15)

⁶⁶ While Peter was below in the courtyard, a servant-girl of the High Priest came by. ⁶⁷ Noticing Peter beside the fire, she looked straight at him and said, "You also were with Jesus, the Nazarene." ⁶⁸ But he denied it, "I don't know or understand what you are talking about." And he went out through the gateway and a cock crowed.

⁶⁹ The servant-girl saw him there and told the bystanders, "This man is one of them." ⁷⁰ But Peter denied it again. After a little while, those standing nearby said to Peter, "Of course you are one of them; you are a Galilean, aren't you?" ⁷¹ And Peter began to justify himself with curses and oaths, "I don't know the man you are talking about."

⁷² Just then a cock crowed a second time and Peter remembered what Jesus had said to him, "Before the cock crows twice, you will deny me three times." And he broke down and wept.

MARK 14:32-72

Read: Jesus prays in Gethsemane—he knows that his hour is near—while the most intimate of his disciples sleep. He is arrested and taken to court. There are many who accuse him but their testimonies do not match. He proclaims himself the Son of God and therefore is condemned to death. Peter denies any link with his Master.

> **Reflect:** Why do you think Jesus' adversaries were looking for his death? Are you listening for the Lord's call, or do you sleep like the disciples? Being in Peter's place, what would you have done?
>
> **Pray:** Ask for grace so that you can proclaim at all times that you are a disciple of Jesus, not only with words but, above all, with your way of life. Also ask for forgiveness if you think you have ever denied him.
>
> **Act:** Share with someone what it means for you to be a disciple of Jesus. Do not be afraid to talk about your faith.

Jesus before Pilate
(Mt 27:11; Lk 23:2; Jn 18:28)

15 ¹Early in the morning, the chief priests, the elders and the teachers of the law (that is, the whole Council or Sanhedrin) had their plan ready. They put Jesus in chains, led him away and handed him over to Pilate.

²Pilate asked him, "Are you the King of the Jews?" Jesus answered, "You say so." ³As the chief priests accused Jesus of many things, ⁴Pilate asked him again, "Have you no answer at all? See how many charges they bring against you." ⁵But Jesus gave no further answers, much to Pilate's surprise.

⁶At every Passover festival, Pilate used to free any prisoner the people asked for. ⁷Now there was a man called Barabbas, jailed with the rioters who had committed murder in the uprising. ⁸When the crowd went up to ask Pilate the usual favor, ⁹he said to them, "Do you want me to set free the King of the Jews?" ¹⁰for he realized that the chief priests had handed Jesus over to him out of envy. ¹¹But the chief priests stirred up the crowd to ask instead, for the release of Barabbas. ¹²Pilate replied, "And what shall I do with the man you call King of the Jews?" ¹³The crowd shouted back, "Crucify him!" ¹⁴Pilate asked, "What evil has he done?" But they shouted the louder, "Crucify him!"

Jesus crowned with thorns
(Mt 27:27; Jn 19:1)

¹⁵As Pilate wanted to please the people, he freed Barabbas; and, having had Jesus flogged, Pilate handed him over to be crucified.

¹⁶ The soldiers took him inside the courtyard, known as the praetorium, and called the rest of their companions. ¹⁷ They clothed him in a purple cloak, and twisting a crown of thorns, they forced it onto his head. ¹⁸ Then they began saluting him, "Long life to the King of the Jews!" ¹⁹ With a stick they gave him blows on the head and spat on him; then they knelt down, pretending to worship him.

²⁰ When they had finished mocking him, they pulled off the purple cloak and put his own clothes on him.

The crucifixion

The soldiers led him out of the city to crucify him. ²¹ On the way, they met Simon of Cyrene, father of Alexander and Rufus, who was coming in from the country and forced him to carry the cross of Jesus.

²² When they had led him to the place called Golgotha, which means the Skull, ²³ they offered him wine mixed with myrrh, but he would not take it. ²⁴ Then they nailed him to the cross and divided his clothes among themselves, casting lots to decide what every man should take.

²⁵ It was about nine o'clock in the morning when they crucified him. ²⁶ The statement of his offense was displayed above his head and it reads, "The King of the Jews." ²⁷ They also crucified two robbers with him, one on his right and one on his left. ²⁸ And the Scripture was fulfilled which says: And with lawless ones, he was numbered.

²⁹ People passing by laughed at him, shook their heads and jeered, "Aha! So, you are able to tear down the temple and build it up in three days? ³⁰ Save yourself now and come down from the cross!"

³¹ In the same way, the chief priests and the teachers of the law mocked him, saying to one another, "The man who saved others cannot save himself. ³² Let's see the Messiah, the King of Israel, come down from his cross and then we will believe in him." Even the men who were crucified with Jesus insulted him.

The death of Jesus
(Mt 27:45; Lk 23:44; Jn 19:28)

³³ When noon came, darkness fell over the whole land and lasted until three o'clock; ³⁴ and at three o'clock Jesus cried out in a loud voice, "*Eloi, Eloi, lamma sabachthani?*" which means, "My God, my God, why have you deserted me?" ³⁵ As soon as they heard these words, some of the bystanders said, "Listen! He is calling for Elijah." ³⁶ And one of them

went quickly to fill a sponge with bitter wine and, putting it on a reed, gave it to him to drink, saying, "Now let's see whether Elijah comes to take him down."

[37] But Jesus uttered a loud cry and gave up his spirit. [38] And immediately, the curtain that enclosed the temple Sanctuary was torn in two, from top to bottom.

[39] The captain, who was standing in front of him, saw how Jesus died and heard the cry he gave; and he said, "Truly, this man was the Son of God."

[40] There were also some women watching from a distance; among them were Mary Magdalene, Mary the mother of James the younger and of Joses, and Salome, [41] who had followed Jesus when he was in Galilee and saw to his needs. There were also others who had come up with him to Jerusalem.

The burial

[42] It was now evening and, as it was Preparation Day, that is the day before the Sabbath, [43] Joseph of Arimathea boldly went to Pilate and asked for the body of Jesus. Joseph was a respected member of the Council, who was himself, waiting for the kingdom of God.

[44] Pilate was surprised that Jesus should have died so soon; so he summoned the captain and inquired if Jesus was already dead. [45] After hearing the captain, he let Joseph have the body.

[46] Joseph took it down and wrapped it in the linen sheet he had bought. He laid the body in a tomb that had been cut out of the rock and rolled a stone across the entrance to the tomb. [47] Now Mary of Magdala and Mary the mother of Joses took note of where the body had been laid.

MARK 15:1-47

Read: The religious authorities give Jesus to the Roman political authority to condemn him. Pilate gives in to the pressure of the crowd. The soldiers make fun of Jesus and then crucify him on Golgotha, where he dies. A centurion proclaims him "Son of God." Some followers remain faithful to the Master, and Joseph of Arimathea buries him.

Reflect: Do you consider that Jesus was abandoned by God?

> Was Pilate a weak man? As a disciple of Jesus, how would you act in such circumstances? In your opinion, what is the hardest part in following Jesus today?
>
> **Pray:** Look at a crucifix and pray for all the men and women who suffer unjust sentences. Pray also that Christians will be faithful followers of the Lord: righteous and in solidarity with others.
>
> **Act:** Approach a church and pray the Via Crucis (Way of the Cross).

He has been raised; he is not here
(Mt 28; Lk 24; Jn 20)

16 ¹When the Sabbath was over, Mary of Magdala, Mary the mother of James, and Salome bought spices so that they might go and anoint the body. ²And very early in the morning, on the first day of the week, just after sunrise, they came to the tomb.

³They were saying to one another, "Who will roll back the stone for us from the entrance to the tomb?" ⁴But, as they looked up, they noticed that the stone had already been rolled away. It was a very big stone.

⁵As they entered the tomb, they saw a young man in a white robe seated on the right, and they were amazed. ⁶But he said to them, "Don't be alarmed; you are looking for Jesus of Nazareth who was crucified; he has been raised and is not here. This is, however, the place where they laid him. ⁷Now go, and tell his disciples and Peter: Jesus is going ahead of you to Galilee; you will see him there, just as he told you." ⁸The women went out and fled from the tomb for terror and amazement had seized them. And they were so afraid that they said nothing to anyone.

Another conclusion of Mark's gospel

⁹After Jesus rose early on the first day of the week, he appeared first to Mary of Magdala, from whom he had driven out seven demons. ¹⁰She went and reported the news to his followers who were now mourning and weeping. ¹¹But when they heard that he lived and had been seen by her, they would not believe it.

¹²After this he showed himself in another form to two of them as they were walking into the country. ¹³These men also went back and told the others, but they did not believe them.

¹⁴Later Jesus showed himself to the Eleven while they were at table. He reproached them for their unbelief, and hardness of heart, in refusing to believe those who had seen him after he had risen.

¹⁵Then he told them, "Go out to the whole world and proclaim the Good News to all creation. ¹⁶The one who believes and is baptized will be saved; the one who refuses to believe will be condemned. ¹⁷Signs like these will accompany those who have believed: in my name they will cast out demons and speak new languages; ¹⁸they will pick up snakes, and if they drink anything poisonous, they will be unharmed; they will lay their hands on the sick and they will be healed."

¹⁹So then, after speaking to them, the Lord Jesus was taken up into heaven and took his place at the right hand of God. ²⁰The Eleven went forth and preached everywhere, while the Lord worked with them and confirmed the message by the signs that accompanied it.

MARK 16:1-20

Read: Probably the Gospel ended in verse 8. The women find the tomb empty, an angel announces the resurrection of the Lord and tells them to announce it to the other disciples. They leave scared, and do not say anything to anyone. To give a proper conclusion, later the other verses would have been added.

Reflect: Do you feel in your daily life the presence of the risen Jesus? How? What is the hardest part in announcing the resurrection of Jesus? What does the unfinished end of the Gospel of Mark suggest to you?

Pray: Pray to God so that Christians can bear witness with our lives that Jesus has conquered death. May we proclaim that the God of our faith is a God of life.

Act: Celebrate the Lord's resurrection by participating in an activity that takes place in your parish in favor of life.

LUKE

The third Gospel is the work of a disciple of Paul, probably a physician (Col 4:14) of Syrian origin. He must have converted to the Christian faith in the 40's when the persecuted Christians of Jerusalem and Caesarea took refuge outside Palestine, bringing the message with them. As early as the year 50 A.D., Luke accompanied Paul in his missions (Acts 16:10).

Luke may have concluded his Gospel and Acts in Greece. For him, these books were two halves of the same work and they were probably finished between the years 63–64 A.D.

Luke tells us that he went to seek the testimonies of the first servants of the word, namely, the apostles (1:1-5). In fact, more than once, Luke went with Paul to Jerusalem and Caesarea, two great centers of the Church in Palestine, and these first communities kept the documents that the first three Gospels used.

Luke, the same as Mark, kept the two main sections that served as the basis of the Church's early catechesis, namely: the activity of Jesus in Galilee and his final days in Jerusalem. But between them, Luke inserted the content of another document with many sayings of Jesus. He intentionally placed them during Jesus' journey from Galilee to Jerusalem to show that Christian life is placed under the sign of the cross.

Other documents of the first Christian communities of Palestine provided Luke with the content of his first two chapters devoted to the infancy of Jesus. It is the testimony of the primitive community of which Mary was a member. From the very start, these chapters give to the Gospel of Luke its own personality. If we had to characterize it in one word, we would have to say that it is the most human of the four.

We can see this profoundly human aspect of Luke in his care to recall the attitude of Jesus toward women. Luke had left his family to follow Paul in his missions and, as a result, he always lived with insecurity and provisionally and more than others, he underlined the incompatibility of the Gospel with possessions.

Luke learned a great deal from Paul, his teacher. He emphasized the words of Jesus that remind us that salvation is always, first and foremost, a personal gift of God rather than a reward for our merits. This highlighting of the strange mercy of God has given us the unforgettable parables of Chapter 15.

After the infancy narrative (1–2), and the account of the Baptism of Jesus in Judea, the Gospel of Luke is made up of three sections:

– The ministry of Jesus in Galilee: 3:1—9:56;
– The journey through Samaria to Jerusalem: 9:57—18:17;
– The events of Jerusalem: 18:18-24.

The last chapter on the apparitions of the risen Jesus will serve as an invitation to read the Book of Acts, which is a continuation of Luke's Gospel.

LUKE

1 [1]Several people have set themselves to relate the events that have taken place among us [2]as they were told by the first witnesses who later became ministers of the word. [3]After I, myself, had carefully gone over the whole story from the beginning, it seemed right for me to give you, Theophilus, an orderly account [4]so that your Excellency may know the truth of all you have been taught.

The birth of John the Baptist foretold

[5]In the days of Herod, king of Judea, there lived a priest named Zechariah, belonging to the priestly clan of Abiah. Elizabeth, Zechariah's wife, also belonged to a priestly family. [6]Both of them were upright in the eyes of God and lived blamelessly in accordance with all the laws and commands of the Lord, [7]but they had no child. Elizabeth could not have any and now they were both very old.

[8]Now, while Zechariah and those with him were fulfilling their office, [9]it fell to him by lot, according to the custom of the priests, to enter the Sanctuary of the Lord and burn incense. [10]At the time of offering incense, all the people were praying outside; [11]it was then that an angel of the Lord appeared to him, standing on the right side of the altar of incense. [12]On seeing the angel, Zechariah was deeply troubled, and fear took hold of him.

[13]But the angel said to him, "Don't be afraid, Zechariah, be assured that your prayer has been heard. Your wife Elizabeth will bear you a son, and you shall name him John. [14]He will bring joy and gladness to you and many will rejoice at his birth.

[15]This son of yours will be great in the eyes of the Lord. Listen: he shall never drink wine or strong drink, but he will be filled with the Holy

Spirit even from his mother's womb. [16] Through him, many of the people of Israel will turn to the Lord their God. [17] He, himself, will open the way to the Lord with the spirit and power of the prophet Elijah; he will reconcile fathers and children, and lead the disobedient to wisdom and righteousness in order to make ready a people prepared for the Lord."

[18] Zechariah said to the angel, "How can I believe this? I am an old man and my wife is elderly, too." [19] The angel replied, "I am Gabriel, who stands before God; and I am the one sent to speak to you and to bring you this good news! My words will come true in their time. [20] But you would not believe; and now, you will be silent and unable to speak until this has happened."

[21] Meanwhile, the people waited for Zechariah; and they were surprised that he delayed so long in the Sanctuary. [22] When he finally appeared, he could not speak to them; and they realized that he had seen a vision in the Sanctuary. He remained dumb and made signs to them.

[23] When his time of service was completed, Zechariah returned home; [24] and, some time later, Elizabeth became pregnant. For five months she kept to herself, remaining at home, and thinking, [25] "This, for me, is the Lord's doing! This is his time for mercy and for taking away my public disgrace."

LUKE 1:1-25

Read: Luke presents the goal of his work "to clearly understand the lessons learned" (4). God acts in history, hears the prayer of the faithful (13), and nothing is impossible for Him (19-20). John the Baptist is the precursor of the Lord.

Reflect: What does all this tells you? Is it possible to contemplate God's action in history? How?

Pray: I ask you, O Lord, the grace to recognize your presence in all the events of life and in the face of every person who crosses my path.

Act: Review your history mentally and contemplate God's presence in it. Praise Him with a song of thanksgiving.

The Annunciation
(Mt 1:18)

²⁶ In the sixth month, the angel Gabriel was sent from God to a town of Galilee called Nazareth. He was sent ²⁷ to a virgin who was betrothed to a man named Joseph, of the family of David; and the virgin's name was Mary.

²⁸ The angel came to her and said, "Rejoice, full of grace, the Lord is with you!" ²⁹ Mary was troubled at these words, wondering what this greeting could mean.

³⁰ But the angel said, "Do not fear, Mary, for God has looked kindly on you. ³¹ You shall conceive and bear a son; and you shall call him Jesus. ³² He will be great, and shall rightly be called Son of the Most High. The Lord God will give him the kingdom of David, his ancestor; he will rule over the people of Jacob forever; ³³ and his reign shall have no end."

³⁴ Then Mary said to the angel, "How can this be since I am a virgin?" ³⁵ And the angel said to her, "The Holy Spirit will come upon you and the power of the Most High will overshadow you; therefore, the holy child to be born of you shall be called Son of God. ³⁶ Even your relative, Elizabeth, is expecting a son in her old age, although she was unable to have a child; and she is now in her sixth month. ³⁷ With God nothing is impossible."

³⁸ Then Mary said, "I am the handmaid of the Lord, let it be done to me as you have said." And the angel left her.

LUKE 1:26-38

Read: The difference between the birth of John and of Jesus is surprising. John will be great before the Lord; Jesus will be great and is also the Son of the Most High. John prepares the people; Jesus will rule them. John's mission is temporal; the reign of Jesus lasts forever. Mary responds generously to God's plan: "Let it be done to me as you have said."

Reflect: Do you trust in the power of God? How? Do you believe in his word? How do you respond to the call that God makes you every day to love and serve Him in the brothers and sisters?

> **Pray:** I ask from you, O Lord, the strength to trust in your Word, respond to your call and do your will.
>
> **Act:** Review the things you do every day and see how many of them do you do the will of God.

Mary visits Elizabeth

³⁹ Mary then set out for a town in the hill country of Judah. ⁴⁰ She entered the house of Zechariah and greeted Elizabeth. ⁴¹ When Elizabeth heard Mary's greeting, the baby leaped in her womb. Elizabeth was filled with the Holy Spirit and, ⁴² giving a loud cry, said, "You are most blessed among women, and blessed is the fruit of your womb! ⁴³ How is it that the mother of my Lord comes to me? ⁴⁴ The moment your greeting sounded in my ears, the baby within me suddenly leaped for joy. ⁴⁵ Blessed are you who believed that the Lord's word would come true!"

⁴⁶ And Mary said,

> "My soul proclaims the greatness of the Lord,
> ⁴⁷ my spirit exults in God, my savior!
> ⁴⁸ He has looked upon his servant in her lowliness,
> and people, forever, will call me blessed.
> ⁴⁹ The Mighty One has done great things for me,
> Holy is his Name!
> ⁵⁰ From age to age, his mercy extends
> to those who live in his presence.
> ⁵¹ He has acted with power and done wonders,
> and scattered the proud with their plans.
> ⁵² He has put down the mighty from their thrones,
> and lifted up those who are downtrodden.
> ⁵³ He has filled the hungry with good things,
> but has sent the rich away empty.
> ⁵⁴ He held out his hand to Israel, his servant,
> for he remembered his mercy,
> ⁵⁵ even as he promised to our fathers,
> to Abraham and his descendants forever."

⁵⁶ Mary remained with Elizabeth for about three months, and then returned home.

LUKE 1:39-56

Read: Mary hurried to go visit her cousin Elizabeth who will give birth in her old age. Elizabeth praises Mary, and Mary praises God with the "Magnificat": praise to God that becomes present in history, showing His power by saving us.

Reflect: What does the attitude of Mary and Elizabeth suggest to you? Could you make a song of praise like Mary? What implications does this expression have today: "He has put down the mighty from their thrones, and lifted up those who are downtrodden"?

Pray: Oh God, help me to contemplate you in the daily events of life, and help me to make of my life a song of praise for your nearness.

Act: Discreetly, offer to help a friend or family member in need. Let this gesture be a way to thank God for His closeness.

Birth of John the Baptist

[57] When the time came for Elizabeth, she gave birth to a son. [58] Her neighbors and relatives heard that the merciful Lord had done a wonderful thing for her and they rejoiced with her.

[59] When, on the eighth day, they came to attend the circumcision of the child, they wanted to name him Zechariah after his father. [60] But his mother said, "Not so; he shall be called John." [61] They said to her, "But no one in your family has that name!" [62] and they made signs to his father for the name he wanted to give him. [63] Zechariah asked for a writing tablet, and wrote on it, "His name is John;" and they were very surprised. [64] Immediately, Zechariah could speak again and his first words were in praise of God.

[65] A holy fear came on all in the neighborhood, and throughout the hill country of Judea, the people talked about these events. [66] All who heard of it, pondered in their minds and wondered, "What will this child be?" For they understood that the hand of the Lord was with him.

[67] Zechariah, filled with the Holy Spirit, sang this canticle:

[68] "Blessed be the Lord God of Israel,
for he has come and redeemed his people.
[69] In the house of David his servant,

he has raised up for us a victorious Savior;

70 as he promised through his prophets of old,

71 salvation from our enemies

and from the hand of our foes.

72 He has shown mercy to our fathers;

and remembered his holy Covenant,

73 the oath he swore to Abraham, our father,

74 to deliver us from the enemy,

75 that we might serve him fearlessly

as a holy and righteous people,

all the days of our lives.

76 And you, my child,

shall be called Prophet of the Most High,

for you shall go before the Lord

to prepare the way for him,

77 and to enable his people to know of their salvation

when he comes to forgive their sins.

78 This is the work of the mercy of our God,

who comes from on high as a rising sun,

79 shining on those who live in darkness

and in the shadow of death,

and guiding our feet into the way of peace."

80 As the child grew up, he was seen to be strong in the Spirit; and he lived in the desert until the day when he appeared openly in Israel.

LUKE 1:57-80

Read: The text tells of the birth of John the Baptist and presents the song of Zechariah: God does not forget His people; His action is salvation for all.

Reflect: Have you contrasted your projects with God's plans? Do they relate? Do you feel the nearness of God in your life?

Pray: I ask from you, O God, the gift of discernment to know what you want from me. I also ask for strength to do your will.

Act: Go to a church and there offer to the Lord your personal projects.

The birth of Jesus

2 ¹At that time, the emperor issued a decree for a census of the whole empire to be taken. ²This first census was taken when Quirinus was governor of Syria. ³Everyone had to be registered in his own town. So everyone set out for his own city. ⁴Joseph, too, set out from Nazareth of Galilee. As he belonged to the family of David, being a descendant of his, he went to Judea, to David's town of Bethlehem, ⁵to be registered with Mary, his wife, who was with child.

⁶They were in Bethlehem when the time came for her to have her child; ⁷and she gave birth to a son, her firstborn. She wrapped him in torn rags and laid him in a feeding trough because there was no place for them in the inn.

The shepherds and the angels

⁸There were shepherds camping in the countryside, taking turns to watch over their flocks by night. ⁹Suddenly, an angel of the Lord appeared to them with the glory of the Lord shining around them.

As they were terrified, ¹⁰the angel said to them, "Don't be afraid; I am here to give you good news, great joy for all the people. ¹¹Today, a Savior has been born to you in David's town; he is the Messiah and the Lord. ¹²Let this be a sign to you: you will find a baby wrapped in torn rags and lying in a feeding trough."

¹³Suddenly, the angel was surrounded by many more heavenly spirits praising God and saying, ¹⁴"Glory to God in the highest and Peace on earth to those whom God loves."

¹⁵When the angels had left them and gone back to heaven, the shepherds said to one another, "Let us go as far as Bethlehem and see what the Lord has made known to us." ¹⁶So they came hurriedly and found Mary and Joseph, and the baby lying in the feeding trough. ¹⁷On seeing him, they related what they had been told about the child; ¹⁸and all were astonished on hearing the shepherds.

¹⁹As for Mary, she treasured all these words and pondered them in her heart.

²⁰The shepherds then returned, giving glory and praise to God for all they had heard and seen, just as the angels had told them.

²¹On the eighth day, the circumcision of the baby had to be performed; he was named Jesus, the name the angel had given him before he was conceived.

LUKE 2:1-21

Read: The birth of Jesus in a manger is not just a circumstantial data, but expresses God's option for the simple and the poor, as Mary, Joseph and the shepherds who come near the child. Luke highlights another detail: "Mary kept and pondered everything in her heart."

Reflect: The desire to gain prestige and social recognition is somewhat inappropriate. What does the birth of Jesus in the midst of poverty suggest to you? And, what about the attitude of Mary?

Pray: O God, may I ask for the grace to recognize your presence in simple things and contemplate your birth in everyday life.

Act: Make a list of birthdays of your loved ones. Remember how you celebrate the birthday of each of them and thank God for the gift of life.

Jesus is presented in the temple

²²When the day came for the purification according to the law of Moses, they brought the baby up to Jerusalem to present him to the Lord, ²³as it is written in the law of the Lord: *Every firstborn male shall be consecrated to God.* ²⁴And they offered a sacrifice as ordered in the law of the Lord: *a pair of turtledoves or two young pigeons.*

²⁵There lived in Jerusalem, at this time, a very upright and devout man named Simeon; the Holy Spirit was in him. He looked forward to the time when the Lord would comfort Israel; ²⁶and he had been assured by the Holy Spirit that he would not die before seeing the Messiah of the Lord. ²⁷So, he was led into the temple by the Holy Spirit at the time the parents brought the child Jesus to do for him according to the custom of the law.

²⁸Simeon took the child in his arms and blessed God, saying,

²⁹"Now, O Lord, you can dismiss
your servant in peace,
for you have fulfilled your word
³⁰and my eyes have seen your salvation,

[31] which you display for all the people to see.
[32] Here is the light you will reveal to the nations,
and the glory of your people Israel."

[33] His father and mother wondered at what was said about the child. [34] Simeon blessed them and said to Mary, his mother, "Know this: your son is a sign; a sign established for the falling and rising of many in Israel, a sign of contradiction; [35] and a sword will pierce your own soul so that out of many hearts thoughts may be revealed."

[36] There was also a prophetess named Anna, daughter of Phanuel, of the tribe of Asher. After leaving her father's home, she had been seven years with her husband; and since then, she had been continually about the temple, serving God as a widow, night and day, in fasting and prayer. [37] She was now eighty-four. [38] Coming up at that time, she gave praise to God and spoke of the child to all who looked forward to the deliverance of Jerusalem.

[39] When the parents had fulfilled all that was required by the law of the Lord, they returned to their town, Nazareth in Galilee. [40] There, the child grew in stature and strength and was filled with wisdom: the grace of God was upon him.

LUKE 2:22-40

Read: Mary and Joseph, as faithful Jews, had Jesus circumcised and presented him to the Lord, as prescribed by the Law. Simeon proclaims the universality of salvation that Jesus brings.

Reflect: Do you observe the commandments of God and the Church? Do you consider them necessary for salvation? Does God want the salvation of a few or of all?

Pray: O God, I ask for your help to do what you command us and to contemplate everywhere your saving presence.

Act: Promote family participation in your parish activities.

I must be in my Father's house

[41] Every year, the parents of Jesus went to Jerusalem for the Feast of the Passover, as was customary. [42] And when Jesus was twelve years old, he went up with them according to the custom of this feast. [43] After

the festival was over they returned, but the boy Jesus remained in Jerusalem and his parents did not know it.

[44] They assumed that he was in their group of travelers and, after walking the whole day, they looked for him among their relatives and friends. [45] As they did not find him, they went back to Jerusalem searching for him; [46] and on the third day, they found him in the temple, sitting among the teachers, listening to them and asking questions. [47] And all the people were amazed at his understanding and his answers.

[48] His parents were very surprised when they saw him; and his mother said to him, "Son, why have you done this to us? Your father and I were very worried while searching for you." [49] Then he said to them, "Why were you looking for me? Did you not know that I must be in my Father's house?" [50] But they did not understand this answer.

[51] Jesus went down with them, returning to Nazareth, and he continued to be obedient to them. As for his mother, she kept all these things in her heart.

[52] And Jesus increased in wisdom and age, and in divine and human favor.

LUKE 2:41-52

Read: On the occasion of the pilgrimage to Jerusalem for the Passover feast, Jesus stays in the Temple without Joseph and Mary knowing it. Through this story, Luke presents the divine sonship of Jesus and his mission: "My Father's affairs."

Reflect: Do you realize that by baptism you are a child of God? In your opinion, what mission has God entrusted you?

Pray: Lord Jesus, help me to be ever more aware of my condition as a child of God, and the mission that as such I have: building up your kingdom.

Act: Support any initiative of your diocese or parish that promotes respect for human rights.

John the Baptist prepares the way
(Mk 1:1; Mt 3:1; Jn 1:19)

3 [1] It was the fifteenth year of the rule of the Emperor Tiberius: Pontius Pilatus was governor of Judea; Herod ruled over Galilee, his brother

Philip ruled over the country of Iturea and Trachonitis; and Lysanias ruled over Abilene. ²Annas and Caiaphas were the High Priests at the time when the word of God came to John, the son of Zechariah, in the desert.

³John proclaimed a baptism for repentant people to obtain forgiveness of sins and he went through the whole country bordering the Jordan River. ⁴It was just as is written in the book of the prophet Isaiah: *Listen to this voice crying out in the desert, 'Prepare the way of the Lord, make his path straight!* ⁵ *The valleys will be filled and the mountains and hills made low. Everything crooked will be made straight and the rough paths smooth;* ⁶ *and every human being will see the salvation of God!'*

⁷John said to the crowds who came out to be baptized by him, "You brood of vipers! How will you escape when divine punishment comes? ⁸Produce now the fruits of a true change of heart; and do not deceive yourselves by saying, 'We have Abraham for our ancestor!' For I tell you, God can make children of Abraham from these stones. ⁹The ax is already laid to the root of the tree and every tree that fails to produce good fruit will be cut down and thrown into the fire."

¹⁰The people asked him, "What are we to do?" ¹¹And John answered, "If you have two coats, give one to the person who has none; and if you have food, do the same."

¹²Even tax collectors came to be baptized and asked him, "Master, what must we do?" ¹³John said to them, "Collect no more than your fixed rate." ¹⁴Then some soldiers asked John, "What about us? What are we to do?" And he answered, "Don't take anything by force, or threaten the people by denouncing them falsely. Be content with your pay."

¹⁵The people were wondering about John's identity, "Could he be the Messiah?" ¹⁶Then John answered them, "I baptize you with water, but the one who is coming will do much more: he will baptize you with the Holy Spirit and fire. As for me, I am not worthy to untie his sandal. ¹⁷He comes with a winnowing fan to clear his threshing floor and gather the grain into his barn. But the chaff he will burn with fire that never goes out."

¹⁸With these and many other words, John announced the Good News to the people ¹⁹until Herod put him in prison. For John had reproached Herod for living with Herodias, his brother's wife, and for his evil deeds. ²⁰Then Herod added another crime to all the rest he had committed: he put John in prison.

LUKE 3:1-20

Read: Presentation of John the Baptist and his ministry. John announces the coming of the Lord and prepares his mission.

Reflect: John proclaims the coming of the Lord boldly, and so is imprisoned. Do you think that we Christians are bold enough in proclaiming the Gospel of the Lord? How should we do it?

Pray: I ask you, Jesus, for strength to proclaim your Gospel with courage.

Act: Find out more about the Church's option in favor of life, and decide how to live the Gospel today.

Jesus is baptized by John
(Mt 3:13; Mk 1:9; Jn 1:29)

²¹ Now, with all the people who came to be baptized, Jesus, too, was baptized. Then, while he was praying, the heavens opened: ²² the Holy Spirit came down upon him in the bodily form of a dove and a voice from heaven was heard, "You are my Son in whom I am well pleased."

²³ When Jesus made his appearance, he had reached the age of thirty years. He was known as the Son of Joseph, whose father and forefathers were:

Heli, ²⁴ Matthat, Levi, Melchi, Jannai, Joseph, ²⁵ Matthathias, Amos, Nahum, Esli, Naggai, ²⁶ Maath, Mattathias, Semein, Josech, Joda, ²⁷ Joanan, Rhesa, Zerubbabel, Shealtiel, Neri, ²⁸ Melchi, Addi, Cosam, Elmadam, Er, ²⁹ Joshua, Eliezer, Jorim, Matthat, Levi, ³⁰ Simeon, Judah, Joseph, Jonam, Eliakim, ³¹ Melea, Menna, Mattatha, Nathan, David, ³² Jesse, Obed, Boaz, Salmon, Nahson, ³³ Amminadab, Adnim, Arni, Hezron, Perez, Judah, ³⁴ Jacob, Isaac, Abraham, Terah, Nahor, ³⁵ Serug, Reu, Peleg, Eber, Shelah, ³⁶ Cainan, Arphaxad, Shem, Noah, Lamech, ³⁷ Methuselah, Enoch, Jared, Malaleel, Cainan, ³⁸ Enos, Seth, and Adam—who was from God.

LUKE 3:21-38

Read: Luke tells of the baptism of the Lord and his genealogy. Unlike Matthew, whose genealogy stretches back to Abraham, the Gospel of Luke extends it to Adam, the father of all humankind.

Reflect: What does the genealogy that Luke presents suggest to you? Do you see in every person who crosses your path a brother and a sister?

Pray: Lord Jesus, I thank you for having become one of us and, thus, we all become brothers and sisters, and together with love, we may build a better world.

Act: Promote among your peers actions that help to treat others as real brothers and sisters: sons and daughters of the one Father/Mother God.

Jesus tempted in the wilderness
(Mt 4:1; Mk 1:12)

4 [1] Jesus was now full of the Holy Spirit. As he returned from the Jordan, the Spirit led him into the desert [2] where he was tempted by the devil for forty days. He did not eat anything during that time and at the end he was hungry. [3] The devil then said to him, "If you are the Son of God, tell this stone to turn into bread." [4] But Jesus answered, "Scripture says: People cannot live on bread alone."

[5] Then the devil took him up to a high place and showed him, in a flash, all the nations of the world. [6] And he said to Jesus, "I can give you power over all the nations; and their wealth will be yours; for power and wealth have been delivered to me; and I give them to whom I wish. [7] All this will be yours, provided you worship me." [8] But Jesus replied, "Scripture says: *You shall worship the Lord your God and serve him alone.*"

[9] Then the devil took him up to Jerusalem and set him on the highest wall of the temple; and he said, "If you are God's Son, throw yourself down from here; [10] for it is written: *God will order his angels to take care of you;* [11] and again: *They will hold you in their hands, lest you hurt your foot on the stones.*" [12] But Jesus replied, "It is written: *You shall not challenge the Lord your God.*"

[13] When the devil had exhausted every way of tempting Jesus, he left him to return another time.

LUKE 4:1-13

Read: Jesus is tested by Satan in the wilderness. Filled with the Holy Spirit, he confronts temptations and always chooses God's plan.

Reflect: What temptations are you facing and how do you deal with them? Do you ask the help of the Holy Spirit to overcome them?

Pray: O God, may your Spirit assist me in times of temptation, helping me always to choose your path of service, love and, self-giving.

Act: Identify the temptation that creates the most problems in your life. Do you have a plan to overcome them? Do you ever ask someone for help?

Jesus proclaims his mission at Nazareth
(Mt 13:53)

¹⁴ Jesus acted with the power of the Spirit; and on his return to Galilee, the news about him spread throughout all that territory. ¹⁵ He began teaching in the synagogues of the Jews and everyone praised him.

¹⁶ When Jesus came to Nazareth, where he had been brought up, he entered the synagogue on the Sabbath as he usually did. ¹⁷ He stood up to read, and they handed him the book of the prophet Isaiah.

Jesus then unrolled the scroll and found the place where it is written: ¹⁸ "*The Spirit of the Lord is upon me. He has anointed me to bring good news to the poor; to proclaim liberty to captives, and new sight to the blind; to free the oppressed;* ¹⁹ *and to announce the Lord's year of mercy.*"

²⁰ Jesus then rolled up the scroll, gave it to the attendant, and sat down; and the eyes of all in the synagogue were fixed on him. ²¹ Then he said to them, "Today, these prophetic words come true even as you listen."

²² All agreed with him and were lost in wonder while he spoke of the grace of God. Nevertheless, they asked, "Who is this but Joseph's Son?" ²³ So he said, "Doubtless you will quote me the saying: Doctor, heal yourself! Do here, in your town, what they say you did in Capernaum."

²⁴ Jesus added, "No prophet is honored in his own country. ²⁵ Truly, I say to you, there were many widows in Israel in the days of Elijah, when

the heavens withheld rain for three years and six months and a great famine came over the whole land. ²⁶Yet, Elijah was not sent to any of them, but to a widow of Zarephath, in the country of Sidon. ²⁷There were also many lepers in Israel in the time of Elisha, the prophet; and no one was healed except Naaman, the Syrian."

²⁸On hearing these words, the whole assembly became indignant. ²⁹They rose up and brought him out of the town, ³⁰to the edge of the hill on which Nazareth is built, intending to throw him down the cliff. But he passed through their midst and went his way.

LUKE 4:14-30

Read: Jesus announces his mission in his own town, Nazareth, but they reject him.

Reflect: How do you see the saving actions of God in your life? How do you think that Jesus fulfills his mission today? What does this expression suggest to you: "Today, in your presence, this passage of the Scripture has been fulfilled"?

Pray: O Jesus, may we contemplate on your saving action among us. Free us from our bias, and may your Spirit encourage us to work in your mission.

Act: Encourage your family to become aware of the mission of Jesus.

With the power of the spirit
(Mk 1:23; Mt 4:24; 8:14)

³¹Jesus went down to Capernaum, a town of Galilee, and began teaching the people at the Sabbath meetings. ³²They were astonished at the way he taught them, for his word was spoken with authority.

³³In the synagogue, there was a man possessed by an evil spirit who shouted in a loud voice, ³⁴"What do you want with us, Jesus of Nazareth? Have you come to destroy us? I recognize you: you are the Holy One of God." ³⁵Then Jesus said to him sharply, "Be silent and leave this man!" The evil spirit then threw the man down in front of them and came out of him without doing him harm.

³⁶Amazement seized all these people, and they said to one another, "What does this mean? He commands the evil spirits with authority and

power. He orders and you see how they come out!" ³⁷ And news about Jesus spread throughout the surrounding area.

³⁸ Leaving the synagogue, Jesus went to the house of Simon. His mother-in-law was suffering from high fever and they asked him to do something for her. ³⁹ Bending over her, he rebuked the fever, and it left her. Immediately, she got up and waited on them.

⁴⁰ At sunset, people suffering from many kinds of sickness were brought to Jesus. Laying his hands on each one, he healed them. ⁴¹ Demons were driven out, howling as they departed from their victims, "You are the Son of God!" He rebuked them and would not allow them to speak, for they knew he was the Messiah.

⁴² Jesus left at daybreak and looked for a solitary place. People went out in search of him, and finding him, they tried to dissuade him from leaving. ⁴³ But he said, "I have to go to other towns to announce the good news of the kingdom of God. That is what I was sent to do." ⁴⁴ And Jesus continued to preach in the synagogues of Galilee.

LUKE 4:31-44

Read: In Capernaum, Jesus exorcizes, heals Peter's mother-in-law and all the sick brought to him.

Reflect: The example of Peter's mother-in-law is very instructive. As soon as she feels healthy, she gets up and serves Jesus. She shows in this way her gratitude. Has God healed you of something? How do you give thanks?

Pray: Dear Jesus, I give thanks to you for all that you do for me. May your Spirit teach me to be generous with others as you are with me.

Act: Perform an act of charity as gratitude for what God has done for you.

You will catch people
(Mt 4:18; Mk 1:16)

5 ¹ One day, as Jesus stood by the Lake of Gennesaret, with a crowd gathered around him listening to the word of God, ² he caught sight of two boats left at the water's edge by fishermen now washing their nets. ³ He got into one of the boats, the one belonging to Simon, and asked him to pull out a little from the shore. There he sat and continued to teach the crowd.

⁴When he had finished speaking, he said to Simon, "Put out into deep water and lower your nets for a catch." ⁵Simon replied, "Master, we worked hard all night and caught nothing. But if you say so, I will lower the nets." ⁶This they did, and caught such a large number of fish that their nets began to break. ⁷They signaled their partners in the other boat to come and help them. They came and they filled both boats almost to the point of sinking.

⁸Upon seeing this, Simon Peter fell at Jesus' knees, saying, "Leave me, Lord, for I am a sinful man!" ⁹For he and his companions were amazed at the catch they had made ¹⁰and so were Simon's partners, James and John, Zebedee's sons.

Jesus said to Simon, "Do not be afraid. You will catch people from now on." ¹¹So they brought their boats to land and followed him, leaving everything.

Cure of a leper
(Mk 1:40; Mt 8:2)

¹²One day, in another town, a man came to Jesus covered with leprosy. On seeing Jesus, the man bowed down to the ground and said, "Lord, if you want to, you can make me clean."

¹³Stretching out his hand, Jesus touched the man and said, "Yes, I want to. Be clean." In an instant, the leprosy left him. ¹⁴Then Jesus instructed him, "Tell this to no one. But go and show yourself to the priest. Make an offering for your healing as Moses prescribed; that will serve as evidence for them."

¹⁵But the news about Jesus spread all the more; and large crowds came to him, to listen and to be healed of their sickness. ¹⁶As for Jesus, he would often withdraw to solitary places and pray.

The paralytic saved
(Mk 2:1; Mt 9:1)

¹⁷One day, Jesus was teaching and many Pharisees and teachers of the law had come from every part of Galilee and Judea, and even from Jerusalem. They were sitting there while the power of the Lord was at work to heal the sick. ¹⁸Then some men brought a paralyzed man who lay on his mat. They tried to enter the house to place him before Jesus,

¹⁹ but they couldn't find a way through the crowd. So they went up on the roof and, removing the tiles, they lowered him on his mat into the middle of the crowd in front of Jesus.

²⁰ When Jesus saw their faith, he said to the man, "My friend, your sins are forgiven." ²¹ At once the teachers of the law and the Pharisees began to wonder, "This man insults God! Who can forgive sins but God alone?"

²² But Jesus knew their thoughts and asked them, "Why are you reacting like this? ²³ Which is easier to say: 'Your sins are forgiven' or 'Get up and walk'? ²⁴ Now you shall know that the Son of Man has authority on earth to forgive sins." And Jesus said to the paralyzed man, "Get up, take your mat and go home." ²⁵ At once, the man stood before them. He took up the mat he had been lying on and went home praising God.

²⁶ Amazement seized the people and they praised God. They were filled with holy fear and said, "What wonderful things we have seen today!"

LUKE 5:1-26

Read: Simon had been trying all night fishing with no success. Jesus asks him to throw their nets one more time. He does and gets a great catch. Jesus calls Simon and his companions and from here on they follow him as his disciples. Jesus' healing reveals God's liberating power in the world.

Reflect: Simon trusts in the words of Jesus despite his initial failure. Do you trust in the Word of God? Do you feel called by the Lord? What for? From what does the Lord liberates us today?

Pray: Lord Jesus, may your Spirit increase my faith to always trust in your Word and be your disciple.

Act: Talk to your family about what it means to have faith in Jesus, and about the mission that he calls us to: the kingdom of God.

Call of Levi
(Mk 2:13; Mt 9:9)

²⁷ After this, Jesus went out, and noticing a tax collector named Levi sitting in the tax office, he said to him, "Follow me!" ²⁸ So Levi, leaving everything, got up and followed Jesus.

²⁹Levi gave a great feast for Jesus and many tax collectors came to his house and took their places at the table with the other people. ³⁰Then the Pharisees and their followers complained to Jesus' disciples, "How is it, that you eat and drink with tax collectors and sinners?" ³¹But Jesus spoke up, "Healthy people don't need a doctor but sick people do. ³²I have not come to call the just, but sinners to a change of heart."

³³Some people asked him, "The disciples of John fast often and say long prayers and so do the disciples of the Pharisees. Why is it that your disciples eat and drink?" Then Jesus said to them, ³⁴"You can't make wedding guests fast while the bridegroom is with them. ³⁵But later the bridegroom will be taken from them and they will fast in those days."

³⁶Jesus also told them this parable: "No one tears a piece from a new coat to put it on an old one; otherwise, the new coat will be torn and the piece taken from the new coat will not match the old coat. ³⁷No one puts new wine into old wineskins; otherwise, the new wine will burst the skins and be spilled and the skins will be destroyed as well. ³⁸But new wine must be put into fresh skins. ³⁹Yet, no one who has tasted old wine is eager to drink new wine, but says, 'The old is good.'"

LUKE 5:27-39

Read: Jesus calls Levi (Matthew), a publican. Immediately, he leaves everything to follow the Master. Levi welcomes Jesus into his home and shares the table with him and with other tax collectors. This scandalized the Pharisees and the scribes.

Reflect: Would you be able to share your table with the marginalized? What do you make of Jesus' comparisons on the piece of new garment to patch an old one? What is new in the message of Jesus?

Pray: Give me, Lord Jesus, a generous heart to welcome you without prejudice in my brothers and sisters, especially those who are despised and marginalized by society.

Act: Share your table with the people considered marginalized by your society, at least once a year. Receive them as you would receive Jesus himself.

Jesus, Lord of the Sabbath
(Mk 2:23; Mt 12:1; Mk 3:1)

6 ¹One Sabbath, Jesus was going through a field of grain, and his disciples began to pick heads of grain crushing them in their hands for
food. ²Some of the Pharisees asked them, "Why do you do what is forbidden on the Sabbath?" ³Then Jesus spoke up and asked them, "Have
you never read what David did when he and his men were hungry? ⁴He
entered the house of God, took and ate the bread of the offering and even
gave some to his men, though only priests are allowed to eat that bread."
⁵And Jesus added, "The Son of Man is Lord and rules over the Sabbath."

⁶On another Sabbath, Jesus entered the synagogue and began teaching. There was a man with a paralyzed right hand ⁷and the teachers of
the law and the Pharisees watched him: Would Jesus heal the man on
the Sabbath? If he did, they could accuse him.

⁸But Jesus knew their thoughts and said to the man, "Get up and
stand in the middle." ⁹Then he spoke to them, "I want to ask you: what
is allowed by the law on the Sabbath? To do good or to do harm, to save
life or to destroy it?" ¹⁰And Jesus looked around at them all.

Then he said to the man, "Stretch out your hand." He stretched it out
and his hand was restored, becoming as healthy as the other. ¹¹But they
were furious and began to discuss with one another how they could deal
with Jesus.

The Twelve
(Mk 3:13; Mt 10:1)

¹²At this time, Jesus went out into the hills to pray, spending the whole
night in prayer with God. ¹³When day came, he called his disciples to
him and chose Twelve of them whom he called 'apostles': ¹⁴Simon,
whom he named Peter, and his brother Andrew; James and John; Philip
and Bartholomew; ¹⁵Matthew and Thomas; James son of Alpheus and
Simon called the Zealot; ¹⁶Judas son of James and Judas Iscariot, who
would be the traitor.

LUKE 6:1-16
Read: Jesus teaches us to be merciful, even on the Sabbath.
He calls the Twelve. The lawyers, who did not approve of his ac-
tions, plot against Him.

> **Reflect:** What does the following question suggests to you: "What is lawful to do on the Sabbath: to do good or to do evil? To save life or to destroy it?" Do you feel called by Jesus by your own name?
>
> **Pray:** I recognize, Lord Jesus, how good you are with me; so I ask for the grace of sharing your goodness with all those in my path.
>
> **Act:** Evaluate yourself for a week, every evening. Consider if you have been kind to others as God is good to you.

Blessings and woes
(Mt 5–7)

¹⁷ Coming down the hill with them, Jesus stood in an open plain. Many of his disciples were there and a large crowd of people who had come from all parts of Judea and Jerusalem, and from the coastal cities of Tyre and Sidon. ¹⁸ They gathered to hear him and to be healed of their diseases. And people troubled by unclean spirits were cured. ¹⁹ The entire crowd tried to touch him, because of the power that went out from him and healed them all.

²⁰ Then, looking at his disciples, Jesus said,

"Fortunate are you who are poor, for the kingdom of God is yours.

²¹ Fortunate are you who are hungry now, for you will be filled.

Fortunate are you who weep now, for you will laugh.

²² Fortunate are you when people hate you, when they reject you and insult you and number you among criminals, because of the Son of Man. ²³ Rejoice in that day and leap for joy, for a great reward is kept for you in heaven. Remember, that is how the ancestors of the people treated the prophets.

²⁴ But alas for you who have wealth, for you have been comforted now.

²⁵ Alas for you who are full, for you will go hungry.

Alas for you, who laugh now, for you will mourn and weep.

²⁶ Alas for you when people speak well of you, for that is how the ancestors of the people treated the false prophets.

Love of enemies
(Mt 5:38)

²⁷ But I say to you who hear me: Love your enemies, do good to those who hate you. ²⁸ Bless those who curse you and pray for those who treat you badly. ²⁹ To the one who strikes you on the cheek, turn the other cheek; from the one who takes your coat, do not keep back your shirt. ³⁰ Give to the one who asks, and if anyone has taken something from you, do not demand it back.

³¹ Do to others, as you would have others do to you. ³² If you love only those who love you, what kind of grace is yours? Even sinners love those who love them. ³³ If you do favors to those who are good to you, what kind of grace is yours? Even sinners do the same. ³⁴ If you lend only when you expect to receive, what kind of grace is yours? For sinners also lend to sinners expecting to receive something in return.

³⁵ But love your enemies and do good to them and lend when there is nothing to expect in return. Then will your reward be great and you will be sons and daughters of the Most High, for he is kind toward the ungrateful and the wicked. ³⁶ Be merciful, just as your Father is merciful.

LUKE 6:17-36

Read: Just after calling the Twelve, Jesus sets the lifestyle that his disciples should aspire to: the Beatitudes. The community of Jesus' disciples is to rule by love.

Reflect: What is the following expression suggesting to you: "Love your enemies, do good, and lend, expecting nothing in return... Be merciful as your Father is compassionate"?

Pray: Lord Jesus, help me to live by the Beatitudes, to be able to share your love with everyone who comes close to me.

Act: Today try to interiorize the Beatitudes deeply in yourself. At the end of the day, thank God for the experience and for His help to try it again tomorrow.

---

³⁷ Don't be a judge of others and you will not be judged; do not condemn, and you will not be condemned; forgive, and you will be forgiven; ³⁸ give and it will be given to you and you will receive in your sack good

measure, pressed down, full and running over. For the measure you give will be the measure you receive back."

³⁹ And Jesus offered this example, "Can a blind person lead another blind person? Surely both will fall into a ditch. ⁴⁰ A disciple is not above the master; but when fully trained, he will be like the master. ⁴¹ So why do you pay attention to the speck in your brother's eye while you have a log in your eye and are not conscious of it? ⁴² How can you say to your neighbor, 'Friend, let me take this speck out of your eye,' when you can't remove the log in your own? You hypocrite! First, remove the log from your own eye, and then you will see clearly enough to remove the speck from your neighbor's eye.

⁴³ No healthy tree bears bad fruit, no poor tree bears good fruit. ⁴⁴ And each tree is known by the fruit it bears: you don't gather figs from thorns or grapes from brambles. ⁴⁵ Similarly, the good person draws good things from the good stored in his heart, and an evil person draws evil things from the evil stored in his heart. For the mouth speaks from the fullness of the heart.

⁴⁶ Why do you call me, 'Lord! Lord!' and do not do what I say? ⁴⁷ I will show you what the one is like who comes to me and listens to my words and acts accordingly. ⁴⁸ That person is like the builder who dug deep and laid the foundations of his house on the rock. The river overflowed and the stream dashed against the house but could not carry it off because the house had been well built.

⁴⁹ But the one who listens and does not act is like a man who built his house on the ground without a foundation. The flood burst against it and the house fell at once: and what a terrible disaster that was!"

LUKE 6:37-49

Read: Jesus asks his disciples to be merciful to others, not to judge or condemn, but know how to forgive. Building up your life on the teachings of Jesus is like building a house on a rock.

Reflect: Do you root your life on the teachings of Jesus? How concretely do you do that?

Pray: Change, Lord Jesus, my life, to be rooted in the love with which you love us.

Act: Review your actions and see what are at the root of them.

Cure of the centurion's servant
(Mt 8:5; Jn 4:46)

7 [1] When Jesus had finished teaching the people, he went to Capernaum.

[2] A Roman military officer lived there whose servant was very sick and near to death, a man very dear to him. [3] So when he heard about Jesus, he sent some elders of the Jews to persuade him to come and save his servant's life. [4] The elders came to Jesus and begged him earnestly, saying, [5] "He deserves this of you, for he loves our people and even built a synagogue for us."

[6] Jesus went with them. He was not far from the house when the Roman officer sent friends to give this message, "Sir, do not trouble yourself, for I am not worthy to welcome you under my roof. [7] You see, I didn't approach you myself. Just give the order and my servant will be healed. [8] For I myself, a junior officer, give orders to my soldiers and I say to this one, 'Go!' and he goes; and to the other, 'Come!' and he comes; and to my servant, 'Do this!' and he does it."

[9] On hearing these words, Jesus was filled with admiration. He turned and said to the people with him, "I say to you, not even in Israel have I found such great faith." [10] The people sent by the captain went back to his house; there they found that the servant was well.

The son of a widow restored to life

[11] A little later, Jesus went to a town called Naim. He was accompanied by his disciples and a great number of people. [12] As he reached the gate of the town, a dead man was being carried out. He was the only son of his mother and she was a widow; there followed a large crowd of townspeople.

[13] On seeing her, the Lord had pity on her and said, "Don't cry." [14] Then he came up and touched the stretcher and the men who carried it stopped. Jesus then said, "Young man, I say to you, wake up!" [15] And the dead man sat up and began to speak and Jesus gave him to his mother. [16] A holy fear came over them all and they praised God saying, "A great prophet has appeared among us. God has visited his people." [17] This news spread throughout Judea and the surrounding places.

LUKE 7:1-17

Read: The healing of the centurion's servant and the resurrection of the son of the widow express the closeness that God has for His people, especially to the marginalized and needy.

Reflect: If Jesus manifested the love of God by caring for the suffering, how do we, his disciples, express that love?

Pray: Father, forgive me for being indifferent to the suffering of those around me. May your grace help me to be caring and compassionate to others.

Act: Express the compassionate love of God concretely by helping someone who is suffering or needing help.

Jesus answers the messengers of John
(Mt 11:2)

[18] John's disciples informed him about all these things. So John called two of his disciples [19] and sent them to the Lord with this message, "Are you the one we are expecting, or should we wait for another?" [20] These men came to Jesus and said, "John the Baptist sent us to ask you: Are you the one we are to expect, or should we wait for another?"

[21] At that time, Jesus healed many people of their sicknesses and diseases; he freed them from evil spirits and he gave sight to the blind. [22] Then he answered the messengers, "Go back and tell John what you have seen and heard: the blind see again, the lame walk, lepers are made clean, the deaf hear, the dead are raised to life, and the poor are given good news. Now, listen: [23] Fortunate are those who meet me, and are not offended by me."

[24] When John's messengers had gone, Jesus began speaking to the people about John. And he said, "What did you want to see when you went to the desert? A reed blowing in the wind? [25] What was there to see? A man dressed in fine clothes? But people who wear fine clothes and enjoy delicate food are found in palaces. [26] What did you go out to see? A prophet? Yes, I tell you, and more than a prophet. [27] For John is the one foretold in Scripture in these words: *I am sending my messenger ahead of you to prepare your way.* [28] No one may be found greater than

John among those born of women; but, I tell you, the least in the kingdom of God is greater than he.

29 All the people listening to him, even the tax collectors, had acknowledged the will of God in receiving the baptism of John, 30 whereas the Pharisees and the teachers of the law, in not letting themselves be baptized by him, ignored the will of God.

31 And Jesus said, "What comparison can I use for the people? What are they like? 32 They are like children sitting in the marketplace about whom their companions complain, 'We piped you a tune and you wouldn't dance; we sang funeral songs and you wouldn't cry.'

33 Remember John: he didn't eat bread or drink wine and you said, 'He has an evil spirit.' 34 Next, came the Son of Man, eating and drinking; and you say, 'Look, a glutton for food and wine, a friend of tax collectors and sinners.' 35 But the children of Wisdom always recognize her work."

LUKE 7:18-35

Read: The message of John the Baptist is accepted by all the people, even by tax collectors. But religious authorities, as wayward children, reject it, closing themselves to all manifestations of God that does not conform to their expectations.

Reflect: Are you open to see the manifestation of God's saving deeds beyond your own prejudices and considerations? At present, how is God's saving action manifested?

Pray: O God, may I see your saving presence in all times and places, and to be imbued by it.

Act: Be aware of the signs of God's saving presence in your life. Give thanks for this by sharing it with your people.

Jesus, the woman, and the Pharisee

36 One of the Pharisees asked Jesus to share his meal, so he went to the Pharisee's home, and as usual reclined at the table to eat. 37 And it happened that a woman of this town, who was known as a sinner, heard that he was in the Pharisee's house. She brought an alabaster jar of perfume 38 and stood behind him, at his feet, weeping. She wet his feet with tears; she dried them with her hair; she kissed his feet and poured the perfume on them.

[39] The Pharisee who had invited Jesus was watching and thought, "If this man were a prophet, he would know what sort of person is touching him; isn't this woman a sinner?"

[40] Then Jesus spoke to the Pharisee and said, "Simon, I have something to ask you." He answered, "Speak, master." And Jesus said, [41] "Two people were in debt to the same creditor. One owed him five hundred silver coins and the other fifty. [42] As they were unable to pay him back, he graciously canceled the debts of both. Now, which of them will love him more?"

[43] Simon answered, "The one, I suppose, who was forgiven more." And Jesus said, "You are right." [44] And turning toward the woman, he said to Simon, "Do you see this woman? [45] You gave me no water for my feet when I entered your house, but she has washed my feet with her tears and dried them with her hair. You didn't welcome me with a kiss, but she has not stopped kissing my feet since she came in. [46] You provided no oil for my head, but she has poured perfume on my feet. [47] This is why, I tell you, her sins, her many sins, are forgiven, because of her great love. But the one who is forgiven little has little love."

[48] Then Jesus said to the woman, "Your sins are forgiven." [49] The others reclining with him at the table began to wonder, "Now this man claims to forgive sins!" [50] But Jesus again spoke to the woman, "Your faith has saved you; go in peace!"

LUKE 7:36-50

Read: Jesus has dinner at Simon's house, the Pharisee, where a woman washes and kisses his feet. Simon is shocked that Jesus did not notice that the woman is a "sinner," but Jesus reproaches the mediocrity of the Pharisee's love, and praises the generosity of love of the sinner: "She has been forgiven many sins, for she showed a great love."

Reflect: A superficial commitment to Jesus and his teachings—like the one of the Pharisee—is not enough. Jesus wants deep commitments: of heart, conversion, gratitude, and compassion, as the one shown by the woman.

Pray: Lord Jesus, transform our lives by the power of your love, that we may love others as you love us.

Act: As the woman of this passage, adhere strongly to the love of Jesus. Wash his feet by doing a gesture of love with somebody.

The women who followed Jesus

8 [1] Jesus walked through towns and countryside, preaching and giving the good news of the kingdom of God. The Twelve followed him, [2] and also some women who had been healed of evil spirits and diseases: Mary called Magdalene, who had been freed of seven demons; [3] Joanna, wife of Chuza, Herod's steward; Suzanna; and others who provided for them out of their own funds.

The parable of the sower
(Mk 4:1; Mt 13:1)

[4] As a great crowd gathered and people came to him from every town, Jesus began teaching them with a story: [5] "The sower went out to sow the seed. And as he sowed, some of the seed fell along the way was trodden on, and the birds of the sky ate it up. [6] Some seed fell on rocky ground, and no sooner had it come up than it withered because it had no water. [7] Some seed fell among thorns; the thorns grew up with the seed and choked it. [8] But some seed fell on good soil and grew, producing fruit a hundred times as much!" And Jesus cried out, "Listen then, if you have ears to hear!"

[9] The disciples asked him, "What does this story mean?" [10] And Jesus answered, "To you, it has been given to know the mystery of the kingdom of God. But to others, it is given in the form of stories, or parables, so that, *seeing, they may not perceive; and hearing, they may not understand.*

[11] Now, this is the point of the parable:

The seed is the word of God. [12] Those along the wayside are people who hear it; but immediately, the devil comes and takes the word from their minds, for he doesn't want them to believe and be saved. [13] Those on the rocky ground are people who receive the word with joy, but they have no root; they believe for a while and give way in time of trial. [14] Among the thorns are people who hear the word, but as they go their way, they are choked by worries, riches, and the pleasures of life; they bring no fruit to maturity. [15] The good soil, instead, are people who receive the word and keep it, in a gentle and generous mind and, persevering patiently, they bear fruit.

[16] No one, after lighting a lamp, covers it with a bowl or puts it under the bed; rather, he puts it on a lampstand so that people coming in may see the light. [17] In the same way, there is nothing hidden that shall not be uncovered; nothing kept secret that shall not be known clearly. [18] Now, pay attention and listen well, for whoever produces, will be given more; but from those who do not produce, even what they seem to have will be taken away from them."

Jesus' mother and brothers
(Mk 3:31; Mt 12:46)

[19] Then his mother and his relatives came to him but they could not get to him because of the crowd. [20] Someone told him, "Your mother and your brothers are standing outside and wish to meet you." [21] Then Jesus answered, "My mother and my brothers are those who hear the word of God and do it."

LUKE 8:1-21

Read: Jesus, along with some disciples, men and women, goes through the region successfully preaching the Gospel. The parable suggests several kinds of responses to the Word of God. The seed that falls on fertile soil produces a hundredfold.

Reflect: As you look at your life, can you identify times when you have been like each of the soils in the parable receiving and responding to God?

Pray: Grant me, Lord Jesus, the grace to receive your Word. May it produce much fruit in my life and in the life of others.

Act: Set aside time in your daily life to listening and meditating on the Word of God.

Jesus calms the storm
(Mk 4:35; Mt 8:23)

[22] One day, Jesus got into a boat with his disciples and said to them, "Let us go across to the other side of the lake." [23] So they set out, and

as they sailed he fell asleep. Suddenly, a storm came down on the lake and the boat began to fill with water; and they were in danger. ²⁴ The disciples then went to Jesus to wake him saying, "Master! Master! We are sinking!" Jesus woke up. He rebuked the wind and the rolling waves; the storm subsided, and all was quiet.

²⁵ Then Jesus said to them, "Where is your faith?" They had been afraid; now they were astonished and said to one another, "Who can this be? See, he commands even the wind and the sea and they obey him!"

The possessed man and the pigs
(Mk 5:1; Mt 8:28)

²⁶ And they sailed to the country of the Gerasenes, which is across the lake from Galilee. ²⁷ As Jesus stepped ashore, a man from the town approached him. This man was possessed by demons and for a long time he had not worn any clothes. He would not live in a house but stayed among the tombstones. ²⁸ When he came nearer to Jesus, he screamed and threw himself on the ground before him; and then he shouted, "What do you want with me, Jesus, Son of the Most High God? I beg you, do not torment me," ²⁹ for Jesus had ordered the evil spirit to leave the man.

This spirit had seized him many times when he had been bound with ropes and chains and kept under control. He would then suddenly break the chains and be driven by the evil spirit into wild places.

When Jesus asked him, ³⁰ "What is your name?" the man said, "I am Legion," because many demons had entered into him. ³¹ And they begged Jesus not to command them to go into the bottomless pit. ³² Nearby on the hillside, a great herd of pigs was feeding; so the demons asked to be allowed to enter the pigs and Jesus gave them permission. ³³ The demons then left the man and entered the pigs and the herd rushed down the hillside into the lake and was drowned.

³⁴ When the herdsmen saw what had happened, they fled and reported it in the town and in the countryside. ³⁵ Then people went out to see what had happened and came to Jesus. There they saw the man from whom the demons had been driven out. He was clothed and in his right mind and was sitting at the feet of Jesus. They were afraid. ³⁶ Then people who had seen it told them how the man had been healed; ³⁷ and all this crowd from the Gerasene country asked Jesus to depart from them, for a great fear took hold of them. So Jesus got into the boat to return.

³⁸ It was then that the man freed of the demons asked Jesus if he could stay with him. ³⁹ But Jesus sent him on his way; "Go back to your family and tell them how much God has done for you." So the man went away, proclaiming through the whole town how much Jesus had done for him.

LUKE 8:22-39

Read: Jesus calms a storm and rebukes the disciple's unbelief. They are astonished to see his power over nature. Closer to home, Jesus frees a man possessed by a "legion" of demons. His power scares locals, and although the liberated man wants to follow him, Jesus tells him to announce what God has done for him.

Reflect: Do you trust in the saving power of God? Do you think there may be some sin that God cannot forgive? What kind of sin? Why?

Pray: Thanks, Lord Jesus, for the gifts of faith and forgiveness. May the Spirit help us in moments of doubt and confusion. May we be able to tell "to our people" what God does for us.

Act: Tell your companions any situation where you experienced God's saving action. Promote faith in them.

A woman is healed and a child, raised to life
(Mk 5:21; Mt 9:18)

⁴⁰ When Jesus returned, the people welcomed him, for all had been waiting for him. ⁴¹ At that time, a man named Jairus, an official of the synagogue, threw himself at Jesus' feet and begged him to come to his house ⁴² because his only daughter, about twelve years old, was dying.

As Jesus was on his way the crowd pressed from every side. ⁴³ There was a woman who had suffered from a bleeding for twelve years. This woman had spent everything she had on doctors, but none of them had been able to cure her. ⁴⁴ Now, she came up behind Jesus and touched the fringe of his cloak and her bleeding stopped at once. ⁴⁵ Jesus said, "Who touched me?" Everyone denied it; and Peter said, "Master, the crowd is pushing all around you." ⁴⁶ But Jesus insisted, "Someone touched me, for I felt power go out from me."

⁴⁷ The woman knew she had been discovered. She came trembling and knelt before Jesus. Then she openly confessed why she had touched

him and how she had been instantly cured. [48] And Jesus said to her, "Daughter, your faith has saved you. Go in peace."

[49] While Jesus was still speaking, a messenger arrived from the official's home to tell him, "Your daughter has just died; don't trouble the master any further." [50] But Jesus heard the news, and said to the official, "Do not fear, only believe."

[51] When he entered the house, Jesus allowed no one to follow him, except Peter, James, and John, with the father and mother of the child. [52] As all the people were weeping and wailing loudly, Jesus said to them, "Do not weep, she is not dead but asleep." [53] And they laughed at him, knowing that she was dead. [54] As for Jesus, he took the child by the hand and said to her, "Child, wake up!" [55] And her spirit returned and she got up at once; then Jesus told them to give her something to eat. [56] The parents were amazed, but Jesus ordered them not to let anyone know what had happened.

LUKE 8:40-56

Read: Luke highlights the faith and courage of those who come to Jesus. Jairus, who is not afraid of what people will say because he is the chief of the synagogue, pleads for his daughter. Similarly, the woman suffering from hemorrhages does not fear being discovered and punished for being impure comes to touch Jesus' cloak. Both get what they expect.

Reflect: Do you think that we, Christians of today, are daring to express our faith? Why? Does the saving action of God have limits? Can you see God acting it in other denominations and religions, and even in the activity of those who do not believe in God?

Pray: Lord Jesus, increase our faith. May we bear witness of your saving presence in the world.

Act: Share in your community what in your time of prayer the Holy Spirit has inspired you about faith.

Jesus sends the Twelve on a mission
(Mt 10:5; Mk 6:7)

9 ¹Then Jesus called his Twelve disciples and gave them power and authority to drive out all evil spirits and to heal diseases. ²And he sent them to proclaim the kingdom of God and to heal the sick. ³He instructed them, "Don't take anything for the journey, neither staff, nor bag, nor bread, nor money; and don't even take a spare tunic. ⁴Whatever house you enter, remain there until you leave that place. ⁵And wherever they don't welcome you, leave the town and shake the dust from your feet: it will be as a testimony against them."

⁶So they set out and went through the villages, proclaiming the good news and healing people everywhere.

⁷King Herod heard of all this and did not know what to think, for people said, "This is John, raised from the dead." ⁸Others believed that Elijah, or one of the ancient prophets, had come back to life. ⁹As for Herod, he said, "I had John beheaded. Who is this man, about whom I hear such wonders?" And he was anxious to see him.

¹⁰On their return, the apostles told Jesus everything they had done. Then he took them with him and they withdrew by themselves to a town called Bethsaida. ¹¹But the crowd heard of this and caught up with him. So he welcomed them and began speaking about the kingdom of God, curing those who needed healing.

The miracle of the loaves
(Mk 6:30; Mt 14:13; Jn 6:1)

¹²The day was drawing to a close, and the Twelve drew near to tell him, "Send the crowd away and let them go into the villages and farms around to find lodging and food, for we are here in a lonely place." ¹³But Jesus replied, "You, yourselves, give them something to eat." They answered, "We have only five loaves and two fish. Do you want us to go and buy food for all this crowd?" ¹⁴for there were about five thousand men. Then Jesus said to his disciples, "Make them sit down in groups of fifty."

¹⁵So they made all of them sit down. ¹⁶Jesus then took the five loaves and two fish and, raising his eyes to heaven, pronounced a blessing over them; he broke them and gave them to the disciples to distribute to the crowd. ¹⁷They ate and everyone had enough; and when they gathered up what was left, twelve baskets were filled with broken pieces.

LUKE 9:1-17

Read: Jesus sends the Twelve to proclaim by word and deed the kingdom of God, and this perplexes Herod. When the Twelve return, a crowd follows them. By nightfall, they are in a deserted place and Jesus feeds the multitude miraculously.

Reflect: Do you feel called to proclaim the kingdom of God? How do you announce it? Do you trust in the generosity of God and people? Do you consider possible the miracle of "sharing" the bread in our present circumstances?

Pray: Thanks, Lord Jesus, for sharing your mission and provide us with food that generates life.

Act: Work with institutions seeking to eradicate hunger and poverty. Make a donation according to your means.

Peter's profession of faith
(Mk 8:27; Mt 16:18)

¹⁸ One day, when Jesus was praying alone, not far from his disciples, he asked them, "What do people say about me?" ¹⁹ And they answered, "Some say that you are John the Baptist; others say that you are Elijah, and still others, that you are one of the prophets of old, risen from the dead." Again Jesus asked them, ²⁰ "But who do you say that I am?" Peter answered, "The Messiah of God." ²¹ Then Jesus spoke to them giving them strict orders not to tell this to anyone.

²² And he added, "The Son of Man must suffer many things. He will be rejected by the elders and chief priests and teachers of the law and be put to death. Then after three days, he will be raised to life."

²³ Jesus also said to all the people, "If you wish to be a follower of mine, deny yourself and take up your cross each day and follow me! ²⁴ For if you choose to save your life, you will lose it; but if you lose your life for my sake, you will save it. ²⁵ What does it profit you to gain the whole world if you destroy or damage yourself? ²⁶ If someone feels ashamed of me and of my words, the Son of Man will be ashamed of him when he comes in his glory and in the glory of his Father with his holy angels. ²⁷ Truly, I say to you, there are some here who will not taste death before they see the kingdom of God."

The transfiguration
(Mk 9:2; Mt 17:1; Jn 12:28)

²⁸ About eight days after Jesus had said all this, he took Peter, John, and James, and went up the mountain to pray. ²⁹ And while he was praying, the aspect of his face was changed and his clothing became dazzling white. ³⁰ Two men were talking with Jesus: Moses and Elijah. ³¹ Appearing in the glory of heaven, Moses and Elijah spoke to Jesus about his departure from this life, which was to take place in Jerusalem.

³² Peter and his companions had fallen asleep but they awoke suddenly and they saw his glory and the two men standing with him. ³³ As Moses and Elijah were about to leave, Peter—not knowing what to say—said to Jesus, "Master, how good it is for us to be here! Let us make three tents, one for you, one for Moses and one for Elijah." ³⁴ And no sooner had he spoken, than a cloud appeared and covered them; and the disciples were afraid as they entered the cloud. ³⁵ Then these words came from the cloud, "This is my Son, my Beloved, listen to him." ³⁶ And after the voice had spoken, Jesus was there alone.

The disciples kept this to themselves at the time, telling no one of anything they had seen.

LUKE 9:18-36

Read: Jesus asks his disciples, "Who do people say that I am?" Peter recognizes him as the Messiah and then he speaks about the requirements to follow him. Subsequently, Jesus takes Peter, James, and John up to the mountain to pray. There, they listen: "This is my chosen Son; listen to him."

Reflect: Who is Jesus for you? Are you willing to accept the conditions to follow him? How do you hear the voice inside you saying, "This is my chosen Son, listen to him"?

Pray: Lord Jesus, help my life may bear witness that you are the Messiah, that I may proclaim your Gospel, announcing and building the kingdom of God.

Act: Participate in activities in your parish that promote Christian formation. Share the faith with your people, tell them what Jesus means to you.

The epileptic demoniac
(Mk 9:14; Mt 17:14)

³⁷ The next day, when they came down from the mountain, a large crowd met Jesus. ³⁸ A man among them called out, "Master, I beg you to look at my son, my only child. ³⁹ When the evil spirit seizes him, he suddenly screams. The spirit throws him into a fit and he foams at the mouth; it scarcely ever leaves him after wearing him out. ⁴⁰ I begged your disciples to drive it out, but they could not."

⁴¹ Jesus answered, "You faithless people! How disoriented you are! How long must I be with you and put up with you? Bring your son here." ⁴² And while the boy was being brought, the demon beat him to the ground and threw him into a fit. But Jesus spoke sharply to the evil spirit, healed the boy, and gave him back to his father. ⁴³ And all who saw it were astonished at God's wonderful work.

(Mk 9:30)

But while all were amazed at everything Jesus did, he said to his disciples, ⁴⁴ "Listen, and remember what I tell you now: The Son of Man will be betrayed into the hands of men." ⁴⁵ But the disciples didn't understand this saying; something prevented them from grasping what he meant and they were afraid to ask him about it.

Who is the greatest?

⁴⁶ One day, the disciples were arguing about which of them was the most important. ⁴⁷ But Jesus knew their thoughts, so he took a little child and stood him by his side. ⁴⁸ Then he said to them, "Whoever welcomes this little child in my name, welcomes me; and whoever welcomes me, welcomes the one who sent me. And listen: the one who is found to be the least among you all is the one who is the greatest."

⁴⁹ Then John spoke up, "Master, we saw someone who drives out demons by calling upon your name and we tried to forbid him because he doesn't follow you with us." ⁵⁰ But Jesus said, "Don't forbid him. He who is not against you is for you."

LUKE 9:37-50

Read: Jesus exorcizes a boy. He announces a second time his passion, but his disciples still do not understand and even argue over who is the most important. Jesus corrects and teaches them: "Whoever is not against you is with you."

Reflect: Do you feel possessed by any concern, worry or distress? Have you asked Jesus for help? What should be the greatest desire of a Christian: service or fame? Do you think that God's action in your life has no limits?

Pray: Lord Jesus, deliver me from all that binds and prevents me from following you with love and freedom. May I serve always and everywhere.

Act: Today try to see the presence of God in all things and thank Him by serving others.

Jesus unwelcome in a Samaritan village

⁵¹ As the time drew near when Jesus would be taken up to heaven, he made up his mind to go to Jerusalem. ⁵² He sent ahead of him some messengers who entered a Samaritan village to prepare a lodging for him. ⁵³ But the people would not receive him because he was on his way to Jerusalem. ⁵⁴ Seeing this, James and John, his disciples, said, "Lord, do you want us to call down fire from heaven to reduce them to ashes?" ⁵⁵ Jesus turned and rebuked them, ⁵⁶ and they went on to another village.

The cost of following Jesus
(Mt 8:19)

⁵⁷ As they went on their way, a man said to him, "I will follow you wherever you go." ⁵⁸ Jesus said to him, "Foxes have holes and the birds of the air have nests, but the Son of Man has nowhere to lay his head."

⁵⁹ To another, Jesus said, "Follow me!" But he answered, "Let me go back now, for first, I want to bury my father." ⁶⁰ And Jesus said to him, "Let the dead bury their dead; as for you, leave them and proclaim the kingdom of God."

⁶¹ Another said to him, "I will follow you, Lord, but first let me say goodbye to my family." ⁶² And Jesus said to him, "Whoever has put his hand to the plow and looks back, is not fit for the kingdom of God."

LUKE 9:51-62

Read: Jesus goes to Jerusalem and sends his disciples to prepare the way for him in a Samaritan village, but they are rejected. Jesus talks about the risks and dangers involved in following him.

Reflect: For you, what is the hardest thing about following Jesus? Is it achievable? Yes? No? Why?

Pray: Lord Jesus, I ask you for strength to face the challenges of each day that your follow-up demands from me. I trust in your Word and in your presence.

Act: What is the most difficult commitment you are taking on this day? Do your best.

Jesus sends out the seventy-two
(Mt 10:5; Mk 6:7)

10 ¹After this, the Lord appointed seventy-two other disciples and sent them, two by two, ahead of him to every town and place where he himself was to go. ²And he said to them, "The harvest is plentiful, but the workers are few. So you must ask the Lord of the harvest to send workers to his harvest. ³Courage! I am sending you like lambs among wolves. ⁴Set off without purse or bag or sandals, and do not stop at the homes of those you know.

⁵Whatever house you enter, first bless them, saying, 'Peace to this house!' ⁶If a friend of peace lives there, the peace shall rest upon that person. But if not, the blessing will return to you. ⁷Stay in that house, eating and drinking at their table, for the worker deserves to be paid. Do not move from house to house.

⁸When they welcome you to any town, eat what they offer you. ⁹Heal the sick who are there and say to them: 'The kingdom of God has drawn near to you.'

¹⁰But in any town where you are not welcome, go to the marketplace and proclaim: ¹¹'Even the dust of your town that clings to our feet, we wipe off and leave with you. But know for a certainty that the kingdom of God has drawn near to you.' ¹²I tell you, that on the Day of Judgment it will be better for Sodom than for this town.

[13] Alas for you, Chorazin! Alas for you, Bethsaida! So many miracles have been worked in you! If the same miracles had been performed in Tyre and Sidon, they would already be sitting in ashes and wearing the sackcloth of repentance. [14] Surely for Tyre and Sidon, it will be better on the Day of Judgment than for you. [15] And what of you, city of Capernaum? Will you be lifted up to heaven? You will be thrown down to the place of the dead.

[16] Whoever listens to you listens to me and whoever rejects you rejects me, and he who rejects me rejects the one who sent me."

Jesus gives thanks to the Father
(Mt 11:25)

[17] The seventy-two disciples returned full of joy. They said, "Lord, even the demons obeyed us when we called on your name." [18] Then Jesus replied, "I saw Satan fall like lightning from heaven. [19] You see, I have given you authority to trample on snakes and scorpions and to overcome all the power of the Enemy so that nothing will harm you. [20] Nevertheless, don't rejoice because the evil spirits submit to you; rejoice, rather, that your names are written in heaven."

[21] At that time, Jesus was filled with the joy of the Holy Spirit and said, "I praise you, Father, Lord of heaven and earth, for you have hidden these things from the wise and learned and made them known to little ones. [22] Yes, Father, such has been your gracious will. I have been given all things by my Father so that no one knows the Son except the Father, and no one knows the Father except the Son and he to whom the Son chooses to reveal him."

[23] Then Jesus turned to his disciples and said to them privately, "Fortunate are you to see what you see, [24] for I tell you that many prophets and kings would have liked to see what you see, but did not see it; and to hear what you hear, but did not hear it."

LUKE 10:1-24

Read: Jesus appoints seventy-two disciples to prepare the way for him. They must travel without belongings and their mission is the proclamation of the kingdom. Upon their return, Jesus gives thanks to God because he reveals himself to the humble and simple.

> **Reflect:** How do you prepare the way of the Lord? How? Can you contemplate the liberating action of God in the simple and humble?
>
> **Pray:** Here I am, Lord Jesus. May my life always announce your good news, your Gospel: the kingdom of God.
>
> **Act:** Collaborate in an initiative of your parish or diocese that promotes missionary action.

The good Samaritan
(Mt 22:34; Mk 12:28)

²⁵ Then a teacher of the law came and began putting Jesus to the test. And he said, "Master, what shall I do to receive eternal life?" ²⁶ Jesus replied, "What is written in the law? How do you understand it?" ²⁷ The man answered, "*It is written: You shall love the Lord your God with all your heart, with all your soul, with all your strength, and with all your mind. And you shall love your neighbor as yourself.*" ²⁸ Jesus replied, "What a good answer! Do this and you shall live." ²⁹ The man wanted to justify his question, so he asked, "Who is my neighbor?"

³⁰ Jesus then said, "There was a man going down from Jerusalem to Jericho, and he fell into the hands of robbers. They stripped him, beat him and went off, leaving him half-dead.

³¹ It happened that a priest was going along that road and saw the man, but passed by on the other side. ³² Likewise, a Levite saw the man and passed by on the other side. ³³ But a Samaritan also was going that way, and when he came upon the man he was moved with compassion. ³⁴ He went over to him and cleaned his wounds with oil and wine and wrapped them in bandages. Then he put him on his own mount and brought him to an inn, where he took care of him.

³⁵ The next day, he had to set off; but he gave two silver coins to the innkeeper and said, 'Take care of him and whatever you spend on him, I will repay when I return.'"

³⁶ Jesus then asked, "Which of these three, do you think, made himself neighbor to the man who fell into the hands of robbers?" ³⁷ The teacher of the law answered, "The one who had mercy on him." And Jesus said, "Then go and do the same."

Martha and Mary

[38] As Jesus and his disciples were on their way, he entered a village and a woman called Martha welcomed him to her house. [39] She had a sister named Mary, who sat down at the Lord's feet to listen to his words. [40] Martha, meanwhile, was busy with all the serving and finally, she said, "Lord, don't you care that my sister has left me to do all the work? Tell her to help me!"

[41] But the Lord answered, "Martha, Martha, you worry and are troubled about many things [42] whereas only one thing is needed. Mary has chosen the better part and it will not be taken away from her."

LUKE 10:25-42

Read: Before the question "Who is my neighbor?" Jesus tells the parable of the Good Samaritan and urges us to follow his example.

Reflect: Do you feel you are a member of a single family: the human family? Can you contemplate the face of God in the face of the suffering brother or sister? What prevents you from being like the Good Samaritan?

Pray: I ask you, Lord, to transform my life. May I follow your example of love, and be able to love all human beings as you love me.

Act: Pray for someone in need, go and offer your support.

Lord, teach us to pray
(Mt 6:9; 7:7)

11 [1] One day, Jesus was praying in a certain place; and when he had finished, one of his disciples said to him, "Lord, teach us to pray, as John also taught his disciples." [2] And Jesus said to them, "When you pray, say this:

Father, may your name be held holy,
may your kingdom come;
[3] give us, each day, the kind of bread we need,
[4] and forgive us our sins; for we also forgive all who do us wrong;
and do not bring us to the test."

[5] Jesus said to them, "Suppose one of you has a friend, and goes to

his house in the middle of the night and says, 'Friend, lend me three loaves, [6]for a friend of mine who is traveling has just arrived, and I have nothing to offer him.' [7]Maybe your friend will answer from inside, 'Don't bother me now; the door is locked, and my children and I are in bed, so I can't get up and give you anything.' [8]But I tell you, even though he will not get up and attend to you because you are a friend, yet he will get up because you are a bother to him, and he will give you all you need.

[9]And so I say to you, 'Ask, and it will be given to you; seek, and you will find; knock, and it will be opened to you. [10]For the one who asks receives, and the one who searches finds, and to him who knocks the door will be opened.

[11]If your child asks for a fish, will you give him a snake instead? [12]And if your child asks for an egg, will you give him a scorpion? [13]If you sinful people know how to give good gifts to your children, how much more will your heavenly Father give the Holy Spirit to those who ask him."

LUKE 11:1-13

Read: Jesus teaches his disciples to pray the Our Father. Then he illustrates with a parable the persistence with which his disciples should beg God. The promptness of the divine response.

Reflect: Prayer is important in Christian following. Do you spend a few moments of your daily life praying with God?

Pray: O God, thank you for your love, which makes us your children. May the consolation and confidence I receive from you in prayer enable me to share your love with everyone who approaches me.

Act: Reserve a time from your daily life for personal prayer.

Jesus and Beelzebul
(Mk 3:22; Mt 12:23; Mk 4:21; 9:40)

[14]One day, Jesus was driving out a demon, which was mute. When the demon had been driven out, the mute person could speak and the people were amazed. [15]Yet some of them said, "He drives out demons by the power of Beelzebul, the chief of the demons." [16]Others wanted to put him to the test by asking him for a heavenly sign.

[17]But Jesus knew their thoughts and said to them, "Every nation

divided by civil war is on the road to ruin and will fall. ¹⁸ If Satan also is divided, his empire is coming to an end. How can you say that I drive out demons by calling upon Beelzebul? ¹⁹ If I drive them out by Beelzebul, by whom do your sons drive out demons? They will be your judges, then.

²⁰ But if I drive out demons by the finger of God, would not this mean that the kingdom of God has come upon you? ²¹ As long as a man, strong and well armed, guards his house, his goods are safe. ²² But when a stronger man attack and overcomes him, the challenger takes away all the weapons he relied on and disposes of his spoils.

²³ Whoever is not with me is against me and whoever does not gather with me, scatters.

²⁴ When the evil spirit goes out of a person, it wanders through dry lands looking for a resting place; and finding none, it says, 'I will return to my house from which I came.' ²⁵ When it comes, it finds the house swept and everything in order. ²⁶ Then it goes to fetch seven other spirits even worse than itself. They move in and settle there so that the last state of that person is worse than the first."

²⁷ As Jesus was speaking, a woman spoke from the crowd and said to him, "Blessed is the one who gave you birth and nursed you!" ²⁸ Jesus replied, "Truly blessed are those who hear the word of God, and keep it as well."

²⁹ As the crowd increased, Jesus spoke the following words: "People of the present time are troubled people. They ask for a sign, but no sign will be given to them except the sign of Jonah. ³⁰ As Jonah became a sign for the people of Nineveh, so will the Son of Man be a sign for this generation. ³¹ The Queen of the South will rise up on Judgment Day with the people of these times and accuse them, for she came from the ends of the earth to hear the wisdom of Solomon and here there is greater than Solomon. ³² The people of Nineveh will rise up on Judgment Day with the people of these times and accuse them, for Jonah's preaching made them turn from their sins and here there is greater than Jonah.

³³ You do not light a lamp to hide it; rather, you put it on a lampstand, so that people coming in may see the light.

³⁴ Your eye is the lamp of your body. If your eye sees clearly, your whole person benefits from the light; but if your eyesight is poor, your whole person is without light. ³⁵ So be careful, lest the light inside you

become darkness. ³⁶If your whole person receives the light, having no part that is dark, you will become light, as when a lamp shines on you."

Woe to you, Pharisees!
(Mt 23:13)

³⁷As Jesus was speaking, a Pharisee asked him to have a meal with him. So he went and sat at table. ³⁸The Pharisee then wondered why Jesus did not first wash his hands before dinner. ³⁹But the Lord said to him, "So then, you Pharisees, you clean the outside of the cup and the dish, but inside yourselves you are full of greed and evil. ⁴⁰Fools! He who made the outside also made the inside. ⁴¹But according to you, by the mere giving of alms everything is made clean.

⁴²A curse is on you, Pharisees! To the temple you give a tenth of all, including mint and rue and other herbs, but you neglect justice and the love of God. These ought to be practiced, without neglecting the other obligations. ⁴³A curse is on you, Pharisees, for you love the best seats in the synagogues and to be greeted in the marketplace. ⁴⁴A curse is on you, for you are like tombstones of the dead which can hardly be seen; people don't notice them and make themselves unclean by stepping on them."

⁴⁵Then a teacher of the law spoke up and said, "Master, when you speak like this, you insult us too." ⁴⁶And Jesus answered, "A curse is on you also, teachers of the law. For you prepare unbearable burdens and load them on the people, while you yourselves do not move a finger to help them. ⁴⁷A curse is on you, for you build monuments to the prophets your ancestors killed. ⁴⁸So you approve and agree with what your ancestors did. Is it not so? They got rid of the prophets, and you build monuments to them!

⁴⁹For that reason, the wisdom of God also said: I will send prophets and apostles and these people will kill and persecute some of them. ⁵⁰But the present generation will have to answer for the blood of all the prophets that has been shed since the foundation of the world, ⁵¹from the blood of Abel to the blood of Zechariah, who was murdered between the altar and the Sanctuary. Yes, I tell you, the people of this time will have to answer for them all.

⁵²A curse is on you, teachers of the law, for you have taken the key of knowledge. You yourselves have not entered, and you prevented others from entering."

[53] As Jesus left that place, the teachers of the law and the Pharisees began to harass him, [54] asking him endless questions, setting traps to catch him in something he might say.

LUKE 11:14-54

Read: Jesus exorcizes demons and his adversaries accuse him of being a demon himself. Jesus fights back: his power is the manifestation of the presence of the kingdom of God. Those honestly looking for God will see his power in Jesus' actions, even if they contradict their preconceived expectations.

Reflect: What does all this suggest? Is it difficult to distinguish a good action from a bad one? Do Christians repeat the same attitudes that Jesus reproaches the Pharisees and doctors of the law?

Pray: My incessant supplication, Lord, is this: "In you I trust. Deliver me from evil."

Act: Be alert to the saving manifestations of God that occur in your day to day. Do not close your eyes before them; give thanks to God for this and promote them in your family environment.

Open and fearless speech
(Mk 3:28; Mt 10:19; 12:31; Mk 8:38)

12 [1] Meanwhile, such a numerous crowd had gathered that they crushed one another. Then Jesus spoke to his disciples in this way,

"Beware of the yeast of the Pharisees, which is hypocrisy. [2] Nothing is covered that will not be uncovered; or hidden, that will not be made known. [3] Whatever you have said in the darkness will be heard in the light, and what you have whispered in hidden places, will be proclaimed from housetops.

[4] I tell you, my friends, do not fear those who put to death the body and, after that, can do no more. [5] But I will tell you whom to fear: Fear the one who, after killing you, is able to throw you into hell. This one you must fear. [6] Don't you buy five sparrows for two pennies? Yet not one of them has been forgotten by God. [7] Even the hairs of your head

have been numbered. Don't be afraid! Are you less worthy in the eyes of God than many sparrows?

⁸ I tell you, whoever acknowledges me before people, the Son of Man will also acknowledge before the angels of God. ⁹ But the one who denies me before others will be denied before the angels of God.

¹⁰ There will be pardon for the one who criticizes the Son of Man, but there will be no pardon for the one who slanders the Holy Spirit.

¹¹ When you are brought before the synagogues, and before governors and rulers, don't worry about how you will defend yourself, or what to say; ¹² for the Holy Spirit will teach you at that time what you have to say."

LUKE 12:1-12

Read: Jesus warns his disciples of hypocrisy, urges them to be sincere and courageous in proclaiming the Gospel.

Reflect: What are the biggest difficulties in proclaiming the Gospel day after day? What difficulty, in particular, do you experience?

Pray: Lord Jesus, may your Spirit accompany us at all times, to confess with courage the faith we profess.

Act: May your life bear witness to the faith of Jesus in welcoming and serving others.

The rich fool

¹³ Someone in the crowd spoke to Jesus, "Master, tell my brother to share with me the family inheritance." ¹⁴ He replied, "My friend, who has appointed me as your judge or your attorney?" ¹⁵ Then Jesus said to the people, "Be on your guard and avoid every kind of greed, for even though you have many possessions, it is not that which gives you life."

¹⁶ And Jesus continued, "There was a rich man and his land had produced a good harvest. ¹⁷ He thought, 'What shall I do, for I am short of room to store my harvest? ¹⁸ Alright, I know what I shall do: I will pull down my barns and I will build bigger ones to store all this grain, which is my wealth. ¹⁹ Then I will say to myself: My friend, you have a lot of good things put by for many years. Rest, eat, drink and enjoy yourself.' ²⁰ But God said to him, 'You fool! This very night your life will be taken

from you. Tell me, who shall get all you have put aside?' ²¹This is the lot of the one who stores up riches for himself and is not wealthy in the eyes of God."

Do not worry!
(Mt 6:25)

²²Then Jesus said to his disciples, "I tell you not to worry about your life: What are we to eat? Or about your body: What are we to wear? ²³For life is more than food and the body more than clothing. ²⁴Look at the crows: they neither sow nor reap; they have no storehouses and no barns, yet God feeds them. In so much, truly, are you different from birds! ²⁵Which of you, for all your worrying, can add a moment to your span of life? ²⁶And if you are not able to control such a small thing, why do you worry about the rest?

²⁷Look at the wildflowers: they do not spin or weave; but I tell you, even Solomon with all his wealth was not clothed as one of these flowers. ²⁸If God so clothes the grass in the fields, which is alive today and to-morrow is thrown into the oven, how much more will he clothe you, people of little faith.

²⁹Do not set your heart on what you are to eat and drink; stop worry-ing! ³⁰Let all the nations of the world run after these things; your Father knows that you need them. ³¹Seek, rather, his kingdom, and these things will be given to you as well.

³²Do not be afraid, little flock, for it has pleased your Father to give you the kingdom. ³³Sell what you have and give alms. Get yourselves purses that do not wear out, and an inexhaustible treasure in the heavens, where no thief comes and no moth destroys. ³⁴For where your treasure is, there will your heart be also.

LUKE 12:13-34

Read: Jesus exhorts his disciples to trust in God, to seek above all His kingdom, which others will receive in addition.

Reflect: Life is a free gift from God. An opportunity to be happy and to make others happy. There is no point worrying about riches. A Christian must first seek the kingdom of God.

Pray: Lord Jesus, save me from the foolishness of striving for riches rather than for your kingdom and justice.

> **Act:** Mentally review all your daily worries and trust them to
> the teaching of the Gospel. Thank God for the good in life and
> ask God for help to remedy the bad.

Be ready
(Mk 13:33; Mt 24:43; 6:19)

³⁵ Be ready, dressed for service, and keep your lamps lit ³⁶ like people waiting for their master to return from the wedding. As soon as he comes and knocks, they will open the door to him. ³⁷ Happy are those servants whom the master finds wide-awake when he comes. ³⁸ Truly, I tell you, he will put on an apron and have them sit at table and he will wait on them. Happy are those servants if he finds them awake when he comes at midnight or daybreak!

³⁹ Pay attention to this: If the master of the house had known at what time the thief would come, he would not have let his house be broken into. ⁴⁰ You also must be ready, for the Son of Man will come at an hour you do not expect."

⁴¹ Peter said, "Lord, did you tell this parable only for us, or for everyone?" ⁴² And the Lord replied, "Imagine, then, the wise and faithful steward, whom the master sets over his other servants to give them wheat at the proper time. ⁴³ Fortunate is this servant if his master, on coming home, finds him doing his work. ⁴⁴ Truly, I say to you, the master will put him in charge of all his property.

⁴⁵ But it may be that the steward thinks, 'My Lord delays in coming,' and he begins to abuse the male servants and the servant girls, eating and drinking and getting drunk. ⁴⁶ Then the master will come on a day he does not expect and at an hour he doesn't know. He will cut him off and send him to the same fate as the unfaithful.

⁴⁷ The servant who knew his master's will, but did not prepare and do what his master wanted, will be soundly beaten; ⁴⁸ but the one who does unconsciously what deserves punishment, shall receive fewer blows. Much will be required of the one who has been given much and more will be asked of the one who has been entrusted with more.

(Mt 10:34; 5:25; 16:2)

⁴⁹ I have come to bring fire upon the earth and how I wish it were

already kindled! ⁵⁰But I have a baptism to undergo and what anguish I feel until it is finished!

⁵¹Do you think that I have come to bring peace on earth? No, I tell you, but rather division. ⁵²From now on, in one house five will be divided: three against two and two against three. ⁵³They will be divided father against son and son against father; mother against daughter and daughter against mother; mother-in-law against her daughter-in-law and daughter-in-law against her mother-in-law."

⁵⁴Jesus said to the crowds, "When you see a cloud rising in the west, you say at once, 'A shower is coming'; and so it happens. ⁵⁵And when the wind blows from the south, you say, 'It will be hot'; and so it is. ⁵⁶You superficial people! You understand the signs of the earth and the sky, but you don't understand the present times. ⁵⁷And why do you not judge for yourselves what is fit? ⁵⁸When you go with your accuser before the court, try to settle the case on the way, lest he drags you before the judge and the judge deliver you to the jailer and the jailer throw you into prison. ⁵⁹I tell you, you will not get out until you have paid the very last penny."

LUKE 12:35-59

Read: After warning his disciples about undue desire for riches, Jesus now calls them to wait for upon his return, be attentive to his presence, and ready to answer his call.

Reflect: Do you consider yourself ready for a definitive encounter with the Lord? If not, what would it be missing? How should we prepare Christians for the encounter with the Lord?

Pray: O God, grant me the grace to perceive death as a close encounter with you, and not as a moment of judgment and punishment. May your Spirit help me to always be ready for meeting you.

Act: Spend more time on those things and situations that help you be prepared for your final encounter with the Lord.

The fig tree without fruit

13 ¹One day, some people told Jesus what had occurred in the temple: Pilate had had Galileans killed and their blood mingled with the blood of their sacrifices. ²Jesus asked them, "Do you think that these Galileans were worse sinners than all other Galileans because they suffered this? ³No, I tell you. But unless you change your ways, you will all perish as they did.

⁴And those eighteen persons in Siloah, who were crushed when the tower fell, do you think they were more guilty than all the others in Jerusalem? ⁵I tell you: no. But unless you change your ways, you will all perish, as they did."

⁶And Jesus continued, "A man had a fig tree growing in his vineyard, and he came looking for fruit on it but found none. ⁷Then he said to the gardener, 'Look here, for three years now I have been looking for figs on this tree and I have found none. Cut it down, why should it continue to deplete the soil?' ⁸The gardener replied, 'Leave it one more year, so that I may dig around it and add some fertilizer, ⁹perhaps it will bear fruit from now on. But if it doesn't, you can cut it down.'"

The healing on a Sabbath day

¹⁰Jesus was teaching in a synagogue on the Sabbath ¹¹and a crippled woman was there. An evil spirit had kept her bent for eighteen years so that she could not straighten up at all. ¹²On seeing her, Jesus called her and said, "Woman, you are freed from your infirmity." ¹³Then he laid his hands upon her and immediately she was made straight and praised God.

¹⁴But the ruler of the synagogue was indignant because Jesus had performed this healing on the Sabbath day and he said to the people, "There are six days in which to work. Come on those days to be healed and not on the Sabbath!"

¹⁵But the Lord replied, "You hypocrites! Every one of you unties his ox or his donkey on the Sabbath and leads it out of the barn to give it water. ¹⁶And here you have a daughter of Abraham, whom Satan had bound for eighteen years. Should she not be freed from her bonds on the Sabbath?"

¹⁷When Jesus said this, all his opponents felt ashamed. But the people rejoiced at the many wonderful things that happened because of him.

Two parables
(Mt 13:31; Mk 4:30)

¹⁸And Jesus continued, "What is the kingdom of God like? What shall

I compare it to? ¹⁹Imagine a person who has taken a mustard seed and planted it in his garden. The seed has grown and become like a small tree so that the birds of the air shelter in its branches."

²⁰And Jesus said again, "What is the kingdom of God like? ²¹Imagine a woman who has taken yeast and hidden it in three measures of flour until it is all leavened."

LUKE 13:1-21

Read: The exhortation to repentance (1–4) contrasts with the patience and mercy of God toward His people (parable of the fig tree without figs). God always watches over His people, even on the Sabbath. His liberating presence is simple but powerful (18-21).

Reflect: What do you need to change in your life? Why? Do you trust in the mercy of God? What do the parables of the mustard seed and the leaven have to do with you?

Pray: Lord, I trust you. Transform my life according to your Gospel.

Act: Promote in your family those gestures that manifest the saving presence of God, such as knowing how to ask for forgiveness and to forgive others.

---

²²Jesus went through towns and villages, teaching and making his way to Jerusalem. ²³Someone asked him, "Lord, is it true that few people will be saved?"

And Jesus answered, ²⁴"Do your best to enter by the narrow door; for many, I tell you, will try to enter and will not be able. ²⁵When once the master of the house has gone inside and locked the door, you will stand outside. Then you will knock at the door, calling, 'Lord, open to us!' But he will say to you, 'I do not know where you come from.'

²⁶Then you will say, 'We ate and drank with you and you taught in our streets!' ²⁷But he will reply, 'I don't know where you come from. *Away from me, all you workers of evil.*'

²⁸You will weep and grind your teeth when you see Abraham, Isaac, and Jacob and all the prophets in the kingdom of God and you yourselves left outside. ²⁹Others will sit at table in the kingdom of God, people

coming from east and west, from north and south. ³⁰Some who are among the last will be first, and some who are among the first will be last!"

³¹At that time some Pharisees came to Jesus and gave him this warning, "Leave this place and go on your way, for Herod wants to kill you." ³²Jesus said to them, "Go and give that fox my answer: 'I drive out demons and I heal today and tomorrow and on the third day I finish my course!' ³³Nevertheless, I must go on my way today and tomorrow and for a little longer; for it would not be fitting for a prophet to be killed outside Jerusalem.

Alas for you, Jerusalem

³⁴O Jerusalem, Jerusalem, you slay the prophets and stone those who are sent to you! How often have I tried to bring together your children as a bird gathers her young under her wings? But you refused! ³⁵From now on, *you will be left with your temple.* And you will no longer see me until the time when you will say, "*Blessed is he who comes in the name of the Lord!*"

LUKE 13:22-35

Read: Jesus invites his disciples to persevere in their vocation, to enter through "the narrow door," and image that reveals following Jesus is not easy. God wants everyone to be saved. Jesus laments for his people because they did not know how to accept his Gospel.

Reflect: What does the expression "enter through the narrow door" mean in your life? Is it difficult to live the values of the Gospel in our current society? Why?

Pray: Lord Jesus, may your Spirit give me the strength to accept your Word with courage and live according to it.

Act: Make a list of the five situations that you consider most difficult for a Christian in our current society. In your daily life, try to overcome them with the values that the Gospel proposes.

---

14 ¹One Sabbath Jesus had gone to eat a meal in the house of a leading Pharisee and he was carefully watched. ²In front of him was a man suffering from dropsy; ³so Jesus asked the teachers of the law and the Pharisees, "Is it lawful to heal on the Sabbath, or not?" [4] But no one answered. Jesus then took the man, healed him and sent him away. [5] And he said to them, "If your lamb or your ox falls into a well on a Sabbath day, who among you doesn't hurry to pull it out?" [6] And they could not answer.

The first places

[7] Jesus then told a parable to the guests, for he had noticed how they tried to take the places of honor. And he said, [8] "When you are invited to a wedding party, do not choose the best seat. It may happen that someone more important than you has been invited; [9] and your host, who invited both of you, will come and say to you, 'Please give this person your place.' What shame is yours when you take the lowest seat!

[10] Whenever you are invited, go rather to the lowest seat so that your host may come and say to you, 'Friend, you must come up higher.' And this will be a great honor for you in the presence of all the other guests. [11] For whoever makes himself out to be great will be humbled, and whoever humbles himself will be exalted."

[12] Jesus also addressed the man who had invited him and said, "When you give a lunch or a dinner, don't invite your friends, or your brothers and relatives, or your wealthy neighbors. For surely they will also invite you in return and you will be repaid. [13] When you give a feast, invite instead the poor, the crippled, the lame and the blind. [14] Fortunate are you then because they cannot repay you. You will be repaid at the resurrection of the upright."

LUKE 14:1-14

Read: Jesus, on the Sabbath, in the midst of a meal offered by a Pharisee, heals a suffering person. It reveals his choice for life and his authority over the Sabbath (Law). Immediately after, he criticizes the attitude of those who strive for public recognition, fame, and honor.

Reflect: What does the following expression suggest: "When you give a feast, invite instead the poor, the crippled, the lame and the blind. Fortunate are you because they cannot repay you. You will be repaid at the resurrection of the upright"?

> **Pray:** Lord Jesus, may your Spirit help me to follow your example of courage, humility, and generosity; always to choose to do good, and do not try to gain fame, but manifest your saving presence in the world.
>
> **Act:** Perform an act of charity with anonymity, with humility and generosity. This will follow the example of Jesus.

A man once gave a feast
(Mt 22:1)

¹⁵ Upon hearing these words, one of those at the table said to Jesus, "Happy are those who eat at the banquet in the kingdom of God!"

¹⁶ Jesus replied, "A man once gave a feast and invited many guests. ¹⁷ When it was time for the feast, he sent his servant to tell those he had invited to come, for everything was ready. ¹⁸ But all alike began to make excuses. The first said, 'Please excuse me. I must go and see the piece of land I have just bought.' ¹⁹ Another said: 'I am sorry, but I am on my way to try out the five yoke of oxen I have just bought.' ²⁰ Still, another said, 'How can I come, when I've just got married?'

²¹ The servant returned alone and reported this to his master. Upon hearing his account, the master of the house flew into a rage and ordered his servant, 'Go out quickly, into the streets and alleys of the town and bring in the poor, the crippled, the blind and the lame.'

²² The servant reported after a while, 'Sir, your orders have been carried out, but there is still room.' ²³ The master said, 'Go out to the highways and country lanes and force people to come in to ensure that my house is full. ²⁴ I tell you, none of those invited will have a morsel of my feast.'"

The cost of following Jesus
(Mt 10:37)

²⁵ One day, when large crowds were walking along with Jesus, he turned and said to them, ²⁶ "If you come to me, unwilling to sacrifice your love for your father and mother, your spouse and children, your brothers and sisters and indeed yourself, you cannot be my disciple. ²⁷ Whoever does not follow me carrying his own cross, cannot be my disciple.

²⁸ Do you build a house without first sitting down to count the cost to

see whether you have enough to complete it? [29] Otherwise, if you have laid the foundation and are not able to finish it, everyone will make fun of you: [30] 'This fellow began to build and was not able to finish.'

[31] And when a king wages war against another king, does he go to fight without first sitting down to consider whether his ten thousand can stand against the twenty thousand of his opponent? [32] And if not, while the other is still a long way off, he sends messengers for peace talks. [33] In the same way, none of you may become my disciple if he doesn't give up everything he has.

[34] However good the salt may be, if the salt has lost taste you cannot make it salty again. [35] It is fit for neither soil nor manure. Let them throw it away. Listen then, if you have ears!"

LUKE 14:15-35

Read: Jesus tells the parable of the wedding feast. He expresses the universality and urgency of the salvation that God offers. Everyone must decide if they will accept or reject God's invitation. Jesus speaks about the need to continually reflect on the willingness to be his disciple.

Reflect: Are you willing to shape your life with the demands of following Jesus? Or do you have a limit that you are not willing to go beyond? What does the expression suggest: "Whoever does not carry his cross and follow me cannot be my disciple"?

Pray: Lord, give me what you ask from me and ask me what you want (St. Augustine).

Act: Make a list of five crosses you carry as you follow Jesus. Do your best with them this day.

The lost sheep
(Mt 18:12)

15 [1] Meanwhile tax collectors and sinners were seeking the company of Jesus, all of them eager to hear what he had to say. [2] But the Pharisees and the teachers of the law frowned at this, muttering, "This man welcomes sinners and eats with them." [3] So Jesus told them this parable:

⁴"Who among you, having a hundred sheep and losing one of them, will not leave the ninety-nine in the wilderness and seek the lost one till he finds it? ⁵And finding it, will he not joyfully carry it home on his shoulders? ⁶Then he will call his friends and neighbors together and say, 'Celebrate with me, for I have found my lost sheep!' ⁷I tell you, in the same way, there will be more rejoicing in heaven over one repentant sinner, than over ninety-nine decent people, who do not need to repent.

⁸What woman, if she has ten silver coins and loses one, will not light a lamp and sweep the house in a thorough search till she finds the lost coin? ⁹And finding it, she will call her friends and neighbors and say, 'Celebrate with me, for I have found the silver coin I lost!' ¹⁰I tell you, in the same way, there is rejoicing among the angels of God over one repentant sinner."

The parable of the lost sons

¹¹Jesus continued, "There was a man with two sons. ¹²The younger said to his father, 'Give me my share of the estate.' So the father divided his property between them.

¹³Some days later, the younger son gathered all his belongings and started off for a distant land where he squandered his wealth in loose living. ¹⁴Having spent everything, he was hard pressed when a severe famine broke out in that land. ¹⁵So he hired himself out to a well-to-do citizen of that place and was sent to work on a pig farm. ¹⁶So famished was he that he longed to fill his stomach even with the food given to the pigs, but no one offered him anything.

¹⁷Finally coming to his senses, he said, 'How many of my father's hired workers have food to spare and here I am starving to death! ¹⁸I will get up and go back to my father, and say to him, Father, I have sinned against God and before you. ¹⁹I no longer deserve to be called your son. Treat me then as one of your hired servants.' With that thought in mind, he set off for his father's house.

²⁰He was still a long way off when his father caught sight of him. His father was so deeply moved with compassion that he ran out to meet him, threw his arms around his neck and kissed him. ²¹The son said, 'Father, I have sinned against Heaven and before you. I no longer deserve to be called your son.'

²²But the father turned to his servants: 'Quick!' he said. 'Bring out the

finest robe and put it on him! Put a ring on his finger and sandals on his feet! ²³Take the fattened calf and kill it! We shall celebrate and have a feast, ²⁴for this son of mine was dead and has come back to life; he was lost and is found!' And the celebration began.

²⁵Meanwhile, the elder son had been working in the fields. As he returned and approached the house, he heard the sound of music and dancing. ²⁶He called one of the servants and asked what it was all about. ²⁷The servant answered, 'Your brother has come home safe and sound and your father is so happy about it that he has ordered this celebration and killed the fattened calf.'

²⁸The elder son became angry and refused to go in. His father came out and pleaded with him. ²⁹The son, very indignant, said, 'Look, I have slaved for you all these years. Never have I disobeyed your orders. Yet you have never given me even a young goat to celebrate with my friends. ³⁰But when this son of yours returns, after squandering your property with loose women, you kill the fattened calf for him!'

³¹The father said, 'My son, you are always with me and everything I have is yours. ³²But this brother of yours was dead and has come back to life; he was lost and is found. And for that, we had to rejoice and be glad.'"

LUKE 15:1-32

Read: Jesus responds to the criticisms of the Pharisees and lawyers with three parables: the lost sheep, the lost coin and the prodigal son. With them, he justifies his choice for "sinners" and reveals the true face of God: mercy (love).

Reflect: Do you feel the mercy of God in your life? Do you consider that just as God is merciful to you, so God is merciful to every human being? Do you consider yourself merciful toward others, as is God with you?

Pray: How can I reciprocate, O God, the measureless love you offer me every day?

Act: As an expression of gratitude to God, be kind and merciful with that person who has distanced himself from you because of some dispute or quarrel. Call him or her and arrange a meeting to remedy the distances.

The crafty steward

16 [1] At another time Jesus told his disciples, "There was a rich man, whose steward was reported to him because of fraudulent service. [2] He summoned the steward and asked him, 'What is this I hear about you? I want you to render an account of your service, for it is about to be terminated.'

[3] The steward thought to himself, 'What am I to do now? My master will surely dismiss me. I am not strong enough to do hard work, and I am ashamed to beg. [4] I know what I will do: I must make sure that when I am dismissed, there will be people who will welcome me into their homes.'

[5] So he called his master's debtors, one by one. He asked the first debtor, 'How much do you owe my master?' [6] The reply was, 'A hundred jars of oil.' The steward said, 'Here is your bill. Sit down quickly and write fifty.' [7] To the second debtor he put the same question, 'How much do you owe?' The answer was, 'A hundred measures of wheat.' Then the steward said, 'Take your bill and write eighty.'

[8] The master commended the dishonest steward for his astuteness: for the people of this world are more astute in dealing with their own kind than are the people of light. [9] And so I tell you: use filthy money to make friends for yourselves, so that, when it fails, these people may welcome you into the eternal homes.

[10] Whoever can be trusted in little things can also be trusted in great ones; whoever is dishonest in slight matters will also be dishonest in greater ones. [11] So if you have been dishonest in handling filthy money, who would entrust you with true wealth? [12] And if you have been dishonest with things that are not really yours, who will give you that wealth which is truly your own?

[13] No servant can serve two masters. Either he does not like the one and is fond of the other, or he regards one highly and the other with contempt. You cannot give yourself both to God and to Money."

LUKE 16:1-13

Read: Jesus exposes to his disciples the parable of the astute administrator. With it, he invites them to be creative, witty and clever in announcing the kingdom. Then he urges them to take a stance against money (wealth) because you cannot be at the service of two masters. Whoever absolutizes money cannot love God with all their heart.

Reflect: How important is money in your life? Do you try to "win" friends with it, or, on the contrary, does it generate "enemies"? How do you experience "You cannot be at the service of God and money"?

Pray: Oh gracious God, give me the grace to be generous with the goods that I have, that I will be in solidarity with the most needy, and that my heart never moves away from you.

Act: Plan a day in which you dare to live on the charity of others. With what you can save, make a donation to a charity.

[14] The Pharisees, who loved money, heard all this and sneered at Jesus. [15] He said to them, "You do your best to be considered righteous by people. But God knows the heart, and what is highly esteemed by human beings is loathed by God.

[16] The time of the law and the prophets ended with John. Now the kingdom of God is proclaimed and everyone tries to enter it by force.

[17] It is easier for heaven and earth to pass away than for a single letter of Scripture not to be fulfilled.

[18] Anyone who divorces his wife and marries another commits adultery, and whoever marries a woman divorced by her husband also commits adultery.

The rich man and Lazarus

[19] Once there was a rich man who dressed in purple and fine linen and feasted every day. [20] At his gate lay Lazarus, a poor man covered with sores, [21] who longed to eat just the scraps falling from the rich man's table. Even dogs used to come and lick his sores. [22] It happened that the poor man died and the angels carried him to take his place with Abraham. The rich man also died and was buried. [23] From the netherworld where he was in torment, the rich man looked up and saw Abraham afar off and with him Lazarus at rest.

[24] He called out, 'Father Abraham, have pity on me and send Lazarus, with the tip of his finger dipped in water, to cool my tongue, for I suffer so much in this fire!'

²⁵ Abraham replied, 'My son, remember that in your lifetime you were well-off, while the lot of Lazarus was a misfortune. Now he is in comfort and you are in agony. ²⁶ But that is not all. Between your place and ours, a great chasm has been fixed so that no one can cross over from here to you, or from your side to us.'

²⁷ The rich man implored once more, 'Then I beg you, Father Abraham, send Lazarus to my father's house ²⁸ where my five brothers live. Let him warn them so that they may not end up in this place of torment.' ²⁹ Abraham replied, 'They have Moses and the prophets. Let them listen to them.' ³⁰ But the rich man said, 'No, Father Abraham; but if someone from the dead goes to them, they will repent.'

³¹ Abraham said, 'If they will not listen to Moses and the prophets, they will not be convinced, even if someone rises from the dead.'"

LUKE 16:14-31

Read: To round off the issue of the incompatibility between service to God and money, Jesus exposes the parable of the rich man and Lazarus. A life lived in service to money is a slavery that makes a person lose the sense and the purpose of life: the definitive encounter with complete happiness is God.

Reflect: What do you think about hunger and misery in the world? Do you feel committed by the words of the Gospel to doing something about it? What should we Christians do?

Pray: I ask you, Lord, the grace to be in solidarity with the needs of others; may I not be indifferent to the pain of those who suffer.

Act: Do something to help some "Lazarus" you know up close.

---

17 ¹ Jesus said to his disciples, "Scandals will necessarily come and cause people to fall, but woe to the one who brings them about. ² It would be better for him to be thrown into the sea with a millstone around his neck. Truly, this would be better for that person, than to cause one of these little ones to fall.

³ Listen carefully: if your brother offends you, tell him, and if he is sorry, forgive him. ⁴ And if he offends you seven times in one day, but seven times he says to you, 'I'm sorry,' forgive him."

⁵ The apostles said to the Lord, "Increase our faith." And the Lord said, ⁶ "If you have faith, even the size of a mustard seed, you may say to this tree, 'Be uprooted, and plant yourself in the sea!' and it will obey you.

⁷ Who among you would say to your servant, coming in from the fields after plowing or tending sheep, 'Go ahead and have your dinner'? ⁸ No, you tell him, 'Prepare my dinner. Put on your apron and wait on me while I eat and drink. You can eat and drink afterward.' ⁹ Do you thank this servant for doing what you told him to do? ¹⁰ I don't think so. And therefore, when you have done all that you have been told to do, you should say, 'We are no more than servants; we have only done our duty.'"

The ten lepers

¹¹ On the way to Jerusalem, Jesus passed through Samaria and Galilee and ¹² as he entered a village, ten lepers came to meet him. ¹³ Keeping their distance, they called to him, "Jesus, Master, have pity on us!" ¹⁴ Jesus said to them, "Go, and show yourselves to the priests." Then, as they went on their way, they found they were cured. ¹⁵ One of them, as soon as he saw that he was cleansed, turned back, praising God in a loud voice; and ¹⁶ throwing himself on his face before Jesus, he gave him thanks. This man was a Samaritan.

¹⁷ Then Jesus asked him, "Were not all ten healed? Where are the other nine? ¹⁸ Did none of them decide to return and give praise to God, but this foreigner?" ¹⁹ And Jesus said to him, "Stand up and go your way; your faith has saved you."

LUKE 17:1-19

Read: Jesus instructs his disciples on the importance of faith. Faith is developed in a community environment, hence the care not to scandalize the "little ones" and to forgive those who offend us. Faith, moreover, is a free gift, we do not earn it by merit, so we must always ask for it and give thanks to God for it.

Reflect: Do you consider it important to have faith in life? Are you careful to practice it in community? How do you thank God for it?

Pray: Thank you, Lord, for the gift of faith; for your call to follow you and proclaim your Gospel with my life to others.

Act: Share your faith with others, telling them how God is present in your daily life.

The coming of the kingdom of God
(Mt 24:17)

²⁰ The Pharisees asked Jesus when the kingdom of God was to come. He answered, "The kingdom of God is not like something you can observe, ²¹ and say of it, 'Look, here it is!' or 'See, there it is!' for the kingdom of God is within you."

²² And Jesus said to his disciples, "The time is at hand when you will long to see one of the glorious days of the Son of Man, but you will not see it. ²³ Then people will tell you, 'Look there! Look here!' 'Do not go with them, do not follow them.' ²⁴ As lightning flashes from one end of the sky to the other, so will it be with the Son of Man; ²⁵ but first he must suffer many things and be rejected by this generation.

²⁶ As it was in the days of Noah, so will it be on the day the Son of Man comes. ²⁷ In those days people ate and drank and got married; but on the day Noah entered the ark, the flood came and destroyed them all. ²⁸ So it was in the days of Lot: people ate and drank, and bought and sold, and planted and built; ²⁹ but on the day Lot left Sodom, God made fire and sulfur rain down from heaven which destroyed them all. ³⁰ So will it be on the day the Son of Man is revealed.

³¹ On that day, if you are on the rooftop, don't go down into the house to get your belongings; and if you happen to be in the fields, do not turn back. ³² Remember Lot's wife! ³³ Whoever tries to save his life will lose it, but whoever gives his life will be born again.

³⁴ I tell you, though two men are sharing the same bed, it might happen that one will be taken and the other left; ³⁵ though two women are grinding meal together, one might be taken and the other left."

³⁷ Then they asked Jesus, "Where will this take place, Lord?" And he answered, "Where the body is, there too will the vultures gather."

LUKE 17:20-37

Read: Jesus speaks about the coming of the kingdom of God: it is not subject to calculations, because it is "among us," and of the future will be fully expressed.

Reflect: Do you perceive the manifestation of the kingdom of God in your life? How? Are you ready for the final encounter with the Lord? How?

Pray: Lord God, help me to be attentive to the manifestation of your kingdom and to be prepared for your encounter. Do not allow what is ephemeral to distract me, and drift away from you.

Act: Reflect on the biggest concerns you have in your life. Do they help you be prepared for your encounter with the Lord?

Pray and never lose heart

18 [1] Jesus told them a parable to show them that they should pray continually and not lose heart. [2] He said, "In a certain town there was a judge who neither feared God nor people. [3] In the same town there was a widow who kept coming to him, saying, 'Defend my rights against my adversary!' [4] For a time he refused, but finally he thought, 'Even though I neither fear God nor care about people, [5] this widow bothers me so much I will see that she gets justice; then she will stop coming and wearing me out."

[6] And Jesus said, "Listen to what the evil judge says. [7] Will God not do justice for his chosen ones, who cry to him day and night, even if he delays in answering them? [8] I tell you, he will speedily do them justice. But, when the Son of Man comes, will he find faith on earth?"

The Pharisee and the tax collector

[9] Jesus told another parable to some people fully convinced of their own righteousness, who looked down on others: [10] "Two men went up to the temple to pray; one was a Pharisee and the other a tax collector. [11] The Pharisee stood by himself and said, 'I thank you, God, that I am not like other people, grasping, crooked, adulterous, or even like this tax collector. [12] I fast twice a week and give a tenth of all my income to the temple.'

¹³In the meantime the tax collector, standing far off, would not even lift his eyes to heaven, but beat his breast, saying, 'O God, be merciful to me, a sinner.'

¹⁴I tell you, when this man went back to his house, he had been reconciled with God, but not the other. For whoever makes himself out to be great will be humbled, and whoever humbles himself will be raised up."

> **LUKE 18:1-14**
>
> **Read:** Jesus tells the parables of the judge and the widow, and of the Pharisee and the tax collector, to invite his listeners to be persevering and humble in prayer.
>
> **Reflect:** Do you pray to God often? Do you consider yourself worthy of divine grace for being a regular in prayer? Do you talk to God about your worries, problems, and desires? How do you trust in God's mercy?
>
> **Pray:** Lord, from my littleness, I recognize your greatness and kindness by taking seriously, as you do, my needs, concerns, problems, and desires.
>
> **Act:** As thanks for the mercy of God, get close to your family and friends, and share with them a time of attentive listening to their needs and desires.

¹⁵People even brought little children to Jesus to have him touch them, but seeing it the disciples rebuked these people. ¹⁶So Jesus called the children to him and said, "Let the children come to me and don't stop them, for the kingdom of God belongs to such as these. ¹⁷Truly I tell you, whoever does not receive the kingdom of God like a child will not enter it."

Jesus and the rich ruler
(Mk 10:17; Mt 19:16)

¹⁸A ruler asked Jesus, "Good master, what shall I do to inherit eternal life?" ¹⁹Jesus said to him, "Why do you call me good? No one is good but God alone. ²⁰You know the commandments: *Do not commit adultery; do not kill; do not steal; do not accuse falsely; honor your father and your mother.*" ²¹And the man said, "I have kept all these commandments from my youth."

²²Then Jesus answered, "There is still one thing you lack. Sell all you have and give the money to the poor, and you will have riches in Heaven. And then come, follow me!" ²³When he heard these words, the man became sad, for he was very rich. ²⁴Jesus noticing this said, "How hard it is for people who have riches to enter the kingdom of God! ²⁵It is easier for a camel to pass through the eye of a needle than for a rich person to enter the kingdom of God." ²⁶The bystanders said, "Who then can be saved?" ²⁷And Jesus replied, "What is impossible for human beings is possible for God."

²⁸Then Peter said, "We left everything we had and followed you." ²⁹Jesus replied, "Truly, I tell you, whoever has left home or wife, or brothers or parents or children, for the sake of the kingdom of God, ³⁰will receive much more in this present time, and eternal life in the world to come."

³¹Jesus then took the Twelve aside, and told them, "Now we are going up to Jerusalem, and everything the Prophets have written about the Son of Man will be fulfilled. ³²He will be delivered up to the foreign power. People will mock him, insult him and spit on him. ³³After they have scourged him, they will kill him, but he will be raised on the third day." ³⁴The apostles could make nothing of this; the meaning of these words remained a mystery to them and they did not understand what he said.

LUKE 18:15-34

Read: Jesus blesses some children, and presents them as an example of welcome to the kingdom of God. When somone refuses an invitation to give up his riches and follow him, Jesus declares that for the rich it is difficult to enter the kingdom. A disciples rewards are found in the kingdom of God.

Reflect: Why do you think that Jesus presents children as an example of welcome to the kingdom of God? What are your greatest riches? Do you feel subject to them? Do you already perceive the enjoyment of the rewards offered by Jesus?

Pray: Lord Jesus, transform my heart to welcome with joy and detachment your kingdom, which you offer us generously, abundant and free.

Act: Live your vocation in constant thanksgiving. Do not cling to what you consider "your riches." Be supportive and generous.

The blind man of Jericho
(Mk 10:46; Mt 20:29)

³⁵ When Jesus drew near to Jericho, a blind man was sitting by the road begging. ³⁶ As he heard the crowd passing by, he inquired what was happening ³⁷ and they told him that Jesus of Nazareth was going by. ³⁸ Then he cried out, "Jesus, Son of David, have mercy on me!" ³⁹ The people in front of him scolded him. "Be quiet!" they said, but he cried out all the more, "Jesus, Son of David, have mercy on me!"

⁴⁰ Jesus stopped and ordered the blind man to be brought to him; and when he came near, Jesus asked him, ⁴¹ "What do you want me to do for you?" And the man said, "Lord, that I may see!" ⁴² Jesus said, "Receive your sight, your faith has saved you." ⁴³ At once the blind man was able to see and he followed Jesus, giving praise to God. And all the people who were there also praised God.

Jesus and Zaccheus

19 ¹ Jesus entered Jericho and was passing through it. ² A man named Zaccheus lived there. He was a tax collector and a wealthy man. ³ He wanted to see what Jesus was like, but he was a short man and could not see him because of the crowd. ⁴ So he ran ahead and climbed up a sycamore tree. From there he would be able to see Jesus who was going to pass that way. ⁵ When Jesus came to the place, he looked up and said to him, "Zaccheus, come down quickly for I must stay at your house today." ⁶ So Zaccheus climbed down and received him joyfully.

⁷ All the people who saw it began to grumble and said, "He has gone as a guest to the house of a sinner." ⁸ But Zaccheus spoke to Jesus, "Half of what I own, Lord, I will give to the poor, and if I have cheated anyone, I will pay him back four times as much." ⁹ Looking at him Jesus said, "Salvation has come to this house today, for he is also a true son of Abraham. ¹⁰ The Son of Man has come to seek and to save the lost."

LUKE 18:35—19:10

Read: On the way to Jerusalem, in Jericho, Jesus heals a blind man and forgives Zacchaeus. Both, despite their physical limitations, want to be close to him. Jesus gives them what they crave most: sight and forgiveness. Then the blind man, giving glory to God, follows him, and Zacchaeus reforms his life.

> **Reflect:** How do you meet the Risen Jesus in your life? How do you go out to meet him? What do you ask? Do you feel welcomed by him?
>
> **Pray:** Help me, Lord, to feel your presence in every person that I find on my path and in every situation of life that I have to face.
>
> **Act:** In prayer, manifest to the Lord the most serious concern you have right now. Like the blind man, ask him "to see," and like Zacchaeus, let him enter "your house."

The ten pounds
(Mt 25:14)

[11] Jesus was now near Jerusalem and the people with him thought that God's reign was about to appear. So as they were listening to him, Jesus went on to tell them a parable. [12] He said, "A man of noble birth went to a distant country in order to be crowned king, after which he planned to return home. [13] Before he left, he summoned ten of his servants and gave them ten pounds of silver. He said, 'Put this money to work until I get back.' [14] But his compatriots, who disliked him, sent a delegation after him with this message, 'We do not want this man to be our king.'

[15] He returned, however, appointed as king. At once he sent for the servants, to whom he had given the money, to find out what profit each had made. [16] The first came in and reported, 'Sir, your pound of silver has earned ten more pounds of silver.'

[17] The master replied, 'Well done, my good servant! Since you have proved yourself faithful in a small matter, I can trust you to take charge of ten cities.' [18] The second reported, 'Sir, your pound of silver earned five more pounds of silver.' [19] The master replied, 'And you, take charge of five cities!'

[20] The third came in and said, 'Sir, here is your money, which I hid for safekeeping. [21] I was afraid of you, for you are an exacting person: you take up what you did not lay down and you reap what you did not sow.'

[22] The master replied, 'You worthless servant, I will judge you by your own words! So you knew I was an exacting person, taking up what I did not lay down and reaping what I did not sow? [23] Why, then, did you not put my money on loan, so that when I got back, I could have collected it with interest?'

²⁴ Then the master said to those standing by, 'Take from him that pound and give it to the one with ten pounds.' ²⁵ But they objected, 'Sir, he already has ten pounds!'

²⁶ The master replied, 'I tell you, everyone who has will be given more; but from those who have nothing, even what they have will be taken away. ²⁷ As for my enemies who did not want me to be their king, bring them in and execute them right here in front of me!'"

LUKE 19:11-27

Read: As Jesus and his disciples draw closer to Jerusalem people think the kingdom of God will come immediately. Jesus tells the parable of the king and the money given to his servants. He exhorts us not to be passive with the gifts received by God; we must invest them and produce, which in the context of the Gospel means giving life in service to others.

Reflect: What are the gifts you consider received from the Lord? What have you done with them? How are you tempted to keep them hidden? What are the risks of investing them in others?

Pray: Lord, may I be fully aware of the gifts and talents you have bestowed upon me. Help me to use them for the greater glory of you: your kingdom.

Act: Identify a gift or talent received from the Lord and use it practically in service to others.

Jesus enters Jerusalem
(Mk 11:1; Mt 21:1; Jn 12:12; Mt 24:2)

²⁸ So Jesus spoke, and then he passed on ahead of them, on his way to Jerusalem. ²⁹ When he drew near to Bethphage and Bethany, close to the Mount of Olives, he sent two of his disciples with these instructions, ³⁰ "Go to the village opposite; and, as you enter it, you will find a colt tied up that no one has yet ridden. Untie it and bring it here. ³¹ And if anyone says to you, 'Why are you untying this colt?' You shall say, 'The Master needs it.'"

³² So the two disciples went and found things just as Jesus had said. ³³ As they were untying the colt, the owner said to them, "Why are you

untying the colt?" [34] And they answered, "The Master needs it." [35] So they brought it to Jesus and throwing their cloaks on the colt, they mounted Jesus on it. [36] And as he went along, people spread their cloaks on the road.

[37] When Jesus came near Jerusalem to the place where the road slopes down from the Mount of Olives, the whole multitude of his disciples began to rejoice and to praise God with a loud voice for all the miracles they had seen; [38] and they cried out, "*Blessed is he who comes as king in the name of the Lord.* Peace in heaven and glory in the highest heavens."

[39] Some Pharisees in the crowd said to him, "Master, rebuke your disciples!" [40] But Jesus answered, "I tell you, if they were to remain silent, the stones would cry out."

[41] When Jesus had come in sight of the city, he wept over it [42] and said, "If only today you knew the ways of peace! But now they are hidden from your eyes. [43] Yet days will come upon you when your enemies will surround you with barricades and shut you in and press on you from every side. [44] And they will dash you to the ground and your children with you and not leave a stone upon stone within you, for you did not recognize the time and the visitation of your God."

[45] Then Jesus entered the temple area and began to drive out the merchants. [46] And he said to them, "God says in the Scriptures, '*My house shall be a house of prayer,*' but you have turned it into a den of robbers!"

[47] Jesus was teaching every day in the temple. The chief priests and teachers of the law wanted to kill him and the elders of the Jews as well, [48] but they were unable to do anything, for all the people were listening to him and hanging on his words.

LUKE 19:28-48

Read: Jesus arrives in Jerusalem. He enters in the midst of praises and blessings. He weeps for the future of the city. Then, he expels the merchants from the Temple. The high priests, the scribes and the chiefs of the people look for a way to kill him.

Reflect: How does your "waiting" for Jesus shows in your daily life? What does the following expression suggest: "My house shall be a house of prayer, but you have turned it into a den of robbers"?

Pray: Lord Jesus, help me to be always attentive to your coming, to receive you with joy, to recognize your presence in my life and in the life of the community.

Act: Encourage someone to participate in a parish group, or a prayer group at work.

20 ¹One day, when Jesus was teaching the people in the temple and proclaiming the good news, the chief priests and the teachers of the law came with the elders of the Jews ²and said to him, "Tell us, what right have you to act like this? Who gives you authority to do all this?"

³Jesus said to them, "I also will ask you a question. Tell me: ⁴was John's baptism of heavenly or of human origin?" ⁵And they argued among themselves, "If we answer that it was a work of God, he will say, 'Why then did you not believe him?' ⁶But if we answer that it was merely something human, the people will stone us, for they all regard John as a prophet." ⁷So they answered Jesus, "We don't know," ⁸and Jesus said to them, "Neither will I tell you what right I have to act like this."

The murderous tenants
(Mk 12:1; Mt 21:33)

⁹Jesus went on to tell the people this parable, "A man planted a vineyard and let it out to tenants before going abroad for a long time.

¹⁰In due time, he sent a servant to the tenants to get some fruit from the vineyard. But the tenants beat him and sent him back empty-handed. ¹¹Again the man sent another servant; they beat him as well and treated him shamefully, and finally sent him back empty-handed. ¹²The owner then sent a third servant, but him they injured and threw out of the vineyard.

¹³The owner then thought, 'What shall I do? I will send my beloved son; surely they will respect him.' ¹⁴However the tenants, as soon as they saw him, said to one another, 'This is the one who will inherit the vineyard. Let us kill him and the property will be ours!' ¹⁵So they threw him out of the vineyard and killed him. ¹⁶Now, what will the owner of the vineyard do to them? He will come and destroy those tenants and give the vineyard to others."

On hearing this, some said, "God forbid!" ¹⁷Then Jesus looked directly at them and said, "What does this text of the Scriptures mean: *The stone which the builders rejected has become the keystone?* ¹⁸ *Everyone who falls on that stone will be broken to pieces and anyone that stone falls on will be crushed.*"

¹⁹ The teachers of the law and the chief priests would have liked to arrest him right there, for they realized that Jesus meant this parable for them, but they were afraid of the crowd. ²⁰ So they left, looking for another opportunity.

LUKE 20:1-20

Read: Jesus thwarts the attempt of the high priests and lawyers to disavow him. The parable of the evil vinedressers is addressed to them. The biblical quote: "The stone which the builders rejected has become the keystone" is the point.

Reflect: Does current Christian witness validate the authority of Jesus and the Gospel? Why or why not? What things should we improve so that Christian witness be authentic and prophetic.

Pray: O God, I ask you for courage and wisdom to bear faithful witness to the teachings of the Gospel in the world.

Act: Do not be afraid to express your faith in the midst of adverse or compromising situations. Remember that your witness expresses the teachings of the Gospel.

Paying taxes to Caesar
(Mk 12:13; Mt 22:15)

They sent spies who pretended to be honest men, in order to trap him in his words and deliver him to the authority and power of the Roman governor. ²¹ They said to him, "Master, we know that you are true in your words and in your teaching and your answers do not vary according to who is listening to you; for you truly teach the way of God. Tell us: ²² are we allowed to pay taxes to Caesar or not?"

²³ But Jesus saw through their cunning and said, ²⁴ "Show me a silver coin. Whose image is this, and whose title does it bear?" They answered, "Caesar's." ²⁵ And Jesus said to them, "Return to Caesar the things that are Caesar's and to God what is God's."

²⁶ So they were unable to trap him in what he said publicly; they were surprised at his answer and kept silent.

The resurrection of the dead
(Mk 12:18)

²⁷ Then some Sadducees arrived. These people claim that there is no resurrection, ²⁸ and they asked Jesus this question, "Master, the law Moses told us, 'If anyone dies, leaving a wife but no children, his brother must take the wife and any child born to them will be regarded as the child of the deceased.' ²⁹ Now, there were seven brothers: the first married but died without children. ³⁰ The second married the woman, but also died childless. ³¹ And then the third married her and in this same way, all seven died, leaving no children. ³² Last of all, the woman died. ³³ On the day of the resurrection, to which of them will the woman be a wife? For all seven had her as a wife."

³⁴ And Jesus replied, "Taking a husband or a wife is proper to people of this world, ³⁵ but for those who are considered worthy of the world to come and of resurrection from the dead, there is no more marriage. ³⁶ Besides, they cannot die, for they are like angels. They are sons and daughters of God because they are born of the resurrection.

³⁷ Yes, the dead will be raised, as Moses revealed at the burning bush when he called the Lord *the God of Abraham and the God of Isaac and the God of Jacob*. ³⁸ For God is God of the living and not of the dead, for to him everyone is alive."

³⁹ Some teachers of the law then agreed with Jesus, "Master, you have spoken well." ⁴⁰ They didn't dare ask him anything else. ⁴¹ So Jesus said to them, "How can people say that the Messiah is the Son of David? ⁴² For David himself says in the book of Psalms, *The Lord said to my Lord: Sit at my right hand,* ⁴³ *until I put your enemies under your feet!* ⁴⁴ David, there, calls him Lord; how then can he be his Son?"

⁴⁵ Jesus also said to his disciples before all the people, ⁴⁶ "Beware of those teachers of the law, who like to be seen in long robes, and love to be greeted in the marketplaces and to take the reserved seats in the synagogues and the places of honor at feasts. ⁴⁷ While making a show of long prayers, they devour the property of widows. They will receive a very severe sentence!"

The widow's mite
(Mk 12:41)

21 ¹Jesus looked up and saw rich people putting their gifts into the treasury of the temple. ²He also saw a poor widow, who dropped in two small coins. ³And he said, "Truly, I tell you, this poor widow put in more than all of them. ⁴For all of them gave an offering from their plenty; but she, out of her poverty, gave all she had to live on."

LUKE 20:20—21:4

Read: The adversaries of Jesus try to discredit him before the people with trick questions. Jesus answers them definitively and denounces their hypocrisy. He praises the attitude of a widow who offers God not what she has extra, but all that she has.

Reflect: Do you believe that today the Christian faith has adversaries? Who are they? In your opinion, what most discredits the message of the Gospel? What shows the truth of the Gospel?

Pray: Lord Jesus, give us courage and wisdom so that we Christians can give authentic witness to your Gospel in the world.

Act: See how you can help the catechists in your parish. Offer them your support.

Signs before the destruction of Jerusalem
(Mk 13:1; Mt 24:1)

⁵While some people were talking about the temple, remarking that it was adorned with fine stonework and rich gifts, Jesus said to them, ⁶"The days will come when there shall not be left one stone upon another of all that you now admire; all will be torn down." ⁷And they asked him, "Master, when will this be and what will be the sign that this is about to take place?"

⁸Jesus said, "Take care not to be deceived, for many will come in my name, saying, 'I am he; the time is near at hand!' Do not follow them. ⁹When you hear of wars and troubled times, don't be frightened; for all these things must happen first, even though the end is not so soon."

¹⁰And Jesus said, "Nations will fight each other and kingdom will oppose kingdom. ¹¹There will be great earthquakes, famines, and plagues; in many places, strange and terrifying signs from heaven will be seen.

¹²Before all these things happen, people will lay their hands on you and persecute you; you will be delivered to the synagogues and put in prison and for my sake, you will be brought before kings and governors. ¹³This will be your opportunity to bear witness.

¹⁴So keep this in mind: do not worry in advance about what to say, ¹⁵for I will give you words and wisdom that none of your opponents will be able to withstand or contradict.

¹⁶You will be betrayed even by parents and brothers, by relatives and friends and some of you will be put to death. ¹⁷But even though, because of my name, you will be hated by everyone, ¹⁸not a hair of your head will perish. ¹⁹By your patient endurance, you will save your souls.

²⁰When you see Jerusalem surrounded by armies, know then that the time has come when it will be reduced to a wasteland. ²¹If you are in Judea, flee to the mountains! If you are in Jerusalem, leave! If you are outside the city, don't enter it!

²²For these will be the days of its punishment and all that was announced in the Scriptures will be fulfilled. ²³How hard will it be for pregnant women and for mothers with babies at the breast! For a great calamity will come upon the land and wrath upon this people. ²⁴They will be put to death by the sword, or taken as slaves to other nations; and Jerusalem will be trampled upon by the pagans until the time of the pagans is fulfilled.

LUKE 21:5-24

Read: Jesus predicts the destruction of Jerusalem. He urges his disciples to be attentive, not to be deceived by things that won't help them but rather, to trust in him.

Reflect: Are you aware of what happens in your social, political, economic and cultural environment? Can you perceive the voice of Jesus that invites you to have confidence in him despite the tribulations?

Pray: Lord Jesus, may your Spirit encourage and strengthen us to live the message of your Gospel at all times, especially in times of adversity.

Act: Express to your parish priest or someone who works in your parish gratitude for the service they give to the community in the midst of so much adversity.

The coming of the Son of Man

[25] Then there will be signs in the sun and moon and stars, and on the earth anguish of nations, perplexed when they hear the roaring of the sea and its waves. [26] People will faint with fear at the mere thought of what is to come upon the world, for the forces of the universe will be shaken. [27] Then, at that time, they will see the Son of Man coming in a cloud with power and great glory.

The signs of the times

[28] So, when you see things begin to happen, stand erect and lift up your heads, for your deliverance is drawing near." [29] And Jesus added this comparison, "Look at the fig tree and all the trees. [30] As soon as their buds sprout, you know that summer is near. [31] In the same way, when you see these things happening, know that the kingdom of God is near. [32] Truly, I tell you, this generation will not pass away until all this has happened. [33] Heaven and earth will pass away, but my words will not pass away.

[34] Be on your guard: don't immerse yourselves in a life of pleasure, drunkenness and worldly cares, lest that day catch you unaware, like a trap! [35] For, like a snare, will that day come upon all the inhabitants of the earth. [36] But watch at all times and pray, that you may be able to escape all that is going to happen and to stand before the Son of Man."

[37] In the daytime Jesus used to teach in the temple; then he would leave the city and pass the night on the Mount of Olives. [38] Early in the morning, the people would come to the temple to hear him.

LUKE 21:25-38

Read: Jesus talks about the destruction of Jerusalem and the hope of the coming of the Son of Man. Again he exhorts his disciples to be attentive, ready to resist difficult times and prepared to meet the Son of Man on the last day.

Reflect: Are you aware of the fragility of life? What is really most important in your life? Are you living in a way that prepares you for the final encounter with the Lord?

Pray: Lord Jesus, may your Spirit help me to live the teachings of your Gospel and be prepared for the final encounter with you.

> **Act:** Make a list of what you feel needs to happen in your life
> to prepare you for your final encounter with the Lord whenever
> that happens. Do one of those things today.

The conspiracy against Jesus
(Mk 14:1; Mt 26:1)

22 [1] The feast of Unleavened Bread, which is called the Passover, was now drawing near, [2] and the chief priests and the teachers of the law wanted to kill Jesus. They were looking for a way to do this because they were afraid of the people. [3] Then Satan entered into Judas, called Iscariot, one of the Twelve, [4] and he went off to discuss with the chief priests and the officers of the guard how to deliver Jesus to them. [5] They were delighted and agreed to give him money; [6] so he accepted and from that time he waited for an opportunity to betray him without the people knowing.

[7] Then came the feast of the Unleavened Bread, in which the Passover lamb had to be sacrificed. [8] So Jesus sent Peter and John, saying, "Go and get everything ready for us to eat the Passover meal." [9] They asked him, "Where do you want us to prepare it?" [10] And he said, "When you enter the city, a man will come to you carrying a jar of water. Follow him to the house he enters, [11] and say to the owner, 'The master asks: Where is the room where I may take the Passover meal with my disciples?' [12] He will show you a large, furnished room upstairs, and there you will prepare for us."

[13] Peter and John went off and having found everything just as Jesus had told them, they prepared the Passover meal.

The supper of the Lord
(Mk 14:12; Mt 26:17)

[14] When the hour came, Jesus took his place at the table and the apostles with him. [15] And he said to them, "I was eager to eat this Passover with you before I suffer; [16] for I tell you, I shall not eat it again until it is fulfilled in the kingdom of God."

[17] Then they passed him a cup, and when he had given thanks, he said, "Take this, and share it among yourselves; [18] for I tell you that, from now on, I will not drink of the fruit of the vine until the kingdom of God

comes." ¹⁹ Jesus also took bread, and after giving thanks, he broke it and gave it to them, saying, "This is my body which is given for you. Do this in remembrance of me." ²⁰ And after the supper, he did the same with the cup, saying, "This cup is the new Covenant, sealed in my blood, which is poured out for you.

²¹ Yet the hand of the traitor is with me on the table. ²² Know that the Son of Man is going the way marked out for him. But alas for that one who betrays him!" ²³ They began to ask one another which of them could do such a thing.

> **LUKE 22:1-23**
>
> **Read:** Jesus celebrates Passover with his disciples, and in that context, he institutes the Eucharist: the giving of his life for all of humanity.
>
> **Reflect:** Do you consider that the gesture of Jesus in this paschal meal is reproduced in your daily life? How is your life bread broken for others? How do you share your life and your gifts beyond your family environment?
>
> **Pray:** O God, may I be generous with my life and with my gifts in service to others. May I share your Eucharist with those I meet in my day to day life.
>
> **Act:** Invite someone you think might be lonely to dinner in your home. Treat them as if Jesus himself were present in them.

Last conversation with Jesus
(Mk 10:42; Jn 13:1)

²⁴ They also began to argue among themselves, which of them should be considered the most important. ²⁵ Jesus said, "The kings of the pagan nations rule over them as lords, and the most hard-hearted rulers claim the title, 'Gracious Lord.' ²⁶ But not so with you; let the greatest among you become as the youngest and the leader as the servant. ²⁷ For who is the greatest, he who sits at the table or he who serves? He who is seated, isn't it? Yet I am among you as one who serves.

²⁸ You are the ones who have been with me and stood by me through my troubles; ²⁹ because of this, just as the kingship has been given to me by my Father so I give it to you. ³⁰ You will eat and drink at my table

in my kingdom, and you will sit on thrones and govern the twelve tribes of Israel.

³¹ Simon, Simon, Satan has demanded to sift you like grain, ³² but I have prayed for you that your faith may not fail. And when you have recovered, you shall strengthen your brothers." ³³ Then Peter said, "Lord, with you I am ready to go even to prison and death." ³⁴ But Jesus replied, "I tell you, Peter, the cock will not crow this day before you have denied three times that you know me."

³⁵ Jesus also said to them, "When I sent you without purse or bag or sandals, were you short of anything?" They answered, "No." ³⁶ And Jesus said to them, "But now, the one who has a purse or a bag must take it, or even his coat, and sell it and buy a sword. ³⁷ For Scripture says: *He was numbered among criminals.* These words have to be fulfilled in me and everything written about me is now taking place.

³⁸ Then they said, "See, Lord, here are two swords!" but Jesus answered, "That is enough."

LUKE 22:24-38

Read: The disciples of Jesus must have the same aspirations as the Master: service. Jesus announces the arrival of somber and disturbing moments: they are the moments previous of his passion.

Reflect: As a Christian, what are your greatest aspirations? How is service to others part of them? Do you consider yourself capable of being faithful to the Lord even in adversities?

Pray: Lord Jesus, grant me the grace to always be at the service of others, to aspire to nothing else but to proclaim and live your Gospel, and that in difficult times I can always be by your side.

Act: Resolve to serve God and neighbor with generous dedication, both in good and bad times.

Gethsemane
(Mk 14:32)

³⁹ After this, Jesus left to go as usual to the Mount of Olives and the disciples followed him. ⁴⁰ When he came to the place, he told them, "Pray that you may not be put to the test."

⁴¹ Then he went a little further, about a stone's throw and kneeling down, he prayed, ⁴² "Father, if it is your will, remove this cup from me; however, not my will but yours be done." ⁴³ And from heaven there appeared to him an angel who gave him strength.

⁴⁴ As he was in agony, he prayed even more earnestly and great drops of blood formed like sweat and fell to the ground. ⁴⁵ When he rose from prayer, he went to his disciples but found them worn out with grief and asleep. ⁴⁶ And he said to them, "Why do you sleep? Get up and pray, so that you may not be put to the test."

⁴⁷ Jesus was still speaking when suddenly a crowd appeared and the man named Judas, one of the Twelve, was leading them. He drew near to Jesus to kiss him ⁴⁸ and Jesus said to him, "Judas, with a kiss you betray the Son of Man?"

⁴⁹ Those with Jesus, seeing what would happen, said to him, "Master, shall we use the sword?" ⁵⁰ And one of them struck the High Priest's servant and cut off his right ear. ⁵¹ But Jesus ordered him, "No more of this!" He touched the man's ear and healed him.

⁵² Then Jesus spoke to those coming against him, the chief priests, officers of the temple and elders; and he said to them, "Are you looking for a thief, a robber? Do you really need swords and clubs to arrest me? ⁵³ Day after day I was among you, teaching in the temple and you did not arrest me. But this is the hour of the power of darkness; this is your hour."

LUKE 22:39-53

Read: Jesus goes to his usual place of prayer and asks his disciples to pray that they will not fall into temptation, but they fall asleep. He, on the other hand, abandons himself to the will of the Father who sends an angel to comfort and prepare him. Judas betrays Jesus and he is taken to the house of the high priest.

Reflect: Do you trust the strength of prayer? Do you use it in times of difficulty? In your prayer do you abandon yourself to the will of God, or ask God to do what you want?

Pray: Father, I put myself in your hands. Do what you want, whatever it is I thank you. I accept everything because you are my Father.

> **Act:** Gather your family and pray together with them for people who feel lonely and abandoned.

The trial of Jesus, Peter's denial
(Mk 14:53; Mt 26:57)

⁵⁴ Then they seized him and took him away, bringing him to the High Priest's house. Peter followed at a distance.

⁵⁵ A fire was kindled in the middle of the courtyard where people were gathered and Peter sat among them. ⁵⁶ A maidservant noticed him. Looking at him intently in the light of the fire, she exclaimed, "This man also was with him!" ⁵⁷ But he denied it, saying, "Woman, I do not know him!"

⁵⁸ A little later someone who saw him said, "You are also one of them!" Peter replied, "My friend, I am not!" ⁵⁹ After about an hour another asserted, "Surely this man was with him, for he is a Galilean."

⁶⁰ Again Peter denied it: "My friend, I don't know what you are talking about!" He had not finished saying this when a cock crowed. ⁶¹ The Lord turned around and looked at Peter and Peter remembered the word which the Lord had spoken: "Before the cock crows, you will deny me three times." ⁶² Peter went outside, weeping bitterly.

⁶³ Now the guards who had arrested Jesus mocked and beat him. ⁶⁴ They blindfolded him, struck him and then asked him, "Who hit you? Tell us, prophet!" ⁶⁵ And they hurled many other insulting words at him.

⁶⁶ At daybreak, the council of the elders of the people, among whom were the chief priests and the teachers of the law, assembled again. Then they had Jesus brought before them and they began questioning him, ⁶⁷ "Tell us, are you the Christ?" Jesus replied, "You will not believe if I tell you ⁶⁸ and neither will you answer if I ask you. ⁶⁹ But from now on, *the Son of Man will be seated at the right hand* of the power of God."

⁷⁰ In chorus, they asked, "So you are the Son of God?" And Jesus said to them, "You are right, I am."

⁷¹ Then they said, "What need have we of witnesses? We have heard it from his own lips."

LUKE 22:54-71

Read: Peter denies Jesus three times. As Jesus looks at Peter, he runs away and weeps for his cowardice. Jesus, on the other hand, despite the insults of his adversaries, reaffirms himself as the Son of God.

Reflect: Is it easy to feel empathy with Peter? What would you do in such circumstances? Is it difficult for you to share your faith in your environment? Do you try to hide that you are a Christian?

Pray: Lord Jesus, may your Spirit help me to proclaim at all times my condition as a disciple of yours, not only with words, but above all with my way of life.

Act: Share with someone what it means for you to be a disciple of Jesus. Do not be afraid to talk about your faith.

Jesus before Pilate
(Mt 27:11; Mk 15:1; Jn 18:28)

23 ¹ The whole council rose and brought Jesus to Pilate. ² They gave their accusation: "We found this man subverting our nation, opposing payment of taxes to Caesar, and claiming to be Christ the King."

³ Pilate asked Jesus, "Are you the King of the Jews?" Jesus replied, "You said so." ⁴ Turning to the chief priests and the crowd, Pilate said, "I find no basis for a case against this man." ⁵ But they insisted, "All the country of the Jews is being stirred up by his teaching. He began in Galilee and now he has come all the way here."

⁶ When Pilate heard this, he asked if the man was a Galilean. ⁷ Finding the accused to come under Herod's jurisdiction, Pilate sent Jesus over to Herod who happened to be in Jerusalem at that time.

⁸ Herod was delighted to have Jesus before him; for a long time he had wanted to see him because of the reports about him and he was hoping to see Jesus work some miracle. ⁹ He piled up question upon question but got no reply from Jesus.

¹⁰ All the while the chief priests and the scribes remained standing there, vehemently pressing their accusations. ¹¹ Finally, Herod ridiculed him and with his guards mocked him. And when he had put a rich cloak

on him, he sent him back to Pilate. [12] Pilate and Herod, who were enemies before, became friends from that day.

LUKE 23:1-12

Read: Jesus is led before Pilate and then before Herod, the political authorities of Judea and Galilee respectively. They do not find any guilt in Jesus, but this does not change their minds.

Reflect: Can a Christian proclaim the Gospel and not commit to justice? Can we be indifferent to the hunger, misery, and suffering of the poorest? What can we Christians do in these circumstances?

Pray: Oh Father, may the power of your Spirit encourage us to assume the inescapable commitments that faith in your Son Jesus implies.

Act: Talk to your people about how important it is for the Christian to practice justice.

---

[13] Pilate then called together the chief priests and the elders and the people [14] and said to them, "You have brought this man before me and accused him of subversion. In your presence I have examined him and found no basis for your charges; [15] and neither has Herod, for he sent him back to me. It is quite clear that this man has done nothing that deserves a death sentence. [16] I will, therefore, have him scourged and then release him." ([17] At Passover, Pilate had to release a prisoner.)

[18] Shouting as one man, the crowd protested, "No! Away with this man! Release Barabbas instead!" [19] This man had been thrown into prison for an uprising in the city and for murder.

[20] Since Pilate wanted to release Jesus, he appealed to the crowd once more, [21] but they shouted back, "Crucify him! Crucify him!" [22] A third time Pilate said to them, "Why, what evil has he done? Since no crime deserving death has been proved, I shall have him scourged and let him go."

[23] But they went on shouting and demanding that Jesus be crucified, and their shouts grew louder. [24] So Pilate decided to pass the sentence they demanded. [25] He released the man they asked for, the one who was in prison for rebellion and murder, and he handed Jesus over in accordance with their wishes.

LUKE 23:13-25

Read: Jesus is condemned to death. Pilate succumbs to the pressure of the crowd and condemns the innocent Jesus to be crucified.

Reflect: Do you know cases of people unjustly condemned? Have you ever felt pressured by the opinion of others and have not done what justice should do? Is it easy for a Christian to act with justice in the current circumstances?

Pray: O God, as disciples of your Son, animated by your Spirit, let us always work for your kingdom and its justice, and make our world a world that is more just, more human.

Act: Collaborate with institutions and agencies that promote justice and reconciliation in your city or country. Pray for those people who are unjustly condemned.

The way of Calvary
(Mt 27:32; Mk 15:16)

[26] When they led Jesus away, they seized Simon of Cyrene, arriving from the countryside, and laid the cross on him to carry it behind Jesus.

[27] A large crowd of people followed him; among them were women beating their breasts and grieving for him, [28] but Jesus turned to them and said, "Women of Jerusalem, do not weep for me! Weep rather for yourselves and for your children, [29] for the days are coming when people will say, 'Happy are the women without child! Happy are those who have not given birth or nursed a child!' [30] And they will say to the mountains, '*Fall on us!*' and to the hills, '*Cover us!*' [31] For if this is the lot of the green wood, what will happen to the dry?"

[32] Along with Jesus, two criminals also were led out to be executed. [33] There, at the place called the Skull, he was crucified together with two criminals—one on his right and another on his left. ([34] Jesus said, "Father, forgive them, for they do not know what they are doing.") And the guards *cast lots to divide his clothes among themselves.*

[35] The people stood by, watching. As for the rulers, they jeered at him, saying to one another, "Let the man who saved others now save himself, for he is the Messiah, the chosen one of God!"

³⁶The soldiers also mocked him and, when they drew near to offer him bitter wine, ³⁷they said, "So you are the King of the Jews? Save yourself!" ³⁸Above Jesus, there was an inscription in Greek, Latin, and Hebrew, which read, "This is the King of the Jews."

³⁹One of the criminals hanging with Jesus insulted him, "So you are the Messiah? Save yourself, and us as well!" ⁴⁰But the other rebuked him, saying, "Have you no fear of God, you who received the same sentence as he did? ⁴¹For us, it is just: this is payment for what we have done. But this man has done nothing wrong." ⁴²And he said, "Jesus, remember me when you come into your kingdom." ⁴³Jesus replied, "In truth I tell you, today you will be with me in paradise."

⁴⁴It was almost midday. ⁴⁵The sun was hidden, and darkness came over the whole land until mid-afternoon, and at that time the curtain of the Sanctuary was torn in two. ⁴⁶Then Jesus gave a loud cry, "Father, into your hands I commend my spirit." And saying that, he gave up his spirit.

⁴⁷The captain, on seeing what had happened, acknowledged the hand of God. "Surely this was an upright man!" he said. ⁴⁸And all the people who had gathered to watch the spectacle, as soon as they saw what had happened, went home beating their breasts. ⁴⁹But those who knew Jesus, and the women who had followed him from Galilee, remained there at a distance. They witnessed all these things.

LUKE 23:26-49

Read: Crucifixion and death of Jesus. Jesus reveals his power by comforting the women who mourn for him, welcoming the repentant thief, forgiving his executioners, and surrendering to the Father.

Reflect: What does Jesus' attitude suggest? Can mercy overcome injustice? Can evil be overcome by doing good? What does the phrase "Father, in your hands I commend my spirit" suggest?

Pray: Lord Jesus! I put all my trust in you. From my weakness, I fear everything, but I expect everything from your kindness. May Christians continue to bear witness to your love in the world.

Act: Support without fear and with conviction everything that promotes and defends life, even when it is publicly rejected by others.

⁵⁰ Then a member of the Jewish supreme council intervened, a good and righteous man named Joseph, ⁵¹ from the Judean town of Arimathea. He had not agreed with the decision and action of his fellow members, and he lived uprightly in the hope of seeing the kingdom of God. ⁵² Joseph went to Pilate and asked for Jesus' body. ⁵³ He then took it down, wrapped it in a linen cloth and laid it in a yet unused tomb cut out of a rock.

⁵⁴ It was the day of preparation and the Sabbath was beginning. ⁵⁵ So the women, who had come with Jesus from Galilee, followed Joseph to see the tomb and how his body was laid. ⁵⁶ Returning home, they prepared perfumes and ointments. And on the Sabbath day, they rested, as the law required.

LUKE 23:50-56

Read: Joseph of Arimathea, a member of the Jewish Council, claims the body of Jesus to give him a worthy burial. The women (disciples) who had accompanied the Master from Galilee are present.

Reflect: And the disciples, the males, where are they? Is not the same thing happening in our current parishes? Are not women (our grandmothers, mothers, wives, and daughters) the ones who participate the most and make ecclesial life possible? What does all this suggest?

Pray: Lord, give me courage and deep inner attitude to bear witness to you, and to actively collaborate in the life of my parish.

Act: Speak openly and joyfully to your own people of the necessary participation of all in the parish life. The Christian faith is a faith that is lived in community.

The Lord has risen
(Mk 16:1; Mt 28:1; Jn 20:1)

24 ¹ On the Sabbath the women rested according to the commandment, but the first day of the week, at dawn, the women went to the tomb with the perfumes and ointments they had prepared. ² Seeing the stone rolled away from the opening of the tomb, ³they entered and were amazed to find that the body of the Lord Jesus was not there.

⁴As they stood there wondering about this, two men in dazzling garments suddenly stood before them. ⁵In fright, the women bowed to the ground. But the men said, "Why look for the living among the dead? ⁶You won't find him here. He is risen. Remember what he told you in Galilee, ⁷that the Son of Man had to be given into the hands of sinners, to be crucified and to rise on the third day." ⁸And they remembered Jesus' words.

⁹Returning from the tomb, they told the Eleven and all the others about these things. ¹⁰Among the women who brought the news, were Mary Magdalene, Joanna, and Mary the mother of James. ¹¹But, however much they insisted, those who heard did not believe the seemingly nonsensical story. ¹²Then Peter got up and ran to the tomb. All he saw, when he bent down and looked into the tomb, were the linen cloths laid by themselves. He went home wondering.

LUKE 24:1-12

Read: The women come to the tomb to anoint Jesus' body and hear the news he has been raised from the dead. They become the first apostles who announce Jesus is risen. When they tell the disciples Jesus is risen from the dead, their message is disregarded as idle tales women tell.

Reflect: When you hear that Jesus is risen, what do you think? What do you believe? What do you doubt? Can God triumph over evil? Notice the women are the first ones entrusted with the news of the resurrection.

Pray: Lord, I believe. But increase my faith!

Act: Read something today that will help you deepen and expand your faith.

The road to Emmaus
(Mk 16:12)

¹³That same day, two followers of Jesus were going to Emmaus, a village seven miles from Jerusalem ¹⁴and they were talking to each other about all the things that had happened. ¹⁵While they were talking and

debating these things, Jesus himself approached and began to accompany them, ¹⁶but their eyes were not able to recognize him.

¹⁷He asked, "What is it you are talking about?" The two stood still, looking sad. ¹⁸Then the one named Cleophas answered, "Why, it seems you are the only traveler to Jerusalem who doesn't know what has happened there these past few days." ¹⁹And he asked, "What is it?"

They replied, "It is about Jesus of Nazareth. He was a prophet, you know, mighty in word and deed before God and the people. ²⁰But the chief priests and our rulers sentenced him to death. They handed him over to be crucified. ²¹We had hoped that he would redeem Israel.

It is now the third day since all this took place. ²²It is also true that some women of our group have disturbed us. When they went to the tomb at dawn, ²³they did not find his body; and they came and told us that they had had a vision of angels, who said that Jesus was alive. ²⁴Some of our people went to the tomb and found everything just as the women had said, but they did not find a body in the tomb."

²⁵He said to them, "How dull you are, how slow of understanding! Is the message of the prophets too difficult for you to understand? ²⁶Is it not written that the Christ should suffer all this and then enter his glory?" ²⁷Then, starting with Moses and going through the prophets, he explained to them everything in the Scriptures concerning himself.

²⁸As they drew near the village they were heading for, Jesus made as if to go farther. ²⁹But they prevailed upon him, "Stay with us, for night comes quickly. The day is now almost over." So he went in to stay with them. ³⁰When they were at table, he took the bread, said a blessing, broke it, and gave each a piece.

³¹Then their eyes were opened, and they recognized him, but he vanished out of their sight. ³²And they said to one another, "Were not our hearts burning within us when he was talking to us on the road and explaining the Scriptures?"

³³They immediately set out and returned to Jerusalem. There they found the Eleven and their companions gathered together. ³⁴They were greeted by these words: "Yes, it is true, the Lord is risen! He has appeared to Simon!" ³⁵Then the two told what had happened on the road to Emmaus and how Jesus had made himself known when he broke bread with them.

LUKE 24:13-35

Read: Two disciples return disillusioned to their village after the death of Jesus. But Jesus meets them and on the way, he explains the Scriptures. Afterward, they invite him to stay and at the table, when he breaks the bread, they recognize his presence and immediately return to Jerusalem to announce what happened.

Reflect: Do you discover the presence of God in the difficult moments of your life? How? Is the Eucharist a central event in your experience of faith? Which of the details in this story resonate with you, and why do you think that is?

Pray: Stay with us, Lord! Enter our home, share our table, open our eyes to discover your life-giving and close presence, which encourages us to witness to your resurrection.

Act: Go to Mass and then, at mealtime, share with your family how you recognize Jesus in the breaking of the bread.

Jesus appears to the apostles
(Jn 20:19)

³⁶ While they were still talking about this, Jesus himself stood in their midst. (He said to them, "Peace to you.") ³⁷ In their panic and fright, they thought they were seeing a ghost, ³⁸ but he said to them, "Why are you upset, and how does such an idea cross your minds? ³⁹ Look at my hands and feet, and see that it is I myself! Touch me and see for yourselves, for a ghost has no flesh and bones as I have!" ⁴⁰ (As he said this, he showed his hands and feet.)

⁴¹ Their joy was so great that they still could not believe it as they were astonished; so he said to them, "Have you anything to eat?" ⁴² And they gave him a piece of broiled fish. ⁴³ He took it and ate it before them.

Last instructions

⁴⁴ Then Jesus said to them, "Remember the words I spoke to you when I was still with you: Everything written about me in the law of Moses, in the prophets and in the psalms must be fulfilled." ⁴⁵ Then he opened their minds to understand the Scriptures.

And he said, [46] "So it was written: the Messiah had to suffer and on the third day rise from the dead. [47] Then repentance and forgiveness in his name would be proclaimed to all nations beginning from Jerusalem. [48] And you are witnesses of these things. [49] And that is why I will send you what my Father promised. So remain in the city until you are clothed with power from on high."

[50] Jesus led them almost as far as Bethany; then he lifted up his hands and blessed them. [51] And as he blessed them, he withdrew and was taken to heaven. [52] They worshiped him and then returned to Jerusalem full of joy; [53] and they were continually in the temple, praising God.

LUKE 24:36-53

Read: Jesus appears to the disciples, gives them a guarantee of his resurrected presence, and after leading them to Bethany, blesses them and ascends to heaven. The disciples, on the other hand, return to Jerusalem and spend their time blessing God.

Reflect: Since you have not enjoyed the opportunity of touching the Risen Lord's body and having lunch with him, why do you believe in the resurrection of Jesus? Do you feel the living presence of the Lord in the midst of your life? How? How do you share your experience of the Risen Lord with others?

Pray: Lord Jesus, may your Spirit encourage us so that we can bear witness with our lives that you are alive and risen, that you have conquered death, and that the kingdom of your Father becomes more and more present in our world.

Act: May your life witness at every moment the victory of Jesus, of life over death. Alleluia!

JOHN

At the outset, the first three Gospels may have us overlook the work and skills of its writers. Whatever vision they wanted to transmit about their Savior, they dealt so plainly with the witnesses that oftentimes we seem to have seen and heard Jesus himself.

The fourth Gospel unfolds in a different setting than the other three. To start with, while Jesus' activity in Galilee occupied a major part of the Synoptics, the fourth Gospel does not say much about it. It deals with what Jesus did between his baptism by John and his return to Galilee (Jn 1–3) and after that, almost everything takes place in Jerusalem. There, within the framework of the pilgrimage feasts, our author observes the mounting conflicts between Jesus and Jewish authorities. He seems to be at home, aware of what is going on behind the scenes of power, namely among the priests.

The difference in tone is even more important. Whether John is dealing with scenes or miracles of Jesus or with the discourses that accompany them, everything bars the seal of a personal eyewitness. This is especially true for the discourses that the evangelist builds upon authentic words of Jesus, but thanks to John's prophetic gift, he is able to develop the intentions of Jesus and the deep meaning of his words and gestures. John does not let us ignore his purpose: "*These are recorded so that you may believe that Jesus is the Christ, the Son of God*" (Jn 20:31). The faith of the Church proclaimed Jesus as the Son of God. But how should we understand this term? Though Jesus' resurrection had manifested the divine character of his person, one could wonder how and from what moment was Jesus Son of God and to what extent was he identified with God. John's Gospel clearly asserts that Jesus' existence was forever in God. This assertion on Jesus' origin helps us understand the range of his work. His discourses reaffirm the incredible promises of Jesus to those who believe in him, promises that, for John, became a reality.

The Gospel of John proclaims the existence of the Son of God *from all eternity*, and this light on the origin of Jesus immediately enlightens the scope of his work. Jesus, the eternal Son of God who became man, did not come to just teach us to be better but he came to transform creation.

This Gospel seems to have accompanied John throughout his life. He reworked it several times. A small paragraph added at the end suggests that the Gospel was published after the death of its author, about the year 95 A.D. Here we find an important element to understand John's mind. He finished writing twenty years after the destruction of Jerusalem and the temple by the Roman armies. John knows as well as Paul that Jesus' Resurrection originated a new age. The revelation to the Jewish people and the great liturgies in the temple belong, to a certain extent to the past, but in this first Covenant that has become the old Covenant are found the keys to the understanding of Jesus' achievements. This is why John will call to mind the Jewish feasts and religious symbols such as the water, the palms, the lamb... and he will show how these are transfigured in the Christian life and liturgy.

This is why three sections can be gleaned after an opening that we call the week of discovery (until 2:16). These are:

– In 2:17 Jesus goes up to the temple for the Passover: Chapters 2–5 develop the sign of the temple.

– In 6:4 the Passover is mentioned again and John develops the sign of bread.

– In 13:1 we find the third Passover, when Jesus is put to death at the moment in which the lambs are sacrificed in the temple. The lamb will be the third sign.

Is John the Author of the Gospel Called by His Name?

This question is very difficult to answer. There are many reasons to doubt the authorship of the Apostle John, but there can be found as many reasons to vindicate the traditional attribution to John. John's message is so clear that it sets us on fire. Telling us that the one who marked him forever, the one he loved and who loved him, was the eternal Word of God, is really an astounding statement. Some would prefer someone else, not an eyewitness, to have written the Gospel. It could have been some theologian who might have more readily idealized Jesus because from a distance, he would not have had all the evidence of his human presence, his way of looking, eating, and the smell of his sweat…

This explains, for the most part, the countless hypotheses that have been built up for a century to attribute this Gospel to a theologian from the second generation after Jesus. None of these have gathered convincing proofs.

However, we have to admit that there are many reasons to doubt that the author is John the Apostle. The main reason is the following: could John, the Galilean fisherman, have written the theological and mystical discourses proper of this Gospel? Naturally, it is not impossible.

But there is still more! The one who gave their final shape to the discourses, in the years 70–80 A.D., probably near Ephesus where an ancient tradition asserts that John had retired, is not only a theologian but he must also have been a priest (18:15) because of his interest for the liturgy and the temple. Can this fit with the person of John, Zebedee's son, a fisherman of Tiberiadis? Is it possible that such a vision of Jesus, the Messiah, and then the Son of God, Savior of the world, had been borne in him and that he has expressed it in his Gospel?

The Disciple Whom Jesus Loved

We have always thought that the fourteen mentions (2 x 7) *of the disciple whom Jesus loved* in the latter part of the Gospel referred to the author himself. Verse 21:24, added after his death, state it explicitly. This beloved disciple was identified with John the Apostle, the brother of James and the son of Zebedee and he was thought to be the youngest of the Twelve. But what was actually known about it?

Zebedee the fisherman might have been a priest. However, the evangelist says nothing about part of the ministry of Jesus in Galilee, about the transfiguration… and even in 21:2, he appears to have been one of the *two disciples* (as in 1:35) and therefore, not the son of Zebedee.

It is only at the Last Supper that the author really enters into the Gospel. We see him in the seat of honor, the seat that rightfully belonged to the host. Could he have been the owner who welcomed Jesus and his disciples (Lk 22:12)? And from then on, he could have accompanied Peter. He can venture to be at the foot of the cross while the Galilean group thought only about escaping from reprisal. Jesus entrusted Mary to him and a few moments later, he understood everything.

The indications that would allow to attribute this Gospel to another John, a priest from Jerusalem and different from Zebedee's son are, then as numerous as the ones that give preference to the latter one and it is difficult to give preference to one of them. However, it is a very interesting clue that leads to many discoveries. Specifically, in Chapter 19:31-37, the author of the Gospel reports the precise event that so deeply moved him and gave him access to the mystery of Jesus. He was really a priest.

We may have met believers who are deeply and truly theologians though they have not passed through university. They encountered some outstanding personality and this was enough to awaken their gifts. Later they became one of these few apostles who continually go over the events and the discoveries of this ministry, always eager to understand the ways of God. Do they need some books, some friends to help them to mature in their thinking? The same God who pours in them wisdom will direct to them this kind of help.

Can't this be the case of John, so close to Jesus and then Apostle for some sixty years? He did not go, as Paul did through rabbinical schools, and this is why he does not use sophisticated arguments, but ever so, couldn't he be a theologian, this someone who knows God?

Composition of the Gospel of John

There have been many attempts to determine the structure of the Gospel of John. We present here a division in three great sessions. These all begin with the expression: the time/hour that appears three times.

It is also important to bear in mind the frequency of Jewish feasts. The Passover appears three times, and then a "feast," the Tents, the Dedication of the Temple.

Prologue: The first week: 1:1—2:11.

First Part: The presentation of God's gift: 2:12—6:71.

Second Part: Rejection of the world and homicidal attempts: 7:1—12:50.

Third Part: Jesus completes his work bringing to perfection the love for his people: Chapters 13–20.

Conclusion: The author's purpose: 20:30-31.

Epilogue: Until his return.

JOHN

The Word became a human

1 ¹ In the beginning was the Word.

And the Word was with God
and the Word was God;
² he was in the beginning with God.

³ All things were made through him,
and without him nothing came to be.
Whatever has come to be, ⁴ found life in him;
life, which for human beings was also light,
⁵ light that shines in darkness,
light that darkness could not overcome.

⁶ A man came, sent by God;
his name was John.
⁷ He came to bear witness,
as a witness to introduce the Light,
so that all might believe through him.
⁸ He was not the Light,
but a witness to introduce the Light;

⁹ for the Light was coming into the world
the true Light that enlightens everyone.
¹⁰ He was in the world
and through him, the world was made,
the very world that did not know him.

¹¹ He came to his own,
yet his own people did not receive him;
¹² but to all who received him,
he empowers to become children of God,
for they believe in his name.

¹³These are born, but not by seed
or carnal desire, nor by the will of man:
they are born of God.

¹⁴And the Word was made flesh and dwelt among us;
and we have seen his glory, the glory of the only Son of the Father:
fullness of truth and loving-kindness.

¹⁵John bore witness to him openly saying,
"This is the one who comes after me,
but he is already ahead of me,
for he was before me."

¹⁶From his fullness we have all received
favor upon favor.
¹⁷For God had given us the law through Moses,
but Truth and Loving-kindness
came through Jesus Christ.
¹⁸No one has ever seen God,
but God-the-only-Son made him known:
the one who is in and with the Father.

JOHN 1:1-18

Read: The prologue provides the theological key to the whole Gospel: Jesus Christ is the incarnate Word who reveals the glory of God in the world. He came to his own and his own did not receive him, but those who welcomed him he "made them able to become children of God." The prologue is poetry and can only be appreciated after several readings.

Reflect: Can you feel and recognize the close presence of the Word of God in your life?

Pray: The Christian prays to God the Father through the Son. Give thanks to the Father for the gift of the Word. Ask the Spirit to accompany you to understand the Word of God.

Act: Reread the prologue at a leisurely pace and allow it to resonate inside you. Notice individual words that catch your attention: Beginning, Word, be with God, all, none, light, darkness.

FIRST PART:
JESUS REVEALS HIMSELF THROUGH SIGNS

John the Baptist presents Jesus, the Lamb of God

[19] This was the testimony of John when the Jews sent priests and Levites to ask him, "Who are you?" [20] John recognized the truth and did not deny it. He said, "I am not the Messiah."

[21] And they asked him, "Then who are you? Elijah?" He answered, "I am not." They said, "Are you the Prophet?" And he answered, "No." [22] Then they said to him, "Tell us who you are so that we can give some answer to those who sent us. How do you see yourself?" [23] And John said, quoting the prophet Isaiah, "I am the *voice of one crying out in the wilderness: Make straight the way of the Lord!*"

[24] Those who had been sent were Pharisees; [25] and they put a further question to John, "Then why are you baptizing if you are not the Messiah, or Elijah, or the Prophet?" [26] John answered, "I baptize you with water, but among you stands one whom you do not know; [27] although he comes after me, I am not worthy to untie the strap of his sandal."

[28] This happened in Bethabara beyond the Jordan, where John was baptizing.

[29] The next day, John saw Jesus coming toward him and said, "There is the Lamb of God who takes away the sin of the world! [30] It is he of whom I said: A man comes after me who is already ahead of me for he was before me. [31] I myself did not know him, but I came baptizing to prepare for him, so that he might be revealed in Israel."

[32] And John also gave this testimony, "I saw the Spirit coming down on him like a dove from heaven and resting on him. [33] I myself did not know him, but God, who sent me to baptize, told me, 'You will see the Spirit coming down and resting on the one who baptizes with the Holy Spirit.' [34] Yes, I have seen! And I declare that this is the Chosen One of God!"

Jesus meets the first disciples

[35] On the following day, John was standing there again with two of his disciples. [36] As Jesus walked by, John looked at him and said, "There is the Lamb of God." [37] On hearing this, the two disciples followed Jesus. [38] He turned and saw them following and he said to them, "What are you looking for?" They answered, "Rabbi (which means Master), where are you staying?" [39] Jesus said, "Come and see." So they went and saw

where he stayed and spent the rest of that day with him. It was about four o'clock in the afternoon.

[40] Andrew, the brother of Simon Peter, was one of the two who heard what John had said and followed Jesus. [41] Early the next morning, he found his brother Simon and said to him, "We have found the Messiah" (which means *the Christ*), [42] and he brought Simon to Jesus. Jesus looked at him and said, "You are Simon, son of John, but you shall be called Cephas" (which means Rock).

[43] The next day, Jesus decided to set off for Galilee. He found Philip and said to him, "Follow me." [44] Philip was from Bethsaida, the town of Andrew and Peter. [45] Philip found Nathanael and said to him, "We have found the one Moses wrote about in the law and the prophets: he is Jesus, son of Joseph, from Nazareth."

[46] Nathanael replied, "Can anything good come from Nazareth?" Philip said to him, "Come and see." [47] When Jesus saw Nathanael coming, he said of him, "Here comes an Israelite, a true one; there is nothing false in him." [48] Nathanael asked him, "How do you know me?" And Jesus said to him, "Before Philip called you, you were under the fig tree and I saw you."

[49] Nathanael answered, "Master, you are the Son of God! You are the king of Israel!" [50] But Jesus replied, "You believe because I said, 'I saw you under the fig tree.' But you will see greater things than that.

[51] Truly, I say to you, you will see the heavens opened and the angels of God ascending and descending upon the Son of Man."

JOHN 1:19-51

Read: John is not the Messiah, but his mission is to announce him: "the Lamb of God who takes away the sin of the world." And upon realizing it, two of his disciples follow Jesus. One of them, Andrew, announces him to his brother Simon, who also follows Jesus. And something similar happens with Philip who presents the Master to his friend Nathaniel.

Reflect: What does the title "Lamb of God" remind you of? How is Jesus your Messiah in daily life? Jesus has already saved the world and through your baptism you participate in the kingdom of God. Do you see yourself in the first disciples who recognized Jesus? How do you communicate and share your faith with others?

Pray: Pray that people recognize they are loved by God in Jesus. Pray that, like the first disciples, you also be eager to meet the Master, the Son of God, and the Word made flesh.

Act: Point out five instances in which you recognized Jesus as the savior, and share it with others.

The wedding at Cana

2 [1] Three days later there was a wedding at Cana in Galilee and the mother of Jesus was there. [2] Jesus was also invited to the wedding with his disciples. [3] When all the wine provided for the celebration had been served and they had run out of wine, the mother of Jesus said to him, "They have no wine." [4] Jesus replied, "Woman, what concern is that to you and me? My hour has not yet come."

[5] However, his mother said to the servants, "Do whatever he tells you."

[6] Nearby were six stone water jars set there for ritual washing as practiced by the Jews; each jar could hold twenty or thirty gallons. [7] Jesus said to the servants, "Fill the jars with water." And they filled them to the brim. [8] Then Jesus said, "Now draw some out and take it to the steward." So they did.

[9] The steward tasted the water that had become wine without knowing from where it had come; for only the servants who had drawn the water knew. Immediately he called the bridegroom [10] and said, "Everyone serves the best wine first, and when people have drunk enough, he serves that which is ordinary. But you have kept the best wine until the end."

[11] This miraculous sign was the first and Jesus performed it at Cana in Galilee. In this way, he showed his glory, and his disciples believed in him.

[12] After this, Jesus went down to Capernaum with his mother, his brothers, and his disciples; and they stayed there for a few days.

JOHN 2:1-12

Read: The Messiah's time will be like a wedding feast in which will be wine in abundance. This Gospel never calls the mother of Jesus by name. Mary responds to the needs of the couple asking Jesus to do something. Jesus resists at first, but then performs the miracle of turning the water into wine, the first sign that he is the Messiah.

Reflect: Think about the relationship between Jesus and his mother. What significance do you attribute to the miracle of water being turned into abundant wine? Have you ever had the experience of being surprised by God?

Pray: Mary asks a favor. In your prayer, ask anything you need. Ask for the intercession of Mary when you pray.

Act: Pray the Rosary or a special prayer to Mary, the Mother of the Lord. As with Mary, may your prayer be an intercession for others.

Jesus clears the temple

¹³ As the Passover of the Jews was at hand, Jesus went up to Jerusalem. ¹⁴ In the temple court, he found merchants selling oxen, sheep, and doves, and moneychangers seated at their tables. ¹⁵ Making a whip of cords, he drove them all out of the temple court, together with the oxen and sheep. He knocked over the tables of the moneychangers, scattering the coins ¹⁶ and ordered the people selling doves, "Take all this away and stop making a marketplace of my Father's house!"

¹⁷ His disciples recalled the words of Scripture: *Zeal for your house devours me like fire.*

¹⁸ The Jews then questioned Jesus, "Where are the miraculous signs which give you the right to do this?" ¹⁹ And Jesus said, "Destroy this temple and in three days I will raise it up." ²⁰ The Jews then replied, "The building of this temple has already taken forty-six years and will you raise it up in three days?"

²¹ Actually, Jesus was referring to the temple of his body. ²² Only when he had risen from the dead did his disciples remember these words; then they believed both the Scripture and the words Jesus had spoken.

²³ Jesus stayed in Jerusalem during the Passover Festival and many believed in his name when they saw the miraculous signs he performed. ²⁴ But Jesus did not trust himself to them, because he knew all of them. ²⁵ He had no need for evidence about anyone for he himself knew what there was in each one.

JOHN 2:13-25

Read: Jesus goes to Jerusalem and cleanses the temple of moneychangers and sellers. Then, he refers to his body as if he was the new temple. People do not know him yet they believe him because of his miracles, but Jesus knows their hearts and does not trust them.

Reflect: Was Jesus, with the cleansing of the temple, the one who started the confrontation with the religious authorities? Could it be that the real conflict begins with those who used the temple for their own purposes? There are two temples, the one Jesus sees needs to be cleansed, and the temple that is Jesus. How can this be applied to the ways in which we worship God today?

Pray: Pray that the temple be always a place of encounter with God, a place of prayer. Pray also that each member of the Body of Christ, each Christian, may honor the Father.

Act: Visit a church and pray for every member of the Body of Christ, especially by their leaders and those who suffer the most.

Jesus and Nicodemus

3 [1] Among the Pharisees there was a ruler of the Jews named Nicodemus. [2] He came to Jesus by night and said, "Rabbi, we know that you have come from God to teach us, for no one can perform miraculous signs like yours unless God is with him."

[3] Jesus replied, "Truly, I say to you, no one can see the kingdom of God unless he is born again from above."

[4] Nicodemus said, "How can there be a rebirth for a grown man? Who could go back to his mother's womb and be born again?" [5] Jesus replied, "Truly, I say to you: No one can enter the kingdom of God without being born of water and Spirit. [6] What is born of the flesh is flesh, and what is born of the Spirit is spirit. [7] Because of this, don't be surprised when I say, 'You must be born again from above.'

[8] The wind blows where it pleases and you hear its sound, but you don't know where it comes from or where it is going. It is like that with everyone who is born of the Spirit."

⁹Nicodemus asked again, "How can this be?" ¹⁰And Jesus answered, "You are a teacher in Israel and you don't know these things!

¹¹Truly, I say to you, we speak of what we know and we witness to the things we have seen, but you don't accept our testimony. ¹²If you don't believe when I speak of earthly things, what then when I speak to you of heavenly things? ¹³No one has ever gone up to heaven except the one who came from heaven, the Son of Man.

¹⁴As Moses lifted up the serpent in the desert, so must the Son of Man be lifted up, ¹⁵so that whoever believes in him may have eternal life.

¹⁶Yes, God so loved the world that he gave his only Son that whoever believes in him may not be lost, but may have eternal life. ¹⁷God did not send the Son into the world to condemn the world; instead, through him, the world is to be saved. ¹⁸Whoever believes in him will not be condemned. He who does not believe is already condemned because he has not believed in the name of the only Son of God.

¹⁹This is how Judgment is made: Light has come into the world, and people loved darkness rather than light because their deeds were evil. ²⁰For whoever does wrong, hates the light and doesn't come to the light for fear that his deeds will be seen as evil. ²¹But whoever lives according to the truth comes into the light so that it can be clearly seen that his works have been done in God."

John the Baptist's last testimony

²²After this, Jesus went into the territory of Judea with his disciples. He stayed there with them and baptized. ²³John was also baptizing in Aenon, near Salim, where water was plentiful; people came to him and were baptized. ²⁴This happened before John was put in prison.

²⁵Now John's disciples had been questioned by a Jew about spiritual cleansing ²⁶so they came to John and said, "Rabbi, the one who was with you across the Jordan and about whom you spoke favorably, is now baptizing and all are going to him."

²⁷John answered, "No one can receive anything except what has been given to him from heaven. ²⁸You yourselves are my witnesses that I said, 'I am not the Christ, but I have been sent before him.' ²⁹Only the bridegroom has the bride, but the friend of the bridegroom stands by and listens and rejoices to hear the bridegroom's voice. My joy is now full. ³⁰It is necessary that he increase, but that I decrease.

[31] He who comes from above is above all; he who comes from the earth belongs to the earth and his words belong to the earth. He who comes from heaven [32] speaks of the things he has seen and heard; he bears witness to these things, but no one accepts his testimony. [33] Whoever does receive his testimony acknowledges the truthfulness of God.

[34] The one sent by God speaks God's words and gives the Spirit unstintingly. [35] The Father loves the Son and has entrusted everything into his hands. [36] Whoever believes in the Son lives with eternal life; but he who will not believe in the Son will never know life and always faces the justice of God."

JOHN 3:1-36

Read: Nicodemus is a religious authority who wants to know Jesus more deeply, but he does not understand all that Jesus said. Jesus tells him to be born again accepting Jesus into his heart. Jesus is the world of God and the light of salvation God has sent into the world.

Reflect: What is the foundation of your faith in Jesus as the Son of God? What does believing in Jesus demands from you? How do you manifest your faith?

Pray: Thank God for the gift of faith and baptism. Ask the Holy Spirit to accompany you in your day to day, and grant you the grace you may need.

Act: At night, light a candle and see how light dispels the darkness. Reflect on how your faith can dispel the darkness of doubt in all areas of your life.

Jesus and the Samaritan woman

4 [1] The Lord knew that the Pharisees were informed about him; people said that Jesus was attracting and baptizing more disciples than John; [2] but in fact, it was not Jesus himself who was baptizing, but his disciples. [3] So Jesus left Judea and returned to Galilee. [4] He had to cross Samaria.

[5] He came to a Samaritan town called Sychar, near the land that Jacob had given to his son Joseph. [6] Jacob's well is there. Tired from his journey, Jesus sat down by the well; it was about noon. [7] Now a Samaritan

woman came to draw water and Jesus said to her, "Give me a drink."
⁸ His disciples had just gone into town to buy some food.

⁹ The Samaritan woman said to him, "How is it that you, a Jew, ask me, a Samaritan and a woman, for a drink?" (For Jews, in fact, have no dealings with Samaritans.) ¹⁰ Jesus replied, "If you only knew the gift of God! If you knew who it is who is asking you for a drink, you yourself would have asked me and I would have given you living water."

¹¹ The woman answered, "Sir, you have no bucket and this well is deep; where is your living water? ¹² Are you greater than our ancestor Jacob, who gave us this well; he drank from it himself together with his sons and his cattle?"

¹³ Jesus said to her, "Those who drink of this water will be thirsty again; ¹⁴ but those who drink of the water that I shall give will never be thirsty; for the water that I shall give will become in them a spring of water welling up to eternal life."

¹⁵ The woman said to him, "Give me this water, that I may never be thirsty and never have to come here to draw water." ¹⁶ Jesus said, "Go, call your husband and come back here." ¹⁷ The woman answered, "I have no husband." And Jesus replied, "You are right to say, 'I have no husband'; ¹⁸ for you have had five husbands and the one you have now is not your husband. What you said is true."

¹⁹ The woman then said to him, "I see you are a prophet; tell me this: ²⁰ Our ancestors came to this mountain to worship God; but you Jews, do you not claim that Jerusalem is the only place to worship God?"

²¹ Jesus said to her, "Believe me, woman, the hour is coming when you shall worship the Father, but that will not be on this mountain nor in Jerusalem. ²² You worship what you do not know; we worship what we know because salvation is from the Jews. ²³ But the hour is coming and is even now here when the true worshipers will worship the Father in Spirit and truth; for that is the kind of worshippers the Father wants. ²⁴ God is Spirit and those who worship him must worship in Spirit and truth."

²⁵ The woman said to him, "I know that the Messiah (that is the Christ) is coming. When he comes, he will tell us everything." ²⁶ And Jesus said, "I who am talking to you, I am he."

²⁷ At this point the disciples returned and were surprised that Jesus was speaking with a woman; however, no one said, "What do you want?" or "Why are you talking with her?" ²⁸ So the woman left her water jar and

ran to the town. There she said to the people, ²⁹"Come and see a man who told me everything I did! Could he not be the Christ?" ³⁰So they left the town and went to meet him.

³¹In the meantime, the disciples urged Jesus, "Master, eat." ³²But he said to them, "I have food to eat that you don't know about." ³³And the disciples wondered, "Has anyone brought him food?" ³⁴Jesus said to them, "My food is to do the will of the one who sent me and to carry out his work.

³⁵You say that in four months there will be the harvest; now, I say to you, look up and see the fields white and ready for harvesting. ³⁶People who reap the harvest are paid for their work and the fruit is gathered for eternal life so that sower and reaper may rejoice together.

³⁷Indeed, the saying holds true: One sows and another reaps. ³⁸I sent you to reap where you didn't work or suffer; others have worked and you are now sharing in their labors."

³⁹In that town, many Samaritans believed in him when they heard the woman who declared, "He told me everything I did." ⁴⁰So when they came to him, they asked him to stay with them and Jesus stayed there for two days. ⁴¹After that, many more believed because of his own words ⁴²and they said to the woman, "We no longer believe because of what you told us; we have heard for ourselves and we know that this is the Savior of the world."

⁴³When the two days were over, Jesus left for Galilee. ⁴⁴Jesus himself said that no prophet is recognized in his own country. ⁴⁵Yet the Galileans welcomed him when he arrived because of all the things which he had done in Jerusalem during the Festival, and which they had seen. For they, too, had gone to the feast.

JOHN 4:1-45

Read: Jews regarded Samaritans heretics, and would never talk to a Samaritan woman alone in public places. However, the saving action of Jesus does not conform to local customs, he reached out to everyone. Unlike Nicodemus, the Samaritan woman accepts the words of the Master and becomes an apostle for the people of her town.

Reflect: What does the expression "God is Spirit and those who worship him must worship in spirit and truth" suggests to you regarding your religious practice?

Pray: Everyone has prejudices. Pray that you may be able to recognize and work to overcome them. May they be recognized and overcome in your daily life. Pray also that within the Church there may not be prejudices but understanding and acceptance for all.

Act: Encourage the recognition of women's work in your community, both social and ecclesial. Approach women pastoral workers, those responsible for administration, pastoral care, liturgy, the choir, the cleaning, etc., of your parish, and thank them for their service to the community.

Jesus cures the son of an official

⁴⁶ Jesus went back to Cana of Galilee, where he had changed the water into wine. At Capernaum, there was an official whose son was ill ⁴⁷ and when he heard that Jesus had come from Judea to Galilee, he went and asked him to come and heal his son, for he was at the point of death.

⁴⁸ Jesus said, "Unless you see signs and wonders, you will not believe!" ⁴⁹ The official said, "Sir, come down before my child dies." ⁵⁰ And Jesus replied, "Go, your son lives!"

The man had faith in the word that Jesus spoke to him and went his way. ⁵¹ As he was approaching his house, his servants met him and gave him the good news, "Your son has recovered!" ⁵² So he asked them at what hour the child began to recover and they said to him, "The fever left him yesterday, at about one o'clock in the afternoon." ⁵³ And the father realized that that was the time when Jesus had told him, "Your son lives!" And he became a believer, he and all his family.

⁵⁴ Jesus performed this second miraculous sign when he returned from Judea to Galilee.

JOHN 4:46-54

Read: On his return to Galilee, Jesus performs his second sign, healing from a distance the son of a royal official. He contrasts the faith of the official and those following him who believe only if they see signs and wonders.

Reflect: What is this passage telling you for your daily faith? Why do you believe in God? Do you really believe in the liberating and saving power of Jesus Christ, or do you place limits to it?

Pray: The world is full of signs that can lead to faith. Pray to the Spirit that your eyes may be opened to the great signs that God gives to grow and mature in your faith experience, which is nothing else than the experience of love and service that Jesus taught.

Act: Look at the creation: the sun, the moon, the sea, the mountains, valleys, animals, people, etc. Give thanks to God for His kindness, contemplating His presence in all beings with whom you meet.

The paralytic at the pool of Bethzatha

5 [1] After this, there was a feast of the Jews and Jesus went up to Jerusalem. [2] Now, by the Sheep Gate in Jerusalem, there is a pool (called Bethzatha in Hebrew) surrounded by five galleries. [3] In these galleries lay a multitude of sick people: blind, lame and paralyzed.

([4] All were waiting for the water to move, for at times an angel of the Lord would descend into the pool and stir up the water; and the first person to enter the pool after this movement of the water, would be healed of whatever disease that he had.)

[5] There was a man who had been sick for thirty-eight years. [6] Jesus saw him and because he knew how long this man had been lying there, he said to him, "Do you want to be healed?" [7] And the sick man answered, "Sir, I have no one to put me into the pool when the water is disturbed; so while I am still on my way, another steps down before me."

[8] Jesus then said to him, "Stand up, take your mat and walk!" [9] And at once the man was healed and he took up his mat and walked.

Now that day happened to be the *Sabbath*. [10] So the Jews said to the man who had just been healed, "It is the *Sabbath* and the law doesn't allow you to carry your mat." [11] He answered them, "The one who healed me said to me, 'Take up your mat and walk!'" [12] They asked him, "Who is the one who said to you: Take up your mat and walk?" [13] But the sick man had no idea who it was who had cured him, for Jesus had slipped away among the crowd that filled the place.

¹⁴Afterward, Jesus met him in the temple court and told him, "Now you are well; don't sin again, lest something worse happen to you." ¹⁵And the man went back and told the Jews that it was Jesus who had healed him. ¹⁶So the Jews persecuted Jesus because he performed healings like that on the *Sabbath*.

¹⁷Jesus replied, "My *Father* goes on working and so do I." ¹⁸And the Jews tried all the harder to kill him, for Jesus not only broke the *Sabbath* observance, but also made himself equal with God, calling God his own *Father*.

The work of the Son is to give life

¹⁹Jesus said to them, "Truly, I assure you, the Son cannot do anything by himself, but only what he sees the *Father* do. And whatever he does, the Son also does. ²⁰The *Father* loves the Son and shows him everything he does; and he will show him even greater things than these so that you will be amazed.

²¹As the *Father* raises the dead and gives them life, so the Son gives life to whom he wills. ²²In the same way, the *Father* judges no one, for he has entrusted all judgment to the Son, ²³and he wants all to honor the Son, as they honor the *Father*. Whoever ignores the Son, ignores as well the *Father* who sent him.

²⁴Truly, I say to you, anyone who hears my word and believes him who sent me has eternal life; and there is no judgment for him because he has passed from death to life.

²⁵Truly, the hour is coming and has indeed come, when the dead will hear the voice of the Son of God and, on hearing it, will live. ²⁶For the *Father* has life in himself and he has given to the Son also to have life in himself. ²⁷And he has empowered him as well to carry out Judgment, for he is Son of Man.

²⁸Do not be surprised at this: the hour is coming when all those lying in tombs will hear my voice ²⁹and come out; those who have done good shall rise to live and those who have done evil will rise to be condemned.

³⁰I can do nothing of myself. As I hear, so I judge, and my judgment is just because I seek not my own will but the will of him who sent me.

³¹ If I bore witness to myself, my testimony would be worthless. ³² But Another One is bearing witness to me and I know that his testimony is true when he bears witness to me. ³³ John also bore witness to the truth when you sent messengers to him, ³⁴ but I do not seek such human testimony; I recall this for you, so that you may be saved.

³⁵ John was a burning and shining lamp and for a while, you were willing to enjoy his light. ³⁶ But I have greater evidence than that of John— the works, which the *Father* entrusted to me to carry out. The very works I do bear witness: the *Father* has sent me. ³⁷ Thus he who bears witness to me is the Father who sent me. You have never heard his voice and have never seen his likeness; ³⁸ therefore, as long as you do not believe his messenger, his word is not in you.

³⁹ You search in the Scriptures, thinking that in them you will find life; yet Scripture bears witness to me. ⁴⁰ But you refuse to come to me that you may live. ⁴¹ I am not seeking human praise; ⁴² but I know that the love of God is not within you, ⁴³ for I have come in my *Father's* name and you do not accept me. If another comes in his own name, you will accept him. ⁴⁴ As long as you seek praise from one another, instead of seeking the glory, which comes from the only God, how can you believe?

⁴⁵ Do not think that I shall accuse you to the *Father*. Moses himself, in whom you placed your hope, accuses you. ⁴⁶ If you believed Moses, you would believe me, for he wrote of me. ⁴⁷ But if you do not believe what he wrote, how will you believe what I say?

JOHN 5:1-47

Read: Jesus violates the Sabbath laws by healing a cripple. God gave Jesus the authority, to give life. Faith in him brings us eternal life. No one needs fear judgment or death since the one who reaches the light (to Jesus) has passed through both.

Reflect: What does "eternal life" mean to you? What about judgment and death? What in this long chapter help you to understand faith? How do you keep the Sabbath holy?

Pray: If eternal life has already begun, you should be happy. Pray to obtain inner peace regarding the future. Pray with

> confidence because God loves you by sending his Son into the world to bring salvation.
>
> **Act:** Behave according to the desires that your heart and your faith dictate. Good deeds are always well received by God.

---

7 [19]Moses gave you the law, didn't he? But none of you keep the law. Why, then, do you want to kill me?"

[20]The people replied, "You have a demon; who wants to kill you?" [21]Jesus said to them, "I performed just one deed and you are all astounded by it. [22]But remember the circumcision ordered by Moses—actually it was not Moses but the ancestors who began this practice. You circumcise a man, even on the Sabbath, [23]and you would break the law if you refused to do so because of the Sabbath. How is it, then, that you are indignant with me because I healed the whole person on the Sabbath? [24]Do not judge by appearances, but according to what is right."

The multiplication of the loaves
(Mk 6:34; Mt 14:13; Lk 9:10)

6 [1]After this, Jesus went to the other side of the Sea of Galilee, near Tiberias [2]and large crowds followed him because of the miraculous signs they saw when he healed the sick. [3]So he went up into the hills and sat down there with his disciples. [4]Now the Passover, the feast of the Jews, was at hand.

[5]Then lifting up his eyes, Jesus saw the crowds that were coming to him and said to Philip, "Where shall we buy bread so that these people may eat?" [6]He said this to test Philip, for he himself knew what he was going to do. [7]Philip answered him, "Two hundred silver coins would not buy enough bread for each of them to have a piece."

[8]Then one of Jesus' disciples, Andrew, Simon Peter's brother, said, [9]"There is a boy here who has five barley loaves and two fish; but what good are these for so many?"

7:19-24: At the end of Chapter 5 we have placed the passage 7:19-24, which concludes the discourses but which, for some unknown reason, was placed after Chapter 6.

[10] Jesus said, "Make the people sit down." There was plenty of grass there, so the people, about five thousand men, sat down. [11] Jesus then took the loaves, gave thanks, and distributed them to those who were seated. He did the same with the fish and gave them as much as they wanted. [12] And when they had eaten enough, he told his disciples, "Gather up the pieces left over, that nothing may be lost."

[13] So they gathered them up and filled twelve baskets with bread, that is, with pieces of the five barley loaves left over by those who had eaten.

[14] When the people saw the miracle, which Jesus had performed, they said, "This is really the Prophet, the one who is to come into the world." [15] Jesus realized that they would come and take him by force to make him king; so he fled to the hills by himself.

[16] When evening came, the disciples went down to the shore. [17] After a while, they got into a boat to make for Capernaum on the other side of the sea, for it was now dark and Jesus had not yet come to them. [18] But the sea was getting rough because a strong wind was blowing.

[19] They had rowed about three or four miles when they saw Jesus walking on the sea and he was drawing near to the boat. They were frightened, [20] but he said to them, "It is I! Don't be afraid!"

[21] They wanted to take him into the boat, but immediately the boat was at the shore to which they were going.

[22] Next day, the people, who had stayed on the other side, realized that only one boat had been there and that Jesus had not entered it with his disciples; but rather, the disciples had gone away alone. [23] Other boats from Tiberias landed near the place where all these people had eaten the bread. [24] When they saw that neither Jesus nor his disciples were there, they got into the boats and went to Capernaum looking for Jesus.

[25] When they found him on the other side of the lake, they asked him, "Master, when did you come here?"

[26] Jesus answered, "Truly, I say to you, you look for me, not because of the signs which you have seen, but because you ate bread and were satisfied. [27] Work then, not for perishable food, but for the lasting food which gives eternal life. The Son of Man will give it to you for he is the one on whom the Father has put his mark."

The bread of life; to believe in the Son of God

[28] Then the Jews asked him, "What shall we do? What are the works that God wants us to do?" [29] And Jesus answered them, "The work God wants is this: that you believe in the One whom God has sent."

[30] They then said, "Show us miraculous signs that we may see and believe you. What sign do you perform? [31] Our ancestors ate manna in the desert; as Scripture says: *They were given bread from heaven to eat.*"

[32] Jesus then said to them, "Truly, I say to you, it was not Moses who gave you the *bread from heaven.* My Father gives you the true *bread from heaven.* [33] The bread God gives is the One who comes from heaven and gives life to the world." [34] And they said to him, "Give us this bread always."

[35] Jesus said to them, "I am the bread of life; whoever comes to me shall never be hungry, and whoever believes in me shall never be thirsty. [36] Nevertheless, as I said, you refuse to believe, even when you have seen. [37] Yet all those whom the Father gives me will come to me, and whoever comes to me, I shall not turn away. [38] For I have come from heaven, not to do my own will, but the will of the One who sent me.

[39] And the will of him who sent me is that I lose nothing of what he has given me, but instead that I raise it up on the last day. [40] This is the will of the Father, that whoever sees the Son and believes in him shall live eternal life; and I will raise him up on the last day."

JOHN 6:1-40

Read: Jesus feeds the crowds. People see the sign and express their belief that Jesus is a prophet, but they mistakenly want to make him king. Jesus goes to the hills alone and then walks on the water. Jesus calls people to work not for the food that perishes but for the one that remains and gives eternal life.

Reflect: Why do you follow Jesus? Who is Jesus for you? What does the following expression suggests for your daily life: "I am the bread of life. Whoever comes to me will never be hungry, and whoever believes in me will never be thirsty."

Pray: Pray that you will have eternal bread in abundance, and also the daily food. Ask the Lord to grant you faith to act according to it. Pray always asking for the good of others.

> **Act:** Seek Jesus in the brothers and sisters and serve them. Participate in the Eucharist to have the necessary food that never perishes and that gives eternal life.

[41] The Jews murmured because Jesus had said, "I am the bread *which comes from heaven*." [42] And they said, "This man is the son of Joseph, isn't he? We know his father and mother. How can he say that he has come from heaven?"

[43] Jesus answered them, "Do not murmur among yourselves. [44] No one can come to me unless he is drawn by the Father who sent me; and I will raise him up on the last day. [45] It has been written in the Prophets: *They shall all be taught by God*. So whoever listens and learns from the Father comes to me.

[46] For no one has seen the Father except the One who comes from God; he has seen the Father. [47] Truly, I say to you, whoever believes has eternal life.

The body of Christ, the bread of life

[48] I am the bread of life. [49] Though your ancestors ate the manna in the desert, they died. [50] But here you have the *bread from heaven*, so that you may eat of it and not die.

[51] I am the living *bread from heaven*; whoever eats of this bread will live forever. The bread I shall give is my flesh, and I will give it for the life of the world."

JOHN 6:41-51

Read: Jesus' discourse generates the murmuring of the people, like the Israelites in the desert. This means that people close themselves to God's action. Jesus calls (it is imperative) not to "gossip" but to be open to the divine presence, for only then will the act of faith that produces life happens.

Reflect: Where does your faith in Jesus lead you? Or are you a Christian by "custom" or "family tradition"? Do you read the bible to nourish your Christian commitment? When you receive holy communion, what does it mean to you?

> **Pray:** In prayer, ask the Lord to guide you in your day to day toward eternal life. At morning ask for help to live and share your faith during the day.
>
> **Act:** Say the prayer that has been suggested to you in your reading of this biblical passage.

⁵²The Jews were arguing among themselves, "How can this man give us his flesh to eat?" ⁵³So Jesus replied, "Truly, I say to you, if you do not eat the flesh of the Son of Man and drink his blood, you have no life in you. ⁵⁴The one who eats my flesh and drinks my blood lives eternal life, and I will raise him up on the last day.

⁵⁵My flesh is true food and my blood is true drink. ⁵⁶Those who eat my flesh and drink my blood live in me and I in them. ⁵⁷Just as the Father, who is life, sent me and I have life from the Father, so whoever eats me will have life from me. ⁵⁸This is the bread from heaven; not like that of your ancestors who ate and later died. Those who eat this bread will live forever."

⁵⁹Jesus spoke in this way in Capernaum when he taught them in the synagogue.

Will you also go away?

⁶⁰After hearing this, many of Jesus' followers said, "This language is very hard! Who can accept it?"

⁶¹Jesus was aware that his disciples were murmuring about this, and so he said to them, "Does this offend you? ⁶²Then how will you react when you see the Son of Man ascending to where he was before? ⁶³It is the spirit that gives life, not the flesh. The words that I have spoken to you are spirit and they are life. ⁶⁴But among you, there are some who do not believe."

From the beginning, Jesus knew who would betray him. ⁶⁵So he added, "As I have told you, no one can come to me unless it is granted by the Father."

⁶⁶After this many disciples withdrew and no longer followed him. ⁶⁷Jesus asked the Twelve, "Will you also go away?" ⁶⁸Peter answered him, "Lord, to whom shall we go? You have the words of eternal life. ⁶⁹We now believe and know that you are the Holy One of God."

⁷⁰ Jesus said to them, "I chose you, the Twelve, did I not? Yet one of you is a devil." ⁷¹ Jesus spoke of Judas Iscariot, the son of Simon. He, one of the Twelve, was to betray him.

JOHN 6:52-71

Read: Here is the reference to the Eucharist in the Gospel of John. Eating the glorious body of Jesus, the bread of life, the believer receives the overabundance of eternal life. This is a life that must be communicated to others. Many have difficulty accepting this teaching of the Teacher and leave. Instead, Peter, the spokesman for the disciples, reaffirms his faith.

Reflect: How does the Eucharist strengthen you? When Jesus says we must eat his flesh and drink his blood to have eternal life, what do you think he means? When asked if he will leave Jesus too, Peter says he has no place to go, Jesus has the words of eternal life. What does that mean for you?

Pray: Pray for growth in the understanding and appreciation of the presence of Jesus in the Eucharist. Pray for those who have difficulty accepting it.

Act: Make your heart a sanctuary of the Eucharist, that the brothers and sisters perceive that it is Jesus Christ who lives in you. Carry everywhere Peter's conviction: "Lord, You have words of eternal life."

Jesus goes up to Jerusalem

7 ¹ After this, Jesus went around Galilee; he would not go about in Judea, because the Jews wanted to kill him. ² Now the Jewish feast of the Tents was at hand. ³ So the brothers of Jesus said to him, "Don't stay here; go instead to Judea and let your disciples see the works you are doing. ⁴ Anyone who wants to be known doesn't work secretly. Since you are able to do these things, show yourself to the world."

⁵ His brothers spoke like this because they didn't believe in him. ⁶ Jesus said to them, "My time has not yet come, but your time is always here.

⁷ The world cannot hate you, but it hates me because I bear witness and I show that its deeds are evil. ⁸ Go up to the feast! I am not going to this feast, because my time has not yet come."

⁹ Jesus said these things and remained in Galilee. ¹⁰ But after his brothers had gone to the festival, he also went up, not publicly but in secret. ¹¹ The Jews were looking for him at the festival and asked, "Where is he?" ¹² There was a lot of talk about him among the people. Some said, "He is a good man," but others replied, "No, he is misleading the people." ¹³ For fear of the Jews, no one spoke openly about him.

¹⁴ When the festival was half over, Jesus went to the temple and began to teach. ¹⁵ The Jews marveled and said, "How is it that he knows Scriptures when he has had no teacher?"

¹⁶ And Jesus answered them, "My teaching is not mine, but it comes from the One who sent me. ¹⁷ Anyone who does the will of God shall know whether my teaching is from God, or whether I speak on my own authority.

¹⁸ Those who speak on their own authority wish to gain honor for themselves. But the one who seeks the glory of him who sent him is truthful and there is no reason to doubt him."

²⁵ Some of the people of Jerusalem said, "Is this not the man they want to kill? ²⁶ And here he is speaking freely and they don't say a word to him? Can it be that the rulers know that this is really the Christ? ²⁷ Yet we know where this man comes from; but when the Christ appears no one will know where he comes from."

²⁸ So Jesus announced in a loud voice in the temple court where he was teaching, "You say that you know me and know where I come from! I have not come of myself; I was sent by the One who is true and you don't know him. ²⁹ I know him for I come from him, and he sent me."

³⁰ They would have arrested him, but no one laid hands on him because his time had not yet come. ³¹ Many people in the crowd, however, believed in him and said, "When the Christ comes, will he give more signs than this man?"

³² The Pharisees heard all these rumors among the people; they and the chief priests sent officers of the temple to arrest him. ³³ Jesus then said, "I shall be with you a little longer; after that, I shall go to him who sent me. ³⁴ You will look for me and you will not find me. Where I am you cannot come."

³⁵ The Jews said to one another, "Where does this man intend to go, where we shall not find him? Will he go abroad to the Jews dispersed among the Greek nations and teach the Greeks also? ³⁶ What does he

mean when he says, 'You will look for me and not find me,' and, 'Where I am going you cannot come'?"

The promise of living water

[37] On the last and greatest day of the festival, Jesus stood up and proclaimed, "Let anyone who is thirsty come to me; [38] and let the one who believes in me drink, for the Scripture says: *Out of the believer's heart shall flow rivers of living water.*"

[39] Jesus was referring to the Spirit, which those who believe in him were to receive; the Spirit had not yet been given, because Jesus had not yet entered into his glory.

Dispute on the origin of Christ

[40] Many who had been listening to these words began to say, "This is the Prophet." [41] Others said, "This is the Christ." But some wondered, "Would the Christ come from Galilee? [42] Doesn't Scripture say that the Christ is a *descendant of David* and *from Bethlehem, the city of David*?" [43] The crowd was divided over him. [44] Some wanted to arrest him, but no one laid hands on him.

[45] The officers of the temple went back to the chief priests who asked them, "Why didn't you bring him?" [46] The officers answered, "No one ever spoke like this man." [47] The Pharisees then said, "So you, too, have been led astray! [48] Have any of the rulers or any of the Pharisees believed in him? [49] Only these cursed people who have no knowledge of the law!"

[50] Yet one of them, Nicodemus, who had gone to Jesus earlier, spoke out, [51] "Does our law condemn people without first hearing them and knowing the facts?" [52] They replied, "Do you, too, come from Galilee? Look it up and see for yourself that no prophet is to come from Galilee."

[53] And they all went home.

JOHN 7:1-53

Read: This chapter has many different events and ideas. Jesus decides not to go to the feast and then changes his mind. He teaches in the temple and people do not understand him. Opposition to Jesus grows. His adversaries want to arrest him.

Even though Jesus is life and salvation, the people "were divided on account of him."

Reflect: At the festival people are divided about Jesus, some think him a good man while others think him a deceiver and seek to kill him. What do people think about Jesus today? Do you feel the thirst for eternal life to come to Jesus every day in the bread of the Word and the bread of the Eucharist? What is this "river of living water" that flows from the hearts of believers?

Pray: When you are thirsty for eternal life, pray to the Spirit who will lead you to Jesus. Pray to be an instrument of the Spirit for others.

Act: From the heart of the believer springs streams of living water. Let your faith find expression in how you live this day; in this way, you will help others to confirm their beliefs, their hopes, and life options.

The adulteress

8 ¹As for Jesus, he went to the Mount of Olives.

²At daybreak, Jesus appeared in the temple again. All the people came to him and he sat down and began to teach them.

³Then the teachers of the law and the Pharisees brought in a woman who had been caught in the act of adultery. They made her stand in front of everyone. ⁴"Master," they said, "this woman has been caught in the act of adultery. ⁵Now, the law of Moses orders that such women be stoned to death; but you, what do you say?" ⁶They said this to test Jesus in order to have some charge against him.

Jesus bent down and started writing on the ground with his finger. ⁷And as they continued to ask him, he straightened up and said to them, "Let anyone among you who has no sin be the first to throw a stone at her." ⁸And he bent down again, writing on the ground.

⁹As a result of these words, they went away one by one, starting with the elders, and Jesus was left alone with the woman standing before him. ¹⁰Then Jesus stood up and said to her, "Woman, where are they?

Has no one condemned you?" [11] She replied, "No one." And Jesus said, "Neither do I condemn you; go away and don't sin again."

I Am the light of the world

[12] Jesus spoke to them again, "I am the Light of the world; the one who follows me will not walk in darkness, but will have light and life." [13] The Pharisees replied, "Now you are speaking on your own behalf, your testimony is worthless."

[14] Then Jesus said, "Even though I bear witness to myself, my testimony is true, for I know where I have come from and where I am going. But you do not know where I came from or where I am going.

[15] You judge by human standards; as for me, I don't judge anyone. [16] But if I had to judge, my judgment would be valid for I am not alone: the Father who sent me is with me. [17] In your law it is written that the testimony of two witnesses is valid; [18] so I am bearing witness to myself, and the Father who sent me bears witness to me."

[19] They asked him, "Where is your Father?" Jesus answered, "You don't know me or my Father; if you knew me, you would know my Father as well."

[20] Jesus said these things when he was teaching in the temple area, in the place where they received the offerings. No one arrested him, because his hour had not yet come.

[21] Again, Jesus said to them, "I am going away and though you look for me, you will die in your sin. Where I am going you cannot come." [22] The Jews wondered, "Why does he say that we can't come where he is going? Will he kill himself?"

[23] But Jesus said, "You are from below and *I am* from above; you are of this world and *I am* not of this world. [24] That is why I told you that you will die in your sins. And you shall die in your sins unless you believe that *I am He.*"

[25] They asked him, "Who are you?"; and Jesus said, "Just what I have told you from the beginning. [26] I have much to say about you and much to condemn; but the One who sent me is truthful and everything I learned from him, I proclaim to the world."

[27] They didn't understand that Jesus was speaking to them about the Father. [28] So Jesus said, "When you have lifted up the Son of Man, then you will know that *I am He* and that I do nothing of myself, but I say just

what the Father taught me. ²⁹He who sent me is with me and has not left me alone; because I always do what pleases him."

The children of truth

³⁰As Jesus spoke like this, many believed in him. ³¹Jesus went on to say to the Jews who believed in him, "You will be my true disciples if you keep my word. ³²Then you will know the truth and the truth will set you free." ³³They answered him, "We are the descendants of Abraham and have never been slaves of anyone. What do you mean by saying: You will be free?"

³⁴Jesus answered them, "Truly, I say to you, whoever commits sin is a slave. ³⁵But the slave doesn't stay in the house forever; the son stays forever. ³⁶So, if the Son makes you free, you will be really free.

³⁷I know that you are the descendants of Abraham, yet you want to kill me because my word finds no place in you. ³⁸For my part, I speak of what I have seen in my Father's presence, but you do what you have learned from your father."

³⁹They answered him, "Our father is Abraham." Then Jesus said, "If you were Abraham's children, you would do as Abraham did. ⁴⁰But now you want to kill me, the one who tells you the truth—the truth that I have learned from God. That is not what Abraham did; ⁴¹what you are doing are the works of your father."

The Jews said to him, "We are not illegitimate children; we have one Father, God." ⁴²Jesus replied, "If God were your Father, you would love me, for I came forth from God and I am here. And I didn't come by my own decision, but it was he himself who sent me. ⁴³Why do you not understand my teaching? It is because you cannot bear my message.

⁴⁴The father you spring from is the devil, and you will carry out the evil wishes of your father who has been a murderer from the beginning. He didn't uphold the truth for, in him, there is no truth; and now, when he speaks for himself, he lies. He is a liar and the father of lies.

⁴⁵Now I speak the truth and you don't believe me. ⁴⁶Who among you can find anything false in me? Then, if I speak the truth, why do you not believe me? ⁴⁷He who is of God hears the words of God; you don't hear because you are not of God."

⁴⁸The Jews retorted, "So we are right in saying that you are a Samaritan and are possessed by a demon." ⁴⁹Jesus said, "I am not possessed,

and you try to shame me when I give honor to my Father. [50] I don't care about my own glory; there is One who cares for me and he will be the judge.

[51] Truly, I say to you, if anyone keeps my word, he will never experience death." [52] The Jews replied, "Now we know that you have a demon. Abraham died and the prophets as well, but you say, 'Whoever keeps my word will never experience death.' Who do you claim to be? [53] Do you claim to be greater than our father Abraham, who died? And the prophets who also died?"

[54] Then Jesus said, "If I were to praise myself, it would count for nothing. But he who gives glory to me is the Father, the very one you claim as your God, [55] although you don't know him. I know him and if I were to say that I don't know him, I would be a liar like you. But I know him and I keep his word.

[56] As for Abraham, your ancestor, he looked forward to the day when I would come; and he rejoiced when he saw it."

[57] The Jews then said to him, "You are not yet fifty years old and you have seen Abraham?" [58] And Jesus said, "Truly, I say to you, before Abraham was, I am." [59] They then picked up stones to throw at him, but Jesus hid himself and left the temple.

JOHN 8:1-59

Read: In this chapter Jesus forgives a guilty woman, declares himself the light his Father sends into the world, and anyone who loves God, will love him. All of these claims are hotly contested by religious people listening to him. Some even call Jesus a demon. In the end, they try to stone him to death but Jesus escapes.

Reflect: Should people avoid judging each other? Are not two people needed for adultery? Why is not man mentioned? Why the discussion on the validity of a "testimony"? What does the Devil have to do with all this? What does "I am the light of the world" mean in the mouth of Jesus?

Pray: People judge others too easily. Pray, so you can avoid making light judgments about others. Give others the benefit of the doubt.

> **Act:** Avoid getting into arguments and judge too easily. Before any discussion, keep a serene attitude and fair spirit, irrespective of prejudices or sympathies. Remember that the only Teacher is Jesus.

Jesus heals the man born blind

9 [1] As Jesus walked along, he saw a man who had been blind from birth. [2] His disciples asked him, "Master, was he born blind because of a sin of his, or of his parents?"

[3] Jesus answered, "Neither was it for his own sin nor for his parents' sin. He was born blind so that God's power might be shown in him. [4] While it is day we must do the work of the One who sent me; for the night will come when no one can work. [5] As long as I am in the world, I am the light of the world."

[6] As Jesus said this, he made paste with spittle and clay and rubbed it on the eyes of the blind man. [7] Then he said, "Go and wash in the Pool of Siloam." (This word means *sent*.) So the blind man went and washed and came back able to see.

[8] His neighbors, and all the people who used to see him begging, wondered. They said, "Isn't this the beggar who used to sit here?" [9] Some said, "He's the one." Others said, "No, but he looks like him." But the man himself said, "I am he." [10] Then they asked him, "How is it that your eyes were opened?" [11] And he answered, "The man called Jesus made a mud paste, put it on my eyes and said to me, 'Go to Siloam and wash.' So I went and washed and I could see." [12] They asked, "Where is he?" And the man answered, "I don't know."

[13] The people brought the man who had been blind to the Pharisees. [14] Now it was a Sabbath day when Jesus made mud paste and opened his eyes. [15] The Pharisees asked him again, "How did you recover your sight?" And he said, "He put paste on my eyes, and I washed, and now I see." [16] Some of the Pharisees said, "That man is not from God, for he works on the Sabbath"; but others wondered, "How can a sinner perform such miraculous signs?" They were divided [17] and they questioned the blind man again, "What do you think of this man who opened your eyes?" And he answered, "He is a prophet!"

[18] After all this, the Jews refused to believe that the man had been blind

and had recovered his sight; so they called his parents ¹⁹and asked them, "Is this your son? You say that he was born blind, how is it that he now sees?" ²⁰The parents answered, "He really is our son and he was born blind; ²¹but how it is that he now sees, we don't know, neither do we know who opened his eyes. Ask him, he is old enough. Let him speak for himself."

²²The parents said this because they feared the Jews, who had already agreed that whoever confessed Jesus to be the Christ was to be expelled from the synagogue. ²³Because of that, his parents said, "He is old enough, ask him."

²⁴So, a second time, the Pharisees called the man who had been blind and they said to him, "Tell us the truth; we know that this man is a sinner." ²⁵He replied, "I don't know whether he is a sinner or not; I only know that I was blind and now I see." ²⁶They said to him, "What did he do to you? How did he open your eyes?" ²⁷He replied, "I have told you already and you would not listen. Why do you want to hear it again? Do you also want to become his disciples?"

²⁸Then they started to insult him. "Become his disciple yourself! We are disciples of Moses. ²⁹We know that God spoke to Moses; but as for this man, we don't know where he comes from."

³⁰The man replied, "It is amazing that you don't know where the man comes from and yet he opened my eyes! ³¹We know that God doesn't listen to sinners, but if anyone honors God and does his will, God listens to him. ³²Never, since the world began, has it been heard that anyone opened the eyes of a person who was born blind. ³³If this man were not from God, he could do nothing."

³⁴They answered him, "You were born a sinner and now you teach us!" And they expelled him.

³⁵Jesus heard that they had expelled him. He found him and said, "Do you believe in the Son of Man?" ³⁶He answered, "Who is he, that I may believe in him?" ³⁷Jesus said, "You have seen him and he is speaking to you." ³⁸He said, "Lord, I believe"; and he worshiped him.

³⁹Jesus said, "I came into this world to carry out a judgment: Those who do not see shall see and those who see shall become blind." ⁴⁰Some Pharisees stood by, and asked him, "So we are blind?" ⁴¹And Jesus answered, "If you were blind, you would not be guilty. But you say, 'We see'; this is the proof of your sin."

JOHN 9:1-41

Read: Jesus cures a blind man from birth on the Sabbath, and again stirring up controversy about the nature of God. In this story, it is actually the blind man who sees God at work, while the religious people are blind to actions of God they do not expect. It is possible that the community of John was thrown out of the synagogue, from Judaism, like the blind man healed by Jesus.

Reflect: Who is blind today in the Church and in the society? Are you blind to others? What do you not want to see? Compare the words of the blind man with the words of the religious authorities. Why do religious authorities refuse to see? Do you accuse others before examining your own motives?

Pray: We all have our blind spots. Pray to recognize those moments when you do not want to see what is obvious. Ask not to accuse others before examining their own points of view.

Act: Be sensitive to anyone who is handicapped. Never treat such a person as being inferior, but recognize their values and capacities, and think in what way they can help you. When that person could help you, ask him or her.

The good shepherd

10 [1] Truly, I say to you, anyone who does not enter the sheepfold by the gate, but climbs in some other way, is a thief and a robber. [2] But the shepherd of the sheep enters by the gate. [3] The keeper opens the gate to him and the sheep hear his voice; he calls each of his sheep by name and leads them out. [4] When he has brought out all his own, he goes before them, and the sheep follow him for they know his voice. [5] A stranger they will not follow, but rather they will run away from him because they don't recognize a stranger's voice."

[6] Jesus used this comparison, but they did not understand what he was saying to them.

[7] So Jesus said, "Truly, I say to you, I am the gate of the sheep. [8] All who came were thieves and robbers and the sheep did not hear them. [9] I am the gate. Whoever enters through me will be saved; he will go in and out freely and find food.

¹⁰ The thief comes to steal and kill and destroy, but I have come that they may have life, life in all its fullness.

¹¹ I am the good shepherd. The good shepherd gives his life for the sheep. ¹² Not so the hired hand, or any other person who is not the shepherd and to whom the sheep do not belong. They abandon the sheep as soon as they see the wolf coming; then the wolf snatches and scatters the sheep. ¹³ This is because the hired hand works for pay and cares nothing for the sheep.

¹⁴ I am the good shepherd. I know my own and my own know me, ¹⁵ as the Father knows me and I know the Father. Because of this, I give my life for my sheep.

¹⁶ I have other sheep, which are not of this fold. These I have to lead as well and they shall listen to my voice. Then there will be one flock since there is one shepherd.

¹⁷ The Father loves me because I lay down my life in order to take it up again. ¹⁸ No one takes it from me, but I lay it down freely. It is mine to lay down and to take up again: this mission I received from my Father."

¹⁹ Because of these words, the Jews were again divided. ²⁰ Many of them said, "He has a demon and is out of his mind. Why listen to him?" ²¹ But others said, "A man possessed doesn't speak in this way. Can a demon open the eyes of the blind?"

Jesus claims to be the Son of God

²² The time came for the feast of the Dedication. It was winter, ²³ and Jesus walked back and forth in the portico of Solomon. ²⁴ The Jews then gathered around him and said to him, "How long will you keep us in doubt? If you are the Messiah, tell us plainly." ²⁵ Jesus answered, "I have already told you, but you do not believe. ²⁶ The works I do in my Father's name, proclaim who I am, but you don't believe because, as I said, you are not my sheep.

²⁷ My sheep hear my voice and I know them; they follow me ²⁸ and I give them eternal life. They shall never perish, and no one will ever steal them from me. ²⁹ What my Father has given me is greater than all things else. To snatch it out of the Father's hand, no one is able! ³⁰ I and the Father are One."

³¹ The Jews then picked up stones to throw at him; ³² so Jesus said, "I

have openly done many good works among you which the Father gave me to do. For which of these do you stone me?"

³³ The Jews answered, "We are not stoning you for doing a good work, but for insulting God; you are only a man and you make yourself God."

³⁴ Then Jesus replied, "Is this not written in your law: *I said, you are gods*? ³⁵ So those who received this word of God were called gods and the Scripture is always true. ³⁶ What then should be said of the one anointed, and sent into the world by the Father? Am I insulting God when I say, 'I am the Son of God'?

³⁷ If I am not doing the works of my Father, do not believe me. ³⁸ But if I do them, even if you have no faith in me, believe because of the works I do; and know that the Father is in me and I in the Father."

³⁹ Again they tried to arrest him, but Jesus escaped from their hands. ⁴⁰ He went away again to the other side of the Jordan, to the place where John had baptized and there he stayed.

⁴¹ Many people came to Jesus and said, "John worked no miracles, but he spoke about you and everything he said was true." ⁴² And many in that place became believers.

JOHN 10:1-42

Read: Jesus is presented as the true shepherd of his people, who gives them food and security, who knows the sheep by name and gives his life for them. They know his voice and follow him. The controversy with religious leaders continues, up to the point of trying to stone him. When in John's Gospel you read, "the Jews" remember he is talking about the religious leaders who were opposed to Jesus, not the Jewish people chosen by God.

Reflect: Do you hear the voice of the Good Shepherd? Since he knows you by name, does this make you feel good? What do you think of the opponents of Jesus? What could their motives be? What teachings of Jesus you particularly like in this passage?

Pray: The Good Shepherd calls you by name. Ask for an attentive ear to listen to his voice in everyday life.

Act: Pay attention to learn or remember the names of acquaintances. Call them by name, and treat them as what they are: sons and daughters of God, your brothers and sisters, sheep of the same fold.

The raising of Lazarus

11 ¹There was a sick man named Lazarus who was from Bethany, the village of Mary and her sister Martha. ²This is the same Mary, who anointed the *Lord* with perfume and wiped his feet with her hair. Her brother Lazarus was sick.

³So the sisters sent this message to Jesus, "*Lord*, the one you love is sick." ⁴On hearing this, Jesus said, "This illness will not end in death; rather it is for God's glory and the Son of God will be glorified through it."

⁵It is a fact that Jesus loved Martha and her sister and Lazarus; ⁶yet, after he heard of the illness of Lazarus, he stayed two days longer in the place where he was. ⁷Only then did he say to his disciples, "Let us go into Judea again." ⁸They replied, "Master, recently the Jews wanted to stone you. Are you going there again?"

⁹Jesus said to them, "Are not twelve working hours needed to complete a day? Those who walk in the daytime shall not stumble, for they see the light of this world. ¹⁰But those who walk at night stumble, for there is no light in them."

¹¹After that, Jesus said to them, "Our friend Lazarus has fallen asleep, but I am going to wake him up." ¹²The disciples replied, "*Lord*, a sick person who sleeps will recover." ¹³But Jesus had referred to Lazarus' death, while they thought that he had meant the repose of sleep. ¹⁴So Jesus said plainly, "Lazarus is dead; ¹⁵and for your sake, I am glad I was not there, so that you may believe. But let us go to him." ¹⁶Then Thomas, called the Twin, said to his fellow disciples, "Let us also go, that we may die with him."

¹⁷When Jesus came, he found that Lazarus had been in the tomb for four days. ¹⁸As Bethany is near Jerusalem, about two miles away, ¹⁹many Jews had come to Martha and Mary after the death of their brother to comfort them.

²⁰When Martha heard that Jesus was coming, she went to meet him while Mary remained sitting in the house. ²¹Martha said to Jesus, "If you had been here, my brother would not have died. ²²But I know that whatever you ask from God, God will give you." ²³Jesus said, "Your brother will rise again."

²⁴Martha replied, "I know that he will rise in the resurrection, at the last day." ²⁵But Jesus said to her, "I am the resurrection. Whoever

believes in me, though he dies, shall live. [26]Whoever lives and believes in me will never die. Do you believe this?"

[27]Martha then answered, "Yes, *Lord*, I have come to believe that you are the Christ, the Son of God, he who is coming into the world."

[28]After that, Martha went and called her sister Mary secretly, saying, "The Master is here and is calling for you." [29]As soon as Mary heard this, she rose and went to him. [30]Jesus had not yet come into the village but was still in the place where Martha had met him.

[31]The Jews, who were with Mary in the house consoling her, also came. When they saw her get up and go out, they followed her, thinking that she was going to the tomb to weep.

[32]When Mary came to the place where Jesus was and saw him, she fell at his feet and said, "*Lord*, if you had been here, my brother would not have died." [33]When Jesus saw her weeping, and the Jews also weeping, who had come with her, he was moved to the depths of his spirit and troubled. [34]Then he asked, "Where have you laid him?" They answered, "*Lord*, come and see." [35]Jesus wept.

[36]The Jews said, "See how he loved him!" [37]But some of them said, "If he could open the eyes of the blind man, could he not have kept this man from dying?"

[38]Jesus, again deeply moved, drew near to the tomb. It was a cave with a stone laid across the entrance. [39]Jesus said, "Take the stone away." Martha said to him, "*Lord*, by now he will smell, for this is the fourth day." [40]Jesus replied, "Have I not told you that, if you believe, you will see the glory of God?" [41]So they removed the stone.

Jesus raised his eyes and said, "Father, I thank you for you have heard me. [42]I knew that you hear me always, but my prayer was for the sake of these people that they may believe that you sent me." [43]When Jesus had said this, he cried out in a loud voice, "Lazarus, come out!"

[44]The dead man came out, his hands and feet bound with linen strips and his face wrapped in a cloth. Jesus said to them, "Untie him, and let him go."

JOHN 11:1-44

Read: Jesus resurrects his friend Lazarus, gives him life, and conquers death. This is his last "sign" in the Gospel, and before it, there are two opposing reactions: faith and disbelief. Faith opens the doors of life; disbelief closes them.

Reflect: What does resurrection mean to you? Do you hope in it? What do you think about Jesus' relationship with Lazarus and his sisters? Does it depict the profound humanity of Jesus?

Pray: Ask every night for the grace of a happy death and a deep faith in the resurrection. Also, ask the intercession of those who have preceded you in faith: the saints, family, and friends.

Act: Read this passage again and try to learn more about the Church's teaching on the resurrection of the body.

The plot to kill Jesus

[45] Many of the Jews who had come with Mary believed in Jesus when they saw what he did; [46] but some went to the Pharisees and told them what Jesus had done. [47] So the chief priests and the Pharisees called together the Council.

They said, "What are we to do? For this man keeps on performing many miraculous signs. [48] If we let him go on like this, all the people will believe in him and, as a result of this, the Romans will come and destroy our Holy Place and our nation."

[49] Then one of them, Caiaphas, who was High Priest that year, spoke up, "You know nothing at all! [50] It is better to have one man die for the people than to let the whole nation be destroyed."

[51] In saying this Caiaphas did not speak for himself, but being High Priest that year, he foretold like a prophet that Jesus would die for the nation [52] and not for the nation only but also would die in order to gather into one the scattered children of God. [53] So, from that day on, they were determined to kill him.

[54] Because of this, Jesus no longer moved about freely among the Jews. He withdrew instead to the country near the wilderness and stayed with his disciples in a town called Ephraim.

[55] The Passover of the Jews was at hand and people from everywhere were coming to Jerusalem to purify themselves before the Passover. [56] They looked for Jesus and as they stood in the temple, they talked

with one another, "What do you think? Will he come to the festival?" [57]Meanwhile, the chief priests and the elders had given orders that anyone who knew where he was should let them know so that they could arrest him.

JOHN 11:45-57

Read: The raising of Lazarus brings the opponents of Jesus to a final decision. They are worried that people will believe in Jesus and the Romans will come and destroy them. Caiaphas speaks of the solution: Jesus must die. Jesus withdraws from public life to a country town while the officials look for an opportunity to arrest him.

Reflect: The officials seem more interested in protecting their own position and privileges than to accept the liberating message of Jesus. Does this still happen today? How? Jesus does die for the sake of the people. Have some followers of Jesus done the same thing as Jesus?

Pray: Believers should strive more for others than for themselves. Pray for sincerity and humility to accept your own life, and the necessary strength to care for the common good, the good of others.

Act: Stand up against corrupt religious and civil leaders who are interested only in protecting and maintaining their own power.

The supper at Bethany
(Mt 26:6; Mk 14:3)

12 [1]Six days before the Passover, Jesus came to Bethany, where he had raised Lazarus, the dead man, to life. [2]Now they gave a dinner for him and while Martha waited on them, Lazarus sat at the table with Jesus.

[3]Then Mary took a pound of costly perfume made from genuine spikenard and anointed the feet of Jesus, wiping them with her hair. And the whole house was filled with the fragrance of the perfume.

[4]Judas Iscariot—the disciple who was to betray Jesus—remarked, [5]"This perfume could have been sold for three hundred silver coins and

the money given to the poor." [6] Judas, indeed, had no concern for the poor; he was a thief and as he held the common purse, he used to help himself to the funds.

[7] But Jesus spoke up, "Leave her alone. Was she not keeping it for the day of my burial? [8] (The poor you always have with you, but you will not always have me.)"

[9] Many Jews heard that Jesus was there and they came, not only because of Jesus, but also to see Lazarus whom he had raised from the dead. [10] So the chief priests thought about killing Lazarus as well, [11] for many of the Jews were drifting away because of him and believing in Jesus.

The Messiah enters Jerusalem
(Mt 21:5; Mk 11:1)

[12] The next day, many people who had come for the festival heard that Jesus was to enter Jerusalem. [13] So they took branches of palm trees and went out to meet him. And they cried out, "Hosanna! Blessed is he who comes in the name of the Lord! Blessed is the king of Israel!"

[14] Jesus found a donkey and sat upon it, as Scripture says: [15] *Do not fear, city of Zion! See, your king is coming, sitting on the colt of a donkey!*

[16] The disciples were not aware of this at first, but after Jesus was glorified, they realized that this had been written about him and that this was what had happened to him.

[17] The people who came with him bore witness and told how he had called Lazarus out of the tomb and raised him from the dead. [18] It was because of this miraculous sign, which Jesus had given, that so many people welcomed him. [19] In the meantime, the Pharisees said to one another, "We are getting nowhere; the whole world has gone after him."

Unless the grain dies

[20] There were some Greeks who had come up to Jerusalem to worship during the feast. [21] They approached Philip, who was from Bethsaida in Galilee, and asked him, "Sir, we wish to see Jesus." [22] Philip went to Andrew and the two of them told Jesus.

[23] Then Jesus said, "The hour has come for the Son of Man to be glorified. [24] Truly, I say to you, unless the grain of wheat falls to the earth and dies, it remains alone; but if it dies, it produces much fruit.

²⁵ Those who love their life destroy it and those who despise their life in this world save it even to everlasting life.

²⁶ Whoever wants to serve me, let him follow me; and wherever I am, there shall my servant be also. If anyone serves me, the Father will honor him.

²⁷ Now my soul is in distress. Shall I say, 'Father, save me from this hour'? But, to face all this, I have come to this hour. ²⁸ Father, glorify your name!" Then a voice came from heaven, "I have glorified it, and I will glorify it again."

²⁹ People standing there heard something and said it was thunder; but others said, "An angel was speaking to him." ³⁰ Then Jesus declared, "This voice did not come for my sake but for yours. ³¹ Now sentence is being passed on this world; now the prince of this world is to be cast down. ³² And when I am lifted up from the earth, I shall draw all people to myself." ³³ With these words, Jesus referred to the kind of death he was to die.

³⁴ The crowd answered him, "We have been told in the law that the Messiah stands forever. How can you say that the Son of Man shall be lifted up? What kind of Son of Man is that?"

³⁵ Jesus said to them, "The light will be with you a little longer. Walk while you have the light, lest the darkness overtakes you. If you walk in the darkness, you do not know where you are going. ³⁶ While you have the light, believe in the light and become children of light."

After Jesus had said this, he withdrew and kept himself hidden.

The unbelief of the Jews

³⁷ Even though Jesus had done so many miraculous signs among them, they didn't believe in him. ³⁸ Indeed the words spoken by the prophet Isaiah had to be fulfilled: *Lord, who has believed what we proclaimed? To whom have the ways of God the Savior been made known?*

³⁹ They could not believe. Isaiah had said elsewhere: ⁴⁰ *He let their eyes become blind and their hearts hard, so that they could neither see nor understand, nor be converted—otherwise, I would have healed them.* ⁴¹ Isaiah said this when he saw his glory and his words refer to him.

⁴² Many of them, however, believed in Jesus, even among the rulers, but they did not acknowledge him because of the Pharisees, lest they be put out of the Jewish community. ⁴³ They preferred the favorable opinion of people, rather than God's approval.

[44] Yet Jesus had said and even cried out, "Whoever believes in me, believes not in me, but in him who sent me. [45] And whoever sees me, sees him who sent me. [46] I have come into the world as light so that whoever believes in me may not remain in darkness.

[47] If anyone hears my words and does not keep them, I am not the one to condemn him; for I have come, not to condemn the world, but to save the world. [48] The one who rejects me and does not receive my words already has a judge: the very words I have spoken will condemn him on the last day.

[49] For I have not spoken on my own authority; the Father, who sent me, has instructed me what to say and how to speak. [50] I know that his commandment is eternal life and that is why the message I give, I give as the Father instructed me."

JOHN 12:1-50

Read: This chapter bridges the gap between the "book of signs (2–12) and the "book of passion or glory" (13–21). It highlights the following idea: in the following of Jesus, surrender (death) is the way to life. "If the grain of fallen wheat does not die, it remains alone; but if it dies, it bears much fruit."

Reflect: Why is Judas so worried? Do you think that Christians care much about money rather than the announcement of the kingdom? Why? Is Jesus the human face of God for you? Why should the grain of wheat die? How does shed light on the death of Jesus? What is the relationship between dying to ourselves and giving life to others?

Pray: Pray that you learn to distinguish what is important from what is secondary. Ask the Lord for the grace to have a generous heart to serve and surrender (to die) to Christ and the brethren in your daily life.

Act: Trust in Jesus at all time, even in the face of adversity, and listen to and answer his call to serve him in those who approach you and ask for help.

SECOND PART:
JESUS COMPLETES HIS WORK

13 ¹It was before the feast of the Passover. Jesus realized that his hour had come to pass from this world to the Father; and as he had loved those who were his own in the world, he would love them with perfect love.

Jesus washes his disciples' feet

²They were at supper and the devil had already put into the mind of Judas, son of Simon Iscariot, to betray him. ³Jesus knew that the Father had entrusted all things to him and as he had come from God, he was going to God. ⁴So he got up from the table, removed his garment and taking a towel, wrapped it around his waist. ⁵Then he poured water into a basin and began to wash the disciples' feet and to wipe them with the towel he was wearing.

⁶When he came to Simon Peter, Simon asked him, "Why, *Lord*, do you want to wash my feet?" ⁷Jesus said, "What I am doing you cannot understand now, but afterward you will understand it." ⁸Peter replied, "You shall never wash my feet!"

Jesus answered him, "If I do not wash you, you can have no part with me." ⁹Then Simon Peter said, "*Lord*, wash not only my feet but also my hands and my head!"

¹⁰Jesus replied, "Whoever has taken a bath does not need to wash (except the feet), for he is clean all over. You are clean, though not all of you." ¹¹Jesus knew who was to betray him; because of this he said, "Not all of you are clean."

¹²When Jesus had finished washing their feet, he put on his garment again, went back to the table and said to them, "Do you understand what I have done to you? ¹³You call me Master and Lord, and you are right, for so I am. ¹⁴If I, then, your Lord and Master, have washed your feet, you also must wash one another's feet. ¹⁵I have given you an example, that as I have done, you also may do.

¹⁶Truly, I say to you, the servant is not greater than his master, nor is the messenger greater than he who sent him. ¹⁷Understand this, and blessed are you, if you put it into practice.

¹⁸I am not speaking of you all, because I know the ones I have chosen and the Scripture has to be fulfilled which says: The one who shares my

table will rise up against me. [19] I tell you this now before it happens, so that when it does happen, you may know that I am He.

[20] Truly, I say to you, whoever welcomes the one I send, welcomes me; and whoever welcomes me, welcomes the One who sent me."

[21] After saying this, Jesus was distressed in spirit, and said plainly, "Truly, one of you will betray me." [22] The disciples then looked at one another, wondering whom he meant. [23] One of the disciples, the one Jesus loved, was reclining near Jesus; [24] so Simon Peter signaled him to ask Jesus whom he meant.

[25] And the disciple, who was reclining near Jesus, asked him, "Lord, who is it?" [26] Jesus answered, "I shall dip a piece of bread in the dish and he to whom I give it, is the one."

So Jesus dipped the bread in the dish and gave it to Judas Iscariot, the son of Simon. [27] As Judas took the piece of bread, Satan entered into him. Jesus then said to him, "What you are going to do, do quickly."

[28] None of the others reclining at the table understood why Jesus had said this to Judas. [29] As Judas had the common purse, they may have thought that Jesus was telling him, "Buy what we need for the feast," or, "Give something to the poor." [30] Judas left as soon as he had eaten the bread. It was night.

[31] When Judas had gone out, Jesus said, "Now is the Son of Man glorified, and God is glorified in him. [32] God will glorify him, and he will glorify him very soon.

[33] My children, I am with you for only a little while; you will look for me, but as I already told the Jews, now I tell you: where I am going you cannot come. [34] I give you a new commandment: Love one another! Just as I have loved you, you also must love one another. [35] By this everyone will know that you are my disciples, if you have love for one another."

[36] Simon Peter said to him, "*Lord*, where are you going?" Jesus answered, "Where I am going you cannot follow me now, but afterward you will." [37] Peter said, "*Lord*, why can't I follow you now? I am ready to give my life for you." [38] "To give your life for me?" Jesus asked Peter. "Truly I tell you, the cock will not crow before you have denied me three times."

JOHN 13:1-38

Read: Jesus loves his own to the end of his life and to the end of the possibility of love. He washes their feet and tells them that unless they do the same, in a gesture of service, they have nothing to do with him. With the announcement of the betrayal of Judas and the cowardice of Peter the time of darkness begins.

Reflect: How great is the love of Jesus to his disciples? Does washing of the feet mean something in our contemporary culture? What does Jesus invite us to do? How do we make the commandment of love a reality in our daily life? What does darkness mean in the Gospel?

Pray: Ask the Lord the grace to persevere in the faith. Pray for all those who once believed and have abandoned belief, that with the example of Christians they may feel invited to come back again.

Act: Perform some humble service or favor for another, especially someone who is dear to you.

I'm going to the Father

14 [1] "Do not be troubled! Trust in God and trust in me! [2] In my Father's house there are many rooms; otherwise, I would not have told you that I go to prepare a place for you. [3] After I have gone and prepared a place for you, I shall come again and take you to me, so that where I am, you also may be. [4] Yet you know the way where I am going."

[5] Thomas said to him, "Lord, we don't know where you are going; how can we know the way?" [6] Jesus said, "I am the way, the truth, and the life; no one comes to the Father but through me. [7] If you know me, you will know the Father also; indeed you know him and you have seen him."

[8] Philip asked him, "Lord, show us the Father and that is enough." [9] Jesus said to him, "What! I have been with you so long and you still do not know me, Philip? Whoever sees me sees the Father; how can you say, 'Show us the Father'? [10] Do you not believe that I am in the Father and the Father is in me?

All that I say to you, I do not say of myself. The Father who dwells in me is doing his own work. [11] Believe me when I say that I am in the Father and the Father is in me; at least believe it on the evidence of these works that I do.

[12] Truly, I say to you, the one who believes in me will do the same works that I do; and he will even do greater than these, for I am going to the Father. [13] Everything you ask in my name, I will do, so that the Father may be glorified in the Son. [14] Indeed, anything you ask, calling upon my name, I will do it.

[15] If you love me, you will keep my commandments; [16] and I will ask the Father, and he will give you another Helper to be with you forever, [17] the Spirit of truth whom the world cannot receive because it neither sees him nor knows him. But you know him, for he is with you and will be in you.

[18] I will not leave you orphans, I am coming to you. [19] A little while and the world will see me no more, but you will see me because I live and you will also live. [20] On that day you will know that I am in my Father, and you in me and I in you.

[21] Whoever keeps my commandments is the one who loves me. If he loves me, he will also be loved by my Father; I too shall love him and show myself clearly to him."

[22] Judas—not Judas Iscariot—asked Jesus, "Lord, how can it be that you will show yourself clearly to us and not to the world?" [23] Jesus answered him, "If anyone loves me, he will keep my word and my Father will love him; and we will come to him and live with him. [24] But if anyone does not love me, he will not keep my words; and these words that you hear are not mine, but the Father's who sent me.

[25] I told you all this while I am still with you. [26] From now on the Helper, the Holy Spirit, whom the Father will send in my name, will teach you all things and remind you of all that I have told you.

[27] Peace be with you! My peace I give to you; not as the world gives peace do I give it to you. Do not be troubled! Do not be afraid! [28] You heard me say, 'I am going away, but I am coming to you.' If you loved me, you would be glad that I go to the Father for the Father is greater than I.

[29] I have told you this now before it takes place, so that when it does happen you may believe. [30] There is very little left for me to tell you for

the prince of this world is at hand, although there is nothing in me that he can claim. ³¹But see, the world must know that I love the Father and that I do what the Father has taught me to do. Come now, let us go.

JOHN 14:1-31

Read: Jesus is the way, the truth, and the life. Nobody goes to the Father unless through him. Jesus announces that his hour has come, the hour of his passion, but also promises the coming of the advocate, the Holy Spirit.

Reflect: Why is the crucifixion a sign of God's power and goodness? Is God present in every death, even in that which is cruel and painful? "Advocate" means "defender." Do you think of the Holy Spirit as your "advocate"?

Pray: Ask the Holy Spirit to accompany you at all times and to assist you in particular in difficulties or decision-making situations.

Act: The Holy Spirit leads everyone to the fullness of truth. Encourage those around you to find truth by listening to the Holy Spirit.

The vine and the branches

15 ¹I am the true vine and my Father is the vine grower. ²If any of my branches doesn't *bear fruit*, he breaks it off; and he prunes every branch that does *bear fruit*, that it may bear even *more fruit*.

³You are already made clean by the word I have spoken to you. ⁴Live in me as I live in you. The branch cannot *bear fruit* by itself, but has to remain part of the vine; so neither can you if you don't remain in me.

⁵I am the vine and you are the branches. As long as you remain in me and I in you, you *bear much fruit*; but apart from me, you can do nothing. ⁶Whoever does not remain in me is thrown away as they do with branches and they wither. Then they are gathered and thrown into the fire and burned.

⁷If you remain in me and my words remain in you, you may ask whatever you want and it will be given to you. ⁸My Father is glorified when you *bear much fruit*: it is then that you become my disciples.

⁹As the Father has loved me, so I have loved you. Remain in my love! ¹⁰You will remain in my love if you keep my commandments, just as I have kept my Father's commandments and remain in his love.

¹¹I have told you all this that my own joy may be in you, and your joy may be complete. ¹²This is my commandment: Love one another as I have loved you! ¹³There is no greater love than this, to give one's life for one's friends; ¹⁴and you are my friends if you do what I command you.

¹⁵I shall not call you servants anymore, because servants do not know what their master is about. Instead, I have called you friends, since I have made known to you everything I learned from my Father.

¹⁶You did not choose me; it was I who chose you and sent you to go and *bear fruit*, fruit that will last. And everything you ask the Father in my name, he will give you.

¹⁷This is my command, that you love one another.

The hostile world

¹⁸If the world *hates* you, remember that the world *hated* me before you. ¹⁹This would not be so if you belonged to the world because the world loves its own. But you are not of the world since I have chosen you from the world; because of this, the world *hates* you.

²⁰Remember what I told you: the servant is not greater than his master; if they persecuted me, they will also persecute you. If they kept my word, they will keep yours as well. ²¹All this they will do to you on account of my name because they do not know the One who sent me.

²²If I had not come and spoken to them, they would have no sin, but now they have no excuse for their sin. ²³Those who *hate* me *hate* my Father.

²⁴If I had not done among them what no one else has ever done, they would have no sin. But after they have seen all this, they hate me and my Father ²⁵and the words written in their law become true: *They hated me for no reason.*

JOHN 15:1-25
Read: This chapter stresses the connections created by love. Using the image of a grape vine, disciples must remain with

Jesus and bear much fruit and must take care of each other. They are friends of Jesus and they are friends to each other. They will have problems in the world, but they have the promise of the Holy Spirit who will defend them at all times.

Reflect: The disciples are called to love each other, to love the members of the community. How do you put into practice this commandment? How should it be done within the parish community?

Pray: Pray for the ability to be sensitive to those members of your community who need your help.

Act: Be a volunteer in any ministry in your parish that is serving the poorest ones and invite somebody from your family to come along with you.

The Spirit will come

²⁶ From the Father, I will send you the Spirit of truth. When this Helper has come from the Father, he will be my witness ²⁷ and you, too, will be my witnesses, for you have been with me from the beginning.

16 ¹ I tell you all this to keep you from stumbling and falling away. ² They will put you out of the synagogue. Still more, the hour is coming when anyone who kills you will claim to be serving God; ³ they will do this because they have not known the Father or me. ⁴ I tell you all these things now so that when the time comes, you may remember that I told you about them.

I did not tell you about this in the beginning because I was with you. ⁵ But now I am going to the One who sent me and none of you asks me where I am going; ⁶ instead you are overcome with grief, because of what I have said.

⁷ Believe me, it is better for you that I go away because as long as I do not go away the Helper will not come to you. But if I go away, I will send him to you ⁸ and when he comes he will vindicate the truth before a sinful world; and he will vindicate the paths of righteousness and justice.

⁹ What is the world's sin in regard to me? Disbelief. ¹⁰ What is the path of righteousness? It is the path I walk by which I go to the Father, and

you shall see me no more. [11] What is the path of justice? It is the path on which the prince of this world will always stand condemned.

[12] I still have many things to tell you, but you cannot bear them now. [13] When he, the Spirit of truth comes, he will guide you into the whole truth.

For he will not speak of his own authority but will speak of what he hears, and he will tell you about the things which are to come. [14] He will take what is mine and make it known to you; in doing this he will glorify me. [15] All that the Father has is mine; for this reason, I told you that the Spirit will take what is mine and make it known to you.

The promise of a new presence

[16] A little while and you will see me no more; and then a little while and you will see me."

[17] Some of the disciples wondered, "What does he mean by, 'A little while and you will not see me; and then a little while and you will see me'? And why did he say, 'I go to the Father'?" [18] And they said to one another, "What does he mean by 'a little while'? We don't understand."

[19] Jesus knew that they wanted to question him; so he said to them, "You are puzzled because I told you that in a little while you will see me no more and then a little while later you will see me.

[20] Truly, I say to you, you will weep and mourn while the world rejoices. You will be sorrowful, but your sorrow will turn to joy. [21] A woman in childbirth is in distress because her time is at hand. But after the child is born, she no longer remembers her suffering because of her great joy: a human being is born into the world.

[22] You feel sorrowful now, but I will see you again and your hearts will rejoice; and no one will take your joy from you. [23] When that day comes you will not ask me anything. Truly, I say to you, whatever you ask the Father in my name, he will give you. [24] So far you have not asked for anything in my name; ask and receive, that your joy may be full.

[25] I have taught you all these things in veiled language, but the time is coming when I shall no longer speak in veiled language but will speak to you plainly about the Father.

[26] When that day comes, you will ask in my name; and it will not be necessary for me to ask the Father for you, [27] for the Father himself loves you, because you have loved me and you believed that I came from the

Father. ²⁸ As I came from the Father and have come into the world, so I am leaving the world and going to the Father."

²⁹ The disciples said to him, "Now you are speaking plainly and not in veiled language! ³⁰ Now we see that you know all things even before we question you. Because of this, we believe that you came from God."

³¹ Jesus answered them, "You say that you believe? ³² The hour is coming, indeed it has come, when you will be scattered, each one to his home, and you will leave me alone. Yet I am not alone, for the Father is with me.

³³ I have told you all this, so that in me you may have peace. You will have trouble in the world, but courage! I have overcome the world."

JOHN 15:26—16:33

Read: The disciples will suffer persecution. The Advocate, the Helper, will speak the truth to the world regarding sin, justice, and condemnation. He will speak the truth with authority. The disciples will experience sadness, but their sadness will become joy. Jesus will return to the Father, but he will never abandon them. As he has conquered the world, the disciples will always have reason to be joyful.

Reflect: How does the Holy Spirit speak to the world regarding sin, justice, and condemnation today? Does the Holy Spirit speak to you? Do you listen to the Holy Spirit? Can you overcome the world with your good deeds? Do you have peace in your heart?

Pray: When you have problems, or feel down for the bad things happening to you, remember in your prayer the blessings you have received and thank God for them.

Act: Speak to someone about the Holy Spirit and explain what the Holy Spirit means to you.

Prayer of Jesus for the new holy people

17 ¹ After saying this, Jesus lifted up his eyes to heaven and said, "Father, the hour has come! Give glory to your Son that the Son may give glory to you. ² You have given him power over all humanity, so that he may give eternal life to all those you entrusted to him. ³For this is eternal life: to *know* you the only true God and the One you sent, Jesus Christ.

⁴I have glorified you on earth and finished the work that you gave me to do. ⁵Now, Father, give me in your presence the same glory I had with you before the world began.

⁶I have made your name known to those you gave me from the world. They were yours, and you gave them to me and they kept your word. ⁷And now they know that whatever you entrusted to me, is indeed from you. ⁸I have given them the teaching I received from you and they accepted it and know in truth that I came from you, and they believe that you sent me.

⁹I pray for them. I do not pray for the world, but for those who belong to you and whom you have given to me. ¹⁰Indeed, all I have is yours and all you have is mine; and now they are my glory. ¹¹I am no longer in the world, but they are in the world, and I come to you. Holy Father, keep those you have given me in your name, so that they may be one as we also are.

¹²When I was with them, I kept them safe in your name; and not one was lost, except the one who was already lost and in this the Scripture was fulfilled. ¹³And now I come to you; in the world I speak these things, so that those whom you gave me might have joy—all my joy within themselves.

¹⁴I have given them your word; and the world has hated them because they are not of the world, just as I am not of the world. ¹⁵I do not ask you to remove them from the world, but to keep them from the evil one. ¹⁶They are not of the world, just as I am not of the world. ¹⁷Consecrate them in the truth. Your word is truth.

¹⁸I have sent them into the world as you sent me into the world; ¹⁹and for their sake, I go to the sacrifice by which I am consecrated, so that they too may be consecrated in truth.

²⁰I pray not only for these but also for those who through their word will believe in me. ²¹May they all be one as you, Father are in me and I am in you. May they be one in us, so that the world may believe that you have sent me.

²²I have given them the glory you have given me, that they may be one as we are one: ²³I in them and you in me. Thus, they shall reach

perfection in unity; and the world shall know that you have sent me and that I have loved them just as you loved me.

²⁴ Father, since you have given them to me, I want them to be with me where I am and see the glory you gave me, for you loved me before the foundation of the world.

²⁵ Righteous Father, the world has not *known* you, but I have *known* you, and these have *known* that you have sent me. ²⁶ As I revealed your name to them, so will I continue to reveal it so that the love with which you loved me may be in them and I also may be in them."

JOHN 17:1-26

Read: This priestly prayer of Jesus applies to all believers. Eternal life, life with God, begins now with Jesus. Jesus reveals his Father to his followers and asks the Father to protect them and love them. Jesus sends them into the world even as the Father sent Jesus. Jesus prays that the love with which God loved him, may also be in his followers. Thus, he completed his mission. His followers must do the same and seek holiness.

Reflect: The follower is sanctified in the truth and has the mission of helping others to sanctify themselves. What does holiness mean to you? Are you holy? Jesus manifests the love of God to the whole world. His disciples continue his mission. How do you live the mission of Jesus?

Pray: Holiness is being close to God. Pray often. Use the prayer of Jesus: "Jesus, Son of God, have mercy on me."

Act: At night, before sleeping, may your last words be the prayer of Jesus.

The arrest of Jesus

18 ¹ When Jesus had finished speaking, he went with his disciples to the other side of the Kidron Valley. There was a garden there, which Jesus entered with his disciples.

² Now Judas, who betrayed him, knew the place since Jesus had often met there with his disciples. ³ So Judas took soldiers and some servants from the chief priests and Pharisees and they went to the garden with lanterns, torches, and weapons.

⁴ Jesus knew all that was going to happen to him; he stepped forward and asked, "Who are you looking for?" ⁵ They answered, "Jesus the Nazarene." Jesus said, "I am he." Judas, who betrayed him, stood there with them.

⁶ When Jesus said, "I am he," they moved backwards and fell to the ground. ⁷ He then asked a second time, "Who are you looking for?" and they answered, "Jesus the Nazarene." ⁸ Jesus replied, "I told you that I am he. If you are looking for me, let these others go." ⁹ So what Jesus had said came true: "I have not lost one of those you gave me."

¹⁰ Simon Peter had a sword; he drew it and struck Malchus, the High Priest's servant, cutting off his right ear. ¹¹ But Jesus said to Peter, "Put your sword into its sheath! Shall I not drink the cup which the Father has given me?"

¹² The guards and the soldiers, with their commander, seized Jesus and bound him; ¹³ and they took him first to Annas. Annas was the father-in-law of Caiaphas, who was the High Priest that year; ¹⁴ and it was Caiaphas who had told the Jews, "It is better that one man should die for the people."

¹⁵ Simon Peter and another disciple followed Jesus. Because this disciple was known to the High Priest, they let him enter the courtyard of the High Priest along with Jesus, ¹⁶ but Peter had to stay outside at the door. The other disciple, who was known to the High Priest, went out and spoke to the maidservant at the gate and brought Peter in. ¹⁷ Then, this maidservant on duty at the door said to Peter, "So you also are one of his disciples?" But he answered, "I am not."

¹⁸ Now the servants and the guards had made a charcoal fire and were standing and warming themselves because it was cold. Peter was also with them warming himself.

¹⁹ The High Priest questioned Jesus about his disciples and his teaching. ²⁰ Jesus answered him, "I have spoken openly to the world; I have always taught in places where the Jews meet together, either at the assemblies in synagogues or in the temple. I did not teach secretly. ²¹ Why then do you question me? Ask those who heard me, they know what I said."

²² At this reply one of the guards standing there gave Jesus a blow on the face, saying, "Is that the way to answer the High Priest?" ²³ Jesus

said to him, "If I have said something wrong, point it out. But if I spoke correctly, why strike me?"

²⁴ Then Annas sent him, bound, to Caiaphas, the High Priest.

²⁵ Now Simon Peter stood there warming himself. They said to him, "Surely you also are one of his disciples." He denied it, and answered, "I am not!" ²⁶ One of the High Priest's servants, a kinsman of the one whose ear Peter had cut off, asked, "Did I not see you with him in the garden?" ²⁷ Again Peter denied it, and at once the cock crowed.

JOHN 18:1-27

Read: Even when arrested, Jesus seems to be in control of the situation at all times. His answer, "I am," causes the fall of his pursuers and even Annas does not know how to answer the assertive words of Jesus. While Jesus asserts himself even when abused, Peter lies and betrays Jesus and himself.

Reflect: Jesus cares for his disciples and acts with authority. Peter is weak. The rock becomes a pebble. Love and commitment demand perseverance, renewal, and care. How do you renew and care for your faith, love, and hope in the Lord?

Pray: The temptation can be strong. Sometimes the concern for the preservation of life itself can overcome commitment. Pray for your perseverance in the midst of problems.

Act: Jesus has conquered the world. When you find yourself in a difficult situation or in a situation that you cannot control, follow the example of freedom of Jesus and take the correct decision or position, even if it is unpopular.

Jesus before Pilate

²⁸ Then they led Jesus from the house of Caiaphas to the headquarters of the Roman governor. It was now morning. The Jews didn't go inside, lest they be made unclean by entering the house of a pagan and therefore not allowed to eat the Passover meal. ²⁹ So Pilate came outside and asked, "What charge do you bring against this man?"

³⁰ They answered, "If he were not a criminal, we would not be handing him over to you." ³¹ Pilate said, "Take him yourselves and judge him

according to your own law." But they replied, "We ourselves are not allowed to put anyone to death."

³² According to what Jesus himself had foretold, it was clear what kind of death he would die.

³³ Pilate then entered the court again, summoned Jesus and asked him, "Are you the King of the Jews?" ³⁴ Jesus replied, "Are you saying this on your own initiative; or have others told you about me?"

³⁵ Pilate answered, "Am I a Jew? Your own nation and the chief priests have handed you over to me. What have you done?" ³⁶ Jesus answered, "My kingship does not come from this world. If I were a king like those of this world, my servants would have fought to save me from being handed over to the Jews. But my kingship is not of this world."

³⁷ Pilate asked him, "So you are a king?" And Jesus answered, "Just as you say, I am a king. For this, I was born and for this I have come into the world, to bear witness to the truth. Everyone who is on the side of truth hears my voice." ³⁸ Pilate said, "What is truth?"

Pilate then went out to the Jews again and said, "I find no crime in this man. ³⁹ Now, according to custom, I must release a prisoner to you at the Passover. With your agreement, I will release to you the King of the Jews." ⁴⁰ But they insisted and cried out, "Not this man, but Barabbas!" Now Barabbas was a robber.

19 ¹ Then Pilate had Jesus taken away and scourged. ² The soldiers twisted thorns into a crown and put it on his head. They threw a cloak of royal purple around his shoulders; ³ and they began coming up to him and saluting him, "Hail, King of the Jews!" and they struck him on the face.

⁴ Pilate went outside yet another time and said to the Jews, "Look, I am bringing him out and I want you to know that I find no crime in him." ⁵ Jesus then came out wearing the crown of thorns and the purple cloak, and Pilate pointed at him, saying, "Behold the man!"

⁶ On seeing him the chief priests and the guards cried out, "Crucify him! Crucify him!" Pilate said, "Take him yourselves and have him crucified for I find no case against him." ⁷ The Jews then said, "We have a law, and according to the law this man must die because he made himself Son of God."

⁸ When Pilate heard this he was more afraid. ⁹ And coming back into

the court he asked Jesus, "Where are you from?" But Jesus gave him no answer. [10]Then Pilate said to him, "You will not speak to me? Do you not know that I have power to release you, just as I have power to crucify you?" [11]Jesus replied, "You would have no power over me unless it had been given to you from above; therefore the one who handed me over to you is more guilty."

[12]From that moment Pilate tried to release him, but the Jews cried out, "If you release this man, you are no friend of Caesar. Anyone who makes himself a king is defying Caesar."

[13]When Pilate heard this, he had Jesus brought outside to the place called the Stone Floor—in Hebrew Gabbatha—and sat down in the judgment seat. [14]It was the day of preparation for the Passover, about noon. Pilate said to the Jews, "Behold your king!" [15]But they cried out, "Away! Take him away! Crucify him!" Pilate replied, "Shall I crucify your king?" And the chief priests answered, "We have no king but Caesar!"

[16]Then Pilate handed Jesus over to them to be crucified.

JOHN 18:28—19:16a

Read: The trial by Pilate has seven scenes. Pilate continues to go in and out of the praetorium speaking to Jesus and to the Jews. He does not want to crucify Jesus but is weak and tries to placate the crowds. He seems curious about who Jesus is; it is just curiosity and so he does not understand him.

Reflect: Who is really on trial, Pilate or Jesus? This Gospel seems to assume that Jesus is the judge, Pilate is the witness to Jesus' innocence and the crowd is the criminal seeking to put to death the innocent. In the end, Pilate gives into the crowd's demands. Who is responsible for the death of Jesus?

Pray: Pray for persons who, like Jesus, are victims of injustice, the mishandling of power, envy. Ask that these people's faces and words may question us as Christians.

Act: Avoid any slight judgment on others, and check your prejudices, especially if they are prejudices against prisoners or marginalized people.

Jesus is crucified

They took Jesus and led him away. [17] Bearing his cross, Jesus went out of the city to what is called the Place of the Skull, in Hebrew Golgotha. [18] There he was crucified and with him two others, one on either side, and Jesus in the middle.

[19] Pilate had a notice written and fastened to the cross, which read: *Jesus the Nazarene, the King of the Jews.* [20] Many Jewish people saw this title because the place where Jesus was crucified was very close to the city; and the title was written in Hebrew, Latin, and Greek. [21] The chief priests said to Pilate, "Do not write 'The King of the Jews' but, 'This man claimed to be King of the Jews.'" [22] Pilate answered them, "What I have written, I have written."

[23] When the soldiers crucified Jesus, they took his clothes and divided them into four parts, one part for each of them. But as the tunic was woven in one piece from top to bottom, [24] they said, "Let us not tear it, but cast lots to decide who will get it." This fulfilled the words of Scripture: *They divided my clothing among them; they cast lots for my garment. This was what the soldiers did.*

Jesus' last words

[25] Near the cross of Jesus stood his mother, his mother's sister, Mary, who was the wife of Cleophas, and Mary of Magdala. [26] When Jesus saw the mother and the disciple whom he loved, he said to the mother, "Woman, this is your son." [27] Then he said to the disciple, "This is your mother." And from that moment the disciple took her to his own home.

[28] Jesus knew all was now finished and, in order to fulfill what was written in Scripture, he said, I am thirsty. [29] A jar full of bitter wine stood there; so, putting a sponge soaked in the wine on a twig of hyssop, they raised it to his lips. [30] Jesus took the wine and said, "It is accomplished." Then he bowed his head and gave up the spirit.

The pierced Christ

[31] As it was Preparation Day, the Jews did not want the bodies to remain on the cross during the Sabbath, for this Sabbath was a very solemn day. They asked Pilate to have the legs of the condemned men broken so that the bodies might be taken away.

[32] The soldiers came and broke the legs of the first man and of the

other man, who had been crucified with Jesus. [33]When they came to Jesus, they saw that he was already dead, so they did not break his legs. [34]One of the soldiers, however, pierced his side with a lance and immediately there came out blood and water.

[35]The one who saw that has testified to it and his testimony is true; he knows he speaks the truth so that you also might believe. [36]All this happened to fulfill the words of Scripture: *Not one of his bones shall be broken.* [37]Another text says: *They shall look on him whom they have pierced.*

[38]After this, Joseph of Arimathea approached Pilate for he was a disciple of Jesus, though secretly, for fear of the Jews. And he asked Pilate to let him remove the body of Jesus. Pilate agreed; so he came and took away the body.

[39]Nicodemus, the man who first visited Jesus by night, also came and brought a jar of myrrh mixed with aloes, about seventy-five pounds. [40]They took the body of Jesus and wrapped it in linen cloths with the spices, following the burial customs of the Jews.

[41]There was a garden in the place where Jesus had been crucified and, in the garden, a new tomb in which no one had ever been laid. [42]And therefore, because the sepulcher was nearby, and the Jewish day of preparation was coming to a close, they placed the body of Jesus there.

JOHN 19:16b-42

Read: Romans crucify Jesus. On the cross, he delivers the beloved disciple to his mother, and her mother to the beloved disciple. Before he dies, he bows his head and hands over his Spirit. Joseph of Arimathea and Nicodemus bury his body.

Reflect: What does the death of Jesus mean? Some hold that when Jesus gives up his Spirit, the Church is born of water from his body and the Spirit he shares with God. What do you think? Why was Nicodemus there? Did he come to be a believer?

Pray: The Church filled with the Spirit continues the mission of Jesus. Pray for the Church leaders that with their life and preaching they may promote the mission of Jesus: the kingdom of God. Pray that the people who are the Church live the love of Christ in the world.

> **Act:** Faith and holiness manifest in what we do for others. Express your faith in action in favor of a person you do not know.

The Lord is risen

20 ¹Now, on the first day after the Sabbath, Mary of Magdala came to the tomb early in the morning while it was still dark and she saw that the stone blocking the tomb had been moved away. ²She ran to Peter, and the other disciple whom Jesus loved, and she said to them, "They have taken the *Lord* out of the tomb and we don't know where they have laid him."

³Peter then set out with the other disciple to go to the tomb. ⁴They ran together, but the other disciple outran Peter and reached the tomb first. ⁵He bent down and saw the linen cloths lying flat, but he did not enter.

⁶Then Simon Peter came, following him and entered the tomb; he, too, saw the linen cloths lying flat. ⁷The napkin, which had been around his head, was not lying flat like the other linen cloths but lay rolled up in its place. ⁸Then the other disciple, who had reached the tomb first, also went in; he saw and believed. ⁹Scripture clearly said that Jesus must rise from the dead, but they had not yet understood that.

¹⁰The disciples went back to their homes.

¹¹Mary stood weeping outside the tomb; and as she wept, she bent down to look inside. ¹²She saw two angels in white sitting where the body of Jesus had been, one at the head and the other at the feet. ¹³They said, "Woman, why are you weeping?" She answered, "Because they have taken my *Lord* and I don't know where they have put him."

¹⁴As she said this, she turned around and saw Jesus standing there, but she did not recognize him. ¹⁵Jesus said to her, "Woman, why are you weeping? Who are you looking for?" She thought it was the gardener and answered him, "Sir, if you have taken him away, tell me where you have put him and I will go and take him away."

¹⁶Jesus said to her, "Mary!" She turned and said to him, "Rabboni!"— which means *Master.* ¹⁷Jesus said to her, "Do not touch me, because I have not yet ascended to the Father. But go to my brothers and say to

them: I am ascending to my Father, who is your Father, to my God, who is your God."

¹⁸ So Mary of Magdala went and announced to the disciples, "I have seen the *Lord* and this is what he said to me."

¹⁹ On the evening of that day, the first day after the Sabbath, the doors were locked where the disciples were, because of their fear of the Jews. But Jesus came and stood among them and said to them, "Peace be with you!" ²⁰ Then he showed them his hands and his side. The disciples, seeing the *Lord*, were full of joy.

²¹ Again Jesus said to them, "Peace be with you! As the Father has sent me, so I send you." ²² After saying this, he breathed on them and said to them, "Receive the Holy Spirit! ²³ Those whose sins you forgive, they are forgiven; those whose sins you retain, they are retained."

²⁴ Thomas, the Twin, one of the Twelve, was not with them when Jesus came. ²⁵ The other disciples told him, "We have seen the *Lord*." But he replied, "Until I have seen in his hands the print of the nails, and put my finger in the mark of the nails and my hand in his side, I will not believe."

²⁶ Eight days later, the disciples were again inside the house and Thomas was with them. Although the doors were locked, Jesus came and stood in their midst and said, "Peace be with you!" ²⁷ Then he said to Thomas, "Put your finger here and see my hands; stretch out your hand, and put it into my side. Do not continue in your unbelief, but believe!"

²⁸ Thomas said, "You are my *Lord* and my God." ²⁹ Jesus replied, "You believe because you see me, don't you? Happy are those who have not seen and yet have come to believe."

Conclusion

³⁰ There were many other signs that Jesus gave in the presence of his disciples, but they are not recorded in this book. ³¹ These are recorded, so that you may believe that Jesus is the Christ, the Son of God. Believe, and you will have life through his name!

JOHN 20:1-31

Read: Mary Magdalene finds the tomb empty. The Beloved Disciple is the first to believe. Mary recognizes Jesus when he calls her by her name. Jesus appears to the disciples twice. Thomas, seeing the traces of the suffering of Jesus, also believes. Jesus blesses all those who never seeing or touching him come to believe in him. The writer of the Gospel says this book was written so the reader might come to believe in Jesus and share his eternal life.

Reflect: What relationship did Jesus and Magdalene have? Peter and the beloved disciple? What does it mean to you that Jesus is alive? Do you also have doubts like Thomas? Do you need to see to believe? What does the following expression suggest to you: "Happy those who believe without having seen"?

Pray: Faith, like life itself, requires constant care. Ask the Lord the grace of deepening your experience of faith. The beloved disciple saw the bandages and believed. Pray for the people who struggle to preserve their faith in the midst of situations of death, neglect or persecution.

Act: Celebrate the resurrection of Jesus by participating and collaborating in some Easter activity in your parish.

Appendix: the appearance of Jesus by the lake

21 [1] After this, Jesus revealed himself to the disciples by the Lake of Tiberias. He appeared to them in this way: [2] Simon Peter, Thomas who was called the Twin, Nathanael of Cana in Galilee, the sons of Zebedee and two other disciples were together; [3] and Simon Peter said to them, "I'm going fishing." They replied, "We will come with you." And they went out and got into the boat, but that night they caught nothing.

[4] When the sun came up, Jesus was standing on the shore, but the disciples did not know that it was Jesus. [5] Jesus called out, "Friends, have you anything to eat?" They answered, "Nothing." [6] Then he said to them, "Throw the net on the right side of the boat and you will find something." When they had lowered the net, they were not able to pull it in because of the great number of fish.

[7] Then the disciple Jesus loved said to Peter, "It's the Lord!" At these words, "It's the Lord!" Simon Peter put on his clothes, for he was stripped for work, and jumped into the water. [8] The other disciples came in the boat, dragging the net full of fish; they were not far from land, about a hundred meters.

⁹When they landed, they saw a charcoal fire with fish on it and some bread. ¹⁰Jesus said to them, "Bring some of the fish you've just caught." ¹¹So Simon Peter climbed into the boat and pulled the net to shore. It was full of big fish—one hundred and fifty-three—but, in spite of this, the net was not torn.

¹²Jesus said to them, "Come and have breakfast." And not one of the disciples dared to ask him, "Who are you?" for they knew it was the Lord. ¹³Jesus came and took the bread and gave it to them and he did the same with the fish.

¹⁴This was the third time that Jesus revealed himself to his disciples after rising from the dead.

JOHN 21:1-14

Read: This chapter begins with the appearance of Jesus by the lake. The disciples are fishing but catch nothing. However, when they pay attention to Jesus words, they catch more than they can imagine. The beloved disciple recognizes him, and Peter, then, acts with impetuosity. The story ends with Jesus making breakfast, once more feeding his disciples.

Reflect: What image do you have of Peter in all this gospel? What things characterize him? Can you identify with him?

Pray: Ask the Lord for grace so that you can trust in his Word. So that, like Peter, be ready to go to encounter him and available at the service of the community.

Act: Invite your neighbors to a meal and feel the presence of the risen Jesus in them.

---

¹⁵After they had finished breakfast, Jesus said to Simon Peter, "Simon, son of John, do you love me more than these do?" He answered, "Yes, Lord, you know that I love you." And Jesus said, "Feed my lambs."

¹⁶A second time Jesus said to him, "Simon, son of John, do you love me?" And Peter answered, "Yes, Lord, you know that I love you." Jesus said to him, "Look after my sheep." ¹⁷And a third time he said to him, "Simon, son of John, do you love me?"

Peter was saddened because Jesus asked him a third time, "Do you love me?" and he said, "Lord, you know everything; you know that I love you."

Jesus then said, "Feed my sheep! [18]Truly, I say to you, when you were young, you put on your belt and walked where you liked. But when you grow old, you will stretch out your hands, and another will put a belt around you, and lead you where you do not wish to go."

[19]Jesus said this to make known the kind of death by which Peter was to glorify God. And he added, "Follow me!"

[20]Peter looked back and saw that the disciple Jesus loved was following as well, the one who had reclined close to Jesus at the supper and had asked him, "Lord, who is to betray you?" [21]On seeing him, Peter asked Jesus, "Lord, what about him?" [22]Jesus answered, "If I want him to remain until I come, is that any concern of yours? Follow me!"

[23]Because of this, the rumor spread in the community that this disciple would not die. Yet Jesus did not say to Peter, "He will not die," but, "Suppose I want him to remain until I come back, what concern is that of yours?"

[24]It is this disciple who testifies about the things and has written these things down, and we know that his testimony is true. [25]But Jesus did many other things; if all were written down, I think the world itself could not contain the books that should be written.

JOHN 21:15-25

Read: The final scene involves Jesus, Peter, and the Beloved Disciple. Peter makes his profession of love to the Lord and Jesus gives him the mission to care for his sheep. The Beloved Disciple is the one "testifying to these things and has written them, and we know that his testimony is true."

Reflect: What do the attitudes of Peter and the beloved disciple suggest? To what do they invite you? How do you witness the resurrection of the Lord in your family?

Pray: Pray for the leaders of the Church, so that with their life and preaching they may at all times give testimony of their love for Jesus and their faith in the resurrection and eternal life.

Act: Tell your friends the good things that Popes John XXIII, Paul VI, John Paul I, John Paul II, Benedict XVI, and Francis did in favor of the Church and the world. Give thanks to God for them.

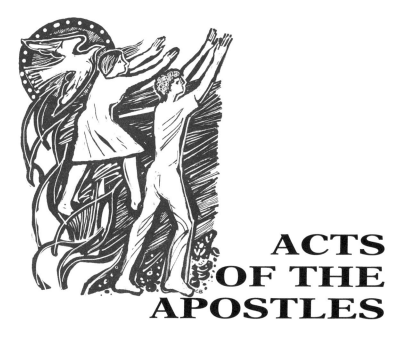

ACTS OF THE APOSTLES

During the three years of public life, Jesus set down the foundations of the Church: he gathered his first disciples and associated them with his mission (Mk 3:13-16). He put Peter in charge of the community (Mt 16:18) and made him the guardian of the faith (Lk 22:31) within the new People of God. He made the Twelve apostles and the disciples a community of witnesses (Jn 15:16) and promised them the gift of the Spirit who would help them come to know the fullness of the Light which Jesus came to bring into the world (Jn 16:13).

Now, the Lord is risen, and from the pierced side of Jesus, a new people, a new world is born, like the child coming to life in the blood and water flowing from its mother's womb (Jn 19:34). This Gospel community, enlightened by the word of Jesus, enlivened by his Spirit, sets out to announce God's marvelous deeds to the ends of the earth and to gather together in unity, the scattered children of God (Jn 11:52).

Two great giants stand out in this evangelization: Peter and Paul. Peter will devote himself in particular to the evangelization of the Jews, while Paul will become the apostle to the Gentiles (Gal 2:7-8).

Luke, the author of the third Gospel, writes about this nascent Church in the Book of Acts of the Apostles, which was probably first called Acts of Apostles. If, as in the case of the Gospels, earlier accounts of the Acts existed which Luke would have drawn upon to write his text, the harmony achieved in editing these various texts is indeed remarkable since it is very difficult to identify these different texts today.

Certain scholars believe that at the outset the Acts of the Apostles and the third Gospel were one and the same text that was only divided up later. One point is certain, however: by the beginning of the second century, the Acts of the Apostles was already a separate text. However, the testimony concerning the beginnings of the Church has come down to us in two different forms: the "current text," coinciding with the majority of ancient manuscripts of Syrian and Egyptian origin, and the said "Western text," which is longer and where the disputes between the Jews and the first Christians are more in evidence.

The Book of Acts does not follow a rigorous outline. One can, however, pick out some clear-cut divisions in the text which allow us to glimpse Luke's project. Without focusing exclusively on Peter and Paul, Luke devoted the greater part of his work to them. In spite of many exceptions, Peter dominates the first twelve chapters, while Paul dominates the second part of the book.

From the geographical point of view, one can notice that the Acts bring us from Jerusalem, through Judea and Samaria, to Rome, thus following the mission to which Jesus appointed his apostles on ascension day (Acts 1:8). In the first seven chapters we are in Jerusalem, then in Chapter 8 and those following, we see—of course, with some exceptions—the Church taking root in Judea, in Samaria, and along the coastal plain; from Chapter 13 onward, we accompany Paul to Asia Minor and to Greece and finally, in Chapter 28, to Rome, to the Palace of the Emperor, that is to say, to the heart of the pagan world.

There, the Book of Acts ends abruptly, as if Luke, like the runner whose job is to carry the Good News of salvation as it is spreading out from Jerusalem to the ends of the earth, has achieved his goal and thus fulfilled his contract. This in itself is sufficient to remind us that the Acts, no more than the Gospels, do not pretend to be a biography of Peter and Paul, or a detailed history of the early Church, but a testimony to the work of the Holy Spirit.

Indeed, the Holy Spirit is the veritable actor in the birth of the Church: this is the reason why many commentators, ever since the first Christian centuries, have not hesitated to call this book "The Gospel of the Holy Spirit." With only slight modification we could use here the words of John in Jn 20:30: "The Spirit has accomplished many other signs which have not been written of in this book. These have been recorded so that you may believe that the Spirit is at work in the Church of Jesus Christ."

Luke's intention in the Acts is to highlight, in particular through the diverse preaching of Peter and Paul, how the mystery of Christ and of the Church has been announced and prepared for in the Old Testament, but also how this double mystery—Christ and the Church—fulfills the Old Testament.

In this perspective, Luke readily highlights the parallels between Jesus and his Church, and also between the people of the Old Testament and the Church: by way of example, let us mention the parallels between the death of Stephen and that of Christ, between the journey to Jerusalem of Paul and that of Christ, but also the opposition between the Tower of Babel and Pentecost.

Continuing in this same line of inquiry, *Jerusalem* constantly flows from the pen of Luke (58 times). As he has done in his Gospel, where the Holy City is mentioned 30 times, Luke points to Jerusalem as the place where salvation is accomplished and from where the Good News is to be taken to all nations.

ACTS OF THE APOSTLES

Jesus taken up to heaven

1 [1] In the first part of my work, Theophilus, I wrote of all that Jesus did and taught from the beginning [2] until the day when he ascended to heaven.

But first, he had instructed, through the Holy Spirit the apostles he had chosen. [3] After his passion, he presented himself to them, giving many signs that he was alive; over a period of forty days he appeared to them and taught them concerning the kingdom of God. [4] Once, when he had been eating with them, he told them, "Do not leave Jerusalem, but wait for the fulfillment of the Father's promise about which I have spoken to you: [5] John baptized with water, but you will be baptized with the Holy Spirit within a few days."

[6] When they had come together, they asked him, "Is it now that you will restore the kingdom of Israel?" [7] And he answered, "It is not for you to know the time and the steps that the Father has fixed by his own authority. [8] But you will receive power when the Holy Spirit comes upon you; and you will be my witnesses in Jerusalem, throughout Judea and Samaria, even to the ends of the earth."

[9] After Jesus said this, he was taken up before their eyes and a cloud hid him from their sight. [10] While they were still looking up to heaven, where he went, suddenly, two men dressed in white stood beside them [11] and said, "Men of Galilee, why do you stand here looking up at the sky? This Jesus, who has been taken from you into heaven, will return in the same way as you have seen him go there."

ACTS 1:1-11

Read: Acts is a second volume, a continuation written by the author of the Gospel of Luke. The intended recipient is

"Theophilus," a name based on two Greek words, *theos* (God) and *philos* (love). For forty days, Jesus appeared to his followers before ascending to heaven. The mission of proclaiming the gospel continues after Jesus' ascension.

Reflect: When Jesus ascends into heaven he leaves a mission to each of his followers, everyone knows his Good News. How do you follow that mission? Are you encouraged to talk about Jesus with others?

Pray: Pray for courage to face the difficulties of the mission received. Also, pray for the willingness to deal with future uncertainties. Thank for the gift of the Holy Spirit who is always with us.

Act: Make a plan detailing how things should be amended for you to be a true disciple and missionary of Jesus Christ. Rely on the power of the Spirit and follow that plan.

The disciples await the Holy Spirit

[12] Then they returned to Jerusalem from the Mount called Olives, which is a fifteen-minute walk away. [13] On entering the city they went to the room upstairs where they were staying. Present there were Peter, John, James, and Andrew; Philip and Thomas, Bartholomew and Matthew, James, son of Alpheus; Simon the Zealot and Judas son of James. [14] They all met together and were constantly united in prayer. With them were some women, and also Mary, the mother of Jesus, and his brothers.

Matthias elected

[15] It was during this time that Peter stood up in the midst of the community—about one hundred and twenty in all—[16] and he said,

"Brothers, it was necessary that the Scriptures referring to Judas be fulfilled. The Holy Spirit had spoken through David about the one who would lead the crowd coming to arrest Jesus. [17] He was one of our number and had been called to share our common ministry.

[18] (We know that he bought a field with the reward of his sin; yet, he threw himself headlong to his death; his body burst open and all his bowels spilled out. [19] This event became known to all the people living in

Jerusalem and they named that field *Akeldama* in their own language, which means Field of Blood).

²⁰ In the Book of Psalms it is written: *Let his house become deserted and may no one live in it.* But it is also written: *May another take his office.* ²¹ Therefore, we must choose someone from among those who were with us during all the time that the Lord Jesus moved about with us, ²² beginning with John's baptism until the day when Jesus was taken away from us. One of these has to become with us a witness to his resurrection."

²³ Then they proposed two: Joseph, called Barsabbas, also known as Justus, and Matthias. ²⁴ They prayed: "You know, Lord, what is in the hearts of all. Show us, therefore, which of the two you have chosen ²⁵ to replace Judas in this apostolic ministry which he deserted to go to the place he deserved."

²⁶ Then they drew lots between the two and the choice fell on Matthias who was added to the eleven apostles.

ACTS 1:12-26

Read: The disciples remain united in prayer. Peter explains that because of the death of Judas, and as announced in the Scripture, it is necessary to replace him in the group of the apostles. After discernment, prayer and drawing lots, the apostles chose Matthias.

Reflect: See if your prayer is in communion with the Church and her community. When you pray, with whom do you feel intimately connected? Do you rely on the light of the Spirit when you need to make important decisions?

Pray: Pray in a way that prayer unites you with God and your neighbor. Rely on the help of the Holy Spirit in your life.

Act: Renew your commitment to pray every day and be a disciple and missionary of Jesus Christ. Like St. Therese, transform your works and daily prayers into a missionary act.

The coming of the Holy Spirit

2 ¹ When the day of Pentecost came, they were all together in one place. ² And suddenly, out of the sky, came a sound like a strong rushing wind; and it filled the whole house where they were sitting. There appeared [3] tongues as if of fire, which parted and came to rest upon each one of them. [4] All were filled with the Holy Spirit and began to speak other languages, as the Spirit enabled them to speak.

[5] Staying in Jerusalem were religious Jews from every nation under heaven. [6] When they heard this sound, a crowd gathered all excited, because each heard them speaking in his own language. [7] Full of amazement and wonder, they asked, "Are not all these who are speaking Galileans? [8] How is it that we hear them in our own native language? [9] Here are Parthians, Medes and Elamites; and residents of Mesopotamia, Judea and Cappadocia; Pontus and Asia; [10] Phrygia, Pamphylia, Egypt; and the parts of Libya belonging to Cyrene; and visitors from Rome; [11] both Jews and foreigners who accept Jewish beliefs, Cretans and Arabians; and all of us hear them proclaiming in our own language what God the Savior does."

[12] They were amazed and greatly confused, and they kept asking one another, "What does this mean?" [13] But others laughed and said, "These people are drunk."

ACTS 2:1-13

Read: The promised Holy Spirit descends upon the disciples in a dramatic way during the feast of Pentecost. Bold deeds result. From that moment, they openly announce the Good News, which is welcomed by many people.

Reflect: Are you a courageous witness of the Good News of Jesus Christ, like Peter and the other apostles after Pentecost? Have you ever felt the power of the Holy Spirit in your life? How do you announce the Good News?

Pray: Allow yourself to be carried away by the Holy Spirit when it breaks into your life. Cowardice is not a reason to stop you from doing your mission. Thank Jesus Christ for being one of his disciples.

Act: Write down everything important that God has done in your life and share it with others.

Peter addresses the crowd

[14] Then Peter stood up with the Eleven and, with a loud voice, addressed them, "Fellow Jews and all foreigners now staying in Jerusalem, listen to what I have to say. [15] These people are not drunk as you suppose, for it is only nine o'clock in the morning. [16] Indeed what the prophet Joel spoke about has happened:

[17] *In the last days, God says, I will pour out my Spirit on every mortal. Your sons and daughters will speak through the Holy Spirit; your young men will see visions and your old men will have dreams.*

[18] *In those days I will pour out my Spirit even on my servants, both men and women, and they will be prophets.*

[19] *I will perform miracles in the sky above and wonders on the earth below.* [20] *The sun will be darkened and the moon will turn red as blood before the great and glorious Day of the Lord comes.*

[21] *And then whoever calls upon the Name of the Lord will be saved.*

[22] Fellow Israelites, listen to what I am going to tell you about Jesus of Nazareth. God accredited him and through him did powerful deeds and wonders and signs in your midst, as you well know. [23] You delivered him to sinners to be crucified and killed, and in this way, the purpose of God from all times was fulfilled. [24] But God raised him to life and released him from the pain of death; because it was impossible for him to be held in the power of death. [25] David spoke of him when he said: *I saw the Lord before me at all times; he is by my side, that I may not be shaken.* [26] *Therefore, my heart was glad and my tongue rejoiced; my body, too, will live in hope.* [27] *Because you will not forsake me in the abode of the dead, nor allow your Holy One to experience corruption.* [28] *You have made known to me the paths of life, and your presence will fill me with joy.*

[29] Friends, I don't need to prove that the patriarch David died and was buried; his tomb is with us to this day. [30] But he knew that God had sworn to him, that one of his descendants would sit upon his throne and, [31] as he was a prophet, he foresaw and spoke of the resurrection of the Messiah. So he said that *he would not be left in the region of the dead, nor would his body experience corruption.*

[32] This Messiah is Jesus, and we are all witnesses that God raised him to life. [33] He has been exalted at God's right side and the Father has entrusted the Holy Spirit to him; this Spirit he has just poured upon us, as you now see and hear.

³⁴ And look: David did not ascend into heaven, but he himself said: *The Lord said to my Lord: sit at my right side,* ³⁵ *until I make your enemies a stool for your feet.* ³⁶ Let Israel, then know for sure that God has made Lord and Christ, this Jesus whom you crucified."

³⁷ When they heard this, they were deeply troubled. And they asked Peter and the other apostles, "What shall we do, brothers?"

³⁸ Peter answered: "Each of you must repent and be baptized in the name of Jesus Christ, so that your sins may be forgiven. Then, you will receive the gift of the Holy Spirit. ³⁹ For the promise of God was made to you and your children and to all those from afar, whom our God may call."

⁴⁰ With many other words Peter gave the message; and appealed to them, saying, "Save yourselves from this crooked generation." ⁴¹ So those who accepted his word were baptized; some three thousand persons were added to their number that day.

ACTS 2:14-41

Read: Peter delivers a speech in which the Pentecost event is explained as the fulfillment of the prophecy of Joel. Convincing proof that Jesus is indeed the Messiah results in the conversion of about three thousand people.

Reflect: Are you prepared to give reasons for your faith, as Peter did? Is your way of life encouraging others to believe in Jesus Christ?

Pray: Pray that your life testimony helps those who are confused and wander from religion to religion. May they find Jesus Christ in the Church. Pray for the missionaries who are persecuted for proclaiming the Gospel.

Act: Perform actions that give testimony to your faith in Jesus Christ. To the extent of your capability, be in solidarity with the missionary works.

The first community

⁴² They were faithful to the teaching of the apostles, the common life of sharing, the breaking of bread and the prayers.

⁴³ A holy fear came upon all the people, for many wonders and miraculous signs were done by the apostles. ⁴⁴ Now, all the believers lived

together and shared all their belongings. ⁴⁵ They would sell their property and all they had and distribute the proceeds to others, according to their need. ⁴⁶ Each day they met together in the temple area; they broke bread in their homes; they shared their food with great joy and simplicity of heart; ⁴⁷ they praised God and won the people's favor. And every day the Lord added to their number those who were being saved.

ACTS 2:42-47

Read: An ideal Christian community life is summarized and presented: to learn who Jesus Christ is; to help one another; and, to pray and celebrate the Eucharist together.

Reflect: Do you regularly attend the Holy Eucharist to hear the Word? Do you participate in the Eucharist and pray in your parish? Do you share your goods with those who have less than you?

Pray: Pray for those who suffer due to lack of education, hunger, abandonment, and loneliness. Pray also for those who do not know Jesus Christ. Ask the Spirit to help you not to be indifferent to these problems.

Act: Participate in any volunteer activity in your community. Commit as a catechist in the parish or in some bible study or prayer group. Share your bread with a neighbor in need.

Peter and John cure a lame man

3 ¹ Once when Peter and John were going up to the temple at three in the afternoon, the hour for prayer, ² a man crippled from birth was being carried in. Every day they would bring him and put him at the temple gate called "Beautiful;" there, he begged from those who entered the temple.

³ When he saw Peter and John on their way into the temple, he asked for alms. ⁴ Then Peter, with John at his side, looked straight at him and said, "Look at us." ⁵ So he looked at them, expecting to receive something from them. ⁶ But Peter said, "I have neither silver nor gold, but what I have I give you: In the name of Jesus of Nazareth, the Messiah, walk!"

⁷ Then, he took the beggar by his right hand and helped him up. At

once his feet and ankles became firm ⁸and jumping up, he stood on his feet and began to walk. And he went with them into the temple, walking and leaping and praising God.

⁹All the people saw him walking and praising God; ¹⁰they recognized him as the one who used to sit begging at the Beautiful Gate of the temple and they were all astonished and amazed at what had happened to him.

ACTS 3:1-10

Read: Peter and John heal a beggar who has asked for alms by invoking the name of Jesus.

Reflect: There are sick or disabled people around us. How can we help them? Should we all, including the government, be more supportive of them? How do you share with others the gift of faith?

Pray: Pray that we all be more sympathetic to those who cannot help themselves. Ask for inspiration to discover how and with whom you can collaborate.

Act: Consider taking time to help an organization that works with people with disabilities. Check with your community.

---

¹¹While he clung to Peter and John, all the people struck with astonishment, came running to them in Solomon's Porch as it was called. ¹²When Peter saw the people, he said to them,

"Fellow Israelites, why are you amazed at this? Why do you stare at us, as if it was by some power or holiness of our own that we made this man walk? ¹³The God of Abraham, of Isaac and of Jacob, the God of our ancestors has glorified his servant Jesus, whom you handed over to death and denied before Pilate, when even Pilate had decided to release him. ¹⁴You rejected the Holy and Just One and you insisted that a murderer be released to you. ¹⁵You killed the Master of life, but God raised him from the dead and we are witnesses to this. ¹⁶It is his Name, and faith in his Name, that has healed this man whom you see and recognize. The faith that comes through Jesus has given him wholeness in the presence of all of you.

¹⁷Yet, I know that you acted out of ignorance as did your leaders.

¹⁸ God has fulfilled, in this way, what he had foretold through all the prophets, that his Messiah would suffer.

¹⁹ Repent, then, and turn to God so that your sins may be wiped out; ²⁰ and the time of refreshment may come by the mercy of God, when he sends the Messiah appointed for you, Jesus. ²¹ For he must remain in heaven until the time of the universal restoration, which God spoke of long ago, through his holy prophets.

²² Moses foretold this when he said: *The Lord God will raise up for you a prophet, like me, from among your own people; you shall listen to him in all that he says to you.* ²³ *Whoever does not listen to that prophet is to be cut off from among his people.*

²⁴ In fact, all the prophets who have spoken, from Samuel onward, have announced the events of these days. ²⁵ You are the children of the prophets and heirs of the Covenant that God gave to your ancestors when he said to Abraham: *All the families of the earth will be blessed through your descendant.* ²⁶ It is to you, first, that God sends his Servant; he raised him to life to bless you, by turning each of you from your wicked ways."

ACTS 3:11-26

Read: Peter explains that it is Jesus Christ who acts through him. Jesus Christ is the Messiah and Lord whom we accept.

Reflect: Is it important for you to believe in Jesus Christ and his works? How can you share with your people your faith in the Risen Lord?

Pray: Ask God to help you continue to grow in faith and to be a courageous witness of the resurrection of Jesus Christ, Messiah and Lord.

Act: Ask in your parish or community where and how to deepen your faith in Jesus Christ.

Peter and John are arrested

4 ¹ While Peter and John were still speaking to the people, the priests, the captain of the temple guard and the Sadducees came up to them. ² They were greatly disturbed because the apostles were teaching the people and proclaiming that resurrection from the dead had been proved in the case of Jesus. ³Since it was already evening, they arrested them and put them in custody until the following day. ⁴But despite this, many of those who heard the Message, believed, and their number increased to about five thousand.

⁵The next day, the Jewish leaders, elders, and teachers of the law assembled in Jerusalem. ⁶Annas, the High Priest, Caiaphas, John, Alexander, and all who were of the high priestly class were there. ⁷They brought Peter and John before them; and began to question them, "How did you do this? Whose name did you use?"

⁸Then Peter, filled with the Holy Spirit, spoke up, "Leaders of the people! Elders! ⁹It is a fact that we are being examined today for a good deed done to a cripple. How was he healed? ¹⁰You and all the people of Israel must know that this man stands before you cured through the name of Jesus Christ, the Nazorean. You had him crucified. But God raised him from the dead. ¹¹Jesus is *the stone rejected by you, the builders, which has become the cornerstone.* ¹²There is no salvation in anyone else; for there is no other Name given to humankind all over the world, by which we may be saved."

¹³They were astonished at the boldness of Peter and John, considering that they were uneducated and untrained men. They also recognized that they had been with Jesus, ¹⁴but, as the man who had been cured stood beside them, they could make no reply.

¹⁵So they ordered them to leave the council room while they consulted with one another. ¹⁶They asked, "What shall we do with these men? Everyone who lives in Jerusalem knows that a remarkable sign has been given through them and we cannot deny it. ¹⁷But to stop this from spreading any further among the people, let us warn them never again to speak to anyone in the name of Jesus." ¹⁸So they called them back and charged them not to speak, or teach at all, in the name of Jesus.

¹⁹But Peter and John answered them, "Judge for yourselves, whether it is right in God's eyes for us to obey you rather than God. ²⁰We cannot stop speaking about what we have seen and heard." ²¹Then the council threatened them once more and let them go. They could find no way of punishing them because of the people who glorified God for what had happened; ²²for the man who had been miraculously healed was over forty years old.

ACTS 4:1-22

Read: Peter and John were arrested by the religious authorities, and were questioned: With what power or in whose name was the paralytic been healed? They respond that what happened is the work of the Risen Christ. This great news is well received by simple people.

Reflect: In what places or environment does the existence and power of Jesus Christ continue to be questioned? Under what circumstances do you feel embarrassed to express your faith? Why?

Pray: Pray for those who are persecuted for believing in the Risen Jesus Christ. Ask for strength to never betray your faith, even amid difficulties. Pray for the authorities of the Church to promote evangelization through the continuing formation of the people of God.

Act: Find ways to deepen your faith and share it with others. Be an apostle at home.

The prayer of the community

²³ As soon as Peter and John were set free, they went to their friends and reported what the chief priests and elders had said to them.

²⁴ When they heard it, they raised their voices as one and called upon God, "Sovereign Lord, maker of heaven and earth, of the sea and everything in them, ²⁵ you have put these words in the mouth of David our father and your servant through the Holy Spirit: *Why did the pagan nations rage and the people conspire in folly?* ²⁶ *The kings of the earth were aligned and the princes gathered together against the Lord and against his Messiah.*

²⁷ For indeed, in this very city, Herod, with Pontius Pilate and the pagans, together with the people of Israel, conspired against your holy servant, Jesus, whom you anointed. ²⁸ Thus, indeed, they brought about whatever your powerful will had decided from all time would happen. ²⁹ But now, Lord, see their threats against us; and enable your servants to speak your word with all boldness. ³⁰ Stretch out your hand to heal and to work signs and wonders through the name of Jesus, your holy servant."

³¹ When they had prayed, the place where they were gathered together shook; and they were all filled with the Holy Spirit and began to speak the word of God boldly.

An attempt to share everything

³² The whole community of believers was one in heart and mind. No one claimed private ownership of any possessions; but rather, they shared all things in common. ³³ With great power, the apostles bore witness to the resurrection of the Lord Jesus, for all of them were living in an exceptional time of grace.

ACTS 4:23-33

Read: The community thanks God that Peter and John have overcome the threats of the Sanhedrin. A second "Pentecost experience" occurs. The community of believers is described as being "of one heart and soul."

Reflect: Do you recognize any gift of the Holy Spirit in your life? How is the Spirit working in your community? Do you know of a community of believers who "have one mind and one heart"?

Pray: Ask the Holy Spirit to pour out his gifts upon your community to bear witness to Jesus Christ. Pray that those who have more share with the hungry. Remember in prayer the neediest members of your community.

Act: Encourage members of your community to reflect on how best to give testimony of Jesus Christ. Empathize with those suffering from cold, hunger and loneliness, especially within your community.

---

³⁴ There was no needy person among them, for those who owned land or houses sold them and brought the proceeds of the sale. ³⁵ And they laid it at the feet of the apostles who distributed it according to each one's need. ³⁶ This is what a certain Joseph did. He was a Levite from Cyprus, whom the apostles called Barnabas, meaning: "The encouraging one." ³⁷ He sold a field, which he owned and handed the money to the apostles.

The fraud of Ananias and Sapphira

5 [1] Another man, named Ananias, in agreement with his wife Sapphira, likewise sold a piece of land; [2] with his wife's knowledge he put aside some of the proceeds and the rest he turned over to the apostles.

[3] Then, Peter said to him, "Ananias, how is it that you let Satan fill your heart; and why do you intend to deceive the Holy Spirit by keeping some of the proceeds of your land for yourself? [4] Who obliged you to sell it? And, after it was sold, could you not have kept all the money? How could you think of such a thing? You have not deceived us but God."

[5] Upon hearing these words, Ananias fell down and died. Great fear came upon all who heard of it; [6] the young men stood up, wrapped his body and carried it out for burial.

[7] About three hours later, Ananias's wife came, but she was not aware of what had happened. [8] Peter challenged her, "Tell me whether you sold that piece of land for this price?" She said, "Yes, that was the price." [9] Peter replied, "How could you two agree to put the Holy Spirit to the test? Those who buried your husband are at the door and they will carry you out as well."

[10] With that, she fell dead at his feet. The young men came in, found her dead and carried her out for burial beside her husband. [11] And great fear came upon the whole church and upon all who heard of it.

[12] Many miraculous signs and wonders were done among the people through the hands of the apostles. The believers, of one accord, used to meet in Solomon's Porch. [13] None of the others dared to join them, but the people held them in high esteem. [14] So, an ever-increasing number of men and women believed in the Lord. [15] The people carried the sick into the streets and laid them on cots and on mats, so that, when Peter passed by, at least his shadow might fall on some of them. [16] The people gathered from the towns around Jerusalem, bringing their sick and those who were troubled by unclean spirits; and all of them were healed.

ACTS 4:34—5:16

Read: The generosity of Joseph/Barnabas is contrasted with the plot of Ananias and Sapphira to deceive and attempt to undermine the sense of unity in the community.

Reflect: Are you a person detached from material goods? Are you tempted to hold on to things rather than sharing them to benefit your community?

Pray: Pray to God to give you the grace to be generous and supportive to others, especially those most in need in your community.

Action: Following the example of Barnabas, consider making an additional donation to your local church community, to a children's home, a home for the elderly or any other place in need.

The apostles arrested again

¹⁷ The High Priest and all his supporters, that is the party of the Sadducees, became very jealous of the apostles; ¹⁸ so they arrested them and had them thrown into the public jail. ¹⁹ But an angel of the Lord opened the door of the prison during the night, brought them out, and said to them, ²⁰ "Go and stand in the temple court and tell the people the whole of this living message." ²¹ Accordingly, they entered the temple at dawn and resumed their teaching.

When the High Priest and his supporters arrived, they called together the Sanhedrin that is the full Council of the elders of Israel. They sent word to the jail to have the prisoners brought in. ²² But when the temple guards arrived at the jail, they did not find them inside; so they returned with the news, ²³ "We found the prison securely locked and the prison guards at their post outside the gate; but when we opened the gate, we found no one inside."

²⁴ Upon hearing these words, the captain of the temple guard and the high priests were baffled, wondering where all of this would end. ²⁵ Just then, someone arrived with the report, "Look, those men whom you put in prison are standing in the temple, teaching the people." ²⁶ Then the captain went off with the guards and brought them back, but without any show of force for fear of being stoned by the people.

²⁷ So they brought them in and made them stand before the Council, and the High Priest questioned them, ²⁸ "We gave you strict orders not to preach such a Savior but you have filled Jerusalem with your teaching; and you intend charging us with the killing of this man." ²⁹ To this, Peter and the apostles replied, "Better for us to obey God, rather than any human authority!

[30] The God of our ancestors raised Jesus, whom you killed by hanging him on a wooden post. [31] God set him at his right hand as Leader and Savior, to grant repentance and forgiveness of sins to Israel. [32] We are witnesses to all these things, as well as the Holy Spirit, whom God has given to those who obey him."

[33] When the Council heard this, they became very angry and wanted to kill them. [34] But one of them, a Pharisee named Gamaliel, a teacher of the law highly respected by the people, stood up in the Sanhedrin. He ordered the men to be taken outside for a few minutes [35] and then he spoke to the assembly.

"Fellow Israelites, consider well what you intend to do to these men. [36] For some time ago, Theudas came forward claiming to be somebody, and about four hundred men joined him. But he was killed and all his followers were dispersed or disappeared. [37] After him, Judas the Galilean appeared at the time of the census and persuaded many people to follow him. But he, too, perished; and his whole following was scattered. [38] So, in this present case, I advise you to have nothing to do with these men. Leave them alone. If their project or activity is of human origin, it will destroy itself. [39] If, on the other hand, it is from God, you will not be able to destroy it; and you might indeed find yourselves fighting against God."

The Council let themselves be persuaded. [40] They called in the apostles and had them whipped; and ordered them not to speak again of Jesus, the Savior. Then they set them free.

[41] The apostles went out from the Council, rejoicing that they were considered worthy to suffer disgrace for the sake of the Name. [42] Day after day, both in the temple and in people's homes, they continued to teach and to proclaim that Jesus was the Messiah.

ACTS 5:17-42

Read: God protects the apostles to continue preaching the Gospel. Gamaliel, a Pharisee and a distinguished scholar of the law, advises the council not to persecute the Christian movement: if it is of human origin it will destroy itself, if it is from God, it cannot be destroyed.

Reflect: Gamaliel requests patience to discern the mysterious actions of God in life: How to obey God rather than people without falling into provocation or even in disobedience? How to know that a personal position is from God and not stubbornness?

Pray: Pray for wisdom and a deeper understanding of God's plan for your life and that of your community.

Act: Offer the practical words of Gamaliel's advice to a person who is troubled about some type of religious controversy.

The choosing of assistants

6 ¹In those days, as the number of disciples grew, the so-called *Hellenists* complained against the so-called *Hebrews*, because their widows were being neglected in the daily distribution. ²So the Twelve summoned the whole body of disciples together, and said, "It is not right that we should neglect the word of God to serve at tables. ³So, friends, choose from among yourselves seven respected men, full of Spirit and wisdom, that we may appoint them to this task. ⁴As for us, we shall give ourselves to prayer and to the ministry of the word."

⁵The whole community agreed; and they chose Stephen, a man full of faith and the Holy Spirit; Philip, Prochorus, Nicanor, Timon, Parmenus and Nicolaus of Antioch, who was a proselyte. ⁶They presented these men to the apostles, who first prayed over them and then laid hands upon them.

⁷The word of God continued to spread, and the number of the disciples in Jerusalem increased greatly, and even many priests accepted the faith.

ACTS 6:1-7

Read: The community is faced with a practical problem and found a solution. They elect the first seven deacons, including Stephen, who will be the first martyr.

Reflect: Do you know how to give practical solutions to family or community problems? Do you consider yourself a positive person or are you putting obstacles to good works?

Pray: The elect were "endowed with the Spirit and wisdom." Pray that people with these gifts arise in our communities.

> **Act:** Respond actively to the power of the Spirit in your life. Lead or participate in your neighborhood in an initiative that benefits the community.

The story of Stephen

[8] Stephen, full of grace and power, did great wonders and miraculous signs among the people. [9] Some persons, then came forward, who belonged to the so-called Synagogue of Freedmen from Cyrene, Alexandria, Cilicia, and Asia. [10] They argued with Stephen. But they could not match the wisdom and the spirit with which he spoke. [11] As they were unable to face the truth, they bribed some men to say, "We heard him speak against Moses and against God."

[12] So they stirred up the people, the elders and the teachers of the law; they took him by surprise, seized him and brought him before the Council. [13] Then they produced false witnesses who said, "This man never stops speaking against our Holy Place and the law. [14] We even heard him say that Jesus, the Nazorean, will destroy our Holy Place and change the customs which Moses handed down to us." [15] And all who sat in the Council fixed their eyes on him, and his face appeared to them like the face of an angel.

7 [1] So the High Priest asked him: "Is it true?" He answered, "Brothers and fathers, listen to me.

[2] The God of glory appeared to our father Abraham when he was in Mesopotamia before he went to live in Haran. And he said to him: [3] 'Leave your land and your relatives and go to the land which I will show you.' [4] So he left the land of the Chaldeans and settled in Haran. After the death of his father, God made him move to this land in which you now dwell. [5] And there, he did not give him anything that was his own, not even the smallest portion of land to put his foot on; but promised to give it to him, in possession, and to his descendants, though he had no child. [6] So God spoke: 'Your descendants shall live in a strange land. They shall be enslaved and maltreated for four hundred years. [7] So, I shall call the nation, which they serve as slaves, to render an account for it. They will come out and worship me in this place.'

[8] He made with him, the Covenant of circumcision. And so, at the birth

of his son Isaac, Abraham circumcised him on the eighth day. Isaac did the same to Jacob, and Jacob, to the twelve patriarchs.

⁹ The patriarchs envied Joseph, so they sold him into Egypt. But God was with him. ¹⁰ He rescued him from all his afflictions, granted him wisdom, and made him please Pharaoh, king of Egypt, who appointed him governor of Egypt, and of the whole of his household. ¹¹ Then there was famine in all the land of Egypt and Canaan; it was a great misery, and our ancestors did not have anything to eat. ¹² Upon learning that there was wheat in Egypt, Jacob sent our ancestors there on their first visit. ¹³ On the second visit, Joseph made himself known to his brothers and Pharaoh came to know the family of Joseph. ¹⁴ Joseph commanded that his father Jacob be brought to him, with the whole of his family of seventy-five persons. ¹⁵ Jacob then went down to Egypt, where he and our ancestors died. ¹⁶ They were transferred to Shechem and laid in the tomb that Abraham had bought for a sum of silver from the sons of Hamor at Shechem.

¹⁷ As the time of promise drew near, which God had made to Abraham, the people increased, and multiplied in Egypt ¹⁸ until came another king who did not know Joseph. ¹⁹ Dealing cunningly with our race, he forced our ancestors to abandon their newborn infants and let them die. ²⁰ At that time, Moses was born and God looked kindly on him. For three months he was nursed in the home of his father; ²¹ and when they abandoned him, Pharaoh's daughter took him and raised him as her own son. ²² So, Moses was educated in all the wisdom of the Egyptians. He was mighty in word and deed. ²³ And when he was forty years old, he wanted to visit his own people, the Israelites. ²⁴ When he saw one of them being wronged, he defended the oppressed man and killed the Egyptian. ²⁵ He thought his kinsfolk would understand that God was sending him to them as a liberator, but they did not understand. ²⁶ On the following day, he came to them as they were fighting and tried to reconcile them, saying: 'You are brothers, why do you hurt each other?' ²⁷ At that moment, the one who was injuring his companion rebuffed him, saying: 'Who appointed you as our leader and judge? ²⁸ Do you want to kill me, as you killed the Egyptian yesterday?' ²⁹ When Moses heard this, he fled and went to live as a stranger in the land of Midian, where he had two sons.

³⁰ After forty years, an angel appeared to him in the desert of Mount Sinai in the flame of a burning bush. ³¹ Moses was astonished at the

vision. And as he approached to look at it, he heard the voice of the Lord: ³²'I am the God of your fathers, the God of Abraham, Isaac, and Jacob.' Moses was filled with fear and did not dare look at it. ³³But the Lord said to him: 'Take off your sandals, for the place where you stand is holy ground. ³⁴I have seen the affliction of my people in Egypt and heard them weeping, and I have come down to free them. And now, get up! I am sending you to Egypt.'

³⁵This Moses, whom they rejected, saying: 'Who appointed you leader and judge?' God sent, as leader and liberator with the assistance of the angel who appeared to him in the bush. ³⁶He led them out, performing signs and wonders in Egypt at the Red Sea and in the desert for forty years. ³⁷This Moses is the one who said to the Israelites: 'God will give you a prophet like me, from among your own people.' ³⁸This is the one who, in the assembly in the desert, became the mediator between the angel who spoke to him on Mount Sinai and our ancestors; and he received the words of life, that he might communicate them to us.

³⁹But our ancestors refused to obey, they rejected him and turned their hearts to Egypt, saying to Aaron: ⁴⁰'Give us gods to lead us, since we do not know what has happened to that Moses, who brought us out of Egypt.' ⁴¹So, in those days, they fashioned a calf, offered sacrifices to their idol and rejoiced in the work of their hands. ⁴²So God departed from them and let them worship the stars of heaven, as it is written in the Book of the Prophets: 'People of Israel, did you offer me burnt offerings and sacrifices for forty years in the desert? ⁴³No, you carried instead the tent of Moloch and the star of the god Rehan; images you made to worship; for this, I will banish you farther than Babylon.'

⁴⁴Our ancestors had the Tent of Meeting in the desert, for God had directed Moses to build it according to the pattern he had seen. ⁴⁵Our ancestors received it and brought it under the command of Joshua into the lands of the pagans that they conquered and whom God expelled before them. They kept it until the days of David, ⁴⁶who found favor with God; and asked him to let him build a house for the God of Jacob. ⁴⁷However, it was Solomon who built that temple.

⁴⁸In reality, the Most High does not dwell in houses made by human hands, as the Prophet says: ⁴⁹*'Heaven is my throne and earth is my footstool. What house will you build for me, says the Lord, how could you give me a dwelling place? ⁵⁰Was it not I who made all these things?'*

⁵¹ But you are a stubborn people. You hardened your hearts and closed your ears. You have always resisted the Holy Spirit, just as your fathers did. ⁵² Was there a prophet whom your ancestors did not persecute? They killed those who announced the coming of the Just One, whom you have now betrayed and murdered; ⁵³ you who received the law through the angels but did not fulfill it."

ACTS 6:8—7:53

Read: Stephen is arrested and brought to trial. In court, he reviews the history of salvation and how Israel did not recognize the presence of God in Jesus and killed him.

Reflect: Why throughout history so many people who acted in the name of God have been killed? How do you act in this situation? Do you rely more on dialogue rather than violence?

Pray: Remember past experiences, and ask the Spirit to give you light to discover the presence of God in them and even learn from your own mistakes.

Act: If you have a conflict with someone discuss it, apologize if necessary, and see in it the presence of God in your life.

---

⁵⁴ When they heard this reproach, they were enraged; and they gnashed their teeth against Stephen. ⁵⁵ But he, full of the Holy Spirit, fixed his eyes on heaven and saw the glory of God and Jesus at God's right hand; ⁵⁶ so he declared: "I see the heavens open and the Son of Man at the right hand of God."

⁵⁷ But they shouted and covered their ears with their hands and rushed together upon him. ⁵⁸ They brought him out of the city and stoned him, and the witnesses laid down their cloaks at the feet of a young man named Saul. ⁵⁹ As they were stoning him, Stephen prayed, saying: "Lord Jesus, receive my spirit." ⁶⁰ Then he knelt down and said in a loud voice: "Lord, do not hold this sin against them." And when he had said this, he died.

8 ¹ Saul was there, approving his murder. This was the beginning of a great persecution against the Church in Jerusalem. All except the apostles were scattered throughout the region of Judea and Samaria.

²Devout men buried Stephen and mourned deeply for him. ³Saul, meanwhile, was trying to destroy the church. He entered house after house and dragged off men and women and had them put in jail.

ACTS 7:54–8:3

Read: After his testimony of faith, Stephen is martyred. A great persecution of Christians takes place in which Saul, the future Paul, actively collaborates.

Reflect: Martyr is one who bears witness of Jesus Christ up to death. Are there still martyrs nowadays? Would you give your life for Jesus?

Pray: Pray that, like Stephen, you will also have the strength to speak and act as Jesus did.

Act: Do not be embarrassed to be a Christian to people who deny the faith. Like Stephen, be consistent and give reasons for it. Look for the opportunity to talk about your faith with someone you know who does not believe in Jesus Christ.

Philip proclaims the word in Samaria

⁴At the same time, those who were scattered went about preaching the word. ⁵Philip went down to a town of Samaria and proclaimed the Christ there. ⁶All the people paid close attention to what Philip said as they listened to him and saw the miraculous signs that he did. ⁷For, in cases of possession the unclean spirits came out shrieking loudly. Many people who were paralyzed or crippled were healed. ⁸So there was great joy in that town.

Simon the magician

⁹A certain man named Simon had come to this town practicing magic. He held the Samaritans spellbound; and passed himself off as a very important person. ¹⁰All the people from the least to the greatest put their trust in him saying, "This is the Power of God, the Great One." ¹¹And they followed him because he had held them under the spell of his magic for a long time. ¹²But when they came to believe Philip, who announced to them the kingdom of God and Jesus Christ as Savior, both men and women were baptized.

[13] Simon himself, believed, and was baptized, and would not depart from Philip. He was astonished when he saw the miraculous signs and wonders that happened.

[14] Now, when the apostles in Jerusalem heard that the Samaritans had accepted the word of God, they sent Peter and John to them. [15] They went down and prayed for them that they might receive the Holy Spirit; [16] for he had not as yet come down upon any of them since they had only been baptized in the name of the Lord Jesus. [17] So Peter and John laid their hands on them and they received the Holy Spirit.

[18] When Simon saw that the Spirit was given through the laying on of the apostles' hands, he offered them money, [19] saying, "Give me also this power, so that anyone upon whom I lay my hands may receive the Holy Spirit."

[20] Peter replied, "May you and your money perish for thinking that the gift of God could be bought with money! [21] You cannot share in this since you do not understand the things of God. [22] Repent, therefore, of this wickedness of yours and pray to the Lord that you may be forgiven such a wrong way of thinking; [23] I see you are poisoned with bitterness and in the grip of sin." [24] Simon answered, "Pray to the Lord for me yourselves so that none of these things you spoke of will happen to me."

[25] Peter and John gave their testimony and spoke the word of the Lord. And they went back to Jerusalem, bringing the Good News to many Samaritan villages along the way.

Philip baptizes the Ethiopian

[26] An angel of the Lord said to Philip, "Go south, toward the road that goes down from Jerusalem to Gaza, the desert road." [27] So he set out and it happened that an Ethiopian was passing along that way. He was an official in charge of the treasury of the queen of the Ethiopians. He had come on pilgrimage to Jerusalem [28] and was on his way home. He was sitting in his carriage and reading the prophet Isaiah.

[29] The Spirit said to Philip, "Go and catch up with that carriage." [30] So Philip ran up and heard the man reading the prophet Isaiah; and he asked, "Do you really understand what you are reading?" The Ethiopian replied, [31] "How can I, unless someone explains it to me?" He then invited Philip to get in and sit beside him. [32] This was the passage of Scripture he was reading:

He was led like a sheep to be slaughtered; like a lamb that is dumb before the shearer, he did not open his mouth. [33] *He was humbled and deprived of his rights. Who can speak of his descendants? For he was uprooted from the earth.*

[34] The official asked Philip, "Tell me, please, does the prophet speak of himself or of someone else?"

[35] Then Philip began to tell him the Good News of Jesus using this text of Scripture as his starting point. [36] As they traveled down the road, they came to a place where there was some water. Then the Ethiopian official said, "Look, here is water; what is to keep me from being baptized?" ([37])

[38] Then he ordered the carriage to stop. Both Philip and the Ethiopian went down into the water and Philip baptized him. [39] When they came out of the water, the Spirit of the Lord took Philip away. The Ethiopian saw him no more, but he continued on his way full of joy.

[40] Philip found himself at Azotus, and he went about announcing the Good News in all the towns until he reached Caesarea.

ACTS 8:4-40

Read: Philip preached in Samaria, where the magician Simon is cursed for trying to buy the power to heal from Peter and John. The Ethiopian eunuch gets converted when Philip explains to him that the promises of Scripture are fulfilled in Jesus Christ.

Reflect: Should we still proclaim the Gospel message outside the community of believers? Why? Are you able to differentiate faith and superstitions? Do you think your faith has something of superstition? Why?

Pray: Pray that your testimony of life attracts others to Christianity.

Act: Like Philip, take the time to listen and patiently explain the faith to someone who would like to learn about it.

Saul meets Jesus

9 [1] Meanwhile, Saul considered nothing but violence and death for the disciples of the Lord. [2] He went to the High Priest and asked him for letters to the synagogues of Damascus that would authorize him to arrest, and bring to Jerusalem, anyone he might find, man or woman, belonging to the Way.

³As he traveled along and was approaching Damascus, a light from the sky suddenly flashed around him. ⁴He fell to the ground and heard a voice saying to him, "Saul, Saul! Why do you persecute me?" ⁵And he asked, "Who are you, Lord?" The voice replied, "I am Jesus, whom you persecute. ⁶Now get up and go into the city; there, you will be told what you are to do."

⁷The men who were traveling with him stood there speechless: they had heard the sound but could see no one. ⁸Saul got up from the ground and, opening his eyes, he could not see. They took him by the hand and brought him to Damascus. ⁹He was blind, and he did not eat or drink for three days.

¹⁰There was a disciple in Damascus named Ananias, to whom the Lord called in a vision, "Ananias!" He answered, "Here I am, Lord!" ¹¹Then the Lord said to him, "Go at once to Straight Street and ask at the house of Judas for a man of Tarsus named Saul. You will find him praying, ¹²for he has just seen in a vision that a man named Ananias has come in and placed his hands upon him to restore his sight."

¹³Ananias answered, "Lord, I have heard from many sources about this man, and all the harm he has done to your saints in Jerusalem; ¹⁴and now he is here with authority from the High Priest, to arrest all who call upon your name." ¹⁵But the Lord said to him, "Go! This man is my chosen instrument to bring my name to the pagan nations and their kings and the people of Israel as well. ¹⁶I myself will show him how much he will have to suffer for my name."

¹⁷So Ananias left and went to the house. He laid his hands upon Saul and said, "Saul, my brother, the Lord Jesus who appeared to you on your way here, has sent me to you so that you may receive your sight, and be filled with the Holy Spirit." ¹⁸Immediately, something like scales fell from his eyes and he could see; he got up and was baptized. ¹⁹Then he took food and was strengthened.

ACTS 9:1-19a

Read: After having been present at the stoning of Stephen, Saul experiences a profound conversion on the road to Damascus.

Ananias is initially reluctant to welcome him; however, the Lord reassures Ananias that Saul has been chosen for a special role.

Reflect: What would actually be Paul's conversion experience? Have you experienced something similar? As Ananias, would you be willing to welcome a former persecutor of the Christian faith?

Pray: Be thankful for moments or processes of conversion to faith. Ask also for the grace to overcome prejudices and be open to new ways of relating to others.

Act: Saul is helped by others and led by the hand to Ananias. Seek out an individual to whom you can lend a helping hand on the road to faith.

For several days Saul stayed with the disciples at Damascus, ²⁰ and he soon began to proclaim in the synagogues that Jesus was the Son of God. ²¹ All who heard were astonished and said, "Is this not the one who cast out in Jerusalem all those calling upon this Name? Did he not come here to bring them bound before the chief priests?"

²² But Saul grew more and more powerful and he confounded the Jews living in Damascus when he proved that Jesus was the Messiah.

²³ After a fairly long time, the Jews conspired together to kill him. ²⁴ But Saul became aware of their plan: Day and night they kept watch at the city gate in order to kill him. ²⁵ So his disciples took him one night and let him down from the top of the wall, lowering him in a basket.

²⁶ When Saul came to Jerusalem, he tried to join the disciples there, but they were afraid of him because they could not believe that he was a disciple. ²⁷ But Barnabas took him and brought him to the apostles. He recounted to them how Saul had seen the Lord on his way and the words the Lord had spoken to him. He told them also, how Saul had preached boldly in the name of Jesus.

²⁸ Then Saul began to live with them. He moved about freely in Jerusalem and preached openly in the name of the Lord. ²⁹ He also spoke to the Hellenists, and argued with them. But they wanted to kill him. ³⁰ When the believers learned of this, they took him down to Caesarea and sent him off to Tarsus.

³¹ Meanwhile, the Church had peace. It was building up throughout all

Judea and Galilee and Samaria, with eyes turned to the Lord and filled with comfort from the Holy Spirit.

> ## ACTS 9:19b-31
>
> **Read:** Saul spends time in Damascus and his presence creates confusion in others because of the radical change he has experienced. After escaping from there, he is presented to the apostles in Jerusalem. He preaches the Gospel fearlessly and is recognized as a Christian.
>
> **Reflect:** No one should be condemned for their past, it is necessary to listen, to help, to understand and to guide the person to Jesus Christ. Why is it so hard to accept and believe in someone whose life has changed? What can you do to make others believe in Jesus Christ?
>
> **Pray:** Ask God to help you change aspects of your life that require conversion. Ask also for a willingness to welcome and accept new converts to the faith.
>
> **Act:** Like Barnabas, take the initiative to introduce a person who is unknown to others. Speak favorably and in a positive way about this individual and help him or her feel welcome.

Peter visits the churches

³²As Peter traveled around, he went to visit the saints who lived in Lydda. ³³There he found a man named Aeneas, who was paralyzed and had been bedridden for eight years. ³⁴Peter said to him, "Aeneas, Jesus Christ heals you; get up and make your bed!" And the man got up at once. ³⁵All the people living in Lydda and Sharon saw him and turned to the Lord.

³⁶There was a disciple in Joppa named Tabitha, which means Dorcas, or Gazelle. She was always doing good works and helping the poor. ³⁷At that time she fell sick and died. After having washed her body, they laid her in the upstairs room.

³⁸As Lydda is near Joppa, the disciples, on hearing that Peter was there, sent two men to him with the request, "Please come to us without delay."

³⁹So Peter went with them. On his arrival, they took him upstairs to

the room. All the widows crowded around him in tears, showing him the clothes that Dorcas had made while she was with them. ⁴⁰Peter made them all leave the room, and then he knelt down and prayed. Turning to the dead body, he said, "Tabitha, stand up." She opened her eyes, looked at Peter and sat up. ⁴¹Peter gave her his hand and helped her up. Then he called in the saints and widows and presented her to them alive. ⁴²This became known throughout all Joppa and many people believed in the Lord because of it. ⁴³As for Peter, he remained for some time in Joppa at the house of Simon a tanner of leather.

ACTS 9:32-43

Read: Peter performs healing miracles in Lydda and Jaffa in the name of Jesus Christ. Because of this, many welcome the announcement of the Good News.

Reflect: What does Jesus need to heal you from your paralytic faith? What work can you do to help others deepen their beliefs and live in a manner more consistent with the Gospel?

Pray: Ask God to help you overcome what paralyzes you. In a special way, pray for the sick and the afflicted.

Act: Make a kind gesture that will bring the presence of God to a sick person. Find someone who lives sad and hopeless, and share the joy of knowing that God is always with us.

The baptism of Cornelius

10 ¹There was in Caesarea a man named Cornelius, captain of what was called the Italian Battalion. ²He was a religious and God-fearing man, together with his whole household. He gave generously to the people and constantly prayed to God.

³One afternoon, at about three, he had a vision in which he clearly saw an angel of God coming toward him and calling him, "Cornelius!" ⁴He stared at the vision with awe and said, "What is it, sir?" And the angel answered, "Your prayers and your alms have just been recalled before God. ⁵Now send some men to Joppa, and summon a certain Simon, also known as Peter; ⁶he is the guest of Simon, a tanner, who lives beside the sea."

[7] As soon as the angel who spoke to him departed, Cornelius called two of his servants and a devout soldier from among those attached to his service [8] and, after having explained everything to them, he sent them to Joppa.

[9] The next day, while they were on their journey and approaching the city, Peter went up to the roof at about noon to pray. [10] He became hungry and wished to eat, but while they were preparing food, he fell into a trance. [11] The heavens were opened to him and he saw an object that looked like a large sheet coming down until it rested on the ground by its four corners. [12] In it were all kinds of four-legged animals of the earth, reptiles, and birds.

[13] Then a voice said to him, "Get up, Peter, kill and eat!" [14] But Peter replied, "Certainly not, Lord! I have never eaten any defiled or unclean creature." [15] And again a second time the voice spoke, "What God has made clean you must not call unclean." [16] This happened three times, and then the sheet was taken up again into the sky.

[17] While Peter was still puzzling over the meaning of the vision he had seen, the messengers of Cornelius arrived at the gate asking for the house of Simon. [18] They called out to inquire whether Simon, also known as Peter, was staying there. [19] At that moment, as Peter continued pondering on the vision, the Spirit spoke to him, "There are men looking for you; [20] get up and go downstairs and follow them without hesitation, for I have sent them."

[21] So Peter went and said to the men, "I am the one you are looking for. What brings you here?" They answered, [22] "He who sent us is Captain Cornelius. He is an upright and God-fearing man, well respected by all the Jewish people. He has been instructed by a holy angel to summon you to his house, so that he may listen to what you have to say." [23] So Peter invited them in and put them up for the night.

The next day, he went off with them and some of the believers from Joppa accompanied him. [24] The following day, he arrived in Caesarea, where Cornelius was expecting them; he had called together his relatives and close friends. [25] As Peter was about to enter, Cornelius went to him, fell on his knees and bowed low. [26] But Peter lifted him up, saying, "Stand up, for I too am a human being."

[27] After talking with him, Peter entered and found many people assembled there. [28] Then he said to them, "You know that it is forbidden for

Jews to associate with anyone of another nation, or to enter their houses. But God has made it clear to me that no one should call any person common or unclean; [29] because of this, I came at once when I was sent for. Now, I should like to know why you sent for me."

[30] Cornelius then answered, "Just three days ago at this time, about three in the afternoon, I was praying in my house when a man in shining clothes stood before me [31] and said to me: 'Cornelius, God has heard your prayer, and your alms have been remembered before him. [32] Send someone, therefore, to Joppa and ask for Simon, also known as Peter, who is guest at the house of Simon the tanner by the sea.' [33] So I sent for you at once and you have been kind enough to come. Now we are all here in God's presence, waiting to hear all that the Lord has commanded you to say."

ACTS 10:1-33

Read: During prayer, both Cornelius and Peter experience profound visions that offer new insides into their lives. Everything God has made is good, and we cannot judge it as bad.

Reflect: Why is it important to grow in faith and expand our view of the world? Can a Christian prejudge people by their race when Jesus Christ came to save all humankind? Do you have a need to eradicate any prejudice?

Pray: Ask for the help of the Spirit to be always open to new and different perceptions of God and the world. Pray that all kinds of prejudice be banished in your community.

Act: Empty your mind of any kind of racism or prejudice. Be a welcoming person performing a specific gesture to someone who may feel marginalized.

---

[34] Peter then spoke to them, "Truly, I realize that God does not show partiality, [35] but in all nations, he listens to everyone who fears God and does good. [36] And this is the message he has sent to the children of Israel, the good news of peace he has proclaimed through Jesus Christ, who is the Lord of all. [37] No doubt you have heard of the event that occurred throughout the whole country of the Jews beginning from Galilee, after the baptism John preached. [38] You know how God anointed Jesus

the Nazorean with the Holy Spirit and power. He went about doing good and healing all who were under the devil's power because God was with him; ³⁹ we are witnesses of all that he did throughout the country of the Jews and in Jerusalem itself. Yet, they put him to death by hanging him on a wooden cross.

⁴⁰ But God raised him to life on the third day and let him manifest himself, ⁴¹ not to all the people, but to the witnesses that were chosen beforehand by God—to us who ate and drank with him after his resurrection from death. ⁴² And he commanded us to preach to the people and to bear witness, that he is the one appointed by God to judge the living and the dead. ⁴³ All the prophets say of him, that everyone who believes in him has forgiveness of sins through his name."

⁴⁴ Peter was still speaking when the Holy Spirit came upon all who listened to the word. ⁴⁵ And the believers of Jewish origin who had come with Peter were amazed, "Why! God gives and pours the Holy Spirit on foreigners also!" ⁴⁶ For indeed, this happened: they heard them speaking in tongues and praising God.

⁴⁷ Then Peter declared, "Can we refuse to baptize with water these people who have received the Holy Spirit just as we have?" ⁴⁸ So he had them baptized in the name of Jesus Christ. After that, they asked him to remain with them for some days.

ACTS 10:34-48

Read: In his speech, Peter explains to Cornelius and his family, a non-Jewish people, what the Christian faith is and that we are all equal. After listening to him, all receive the Holy Spirit.

Reflect: Why is the sentence "God does not show partiality" at the beginning of Peter's speech? Do all people have the right to receive Jesus Christ in their life? Can anyone be excluded from salvation?

Pray: Support the missionaries, through prayers, in their efforts to evangelize those who are further away from the faith. Ask for the willingness to understand all people.

Act: Many who are not Christians live a Christian life. Do you know any of these people? Talk and learn from them.

Peter justifies his conduct

11 [1] News came to the apostles and the brothers and sisters in Judea that even foreigners had received the word of God. [2] So, when Peter went up to Jerusalem, these Jewish believers began to argue with him, [3] "You went to the home of uncircumcised people and ate with them!"

[4] So Peter began to give them the facts as they had happened, [5] "I was at prayer in the city of Joppa when, in a trance, I saw a vision. Something like a large sheet came down from the sky and drew near to me, landing on the ground by its four corners. [6] As I stared at it, I saw four-legged creatures of the earth, wild beasts and reptiles, and birds of the sky. [7] Then I heard a voice saying to me: 'Get up, Peter, kill and eat!' [8] I replied, 'Certainly not, Lord! No common or unclean creature has ever entered my mouth.' [9] A second time the voice from the heavens spoke, 'What God has made clean, you must not call unclean.' [10] This happened three times, and then it was all drawn up into the sky. [11] At that moment, three men, who had been sent to me from Caesarea, arrived at the house where we were staying. [12] The Spirit instructed me to go with them without hesitation; so these six brothers came along with me and we entered into the man's house. [13] He told us how he had seen an angel standing in his house and telling him: 'Send someone to Joppa and fetch Simon, also known as Peter. [14] He will bring you a message by which you and all your household will be saved.'

[15] I had begun to address them when suddenly the Holy Spirit came upon them, just as it had come upon us at the beginning. [16] Then I remembered what the Lord had said: 'John baptized with water, but you shall be baptized with the Holy Spirit.' [17] If, then, God had given them the same gift that he had given us when we believed in the Lord Jesus Christ, who was I to resist God?"

[18] When they heard this they set their minds at rest and praised God saying, "Then God has granted life-giving repentance to the pagan nations as well."

ACTS 11:1-18

Read: Peter is questioned in Jerusalem because he got together with the Gentiles. He uses his latest vision to support his actions: God has also granted to the Gentiles the repentance that leads to life.

Reflect: What is the similarity of the coming of the Holy Spirit to the Gentiles, and what happened on Pentecost? Does anyone have the authority to remove/separate a faithful from the faith of the Church?

Pray: Pray that the Holy Spirit fill you and allow you to see life from a new perspective. Ask God to help you understand that all can be a Christian if someone talks to them about faith that leads them to conversion.

Act: Like Peter, be willing to accept a new spiritual perception to change your attitude toward others. Have a gesture of harmony with someone who does not share your political, social or religious views.

The foundation of the Church at Antioch

[19] Those who had been scattered, because of the persecution over Stephen, traveled as far as Phoenicia, Cyprus, and Antioch, proclaiming the message, but only to the Jews. [20] But there were some natives of Cyprus and Cyrene among them who, on coming into Antioch, spoke also to the Greeks giving them the good news of the Lord Jesus. [21] The hand of the Lord was with them so that a great number believed and turned to the Lord.

[22] News of this reached the ears of the Church in Jerusalem, so they sent Barnabas to Antioch. [23] When he arrived and saw the manifest signs of God's favor, he rejoiced and urged them all to remain firmly faithful to the Lord; [24] for he, himself, was a good man, filled with the Holy Spirit and faith. Thus large crowds came to know the Lord.

[25] Then Barnabas went off to Tarsus, to look for Saul; [26] and when he found him, he brought him to Antioch. For a whole year, they had meetings with the Church and instructed many people. It was in Antioch that the disciples were first called *Christians*.

[27] At that time, some prophets went down from Jerusalem to Antioch; [28] and one of them named Agabus, inspired by the Holy Spirit, foretold that a great famine would spread over the whole world. This actually happened in the days of Emperor Claudius. [29] So the disciples decided,

within their means, to set something aside and to send relief to the brothers and sisters who were living in Judea. ³⁰ They did this and sent their donations to the elders by Barnabas and Saul.

ACTS 11:19-30

Read: The early Church continues to grow, expanding with Gentile converts in Antioch. Barnabas is sent from Jerusalem to investigate. He goes to Tarsus seeking Saul and brings him back to Antioch, where the disciples are called Christians for the first time.

Reflect: Why do so many people embrace the faith proclaimed by the early Church? What does it mean to you to be "Christian"?

Pray: Pray that every day many people may know Jesus Christ and embrace him as their Savior. Pray for those who are considering becoming Christians and for the catechumens, that they may not be discouraged by difficulties and always receive the power of the Spirit.

Act: Be consistent with the Christian faith you profess. Let your faith shine by your testimony, especially before those who doubt. Perform an act of solidarity with the community when the occasion arises.

James is put to death; Peter's miraculous escape

12 ¹ About that time, King Herod decided to persecute some members of the Church. ² He had James, the brother of John, killed with the sword, ³ and when he saw how it pleased the Jews, he proceeded to arrest Peter also.

This happened during the festival of the Unleavened Bread. ⁴ Herod had him seized and thrown into prison with four squads, each of four soldiers, to guard him. He wanted to bring him to trial before the people after the Passover feast, ⁵ but while Peter was kept in prison, the whole Church prayed earnestly for him.

⁶ On the very night before Herod was to bring him to trial, Peter was sleeping between two soldiers, bound by a double chain, while guards kept watch at the gate of the prison.

⁷ Suddenly, an angel of the Lord stood there and a light shone in the

prison cell. The angel tapped Peter on the side and woke him saying, "Get up quickly!" At once, the chains fell from Peter's wrists. The angel said, "Put on your belt and your sandals." Peter did so; [8] and the angel added, "Now, put on your cloak and follow me."

[9] Peter followed him out, yet he did not realize that what was happening with the angel was real; he thought he was seeing a vision. [10] They passed the first guard and then the second, and they came to the iron door leading out to the city, which opened by itself for them. They went out and made their way down a narrow alley when suddenly the angel left him.

[11] Then Peter recovered his senses and said, "Now I know that the Lord has sent his angel and has rescued me from Herod's clutches and from all that the Jews had in store for me."

[12] Peter then found his bearings and came to the house of Mary, the mother of John also known as Mark, where many were gathered together and were praying. [13] When he knocked at the outside door, a maid named Rhoda came to answer it. [14] On recognizing the voice of Peter she was so overcome with joy that, instead of opening the door, she ran in to announce that Peter was at the door. [15] They said to her, "You are crazy!" And as she insisted, they said, "It must be his angel."

[16] Meanwhile, Peter continued knocking and, when they finally opened the door, they were amazed to see him. [17] He motioned to them with his hand to be quiet and told them how the Lord had brought him out of prison. And he said to them, "Report this to James and to the brothers." Then he left and went to another place.

[18] At daybreak, there was a great commotion among the soldiers over what had become of Peter. [19] Herod began a search for him and, not finding him, had the guards questioned and executed. After that, he came down from Judea to Caesarea and stayed there.

Herod's death

[20] At that time, Herod was angry with the people of Tyre and Sidon. By general agreement they appeared before him and, after having won over Blastus, the king's treasurer, they asked for peace, for their country was supplied with food from the territory of Herod. [21] On the appointed day Herod, clothed in royal robes, sat on his throne and addressed them. [22] So the assembled crowd shouted back, "A god is speaking, not a man!"

[23] The angel of the Lord immediately struck Herod for he did not return the honor to God, and he died eaten by worms.

[24] Meanwhile, the word of God was increasing and spreading. [25] Barnabas and Saul carried out their mission and then came back to Jerusalem, taking with them John, also called Mark.

ACTS 12:1-25

Read: King Herod has James, the brother of John, put to death and Peter, imprisoned. Peter's unexpected release from prison results in a humorous scene. He then goes to the community who is praying for him. We also learn of Herod's gruesome death.

Reflect: Martyrdom is a seed that converts new people to Christianity. What difficulties can "prevent us" from witnessing our faith? Have you ever felt liberated by God?

Pray: Ask for the courage of the martyrs so that nothing prevents you from witnessing your faith in adverse situations. Pray to God to protect the missionaries from dangers.

Act: Do not be afraid to give testimony to your faith in difficult situations. Trust in the care and protection that God offers to His followers.

Paul sent by the Church

13 [1] There were at Antioch—in the Church which was there—prophets and teachers: Barnabas, Symeon known as Niger, Lucius of Cyrene, Manaen who had been brought up with Herod, and Saul. [2] On one occasion, while they were celebrating the Lord and fasting, the Holy Spirit said to them, "Set apart for me Barnabas and Saul to do the work for which I have called them." [3] So, after fasting and praying, they laid their hands on them and sent them off.

Paul's first mission

[4] These then, sent by the Holy Spirit, went down to the port of Seleucia and from there sailed to Cyprus. [5] Upon their arrival in Salamis, they proclaimed the word of God in the Jewish synagogue; John was with them as an assistant.

⁶ They traveled over the whole island as far as Paphos, where they met a certain magician named Bar-Jesus, a Jewish false prophet, ⁷ who lived with the governor Sergius Paulus, an intelligent man. He had summoned Barnabas and Saul, and wanted to hear the word of God. ⁸ But they were opposed by the Elymas (that is, the magician) who tried to turn the governor from the faith.

⁹ Then Saul, also known as Paul, full of the Holy Spirit, looked intently at him ¹⁰ and said, "You son of the devil, full of all kinds of deceit, and enemy of all that is right! Will you never stop perverting the straight paths of the Lord? ¹¹ Now, the Lord's hand is upon you; you will become blind and, for a time, you will not see the light of day." At once, a misty darkness came upon him and he groped about for someone to lead him by the hand.

¹² The governor saw what had happened; he believed and was deeply impressed by the teaching about the Lord.

ACTS 13:1-12

Read: After spending time in prayer and fasting, the Holy Spirit chooses Barnabas and Paul to proclaim the Gospel beyond the Church of Antioch, which is a pagan territory.

Reflect: Is it important that the community takes time for prayer and fasting before sending their missionaries? Why? How do you collaborate with this endeavor?

Pray: There are false prophets, people who would deliberately deceive others. Pray that they change their attitudes. Ask for light to distinguish God's words from the words of people, and courage to denounce those that are false.

Act: In times of adversity, challenge your community to always pray to God to help them discern for the best decision.

Paul in the capital of Pisidia

¹³ From Paphos, Paul and his companions set sail and came to Perga in Pamphylia. There, John left them and returned to Jerusalem, ¹⁴ while they went on from Perga and came to Antioch in Pisidia. On the Sabbath day, they entered the synagogue and sat down. ¹⁵ After the reading of the law and the prophets, the officials of the synagogue sent this

message to them, "Brothers, if you have any word of encouragement for the assembly, please speak up."

¹⁶ So Paul arose, motioned to them for silence and began, "Fellow Israelites and also all you who fear God, listen. ¹⁷ The God of our people Israel chose our ancestors; and after he had made them increase during their stay in Egypt, he led them out by powerful deeds. ¹⁸ For forty years he fed them in the desert; ¹⁹ and after he had destroyed seven nations in the land of Canaan, he gave them their land as an inheritance. ²⁰ All this took four hundred and fifty years. ²¹ After that, he gave them Judges, until Samuel the prophet. Then they asked for a king; and God gave them Saul, son of Kish, of the tribe of Benjamin; and he was king for forty years. ²² After that time, God removed him and raised up David as king, to whom he bore witness saying: *I have found David, the son of Jesse, a man after my own heart, who will do all I want him to do.*

²³ It is from the descendants of David that God has now raised up the promised Savior of Israel, Jesus. ²⁴ Before he appeared, John proclaimed a baptism of repentance for all the people of Israel. ²⁵ As John was ending his life's work, he said: 'I am not what you think I am, for after me another one is coming, whose sandal I am not worthy to untie.'

²⁶ Brothers, children, and descendants of Abraham, and you also who fear God, it is to you that this message of salvation has been sent. ²⁷ It is a fact, that the inhabitants of Jerusalem and their leaders did not recognize Jesus. Yet, in condemning him, they fulfilled the words of the prophets that are read every Sabbath, but not understood. ²⁸ Even though they found no charge against him that deserved death, they asked Pilate to have him executed. ²⁹ And after they had carried out all that had been written concerning him, they took him down from the cross and laid him in a tomb.

³⁰ But God raised him from the dead, ³¹ and for many days thereafter he showed himself to those who had come up with him from Galilee to Jerusalem. They have now become his witnesses before the people. ³² We, ourselves, announce to you this Good News: All that God promised our ancestors, ³³ he has fulfilled for us, their descendants, by raising Jesus, according to what is written in the second Psalm: *You are my Son, today I have begotten you.* ³⁴ On raising him from the dead, so that he would never know the decay of death, God fulfilled his promise: *I will give you the holy blessings, the sure ones that I kept for David.*

^{35} Moreover, in another place it is said: *You will not allow your holy one to suffer corruption.* ^{36} Now David was subjected to corruption for he died and was laid beside his ancestors after having served God's purpose in his own time. ^{37} But the one God raised up—Jesus—did not know corruption. $^{38-39}$ Through him, fellow Israelites, you have forgiveness of sins, and this is our good news. Whoever believes in him is freed of everything from which you could not be freed by the law of Moses.

^{40} Now, watch out, lest what was said by the prophet happens to you: ^{41} *Take care, you cynics; be amazed and disappear! For I am about to do something in your days which you would never believe even if you had been told."*

^{42} As Paul and Barnabas withdrew, they were invited to speak again on the same subject the following Sabbath. ^{43} After that, when the assembly broke up, many Jews and devout God-fearing people followed them; and to these they spoke, urging them to hold fast to the grace of God.

ACTS 13:13-43

Read: Paul arrives with his companions in Antioch in Pisidia and delivered an important sermon at the synagogue. He explains how the history of Israel is fulfilled in Jesus Christ. Many Jews are converted.

Reflect: Compare this discourse of Paul with Peter's discourse on Pentecost (Acts 2:14-40). Early Christianity made its way with the proclamation of Jesus Christ, who died on the cross, and whom God resurrected. Christianity is primarily witnessing life and faith.

Pray: Pray that the cross of Jesus Christ gives meaning to your life and to the suffering of so many people in history. Ask for the grace of being able to contemplate the victory of life over death.

Act: In suffering, remember the cross of Jesus Christ and live it with courage and without fear, knowing that with Christ's resurrection life triumphs over death.

⁴⁴ The following Sabbath almost the entire city gathered to listen to Paul, who spoke a fairly long time about the Lord. ⁴⁵ But the presence of such a crowd made the Jews jealous. So they began to oppose with insults, whatever Paul said.

⁴⁶ Then Paul and Barnabas spoke out firmly, saying, "It was necessary that God's word be first proclaimed to you, but since you now reject it and judge yourselves to be unworthy of eternal life, we turn to non-Jewish people. ⁴⁷ For thus we were commanded by the Lord: *I have set you as a light to the pagan nations, so that you may bring my salvation to the ends of the earth.*"

⁴⁸ Those who were not Jews rejoiced, when they heard this, and praised the message of the Lord; and all those destined for everlasting life believed in it. ⁴⁹ Thus the word spread, throughout the whole region.

⁵⁰ Some of the Jews, however, incited God-fearing women of the upper class and the leading men of the city as well and stirred up an intense persecution against Paul and Barnabas. Finally, they had them expelled from their region. ⁵¹ The apostles shook the dust from their feet in protest against this people and went to Iconium, ⁵² leaving the disciples filled with joy and the Holy Spirit.

ACTS 13:44-52

Read: The Jews reject the preaching of Paul and Barnabas, and so they start to preach to the Gentiles, who rejoice and welcome this Good News.

Reflect: Why can the Christian message be rejected? Have you ever done it? How was your initiation to the faith?

Pray: Give thanks for your faith in Jesus Christ and ask for courage to never reject him, even in situations that may cause your rejection because of him.

Act: Celebrate often your faith in community and talk about it without fear.

Iconium is evangelized

14 ¹ In Iconium Paul and Barnabas likewise went into the Jewish synagogue and preached in such a manner that a great number of Jews and Greeks believed. ² But the Jews, who would not believe, stirred up the pagan people and poisoned their minds against the brothers. ³In spite of this, Paul and Barnabas spent considerable time there. They spoke fearlessly of the Lord who confirmed the message of his grace with the miraculous signs and wonders he gave them the power to do.

⁴But the people of the city were divided, some siding with the Jews and some with the apostles. ⁵A move was made by pagans and Jews, together with their leaders, to harm the apostles and to stone them. ⁶But Paul and Barnabas learned of this and fled to the Lycaonian towns of Lystra and Derbe and to the surrounding countryside, ⁷where they continued preaching the Good News.

Lystra and Derbe

Paul and Barnabas spent a fairly long time at Lystra. ⁸There was a crippled man in Lystra who had never been able to stand or walk. ⁹One day, as he was listening to the preaching, Paul looked intently at him and saw that he had the faith to be saved. ¹⁰So he said with a loud voice, "Stand upright on your feet." And the man leaped up and began walking.

¹¹When the people saw what Paul had done, they cried out in the language of Lycaonia, "The gods have come to us in human likeness!" ¹²They named Barnabas Zeus, and Paul they called Hermes since he was the chief speaker. ¹³Even the priest of the temple of Zeus, which stood outside the town, brought oxen and garlands to the gate; together with the people, he wanted to offer sacrifice to them.

¹⁴When Barnabas and Paul heard this, they tore their garments to show their indignation and rushed into the crowd, shouting, ¹⁵"Friends, why are you doing this? We are human beings, with the same weakness you have, and we are now telling you to turn away from these useless things, to the living God who made the heavens, the earth, the sea and all that is in them. ¹⁶In past generations he allowed each nation to go its own way, ¹⁷though he never stopped making himself known; for he is continually doing good, giving you rain from heaven and fruitful seasons, providing you with food and filling your hearts with gladness."

¹⁸Even these words could hardly keep the crowd from offering sacrifice to them.

¹⁹Then some Jews arrived from Antioch and Iconium and turned the people against them. They stoned Paul and dragged him out of the town,

leaving him for dead. [20] But, when his disciples gathered around him, he stood up and returned to the town. And the next day, he left for Derbe with Barnabas.

ACTS 14:1-20

Read: Paul and Barnabas continue their mission. Their preaching generates conflicts. They are deified by the powerful works they perform, but they are also mistreated. And still, they continue.

Reflect: God works wonders through his servants. By their works, they can either be deified or despised. Have you felt praise and scorn for expressing your faith? Where do you get the strength to get up?

Pray: Ask a courageous attitude like the one of Paul and Barnabas to proclaim your faith. Ask also for the grace to express through your work the presence of God in the world.

Act: Perform a gesture for which God can be present among others. Like Paul, get up and start again before the next problem comes.

Return to Antioch

[21] After proclaiming the gospel in that town and making many disciples, they returned to Lystra and Iconium, and on to Antioch. [22] They were strengthening the disciples and encouraging them to remain firm in the faith; for they said, "We must go through many trials to enter the kingdom of God." [23] In each church they appointed elders and, after praying and fasting, they commended them to the Lord in whom they had placed their faith.

[24] Then they traveled through Pisidia and came to Pamphylia. [25] They preached the word in Perga and went down to Attalia. [26] From there, they sailed back to Antioch, where they had first been commended to God's grace for the task they had now completed.

[27] On their arrival, they gathered the Church together and told them all that God had done through them, and how he had opened the door of faith to the non-Jews. [28] They spent a fairly long time there with the disciples.

ACTS OF THE APOSTLES 15

> **ACTS 14:21-28**
>
> **Read:** The first missionary journey ends with a positive and encouraging evaluation, with a good number of communities organized in distant cities. The Church has opened the door to the Gentiles since most of the Jews despise faith in Jesus Christ.
>
> **Reflect:** "Reminding them that they had to go through many trials to enter the kingdom of God" (v. 22). Have you experienced that the kingdom of God enters through the narrow gate, with work and daily witness? In a matter of faith, where do you feel "at home"?
>
> **Pray:** Give thanks for your church community. If you feel distant to it, ask for courage to approach it. Ask to have no fear of adversity.
>
> **Act:** Thank publicly the presence of the community in your faith experience. Share with someone the good things God has done for you.

The council at Jerusalem

15 ¹Some persons who had come from Judea to Antioch were teaching the brothers in this way, "Unless you are circumcised, according to the law of Moses, you cannot be saved."

²Because of this, there was trouble; and Paul and Barnabas had fierce arguments with them. For Paul told the people to remain as they were when they became believers. Finally, those who had come from Jerusalem suggested that Paul and Barnabas and some others go up to Jerusalem, to discuss the matter with the apostles and elders.

³They were sent on their way by the Church. As they passed through Phoenicia and Samaria they reported how the non-Jews had turned to God; and there was great joy among all the brothers and sisters.

⁴On their arrival in Jerusalem, they were welcomed by the Church, the apostles and the elders, to whom they told all that God had done through them. ⁵Some believers, however, who belonged to the party of the Pharisees, stood up and said that non-Jewish men must be circumcised and instructed to keep the law of Moses. ⁶So the apostles and elders met together to consider this matter.

⁷ As the discussions became heated, Peter stood up and said to them, "Brothers, you know that from the beginning, God chose me among you, so that non-Jews could hear the Good News from me and believe. ⁸ God, who can read hearts, put himself on their side by giving the Holy Spirit to them, just as he did to us. ⁹ He made no distinction between them and us, and cleansed their hearts through faith. ¹⁰ So, why do you want to put God to the test? Why do you lay on the disciples a burden that neither our ancestors nor we, ourselves, were able to carry? ¹¹ We believe, indeed, that we are saved through the grace of the Lord Jesus, just as they are."

¹² The whole assembly kept silent as they listened to Paul and Barnabas tell of all the miraculous signs and wonders that God had done, through them, among the non-Jews.

¹³ After they had finished, James spoke up, "Listen to me, brothers. ¹⁴ Symeon has just explained how God first showed his care by taking a people for himself from non-Jewish nations. ¹⁵ And the words of the prophets agree with this, for Scripture says,

¹⁶ *After this I will return and rebuild the booth of David which has fallen; I will rebuild its ruins and set it up again.* ¹⁷ *Then, the rest of humanity will look for the Lord, and all the nations will be consecrated to my Name. So says the Lord, who does today* ¹⁸ *what he decided from the beginning.*

¹⁹ Because of this, I think that we should not make difficulties for those non-Jews who are turning to God. ²⁰ Let us just tell them not to eat food that is unclean from having been offered to idols; to keep themselves from prohibited marriages; and not to eat the flesh of animals that have been strangled; or any blood. ²¹ For, from the earliest times, Moses has been taught in every place, and every Sabbath his laws are recalled."

ACTS 15:1-21

Read: There were complaints from some Jewish Christians. The issue of how to accept gentile converts is addressed in Jerusalem. Finally, it was decided to allow them to embrace the faith without having to meet all Jewish precepts.

Reflect: Do we need many precepts to be a good Christian? Where do these demands come from at times?

> **Pray:** Ask the Spirit for light to differentiate the essential from the secondary in the experience of faith. Ask for an open mind and heart to accept other Christians who live their faith differently.
>
> **Act:** Approach someone in your community whom you secretly reproach of something. Talk to him or her and try to understand and accept the person.

The council's letters

²²Then the apostles and elders, together with the whole Church, decided to choose representatives from among them to send to Antioch with Paul and Barnabas. These were Judas, known as Barsabbas, and Silas, both leading men among the brothers. ²³They took with them the following letter:

"Greetings from the apostles and elders, your brothers, to the believers of non-Jewish birth in Antioch, Syria and Cilicia. ²⁴We have heard, that some persons from among us have worried you with their discussions, and troubled your peace of mind. They were not appointed by us. ²⁵But now, it has seemed right to us, in an assembly, to choose representatives and to send them to you, along with our beloved Barnabas and Paul, ²⁶who have dedicated their lives to the service of our Lord Jesus Christ. ²⁷We send you then, Judas and Silas, who, themselves, will give you these instructions by word of mouth.

²⁸We, with the Holy Spirit, have decided not to put any other burden on you except what is necessary: ²⁹You are to abstain from blood; from the meat of strangled animals; and from prohibited marriages. If you keep yourselves from these, you will do well. Farewell."

³⁰After saying good-bye, the messengers went to Antioch where they assembled the community and handed them the letter. ³¹When they read the news, all were delighted with the encouragement it gave them. ³²Judas and Silas, who were themselves prophets, spoke at length to encourage and strengthen them. ³³After they had spent some time there, the messengers were sent off in peace by the believers; ³⁴Silas, however, preferred to stay with them and only Judas went off. ³⁵So Paul and Barnabas continued in Antioch, teaching and preaching with many others, the word of God.

ACTS 15:22-35

Read: The Jerusalem Church, the Mother Church, informs the Gentiles, that they are welcomed into Christianity only by following the essential precepts.

Reflect: What is the role of the Spirit in the decision of the Church? How does the Spirit operate in your life? Do you feel how the Spirit frees you from worries?

Pray: Ask the inspiration of the Holy Spirit when you need to resolve conflicts at home, at work or in the community. Give thanks for the diversity of people who make up your environment.

Act: Identify the secondary aspects of Christian life and place them after the important ones.

Paul's second mission

[36] After some days, Paul said to Barnabas, "Let us return and visit the believers in every town where we proclaimed the word of the Lord, to see how they are getting on." [37] Barnabas wanted to take with them John, also called Mark, [38] but Paul did not think it right to take him, since he had not stayed with them to the end of their mission, but had turned back and left them in Pamphylia. [39] Such a sharp disagreement resulted that the two finally separated. Barnabas took Mark along with him and sailed for Cyprus. [40] Paul, for his part, chose Silas and left commended by the brothers and sisters to the grace of the Lord.

[41] He traveled throughout Syria and Cilicia, strengthening the churches there.

ACTS 15:36-41

Read: Determined to start their second voyage, a dispute between Paul and Barnabas over John, also called Mark, causes separation. Each follows his own path.

Reflect: What does the situation described in the text reveal regarding human nature? Have you experienced any similar situation? Can anything positive come out of that?

Pray: Ask for light to sense the presence of God amidst human

> misunderstandings and disagreements. Give thanks for the times
> when this has happened and pray that you may continue to ex-
> perience it.
>
> **Act:** Overcome pride and try to reconcile with that person with
> whom you had any misunderstanding. If possible, look for the
> positive side of the situation.

Paul recruits Timothy

16 [1] Paul traveled on to Derbe and then to Lystra. A disciple named Timothy lived there whose mother was a believer of Jewish origin but whose father was a Greek. [2] As the believers at Lystra and Iconium spoke well of him, Paul wanted Timothy to accompany him. [3] So he took him and because of the Jews of that place who all knew that his father was a Greek, he circumcised him.

[4] As they traveled from town to town, they delivered the decisions of the apostles and elders in Jerusalem, for the people to obey. [5] Meanwhile, the churches grew stronger in faith and increased in number every day.

[6] They traveled through Phrygia and Galatia, because they had been prevented by the Holy Spirit from preaching the message in the province of Asia. [7] When they came to Mysia, they tried to go on to Bithynia, but the Spirit of Jesus did not allow them to do this. [8] So passing by Mysia, they went down to Troas.

Paul goes to Macedonia

[9] There, one night, Paul had a vision. A Macedonian stood before him and begged him, "Come over to Macedonia and help us!" [10] When he awoke, he told us of this vision; and we understood that the Lord was calling us to give the Good News to the Macedonian people.

[11] So we put out to sea from Troas and sailed straight across to Samothrace Island and the next day to Neapolis. [12] From there, we went inland to Philippi, the leading city of the district of Macedonia and a Roman colony. We spent some days in that city.

[13] On the Sabbath, we went outside the city gate to the bank of the river, where we thought the Jews would gather to pray. We sat down and

began speaking to the women who were gathering there. [14]One of them was a God-fearing woman named Lydia, from the city of Thyatira, a dealer in purple cloth.

As she listened, the Lord opened her heart to respond to what Paul was saying. [15]After she had been baptized, together with her household, she invited us to her house, "If you think I am faithful to the Lord, come and stay at my house." And she persuaded us to accept her invitation.

ACTS 16:1-15

Read: While traveling, Paul chooses Timothy as a companion, a member of his community. In his company, he will be sent to Macedonia. In Philippi, Lydia, a rich merchant, and her family welcome the Good News and are baptized.

Reflect: How to choose the right traveling companions? Are you receptive, like Paul, to all the signs that God puts in your life? How do you welcome and listen to people who speak to you of God?

Pray: Thank God for the signs and the people He places on your way. Pray to be enlightened to continue discovering His will in everyday life.

Act: When the opportunity arises, speak well of another person, so as to help that person grow and achieve his or her goals in life. Ask for help from others when needed.

Paul and Silas in prison

[16]One day, as we were on our way to the place of prayer, we were met by a slave girl who had a spirit of divination and gained much profit for her owners by her fortune-telling.

[17]She followed Paul and the rest of us, shouting: "These people are servants of the Most High God. They will make known to you a way of salvation." [18]The girl did this for several days, until Paul was annoyed. Then he turned around and said to the spirit, "In the name of Jesus Christ, I command you, come out of her!" The spirit went out of her that very moment.

[19]When her owners realized that all the profits they expected had gone, they seized Paul and Silas and dragged them into the marketplace,

before the local authorities. [20] And when they had turned them over to the officials, they said, [21] "These people are Jews and they are disturbing our city. They have come here to introduce customs which are not lawful for us Romans to adopt or practice."

[22] So they set the crowd against them; and the officials tore the clothes off Paul and Silas and ordered them to be flogged. [23] And after inflicting many blows on them, they threw them into prison, charging the jailer to guard them safely. [24] Upon receiving these instructions, he threw them into the inner cell and fastened their feet in the stocks.

A miraculous deliverance

[25] About midnight, Paul and Silas were praying and singing hymns to God, and the other prisoners were listening. [26] Suddenly, a severe earthquake shook the place, rocking the prison to its foundations. Immediately, all the doors flew open and the chains of all the prisoners fell off. [27] The jailer woke up to see the prison gates wide open. Thinking that the prisoners had escaped, he drew his sword to kill himself, [28] but Paul shouted to him, "Do not harm yourself! We are all still here."

[29] The jailer asked for a light, then rushed in, and fell at the feet of Paul and Silas. [30] After he had secured the other prisoners, he led them out and asked, "Sirs, what must I do to be saved?" [31] They answered, "Believe in the Lord Jesus Christ and you, and your household, will be saved." [32] Then they spoke the word of God to him and to all his household.

[33] Even at that hour of the night, the jailer took care of them and washed their wounds; and he and his whole household were baptized at once. [34] He led them to his house, spread a meal before them and joyfully celebrated with his whole household his new found faith in God.

[35] The next morning, the officials sent police officers with the order, "Let those men go." [36] So the jailer said to Paul and Silas, "The officials have sent an order for you and Silas to be released. You may leave and go in peace."

[37] But Paul said to him, "They flogged us publicly, and jailed us without trial, men who are Roman citizens; and now they want to smuggle us out secretly? Oh no! Let them come themselves and lead us out."

[38] The police officers reported this to the officials, who were afraid when they heard that Paul and Silas were Roman citizens. [39] So they

came and apologized to them, took them out and asked them to leave the town.

⁴⁰ Once outside the prison, Paul and Silas went to Lydia's house, where they met and encouraged the brothers and sisters, and then departed.

ACTS 16:16-40

Read: Paul and Silas are arrested and punished for "disturbing the city" with the announcement of the Good News. Soon after, with the help of the Lord, they are released, take refuge in the home of Lydia and leave the city.

Reflect: What does the hospitality that Paul and his companions receive, mean? How should you behave in difficult times? To whom should you provide hospitality?

Pray: Pray for the missionaries who are faced with difficulties, and all the prisoners in just or unjust causes. Ask God to be always present in their lives.

Act: Provide hospitality with joy. Embrace people as sent by the Lord himself. If you know a person in prison, visit him/her.

Difficulties in Thessalonica

17 ¹ Paul and Silas took the road through Amphipolis and Apollonia and came to Thessalonica, where there was a Jewish synagogue. ² As Paul used to do, he went to the synagogue; and on three Sabbaths he held discussions with them about the Scriptures. ³ He explained, and proved to them, that the Messiah had to suffer and rise from the dead, and he said, "Such a Messiah is this Jesus whom I am proclaiming to you."

⁴ Some of them were convinced and joined Paul and Silas. So too, did a great number of Greeks sympathetic to Judaism, and many prominent women.

⁵ This only made the Jews jealous; so they gathered some of the good-for-nothing street loafers and formed a mob to start a riot in the town. They came to the house of Jason, in an attempt to bring Paul and Silas before the people's assembly. ⁶ Not finding them there, they dragged off Jason and some believers to the city authorities shouting, "These people

who have turned the world upside down, have come here also, [7]and Jason has given them hospitality. They all disregard the decrees of the Emperor and claim that there is another King, Jesus."

[8]In this way, they upset the crowd and the city officials who heard them. [9]The officials released Jason and the others on bail.

[10]As soon as night fell, the believers sent Paul and Silas off to Beroea. On their arrival, they went to the Jewish synagogue. [11]Its members were more open-minded than those in Thessalonica and welcomed the message with great enthusiasm. Each day they examined the Scriptures to see if these things were so. [12]Many of them came to believe, as did numerous influential Greek women and many men as well.

[13]But when the Jews of Thessalonica came to know that the word of God had been proclaimed by Paul in Beroea also, they hurried there to cause a commotion and stir up the crowds. [14]At once, the believers sent Paul away to the coast; but both Silas and Timothy stayed in Beroea. [15]Paul was taken as far as Athens by his escort, who then returned to Beroea with instructions for Silas and Timothy to come to him as soon as possible.

ACTS 17:1-15

Read: The mixed responses to the missionary proclamation continue in the journeys to Thessalonica and Beroea. Antagonism toward Paul and Silas escalates, crowds are stirred up, and the missionaries need to depart.

Reflect: Are only religious issues that cause shock and irritate the people? Do you mind if others think, believe or act differently from you? Do you know how to stand firm in your Christian convictions?

Pray: Ask God to help you overcome the feelings that make you act badly toward others, such as envy and anger. Also, ask for strength to compensate for the damage caused.

Act: Approach a person you have offended with your prejudices, with your feelings of envy or anger. Reconcile with her/him.

Paul in Athens

[16] While Paul was waiting for them in Athens, he felt very uneasy at the sight of a city full of idols. [17] He held discussions in the synagogue with the Jews and the God-fearing people, as well as daily debates in the public square with ordinary passersby.

[18] Epicureans and Stoic philosophers debated with him, some of them asking, "What is this babbler trying to say?" Others commented, "He sounds like a promoter of foreign gods," because he was heard to speak of Jesus and 'the Resurrection.' [19] So they took Paul and led him off to the Areopagus hall, and said, "We would like to know what this new teaching is that you are talking about. [20] Some of the things we hear you say sound strange to us and we would like to know what they mean."

[21] Indeed, all Athenian citizens, as well as the foreigners who live there, have as their favorite occupation talking about or listening to the latest news.

[22] Then Paul stood up in the Areopagus hall and said, "Athenian citizens, I note that in every way you are very religious. [23] As I walked around looking at your shrines, I even discovered an altar with this inscription: *To an unknown God.* Now, what you worship as unknown, I intend to make known to you.

[24] God, who made the world and all that is in it, does not dwell in sanctuaries made by human hands, being as he is Lord of heaven and earth. [25] Nor does his worship depend on anything made by human hands, as if he were in need. Rather, it is he who gives life and breath and everything else to everyone. [26] From one stock he created the whole human race, to live throughout all the earth, and he fixed the time and the boundaries of each nation. [27] He wanted them to seek him by themselves, even if it was only by groping for him, that they succeed in finding him.

Yet, he is not far from any one of us. [28] For, in him, we live and move and have our being, as some of your poets have said: *for we, too, are his offspring.* [29] If we are indeed God's offspring, we ought not to think of divinity as something like a statue of gold or silver or stone, a product of human art and imagination.

[30] But now, God prefers to overlook this time of ignorance; and he calls on all people to change their ways. [31] He has already set a day on which he will judge the world with justice through a man he has appointed. And

so that all may believe it, he has just given a sign, by raising this man from the dead."

³²When they heard Paul speak of a resurrection from death, some made fun of him, while others said, "We must hear you on this topic some other time." ³³At that point Paul left. ³⁴But a few did join him, and believed. Among them were Dionysius, a member of the Areopagus court, a woman named Damaris, and some others.

ACTS 17:16-34

Read: In Athens, Paul speaks to the Jews in the synagogue and to the Gentiles in the marketplace. To the latter, he explains that the God of the Jews is the one who created the world and keeps it; he is offering salvation to all through Jesus Christ, crucified and risen.

Reflect: Paul speaks to the Jews and the Gentiles, to each group in their own language and in their context. What is our context today to accept faith? Do we need something more than the reason to believe? What does it mean in our daily life to believe in Jesus, dead and risen, as the savior of the world?

Pray: Pray for a deeper faith, to seek a better understanding of human situations. Give thanks to God for all great and incomprehensible things that He does in life.

Act: Encourage conversations about the relationship that should exist between faith and reason. Do not hesitate to express your doubts of faith with the responsible leaders of your community.

Paul in Corinth

18 ¹After this, Paul left Athens and went to Corinth. ²There he found a Jew named Aquila, a native of Pontus, who had recently come from Italy with his wife Priscilla following a decree of the Emperor Claudius, which ordered all Jews to leave Rome. ³Paul went to visit them and then stayed and worked with them because they shared the same trade of tent making. ⁴Every Sabbath he held discussions in the synagogue, trying to convince both Jews and Greeks.

⁵When Silas and Timothy came down from Macedonia, Paul was able

to give himself wholly to preaching and proving to the Jews that Jesus was the Messiah. ⁶One day, when they opposed him and insulted him, he shook the dust from his clothes in protest saying, "Your blood be on your own heads! I am innocent. I am not to blame if, from now on, I go to the non-Jews."

⁷So Paul left there and went to the house of a God-fearing man named Titus Justus, who lived next door to the synagogue. ⁸A leading man of the synagogue, Crispus, along with his whole household, believed in the Lord. On hearing Paul, many more Corinthians believed and were baptized.

⁹One night, in a vision, the Lord said to Paul, "Do not be afraid, but continue speaking and do not be silent, ¹⁰for many people in this city are mine. I am with you, so no one will harm you." ¹¹So Paul stayed a year and a half in that place teaching the word of God among them.

¹²When Gallio was governor of Achaia, the Jews made a united attack on Paul and brought him before the court. And they accused him, ¹³"This man tries to persuade us to worship God in ways that are against the law."

¹⁴Paul was about to speak in his own defense when Gallio said to the Jews, "If it were a matter of a misdeed or vicious crime, I would have to consider your complaint. ¹⁵But since this is a quarrel about teachings and divine names that are proper to your own law, see to it yourselves: I refuse to judge such matters." ¹⁶And he sent them out of the court.

¹⁷Then the people seized Sosthenes, a leading man of the synagogue, and beat him in front of the tribunal; but Gallio paid no attention to it.

¹⁸Paul stayed on with the disciples in Corinth for many days; he then left them and sailed off with Priscilla and Aquila for Syria. And as he was no longer under a vow he had taken, he shaved his head before sailing from Cenchreae.

ACTS 18:1-18

Read: Paul's missionary journeys bring him to Corinth. There he befriends Aquila and Priscilla, Jews who were exiled from Rome. He works with them and announces the Gospel to the Jews and Gentiles.

Reflect: In his missionary activity, Paul takes care of his own needs. He does not want to be a burden to the community. How do you combine work with the activities of your faith? Does your work allow you to be a witness to the Gospel?

Pray: Ask the Spirit to accompany and guide you in your daily work to enable you to witness your faith in Jesus Christ. Give thanks to the divine omnipresence.

Act: Have Christian attitudes in your work. May this give testimony of your faith.

[19] When they reached Ephesus, he left Priscilla and Aquila behind and entered the synagogue to hold discussions with the Jews. [20] But although they asked him to stay longer, he declined. [21] And he took leave of them saying, "God willing, I will come back to you again." Then he set sail from Ephesus. [22] On landing at Caesarea, he went up to greet the Church, and then went down to Antioch.

[23] After spending some time there, he left and traveled from place to place through Galatia and Phrygia, strengthening the disciples.

[24] A certain Jew named Apollos, a native of Alexandria, arrived at Ephesus. He was an eloquent speaker and an authority on the Scriptures, [25] and he had some knowledge of the way of the Lord. With great enthusiasm he preached, and taught correctly about Jesus, although he knew only of John's baptism. [26] As he began to speak boldly in the synagogue, Priscilla and Aquila heard him; so they took him home with them and explained to him the way more accurately. [27] As Apollos wished to go to Achaia, the believers encouraged him and wrote to the disciples there to welcome him. When he arrived, he greatly strengthened those who, by God's grace, had become believers, [28] for he vigorously refuted the Jews proving from the Scriptures that Jesus is the Messiah.

ACTS 18:19-28

Read: Paul returns to Antioch. While in Ephesus, Priscilla and Aquila instruct Apollo, versed in Scripture, but he knows little about Jesus Christ. They explain to him "more accurately the way of God" and he becomes a disciple.

Reflect: Are you sufficiently trained in all matters relating to

the Gospel? And among those around you, do you think they
need more formation?

Pray: Pray for catechists and religious educators, to be effective in their mission of educating in the faith. Pray also for
priests, that in their formation they soak in the Word of God
and preach and live happily.

Act: Find time to deepen the knowledge of the Gospel and, if
possible, work in the community for the training of its members.

Paul in Ephesus

19 [1] While Apollos was in Corinth, Paul traveled through the interior
of the country and came to Ephesus. There he found some disciples [2] whom he asked, "Did you receive the Holy Spirit when you became believers?" They answered, "We have not even heard that anyone
may receive the Holy Spirit." [3] Paul then asked, "What kind of baptism
have you received?" And they answered, "The baptism of John."

[4] Paul then explained, "John's baptism was for conversion, but he himself said they should believe in the one who was to come and that one
is Jesus." [5] Upon hearing this, they were baptized in the name of the Lord
Jesus. [6] Then Paul laid his hands on them and the Holy Spirit came down
upon them; and they began to speak in tongues and to prophesy. [7] There
were about twelve of them in all.

[8] Paul went into the synagogue; and for three months he preached and
discussed there boldly, trying to convince them about the kingdom of
God. [9] Some of them, instead of believing, grew obstinate, and criticized
the way publicly. So Paul departed from them and took the disciples with
him. He taught daily in the lecture hall of a certain Tyrannus. [10] He did
this for two years, so that all those who lived in the province of Asia,
both Jews and non-Jews, heard the word of the Lord.

ACTS 19:1-10

Read: Paul begins his third missionary journey. In Ephesus, he
instructs some disciples, to whom he explains the difference between John's baptism and being baptized in the name of the

Lord Jesus. Paul lays his hands, the Spirit descends on them and they prophesy.

Reflect: What is the value of Baptism for us? Do we feel the presence of the Spirit in our lives and in our community? How does it manifest?

Pray: The Holy Spirit is often the least known person of the Holy Trinity. When you pray, perceive interiorly the movements and signs that the Spirit awakens in you.

Act: Extend your knowledge of the Holy Spirit through readings that deal with him.

[11] God did extraordinary deeds of power through the hands of Paul. [12] Even handkerchiefs, or cloths that had touched his skin, were laid upon the sick and their illnesses were cured and evil spirits also departed from them.

[13] Some Jews who traveled around driving out evil spirits also tried to use the name of the Lord Jesus over those possessed by evil spirits, saying, "I command you, by this Jesus whom Paul preaches." [14] Among them were the seven sons of a Jewish priest named Sceva. [15] But one day, when they entered a house and dared to do this, the evil spirit said to them, "Jesus I recognize; and Paul I know; but who are you?" [16] Then the man with the evil spirit sprang at them and overpowered, first, one and then, another. And he handled them so violently that they fled from that house naked and mauled. [17] This became known to all the Jews and Greeks living in Ephesus; all of them were very impressed and the name of the Lord Jesus came to be held in great honor.

[18] Many of those who had become believers came forward and openly acknowledged their former practices. [19] Many who had practiced magic arts collected their books and burned them in front of everyone. When the value of these was assessed, it came to fifty thousand silver coins.

[20] In this way, the word of the Lord spread widely and with power.

ACTS 19:11-20

Read: Paul works signs and wonders in the name of Jesus Christ. Some Jewish exorcists try to do the same, but the evil spirit faced them and left them humiliated. The word of Jesus grew and Paul continues his missionary travels.

Reflect: What is the difference between the way of acting of Paul and that of the exorcists? Can one act in a Christian way without following the example of Jesus Christ? Why?

Pray: Pray to God to grant you the grace to profess and live a coherent faith. That your proclamation of faith in Jesus Christ be revealed in your daily work.

Act: Ask your pastor about any questions you may have about your absolute trust in God. Is it possible to be a Christian and consult the tarot? Is it possible to be a Christian and put all hope on money?

The silversmiths' riot

²¹ When all these events were completed, Paul, led by the Holy Spirit, decided to travel through Macedonia and Achaia again; and then go on to Jerusalem. And he said, "After I have been there I must visit Rome also." ²² So he sent two of his assistants, Timothy and Erastus, to Macedonia ahead of him, while he himself stayed on for a time in Asia.

²³ About that time, the city was deeply troubled because of the Way. ²⁴ It all began because of a certain silversmith named Demetrius, who made silver models of the temple of the goddess Artemis, and whose business brought a great deal of profit to the workers. ²⁵ He called them together with others who did similar work, and said, "Friends, you know that our prosperity depends on this work. ²⁶ But as you can see and hear for yourselves, this Paul has led astray a great number of people not only here in Ephesus, but also throughout most of the province of Asia. And he has convinced them that gods made by human hands are no gods at all. ²⁷ The danger grows, that not only our trade will be discredited, but even that the temple of the great goddess Artemis will count for nothing. She whom Asia and all the world worships may soon be stripped of her renown."

²⁸ On hearing this, they became enraged and began shouting, "Great is Artemis of the Ephesians!" ²⁹ The uproar spread throughout the whole city. The mob rushed to the theater, dragging with them Gaius and Aristarchus, two Macedonians, who were Paul's traveling companions.

30 Paul wished to face this crowd, but the disciples would not let him. 31 Some of the officials of the Asian province also, who were friends of Paul, sent him a message begging him not to show himself in the theater.

32 Meanwhile, the whole assembly was in an uproar. Some shouted one thing, and some shouted another; and most of them did not know why they were there. 33 Some of the crowd wanted a certain Alexander to speak, whom the Jews put forward. Alexander intended to make a speech of defense before the crowd, 34 but when they recognized that he was a Jew, they chanted all together for about two hours, "Great is Artemis of the Ephesians!"

35 Finally, the town clerk was able to calm the mob. He said, "Citizens of Ephesus, who does not know that Ephesus is keeper of the temple of the great Artemis, and of her image which fell from the sky? 36 Since these things are undeniable, you must calm yourselves and do nothing rash. 37 These men whom you brought here are not temple-robbers, nor have they spoken ill of our goddess. 38 If Demetrius and his fellow craftsmen want to bring charges against anyone, the courts are open and there are officials. Let them bring charges against each other. 39 If there is anything further that needs to be investigated, let it be done in the lawful assembly. 40 For, as it is today, we are in danger of being charged with rioting, since there is no valid excuse we can give for this wild demonstration." 41 And the town clerk dismissed the assembly.

ACTS 19:21-41

Read: Paul's preaching does not stop despite the discomfort it generates among the great traders of pagan worship. Following this, a riot in Ephesus happens, which is solved by appealing to common sense.

Reflect: Is your practice of faith consistent with the Gospel? How important is money in your life? Does it weigh more than the other aspects of your Christian life? Do you think it is right? Why?

Pray: Ask forgiveness for the times you have put economic interests ahead of the interests of the Gospel. Ask for light and generosity to prioritize the most important thing.

> **Act:** When making a purchase, consider not only the item's price but also fair business practices. Please also note that those who make this product should receive a fair wage for their work.

Paul returns to Macedonia

20 ¹After the uproar died down, Paul called his disciples together to encourage them. Then he said goodbye and set out on his journey to Macedonia. ²He traveled throughout those regions and spent himself in speaking and encouraging them. He finally arrived in Greece.

³When he had been there for three months, he wanted to set sail for Syria; but as the Jews were plotting against him, he decided to return by way of Macedonia. ⁴When he was about to leave for the Asian province, some companions went with him: Sopater, son of Pyrrhus, from Berea, Aristarchus and Secundus from Thessalonica, Gaius from Derbe, Timothy, Tychicus and Trophimus from Asia. ⁵So they went ahead and waited for us in Troas, ⁶while we set sail from Philippi as soon as the festival of Unleavened Bread was over. Five days later, we joined them in Troas, where we spent a week.

The Eucharist at Troas

⁷On the first day of the week we were together for the breaking of the bread, and Paul, who intended to leave the following day, spoke at length. The discourse went on until midnight, ⁸with many lamps burning in the upstairs room where we were gathered. A young man named Eutychius was sitting on the window ledge ⁹and as Paul kept on talking, Eutychius grew more and more sleepy until he finally went sound asleep and fell from the third floor to the ground. There they found him dead.

¹⁰Paul went down, bent over him and took him in his arms. "Do not be alarmed," he said, "there is life in him." ¹¹Then he went back upstairs, broke the bread and ate. After that, he kept on talking with them for a long time until daybreak, and then he left. ¹²As for the young man, they lifted him up alive and were greatly comforted.

¹³We went on ahead to the ship and sailed for Assos, where we were to pick up Paul. This was the arrangement, since Paul intended to travel

by foot. ¹⁴In fact, we met him at Assos and, taking him aboard, we went on to Mitylene. ¹⁵We sailed from there and arrived off Chios the next day. A day later, we came to Samos; and the following day, we reached Miletus.

¹⁶Paul had decided to sail past Ephesus so as not to lose time in Asia, for he was eager to reach Jerusalem by the day of Pentecost, if at all possible.

Paul's farewell to the Ephesian elders

¹⁷From Miletus, Paul sent word to Ephesus summoning the elders of the Church. ¹⁸When they came to him, he addressed them, "You know how I lived among you, from the first day I set foot in the province of Asia; ¹⁹how I served the Lord in humility through the sorrows and trials that the Jews caused me. ²⁰You know that I never held back from doing anything that could be useful for you; I spoke publicly and in your homes; ²¹and I urged Jews and non-Jews alike, to turn to God and believe in our Lord Jesus.

²²But now I am going to Jerusalem, chained by the Spirit, without knowing what will happen to me there. ²³Yet in every city, the Holy Spirit warns me that imprisonment and troubles await me. ²⁴Indeed, I put no value on my life; if only I can finish my race; and complete the service to which I have been assigned by the Lord Jesus to announce the good news of God's grace.

²⁵I now feel sure that none of you, among whom I have gone about proclaiming the kingdom of God, will ever see me again. ²⁶Therefore, I declare to you this day that my conscience is clear with regard to all of you. ²⁷For I have spared no effort in fully declaring to you God's will.

²⁸Keep watch over yourselves and over the whole flock the Holy Spirit has placed into your care. Shepherd the Church of the Lord that he has won at the price of his own blood. ²⁹I know that after I leave ruthless wolves will come among you and not spare the flock. ³⁰And from among you some will arise corrupting the truth, and inducing the disciples to follow them.

³¹Be on the watch, therefore, remembering that for three years, night and day, I did not cease to warn everyone even with tears. ³²Now I commend you to God and to his grace-filled word, which is able to make you grow and gain the inheritance that you shall share with all the saints.

³³ I have not looked for anyone's silver, gold or clothing. ³⁴ You, your-selves, know that these hands of mine have provided for both my needs and the needs of those who were with me. ³⁵ In every way I have shown you that by working hard one must help the weak, remembering the words that the Lord Jesus himself said, 'Happiness lies more in giving than in receiving.'"

³⁶ After this discourse, Paul knelt down with them and prayed. ³⁷ Then they all began to weep and threw their arms around him and kissed him. ³⁸ They were deeply distressed because he had said that they would never see him again. And they went with him even to the ship.

ACTS 20:1-38

Read: Paul leaves Ephesus and departs for Macedonia and Greece. From Miletus he sends a very emotional message to the leaders of the church of Ephesus, reminding them that all Chris-tians should be prepared to overcome the difficulties associated with the proclamation of the Gospel.

Reflect: How is Paul's commitment and affection for the com-munity of Ephesus perceived? How are you preparing yourself for your future? How do you collaborate with your community?

Pray: Remember with gratitude those who have played an im-portant role in your life. Ask the Lord to continue sending lead-ers and collaborators committed to the cause of the Gospel.

Act: Express your gratitude to people who have had or have a role in your Christian life.

On to Jerusalem

21 ¹ When we had finally taken leave of them, we put out to sea and sailed straight to Cos, and the next day to Rhodes; and from there, to Patara. ² There we found a ship that made for Phoenicia; we went aboard and set sail. ³ We caught sight of Cyprus but passed it by on our left as we continued on towards Syria. We landed at Tyre where the ship had to unload cargo. ⁴ There we found the disciples and stayed a week. Warned by the Spirit, they told Paul not to go to Jerusalem.

⁵ But when it was time, we departed and continued on our journey. All of them, wives and children included, came out of the city with us and,

on the beach, we knelt down and prayed. ⁶After that we said good-bye
to one another; we boarded the ship and they returned home.

⁷We continued our journey, sailing from Tyre to Ptolemais, where we
greeted the brothers and sisters and spent a day with them. ⁸On the following day, we left and came to Caesarea. There we entered the house
of Philip, the evangelist; and we stayed with him. He was one of the
Seven; ⁹and had four unmarried daughters who were gifted with
prophecy.

¹⁰We were there some days, when a prophet named Agabus came
down from Judea. Coming to us, he took Paul's belt and bound his own
feet and hands with it saying, ¹¹"Thus speaks the Holy Spirit: 'This is
how the Jews in Jerusalem will bind the owner of this belt and hand him
over to the foreign power.'"

¹²When we heard this, we, together with these people of Caesarea,
begged Paul not to go up to Jerusalem. ¹³Then he answered, "Why are
you weeping and breaking my heart? For I am ready not only to be imprisoned, but also to die in Jerusalem for the name of the Lord Jesus."
¹⁴When he would not be persuaded, we gave up and said, "The Lord's
will be done."

¹⁵After this we got ready and went up to Jerusalem. ¹⁶With us were
some of the disciples of Caesarea who brought us to the house of a
Cypriot, where we were to stay. He was called Mnason and was one of
the early disciples.

Paul is received by the Church of Jerusalem

¹⁷When we arrived in Jerusalem the brothers welcomed us warmly.
¹⁸The next day, Paul went with us to James' house where all the elders
had gathered. ¹⁹After greeting them, Paul began telling them in detail
everything God had done among the non-Jews, through his ministry.

²⁰After hearing this, they all praised God; but they said, "You see,
brother, how many thousands of Jews of Judea have come to believe
and all of them are zealous for the law. ²¹Yet they have heard that you
teach the Jews who live in pagan nations to depart from Moses, telling
them not to have their sons circumcised and to renounce Jewish customs. ²²We shall gather the assembly for, in any case, they will hear that
you have arrived. ²³Then, do as we tell you.

There are four men among us who have made a vow. ²⁴Take them and purify yourself along with them, and pay the sacrifice for them to shave their heads. In that way, everyone will know that there is nothing true in what they have been told about you; but that, you go on keeping the law.

²⁵ As for the non-Jews who have become believers, we sent them a letter to tell them, that they are only obliged not to eat meat offered to idols, or blood, or flesh of strangled animals; and also to avoid prohibited sexual union."

²⁶ So the next day, Paul took the men; together with them, he purified himself and entered the temple to give notice of what day the sacrifice would be offered for each of them to end his time of purification.

ACTS 21:1-26

Read: Paul and his disciples travel to Jerusalem. They know it's a dangerous journey but Paul is determined to continue. In Jerusalem, the Church recommends Paul to follow the Jewish customs to avoid scandal with the Jews.

Reflect: What do you think of the suggestion made by the Church of Jerusalem to Paul? Do you think Paul betrays his convictions? Did you ever find yourself in that situation? What did you do? Had the common good outweighed your own interests?

Pray: Give thanks for the presence of the Christian community in your life, and ask the Holy Spirit for wisdom and humility, for placing the common good ahead of your own.

Act: Learn to trust the decisions of the community, though contrary to your personal opinion. Offer unconditional support to the leaders and promoters of those decisions.

Paul is arrested in the temple

²⁷ When the seven days were almost over, some Jews from Asia who saw Paul in the temple began to stir up the whole crowd. They seized him, ²⁸ shouting, "Fellow Israelites, help! This is the man who is spreading his teaching everywhere against our people, our law and this Sanctuary. And now he has even brought non-Jews into the temple area, defiling this Holy Place." ²⁹ For they thought they had seen him in the city with Trophimus, a Greek man from Ephesus, and they supposed that Paul had introduced him into the temple.

³⁰ Then turmoil spread through the whole city. People came running from all sides. They seized Paul and dragged him outside the temple. At once, the gates were shut.

³¹ They would have killed him, had not a report reached the commander of the Roman troops that all of Jerusalem was rioting. ³² At once the commander took some officers and soldiers and rushed down to the crowd.

When they saw the commander and the soldiers, the crowd stopped beating Paul. ³³ The commander went over to Paul, arrested him, and ordered him to be bound with two chains; then he inquired who he was and what he had done. ³⁴ But some in the crowd shouted one thing and others another. As the commander was unable to find out the facts because of the uproar, he ordered Paul to be brought to the fortress. ³⁵ When Paul reached the steps, he actually had to be carried up by the soldiers because of the violence of the mob, ³⁶ for a multitude of people followed shouting, "Kill him!"

³⁷ Just as he was about to be taken inside, Paul said to the commander, "May I say something to you?" He replied, "So you speak Greek! ³⁸ Are you not the Egyptian, then, who caused a riot some time ago and led a band of four thousand terrorists out into the desert?" Paul answered, ³⁹ "I am a Jew, a citizen of Tarsus, a well-known city in Cilicia. I beg you, let me address these people."

The commander agreed. ⁴⁰ So Paul, standing on the steps, motioned to the people with his hand and, when they were silent, he began to speak to them in Hebrew.

ACTS 21:27-40

Read: Paul goes to the temple in Jerusalem following the advice of the community. The Jews accuse him of desecrating the temple and try to lynch him. The soldiers save him, and Paul decides to talk to the people.

Reflect: Have you ever felt rejected because of your faith? How have you reacted?

Pray: Ask for strength that your deeds be faithful to the will of God, knowing that it can bring rejection and misunderstanding.

Act: Be consistent with the mission you have received, even if that does not entail applause and recognition.

Paul addresses the Jews

22 [1] "Brothers and fathers, listen to what I have to say to you in my defense." [2] When they heard him speaking to them in Hebrew, they became more quiet. So he went on.

[3] "I am a Jew, born in Tarsus in Cilicia, but brought up here in this city, where I was educated in the school of Gamaliel, according to the strict observance of our law. And I was dedicated to God's service, as are all of you today. [4] As for this Way, I persecuted it to the point of death and arrested its followers, both men and women, throwing them into prison.

[5] The High Priest and the whole Council of elders can bear witness to this. From them, I received letters for the Jewish brothers in Damascus; and I set out to arrest those who were there, and bring them back to Jerusalem for punishment. [6] But, as I was traveling along, nearing Damascus at about noon, a great light from the sky suddenly flashed about me. [7] I fell to the ground and heard a voice saying to me: 'Saul, Saul, why do you persecute me?' [8] I answered: 'Who are you, Lord?' And he said to me: 'I am Jesus, the Nazorean, whom you persecute.' [9] The men who were with me saw the light, but they did not understand the voice of the one who was speaking to me. [10] I asked: 'What shall I do, Lord?' And the Lord replied: 'Get up and go to Damascus; there, you will be told all that you are destined to do.' [11] Yet, the brightness of that light had blinded me; and so I was led by the hand into Damascus by my companions.

[12] There, a certain Ananias came to me. He was a devout observer of the law and well spoken of by all the Jews who were living there. [13] As he stood by me, he said: 'Brother Saul, recover your sight.' At that moment, I could see; and I looked at him. [14] He then said, 'The God of our ancestors has chosen you to know his will, to see the Just One, and to hear the words from his mouth. [15] From now on you shall be his witness before all the pagan people and tell them all that you have seen and heard. [16] And now, why delay? Get up and be baptized; and have your sins washed away by calling upon his Name.'

[17] On my return to Jerusalem, I was praying in the temple when I fell into a trance [18] and saw him. He spoke to me: 'Get ready to leave Jerusalem without delay, because they will not accept your testimony about me.' [19] I answered: 'Lord, they know well that I imprisoned those who believed in you and had them beaten in every synagogue; [20] and,

while the blood of your witness Stephen was being poured out, I stood by and approved it and even guarded the cloaks of his murderers.' ²¹Then he said to me: 'Go, for I am sending you far away, to the pagan nations.'"

²²Up to this point the crowd listened to Paul, but on hearing the last words, they began to shout, "Kill him! He does not deserve to live!" ²³They were screaming and waving their cloaks and throwing dust into the air. ²⁴So the commander ordered Paul to be brought inside the fortress and questioned, after flogging, to find out why they made such an outcry against him.

²⁵But when the soldiers had strapped him down, Paul said to the officer standing there, "Is it legal to flog a Roman citizen without a trial?"

²⁶On hearing this, the officer went to the commander and said, "What are you doing? That man is a Roman citizen." ²⁷So the commander came and asked him, "Tell me, are you a Roman citizen?" "Yes," answered Paul. ²⁸The commander then said, "It cost me a large sum of money to become a Roman citizen." Paul answered, "I am one by birth."

²⁹Then those who were about to question him backed away; and the commander himself was alarmed when he realized that he had put a Roman citizen in chains.

Paul appears before the Sanhedrin

³⁰The next day, the commander wanted to know for certain the charges the Jews were making against Paul. So, he released him from prison and called together the High Priest and the whole Council; and they brought Paul down and made him stand before them.

ACTS 22:1-30

Read: Paul explains to the Jews of Jerusalem how his conversion was and why he began to preach to the Gentiles. The Jews reject him and try to kill him again.

Reflect: Why does Paul use as a defense the story of his conversion? Is your witness of life also a testimony of faith to others?

Pray: Give thanks for God's presence in your life. Always put your life into God's hands, especially in times of difficulty.

Act: Tell or write your Christian life story and share it with someone whom you think can do well with it in his/her journey of faith.

23 ¹Paul looked directly at the Council and said, "Brothers, to this day I have lived my life with a clear conscience before God." ²At that, the High Priest Ananias ordered his attendants to strike him on the mouth. ³Then Paul said, "God is about to strike you, you whitewashed wall! You sit there to judge me according to the law and you break the law by ordering me to be struck!" ⁴At this, the attendants protested, "How dare you insult God's High Priest!" ⁵Paul answered, "Brothers, I did not know that he was the High Priest. For Scripture says: *You shall not curse the ruler of your people.*"

⁶Paul knew, that part of the Council were Sadducees and others Pharisees; so he spoke out in the Council, "Brothers, I am a Pharisee, son of a Pharisee. It is for the hope in the resurrection of the dead that I am on trial here."

⁷At these words, an argument broke out between the Pharisees and the Sadducees, and the whole assembly was divided. ⁸For the Sadducees claim that there are neither resurrection, nor angels nor spirits; while the Pharisees acknowledge all these things.

⁹Then the shouting grew louder; and some teachers of the law of the Pharisee party protested, "We find nothing wrong with this man. Maybe a spirit or an angel has spoken to him."

¹⁰With this, the argument became so violent that the commander feared that Paul would be torn to pieces by them. He, therefore, ordered the soldiers to go down and rescue him from their midst, and take him back to the fortress.

¹¹That night, the Lord stood by Paul and said, "Courage! As you have borne witness to me here in Jerusalem, so must you do in Rome."

ACTS 23:1-11

Read: Paul defends himself before the Grand Council of the Jews. Cleverly takes advantage of the division of the Council to vindicate his faith and be free.

Reflect: What is your biggest motivation to bear witness to Christ? What does the expression "be wise as serpents and harmless as doves" (Mt 10:16) suggest to you?

Pray: Present to the Lord any fear, difficulty or challenges you are facing right now, and ask for courage and skill to address it.

> Ask also the ability of Paul to proclaim the saving work of Jesus Christ.
>
> **Act:** Find effective strategies to proclaim Jesus Christ in every moment of your life. Share this reflection with the priest or another leader in your community.

The plot to kill Paul

¹²When it was day, certain Jews formed a conspiracy. They bound themselves by an oath not to eat or drink until they had killed Paul. ¹³There were more than forty of them who joined in this conspiracy.

¹⁴They went to the high priests and the elders and said, "We have bound ourselves by oath not to taste food until we have killed Paul. ¹⁵Now then, it is up to you and the Council together, to convince the Roman commander to bring him down to you on the pretext that you want to investigate his case more thoroughly. We, for our part, are prepared to kill him before he gets there."

¹⁶But the son of Paul's sister heard about the planned ambush. So he went to the headquarters and informed Paul. ¹⁷Paul sent for one of the officers and said, "Take this young man to the commander for he has something to report to him." ¹⁸So the officer took him and brought him to the commander saying, "The prisoner, Paul, called me and asked me to bring this boy to you, because he has something to tell you."

¹⁹The commander took him by the hand and, drawing him aside, asked him privately, "What is it that you have to report to me?" ²⁰The boy replied, "The Jews have agreed among themselves to ask you tomorrow to have Paul brought down to the Council, as if to inquire more thoroughly about him. ²¹But do not be persuaded by them, for there are more than forty of them ready to ambush him having bound themselves by an oath not to eat or drink until they have killed him. They are now ready to do it and are awaiting your decision." ²²The commander let the boy go with this advice, "Do not tell anyone that you gave me this information."

Paul is transferred to Caesarea

²³Then the commander summoned two of his officers and said to them, "Get ready to leave for Caesarea by nine o'clock tonight with two

hundred infantrymen, seventy horsemen and two hundred spearmen. [24] Provide horses also for Paul to ride; so that he may be brought safely to Felix, the governor."

[25] He then wrote the governor a letter to this effect:

[26] "Claudius Lysias greets the Most Excellent Governor Felix, and communicates to him the following: [27] The Jews had arrested this man and were about to kill him when I intervened with my troops and took him out of their hands, since I knew he was a Roman citizen. [28] As I wanted to know what charge they had against him, I presented him before the Sanhedrin; [29] and I discovered that the accusation related to matters of their law; but there was nothing that deserved death or imprisonment. [30] When I was informed that the Jews had prepared a plot against this man, I decided to send him to you and told his accusers to present their complaints before you. Farewell."

[31] The soldiers acted in accordance with these instructions. They took Paul and brought him to Antipatris by night. [32] On the following day, they returned to the fortress, but the horsemen continued journeying with him. [33] Upon entering Caesarea, they handed the letter to the governor and presented Paul to him. [34] When Felix had read the letter, he asked Paul from which province he was; and when he learned that Paul was from Cilicia, [35] he said to him: "I shall hear your accusers when they come." And he ordered that he be kept in custody in the palace of Herod.

ACTS 23:12-35

Read: Paul's nephew intervenes to save his uncle from a new assassination attempt on the part of the Jews. Soldiers defend Paul and transfer him safely to Caesarea.

Reflect: Can one be a Christian without suffering rejection and persecution? Why? What difficulties do you face in your life of faith? Is it easy to be a Christian today?

Pray: Ask the Lord for strength to bear witness to the Gospel even amid difficulties.

Act: Follow the example of Paul's nephew, and support the cause of the persecuted and unjustly accused.

The case before Felix

24 ¹After five days, Ananias the High Priest, came down to Caesarea with some of the elders, and a lawyer named Tertullus. And they presented their case against Paul before the governor. ²Paul was called in and Tertullus accused him in this way:

³"Most Excellent Felix, thanks to you—your labors and your wise reforms—our people now enjoy great peace. We accept all this in every way and in every place, and we are totally grateful to you. ⁴So as not to take more of your time, I beg you to listen briefly to us, with your usual kindness. ⁵We have found that this man is a pest, he creates division among the Jews throughout the world and is a leader of the Nazorene sect. ⁶He even tried to profane the temple. So we seized him. We would have judged him according to our law, ⁷but Lysias, the commandant, intervened in a very violent way and took him from us. ⁸Then he declared that his accusers must present themselves before you. By examining him yourself, you will learn from him about all that we accuse him of."

⁹The Jews confirmed this, firmly maintaining that all this was so.

¹⁰Then the governor motioned to Paul, who said:

"As I know that you have administered this nation for many years, I make my defense with much confidence. ¹¹You, yourself, can ascertain that not more than twelve days ago I went up to Jerusalem to worship; ¹²and that they did not find me disputing with anyone, or inciting the people, either in the temple or in the synagogues or in the city. ¹³So they cannot prove the things of which they now accuse me.

¹⁴But this I admit before you, that I serve the God of our ancestors, according to the Way that they call a sect. I believe everything written in the law and in the prophets; ¹⁵and I have the same hope in God that they have: that there will be a resurrection of the dead, both the good and the sinners. ¹⁶So I strive always to have a clear conscience before God and before people.

¹⁷After many years, I came to bring help to those of my nation and to offer sacrifices. ¹⁸On that occasion, they found me in the temple; I had been purified, according to the law, and there was no crowd or commotion. Yet, all began with some Jews from Asia, ¹⁹who ought to be here before you to accuse me if they have anything against me. ²⁰Let these men say what crime they found in me when I stood before the Sanhedrin;

21 unless it was for having declared in a loud voice, when I was before them: 'Today, I am being judged on account of the resurrection of the dead.'"

22 Felix, who was well informed about the Way, postponed the case, and said to them, "When the commandant, Lysias, comes down, I will examine the case thoroughly." 23 So he ordered the captain to keep Paul under guard, giving him a certain liberty and without preventing his friends from attending to him.

24 After some days, Felix came with his wife Drusilla, who was a Jew. He sent for Paul and let him speak about faith in Christ. 25 But when Paul spoke about justice, self-control and the future judgment, Felix was frightened, and he said to him: "You may leave now; I shall send for you some other time." 26 Felix was hoping that Paul would give him money, so he sent for him often and conversed with him.

27 Two years passed and Felix was succeeded by Porcius Festus; and as Felix wanted to remain on good terms with the Jews, he left Paul in prison.

ACTS 24:1-27

Read: Paul is placed on trial before Felix, the governor. During his defense, he retells everything that happened since his arrival in Jerusalem and declared himself a Christian, believing in God and a man of peace. But Felix, who expects to receive money from Paul, lengthens the trial for two years more.

Reflect: How does Paul defend himself at the trial? How should Christians act with attitudes like that of Felix? Should we promote or denounce corruption? Is it easy to act consistently?

Pray: Ask for the help of the Holy Spirit in those moments when it is difficult to give Christian witness. Pray for Christians, that by our actions, we can eradicate corruption from our society.

Act: Be consistent with the Gospel message: promoting peace, forgiveness, justice, consistency, love, and faith among your people.

The trial before Festus

25 ¹Three days after Festus arrived in the province, he went up from Caesarea to Jerusalem. ²There, the chief priests and the elders accused Paul again. ³In a very hypocritical way they asked, as a favor from Festus, that Paul be brought to Jerusalem; but they were planning to kill him on the way. ⁴Festus answered, that Paul was under custody in Caesarea and, as he, himself, had to go there shortly, he added, ⁵"Let those of you, who have the authority go down with me to Caesarea; and if this man has done anything wrong, let them accuse him."

⁶Festus did not stay in Jerusalem for more than eight or ten days and then he went to Caesarea. The next day, he took his seat on the tribunal and sent for Paul. ⁷When Paul arrived, the Jews who came from Jerusalem stood around him, and presented many serious charges that they could not prove. ⁸Paul defended himself from all these, saying, "I have not committed any offense against the law of the Jews, or against the temple or against Caesar."

⁹Then Festus, who wanted to please the Jews, asked Paul: "Do you wish to go up to Jerusalem to be tried before me?" ¹⁰Paul answered, "I am on trial before Caesar's tribunal; here I have to be tried. I have done no wrong to the Jews: you, yourself, know this very well. ¹¹If I have committed any crime, which deserves death, I accept death. But if I have not done anything of which they accuse me, no one can give me up to them. I appeal to Caesar."

¹²So Festus, after conferring with his council, answered, "You have appealed to Caesar. To Caesar, you shall go."

ACTS 25:1-12

Read: Festus replaces Felix as governor. To curry favor with the Jews, he tries that Paul stands trial in Jerusalem, but he, as a Roman citizen, asks to be judged by the emperor.

Reflect: Paul identifies himself as a Christian believer and as a Roman citizen. How do these two identities relate among themselves? Should a Christian participate in the political life of society? How?

Pray: Pray to the Holy Spirit for strength, like Paul, and be firm in your convictions, that your Christian life be leaven in the transformation of society.

> **Act:** Watch for social and political events around you. Be a responsible citizen and participate, from your Christian values in the political process to enact laws that are increasingly similar to the Gospel values.

[13] Some days later, King Agrippa and his sister Bernice, arrived in Caesarea to greet Festus. As they were to stay there several days, Festus told the king about Paul's case and said to him,

[14] "We have here a man whom Felix left as a prisoner. [15] When I was in Jerusalem, the chief priests and the elders of the Jews accused him, and asked me to sentence him. [16] I told them that it is not the custom of the Romans to hand over a man without giving him an opportunity to defend himself in front of his accusers. [17] So they came, and I took my seat without delay on the tribunal and sent for the man.

[18] When the accusers had the floor, they did not accuse him of any of the crimes that I was led to think he had committed; [19] instead, they quarreled with him about religion and about a certain Jesus, who has died but whom Paul asserted to be alive. [20] I did not know what to do about this case, so I asked Paul if he wanted to go to Jerusalem to be tried there. [21] But Paul appealed to be judged by the emperor. So I ordered that he be kept in custody until I send him to Caesar." [22] Agrippa said to Festus: "I would like to hear that man." Festus answered him: "Tomorrow, you shall."

[23] On the following day, Agrippa and Bernice arrived, with great ceremony and entered the audience hall with the commanders and the elders of the city. Festus ordered that Paul be brought in and said:

[24] "King Agrippa, and all here present; here you see this man, about whom the whole community of the Jews came to see me in Jerusalem, as well as here, protesting loudly that he must not live. [25] I, for my part, am convinced that he has not done anything that deserves death. But, after he appealed to be judged by the emperor, I decided to send him on. [26] Well, if I have no definite information, what can I write to Caesar about him? Therefore, I present him before all of you, and especially before you, King Agrippa, that you may examine him, and that I may know what to write. [27] For it seems absurd to me to send a prisoner without indicating the charges against him."

Paul's speech before King Agrippa

26 [1] Agrippa said to Paul: "You may speak in your own defense." So Paul stretched out his hand and began in this way:

[2] "King Agrippa, you have just heard about the accusations of the Jews. I consider myself fortunate in having the opportunity to defend myself against all this before you today; [3] for you are an expert in the customs of the Jews and their disputes. Therefore, I beg you to listen to me patiently.

[4] All the Jews know how I have lived from my youth; how I have lived among my own people and in Jerusalem. [5] They have always known me; and they can tell you, if they wish, that I have lived as a Pharisee in the most rigorous sect of our religion. [6] If I am now tried here, it is because of the hope I have in the promise made by God to our ancestors. [7] The hope of attaining this promise is behind the fervent worship that our twelve tribes render to God night and day. Yet now, O king, the Jews accuse me for this hope! [8] But why refuse to believe that God raises the dead?

[9] I myself, in the beginning, thought that I had to use all possible means to counteract the Name of Jesus of Nazareth. [10] This I did in Jerusalem; and with the authorization of the chief priests, I put in prison many who believed; and I cast my vote when they were condemned to death.

[11] I went round the synagogues and multiplied punishments against them to force them to renounce their faith; such was my rage against them that I pursued them, even to foreign cities.

[12] With this purpose in mind, I went to Damascus with full authority and commissioned by the chief priests. [13] On the way, O king, at midday, I saw a light from heaven, more brilliant than the sun that dazzled me and those who accompanied me. [14] We all fell to the ground; and I heard a voice saying to me in Hebrew: 'Saul, Saul, why do you persecute me? In vain do you kick against the goad.'

[15] I answered: 'Who are you, Lord?' And the Lord said: 'I am Jesus, whom you persecute. [16] Get up now, and stand on your feet. I have revealed myself to you, to make you servant and witness to what I have just shown you and to what I will show you later on. [17] I will rescue you from all evil that may come from your own people, or from the pagans, to whom I am sending you. [18] For you shall open their eyes, that they may turn from darkness to light, and from the power of Satan to God;

and, through faith in me, may obtain forgiveness of their sins and a place among those who are sanctified.'

[19] Since that time, King Agrippa, I did not stray from this heavenly vision; [20] on the contrary, I began preaching; first, to those in Damascus, then to those in Jerusalem and throughout Judea; and then to the pagan nations that they should repent, and turn to God showing the fruits of true conversion. [21] I was carrying out this mission, when the Jews arrested me in the temple and tried to kill me. But, with the help of God, I still stand here, today, to give my testimony, both to the great and the small.

[22] I do not teach anything other than what Moses and the prophets announced beforehand: [23] the Messiah had to die; and after being the first to be raised from the dead, he would proclaim the light to his people, as well as to all nations."

[24] As Paul came to this point of his defense, Festus said in a loud voice: "Paul, you are mad; your great learning has deranged your mind!" [25] But Paul answered: "I am not mad, Most Excellent Festus, but everything I have said is reliable and true. [26] The king is acquainted with all these things, so to him I speak with such confidence. I am convinced that he knows everything about this case, for these things did not happen in a dark corner. [27] King Agrippa, do you believe the prophets? I know that you do."

[28] Agrippa said to him: "You almost believe that you have already made me a Christian!" [29] Paul answered him: "Whether little or more, I would that not only you, but all who hear me this day, may come to be as I am—except for these chains."

[30] Then the king rose and, with him the governor, Bernice and all the attendants. [31] When they went out, they talked among themselves and said: "This man has done nothing to deserve death or imprisonment." [32] And Agrippa said to Festus: "Had he not appealed to Caesar, he could have been set free."

ACTS 25:13—26:32

Read: Festus invites King Agrippa to hear the case of Paul, who recounts his conversion. He makes sure that all he announces is the realization of the promise that the Jews expected: Jesus Christ. But the Jews do not accept his word.

> **Reflect:** Paul is a missionary in every moment of his life. Do you follow his example or your faith life takes a different level in everyday life? What things cause you to stay away from your Christian convictions?
>
> **Pray:** Ask forgiveness for your possible inconsistencies with faith. Ask for light to recognize the action of God in your life and the courage to express it in any circumstance.
>
> **Act:** A Christian cannot bracket the faith he or she professes. Be consistent, like Paul, in all aspects of your life.

Departure for Rome

27 [1] When it was decided that we should sail for Italy, they handed over Paul and the other prisoners into the care of an officer of the Augustan battalion named Julius. [2] We boarded a ship of Adramyttium, bound for the Asian coasts, and we left, accompanied by Aristarchus, a Macedonian from the city of Thessalonica. [3] We arrived at Sidon on the next day. Julius was very kind to Paul, letting him visit his friends and be cared for by them. [4] From there, we sailed along the sheltered coast of Cyprus because the winds were against us. [5] We sailed across the seas off Cilicia and Pamphylia and arrived at Myra, in Lycia. [6] There, the captain found a ship from Alexandria sailing for Italy, and made us board it.

[7] We sailed slowly for several days, and arrived with great difficulty at Cnidus. As the wind did not allow us to enter that port, we sailed for the shelter of Crete with the Cape of Salmone within sight. [8] We turned with difficulty and arrived at a place called Good Ports, near the city of Lasea.

[9] Time passed, and the crossing began to be dangerous: we had already celebrated the feast of the Fast. [10] Then Paul said to them: "Friends, I believe that it would not be very wise to proceed with our crossing for we could lose not only the cargo and the ship, but also our lives." [11] But the Roman officer relied more on the ship's captain, and the owner of the ship than on the words of Paul. [12] And, as the port was not suitable for wintering, the majority agreed to set out from there in the hope of reaching the harbor of Crete called Phoenix, overlooking Africa and Choros, where they could spend the winter.

Storm and shipwreck

¹³ Then the south wind began to blow; and they thought that they had gained their purpose; they weighed anchor and sailed along the island of Crete. ¹⁴ But a little later, a strong wind called "the northeaster" swept down on them from across the island. ¹⁵ The ship was dragged along and could not face the wind, so that we remained adrift.

¹⁶ As we were crossing under the lee of the small island of Cauda, we managed—but with effort—to secure the lifeboat. ¹⁷ After lifting it aboard, they used cables to undergird the hull, and since we feared running aground on the sands of Syrtis, they lowered the sea anchor. So we continued to be dragged along.

¹⁸ The storm lashed at us so strongly that on the next day they began throwing the cargo overboard. ¹⁹ On the third day, the sailors, with their own hands, threw out the ship's gear. ²⁰ For several days, neither the sun nor the stars could be seen and the tempest had not subsided: we lost all hope of saving ourselves.

²¹ As we had not eaten for days, Paul stood up among them and said: "Friends, if you had followed my advice when I told you not to set sail from Crete, we would not be in such danger now and we could have avoided this loss. ²² But now I invite you to regain courage, for no one among you shall die; only the ship shall be destroyed. ²³ Last night, there appeared to me an angel of my God whom I serve ²⁴ and he said to me: 'Paul, do not be afraid, you must present yourself before Caesar's tribunal; and God has guaranteed you the life of all those who sail with you.'

²⁵ Have courage, therefore, my friends, for I trust in God that it will be just as he told me. ²⁶ But we have to run aground on some island."

²⁷ Near midnight, on the fourteenth night, as we were drifting in the Adriatic Sea, the sailors suspected that land was near. ²⁸ They measured the depth of the water and it was thirty-seven meters. After a while, they measured it again and it was twenty-seven meters. ²⁹ They feared that we might hit some rocks, so they cast out four anchors from the stern and waited anxiously for morning. ³⁰ Then the sailors tried to escape from the ship, under the pretext of extending the cables of the anchors from the bow; so they lowered the lifeboat into the sea. ³¹ But Paul said to the captain, and to the soldiers: "If they leave the ship, you cannot be saved." ³² So the soldiers cut the mooring cables of the boat and let it fall.

³³ As they waited for dawn, Paul urged everyone: "For fourteen days you have not eaten anything because of anxious waiting. ³⁴ I ask you to eat now if you want to live; be sure that not even a hair of your head will be lost." ³⁵ Having said this, he took bread, gave thanks to God in everybody's presence, broke it and began to eat. ³⁶ All were encouraged and they too ate. ³⁷ They were two hundred and seventy-six persons in all. ³⁸ When they had eaten enough, they threw the wheat into the sea to lighten the boat.

³⁹ When morning came, they did not recognize the land, but noticed a bay with a beach; so they decided to run the ship aground, if possible. ⁴⁰ They cast off the anchors and left them in the sea; at the same time, they loosened the ropes of the rudders, hoisted the foresail to the wind and headed for the beach. ⁴¹ But they struck a sandbank and the ship ran aground. The bow stuck and was immovable, while the stern was broken up by the violent waves.

⁴² The soldiers then planned to kill the prisoners, for fear that some of them might escape by swimming. ⁴³ But the captain, who wished to save Paul, did not allow them to do this. He ordered those who knew how to swim to be the first to jump into the water and head for the shore, ⁴⁴ and the rest to hold on to planks or pieces of the ship. So all of us reached land safe and sound.

ACTS 27:1-44

Read: Paul departs by sea to Rome to be tried by the emperor. On the way, the ship sinks, but he is confident at all times that divine providence will save them.

Reflect: What good does Paul get from the heavy storm? What storms shake your life and how do you take advantage of them to grow in faith? Do you trust in God's providence?

Pray: As hard as it is, give thanks to God for the storms in your life. Trust that something positive will come out of them.

Act: Be optimistic about the next difficulty you will face. Thank God for every moment of your life, even if all you can offer is a short and simple prayer.

On Malta

28 ¹ After being saved, we learned that the island was called Malta.
² The natives were very cordial. They lit a big bonfire and took
good care of us all, since it was raining and cold.

³ Paul gathered a bundle of dried twigs; and as he threw them into the
fire, a viper suddenly came out, because of the heat, and entwined itself
around his hand. ⁴ When the natives saw the viper hanging from his
hand, they said to one another: "Surely this man is a murderer: he has
barely escaped from the raging sea, yet divine justice will not allow him
to live." ⁵ But Paul shook off the viper into the fire and did not suffer any
harm. They waited to see him swell and die; ⁶ but after observing him
for a while, they saw that nothing happened to him; so they changed
their minds and began to say that he was a god.

⁷ Near this place was an estate owned by the head of the island, named
Publius. For three days this man welcomed us hospitably. ⁸ It so happened that his father was in bed with fever and dysentery. Paul went to
see him; he prayed and laid his hands on him and healed him. ⁹ Because
of this, the rest of the sick people on the island came to see him and
were cured. ¹⁰ So they showered us with kindness, and on our departure,
they provided us with everything we needed.

From Malta to Rome

¹¹ After three months, we boarded a ship that had spent the winter at
the island. It belonged to an Alexandrian company and carried the fig-
urehead of Castor and Pollux as insignia. ¹² We sailed for Syracuse, staying there for three days; ¹³ and after circling the coast, we arrived at
Rhegium. On the following day, a south wind began to blow, and at the
end of two days we arrived at Puteoli, ¹⁴ where we found some of our
brothers, who invited us to stay with them for a week. And that was how
we came to Rome.

¹⁵ There, the brothers and sisters had been informed of our arrival, and
came out to meet us as far as the Appian Forum and the Three Taverns.
When Paul saw them, he gave thanks to God and took courage. ¹⁶ Upon
our arrival in Rome, the captain turned the prisoners over to the military
governor, but permitted Paul to lodge in a private house with the soldier
who guarded him.

Paul meets the Jews in Rome

[17] After three days, Paul called together the leaders of the Jews. When they had gathered, he said to them: "Brothers, though I have not done anything against our people or against the traditions of our fathers, I was arrested in Jerusalem and handed over to the Romans. [18] They examined me and wanted to set me free, for they saw nothing in my case that deserved death. [19] But the Jews objected, so I was forced to appeal to Caesar without the least intention of bringing any case against my own people. [20] Therefore, I have asked to see you and speak with you, since it is because of the hope of Israel, that I bear these chains."

[21] They answered: "We have not received any letter about you from Judea; and none of the brothers who have come from there have brought any message or said anything against you. [22] But we wish to hear from you what you think; although we know already, that everywhere, people speak against this sect that you belong to."

[23] They set a day for him and came in great numbers to his lodging. So Paul explained everything he wanted to tell them regarding the kingdom of God, and tried to convince them concerning Jesus, taking the law of Moses and the prophets as his starting point. This continued from morning till night. [24] Some were convinced by his words, others were

not. ²⁵Finally, the Jews left, still arguing strongly among themselves; and Paul sent them away with this statement: "What the Holy Spirit said has come true, when he spoke to your ancestors through the prophet Isaiah:

²⁶ *Go to these people and say to them: However much you hear, you will not understand; you will see, and see again, but not perceive.*

²⁷ *The heart of these people have grown hard; they have covered their ears and closed their eyes; lest they should see with their eyes and hear with their ears; lest their spirit understand, and I should heal them.*

²⁸Let it be known to you that this salvation of God has been sent to the pagans: they will listen."

³⁰Paul stayed for two whole years in a house he, himself, rented, where he received, without any hindrance, all those who came to see him. ³¹He proclaimed the kingdom of God and taught the truth about Jesus Christ, the Lord, quite openly and without any hindrance.

ACTS 28:17-31

Read: Paul bears witness to his faith among the Jews of Rome and insists that he is not against the laws, traditions, or Jewish customs. The Jews reject the gospel again, and again Paul states that he will preach to the Gentiles. The book does not relate what happens to Paul after his two-year stay in Rome.

Reflect: The encounter with Jesus changed Paul's life completely: from persecutor to apostle. Why are you a Christian? Do you consider urgent to witness your faith in Christ today? Paul was able to adapt the Gospel to the language and context of his listeners. Do you think the Church adapts the Word of God into the language and context of today's world?

Pray: Thank God for having met the Risen Christ and for the gift of faith. Ask for Paul's strength to face the difficulties, punishment, and rejection because of the Gospel.

Act: Tell the story of your own faith to your own people. Do not be afraid to be rejected, trust in the divine company and providence.

CEREZO BARREDO

LETTERS
OF PAUL

From the beginning, the churches took care to preserve the letters they received from the apostles, since in them they had authoritative witnesses to the faith. It was more difficult then than it is today to gather these documents, and even save the perishable material of papyrus from dampness.

Before long, there was an initial collection of the first seven epistles arranged in the order of decreasing length: the four "great" letters to the Romans, to the Corinthians, and to the Galatians, and "the letters from captivity." Others came to be added: first, those to the Thessalonians which are actually the oldest; and then those that were passed on under the patronage of Paul: the letters to Timothy and Titus which were written some twenty or thirty years later, and the beautiful letter to the Hebrews, written most likely under the influence of Paul but by an unknown author. A phrase from the "second letter of Peter" (not written by himself but about fifty years after his death) is evidence that from this time the letters of Paul were counted among the inspired writings (2 Pt 3:15-16).

Paul saw himself as "the apostle to the pagan nations," seeing there his personal vocation beside Peter (to whom God had confided the charge of evangelizing the Jewish world) not only in Palestine, but also throughout the Roman Empire, wherever they were established. Paul received this mission from Jesus himself at the time of his conversion (Acts 22:21; Gal 2:7); so highly fundamental was it in the divine project of the mission and extension of the Church that it remained unfinished at the time of his death. The spirit of Paul, one of the great manifestations of the spirit of Jesus, is always at work in our midst through his letters.

CEREZO BARREDO

LETTER TO THE
ROMANS

Jesus presented himself as the Savior. First of all, he wanted to save the Jewish people. He spoke to them of the kingdom and they understood that God would reign over them just as he would reign in their lives. Their collective aspirations were not unknown to him, but he oriented them toward a more universal mission: it was truly "good news" for them.

With the beginning of the mission into Roman territory, the Gospel had equally to be good news for the Greeks of the Roman Empire who were listening to the word of the apostles. Protected by solid structures that no one questioned, they did not share the Jewish longing for liberation. In absorbing them the Roman Empire had practically reduced to nothing the pride and ambitions of nations great and small, leaving a void for religious concerns to take root. These people were interested in all that related to the human person and searched high and low in a jumble of doctrines and religions as a means of escaping Fate. So it was essential to speak to them of Christ, as the one who unravels our contradictions and gives us life.

In this letter to the Christians of Rome, capital of the Empire, Paul intends to respond to the concerns of the Greeks but without thereby neglecting the Jews.

The Letter to the Romans is, for the most part, a long exposition about Christian vocation. To us, it will seem difficult because that is what it is. It must be remembered that Paul's teaching does not stem from a doctrinal system or from a theology: rather it constantly springs from his own experience. The encounter with the Risen Christ, the call made to Paul that put him at the service of the Gospel, the long experience as an apostle, the gifts of the Spirit acting in him, and constant communion with Jesus: these were the sources of his vision of faith.

So Paul spoke of God's salvation as if forgetful of the explosive Palestinian context where Jewish nationalism was at grips with the Romans and where all religious hopes were politicized. God's salvation is the salvation of the human race, a total project, but taking place in the heart of people; all will depend on our response to God's call: can we trust him?

Paul, marked by his own history, presents the beginning of faith as a dramatic conversion. People are slaves to sin (it would be necessary to understand what Paul means by that). We have been created to share the life of God, and as long as we do not achieve this we carry within ourselves a conscious or unconscious rebellion against God. Must we turn toward religion? We would gain very little, says Paul, with the insistence that will shock many people: as long as we believe in becoming "good" through religious practices we turn our back on the only power that can free us: God's merciful love. The only response he expects from us is our act of faith, a faith which immediately frees us.

This salvation is the one announced by Scripture, but it will disconcert those believers who do not go beyond religious practices. These belong to a first stage of sacred history that ended with Jesus' death. Our baptism gives us entrance to a mysterious world which is no other than the Risen Christ: from now on we are "in Christ," and living by his Spirit. The gift of the Spirit opens a new era where all is inspired by the law of love, for those who have become true sons and daughters of God.

Why Did Paul Send This Letter?

Paul had decided to leave the Eastern provinces of the empire and to reach its very heart, that is to say, Rome (Rom 15:23). But others had established and formed that community, Peter for sure, and many others who are unknown. These Christians already had their own ways and their customs. Some of them had heard comments that did not predispose them favorably toward Paul and his methods. Therefore, it is understandable that Paul wanted to prepare his coming. He may have been thinking even more about the Jerusalem Christians who were spreading rumors and slandering him (Acts 21:21). Before Paul went to Rome, he had to go to Jerusalem to bring the proceeds of the collection taken in the Greek communities for the poor of Jerusalem. Paul was not too sure of being welcomed as a brother (Rom 15:31). So, he sent this letter to Rome, knowing that it would quickly reach Jerusalem. In this letter, Paul dwells on the complementary vocation of the Jews and the pagans.

His calls for mutual understanding that make up the content of Chapters 13–15 of this letter, were important concerns of Paul at the time. Even if he addressed the Jewish community of Jerusalem in a special way, his remarks were not out of place in Rome. There, like everywhere, it was not easy to gather Jews and converted pagans in the same community. Paul was already preaching what we fail to put into practice, namely, to accept one another with our differences.

Paul probably sent this letter from Corinth in the winter of 57–58.

The Letter to the Romans and the Church

It is now impossible to speak of the letter to the Romans without saying at least a word on the place it has held and continues to hold in Protestant Churches. It has been considered by many as the key to the interpretation of the entire Scriptures.

It is known that Luther deepened the Reformation by commenting on this epistle. He was not wrong in seeing in this letter the condemnation of a Church established in the world, where faith had been degraded, becoming no more than practice devoid of faith which saves. The Christianity of the Middle Ages was, in fact, a people, rather like what the people of Israel had become. A person was a Christian by birth and continued to be one; he/she could be a believer, but as one is in any culture whatever. It was thought that salvation was gained by religious rites and by the practice of good deeds that merited heaven.

It was therefore very important to remember that faith is at the heart of every conversion, and that this conversion is the response to a freely given call from God. This letter emphasizes Christ the Savior and this emphasis was sufficient to devalue the whole religious system which at the time was crushed by tradition and devotions. There was faith, at a time when preaching rarely touched on anything other than morality with its catalogs of moral principles. There was the word of God directed toward the individual person at a time when people were quite happy to trust Church leaders. It was then, a radical criticism of the Church, which ended up looking at itself instead of turning toward God, and of a Church whose whole system—political, doctrinal and repressive—blocked the horizon.

We have said, however, that this letter had its roots in Paul's experience as a Jew, a Pharisee and as an apostle called directly by Christ. It is from that point that Paul spoke of sin and justification, of call, of salvation through faith. For their part, Luther and his contemporaries read this letter against the backdrop of their own problems—or better—of their anguish.

They magnified the perspective of sin and eternal condemnation, victims of a philosophy (nominalism) in which nothing was good or bad in itself but only if God declares it so. Because of that, everything Paul said about the predestination of the Jewish people was interpreted by them as a personal predestination to heaven or hell.

When Paul spoke of justification—a word which at that time had a large and imprecise meaning—he meant that God re-establishes in us an order which is the true one; they understood instead that, if we believe, God will accept us even if nothing has been changed in us. The great perspectives of humankind and history as a battlefield of sin and grace, were reduced to a personal problem: am I really free or am I enslaved to sin or grace. Taking literally Paul's images and comparisons, a doctrine of original sin was developed in which we all pay now and forever, for the sin of our first ancestors.

Several generations of Protestants and Catholics have been marked by these controversies: salvation through faith alone, or through faith and works, or through faith, works, and sacraments? The love of the Father who saves and of Christ the Savior were eclipsed in fact by an obsession for salvation: how can I escape from this rigid frame in which God confines me? The concept of a just God, of inexorable decisions, which so easily condemns people into hell would traumatize the West and prepare a revolt in the next centuries, that of militant atheism.

It is not pointless for us today to know this. We are all children of our time and the remedy, if we do not wish to be enslaved, is to not give over-importance to one biblical text to the detriment of others. When you have become familiar with Paul and first with the letter to the Romans you see that for him the Father of Jesus is really father, and passionately loved. Thousands of details are to be discovered in Paul that disclose his experience of a continual communion and a life "in" the Triune God, an experience very close to that of St. John.

That will not prevent us from finding in this letter just what Luther, after St. Augustine, saw there: a genial presentation of the mystery of humanity redeemed by Christ. There is a certain forgetfulness perhaps of this letter and of this doctrine which too often has allowed Catholics to hem themselves in by their practices and their sacraments, and neglect mission.

LETTER TO THE
ROMANS

1 ¹From Paul, a servant of Jesus Christ,
an apostle called and set apart for God's Good News,

²the very promises he foretold through his prophets in the sacred Scriptures regarding his Son,

³who was born in the flesh a descendant of David,

⁴and has been recognized as the Son of God endowed with Power, upon rising from the dead through the Holy Spirit.

Through him, Jesus Christ our Lord, ⁵and for the sake of his name,

we received grace and mission in all the nations for them to accept the faith.

⁶All of you, the elected of Christ, are part of them;

you, the beloved of God in Rome, called to be holy:

⁷May God our Father and the Lord Jesus Christ give you grace and peace.

Paul longs to visit them

⁸First of all, I give thanks to my God through Jesus Christ for all of you, because your faith is spoken of all over the world. ⁹And God, whom I serve in spirit by announcing the Good News of his Son, is my witness that I remember you in my prayers at all times. ¹⁰I pray constantly that, if it is his will, he makes it possible for me to visit you. ¹¹I long to see you and share some spiritual blessings with you to strengthen you. ¹²In that way, we will encourage each other by sharing our common faith.

¹³You must know, brothers and sisters, that many times, I have made plans to go to you, but till now, I have been prevented. ¹⁴I would like to harvest some fruits among you, as I have done among other nations. Whether Greeks or foreigners, cultured or ignorant, I feel under obligation to all. ¹⁵Hence, my eagerness to proclaim the gospel also to you who are in Rome.

¹⁶For I am not ashamed at all of this Good News; it is God's power, saving those who believe, first the Jews, and then the Greeks. ¹⁷This Good News shows us the saving justice of God; a justice that saves exclusively by faith, as the Scripture says: *The upright one shall live by faith.*

> **ROMANS 1:1-17**
>
> **Read:** Paul begins this letter greeting a community that he had not founded, hence his suggestive presentation: "servant of Jesus Christ," "called to be an apostle," "chosen to announce the Good News." Since only a few in this local church know him, in this letter he summarizes his understanding of the Gospel of Jesus Christ.
>
> **Reflect:** Paul feels chosen to announce the Good News. In one sentence salvation is for all, but do you think people know this? How do you, in your life, share this Good News.
>
> **Pray:** Pray for people of all beliefs, that faith in the Love of God may be strong.
>
> **Act:** Be always willing to learn from others. Share your faith with those who need it; may your life be Good News to them.

Humankind is under God's "wrath"

¹⁸For the wrath of God is being revealed from heaven against all ungodliness and injustice, of those who have silenced the truth by their wicked ways. ¹⁹For everything that could have been known about God was clear to them: God himself made it plain. ²⁰Because his invisible attributes—his everlasting power and divinity—are made visible to reason, by means of his works since the creation of the world.

So they have no excuse, ²¹for they knew God, and did not glorify him as was fitting; nor did they give thanks to him. On the contrary, they lost themselves in their reasoning, and darkness filled their minds.

²²Believing themselves wise, they became foolish: ²³they exchanged the glory of the immortal God for the likes of mortal human beings, birds, animals, and reptiles. ²⁴Because of this, God gave them up to their inner cravings; they did shameful things and dishonored their bodies.

²⁵They exchanged God's truth for a lie; they honored and worshiped

created things instead of the Creator, to whom be praise for ever, Amen! [26] Because of that, God gave them up to shameful passions: their women exchanged natural sexual relations for unnatural ones. [27] Similarly, the men giving up natural sexual relations with women were lustful of each other: they did, men with men, shameful things, bringing upon themselves the punishment they deserve for their wickedness. [28] And since they did not think that God was worth knowing, he gave them up to their senseless minds so that they committed all kinds of obscenities.

[29] And so, they are full of injustice, perversity, greed, evil; they are full of jealousy, murder, strife, deceit, bad will, and gossip. [30] They commit calumny, offend God, are haughty; they are proud, liars, clever in doing evil. They are rebellious toward their parents, [31] senseless, disloyal, cold-hearted and merciless. [32] They know of God's judgment, which declares worthy of death to anyone living in this way; yet, not only do they do all these things, they even applaud anyone who does the same.

ROMANS 1:18-32

Read: Paul reminds the Romans that without God's saving action humanity is lost. Humans tend to replace the true God with false gods in all areas of their lives, even the most intimate.

Reflect: Sin and evil seem everywhere. When you get discouraged by this how do you trust God, and trust God enough to make changes in your own life? What situations of death and sin should Christians condemn and redeem?

Pray: Ask the Holy Spirit to help you to perceive God's saving action in your life, and share it with your loved ones. Ask also for courage to denounce the situations of death that you see around you.

Act: Make an examination of conscience and recognize your weaknesses and avoid judging the weakness of others.

The Jews also must fear judgment

2 [1] Therefore, you have no excuse, whoever you are, if you are able to judge others. For, in judging your neighbor, you condemn yourself, for you practice what you are judging. [2] We know that the condemnation of God will justly reach those who commit these things, [3] and do you think that by condemning others, you will escape from the judgment of God, you who are doing the same?

⁴This would be taking advantage of God and his infinite goodness, patience, and understanding; and not to realize that his goodness is in order to lead you to conversion. ⁵If your heart becomes hard and you refuse to change, then you are storing for yourself a great punishment on the day of judgment, when God will appear as just judge.

⁶He will give each one his due according to his actions. ⁷He will give everlasting life to those who seek glory, honor and immortality, and persevere in doing good. ⁸But anger and vengeance will be the lot of those who do not serve the truth, but injustice. ⁹There will be suffering and anguish for everyone committing evil, first the Jew, then the Greek. ¹⁰But God will give glory, honor, and peace to whoever does good, first the Jew, then the Greek, ¹¹because one is not different from the other before God.

Everyone is judged by his conscience

¹²Those who, without knowing the law, committed sin, will perish without the law; and whoever committed sin, knowing the law, will be judged by that law. ¹³What makes us righteous before God is not hearing the law, but obeying it. ¹⁴When the non-Jews, who do not have the law, practice naturally what the law commands, they are giving themselves a law, ¹⁵showing that the commandments of the law are engraved in their minds. Their conscience speaking within them also shows it when they condemn or approve their actions. ¹⁶The same is to happen on the day when God, according to my gospel, will judge people's secret actions in the person of Jesus Christ.

¹⁷But, suppose you call yourself a Jew: you have the law as foundation and feel proud of your God. ¹⁸You know the will of God and the law teaches you to distinguish what is better, ¹⁹and so, you believe you are the guide for the blind, a light in darkness, ²⁰a corrector of the foolish and the instructor of the ignorant, because you possess in the law the formulation of true knowledge. ²¹Well then, you who teach others, why don't you teach yourself? If you say that one must not steal, why do you steal? ²²You say one must not commit adultery, yet you commit it! You say you hate idols, but you steal into their temples! ²³You feel proud of the law, yet you do not obey it, and you dishonor your God. ²⁴In fact, as

the Scripture says, *the other nations despise the name of God because of you.*

²⁵ Circumcision is of value to you if you obey the law; but if you do not obey, it is as if you were not circumcised. ²⁶ On the contrary, if those who are uncircumcised obey the commandments of the law, do you not think that in spite of them being pagans, they make themselves like the circumcised? ²⁷ The one who obeys the law without being marked in his body with circumcision will judge you who have been marked with circumcision and who have the law, which you do not obey. ²⁸ For external things do not make a true Jew, nor is real circumcision that which is marked on the body. ²⁹ A Jew must be so interiorly; the heart's circumcision belongs to the spirit and not to a written law; he who lives in this way will be praised not by people but by God.

ROMANS 2:1-29

Read: To Paul, the most important thing is not to listen to the Law but to fulfill it. Therefore, those who know it and do not comply with it will be judged. On the other hand, those who do not known it but their lives in a loving fashion will receive glory and honor, because the divine law is engraved in the heart of the human being.

Reflect: The judgment of humanity belongs to God alone. What does the following expression suggest to you: "nobody should judge anyone, because we are all sinners"? Is this how you live as a Christian? How do your behavior and attitudes differ from those proposed by Jesus?

Pray: Ask the Lord strength to live your faith and in so doing be a witness to the salvation that Jesus offers to all those who believe in Him.

Act: Talk to someone you trust, and ask him or her to help you to see what things you should improve in your life so that your faith be consistent with the saving message of the Good News of Jesus.

What advantage is it to be a Jew?

3 ¹ Then, what is the advantage of being a Jew? And what is the use of circumcision? ²It is important from any point of view. In the first place, it was to the Jews that God entrusted his word.

³Well, now, if some of them were not faithful, will their unfaithfulness do away with the faithfulness of God? Of course not! ⁴Rather, it will be proved that God is truthful, *every human a liar*, as the Scripture says: *it will be proved that your words are true and you will be the winner if they want to judge you.*

⁵If our wickedness shows God to be just, would it be right to say that God is unjust when he gets angry and punishes us? (I speak in a human way.)

⁶—Not at all because, otherwise, how could God judge the world?

⁷—But if my lie makes the truth of God more evident, thus increasing his glory, is it correct to call me a sinner?

⁸—Then your only choice would be to sin, so that good may come of it. Some slanderers say that this is my teaching, but they will have to answer for those words.

⁹Do we have, then, any advantage? Not really. For we have just demonstrated that all, Jews and non-Jews, are under the power of sin, ¹⁰as the Scripture says:

Nobody is good, not even one,

¹¹ *no one understands, no one looks for God.*

¹² *All have gone astray and have become base. There is no one doing what is good, not even one.*

¹³ *Their throats are open tombs, their words deceit.*

¹⁴ *Their lips hide the poison of vipers, from their mouths come bitter curses.*

¹⁵ *They run to where they can shed blood,* ¹⁶ *leaving behind ruin and misery.* ¹⁷ *They do not know the way of peace.*

¹⁸ *There is no fear of God before their eyes.*

¹⁹Now, we know that whatever the Scripture says, it is said for the people of the law, that is for the Jews. Let all be silent, then, and recognize that the whole world is guilty before God. ²⁰Still more: *no mortal will be worthy before God* by performing the demands of the law. What comes from the law is the consciousness of sin.

Faith, the way to salvation

[21] But now it has been revealed altogether apart from the law, as it was already foretold in the law and the prophets: [22] God makes us righteous by means of faith in Jesus Christ, and this is applied to all who believe without distinction of persons. [23] Because all have sinned and all fall short of the glory of God; [24] and all are graciously forgiven and made righteous through the redemption effected in Christ Jesus. [25] For God has given him to be the victim whose blood obtains us forgiveness through faith.

So God shows us how he makes us righteous. Past sins are forgiven, which God overlooked till now. [26] For now, he wants to reveal his way of righteousness: how he is just and how he makes us righteous through faith in Jesus.

[27] Then, what becomes of our pride? It is excluded. How? Not through the law and its observances, but through another law, which is faith. [28] For we hold that people are in God's grace by faith, and not because of all the things ordered by the law. [29] Otherwise, God would be the God of the Jews; but is he not God of pagan nations as well? [30] Of course, he is, for there is only one God, and he will save by faith the circumcised Jews, as well as the uncircumcised nations. [31] Do we, then, deny the value of the law because of what we say of faith? Of course not, rather, we place the Law in its proper place.

ROMANS 3:1-31

Read: Jews and gentiles, those who know the Law and those who do not, all sin and will be judged. But Jesus, by his death and resurrection, reconciles all with God. Jesus makes possible for human beings to overcome sin and live according to the divine will.

Reflect: What "guarantee" of salvation does being a Christian offer? Can we truly believe in Jesus without acting as He did? What personal and communitarian commitments are required by the Christian faith?

Pray: Give thanks to God for the salvation offered to humanity through Jesus. Ask him to free you from the pride of thinking and feeling that you can live in fullness by your own.

> **Act:** Live with humility the demands of the Christian faith that this reflection has suggested to you.

Abraham, father of the just

4 ^{1} Let us consider Abraham, our father in the flesh. What has he found? ^{2} If Abraham attained righteousness because of his deeds, he could be proud. But he cannot be this before God ^{3} because Scripture says: *Abraham believed God who took it into account and held him to be a just man.*

^{4} Now, when someone does a work, salary is not given as a favor, but as a debt that is paid. ^{5} Here, on the contrary, someone who has no deeds to show, but believes in him, who makes sinners righteous before him: such faith is *taken into account* and that person is held as righteous. ^{6} David congratulates in this way those who become righteous, by the favor of God and not by their actions: ^{7} *Blessed are those whose sins are forgiven and whose offenses are forgotten*; ^{8} *blessed the one whose sin God does not take into account!*

^{9} Is this blessing only for the circumcised, or is it also for the uncircumcised? We have just said that because of his faith Abraham was made a just man, ^{10} but when did this happen? After Abraham was circumcised or before? Not after, but before. ^{11} He received the rite of circumcision as a sign of the righteousness given him, through faith, when he was still uncircumcised, that he might be the father of all those uncircumcised who come to faith and are made just. ^{12} And he was to be the father of the Jews, provided that, besides being circumcised, they also imitate the faith Abraham showed before being circumcised.

^{13} If God promised Abraham, or rather his descendants, that the world would belong to him, this was not because of his obeying the law, but because he was just and a friend of God, through faith. ^{14} If now the promise is kept for those who rely on the law, then faith has no power and nothing is left of the promise. ^{15} For it is proper of the law to bring punishment, and it is only when there is no law that it is possible to live without breaking the law.

^{16} For that reason, faith is the way, and all is given by grace; and the promises of Abraham are fulfilled for all his descendants, not only for his children, according to the law, but also for all the others who have believed.

Abraham is the father of all of us [17] as it is written: *I will make you the father of many nations.* He is our father in the eyes of Him who gives life to the dead, and calls into existence what does not yet exist, for this is the God in whom he believed.

[18] Abraham believed and hoped against all expectation, thus becoming the father of many nations, as he had been told: *See how many will be your descendants.* [19] He did not doubt, although his body could no longer give life—he was about a hundred years old—and, in spite of his wife, Sarah, being unable to have children. [20] He did not doubt, nor did he distrust the promise of God, and by being strong in faith, he gave glory to God: [21] he was convinced that He who had given the promise had [the] power to fulfill it.

[22] This was taken into account for him to attain righteousness. [23] *This was taken into account*: these words of Scripture are not only for him, [24] but for us too, because we believe in him who raised Jesus, our Lord, from among the dead, [25] he, who was delivered for our sins and raised to life for us to receive true righteousness.

ROMANS 4:1-25

Read: Abraham occupies an important place both for Jews and Christians. God asked him to believe in Him, and he trusted and obeyed, and for that God kept His promise and made Him a model for all those who have faith.

Reflect: God asked Abraham to trust in His word. What does God ask from you?

Pray: Give thanks to God for belonging to the great family of all those who have faith, from Abraham to the present day. Ask the Holy Spirit to help you embrace today the Word of God as Abraham did.

Act: Read the stories that speak of Abraham's faith in the Book of Genesis (12:1-9; 17:1-26). Do any of the conflicts in his journey reflect the questions in your spiritual journey?

Now we are at peace with God

5 [1] By faith, we have received true righteousness, and we are at peace with God, through Jesus Christ, our Lord. [2] Through him, we obtain this favor in which we remain, and we even boast to expect the glory of God.

[3] Not only that, we continue to shout our praise even in trials, knowing that trials produce patience, [4] from patience comes merit; merit is the source of hope [5] and hope does not disappoint us because the Holy Spirit has been given to us, pouring into our hearts the love of God.

[6] Consider, moreover, the time that Christ died for us: when we were still helpless and unable to do anything. [7] Few would accept to die for an upright person; although for a very good person, perhaps someone would dare to die. [8] But see how God manifested his love for us: while we were still sinners, Christ died for us; [9] and we have become just through his blood. With much more reason now he will save us from any condemnation. [10] Once enemies, we have been reconciled with God through the death of his Son; with much more reason, now we may be saved through his life. [11] Not only that, but we even boast in God because of Christ Jesus our Lord, through whom we have been reconciled.

ROMANS 5:1-11

Read: Jesus died on the cross to forgive all sins. The love of God is so great that He offers us His forgiveness even before we ask for it. Jesus reconciles us to God enabling us to trust in God's love completely.

Reflect: Do you really have faith and hope that God intends your salvation and will help you to get it? What does the experience of the forgiveness of the Father and of the goodness of the Son, require from you in your daily life?

Pray: Give thanks for the salvation that God offers to all humanity. Ask to deepen your trust in God's love for you and for all.

Act: Conscious of God's infinite love, try to respond to that love by loving the people around you.

Adam and Jesus Christ

[12] Therefore, sin entered the world through one man; and through sin, death; and later on, death spread to all humankind because all sinned.

¹³ As long as there was no law, they could not speak of disobedience, but sin was already in the world. ¹⁴ This is why, from Adam to Moses, death reigned among them, although their sin was not disobedience as in Adam's case—this was not the true Adam, but foretold the other who was to come.

¹⁵ Such has been the fall, but God's gift goes far beyond. All died because of the fault of one man, but how much more does the grace of God spread when the gift he granted reaches all, from this unique man, Jesus Christ. ¹⁶ Again, there is no comparison between the gift and the offense of one man. The disobedience that brought condemnation was of one sinner, whereas the grace of God brings forgiveness to a world of sinners. ¹⁷ If death reigned through the disobedience of one and only one person, how much more will there be a reign of life for those who receive the grace and the gift of true righteousness through the one person, Jesus Christ!

¹⁸ Just as one transgression brought sentence of death to all, so too, one man's good act has brought justification and light to all; ¹⁹ and, as the disobedience of only one made all sinners, so the obedience of one person allowed all to be made just and holy.

²⁰ The law itself, introduced later on, caused sin to increase; but where sin increased, grace abounded all the more, ²¹ and as sin caused death to reign, so grace will reign in its own time, and after making us just and friends of God, will bring us to eternal life through Jesus Christ, our Lord.

ROMANS 5:12-21

Read: Paul highlights how the first man, Adam, sinned and since then we all sin. Jesus, not Adam, is the model for humanity, and his trust in the love of God saves us all.

Reflect: Jesus shows us that Grace is always stronger than sin, and the love of God stronger than human failing. It is the way of God's love to which we trust our life.

Pray: Prayer is the time to experience God's love for us and to ask for the strength to manifest that love in our daily life.

Act: That your life be always Good News of salvation to all those around you. Share with your own people the gratuitous and generous love of God that you have experienced in prayer.

Through baptism, we died with Christ

6 [1] Then, what shall we say? Shall we keep on sinning so that grace may come more abundantly? [2] Can we live again in sin? Of course not: we are now dead regarding sin.

[3] Don't you know that in baptism, which unites us to Christ, we are all baptized and plunged into his death? [4] By this baptism in his death, we were buried with Christ and, as Christ was raised from among the dead by the glory of the Father, we begin walking in a new life. [5] If we have been joined to him by dying a death like his, so shall we be, by a resurrection like his.

[6] We know that our old self was crucified with Christ so as to destroy what of us was sin, so that we may no longer be in slavery to sin. [7] If we are dead, we are no longer in debt to sin. [8] But if we have died with Christ, we believe we will also live with him. [9] We know that Christ, once risen from the dead, will not die again and death has no more dominion over him. [10] For, by dying, he is dead to sin once and for all, and now, the life that he lives is life with God.

[11] So you, too, must consider yourselves dead to sin and alive to God, in Christ Jesus. [12] Do not allow sin to have control over your mortal bodies; do not submit yourselves to its evil inclinations, [13] and do not give your members over to sin as instruments to do evil. On the contrary, offer yourselves, as persons returned from death to life, and let the members of your body be as holy instruments at the service of God. [14] Sin will not lord it over you again, for you are not under the law, but under grace.

[15] I ask again: are we to sin because we are not under the law but under grace? Certainly not. [16] If you have given yourselves up to someone as his slave, you are to obey the one who commands you, aren't you? Now, with sin, you go to death, and by accepting faith, you go the right way. [17] Let us give thanks to God, for after having sin as your master, you have been given to another, that is, to the doctrine of faith to which you listen willingly. [18] And being free from sin, you began to serve true righteousness—[19] you see that I speak in a very human way taking into account that you are not fully mature.

There was a time when you let your members be slaves of impurity and disorder, walking in the way of sin; convert them now into servants of righteousness, to the point of becoming holy.

²⁰When you were slaves of sin, you did not feel under obligation to righteousness, ²¹but what were the fruits of those actions of which you are now ashamed? Such things bring death. ²²Now, however, you have been freed from sin and serve God. You are bearing fruit and growing in holiness and the result will be life everlasting. ²³So, on one side is sin: its reward, death; on the other side is God: He gives us by grace life everlasting, in Christ Jesus our Lord.

ROMANS 6:1-23

Read: Knowing that God saves us cannot be an excuse to continue sinning. On the contrary, in baptism Christians abandon the life of sin forever and commit themselves to live as Jesus lived.

Reflect: Baptism is how Christians signify that they have embraced the meaning and purpose of life revealed by the Risen Christ. How does Baptism affect how you think about and live your life?

Pray: Pray for the strength to live out the Christian life. Pray also for all those who are searching for the love of God in their lives.

Act: Get the text of the promises of Baptism. Read them by yourself, repeat them, with all your will to be faithful and trusting fully in God.

The Christian is not bound by the Jewish religion

7 ¹You, my friends, understand the law. The law has power only while a person is alive. ²The married woman, for example, is bound by law to her husband while he is alive; but if he dies, she is free from her obligations as a wife. ³If she gives herself to another while her husband is alive, she will be an adulteress; but once the husband dies, she is free, and if she gives herself to another man, she is not an adulteress.

⁴It was the same with you, brothers and sisters: you have died to the law with the person of Christ and you belong to another who has risen from among the dead so that we may produce fruit for God. ⁵When we lived as humans used to do, the law stirred up the desires for all that is sin, and they worked in our bodies with fruits of death. ⁶But we

have died to what was holding us; we are freed from the law and no longer serve a written law—which was the old; with the Spirit, we are in the new.

⁷Then, shall we say that the law is part of sin? Of course not! However, I would not have known sin, had it not been for the law. I would not be aware of greed if the law did not tell me: *Do not covet.* ⁸Sin took advantage of the commandment to stir in me all kinds of greed, whereas, without a law, sin lies dead.

⁹First, there was no law and I lived. Then the commandment came and gave life to sin, ¹⁰and I died. It happened that the law of life had brought me death. ¹¹Sin took advantage of the commandment. It lured me and killed me through the commandment.

¹²But the law itself is holy, just and good. ¹³Is it possible that something good brings death to me? Of course not. This comes from sin that may be seen as sin when it takes advantage of something good to kill: the commandment lets sin appear fully sinful.

The law without Christ makes humans divided

¹⁴We know that the law is spiritual; as for me, I am flesh and have been sold to sin. ¹⁵I cannot explain what is happening to me, because I do not do what I want, but, on the contrary, the very things I hate. ¹⁶Well then, if I do the evil I do not want to do, I agree that the law is good; ¹⁷but, in this case, I am not the one striving toward evil, but it is sin living in me. ¹⁸ I know that what is right does not abide in me, I mean, in my flesh. I can want to do what is right, but I am unable to do it. ¹⁹In fact, I do not do the good I want, but the evil I hate. ²⁰Therefore, if I do what I do not want to do, I am not the one striving toward evil, but sin, which is in me.

²¹I discover, then, this reality: though I wish to do what is right, the evil within me asserts itself first. ²²My inmost self agrees and rejoices with the law of God, ²³but I notice in my body, another law, challenging the law of the spirit and delivering me as a slave to the law of sin, written in my members. ²⁴Alas for me! Who will free me from this being which is only death? ²⁵Let us give thanks to God through Jesus Christ, our Lord!

So, with my conscience, I am a servant of the law of God, and with my mortal body, I serve the law of sin.

ROMANS 7:1-25

Read: Paul details his interpretation of the Law. The Law is good but does not save. God loves us because we are, not because of what we accomplish. Living out of God's love is what helps us reject sin.

Reflect: Have you already experienced this tension of wanting to do one thing and be pushed to do another? In what ways is sin still attractive enough to choose over the love God offers you?

Pray: Ask forgiveness for the times that sin is stronger than love in your daily life, and also ask for the strength to face it and overcome it.

Act: Next time you feel the temptation to do the opposite of what you know is good, entrust yourself to the Lord asking for the strength to do the right thing. Then write the feelings that that has awakened in you.

We have received the spirit

8 ¹ This contradiction no longer exists for those who are in Jesus Christ. ² For in Jesus Christ the law of the spirit of life has set me free from the law of sin and death. ³ The law was without effect, weak as it was through the flesh. God, planning to destroy sin, sent his own Son in the likeness of those subject to the sinful human condition; by doing this he condemned the sin in this human condition. ⁴ Since then, the perfection intended by the law would be fulfilled in those not walking in the way of the flesh but in the way of the spirit.

Life through the spirit

⁵ Those walking according to the flesh tend toward what is flesh; those led by the spirit, to what is spirit. ⁶ The flesh tends toward death, while spirit aims at life and peace. ⁷ What the flesh seeks is against God: it does not agree, it cannot even submit to the law of God. ⁸ So, those walking according to the flesh cannot please God.

⁹ Yet, your existence is not in the flesh, but in the spirit, because the Spirit of God is within you. If you did not have the Spirit of Christ, you

would not belong to him. [10] But Christ is within you; though the body is branded by death, as a consequence of sin, the spirit is life and holiness. [11] And if the Spirit of him, who raised Jesus from the dead, is within you, he who raised Jesus Christ from among the dead will also give life to your mortal bodies. Yes, he will do it through his Spirit who dwells within you.

[12] Then, brothers and sisters, let us leave the flesh and no longer live according to it. [13] If not, we will die. Rather, walking in the Spirit, let us put to death the body's deeds, so that we may live.

[14] All those who walk in the Spirit of God are sons and daughters of God. [15] Then, no more fear: you did not receive a spirit of slavery, but the spirit that makes you sons and daughters, and every time we cry, "Abba! (this is Dad!) Father!" [16] the Spirit assures our spirit that we are sons and daughters of God. [17] If we are children, we are heirs too. Ours will be the inheritance of God and we will share it with Christ; for if we now suffer with him, we will also share glory with him.

ROMANS 8:1-17

Read: When Paul speaks about "the flesh" he means a life lived only for material things, a life without a spiritual dimension of any sort. He contrasts this way of life with the power of God through the Spirit. The Spirit is in us, is stronger than sin, and moves us to call God: "Abba, Father." As children, we are also heirs of His love.

Reflect: How does the Holy Spirit act in your life? Paul is confident that God is a loving parent, do you share his confidence?

Pray: Pray to recognize the Holy Spirit in your life, the Spirit that inspires you to witness to God's love.

Act: Invoke the strength of the Holy Spirit in your life at the start of each day: "Come, Holy Spirit, fill the hearts of your faithful, and kindle in them the fire of your love."

The universe, too, waits for its redemption

[18] I consider that the suffering of our present life cannot be compared with the glory that will be revealed and given to us. [19] All creation is eagerly expecting the birth, in glory, of the children of God. [20] For, if now,

the created world was unable to attain its purpose, this did not come from itself, but from the one who subjected it. But it is not without hope; [21] for even the created world will be freed from this fate of death and share the freedom and glory of the children of God.

[22] We know that the whole creation groans and suffers the pangs of birth. [23] Not creation alone, but even ourselves; although the Spirit was given to us as a foretaste of what we are to receive, we groan in our innermost being, eagerly awaiting the day when God will give us full rights and rescue our bodies as well.

[24] In hope, we already have salvation. But if we saw what we hoped for, there would no longer be hope: how can you hope for what is already seen? [25] So we hope for what we do not see, and we will receive it through patient hope.

[26] Likewise, the Spirit helps us in our weakness; for we do not know how to pray as we ought, but that very Spirit intercedes for us without words, as if with groans. [27] And he, who sees inner secrets, knows the desires of the Spirit, for he asks for the holy ones what is pleasing to God.

Who shall separate us from the love of God?

[28] We know that in everything God works for the good of those who love him, whom he has called according to his plan. [29] Those whom he knew beforehand he has also predestined to be like his Son, similar to him, so that he may be the Firstborn among many brothers and sisters. [30] And so those whom God predestined, he called; and those whom he called, he makes righteous; and to those whom he makes righteous, he will give his glory.

[31] What shall we say after this? If God is with us, who shall be against us? [32] If he did not spare his own Son but gave him up for us all, how will he not give us all things with him? [33] Who shall accuse those chosen by God: He takes away their guilt. [34] Who will dare to condemn them? Christ who died, and better still, rose, and is seated at the right hand of God interceding for us?

[35] Who shall separate us from the love of Christ? Will it be trials, or anguish, persecution or hunger, lack of clothing, or dangers or sword? [36] As the Scripture says: *For your sake, we are being killed all day long; they treat us like sheep to be slaughtered.*

[37] No, in all of this we are more than conquerors, thanks to him who

has loved us. [38] I am certain that neither death, nor life, neither angels nor spiritual powers, neither the present nor the future, nor cosmic powers [39] were they from heaven or from the deep world below, nor any creature whatsoever, will separate us from the love of God, which we have in Jesus Christ, our Lord.

ROMANS 8:18-39

Read: Although we now suffer because of sin, we who believe in Jesus, look forward to the glory of God. The Spirit helps us in our weakness and helps us to seek what is good for us. If we are united to the love of God, no one or nothing can separate us from the Love of God.

Reflect: Much of this world is not encouraging: hunger, war, corruption, injustice and death. Despite this, do you retain the hope in a better world? How should the Christian live in this world?

Pray: Pray for those who work for the betterment of our world and its environment. Pray that rulers will make just decisions that reflect the will of God and care for those who are without.

Act: Do something positive for someone in need. Promote in your family the practice of justice and solidarity toward the most helpless. Do not neglect to protect the environment.

Why have the Jews not believed?

9 [1] I tell you sincerely, in Christ, and my conscience assures me in the Holy Spirit that I am not lying: [2] I have great sadness and constant anguish for the Jews. [3] I would even desire that I myself suffer the curse of being cut off from Christ, instead of my brethren: I mean my own people, my kin. [4] They are Israelites whom God adopted, and on them rests his glory. Theirs are the Covenants, the law, the worship and the promises of God. [5] They are descendants of the patriarchs, and from their race, Christ was born, he who as God is above all distinctions. Blessed be He forever and ever: Amen!

[6] We cannot say that the promise of God has failed. For not all Israelites belong to Israel. [7] And not because they are of the race of Abraham they are all his children, for it was said to him: *The children of Isaac will be*

called your descendants. [8] This means that the children of God are not identified with the race of Abraham, but only with the children born to him because of the promise of God. [9] To such a promise this text refers: *I shall return about this time and Sarah will have a son.* [10] And listen: Rebecca, the wife of our father Isaac, became pregnant, [11] and before the twins were born or had done anything, right or wrong, in order that God's purpose of election might continue [12] not on the merits but of who is called, she was told: *The elder will serve the younger;* [13] as the Scripture says: *I chose Jacob and rejected Esau.*

God is not unjust

[14] Shall we say that God is unjust? Of course not. [15] However, God said to Moses: *I shall forgive whom I forgive, and have pity on whom I have pity.* [16] So what is important is not that we worry or hurry, but that God has compassion. [17] And he says in Scripture to Pharaoh: *I made you, Pharaoh, to show my power in you, and for the whole world to know my name.* [18] And so God takes pity on whom he wishes, and hardens the heart of whomsoever he wishes.

[19] Maybe you say: "Why then, does God complain if it is impossible to evade his decision?" [20] But you, my friend, who are you to call God to account? Should the clay pot say to its maker: Why did you make me like this? [21] Is it not up to the potter to make from the same clay a vessel for beauty and a vessel for menial use?

[22] Thus, God endures, very patiently, vessels that deserve his wrath, fit to be broken, and through them, he wants to show his wrath and the extent of his power. [23] But he also wants to show the riches of his glory in others, in vessels of mercy prepared for glory. [24] And he called us, not only from among the Jews, but from among the pagans too, [25] as he said through the prophet Hosea: *I will call "my people" those that were not my people, and "my beloved" the one who was not beloved.* [26] *And in the same place where they were told, "You are not my people," they will be called children of the living God.*

[27] With regard to Israel, Isaiah proclaims: *Even if the Israelites are as numerous as the sand of the sea, only a few will be saved.* [28] *This is a matter that the Lord will settle in Israel, without fail or delay.* [29] Isaiah also announced: *If the Almighty Lord had not left us some descendants, we would have become like Sodom and similar to Gomorrah.*

³⁰What are we saying, then? That the pagans, who were not aiming at true righteousness, found it (I speak of righteousness through faith); ³¹while Israel, striving to observe a law of righteousness, lost the purpose of the law. ³²Why? Because they relied on the observance of the law, not on faith. And they stumbled over the stumbling stone (Christ), ³³as it was said: *Look, I am laying in Zion a stone, that will make people stumble, a rock that will make them fall; but whoever relies on him will not be deceived.*

ROMANS 9:1-33

Read: Paul's conflict is that God's promises are given to the people of Israel, and through them comes the Messiah. However, most Jews do not recognize Jesus as Messiah. He resolves this struggle with the faith that God can give His mercy to whomever He pleases, Gentiles and Jews alike.

Reflect: This chapter reflects a conflict between Christians and Jews, a difference which led Christians to anti-Semitism, although Jesus himself was a Jew.

Pray: Pray that Christians and Jews recognize they worship the same God, though in different traditions. Pray that religious differences will never be the excuse for violence.

Act: Talk with someone who has a different faith, ask about the fundamentals of his/her faith, on their practices and rites, etc. Share this experience with those close to you.

They tried to achieve their own righteousness

10 ¹My brothers and sisters, I wish with all my heart that the Jews be saved, and I pray to God for them. ²I can testify that they are zealous for God, but this is not the way. ³They don't know God's way of righteousness, and they try to achieve their own righteousness: this is why they did not enter God's way of righteousness. ⁴For Christ is the aim of the law, and it is then that the believer reaches this righteousness.

⁵Moses, indeed, speaks of becoming just through the law; he writes: *The one who obeys the law will find life through it.* ⁶But the righteousness coming from the faith says instead: *Do not say in your heart: Who will go up to heaven?* (because in fact, Christ came down from there)

[7] or *who will go down to the world below?* (because in fact, Christ came up from among the dead). [8] True righteousness, coming from faith, also says: *The word of God is near you, on your lips and in your hearts.* This is the message that we preach and this is faith.

[9] You are saved if you confess with your lips that Jesus is Lord, and in your heart, you believe that God raised him from the dead. [10] By believing from the heart, you obtain true righteousness; by confessing the faith with your lips, you are saved. [11] For Scripture says: *No one who believes in him will be ashamed.* [12] Here, there is no distinction between Jew and Greek; all have the same Lord who is very generous with whoever calls on him. [13] Truly, *all who call upon the name of the Lord will be saved.*

[14] But how can they call upon the name of the Lord without having believed in him? And how can they believe in him without having first heard about him? And how will they hear about him if no one preaches about him? [15] And how will they preach about him if no one sends them? As Scripture says: *How beautiful are the feet of the messenger of good news.* [16] Although, not everyone obeyed the good news, as Isaiah said: *Lord, who has believed in our preaching?* [17] So, faith comes from preaching and preaching is rooted in the word of Christ.

[18] I ask: Have the Jews not heard? But of course, they have. Because the voice of those preaching *resounded all over the earth and their voice was heard to the ends of the world.* [19] Then, I must ask: *Did Israel not understand?* Moses was the first to say: *I will make you jealous of a nation that is not a nation; I will excite your anger against a senseless nation.* [20] Isaiah dares to add more: *I was found by those not looking for me; I have shown myself to those not asking for me.* [21] While referring to Israel, the same Isaiah says: *I hold out my hands the whole day long to a disobedient and rebellious people.*

ROMANS 10:1-21

Read: Paul insists that God's salvation is universal: "all those who invoke the name of the Lord will be saved," and regrets that his countrymen, the Jewish people, do not recognize Jesus as the Messiah.

Reflect: In your everyday life, do you live your faith in a universal way, welcoming all who seek God, or in a sectarian manner, considering companions on the way only those who think and believe like you? Do you cling to your accustomed way of believing, or are you open to what the Word of God inspires, although breaking your own schemes?

Pray: Ask God to help you renew your ideas of what is good, even your idea about Him. Ask God to help you not to fall into the arrogance of thinking yourself an "expert of the divine." Allow yourself to be surprised by God.

Act: Live your faith in a universal manner, as Jesus, our Master did: welcome all those who seek and need God and let yourself be surprised by the unpredictable ways of divine acting. Find an opportunity to visit a synagogue or visit with a rabbi to learn about their tradition of faith.

A remnant of Israel has been saved

11 [1] And so I ask: Has God rejected his people? Of course not! I, myself, am an Israelite, a descendant of Abraham from the tribe of Benjamin. [2] No, God has not rejected the people he knew beforehand. Don't you know what the Scripture says of Elijah when he was accusing Israel before God? [3] He said: "*Lord, they have killed your prophets, destroyed your altars, and I alone remain; and now they want to kill me.*" [4] What was God's answer? "*I kept for myself seven thousand who did not worship Baal.*" [5] In the same way, now there is a remnant in Israel, those who were chosen by grace. [6] It is said: by grace, not because of what they did. Otherwise, grace would not be grace.

[7] What then? What Israel was looking for it did not find, but those whom God elected found it. The others hardened their hearts [8] as Scripture says: *God made them dull of heart and mind; to this day their eyes cannot see nor their ears hear.* [9] David says: *May they be caught and trapped at their banquets; may they fall, may they be punished.* [10] *May their eyes be closed so that they cannot see and their backs be bent forever.*

Do not despise those who stumbled

[11] Again, I ask: Did they stumble so as to fall? Of course not. Their stumbling allowed salvation to come to the pagan nations, and this, in

turn, will stir up the jealousy of Israel. ¹²If Israel's shortcoming made the world rich if the pagan nations grew rich with what they lost, what will happen when Israel is restored?

¹³Listen to me, you who are not Jews: I am spending myself, as an apostle to the pagan nations, ¹⁴but I hope my ministry will be successful enough to awaken the jealousy of those of my race and finally, to save some of them. ¹⁵If the world made peace with God when they remained apart, what will it be when they are welcomed? Nothing less than a passing from death to life.

¹⁶When the first fruits are consecrated to God, the whole is consecrated. If the roots are holy, so will be the branches. ¹⁷Some branches have been cut from the olive tree while you, as a wild olive tree, have been grafted in their stead, and you are benefiting from their roots and sap. ¹⁸Now, therefore, do not be proud and despise the branches, because you do not support the roots, the roots support you. ¹⁹You may say, "They cut off the branches to graft me." ²⁰Well and good! But they were cut off because they did not believe while you stand by faith. Then do not pride yourself on this too much, rather beware: ²¹if God did not spare the natural branches, even less will he spare you.

²²Admire at the same time both the goodness and severity of God: he was severe with the fallen and he is generous with you, as long as you remain faithful. Otherwise, you will be cut off. ²³If they do not keep on rejecting the faith they will be grafted in, for God is able to graft them back again. ²⁴If you were taken from the wild olive tree to which you belonged and, in spite of being a different specie, you were grafted into the good olive tree, how much more will these who are the natural branches be grafted into their own olive tree?

Israel will be saved

²⁵I want you to understand the mysterious decree of God, lest you be too confident: a part of Israel will remain hardened until the majority of pagans have entered. ²⁶Then the whole of Israel will be saved as Scripture says: *From Zion will come the Liberator who will purify the descendants of Jacob from all sin.* ²⁷*And this is the Covenant I will make with them: I will take away from them their sins.*

²⁸Regarding the gospel, the Jews are opponents, but it is for your

benefit. Regarding the election, they are beloved, because of their ancestors; ²⁹ because the call of God and his gifts cannot be nullified.

³⁰ Through the disobedience of the Jews, the mercy of God came to you who did not obey God. ³¹ They, in turn, will receive mercy in due time, after this disobedience that brought God's mercy to you. ³² So, God has submitted all to disobedience, in order to show his mercy to all.

³³ How deep are the riches, the wisdom, and knowledge of God! His decisions cannot be explained, nor his ways understood! ³⁴ *Who has ever known God's thoughts? Who has ever been his adviser?* ³⁵ *Who has given him something first so that God had to repay him?* ³⁶ For everything comes from him, has been made by him and has to return to him. To him be the glory for ever! Amen.

ROMANS 11:1-36

Read: God does not reject His people, but the Jewish people do not accept the offer of salvation. For Paul, this attitude has made it possible for the Gospel to reach the gentiles. Therefore he affirms: "If the pagan nations grew rich with what they (Israel) lost, what will happen when Israel is restored?" Paul believes the Jews are irrevocably God's chosen people, and that God's mercy remains with them.

Reflect: Christians must never adopt an attitude of superiority toward other believers or non-believers. We must be witnesses to God's mercy: "How deep are the riches, the wisdom and the knowledge of God! His decisions cannot be explained, nor his ways understood!"

Pray: Give thanks for the gift of faith. Ask the Holy Spirit light to contemplate the mercy of God and humility to accept His mysteries.

Act: Observe what surrounds you as if your eyes were the eyes of God, full of mercy. Be merciful as God is merciful.

Christian life: be concerned for others

12 [1] I beg you, dearly beloved, by the mercy of God, to give yourselves as a living and holy sacrifice pleasing to God; that is the kind of worship for you as sensible people. [2] Don't let yourselves be shaped by the world where you live, but rather be transformed through the renewal of your mind. You must discern the will of God: what is good, what pleases, what is perfect.

[3] The grace that God has given me allows me to tell each of you: don't pretend too much, but think with sober judgment, each according to the measure of faith that God has assigned.

[4] See, the body is one even if formed by many members, but not all of them with the same function. [5] The same with us; being many, we are one body in Christ depending on one another. [6] Let each one of us, therefore, serve according to our different gifts. Are you a prophet? Then give the insights of faith. [7] Let the minister fulfill his office; let the teacher teach, [8] the one who encourages, convince.

You must, likewise, give with an open hand, preside with dedication, and be cheerful in your works of charity.

[9] Let love be sincere. Hate what is evil and hold to whatever is good. [10] Love one another and be considerate. Outdo one another in mutual respect. [11] Be zealous in fulfilling your duties. Be fervent in the spirit and serve God.

[12] Have hope and be cheerful. Be patient in trials and pray constantly. [13] Share with other Christians in need. With those passing by, be ready to receive them.

[14] Bless those who persecute you; bless and do not wish evil on anyone. [15] Rejoice with those who are joyful, and weep with those who weep. [16] Live in peace with one another. Do not dream of extraordinary things; be humble and do not hold yourselves as wise.

[17] Do not return evil for evil, but let everyone see your good will. [18] Do your best to live in peace with everybody. [19] Beloved, do not avenge yourselves but let God be the one who punishes, as Scripture says: *Vengeance is mine, I will repay, says the Lord.* [20] And it adds: *If your enemy is hungry, feed him; if he is thirsty, give him to drink; by doing this you will heap burning coals upon his head.* [21] Do not let evil defeat you, but conquer evil with goodness.

ROMANS 12:1-21

Read: Paul invites the Romans to offer their lives "as a living and holy sacrifice, pleasing to God; that is the king of worship for you." This spiritual sacrifice means to humbly accept God's gifts and sharing them generously in the community.

Reflect: Is life in community important for a Christian? Why? Do you think that you have some gift that you can share with the community? What does the following expression suggest to you: "Do not let evil defeat you, but conquer evil with goodness"?

Pray: Pray for the unity of your community and also of the Church. Ask for the God's help to always do good and offer your life as a living sacrifice, holy, acceptable to God.

Act: Promote dialogue in your community. Practice hospitality. Bless always and do not condemn others. May your daily life be a sign of the unity of your community and of the Church.

Submission to authority

13 [1] Let everyone be subject to the authorities. For there is no authority that does not come from God, and the offices have been established by God. [2] Whoever, therefore, resists authority, goes against a decree of God, and those who resist deserve to be condemned.

[3] In fact, who fears authority? Not those who do good, but those who do evil. Do you want to be without fear of a person in authority? Do good and you will receive praise. [4] They are the stewards of God, for your good. But if you do not behave, fear them, for they do not carry arms in vain; they are at the service of God when they judge and punish wrongdoers.

[5] It is necessary to obey, not through fear, but as a matter of conscience. [6] In the same way, you must pay taxes and the collectors are God's officials. [7] Pay to all what is due them; to whomsoever you owe contributions, make a contribution; to whom taxes are due, pay taxes; to whom respect is due, give respect; to whom honor is due, give honor.

[8] Do not be in debt to anyone. Let this be the only debt of one to another: Love. The one who loves his or her neighbor fulfills the law. [9] For

the commandments: *Do not commit adultery, do not kill, do not covet,* and whatever else, are summarized in this one: *You will love your neighbor as yourself.* [10] Love cannot do the neighbor any harm; so love fulfills the whole law.

Children of the light

[11] You know what hour it is. This is the time to awake, for our salvation is now nearer than when we first believed; [12] the night is almost over and the day is at hand. Let us discard, therefore, everything that belongs to darkness and let us put on the armor of light. [13] As we live in the full light of day, let us behave with decency; no banquets with drunkenness, no promiscuity or licentiousness, no fighting or jealousy. [14] Put on, rather, the Lord Jesus Christ, and do not be led by the will of the flesh nor follow its desires.

ROMANS 13:1-14

Read: The initial verses may refer to a tax increase in Rome. Like Jesus, Paul advises obedience to civil authorities. In any case, those who act out of love cannot commit evil whatsoever. We Christians must live like Jesus lived: doing good.

Reflect: How should our Christian behavior be with the civil society? How do you love your neighbor as yourself in a complicated civil society? "Owe no one anything, except to love one another" how is this part of your life?

Pray: Ask forgiveness for the times you have failed the law of love and have not given witness of your Christian faith. Ask for the grace to live as a good Christian.

Act: Check how you behave with others in your day to day, and try to live as a good Christian "clothed with the Lord Jesus Christ."

The weak and the strong

14 [1] Welcome those weak in faith and do not criticize their scruples. [2] Some think they can eat any food, while others less liberated eat only vegetables. [3] If you eat, do not despise those who abstain; if you abstain, do not criticize those who eat, for God has welcomed them.

⁴Who are you to pass judgment on the servant of another? Whether he stands or falls, the one concerned is his master. But he will not fall, for his master is able to keep him standing.

⁵Some judge one day to be better than the other; let us act according to our own opinion. ⁶The one who distinguishes among days, does that for the Lord; and the one who eats, eats for the Lord and in eating, gives thanks to the Lord. And the one who does not eat does it for the Lord and gives him thanks as well.

⁷In fact, none of us lives for himself, nor dies for himself. ⁸If we live, we live for the Lord, and if we die, we die for the Lord. Either in life or in death, we belong to the Lord. ⁹It was for this purpose that Christ both died and came to life again, to be Lord both of the living and of the dead.

¹⁰Then you, why do you criticize your brother or sister? And you, why do you despise them? For we will all appear at the tribunal of God. ¹¹It is written: *I swear by myself—word of the Lord—every knee will bend before me and every tongue shall give glory to God.* ¹²So each of us will account for himself before God.

¹³Therefore, let us not continue criticizing one another; let us try, rather, never to put in the way of our brother or sister anything that would make him stumble or fall. ¹⁴I know, I am sure of this in the Lord Jesus, that nothing is unclean in itself, it is only unclean for those who consider it unclean. ¹⁵But if you hurt your brother or sister because of a certain food, you are no longer walking according to love. Let not your eating cause the loss of one for whom Christ died.

¹⁶Don't put yourself in the wrong with something good. ¹⁷The kingdom of God is not a matter of food or drink; it is justice, peace, and joy in the Holy Spirit, ¹⁸and if you serve Christ in this way, you will please God and be praised by people. ¹⁹Let us look then for what strengthens peace and makes us better.

²⁰Do not destroy the work of God because of food. All food is clean, but it is wrong for you to make others fall by what you eat. ²¹And it may be better not to eat meat, or drink wine, or anything else that causes your brother or sister to stumble.

²²Keep your own belief before God, and happy are you if you never act against your own belief. ²³Instead, whoever eats something in spite of his doubt, is condemned by his conscience, because whatever we do against our conscience is sinful.

ROMANS 14:1-23

Read: Paul exhorts to "look for what strengthens peace and makes us better" in the community. We Christians must be tolerant and welcoming those who are different, because "everyone belongs to the Lord."

Reflect: It is easy to judge others. How do you react to attitudes or approaches different from yours within your family or your community? What does the following expression suggest to you: "Let us not continue criticizing one another; let us try, rather, never to put in the way of our brother anything that would make him stumble or fall"?

Pray: Ask the Lord the grace of knowing to look at the qualities of those who think differently from you. Also, ask for humility to recognize your own capabilities and limitations.

Act: Check your prejudices and don't judge anyone without first examining and putting yourself in the place of the other.

---

15 ¹ We, the strong and liberated, should bear the weakness of those who are not strong instead of pleasing ourselves. ² Let each of us bring joy to our neighbors, helping them for the good purpose, for building up. ³ Christ, himself, did not look for his own contentment, as Scripture says: *The insults of those insulting you fell upon me.* ⁴ And we know that whatever was written in the past was written for our instruction, for both perseverance and comfort, given us by the Scripture, to sustain our hope. ⁵ May God, the source of all perseverance and comfort, give to all of you to live in peace in Christ Jesus, ⁶ that you may be able to praise in one voice God, Father of Christ Jesus, our Lord.

⁷ Welcome then one another, as Christ welcomed you for the glory of God. ⁸ Look: Christ put himself at the service of the Jewish world to fulfill the promises made by God to their ancestors; here you see God's faithfulness. ⁹ The pagans instead, give thanks to God for his mercy, as Scripture says: *Because of that, I will sing and praise your name among the pagans.* ¹⁰ And in another place: *Rejoice, pagan nations, with God's people.* ¹¹ And again: *Praise the Lord, all people, and let all nations speak of*

his magnificence. ¹²Isaiah says: *A descendant of Jesse will come who will rule the pagan nations and they will hope in him.*

¹³May God the source of hope, fill you with joy and peace in the faith, so that your hope may increase by the power of the Holy Spirit.

Paul feels responsible for the Christians of Rome

¹⁴As for me, brothers and sisters, I am convinced that you have good-will, knowledge, and the capacity to advise each other; ¹⁵nevertheless, I have written boldly in some parts of this letter to remind you of what you already know. I do this according to the grace God has given to me ¹⁶when I was sent to the pagan nations. I dedicated myself to the service of the Good News of God as a minister of Christ Jesus, in order to present the non-Jews to God as an agreeable offering, consecrated by the Holy Spirit. ¹⁷This service of God is for me a cause of pride, in Christ Jesus.

¹⁸Of course, I would not dare to speak of other things, but what Christ, himself has done through me, my words and my works, ¹⁹with miracles and signs, by the power of the Holy Spirit—so that non-Jews may obey the faith. In this way, I have extended the Good News to all parts, from Jerusalem to Illyricum.

²⁰I have been very careful, however, and I am proud of this, not to preach in places where Christ is already known, and not to build upon foundations laid by others. ²¹Let it be as Scripture says: *Those not told about him will see, and those who have not heard will understand.*

Help for the Christians in Jerusalem

²²This work has prevented me from going to you. ²³But now there is no more place for me in these regions and, as I have wanted for so long to go and see you, ²⁴I hope to visit you when I go to Spain. Then you could help me go to that nation, once I have fully enjoyed your company.

²⁵Right now I am going to Jerusalem to help that community. ²⁶Know that the churches of Macedonia and Achaia have decided to make a contribution for the poor among the believers of Jerusalem. ²⁷They have decided to do that, and in fact, they were indebted to them. For the non-Jews have shared the spiritual goods of the Jews, and now they must help them materially. ²⁸So I am to complete this task and give over the

amount that has been collected. Then I will go to you, and from there, to Spain. [29]And I am sure, that when I go to you, I will go with all the blessings of God.

[30]I beg of you, brothers and sisters, by Christ Jesus our Lord and by the love of the Spirit, to join me in the fight, praying to God for me; [31]pray that I may avoid the snares of the enemies of faith in Judea and that the community of Jerusalem may welcome the help I bring. [32]And so I will go to you with joy and, God willing, be refreshed in your company. [33]The God of peace be with you. Amen.

ROMANS 15:1-33

Read: Christians must be characterized for being solicitous with others, following the example of Jesus. "Welcome one another, as Christ welcomed you for the glory of God," exhorts Paul.

Reflect: What does the following expression suggest to you: "May God, the source of perseverance and comfort, give to all of you, to live in peace in Jesus Christ"?

Pray: Ask, through the intercession of St. Paul, to improve your relationship with people who are not in agreement with you. Ask also for humility to see in them the presence of Jesus.

Act: Foster in your daily life attitudes of acceptance, consent and good manners. Become an apostle of Christian living.

Greetings

16 [1]I recommend to you our sister Phoebe, a deaconess of the church of Cenchreae. [2]Please receive her, in the name of the Lord, as it should be among brothers and sisters in the faith and help her in whatever is necessary, because she helped many; among them, myself.

[3]Greetings to Prisca and Aquilas, my helpers in Christ Jesus. [4]To save my life they risked theirs; I am very grateful to them, as are all the churches of the pagan nations. [5]Greetings also to the church that meets in their house. Greetings to my dear Epaenetus, the first in the province of Asia to believe in Christ. [6]Greet Mary, who worked so much for you.

⁷Greetings to Andronicus and Junia, my relatives and companions in prison; they are well-known apostles and served Christ before I did.

⁸Give greetings to Ampliatus, whom I love so much in the Lord. ⁹Greetings to Urbanus, our fellow worker, and to my dear Stachys. ¹⁰Greetings to Apelles, who suffered for Christ, and the family of Aristobulus. ¹¹Greetings to my relative Herodion and those in the household of Narcissus who work in the Lord's service. ¹²Greetings to Tryphaena and Tryphosa, who toil for the Lord's sake. ¹³Greetings to Rufus, elected of the Lord, and his mother who was a second mother to me. ¹⁴Greetings to Asyncritus, Phlegon, Hermes, Patrobas, Hermas and the brothers and sisters staying with them. ¹⁵Greetings to Philologus and Julia, Nereus and his sister, Olympas and all the holy ones in Christ Jesus with them. ¹⁶Greet one another with a holy kiss. All the churches of Christ send their greetings.

A warning

¹⁷Brothers and sisters, I beg of you, to be careful of those who are causing divisions and troubles in teaching you a different teaching from the one you were taught. Keep away from them, ¹⁸because those persons do not serve Christ our Lord, but their own interests, deceiving with their soft and entertaining language those who are simple of heart. ¹⁹Everybody knows that you are very obedient, and because of that I am happy, but I want you to be sensible in doing good and firm against evil. ²⁰The God of peace will soon crush Satan and place him under your feet.

May Christ Jesus, our Lord, bless you. ²¹Timothy, who is with me, sends you greetings, and so do Lucius, Jason and Sosipatros, my relatives.

²²I, Tertius, the writer of this letter, send you greetings in the Lord.

²³Greetings from Gaius who has given me lodging and in whose house the church meets. Greetings from Erastus, treasurer of the city, and from our brother Quartus. (²⁴)

²⁵Glory be to God!

He is able to give you strength according to the Good News I proclaim, announcing Christ Jesus.

Now is revealed the mysterious plan kept hidden for long ages in the past.

²⁶ By the will of the eternal God, it is brought to light through the prophetic books, and all nations shall believe the faith proclaimed to them.

²⁷ Glory to God who alone is wise, through Christ Jesus, for ever! Amen.

ROMANS 16:1-27

Read: Paul ends his letter showing his gratitude. The list of men and women is long and detailed. Each name is followed by a few words of appreciation and gratitude for the work done in favor of the community, and for the ties of friendship that bind them to the apostle.

Reflect: Do you have friends in the Christian community? Do you feel close to its members? Do you consider the Church as a community of friends in the Lord?

Pray: Pray for your Christian community, that its members may become friends in the Lord and collaborators of a mission that is the responsibility of all: the proclamation of the Gospel.

Act: Make a list with the names of all the friends you have in the Christian community, and write them a letter with much affection for what they mean in your life and in your evangelizing mission.

The Risen Christ:
Has Jesus of Nazareth Been Distorted?

Jesus' figure, as it emerges from the Gospels of Matthew, Mark, and Luke, is the figure of a rabbi, a teacher of the Law in the purest tradition of the people of Israel (Jn 3:2). Although, later on, the first Christian community gave more importance to the conflicts with the Pharisees than actually occurred, they did not forget that Jesus' teaching was very close to the teaching of the Pharisees on many points (Mk 2:16; 12:28; 12:32). Both disciples and opponents saw him as a self-taught master of the law (Jn 7:15). How then did we go from there to the figure of Christ as it appears particularly in Paul's letters: the Lord of history, the new Adam, the one who received the ineffable "Name"?

The apostles believed in the resurrection of Jesus and so did the entire Christian community who were born of this conviction. There was no doubt that he was the Messiah; people also believed that he was God's Son in a very special sense, different from what the Jews understood by this term. A long time was needed to draw all the inferences from this. This passage was undoubtedly more difficult for those who had known Jesus personally and who had seen him through the eyes of their Jewish culture, not because Jesus was not utterly Jewish, including his way of teaching, but because what they loved in him was preventing them from seeing beyond.

They certainly recognized themselves in James' letter, the most "Jewish" of the apostolic writings. While acknowledging Jesus as "our Lord," the author of the letter sees Jesus first as the teacher of a new law which included the best of the Old Testament (2:1 and 8). With the help of the impact of the Nazareth group, the "brothers of Jesus," the Christian communities of Palestine would grow fond of this image they had of the Galilean rabbi. He had risen, of course, but he had not set the world clock back to zero, and his heritage was, first of all, an example of doing *good*, not just teaching the Law.

Within just a few generations, these "Judeo-Christians" would find themselves like strangers to the faith of the Church whose center had moved from Jerusalem to Antioch, then to Rome. It is there that Paul played a decisive role that he himself did not choose. He did not invent Christ the Lord and Redeemer: he was already present in Peter's first proclamations (Acts 2:32-36; 3:15). Paul, however, had not been influenced (and at the same time limited) by the image and the words of the Galilean rabbi. On the contrary, his conversion had been an encounter with God himself in the person of Jesus, and he saw the Master's itinerant preaching as the first stage of a wider destiny (2 Cor 5:16).

If Jesus had not risen, he would have remained a teacher; until then, his words were perhaps more important than he himself was. But his body disappeared from the tomb; this first-ever happening did not fit into the laws of the universe. So the visions of the resurrected one conveyed but one message: Jesus, the Lord! This went far beyond Jeremiah's exultant in glory or Elijah taken up to heaven. On the day of Pentecost, Peter said that God had raised his holy servant (Acts 3:15) and he added: "God has made him Lord." Before long Jesus will be recognized as "the son of the woman taken up to heaven to seize the book of history" (Rev 12:5; 5:7). Paul and John have the authority to speak about him because they are true witnesses; both of them were privileged to get a glimpse of the above (Rev 4:1; 2 Cor 12:2).

From that moment, it was knowing who Jesus was that gave the understanding of his words because he was God born of God. From that point on, his whole human adventure was a new beginning.

Therefore, when Paul speaks of Christ as the "image of God" (Col 1:15), he is not primarily inviting us to find the goodness of the Father in Jesus' gestures: instead he is thinking more directly about the Son who, from the beginning, is the manifestation, the projection and the active wisdom of the forever invisible God. Christ is the one who passed through our history and our time so that, through him, all of creation including humankind would be seen as part of the divine mystery (Col 1:20).

In the gospels, Jesus chose to be the proclaimer of the Reign of God. With Paul, however, there is not just kingdom, but our life in the risen Christ (Col 3:1). There we see the gap between Christian faith and the position of the non-Christian Jews who were the most sympathetic toward Jesus and acknowledged him as one of their own. Paul was not the one who built a wall of misunderstanding; the scandal was found in Jesus' resurrection as well as in his death on the cross.

These are not less scandalous for today's Christians. Although we have faith, at times we are besieged by doubt: is all of that certain? Many books written by unbelievers, or even by educated Christians, will reinforce our doubts: "The resurrection? There is no other basis than an empty tomb—and do we even know that? Yet, all these reasons do not overcome a deep-seated conviction in the hearts of believers. Then, people interpreted; they believed; they saw…. To say that he had risen was a way of exalting him and of reasserting the hope of the community…." A sense of God tells them that truth is found in the mystery rather than in the interpretations that seek to do away with it (1 Jn 2:27).

We have just said "a sense of God," because it is not a matter of human feeling: we believe, which means first of all that we receive the testimony of the apostles and of the Church, and we believe the way they did. If we welcome faith, God will not leave us alone with our doubts, there is also an added promise: the gift of the Holy Spirit (Acts 2:18). There can be no lasting faith without a spiritual experience (Heb 12:18-24), and this is even truer for those living in a culture impervious to faith, as we are.

FIRST LETTER TO THE
CORINTHIANS

Some persons praise the first Christians as if they had been models of all virtue. In fact, there were no more miracles then than now. Here as elsewhere, Paul addresses men and women living in a world as real as our own. Corinth had its own particular character among the Mediterranean cities. Situated on a tongue of land separating two gulfs, it had the best part of its privileged site. The two ports of the east and west had been joined by a kind of paved way on which boats were pulled by means of enormous wagons drawn by bullocks. This spared sailors having to detour to Greece by the south: a very long voyage at the time and very dangerous. Obviously, it had to be paid for; this financially benefited the town; it also needed labor which meant many slaves. The city had a sanctuary dedicated to the goddess Aphrodite, the goddess of "love" for the Greeks, around which had developed (with the help of money) a prostitution that had nothing sacred about it other than its name. The prostitutes were counted in the thousands. Quite near Corinth, there was a sportive celebration—rather similar to the Olympic Games of our day—every two years. This drew large crowds of people. We notice in these two letters of Paul very clear allusions to these different aspects of Corinthian history: slavery, prostitution, stadium sports.

In Corinth, there existed a dynamic, though not well ordered Church, composed of Jews and Greeks converted by Paul. Many of them were in danger of returning to the vices of their former lives, once the enthusiasm of their first years as Christians had worn off. Those responsible in the Church apparently were not capable of dealing with many problems: internal divisions and doubts about faith. They, therefore, called upon Paul, who wrote the present letter, because he could not interrupt his work in Ephesus.

We notice the authority with which Paul, from afar, leads the Church in the name of Christ; also his manner of teaching: before answering any question, he reasserts the foundations of the faith.

The Corinthians, in the midst of a pagan world, were concerned about matters that are again relevant in our times:

– about celibacy and marriage,
– about living together with those who do not share the Christian faith,
– about conducting the assemblies, for both the celebration of the Eucharist and the use of "spiritual gifts,"
– about the resurrection of the dead.

FIRST LETTER TO THE
CORINTHIANS

1 [1]From Paul, called to be an apostle of Christ Jesus by the will of God and from Sosthenes our brother, [2]to God's Church which is in Corinth; to you whom God has sanctified in Christ Jesus and called to be holy together with those who everywhere call upon the name of our Lord Christ Jesus, their Lord and ours.

[3]Receive grace and peace from God, our Father, and Christ Jesus, our Lord.

[4]I give thanks constantly to my God, for you, and for the grace of God given to you in Christ Jesus. [5]For you have been fully enriched in him with words, as well as with knowledge, [6]even as the testimony concerning Christ was confirmed in you. [7]You do not lack any spiritual gift and only await the glorious coming of Christ Jesus, our Lord. [8]He will keep you steadfast to the end, and you will be without reproach on the day of the coming of our Lord Jesus. [9]The faithful God will not fail you after calling you to this fellowship with his Son, Christ Jesus, our Lord.

Divisions among the faithful

[10]I beg of you, brothers and sisters, in the name of Christ Jesus, our Lord, to agree among yourselves and do away with divisions; please be perfectly united with one mind and one judgment.

[11]For I heard from people of Cloe's house about your rivalries. [12]What I mean is this: some say, "I am for Paul," and others: "I am for Apollos," or "I am for Peter," or "I am for Christ." [13]Is Christ divided, or have I, Paul, been crucified for you? Have you been baptized in the name of Paul?

[14]I thank God that I did not baptize any of you except Crispus and

Gaius, [15] so that no one can say that he was baptized in my name. [16] Well, I have also baptized the Stephanas family. Apart from these, I do not recall having baptized anyone else.

The folly of the cross

[17] For Christ did not send me to baptize, but to proclaim his gospel. And not with beautiful words! That would be like getting rid of the cross of Christ. [18] The language of the cross remains nonsense for those who are lost. Yet for us who are saved it is the power of God, [19] as Scripture says: *I will destroy the wisdom of the wise and make fail the foresight of the foresighted.* [20] Masters of human wisdom, educated people, philosophers, you have no reply! And the wisdom of this world? God, let it fail.

[21] At first, God spoke the language of wisdom and the world did not know God through wisdom. Then God thought of saving the believers through the foolishness that we preach.

[22] The Jews ask for miracles and the Greeks for a higher knowledge, [23] while we proclaim a crucified Messiah. For the Jews, what a great scandal! And for the Greeks, what nonsense! [24] But he is Christ, the power of God and the wisdom of God, for those called by God among both Jews and Greeks.

[25] In reality, the "foolishness" of God is wiser than humans and the "weakness" of God is stronger than humans.

[26] Brothers and sisters, look and see whom God has called. Few among you can be said to be cultured or wealthy and few belong to noble families. [27] Yet God has chosen what the world considers foolish to shame the wise; he has chosen what the world considers weak to shame the strong. [28] God has chosen common and unimportant people, making use of what is nothing, to nullify the things that are, [29] so that *no mortal may boast before God.* [30] But by God's grace you are in Christ Jesus who has become our wisdom from God, and who makes us just and holy and free. [31] Scripture says: *Let the one who boasts, boast of the Lord.*

1 CORINTHIANS 1:1-31

Read: Paul, with Sosthenes, writes to a Corinthian community divided into factions. He points the factions to what they have in common, belief in the crucified and Risen Lord. To others this belief is nonsense, but for the Christians in Corinth, this is the meaning of life.

Reflect: Paul tells the Corinthians they are called into community by Jesus Christ, is that your experience? In a world with so many different points of view, is it possible for faith in Jesus Christ to unify Christians?

Pray: Pray that you may be an instrument of peace in the community. Pray that your faith in Christ helps you to build bridges between the gaps that separates people.

Act: Strive to be a person who listens to different points of view. Look for ways to help people discover what they have in common.

2 ¹When I came to reveal to you the mystery of God's plan, I did not count on eloquence or on a show of learning. ²I was determined not to know anything among you but Jesus, the Messiah, and a crucified Messiah. ³I, myself, came weak, fearful and trembling; ⁴my words and preaching were not brilliant or clever to win listeners. It was rather a demonstration of spirit and power, ⁵so that your faith might be a matter, not of human wisdom, but of God's power.

The Spirit teaches us wisdom

⁶In fact, we do speak of wisdom to the mature in faith, although it is not a wisdom of this world or of its rulers who are doomed to perish. ⁷We teach the mystery and secret plan of divine wisdom, which God destined from the beginning, to bring us to glory.

⁸No ruler of this world ever knew this; otherwise, they would not have crucified the Lord of glory. ⁹But as Scripture says: *Eye has not seen, ear has not heard, nor has it dawned on the mind what God has prepared for those who love him.* ¹⁰God has revealed it to us through his Spirit because the Spirit probes everything, even the depth of God.

¹¹Who, but his own spirit, knows the secrets of a person? Similarly, no one but the Spirit of God knows the secrets of God. ¹²We have not received the spirit of the world but the Spirit who comes from God and, through him, we understand what God, in his goodness, has given us.

¹³So we speak of this not in terms inspired by human wisdom, but in

a language taught by the Spirit, explaining a spiritual wisdom to spiritual persons. [14] The one who remains on the psychological level does not understand the things of the Spirit. They are foolishness for him; and he does not understand, because they require a spiritual experience. [15] On the other hand, the spiritual person judges everything, but no one judges him. [16] *Who has known the mind of God so as to teach him?* But we have the mind of Christ.

---

1 CORINTHIANS 2:1-16

Read: Paul came humbly and without pretense to preach the Gospel of Jesus. Truth comes not from the preacher but from the Spirit of God in our midst, opening hearts to the ways God works in people's lives.

Reflect: How should we, Catholics, express our faith? Do you allow the Holy Spirit to be present in your life? How? Paul writes: "We have received the Spirit of God so can understand the gifts bestowed on us from God." How do you interpret that?

Pray: Ask the Holy Spirit to help you understand and use the gifts God has given to you.

Act: Before speaking about matters of faith in your community, ask for the help of the Spirit so that he may be present in your words. May your faith be rooted not in human wisdom but on the power of the Spirit.

There are many workers, the building is one

3 [1] I could not, friends, speak to you as spiritual persons but as fleshly people, for you are still infants in Christ. [2] I gave you milk, and not solid food, for you were not ready for it, and, up to now, you cannot receive it [3] for you are still of the flesh. As long as there are jealousy and strife, what can I say, but that you are at the level of the flesh and behave like ordinary people.

[4] While one says: "I follow Paul," and the other: "I follow Apollos," what are you, but people still at a human level?

[5] For what is Apollos? What is Paul? They are ministers and, through them, you believed, as it was given by the Lord to each of them. [6] I

planted, Apollos watered the plant, but God made it grow. [7]So neither the one who plants nor the one who waters is anything, but God who makes the plant grow.

[8]The one who plants and the one who waters work to the same end, and the Lord will pay each, according to their work. [9]We are fellow-workers with God, but you are God's field and building.

[10]I, as a good architect, according to the capacity given to me, I laid the foundation, and another is to build upon it. Each one must be careful how to build upon it. [11]No one can lay a foundation other than the one which is already laid, which is Jesus Christ. [12]Then, if someone builds with gold upon this foundation, another with silver and precious stones, or with wood, bamboo or straw, [13]the work of each one will be shown for what it is. The day of Judgment will reveal it because the fire will make everything known. The fire will test the work of everyone. [14]If your work withstands the fire, you will be rewarded; [15]but if your work becomes ashes, you will pay for it. You will be saved, but it will be as if passing through fire.

[16]Do you not know that you are God's temple and that God's Spirit abides within you? [17]If anyone destroys the temple of God, God will destroy him. God's temple is holy, and you are this temple.

Do not divide the Church

[18]Do not deceive yourselves. If anyone of you considers himself wise in the ways of the world, let him become a fool so that he may become wise. [19]For the wisdom of this world is foolishness in God's eyes. To this, Scripture says: *God catches the wise in their own wisdom.* [20]It also says: *The Lord knows the reasoning of the wise, that it is useless.*

[21]Because of this, let no one boasts about human beings, for everything belongs to you; [22]Paul, Apollos, Cephas—life, death, the present, and the future. Everything is yours [23]and you, you belong to Christ, and Christ is of God.

---

1 CORINTHIANS 3:1-23

Read: The community appears divided in following one or other preacher. Paul reminds us that a Christian follows only Christ. Christ is the only foundation of the community and of each believer.

> **Reflect:** Who is at the center of your parish community? Is your
> parish is rooted in Christ and his Word in Scripture? Paul tells
> the Corinthian community that they are God's temple and God's
> Spirit dwells within them. Does your community feel that way?
>
> **Pray:** "You belong to Christ," St. Paul says; pray for a deeper
> appreciation of what it means for you to belong to Christ.
>
> **Act:** Paul says, "You are God's field, God's building, God's tem-
> ple." Have a conversation with a member of your community
> about this means to them.

4 ¹Let everyone, then, see us as the servants of Christ and stewards of the secret works of God. ²Being stewards, faithfulness shall be demanded of us; ³but I do not mind if you, or any human court, judges me. I do not even judge myself; ⁴my conscience, indeed, does not accuse me of anything, but that is not enough for me to be set right with God: the Lord is the one who judges me.

⁵Therefore, do not judge before the time, until the coming of the Lord. He will bring to light whatever was hidden in darkness and will disclose the secret intentions of the hearts. Then each one will receive praise from God.

⁶Brothers and sisters, you forced me to apply these comparisons to Apollos and to myself. Learn by this example not to believe yourselves superior by siding with one against the other. ⁷How then are you more than the others? What have you that you have not received? And if you received it, why are you proud as if you did not receive it?

Comforted Christians and harassed apostles

⁸So, then, you are already rich and satisfied and feel like kings, without us! I wish you really were kings so that we might enjoy the kingship with you!

⁹It seems to me that God has placed us, the apostles, in the last place as if condemned to death and as spectacles for the whole world, for the angels as well as for mortals.

¹⁰We are fools for Christ, while you show forth the wisdom of Christ. We are weak, you are strong. You are honored, while we are despised.

¹¹Until now, we hunger and thirst, we are poorly clothed and badly treated while moving from place to place. ¹²We labor, working with our hands. People insult us and we bless them, they persecute us and we endure everything; ¹³they speak evil against us, and ours are works of peace. We have become like the scum of the earth, like the garbage of humankind until now.

¹⁴I do not write this to shame you, but to warn you as very dear children. ¹⁵Because, even though you may have ten thousand guardians in the Christian life, you have only one father and it was I who gave you life in Christ through the gospel. ¹⁶Therefore, I pray you to follow my example. ¹⁷With this purpose, I send to you Timothy, my dear and trustworthy son in the service of the Lord. He will remind you of my way of Christian life, as I teach it in all churches everywhere.

¹⁸Some of you thought that I could not visit you and became very arrogant. ¹⁹But I will visit you soon, the Lord willing, and I will see, not what those arrogant people say, but what they can do. ²⁰Because the kingdom of God is not a matter of words but of power. ²¹What do you prefer, for me to come with a stick, or with love and gentleness?

1 CORINTHIANS 4:1-21

Read: In Corinth, there were some arrogant Christians Who were sure they knew how everyone else should believe and act. Paul exhorts not to judge anyone, to recognize God's gifts and to live in humility remembering their own origins.

Reflect: What is the meaning that preachers are servants of Christ and administrators of the secrets of God? What is most convincing, words or deed?

Pray: Pray that preachers in your community be first of all messengers of the Gospel of Jesus, Uniting people and inspiring them to do the deeds of Christ.

Act: Build up unity with your attitudes and announce the Gospel mainly through the witness of your life.

Expel the immoral brother!

5 ¹You have become news, with a case of immorality, and such a case that is not even found among pagans. Yes, one of you has taken as wife his own stepmother. ² And you feel proud! Should you not be in mourning instead, and expel the one who did such a thing? ³ For my part, although I am physically absent, my spirit is with you and, as if present, I have already passed sentence on the man who committed such a sin. ⁴ Let us meet together, you and my spirit, and in the name of our Lord Jesus, and with his power ⁵ you shall deliver him to Satan for the destruction of the flesh, so that his spirit be saved in the day of Judgment.

⁶ This is not the time to praise yourselves. Do you not know that a little yeast makes the whole mass of dough rise? ⁷ Throw out, then, the old yeast and be new dough. If Christ became our Passover, you should be unleavened bread. ⁸ Let us celebrate, therefore, the Passover, no longer with old yeast which is sin and perversity; let us have unleavened bread, that is purity and sincerity.

⁹ In my last letter, I instructed you not to associate with immoral people. ¹⁰ I did not mean, of course, those who do not belong to the church and who are immoral, exploiters, embezzlers or worshipers of idols. Otherwise, you would have to leave this world. ¹¹ What I really meant was to avoid and not to mingle with anyone who, bearing the name of brother or sister, becomes immoral, exploiter, slanderer, drunkard, embezzler. In which case, you should not even eat with them.

¹² Why should I judge outsiders? But you, are you not to judge those who are inside? ¹³ Let God judge those outside, but as for you, *drive out the wicked person from among you.*

---

1 CORINTHIANS 5:1-13

Read: Evil can exist within the community when greed, idolatry, slander, lying or debauchery is tolerated. These create distrust and abuse within the community. The community must have the courage not to allow this to go uncorrected.

Reflect: What behaviors divide your community? How does your community respond to abuse when it happens? Are injustice and exploitation of others tolerated?

Pray: Ask to be faithful to the Christian principles and values. Ask not to be indifferent when seeing hunger, misery, sicknesses, and distress in the people around you.

> **Act:** Seek ways of ensuring for each person the rights and dignity that God bestows on all. This is a communitarian obligation in which all must be united.

Do not bring another Christian to court

6 [1] When you have a complaint against a brother, how dare you bring it before pagan judges instead of bringing it before God's people? [2] Do you not know that you shall one day judge the world? And if you are to judge the world, are you incapable of judging such simple problems?

[3] Do you not know that we will even judge the angels? And could you not decide everyday affairs? [4] But when you have ordinary cases to be judged, you bring them before those who are of no account in the Church! [5] Shame on you! Is there not even one among you wise enough to be the arbiter among believers?

[6] But no. One of you brings a suit against another one and files that suit before unbelievers. [7] It is already a failure that you have suits against each other. Why do you not rather suffer wrong and receive some damage? [8] But no. You wrong and injure others and those are your brothers and sisters. [9] Do you not know that the wicked will not inherit the kingdom of God?

Make no mistake about it: those who lead sexually immoral lives, or worship idols, or who are adulterers, perverts, sodomites, [10] or thieves, exploiters, drunkards, slanderers or embezzlers will not inherit the kingdom of heaven. [11] Some of you were like that, but you have been cleansed and consecrated to God and have been set right with God by the name of the Lord Jesus and the Spirit of our God.

Sexual immorality

[12] Everything is lawful for me, but not everything is to my profit. Everything is lawful for me, but I will not become a slave of anything. [13] Food is for the stomach as the stomach is for food, and God will destroy them both. Yet the body is not for fornication, but for the Lord, and the Lord is for the body. [14] And God, who raised the Lord, will also raise us with his power.

[15] Do you not know that your bodies are members of Christ? And you would make that part of his body become a part of a prostitute? Never!

¹⁶But you well know that when you join yourselves to a prostitute, you become one with her. For Scripture says: *The two will become one flesh.* ¹⁷On the contrary, anyone united to the Lord becomes one spirit with him.

¹⁸Avoid unlawful sex entirely. Any other sin a person commits is outside the body but those who commit sexual immorality sin against their own body.

¹⁹Do you not know that your body is a temple of the Holy Spirit within you, given by God? You belong no longer to yourselves. ²⁰Remember at what price you have been bought, and make your body serve the glory of God.

---

1 CORINTHIANS 6:1-20

Read: Paul asks the Corinthians to use mediation not punishment when there are disputes among themselves. Avoid what is not beneficial or leads to the debasement of the body or spirit. We must recognize our own dignity and not engage in acts that are unworthy of our calling.

Reflect: How do you deal with situations of conflict regarding moral issues in the community? Am I aware of my own failings toward others? Does the Church have a duty to denounce situations of corruption in society?

Pray: "Your body is a temple of the Holy Spirit," writes St. Paul; pray that your body and spirit always live in harmony.

Act: Try to condemn no one; but, above all, avoid actions that will generate immorality and injustice in the society.

Marriage and abstinence

7 ¹Now I will answer the questions in your letter. It is good for a man not to touch a woman. ²Yet to avoid immorality every man should have his own wife and each woman her own husband. ³Let the husband fulfill his duty of husband and likewise the wife. ⁴The wife is not the owner of her own body: the husband is. Similarly, the husband is not the owner of his own body: the wife is.

⁵Do not refuse each other, except by mutual consent, and only for a time in order to dedicate yourselves to prayer, and then come together again lest you fall into Satan's trap by lack of self-control. ⁶I approve of

this abstention, but I do not order it. [7] I would like everyone to be like me, but each has from God a particular gift, some in one way, others differently.

[8] To the unmarried and the widows, I say that it would be good for them to remain as I am, [9] but if they cannot control themselves, let them marry, for it is better to marry than to burn with passion.

Marriage and divorce

[10] I command married couples—not I but the Lord—that the wife should not separate from her husband. [11] If she separates from him, let her not marry again, or let her make peace with her husband. Similarly, the husband should not divorce his wife.

[12] To the others I say—from me and not from the Lord—if a brother has a wife who is not a believer, but she agrees to live with him, let him not separate from her. [13] In the same manner, if a woman has a husband who is not a believer, but he agrees to live with her, let her not separate from her husband. [14] Because the unbelieving husband is sanctified by the wife, and the unbelieving wife is sanctified by the husband who believes. Otherwise, your children also would be apart from God; but as it is, they are consecrated to God.

[15] Now, if the unbelieving husband or wife wants to separate, let them do so. In this case, the Christian partner is not bound for the Lord has called us to peace. [16] Besides, are you sure, wife, that you could save your husband, and you, husband, that you could save your wife?

[17] Except for this, let each one continue living as he was when God called him as was his lot set by the Lord. This is what I order in all churches. [18] Let the circumcised Jew, not remove the marks of the circumcision when he is called by God and let the non-Jew not be circumcised when he is called. [19] For the important thing is not to be circumcised or not but to keep the commandments of God.

[20] Let each of you, therefore, remain in the state in which you were called by God. [21] If you were a slave when called do not worry; yet if you can gain your freedom, take the opportunity.

[22] The slave called to believe in the Lord is a freed person belonging to the Lord just as whoever has been called while free becomes a slave of Christ. [23] You have been bought at a very great price; do not become slaves of a human being.

²⁴ So then, brothers and sisters, continue living in the state you were before God at the time of his call.

Marriage and virginity

²⁵ With regard to those who remain virgins, I have no special commandment from the Lord, but I give some advice hoping that I am worthy of trust by the mercy of the Lord.

²⁶ I think this is good in these hard times in which we live. It is good for someone to remain as he is. ²⁷ If you are married, do not try to divorce your wife; if you are not married, do not marry. ²⁸ He who marries does not sin, nor does the young girl sin who marries. Yet they will face disturbing experiences and I would like to spare you.

²⁹ I say this, brothers and sisters: time is running out and those who are married must live as if not married; ³⁰ those who weep as if not weeping; those who are happy as if they were not happy; those buying something as if they had not bought it, and those enjoying the present life as if they were not enjoying it. ³¹ For the order of this world is vanishing.

³² I would like you to be free from anxieties. He who is not married is concerned about the things of the Lord and how to please the Lord. ³³ While he who is married is taken up with the things of the world and how to please his wife and he is divided in his interests.

³⁴ Likewise, the unmarried woman and the virgin are concerned with the service of the Lord, to be holy in body and spirit. The married woman instead worries about the things of the world and how to please her husband.

³⁵ I say this for your own good. I do not wish to lay traps for you but to lead you to a beautiful life, entirely united with the Lord.

³⁶ If anyone realizes he will not be behaving correctly with his fiancée because of the ardor of his passion, and that things should take their due course, let him marry; he commits no sin. ³⁷ But if another of firmer heart thinks that he can control his passion and decides not to marry so that his fiancée may remain a virgin, he does better. ³⁸ So then, he who marries does well, and he who does not marry does better.

³⁹ The wife is bound as long as her husband lives. If he dies, she is free to be married to whomsoever she wishes, provided that she does so in the Christian way. ⁴⁰ However, she will be happier if, following my advice, she remains as she is, and I believe that I also have the Spirit of God.

---

1 CORINTHIANS 7:1-40

Read: Paul insists on equality between husband and wife, not only in marriage, but in situations of divorce. He repeats that circumcision is unimportant for Christians, as is social status. Slaves and free persons are equally called by God.

Reflect: What role does marriage play in the spiritual life of partners? In that Paul shortly expected the end of the world he was concerned it would be a distraction, in what ways is it a grace? The Corinthian Church was composed of slaves and free people whom Paul treats equally. Are there issues of social status that divide the Church today?

Pray: Pray that your sexuality be a vehicle for holiness and your relationships an expression of love.

Act: Live your sexuality in an integral way and according to the life option you have chosen. Let it be a witness to the love of God you experience, and an always-valid offer for human realization.

Can we share in pagan customs?

8 ¹Regarding meat from the offerings to idols, we know that all of us have the knowledge, but knowledge puffs up, while love builds. ²If anyone thinks that he has the knowledge, he does not yet know as he should know, ³but if someone loves (God), he has been known (by God).

⁴Can we, then, eat meat from offerings to the idols? We know that an idol is without existence and that there is no God but one. ⁵People speak indeed of other gods in heaven and on earth and in this sense, there are many gods and lords. ⁶Yet for us, there is but one God, the Father, from whom everything comes and to whom we go. And there is one Lord, Christ Jesus, through whom everything exists and through him we exist.

⁷Not everyone, however, has that knowledge. For some persons, who until recently took the idols seriously, that food remains linked to the idol, and eating of it stains their conscience, which is unformed.

⁸It is not food that brings us closer to God. If we eat, we gain nothing, and if we do not eat, we do not lose anything. ⁹We are free, of course, but let not your freedom cause others, who are less prepared, to fall.

[10] What if others with an unformed conscience see you a person of knowledge sitting at the table in the temple of idols? Will not their weak conscience, because of your example, move them to eat also? [11] Then, with your knowledge, you would have caused your weak brother or sister to perish, the one for whom Christ died. [12] When you disturb the weak conscience of your brother or sister and sin against them, you sin against Christ himself. [13] Therefore, if any food will bring my brother or sister to sin, I shall never eat this food, lest my brother or sister fall.

---

1 CORINTHIANS 8:1-13

Read: Paul deals with the problem of conscience that, at that time, generated from eating meat offered to idols. This is not sin in itself since idols are just that: idols and not gods. There is only one God. But one should think about others: "If food is a cause of their falling, I will never eat meat, so that I may not cause one of them to fall," is Paul's conclusion.

Reflect: Do you have any doubt about God's existence? Do you think that society today has idols? Which ones? Are we, Christians, free from them? And you, which idols do you adore?

Pray: Modern life can fall victim to the idols of prestige, money and power. Pray that Christ's love always has first place in your heart.

Act: Let your everyday life manifest Christ's presence; let your deeds reveal the Father's love and may your life example extend the sanctifying work of the Holy Spirit.

Renouncing one's own rights: the example of Paul

9 [1] As for me, am I not free? I am an apostle and I have seen Jesus the Lord, and you are my work in the Lord. [2] Although I may not be an apostle for others, at least I am one for you. You are, in the Lord, evidence of my apostleship.

[3] Now, this is what I answer to those who criticize me: [4] Have we not the right to be fed? [5] Have we not the right to bring along with us a sister as do the other apostles and the brothers of the Lord and Cephas? [6] Am I the only one, with Barnabas, bound to work?

What soldier goes to war at his own expense? [7] What farmer does not eat from the vineyard he planted? Who tends a flock and does not drink from its milk? [8] Are these rights only accepted human practice? No. The law says the same. In the law of Moses it is written: *Do not muzzle the ox which threshes grain.* [9] Does this mean that God is concerned with oxen, [10] or rather with us? Of course, it applies to us. For our sake, it was written that no one plows without expecting a reward for plowing, and no one threshes without hoping for a share of the crop. [11] Then, if we have sown spiritual riches among you, would it be too much for us to reap some material reward? [12] If others have had a share among you, we could have it all the more.

Yet, we made no use of this right and we prefer to endure everything rather than put any obstacle to the gospel of Christ. [13] Do you not know that those working in the sacred service eat from what is offered for the temple? And those serving at the altar receive their part from the altar? [14] The Lord ordered, likewise, that those announcing the gospel live from the gospel. [15] Yet, I have not made use of my rights, and now I do not write to claim them: I would rather die! No one will deprive me of this glory of mine.

[16] Because I cannot boast of announcing the gospel: I am bound to do it. Woe to me if I do not preach the gospel! [17] If I preach voluntarily, I could expect my reward, but I have been trusted with this office against my will. [18] How can I, then, deserve a reward? In announcing the gospel, I will do it freely without making use of the rights given to me by the gospel.

[19] So, feeling free with everybody, I have become everybody's slave in order to gain a greater number. [20] To save the Jews, I became a Jew with the Jews, and because they are under the law, I myself submitted to the law, although I am free from it. [21] With the pagans, not subject to the law, I became one of them, although I am not without a law of God since Christ is my law. Yet, I wanted to gain those strangers to the law. [22] To the weak, I made myself weak to win the weak. So I made myself all things to all people in order to save, by all possible means, some of them. [23] This, I do for the gospel, so that I, too, have a share of it.

Faith demands sacrifice

[24] Have you not learned anything from the stadium? Many run, but only one gets the prize. Run, therefore, intending to win it, [25] as athletes

who impose upon themselves a rigorous discipline. Yet, for them the wreath is of laurels, which wither, while for us it does not wither.

²⁶So then, I run knowing where I go. I box, but not aimlessly in the air. ²⁷I punish my body and control it, lest, after preaching to others, I myself should be rejected.

---

1 CORINTHIANS 9:1-27

Read: Paul declares himself an apostle to the Gentiles. Those who announce the Good News should live from their ministry, this is their right. But Paul preferred not to use this right to avoid placing an obstacle to the Gospel. For him, to announce the Good News is not a reason for pride, but an obligation he cannot renounce. He preaches to reach an incorruptible crown: eternal salvation.

Reflect: It is just to earn a living by working. So, how is it that Paul preaches for free and does not live by it? Can preaching the Gospel be considered a simple work, or rather an obligation for all Christians?

Pray: Pray for those who make out of the preaching of the Gospel their only occupation and work: priests, missionaries, religious men and women... Ask for them the strength of the Spirit.

Act: Help according to your possibilities those who leave everything for the Gospel. Collaborate with your time, talents or treasure.

---

10 ¹Let me remind you, brothers and sisters, about our ancestors. All of them were under the cloud and all crossed the sea. ²All underwent the baptism of the land and of the sea to join Moses; ³and all of them ate from the same spiritual manna; ⁴and all of them drank from the same spiritual drink. For you know that they drank from a spiritual rock following them, and the rock was Christ. ⁵However, most of them did not please God and the desert was strewn with their bodies.

⁶All of this happened as an example for us so that we might not become people of evil desires as they did.

⁷Do not follow idols as some of them did, and Scripture says: *The

people sat down to eat and drink and stood up for orgy. ⁸Let us not fall into sexual immorality, as some of them did, and in one day, twenty-three thousand of them fell dead. ⁹And let us not tempt the Lord, as some of them did, and were killed by serpents; ¹⁰nor grumble, as some of them did, and were cut down by the destroying angel.

¹¹These things happened to them as an example, and they were written as a warning for us as the last times come upon us. ¹²Therefore, if you think you stand, beware, lest you fall. ¹³No trial greater than human endurance has overcome you. God is faithful and will not let you be tempted beyond your strength. He will give you, together with the temptation, the strength to escape and to resist.

¹⁴Therefore, dear friends, shun the cult of idols.

¹⁵I address you as intelligent persons; judge what I say. ¹⁶The cup of blessing that we bless, is it not a communion with the blood of Christ? And the bread that we break, is it not a communion with the body of Christ? ¹⁷The bread is one, and so we, though many, form one body sharing the one bread.

¹⁸Consider the Israelites. For them, to eat of the victim is to come into communion with its altar.

¹⁹What does all that mean? That the meat is really consecrated to the idol, or that the idol is a being. ²⁰However, when the pagans offer a sacrifice, the sacrifice goes to the demons, not to God. I do not want you to come into fellowship with demons. ²¹You cannot drink at the same time from the cup of the Lord and from the cup of demons. You cannot share in the table of the Lord and in the table of the demons. ²²Do we want, perhaps, to provoke the jealousy of the Lord? Could we be stronger than he?

Practical solutions

²³Everything is lawful for me, but not everything is to my profit. Everything is lawful for me, but not everything builds up: ²⁴let no one pursue his own interests, but the interests of the other.

²⁵Eat, then, whatever is sold at the market, and do not raise questions of conscience about it. ²⁶Because: *the earth and whatever is in it belongs to the Lord.* ²⁷If someone who does not share your faith invites you, go and eat of anything served to you without problems of conscience. ²⁸However, if somebody tells you that the meat is from the

offerings to idols, then do not eat out of consideration for those warning you and for the sake of their conscience.

²⁹I say: "In consideration of their conscience," not of yours, for is it convenient that my rights be misinterpreted by them and their conscience? ³⁰Is it good that I bring on me criticism for some good thing I am sharing and for which I will give thanks?

³¹Then, whether you eat or drink, or whatever you do, do it for the glory of God. ³²Give no offense to the Jews or to the Greeks or to the Church of God, ³³just as I try to please everyone in everything. I do not seek my own interest, but that of many, this is: that they be saved.

---

1 CORINTHIANS 10:1-33

Read: Paul exhorts the community of Corinth to avoid idolatry and not to fall in sexual immorality. "All things are lawful, but not all things are beneficial." Christians should do everything for the glory of God, should look for the good of others before their own, and should avoid being a cause of scandals to others.

Reflect: Do you trust that you can overcome all your difficulties with God's help? Do you have any behavior that may scandalize others even if you consider them normal?

Pray: Trust that God listens to your prayers. Ask for help in your difficulties and to give you humility to give up your ways when necessary.

Act: Explore the faiths of other people, not as an alternative of your own but in order to broaden your understanding of the richness of God.

Women's dress and Mediterranean customs

11 ¹Follow my example, as I follow the example of Christ. ²I praise you because you remember me in everything and you keep the traditions that I have given you. ³However, I wish to remind you that every man has Christ as his head, while the wife has her husband as her head; and God is the head of Christ. ⁴If a man prays or prophesies with his head covered, he dishonors his head. ⁵On the contrary, the woman who prays or prophesies with her head uncovered does not respect her head. She might as well cut her hair. ⁶If a woman does not use a veil, let her cut her hair; and if it is a shame for a woman to have her hair cut or shaved, then let her use a veil.

⁷Men do not need to cover their heads, for they are the image of God and reflect his glory, while a woman reflects the glory of man. ⁸Man was not formed from woman, but woman from man. ⁹Nor did God create man for woman, but woman for man. ¹⁰Therefore, a woman must respect the angels, and have on her head the sign of her dependence.

¹¹Anyway, the Christian attitude does not separate man from woman and woman from man, ¹²and if God has created woman from man, man is born of woman and both come from God.

¹³Judge for yourselves: is it proper for a woman to pray without a veil? ¹⁴Common sense teaches us that it is shameful for a man to wear long hair ¹⁵while long hair is the pride of a woman and it has been given to her precisely as a veil.

¹⁶If some of you want to argue, let it be known that it is not our custom, nor the custom in the churches of God.

The Lord's Supper

¹⁷To continue with my advice, I cannot praise you for your gatherings are not for the better but for the worse.

¹⁸First, as I have heard, when you gather together, there are divisions among you and I partly believe it. ¹⁹There may have to be different groups among you so that it becomes clear who among you are genuine.

²⁰Your gatherings are no longer the Supper of the Lord, ²¹for each one eats at once his own food and while one is hungry the other is getting drunk. ²²Do you not have houses in which to eat and drink? Or perhaps you despise the Church of God and desire to humiliate those who have nothing? What shall I say? Shall I praise you? For this, I cannot praise you.

²³This is the tradition of the Lord that I received and that in my turn I have handed on to you; the Lord Jesus, on the night that he was delivered up, took bread and, ²⁴after giving thanks, broke it, saying, "This is my body which is broken for you; do this in memory of me." ²⁵In the same manner, taking the cup after the supper, he said, "This cup is the new Covenant in my blood. Whenever you drink it, do it in memory of

me." ²⁶ So then, whenever you eat of this bread and drink from this cup you are proclaiming the death of the Lord until he comes.

²⁷ Therefore, if anyone eats of the bread or drinks from the cup of the Lord unworthily, he sins against the body and blood of the Lord.

²⁸ Let each one, then, examine himself before eating of the bread and drinking from the cup. ²⁹ Otherwise, he eats and drinks his own condemnation in not recognizing the Body.

³⁰ This is the reason why so many among you are sick and weak and several have died. ³¹ But if we examine ourselves, we will not be examined by God and judged in this way. ³² The Lord's strokes are to correct us so that we may not be condemned with this world.

³³ So then, brothers and sisters, when you gather for a meal, wait for one another ³⁴ and, if someone is hungry, let him eat in his own house. In this way, you will not gather for your common condemnation. The other instructions I shall give when I go there.

---

1 CORINTHIANS 11:1-34

Read: In the Church, we are all united in God, in the same way, that during the Eucharist we should all participate as equals, with the conviction that we form part of the body of Jesus. When we are gathered as Church there should not be any differences.

Reflect: To what does the celebration of the Eucharist commit us? What does this expression suggest to you: "For as often as you eat this bread and drink the cup, you proclaim the Lord's death until he comes"? When you celebrate the Eucharist how are you and your community conscious of the death and resurrection of the Lord? Are there ways in which celebrating the Eucharist could be hypocritical?

Pray: Paul's attitudes toward women are conditioned by his time. Pray that women are seen everywhere as equal disciples of the Lord.

Act: Decide how you are going to live the Eucharist you celebrate.

Spiritual gifts and harmony

12 ¹With respect to spiritual gifts, I will remind you of the following: ²When you were still pagans, you were irresistibly drawn to your dumb idols. ³I tell you that nobody inspired by the Spirit of God may say, "A curse on Jesus," as no one can say, "Jesus is the Lord," except by the Holy Spirit.

⁴There is a diversity of gifts, but the Spirit is the same. ⁵There is a diversity of ministries, but the Lord is the same. ⁶There is a diversity of works, but the same God works in all.

⁷The Spirit reveals his presence in each one with a gift that is also a service. ⁸One is to speak with wisdom through the Spirit. Another teaches according to the same Spirit. ⁹To another is given faith in which the Spirit acts; to another the gift of healing, and it is the same Spirit. ¹⁰Another works miracles, another is a prophet, another recognizes what comes from the good or evil spirit; another speaks in tongues, and still, another interprets what has been said in tongues. ¹¹And all of this is the work of the one and only Spirit, who gives to each one as he so desires.

Comparison with the body

¹²As the body is one, having many members, and all the members while being many form one body, so it is with Christ. ¹³All of us, whether Jews or Greeks, slaves or free, have been baptized in one Spirit to form one body, and all of us have been given to drink from the one Spirit.

¹⁴The body has not just one member, but many. ¹⁵If the foot should say, "I do not belong to the body for I am not a hand," it would be wrong: it is part of the body! ¹⁶Even though the ear says, "I do not belong to the body for I am not an eye," it is part of the body. ¹⁷If all the body were an eye, how would we hear? And if all the body were an ear, how would we smell?

¹⁸God has arranged all the members, placing each part of the body as he pleased. ¹⁹If all were the same part where would the body be? ²⁰But there are many members and one body. ²¹The eye cannot tell the hand, "I do not need you," nor the head tell the feet, "I do not need you."

²²Still more, the parts of our body that we most need are those that seem to be the weakest; ²³the parts that we consider lower are treated with much care ²⁴and we cover them with more modesty because they are less presentable, whereas the others do not need such attention.

²⁵ God himself arranged the body in this way, giving more honor to those parts that need it so that the body may not be divided but rather each member may care for the others. ²⁶ When one suffers all of them suffer, and when one receives honor all rejoice together.

²⁷ Now, you are the body of Christ, and each of you individually is a member of it. ²⁸ So God has appointed us in the Church. First apostles, second prophets, third teachers. Then come miracles, then the gift of healing, material help, administration in the Church and the gift of tongues.

²⁹ Are all apostles? Are all prophets? Are all teachers? Can all perform miracles ³⁰ or cure the sick or speak in tongues or explain what was said in tongues? ³¹ Be that as it may, set your hearts on the most precious gifts and I will show you a much better way.

---

1 CORINTHIANS 12:1-31

Read: Divisions within the community are often based simply on legitimate personal differences. People are different, but the Spirit is one and in that way, we are all members of the one body of Christ.

Reflect: Are you aware of being united by the Holy Spirit to the other members of your community? Which are your gifts for the community? What does the following text suggest to you: "For just as the body is one and has many members, and all the members of the body, though many, are one body, so it is with Christ."

Pray: Ask from the Holy Spirit the grace to strengthen the bonds with the members of your community. Ask also that each member of the community may generously offer their gifts for the benefit of others.

Act: Talk to some people in your community to whom you trust. Tell them about the gifts of the Spirit that you perceive in them and ask them to do the same with you.

No gift higher than love

13 ¹ If I could speak all the human and angelic tongues, but had no love, I would only be sounding brass or a clanging cymbal. ² If I had the gift of prophecy, knowing secret things with all kinds of knowledge and had faith great enough to remove mountains but had no love I would be nothing. ³If I gave everything I had to the poor and even give up my body to be burned if I am without love it would be of no value to me.

⁴Love is patient, kind, without envy. It is not boastful or arrogant. It is not ill-mannered, nor does it seek its own interest. ⁵Love overcomes anger and forgets offenses. ⁶It does not take delight in the wrong but rejoices in the truth. ⁷Love excuses everything, believes all things, hopes all things, endures all things.

⁸Love will never end. Prophecies may cease, tongues will be silent and knowledge, disappear. ⁹For knowledge grasps something of the truth and prophecy as well. ¹⁰And when what is perfect comes, everything imperfect will pass away. ¹¹When I was a child, I thought and reasoned like a child, but when I grew up I gave up childish ways. ¹²Likewise, at present, we see dimly as in a mirror, but then it shall be face to face. Now we know in part, but then I will know as I am known. ¹³Now, we have faith, hope, and love, these three, but the greatest of these is love.

---

1 CORINTHIANS 13:1-13

Read: Paul describes the gift of God whereby Christians imitate Jesus. It's a lifetime of experience wrapped into one statement: faith, hope, and love, with the greatest of these being love.

Reflect: In what ways is your love, patient, kind, not irritable or resentful, never jealous or judgmental, but builds up those you love? How does your Church live the love of which St. Paul speaks?

Pray: Give thanks to God for all the love you received in life, asking that you may share this love with others.

Act: Read again verses 4 to 7. Do something concrete to make your love real to those around you.

Gifts of prophecy and tongues

14 ¹Strive, then, for love and set your hearts on spiritual gifts, especially that you may prophesy. ²The one who speaks in tongues does not speak to people, but to God for no one understands him; the spirit makes him say things that are not understandable. ³The prophet, instead, addresses all people to give them strength, encouragement, and consolation. ⁴He who speaks in tongues strengthens himself, but the prophet builds the Church.

⁵I should like all of you to speak in tongues, but even more to prophesy. The prophet has an advantage over the one who speaks in tongues unless someone explains what was spoken so that the community may profit. ⁶Suppose, brothers and sisters, I go to you and I speak in tongues, of what use will it be to you if I do not bring you some revelation, knowledge, prophecy or teaching?

⁷When someone plays the flute or harp or any musical instrument, if there are no tunes and notes, who will recognize the tune? ⁸And if the bugle call is not clear who will get ready for battle? ⁹The same with you. If your words are not understood, who will know what is said? You will be talking to the moon! ¹⁰There are many languages in the world and each of them has a meaning, ¹¹but if I cannot find any meaning in what is said, I become a foreigner to the speaker and the speaker to me.

¹²As you set your heart on spiritual gifts, be eager to build the Church and you will receive abundantly. ¹³Because of this those who speak in tongues should ask God for the ability to explain what they say.

¹⁴When I am praying in tongues my spirit prays, but my mind remains idle. ¹⁵What shall I do, then? I will pray with the spirit and I will pray with my mind. I will sing with the spirit and I will sing with the mind. ¹⁶If you praise God only with your spirit, how will the ordinary person add the "Amen" to your thanksgiving since the outsider has not understood what you said? ¹⁷Your thanksgiving was indeed beautiful, but it was useless for others.

¹⁸I give thanks to God because I speak in tongues more than all of you, ¹⁹but when I am in the assembly I prefer to say five words from my mind, which may teach others than ten thousand words in tongues.

²⁰Brothers and sisters, do not remain as children in your thinking. Be like infants in doing evil, but mature in your thinking. ²¹God says in the law: *I will speak to this people through those talking other tongues and through lips of foreigners, but even so, they will not listen to me.* ²²So, speaking in tongues is significant for those who refuse to believe, not for those who believe; while prophecy is a sign for those who believe, not for those who refuse to believe.

²³Yet, imagine that the whole Church is gathered together and all speak in tongues when unbelievers and uninformed people enter. What will they think? That you are crazy. ²⁴Instead, suppose that each of you speaks as a prophet; as soon as an unbeliever or an uninformed person enters all of you call him to account and disclose his most secret thinking. ²⁵Then, falling on his face, he would be urged to worship God and declare that God is truly among you.

²⁶What then shall we conclude brothers and sisters? When you gather, each of you can take part with a song, a teaching, or a revelation, by speaking in tongues or interpreting what has been said in tongues. But let all this build up the Church.

²⁷Are you going to speak in tongues? Let two or three at most, speak, each in turn, and let one interpret what has been said. ²⁸If there is no interpreter, hold your tongue in the assembly and speak to God by yourself.

²⁹As for the prophets, let two or three speak with the others commenting on what has been said. ³⁰If a revelation comes to one of those sitting by let the first be silent. ³¹Even all of you could prophesy, one by one, for the instruction and encouragement of all. ³²The spirits, speaking through prophets, are submitted to prophets ³³because God is not a God of confusion, but of peace.

³⁴(Let women be silent in the assemblies as in all the churches of the saints. They are not allowed to speak. Let them be submissive as the law commands. ³⁵If there is anything they desire to know, let them consult their husbands at home. For it is shameful for a woman to speak in Church.)

³⁶Did the word of God perhaps come from you? Or did it come only to you? ³⁷Anyone among you who claims to be a prophet or a spiritual person should acknowledge that what I am writing to you is the Lord's command. ³⁸If he does not recognize that God will not recognize him.

³⁹So, my friends, set your hearts on the gift of prophecy and do not forbid speaking in tongues. ⁴⁰However, everything should be done in a fitting and orderly way.

1 CORINTHIANS 14:1-40

Read: In prayer services, speaking in tongues seems to have been a common practice. Paul recognizes this and doesn't dismiss the practice but puts it below the building up of the Church.

Reflect: The chapter begins: pursue love and strive for the spiritual gifts, how can you do this?

Pray: Give thanks to God for the richness and diversity of gifts you find in your community. Let them be of use for the building up of the Church.

Act: Place at the service of the community the gifts the Lord has given you. If you know how to speak in public, look for the occasion, in coordination with the priest or the ministry of the Word, and comment the Word of God in the assembly.

Resurrection is a fact

15 [1] Let me remind you, brothers and sisters, of the Good News that I preached to you and which you received and on which you stand firm. [2] By that gospel, you are saved provided that you hold to it as I preached it. Otherwise, you will have believed in vain.

[3] In the first place, I have passed on to you what I, myself, received: that Christ died for our sins as Scripture says; [4] that he was buried; that he was raised on the third day according to the Scriptures; [5] that he appeared to Cephas and then to the Twelve. [6] Afterward, he appeared to more than five hundred brothers and sisters together; most of them are still alive although some have already gone to rest. [7] Then he appeared to James and after that to all the apostles. [8] And last of all, he appeared to the most despicable of them, this is to me. [9] For I am the last of the apostles, and I do not even deserve to be called an apostle because I persecuted the Church of God. [10] Nevertheless, by the grace of God, I am what I am, and his grace toward me has not been without fruit. Far from it, I have toiled more than all of them, although not I, rather the grace of God in me.

[11] Now, whether it was I or they, this we preach and this you have believed. [12] Well then, if Christ is preached as risen from the dead, how can some of you say that there is no resurrection of the dead? [13] If there is no resurrection of the dead, then Christ has not been raised. [14] And if Christ has not been raised, our preaching is empty, and our belief comes

to nothing. ¹⁵ And we become false witnesses of God, attesting that he raised Christ, whereas he could not raise him if indeed the dead are not raised. ¹⁶ If the dead are not raised, neither has Christ been raised. ¹⁷ And if Christ has not been raised, your faith gives you nothing and you are still in sin. ¹⁸ Also, those who fall asleep in Christ are lost. ¹⁹ If it is only for this life that we hope in Christ, we are the most unfortunate of all people.

Christ gave us the way

²⁰ But no, Christ has been raised from the dead and he comes before all those who have fallen asleep. ²¹ A human being brought death; a human being also brings resurrection of the dead. ²² For, as in Adam all die, so in Christ, all will be made alive. ²³ However, each one in his own time: first Christ, then Christ's people when he comes.

²⁴ Then, the end will come when Christ delivers the kingdom to God the Father, after having destroyed every rule, authority, and power. ²⁵ For he must reign and put all enemies under his feet. ²⁶ The last enemy to be destroyed will be death. ²⁷ As Scripture says: *God has subjected everything under his feet.*

When we say that everything is put under his feet, we exclude, of course, the Father who subjects everything to him. ²⁸ When the Father has subjected everything to him, the Son will place himself under the One who subjected everything to him. From then on, God will be all in all.

²⁹ Tell me: what are these people doing who are baptized on behalf of the dead? If the dead cannot be raised, why do they want to be baptized for the dead?

³⁰ As for us, why do we constantly risk our lives? For death is my daily companion. ³¹ I say that, brothers and sisters, before you who are my pride in Christ Jesus our Lord. ³² Was it for the human interest that I fought in Ephesus like a lion tamer? If the dead are not raised, *let us eat and drink, for tomorrow we shall die!*

³³ Do not be deceived; bad theories corrupt good morals. Wake up and do not sin, ³⁴ because some of you are outstandingly ignorant about God; I say this to your shame.

The body after the Resurrection

³⁵ Some of you will ask: How will the dead be raised? With what kind of body will they come?

³⁶ You fools! What you sow cannot sprout unless it dies. ³⁷ And what you sow is not the body of the future plant, but a bare grain of wheat or any other seed, ³⁸ and God will give the appropriate body as he gives to each seed its own body. ³⁹ Now, look: not all flesh is the same; one is the flesh of human beings, another the flesh of animals, and still others the flesh of birds and of fish. ⁴⁰ There are, likewise, heavenly bodies and earthly bodies, but the earthly bodies do not shine as do the heavenly ones. ⁴¹ The brightness of the sun differs from the brightness of the moon and the stars, and the stars differ from one another in brightness.

⁴² It is the same with the resurrection of the dead. The body is sown in decomposition; it will be raised never more to die. ⁴³ It is sown in humiliation and it will be raised for glory. It is buried in weakness, but the resurrection shall be with power. When buried, it is a natural body, but it will be raised as a spiritual body. ⁴⁴ For there shall be a spiritual body as there is at present a living body. ⁴⁵ Scripture says that Adam, the first man, became a living being; but the last Adam has become a life-giving spirit.

⁴⁶ The spirit does not appear first but the natural life and afterward comes the spirit. ⁴⁷ The first man comes from the earth and is earthly while the second one comes from heaven. ⁴⁸ As it was with the earthly one so is it with the earthly people. As it is with Christ, so with the heavenly. ⁴⁹ This is why after bearing the image of the earthly one we shall also bear the image of the heavenly one.

The day of Resurrection

⁵⁰ This I say, brothers: Flesh and blood cannot share the kingdom of God; nothing of us that is to decay can reach imperishable life. ⁵¹ So I want to teach you this mystery: although not all of us will die, all of us have to be transformed, ⁵² in an instant, at the sound of the trumpet. You have heard of the last trumpet; then, in the twinkling of an eye, the dead will be raised, imperishable, while we shall be transformed. ⁵³ For it is necessary that our mortal and perishable being put on the life that knows neither death nor decay.

⁵⁴ When our perishable being puts on imperishable life when our mortal being puts on immortality, the word of Scripture will be fulfilled: *Death has been swallowed up by victory.* ⁵⁵ *Death, where is your victory? Death, where is your sting?*

⁵⁶Sin is the sting of death, to kill, and the law is what gives force to sin. ⁵⁷But give thanks to God who gives us the victory through Christ Jesus, our Lord.

⁵⁸So then, my dear brothers and sisters, be steadfast and do not be moved. Improve constantly in the work of the Lord, knowing that, with him, your labor is not without fruit.

---

1 CORINTHIANS 15:1-58

Read: The resurrection is the core belief of Christianity, symbolizing God's merciful and forgiving love. Jesus is raised from the dead, and so will all who follow him experience resurrection to a spiritual body. The resurrection of Christ shows that we do not need to fear death, it only leads to eternal life with Christ.

Reflect: Have you ever questioned the mystery of the resurrection? Even if it cannot be explained, do you believe that there is another life that we do not know, after this one that we know? Does this help to accept the death of your loved ones?

Pray: Allow the rebirth into the love lived by Christ to be the guiding principle of your life. Consider what that means in your everyday life and let the radiance of divine affirmation be real.

Act: Celebrate with your family the gift of life and the triumph over death, giving thanks to God for all the deceased loved ones, be it with a Mass or with dinner.

Commendations and greetings

16 ¹With regard to the collection in favor of the saints, follow the rules that I gave to the churches of Galatia. ²On the first day of the week, let each of you put aside what you are able to spare so that no collection need be made when I come. ³Then, when I arrive, I will send those whom you approve with letters of explanation to carry your gift to Jerusalem. ⁴And if it seems better for me to go they will go with me.

⁵I will visit you after passing through Macedonia for I want to go only through Macedonia. ⁶I would like to stay with you for a while and perhaps I will spend the winter so that you may help me on my way wherever I go. ⁷I do not want to see you now, just in passing, for I really hope

to stay with you, if the Lord permits. [8] But I will stay in Ephesus until Pentecost [9] because I have a door wide open here, even though there are many opponents.

[10] When Timothy comes, make him feel at ease with you. Consider that, like me, he is working for the Lord. [11] Let no one look down on him. Help him continue his journey so that he may return to me without difficulties. I am expecting him with the brothers.

[12] With respect to our brother Apollos, I have strongly urged him to visit you with the brothers, but he did not want to go at all; he will visit you at his first opportunity.

[13] Be alert, stand firm in the faith, be courageous, be strong. [14] Let love be in all. [15] Now, brothers and sisters, you know that in Achaia there is none better than Stephanas and his family and that they have devoted themselves to the service of the holy ones. [16] I urge you to be subject to such persons and to anyone who works and toils with them.

[17] I am glad about the coming of Stephanas, Fortunatus, and Achaicus, who were able to represent you. [18] In fact, they appeased my spirit and yours. Appreciate persons like them.

[19] The churches of Asia greet you. Aquila and Prisca greet you in the Lord as does the church that gathers in their house. [20] All the brothers and sisters greet you. Greet one another with a holy kiss.

[21] The greeting is from me, Paul, in my own hand. [22] A curse on anyone who does not love the Lord! Maranatha! Come, Lord!

[23] The grace of the Lord Jesus be with you. [24] My love to all, in Christ Jesus.

---

1 CORINTHIANS 16:1-24

Read: Paul concludes his letter by asking that a collection be taken up for the Jerusalem Church. He tells them he hopes to visit them again, and to welcome Timothy when he visits. Ge specifically greets specific people, including the married couple Aquila and Prisca, and says how much he enjoyed it when some of their community visited him.

Reflect: Paul says: "Keep alert, stand firm in your faith, be courageous, be strong. Let all that you do be done in love." In what ways does this describe your life?

Pray: Give thanks for the material things, big or small, that you have and pray for those who lack what is necessary: let Christians help one another and share in this way the gift of faith.

Act: Follow Paul's exhortation: "Stand firm in the faith, be courageous, be strong, and do everything with love" Have your church community help poorer or struggling church communities in a practical way.

SECOND LETTER TO THE
CORINTHIANS

At the end of his first letter to the Corinthians Paul expressed the desire to come back and see them soon. He was unable to return, and they took this badly.

"Judaizing" preachers, that is to say, those Jews insufficiently converted to Christ, whom Paul had to face all the time, were trying to undermine his authority. Paul sent a messenger whom the Corinthians deeply offended: some members of the community were openly rebelling against the apostle. Paul responded in a letter "written in the midst of tears" (2:4) whereby he demanded the submission of the community. One of Paul's best assistants, Titus, brought the letter and concluded his mission successfully. Upon Titus' return, Paul, reassured, sent this "second" letter (in fact, it was the third or fourth) to the Corinthians.

What is the content of this letter? What Paul feels with regard to the Corinthians and what he suffers from their lack of understanding. It is not much and yet it is a great deal. Paul is incapable of speaking about

himself without speaking of Christ. This restless man, eager for understanding and affection, is so permeated with the love of Christ, that he
cannot express a suspicion or a reproach without giving the most profound sermons on faith. In trying to justify himself he writes the most
beautiful pages on *evangelization* and on what it means to be an apostle
of Christ.

We shall see that this letter includes pages which were not a part of
it—fragments of other letters or notes sent by Paul to the Church of
Corinth: in particular, 6:14-18 was probably written before our First Letter to the Corinthians; Chapter 9 (see commentary of 9:1); Chapters
10–13 which should contain a good part of the "letter written in tears"
(see preceding paragraph).

SECOND LETTER TO THE
CORINTHIANS

1 ¹ Paul, an apostle of Christ Jesus by the will of God, and Timothy, our brother to the church of God in Corinth and to all the saints in the whole of Achaia. ² May you receive grace and peace from God our Father, and from Christ Jesus, the Lord.

Blessed be God, the source of all comfort

³ Blessed be God the Father of Christ Jesus, our Lord, the all-merciful Father and the God of all comfort! ⁴ He encourages us in all our trials so that we may also encourage those in any trial with the same comfort that we receive from God.

⁵ For whenever the sufferings of Christ overflow to us, so through Christ a great comfort also overflows. ⁶ So, if we are afflicted, it is for your comfort and salvation; and if we receive comfort it is also for you. You may experience the same comfort when you come to endure the same sufferings we endure. ⁷ Our hope for you is most firm; just as you share in our sufferings, so shall you also share in our consolation.

⁸ Brothers and sisters, we want you to know some of the trials we experienced in the province of Asia. We were crushed; it was too much; it was more than we could bear and we had already lost all hope of coming through alive. ⁹ We felt branded for death, but this happened that we might no longer rely on ourselves but on God who raises the dead. ¹⁰ He freed us from such a deadly peril and will continue to do so. We trust he will continue protecting us, ¹¹ but you must help us with your prayers. When such a favor is obtained by the intercession of many, so will there be many to give thanks to God on our behalf.

The plans of Paul

¹²There is something we are proud of: our conscience tells us that we have lived in this world with the openness and sincerity that comes from God. We have been guided, not by human motives, but by the grace of God, especially in relation to you. ¹³There were no hidden intentions in my letter, but only what you can read and understand. ¹⁴I trust that what you now only partly realize, you will come to understand fully and so be proud of us, as we shall also be proud of you on the Day of the Lord Jesus.

¹⁵With this assurance, I wanted to go and visit you first and this would have been a double blessing for you, ¹⁶for I would have left you to go through Macedonia and I would have come back to you on my way back from Macedonia and you would have sent me on my way to Judea. ¹⁷Have I planned this without thinking at all? Or do I change my decisions on the spur of the moment, so that I am between No and Yes?

¹⁸God knows that our dealing with you is not Yes and No, ¹⁹just as the Son of God, Christ Jesus, whom we—Silvanus, Timothy and I—preach to you, was not Yes and No; with him, it was simply Yes. ²⁰In him, all the promises of God have come to be a Yes, and we also say in his name: *Amen!* giving thanks to God. ²¹God, himself, has anointed us and strengthens us with you to serve Christ; ²²he has marked us with his own seal in a first outpouring of the Spirit in our hearts.

Paul refers to a scandal

²³God knows, and I swear to you by my own life, that if I did not return to Corinth, it was because I wanted to spare you. ²⁴I do not wish to lord it over your faith, but to contribute to your happiness; for regarding faith, you already stand firm.

2 CORINTHIANS 1:1-24

Read: Paul is distressed, he is currently suffering and has had an attempt on his life, he has had to postpone his trip to Corinth, and is very sad that there is a rift between himself and them.

Reflect: Have you ever felt the presence of God protecting you in difficulties? Do you feel responsible, in some way, for the life

> of your community? How do you take care of your faith so that
> it will be strong at difficult moments?
>
> **Pray:** Ask that at moments of trials your faith and the faith of
> the community will not decay. Ask also for the leaders in your
> parish that they may fill the support of the community and,
> above all, God's help.
>
> **Act:** Talk to your parish priest, express your thankfulness for
> his ministry, and offer yourself for help in the parish.

2 ¹So I gave up a visit that would again be a distressing one. ²If I make
you sad, who will make me happy, if not you whom I have grieved?
³Remember what I wrote you, "May it be that when I come, I do not feel
sad because of you who should rather make me happy." I trust in everyone and I am sure that my joy will be the joy of you all.

⁴So afflicted and worried was I when I wrote to you, that I even shed
tears. I did not intend to cause you pain but rather to let you know of the
immense love that I have for you.

⁵If anyone has caused me pain, he has hurt not me, but in some measure, (I do not wish to exaggerate) all of you. ⁶The punishment that he
received from the majority is enough for him. ⁷Now you should rather
forgive and comfort him, lest excessive sorrow discourage him. ⁸So I
beg you to treat him with love.

⁹This is why I wrote to you, to test you and to know if you would obey
in everything. ¹⁰The one you forgive, I also forgive. And what I forgave,
if indeed I had anything to forgive, I forgave for your sake in the presence
of Christ, ¹¹lest Satan takes advantage of us, for we know his designs.

We are the fragrance of Christ

¹²So I came to Troas to preach the gospel of Christ and the Lord
opened doors for me. ¹³However, I could not be at peace because I did
not find my brother Titus there. So I took leave of them and went to
Macedonia.

¹⁴Thanks be to God, who always leads us in the triumphant following
of Christ and, through us, spreads the knowledge of him everywhere like
an aroma. ¹⁵We are Christ's fragrance rising up to God and perceived
by those who are saved as well as by those who are lost. ¹⁶To the latter,

it smells of death and leads them to death. To others, it is the fragrance of life and leads to life.

¹⁷ But who is worthy of such a mission? Unlike so many who make money out of the word of God, we speak with sincerity: everything comes from God and is said in his presence in Christ.

---

2 CORINTHIANS 2:1-17

Read: Paul feels hurt because of an unexplained rift between himself and the community. He asks that everyone practice forgiveness, and reminds them that he speaks to them sincerely from his heart and belief in Christ.

Reflect: Have you ever felt offended by somebody you tried to help? How did you react? Have you been able to forgive?

Pray: Ask from God the grace to forgive offenses you received in your life and ask for forgiveness for the ones you have inflicted. Slowly pray the Our Father.

Act: Seek out someone who has caused you distress and find a way to reconcile with forgiveness and love.

The great dignity of Christ's ministers

3 ¹ Am I again commending myself? Or do I need to present to you letters of recommendation as some do; or should I ask you for those letters? ² You are the letter. This letter is written in your inner self, yet all can read and understand it. ³ Yes, who could deny that you are Christ's letter, written by us—a letter written not with ink, but with the Spirit of the living God carved not in slabs of stone but in hearts of flesh.

⁴ This is how we are sure of God through Christ. ⁵ As for us, we would not dare consider that something comes from us: our ability comes from God. ⁶ He has even enabled us to be ministers of a new covenant no longer depending on a written text, but on the Spirit. The written text kills but the Spirit gives life.

⁷ The ministry of the law carved on stones brought death; it was, nevertheless, surrounded by glory, and we know that the Israelites could not fix their eyes on the face of Moses, such was his radiance, though fleeting. ⁸ How much more glorious will the ministry of the Spirit be! ⁹ If there is greatness in a ministry, which used to condemn, how much more will

there be in the ministry that brings holiness? [10]This is such a glorious thing that, in comparison, the former's glory is like nothing. [11]That ministry was provisory and had only moments of glory, but ours endures with a lasting glory.

The veil of Moses

[12]Since we have such a great ambition, we are quite confident—[13]unlike Moses, *who covered his face with a veil.* Otherwise, the Israelites would have seen his passing radiance fade.

[14]They became blind, however; until this day, the same veil prevents them from understanding the Old Covenant and they do not realize that in Christ it is nullified. [15]Up to this very day, whenever they read Moses, the veil remains over their understanding, [16]but for whoever *turns to the Lord, the veil shall be removed.* [17]The Lord is Spirit, and where the Spirit of the Lord is there is freedom.

[18]So, with unveiled faces, we all reflect the glory of the Lord while we are transformed into his likeness, and experience his glory more and more by the action of the Lord who is Spirit.

2 CORINTHIANS 3:1-18

Read: Formalities are hardly needed when personal relationships are strong. We now recognize that sin is not the end. When we are open to God's mercy in and through Christ. Aware of our merciful God, we can only celebrate forgiveness and focus on the enduring bonds that unite us with God and with one another.

Reflect: Paul's stress on God's forgiveness of our sins is applied here to offenses within the believing community. We must not hold grudges but instead seek ways to reconcile, even in instances of broken trust.

Pray: If sinning is human and forgiving divine, we need to seek divine guidance and strength to let forgiveness renew our fractured relationships. Ask for God's help in this.

Act: Seek out a fractured relationship in your life and find ways to mend it with forgiveness and love.

We carry this treasure in vessels of clay

4 [1] Since this is our ministry, mercifully given to us, we do not weaken. [2] We refuse to stay with half-truths through fear; we do not behave with cunning or falsify the message of God, but manifesting the truth, we commend ourselves to the conscience of everyone in the sight of God.

[3] In fact, if the gospel we proclaim remains obscure, it is obscure only for those who go to their own destruction. [4] The god of this world has blinded the minds of these unbelievers, lest they see the radiance of the glorious gospel of Christ who is God's image. [5] It is not ourselves we preach, but Christ Jesus, as Lord; and for Jesus' sake, we are your servants. [6] God who said, "*Let the light shine out of darkness*," has also made the light shine in our hearts to radiate and to make known the glory of God as it shines in the face of Christ.

[7] However, we carry this treasure in vessels of clay so that this all-surpassing power may not be seen as ours, but as God's. [8] Trials of every sort come to us, but we are not discouraged. [9] We are left without an answer, but do not despair; persecuted, but not abandoned, knocked down but not crushed. [10] At any moment, we carry in our person, the death of Jesus, so that the life of Jesus may also be manifested in us. [11] For we, the living, are given up continually to death for the sake of Jesus, so that the life of Jesus may appear in our mortal existence. [12] And as death is at work in us, life comes to you.

[13] We have received the same spirit of faith referred to in Scripture that says: *I believed and so I spoke*. We also believe, and so we speak. [14] We know that he who raised the Lord Jesus, will also raise us with Jesus, and bring us with you into his presence. [15] Finally, everything is for your good so that grace will come more abundantly upon you and great will be the thanksgiving for the glory of God.

We long for our heavenly dwelling

[16] Therefore, we are not discouraged. On the contrary, while our outer being wasted away, the inner self is renewed from day to day. [17] The slight affliction that quickly passes away, prepares us for an eternal wealth of glory, so great and beyond all comparison. [18] So we no longer pay attention to the things that are seen, but to those that are unseen, for the things that we see last for a moment, but that which cannot be seen is eternal.

> ## 2 CORINTHIANS 4:1-18
>
> **Read:** The Good News is only hidden to those who are lost. We are not announcing ourselves, but Jesus; and we are only servants of our brothers and sisters because of the love of Jesus. We carry this treasure in earthen vessels, to show that the power of the Good News does not rest in us but in God. The present anguish prepares us for an eternal glory that surpasses all measures since we have set our eyes on something that will last forever.
>
> **Reflect:** We are destined to live in God's love forever; that's why our faith needs to be nurtured and shared with those who do not know Christ. This is not an easy task, it brings many anxieties, and even suffering, but what awaits us is to be in God's presence forever.
>
> **Pray:** Paul tells us not to lose heart. Pray when you are discouraged.
>
> **Act:** Loving means commitment. Commit yourself to announce with your life the Gospel of Jesus to your people. Don't be afraid of your failures, you are the earthen vessel that contains God's grace.

5 ¹ We know that when our earthly dwelling, or rather our tent, is destroyed, we may count on a building from God, a heavenly dwelling, not built by human hands, that lasts forever. ² Therefore, we long and groan: Why may we not put on this heavenly dwelling over that which we have? ³ (Indeed, are we sure that we shall still be wearing our earthly dwelling and not be unclothed?)

⁴ As long as we are in the field-tent, we indeed bemoan our unbearable fate, for we do not want this clothing to be removed from us; we would rather put the other over it, that the mortal body may be absorbed by true life. ⁵ This is God's purpose for us and he has given us the Spirit as a pledge of what we are to receive.

⁶ So we feel confident always. We know that while living in the body, we are exiled from the Lord, ⁷ living by faith without seeing; ⁸ but we dare to think that we would rather be away from the body to go and live with

the Lord. [9] So, whether we have to keep this house or lose it, we only wish to please the Lord. [10] Anyway, we all have to appear before the tribunal of Christ for each one to receive what he deserves for his good or evil deeds in the present life.

We proclaim the message of reconciliation

[11] So, we know the fear of the Lord and we try to convince people while we live openly before God. And I trust that you know in your conscience what we truly are. [12] Once more, we do not try to win your esteem; we want to give you a reason to feel proud of us that you may respond to those who heed appearances and not the reality. [13] Now, if I have spoken foolishly let God alone hear; if what I have said makes sense take it for yourselves.

[14] Indeed, the love of Christ holds us and we realize that if he died for all, all have died. [15] He died for all so that those who live may live no longer for themselves, but for him who died and rose again for them. [16] And so, from now on, we do not regard anyone from a human point of view; and even if we once knew Christ personally, we should now regard him in another way.

[17] For that same reason, the one who is in Christ is a new creature. For him, the old things have passed away; a new world has come. [18] All this is the work of God who, in Christ, reconciled us to himself and who entrusted to us the ministry of reconciliation. [19] Because in Christ, God reconciled the world with himself, no longer taking into account their trespasses, and entrusting to us the message of reconciliation.

[20] So we present ourselves as ambassadors in the name of Christ, as if God himself makes an appeal to you through us. Let God reconcile you; this we ask you in the name of Christ. [21] He had no sin, but God made him bear our sin so that in him we might share the holiness of God.

2 CORINTHIANS 5:1-21

Read: We can easily be distracted from what is most important in life. We recognize that anyone who is in Christ is a new creation. God has freed us from sin's grip through Christ and has given us a ministry of reconciliation to make all things new in Christ.

> **Reflect:** How does the love of Jesus Christ make you feel new and refreshed? In your heart, do you believe God does not count your offenses against you, but has trusted you with the message of Christ?
>
> **Pray:** In prayer allow the love of Christ to urge you on to share the fruits of the new creation with others.
>
> **Act:** Examine your actions and take steps to eliminate all those that are not giving testimony as a new creation in Christ.

6 [1] Being God's helpers, we beg you: let it not be in vain that you received this grace of God. [2] Scripture says: *At the favorable time I listened to you, on the day of salvation I helped you.* This is the favorable time, this is the day of salvation.

The trials of an apostle

[3] We are concerned not to give anyone an occasion to stumble or criticize our mission. [4] Instead, we prove we are true ministers of God in every way by our endurance in so many trials, in hardships, afflictions, [5] floggings, imprisonment, riots, fatigue, sleepless nights and days of hunger.

[6] People can notice in our upright life, knowledge, patience and kindness, the action of the Holy Spirit, sincere love, [7] words of truth, and power of God. So we fight with the weapons of justice, to attack as well as to defend.

[8] Sometimes we are honored, at other times, insulted; we receive criticism as well as praise. We are regarded as liars, although we speak the truth; [9] as unknown, though we are well known; as dead, and yet we live. Punishments come upon us, but we have not, as yet, been put to death. [10] We appear to be afflicted, yet always joyful; we seem to be poor, but we enrich many; we have nothing, but we possess everything!

[11] Corinthians! I have spoken to you frankly and I have uncovered my inner thought. [12] My heart is wide open to you, but you feel uneasy because of your closed heart: [13] repay us with the same measure—I speak to you as to my children—open wide your hearts also.

Have nothing to do with evil

¹⁴Do not make unsuitable covenants with those who do not believe: can justice walk with wickedness? Or can light coexist with darkness, ¹⁵and can there be harmony between Christ and Satan? What union can there be between one who believes and one who does not believe? ¹⁶God's temple must have no room for idols, and we are the temple of the living God. As Scripture says: "*I will dwell and live in their midst, I will be their God and they shall be my people.*

¹⁷Therefore: *Come out from their midst and separate from them, says the Lord. Do not touch anything unclean* ¹⁸*and I will be gracious to you. I will be a father to you, that you may become my sons* and daughters, *says the all-powerful God.*"

---

2 CORINTHIANS 6:1-18

Read: The time to receive God's grace is now! Paul reminds that he always acted with integrity, being docile to the Holy Spirit. He tells the Corinthians that his heart has expanded to accept them all, even if they have not reciprocated. He asks them to open their hearts.

Reflect: Can you assure that all the brothers and sisters of your community are present in your heart? Is your heart open to a pure and sincere love for all of them?

Pray: Ask the Lord that all the believers in your community be united by love and not separated by divisions.

Act: There is strength in numbers; work with others to renew the face of the earth in love.

---

7 ¹Since we have such promises, dear friends, let us purify ourselves from all defilement of body and spirit, and complete the work of sanctification in the fear of God.

Welcome us in your hearts

²Welcome us in your hearts! We have injured no one. We have harmed no one, we have cheated no one. ³I do not say this to condemn you: I have just said that you are in our heart so that together we live, together we die. ⁴I have great confidence in you and I am indeed proud of you. I

feel very much encouraged and my joy overflows in spite of all this bitterness.

⁵Know that when I came to Macedonia, I had no rest at all, but I was afflicted with all kinds of difficulties: conflict outside and fear within. ⁶But God, who encourages the humble, gave me comfort with the arrival of Titus, ⁷not only because of his arrival but also because you had received him very well. He told me about your deep affection for me; you were affected by what happened. You worried about me and this made me rejoice all the more.

⁸If my letter caused you pain, I do not regret it. Perhaps I did regret it, for I saw that the letter caused you sadness for a moment, but now, I rejoice, ⁹not because of your sadness, but because this sadness brought you to repentance. This was a sadness from God so that no evil came to you because of me. ¹⁰Sadness from God brings firm repentance that leads to salvation and brings no regret, but worldly grief produces death. ¹¹See what this sadness from God has produced in you: What concern for me! What apologies! What indignation and fear! What a longing to see me, to make amends and do me justice!

You have fully proved that you were innocent in this matter. ¹²In reality, I wrote to you not on account of the offender or of the offended, but that you may be conscious of the concern you have for me before God. ¹³I was encouraged by this.

In addition to this consolation of mine, I rejoice especially to see Titus very pleased with the way you all reassured him. ¹⁴I had no cause to regret my praise of you to him. You know that I am always sincere with you; likewise, my praise of you to Titus has been justified. ¹⁵He now feels much more affection for you as he remembers the obedience of all and the respect and humility with which you received him. ¹⁶Really, I rejoice, for I can be truly proud of you.

2 CORINTHIANS 7:1-16

Read: On returning from Corinth, Titus brought good news to Paul regarding the repair of relations there, in response to Paul's earlier communications. Paul rejoices because he has confidence in the Corinthians.

Reflect: Every relationship, family, and community is sometimes faced with conflicts and must find a path to reconciliation. Paul's team worked with the Corinthian community in finding such a path. We also may sometimes need the help of others to repair fractured relations.

Pray: Pray for the openness of heart to be willing to be reconciled with someone with whom you have been in conflict.

Act: If you are aware of having wronged somebody, go and ask for forgiveness.

The collection for those in Jerusalem

8 ¹Now, I want you to know about a gift of divine grace among the Churches of Macedonia. ²While they were so afflicted and persecuted, their joy overflowed and their extreme poverty turned into a wealth of generosity. ³According to their means—even beyond their means—they wanted to share in helping the saints.

⁴They asked us for this favor spontaneously and with much insistence ⁵and, far beyond anything we expected, they put themselves at the disposal of the Lord and of us by the will of God. ⁶Accordingly, I urged Titus to complete, among you, this work of grace since he began it with you. ⁷You excel in everything: in the gifts of faith, speech and knowledge; you feel concern for every cause and, besides, you are first in my heart. Excel also in this generous service.

⁸This is not a command; I make known to you the determination of others to check the sincerity of your fraternal concern. ⁹You know well the generosity of Christ Jesus, our Lord. Although he was rich, he made himself poor to make you rich through his poverty.

¹⁰I only make a suggestion, because you were the first, not only in co-operating but also in beginning this project a year ago. ¹¹So complete this work and, according to your means, carry out what you decided with much enthusiasm. ¹²When there is a good disposition, everything you give is welcomed and no one longs for what you do not have. ¹³I do not mean that others should be at ease and you burdened. Strive for equality; ¹⁴at present, give from your abundance what they are short of, and in some way, they also will give from their abundance what you lack. Then you will be equal ¹⁵and what Scripture says shall come true: *To*

the one who had much, nothing was in excess; to the one who had little, nothing was lacking.

¹⁶ Blessed be God who inspires Titus with such care for you! ¹⁷ He not only listened to my appeal, but he wanted to go and see you on his own initiative. ¹⁸ I am sending with him the brother who has gained the esteem of the churches in the work of the gospel; ¹⁹ moreover, they appointed him to travel with us in this blessed work we are carrying on for the glory of the Lord, but also because of our personal enthusiasm.

²⁰ We decided on this so that no one could suspect us with regard to this generous fund that we are administering. ²¹ *Let us see to it* that all may *appear clean, not only before God but also before people.* ²² We also send with them another brother who, on several occasions, has shown us his zeal and now is more enthusiastic because of his confidence in you.

²³ You, then, have Titus, our companion and minister, to serve you and with him, you have our brothers, representatives of the churches, and a glory to Christ. ²⁴ Show them how you love and prove before the churches all the good things I said to them about you.

---

2 CORINTHIANS 8:1-24

Read: Paul encourages the Corinthians to share their resources with other Christians. He encourages them to strike a fair balance between that others need and their abundance. Titus is coming to see them and they should welcome him.

Reflect: In which acts of generosity have you participated lately? Have you always fulfilled promises you made to someone?

Pray: In addition to being disposed toward what is good, we need strength and endurance. We must rely upon God's graciousness both as a model and pillar for our commitment. Ask the Lord for this to happen.

Act: Seek out support for doing what is good and right. When our commitments are shared, we have a greater likelihood of success.

More about the collection

9¹It is not necessary for me to write to you about assistance to the saints. ²I know your readiness and I praised you before the Macedonians. I said, "In Achaia, they have been ready for the collection since last year." And your enthusiasm carried most of them along. ³So I send you these brothers of ours. May all my praise of you not fall flat in this case! May you be ready, as I said. ⁴If some Macedonians come with me, let them not find you unprepared. What a shame for me—and perhaps for you—after so much confidence!

⁵So I thought it necessary to ask our brothers to go ahead of us and see you, to organize this blessed work you have promised. It shall come from your generosity and not be an imposed task.

⁶Remember: the one who sows meagerly will reap meagerly, and there shall be generous harvests for the one who sows generously. ⁷Each of you should give as you decided personally and not reluctantly as if obliged. *God loves a cheerful giver.* ⁸And God is able to fill you with every good thing so that you have enough of everything at all times and may give abundantly for any good work.

⁹Scripture says: *He distributed, he gave to the poor, his good works last forever.* ¹⁰God, who provides the sower with seed, will also provide him with the bread he eats. He will multiply the seed for you and also increase the interest in your good works. ¹¹Become rich in every way and give abundantly. What you give will become, through us, a thanksgiving to God.

¹²For this sacred relief, after providing the saints with what they need, will result in much thanksgiving to God. ¹³This will be a test for them; they will give thanks because you obey the requirements of Christ's gospel and share generously with them and with all. ¹⁴They shall pray to God for you and feel affection for you because the grace of God overflows in you.

¹⁵Yes, thanks be to God for his indescribable gift!

2 CORINTHIANS 9:1-15

Read: Sending a team of brothers ahead to arrange in advance the collection for the poor, Paul encourages the Corinthians to be generous and mindful of how appropriate and necessary their material help to the Jerusalem community. Paul stimulates generosity reminding them that God is more generous than all of us.

> **Reflect:** What God has blessed you with, you should bless others. Generosity should not be reluctant, but cheerful.
>
> **Pray:** Give thanks to God for the generous people and people of faith that he has placed in your life. Ask for the energy and commitment to be truly generous.
>
> **Act:** If possible, meet some of the people who have been an example in your life. Tell them what you feel and thank them for their constant witness.

Paul's defense and admonition

10 [1] It is I, Paul, who, by the humility and kindness of Christ, appeal to you; the Paul "who is timid among you and bold when far away from you!"

[2] Do not force me to act boldly when I come, as I am determined and will dare to act against some people who think that I act from human motives. [3] Human is our condition, but not our fight.

[4] Our weapons for this fight are not human, but they have divine power to destroy strongholds—those arguments [5] and haughty thoughts that oppose the knowledge of God. We compel all understanding that they obey Christ. [6] So, I am prepared to punish any disobedience when you should show perfect obedience.

[7] See things as they really are. If someone is convinced that he belongs to Christ, let him consider that, just as he is Christ's, so am I. [8] Although I may seem too confident in the authority that the Lord gave me for building you up and not for pulling you down, I will not be put to shame for saying this. [9] Do not think that I can only frighten you with letters. [10] "His letters are severe and strong," some say, "but as he is, he has no presence and he is a poor speaker." [11] To such people, I say, "Be careful: what my letters say from afar is what I will do when I come."

[12] How could I venture to equate or compare myself with some people who proclaim their own merits? Fools! They measure themselves with their own measure and compare themselves with themselves. [13] As for me, I will not boast beyond measure for I will not go past the limits that the God of true measure has set for me: He gave the measuring stick when he made me set foot in your place.

[14]It is not the same when someone goes beyond his field, to where he has not been able to set foot. But I am he who first reached you with the gospel of Christ. [15]I am not making myself important where others have worked. On the contrary, we hope that as your faith increases, so too our area of ministry among you will be enlarged without going beyond our limit. [16]So, we shall bring the gospel to places beyond yours without entering into the field of others, or boasting and making ourselves important where the work is already done. [17]*Let the one who boasts, boast in the Lord.* [18]It is not the one who commends himself, who is approved, but the one whom the Lord commends.

---

2 CORINTHIANS 10:1-18

Read: Paul is not afraid to tell his friends things that are hard to hear, but he speaks from his heart. The most important thing is to belong to Christ.

Reflect: What skills and abilities do you have? Do you recognize those that were given by God, or you think they are of your own merits? What responsibilities does God give you along with those talents?

Pray: Pray for the grace to recognize that everything you have comes from God, and ask for strength and wisdom to fulfill your responsibilities, as God wants.

Act: Discern your abilities and assets. Find ways to share them in meaningful ways with others. Ask about a project where you can participate in or the possibility to start a new one.

---

11 [1]May you bear with me in some little foolishness! But surely you will. [2]I confess that I share the jealousy of God for you, for I have promised you in marriage to Christ, the only spouse, to present you to him as a pure virgin. [3]And this is my fear: the serpent that seduced Eve with cunning, could also corrupt your minds and divert you from Christian sincerity. [4]Someone now comes and preaches another Jesus, different from the one we preach, or you are offered a different spirit from the one you have received with a different gospel from the one you have accepted—and you agree!

[5]I do not see how I am inferior to those super-apostles. [6]Does my

speaking leave much to be desired? Perhaps, but not my knowledge, as I have abundantly shown to you in every way.

Paul commends the apostle Paul

[7] Perhaps my fault was that I humbled myself in order to uplift you, or that I gave you the gospel free of charge. [8] I called upon the services of other churches and served you with the support I received from them. [9] When I was with you, although I was in need, I did not become a burden to anyone. The friends from Macedonia gave me what I needed. I have taken care not to be a burden to you in anything, and I will continue to do so. [10] By the truth of Christ within me, I will let no one in the land of Achaia stop this boasting of mine.

[11] Why? Because I do not love you? God knows that I do! [12] Yet I do and I will continue to do so to silence any people anxious to appear as equal to me: this is my glory. [13] In reality, they are false apostles, deceivers, disguised as apostles of Christ. [14] It is not surprising: if Satan disguises himself as an angel of light, [15] his servants can easily disguise themselves as ministers of salvation until they receive what their deeds deserve.

[16] I say again: Do not take me for a fool, but if you do take me as such, bear with me that I may sing my own praises a little. [17] I will not speak with the Lord's authority, but as a fool bringing my own merits to prominence. [18] As some people boast of human advantages, I will do the same. [19] Fortunately, you bear rather well with fools, you who are so wise! [20] You tolerate being enslaved and exploited, robbed, treated with contempt and slapped in the face. [21] What a shame that I acted so weakly with you!

But if others are so bold, I shall also dare, although I may speak like a fool. [22] Are they Hebrews? So am I. Are they Israelites? So am I. Are they descendants of Abraham? So am I. [23] Are they ministers of Christ? (I begin to talk like a madman) I am better than they.

Better than they, with my numerous labors. Better than they, with the time spent in prison. The beatings I received are beyond comparison. How many times have I found myself in danger of death! [24] Five times the Jews sentenced me to thirty-nine lashes. [25] Three times I was beaten with a rod. Once I was stoned. Three times I was shipwrecked, and once I spent a night and a day adrift on the high seas.

²⁶I have been continually in hazards of traveling; because of rivers, because of bandits, because of my fellow Jews, or because of the pagans; in danger in the city, in the open country, at sea; in danger from false brothers. ²⁷I have worked and often labored without sleep, I have been hungry and thirsty and starving, cold, and without shelter.

²⁸Besides these and other things, there was my daily concern for all the churches. ²⁹Who is weak, that I do not feel weak as well? Whoever stumbles, am I not on hot bricks?

³⁰If it is necessary to boast, let me proclaim the occasions on which I was found weak. ³¹The God and Father of Jesus the Lord—may he be blessed for ever!—knows that I speak the truth. ³²At Damascus, the governor under King Aretas placed the city under guard in order to arrest me, ³³and I had to be let down in a basket, through a window in the wall. In that way, I slipped through his hands.

---

2 CORINTHIANS 11:1-33

Read: Paul is reluctant to ask for support from those he serves in his apostolic mission. Nevertheless, support comes from generous people who are willing to support his other missionary activities. When judging his apostolic service, people should know that he acts with integrity and dedication, no matter how foolish he may seem. He has proven himself through having endured extreme hardships for righteousness.

Reflect: At times, we have to pay a price for our personal commitments. It is during these times that we can assess the extent of our dedication.

Pray: Pray that amidst difficulties you may act like Jesus and Paul: firm in the ministry that you received. Ask for the grace to be able to give witness to Christ at all times.

Act: When the time comes, don't be afraid to be afraid to live your faith openly or to defend others who try to do so.

Extraordinary graces

12 ¹It is useless to boast; but if I have to, I will go on to some visions and revelations of the Lord.

² I know a certain Christian: fourteen years ago he was taken up to the third heaven. ³ Whether in the body or out of the body, I do not know, God knows. But I know that this man, whether in the body or out of the body—I do not know, God knows—⁴ was taken up to Paradise where he heard words that cannot be told: things which humans cannot express.

⁵ Of that man, I can indeed boast, but of myself, I will not boast except of my weaknesses. ⁶ If I wanted to boast, it would not be foolish of me, for I would speak the truth. ⁷ However, I better give up, lest somebody think more of me than what is seen in me, or heard from me. Lest I become proud, after so many and extraordinary revelations, I was given a thorn in my flesh, a true messenger of Satan, to slap me in the face. ⁸ Three times I prayed to the Lord that it might leave me, ⁹ but he answered, "My grace is enough for you; my great strength is revealed in weakness."

Gladly then, will I boast of my weakness, that the strength of Christ may be mine. ¹⁰ So I rejoice when I suffer infirmities, humiliations, want, persecutions: all for Christ! For when I am weak, then I am strong.

¹¹ I have acted as a fool but you forced me. You should have been the ones commending me. Yet I do not feel outdone by those super-apostles, ¹² even though I am nothing. All the signs of a true apostle are found in me: patience in all trials, signs, miracles, and wonders.

¹³ Now, in what way were you not treated like the rest of the churches? Only in this: I was not a burden to you—forgive me for this offense!

This is my third visit to you

¹⁴ For the third time I plan to visit you, and I will not be a burden to you, for I am not interested in what you have, but only in you. Children should not have to collect money for their parents, but the parents for their children. ¹⁵ As for me, I am ready to spend whatever I have and even my whole self, for all of you. If I love you so much, am I to be loved less?

¹⁶ Well, I was not a burden to you, but was it not a trick to deceive you? Tell me: ¹⁷ Did I take money from you through any of my messengers? ¹⁸ I asked Titus to go to you and I sent another brother with him. But did Titus take money from you? Have we not both acted in the same spirit?

¹⁹ Perhaps you think that we are again apologizing; but no: we speak in Christ and before God, and I do this for you, dear friends, to build you up. ²⁰ I fear that if I go and see you, I might not find you as I would wish,

and you, in turn, might not find me to your liking. I might see rivalries, envy, grudges, disputes, slanders, gossip, conceit, disorder. ²¹ Let it not be that in coming again to you, God humbles me because of you, and I have to grieve over so many of you who live in sin, on seeing that they have not yet given up an impure way of living, their wicked conduct, and the vices they formerly practiced.

---

2 CORINTHIANS 12:1-21

Read: Paul boasts of having been called, even if his service can be criticized or faulted. Some may call him foolish, but there is no question that he serves with a firm and sincere heart.

Reflect: Dismissive ridicule can destroy even the best of people. It is easier to undermine than to instill confidence. Ridicule rarely produces a fair assessment of people.

Pray: Pray that you, your local Church and the Holy Father have the strength to ignore ridicule and remain faithful to the light.

Act: Seek to make fair assessments and avoid undermining those who pursue good goals. Rejoice with those who act well for the Gospel's sake. Appreciate the work of every person who works with you.

---

13 ¹ This will be my third visit to you. *Any charge must be decided upon by the declaration of two or three witnesses.* ² I have said and I say again, being still far away, just as I did on my second visit, I say to you who lived in sin, as well as to the rest: when I return to you, I will not have pity. ³ You want to know if Christ is speaking through me? So you will. He is not used to dealing weakly with you, but rather he acts with power. ⁴ If he was crucified in his weakness, now he lives by the strength of God; and so we are weak with him, but we will be well alive with him because God acts powerfully with you.

⁵ Examine yourselves: are you acting according to faith? Test yourselves. Can you assert that Christ Jesus is in you? If not, you have failed the test. ⁶ I hope you recognize that we ourselves have not failed it.

⁷ We pray God that you may do no wrong, not that we wish to be acknowledged, but we want you to do right, even if in this we appear to

have failed. [8]For we do not have power against the truth, but only for the truth. [9]We rejoice if we are weak while you are strong, for all we hope, is that you become perfect. [10]This is why I am writing now so that when I come I may not have to act strictly and make use of the authority the Lord has given me for building up and not for destroying.

[11]Finally, brothers and sisters, be happy, strive to be perfect, have courage, be of one mind and live in peace. And the God of love and peace will be with you. [12]Greet one another with a holy kiss. All the saints greet you.

[13]The grace of Christ Jesus the Lord, the love of God and the fellowship of the Holy Spirit be with you all.

2 CORINTHIANS 13:1-13

Read: For his third visit, Paul asks that the community examine themselves to see if they are still maintaining the Faith. He warns them not to believe rumor and gossip but to insist on reliable testimony. He urges them to remember that the power of Christ is strong within them.

Reflect: In your Christian behavior, where does your own strength ends and where does God's strength begin acting in you? What kind of good deeds does God inspire you to do?

Pray: Give thanks to God for the difficult moments in your life that you would not have been able to overcome by yourself, but you did with His grace. Ask for the acceptance of your weaknesses.

Act: Make a list of all the moments when you felt saved, redeemed and comforted by God. Share it with your people, trying to describe the feelings you experienced on each occasion.

LETTER TO THE
GALATIANS

CEREZO BARREDO

Who were the Galatians? Galatia was a northern province of today's Turkey. Once Paul had stopped there (Acts 16:6) when an illness had prevented him from pursuing his journey (Gal 4:13-14). He had visited the Galatians again (Acts 18:23) before settling in Ephesus (Acts 19:1) and he had asked them to help the poor in Jerusalem (1 Cor 16:1).

Paul is writing because the community is in danger. Strangely enough, Paul does not make any reference to the scandals, laxity or conflicts of authority, as it was the case in Corinth. There were tensions and doubts as some people wanted to go back to Jewish practices. However, it seems that the community was not expecting such a warning from Paul. He had shown greater foresight. Some people wanted to return to religious practices because they had failed to understand that being Christian was primarily living one's faith rather than practicing a religion.

For the Galatians, discovering the Gospel had been like a bath in freedom. Those who were Jewish were freed from the constraint of religious practices and those who were Greek (and pagan) were freed from the prejudices of their society: it was like a great cleansing. But were they able to follow Paul when he declared that Christ was able to fill our lives and that the Spirit is a much better guide than any religious obligations?

At first, the Galatians had experienced what was at the core of Paul's life. But the community found it difficult to maintain itself along such a new line. After their initial enthusiasm, most of these new Christians felt a need for rules and practices. They did have faith in Christ but it was asking for a lot to want all of them to be "spiritual" people.

It was precisely at that time that preachers of Jewish origin were exhorting them to be circumcised and to observe the customs of Israel (4:10) by promising them a life superior to the life obtained by conversion to Christ.

Belonging to Judaism would have brought material security to the Galatians since the Israelite religion was protected by Roman laws. If they refused both idolatry and the Jewish religion, they were running the risk of being persecuted (6:12-14). On the contrary, if they adopted the Jewish nationality and the customs of Israel, they would have avoided persecution but that would have been the same as saying that Christ had died for nothing (2:21).

This is the reason why Paul reacted passionately. All of us, believers and non-believers, are solely saved by the generosity of God who has forgiven our sins and who has given us, along with his Spirit, the freedom of love (5:13-14). When we give too much credit to the rules and practices of a religion, we are locking ourselves into a system, an order in which we expect, even without saying it, a reward for our good deeds. On the contrary, faith means surrendering to God and his mystery that is as awesome as its symbol, the cross. Faith also means believing that God wants the salvation of all human beings, regardless of their nationality (3:9).

This should be enough to understand that this letter to the Galatians is still addressing us in our time when so many people reduce religion to practices. Moreover, it is a fact that to the extent that the Church has to sustain many Christians who have a very limited experience of life in the freedom of the Spirit, it tends to bring itself to their level and to become a religion. This is why the Church has to regain the awareness of its identity and to rediscover the meaning of living by faith.

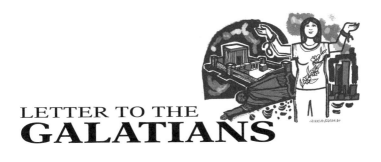

LETTER TO THE
GALATIANS

1 [1] From Paul, an apostle sent, not by humans nor by human mediation, but by Christ Jesus and by God the Father who raised him from the dead;

[2] I, and all the brothers and sisters who are with me, greet the churches in Galatia: [3] may you receive grace and peace from God, our Father and from Christ Jesus, our Lord.

[4] He gave himself for our sins, to rescue us from this evil world in fulfillment of the will of God the Father:

[5] Glory to him for ever and ever. Amen.

There is no other gospel

[6] I am surprised at how quickly you have abandoned God, who called you according to the grace of Christ, and have gone to another gospel. [7] Indeed, there is no other gospel, but some people who are sowing confusion among you want to turn the gospel of Christ upside down.

[8] But even if we, ourselves, were giving you another gospel different from the one we preached to you, or if it were an angel from heaven, I would say: let God's curse be on him! [9] As I have said, I now say again: if anyone preaches the gospel in a way other than you received it, fire that one! [10] Are we to please humans or obey God? Do you think that I try to please people? If I were still trying to please people, I would not be a servant of Christ.

GALATIANS 1:1-10

Read: Paul is annoyed at people who question his apostleship and who have strayed from the gospel of freedom and grace.

> **Reflect:** The Gospel of Jesus recounts a life that makes love the most powerful force, to overcome death. Do you think everyone in the Church preaches and lives this gospel? What changes have you seen creep into the way people talk about Jesus?
>
> **Pray:** Pray that the Gospel continues to motivate your life.
>
> **Act:** Make a gesture of love toward the marginalized people in your community, just as Jesus did to the marginalized of his time.

Paul teaches what he received from God

[11] Let me remind you, brothers and sisters, that the gospel we preached to you is not a human message, [12] nor did I receive it from anyone. I was not taught about it, but it came to me as a revelation from Christ Jesus. [13] You have heard of my previous activity in the Jewish community; I furiously persecuted the Church of God and tried to destroy it. [14] For I was more devoted to the Jewish religion than many fellow Jews of my age, and I defended the traditions of my ancestors more fanatically.

[15] But one day, God called me, out of his great love, he, who *had chosen me from my mother's womb*; and he was pleased [16] to reveal in me his Son, that I might make him known among the pagan nations. Then, I did not seek human advice [17] nor did I go up to Jerusalem to those who were apostles before me. I immediately went to Arabia, and from there, I returned, again to Damascus. [18] Later, after three years, I went up to Jerusalem to meet Cephas, and I stayed with him for fifteen days. [19] But I did not see any other apostle except James, the Lord's brother. [20] On writing this to you, I affirm before God that I am not lying.

[21] After that, I went to Syria and Cilicia. [22] The churches of Christ in Judea did not know me personally; [23] they had only heard of me: "He, who once persecuted us, is now preaching the faith he tried to uproot." [24] And they praised God because of me.

GALATIANS 1:11-24

Read: Paul acknowledges that it is true that he used to persecute Christians. He changed when he received a revelation from the Risen Christ. He lived with Christians in Damascus for three years and then went to see the apostles in Jerusalem.

> **Reflect:** Think about your own life. How and why or by whom are you a Christian? People mediate Jesus to us. Do you have to give thanks to somebody for being a Christian?
>
> **Pray:** Pray for the people who helped you be a Christian asking God to bless their lives.
>
> **Act:** Think of what you can do to support someone in their faith.

Paul with the apostles

2 ¹ After fourteen years, I, again, went up to Jerusalem with Barnabas, and Titus came with us. ² Following a revelation, I went to lay before them the gospel that I am preaching to the pagans. I had a private meeting with the leaders—lest I should be working, or have worked, in a wrong way. ³ But they did not impose circumcision, not even on Titus, who is Greek, and who was with me. ⁴ But there were some intruders and false brothers who had gained access to watch over the way we live the freedom Christ has given us. They would have us enslaved by the law, ⁵ but we refused to yield, even for a moment, so that the truth of the gospel remains intact for you.

⁶ The others, the more respectable leaders—it does not matter what they were before: God pays no attention to the status of a person—gave me no new instructions. ⁷ They recognized that I have been entrusted to give the Good News to the pagan nations, just as Peter has been entrusted to give it to the Jews. ⁸ In the same way that God made Peter the apostle of the Jews, he made me the apostle of the pagans.

⁹ James, Cephas, and John acknowledged the graces God gave me. Those men, who were regarded as the pillars of the Church, stretched out their hand to me and Barnabas, as a sign of fellowship; we would go to the pagans, and they, to the Jews. ¹⁰ We should only keep in mind the poor among them. I have taken care to do this.

> **GALATIANS 2:1-10**
>
> **Read:** Paul reminds the Galatians that his understanding of the Gospel was approved by the apostles in Jerusalem. They are the ones who sent him to preach to Gentiles who do not have to become Jews but do have to care for the poor.

> **Reflect:** Do you consider yourself an apostle of the Lord? What is God calling you to do? Who has God called you to be with? Paul says God shows no partiality, do you think that is true of the Church today?
>
> **Pray:** It is not always easy to know what God wants us to do. Pray for humility in living the faith. Pray that your life is not distracted by the modern idols of money, pleasure, and comfort.
>
> **Act:** Be faithful to the Christian traditions and to the only Gospel that is Christ, and let your every action be a living testimony of your faith.

The conflict with Peter

[11] When, later, Cephas came to Antioch, I confronted him since he deserved to be blamed. [12] Before some of James' people arrived, he used to eat with non-Jewish people. But when they arrived, he withdrew and did not mingle anymore with them for fear of the Jewish group. [13] The rest of the Jews followed him in this pretense, and even Barnabas was part of this insincerity. [14] When I saw that they were not acting in line with the truth of the gospel, I said to Cephas publicly: If you who are Jewish, agreed to live like the non-Jews setting aside the Jewish customs, why do you now compel the non-Jews to live like Jews?

[15] We are Jews by birth; we are not pagan sinners. [16] Yet, we know that a person is justified, not by practicing the law, but by faith in Christ Jesus. So we have believed in Christ Jesus, that we may receive the true righteousness from faith in Christ Jesus, and not from the practices of the law because no one will be justified by the works of the law.

[17] Now, if in our own effort to be justified in Christ, we ourselves have been found to be sinners, then Christ would be at the service of sin. Not so! [18] But look: if we do away with something and then restore it, we admit we did wrong.

[19] As for me, the very law brought me to die to the law that I may live for God. I am crucified with Christ. [20] Do I live? It is no longer me; Christ lives in me. My life in this body is life through faith in the Son of God, who loved me and gave himself for me. [21] In this way, I don't ignore the gift of God, for if justification comes through the practice of the law, Christ would have died for nothing.

GALATIANS 2:11-21

Read: Paul confronts Peter who he thinks is giving in to the pressure of the Jewish Christians that Gentiles for Gentile to believe in Jesus they must first become Jews. Traditions no matter how sacred do not make you a Christian, but only trust in Christ. Paul trusts Christ so completely he says with this faith he has been crucified with Christ and Christ lives in him.

Reflect: Do you cling to any tradition or custom in order not to look bad to others, instead of centering your life to Christ? Have you ever changed your ways for fear of others?

Pray: Ask for forgiveness for the times that you have been carried away by fear of what others may say of you, rather than being true to yourself. Ask for strength to overcome these situations.

Act: If you know someone who speaks badly against you for your faithfulness to the Gospel, approach the person and explain why you do what you do.

We are saved by faith

3 ¹ How foolish you are, Galatians! How could they bewitch you after Jesus Christ has been presented to you as crucified? ² I shall ask you only this: Did you receive the Spirit by the practice of the law, or by believing the message? ³ How can you be such fools: you begin with the Spirit and end up with the flesh!

⁴ So, you have experienced all this in vain! Would that it were not so! ⁵ Did God give you the Spirit, and work miracles among you because of your observance of the *law, or because you believed in his message?* ⁶ *Remember Abraham: he believed God, and because of this, was held to be a just man.* ⁷ Understand, then, that those who follow the way of faith are sons and daughters of Abraham.

⁸ The Scriptures foresaw that, by the way of faith, God would give true righteousness to the non-Jewish nations. For God's promise to Abraham was this: *In you shall all the nations be blessed.* ⁹ So now those who take the way of faith receive the same blessing as Abraham, who believed; ¹⁰ but those who rely on the practice of the law are under a curse, for it

is written: *Cursed is everyone who does not always fulfill everything written in the law.*

[11] It is plainly written that no one becomes righteous in God's way, by the law: *by faith, the righteous shall live.* [12] Yet the law gives no place to faith, for according to it: *the one who fulfills the commandments shall have life through them.*

[13] Now Christ rescued us from the curse of the law by becoming cursed himself, for our sake, as it is written: *there is a curse on everyone who is hanged on a tree.* [14] So the blessing granted to Abraham reached the pagan nations in and with Christ, and we received the promised Spirit through faith.

GALATIANS 3:1-14

Read: Paul begins with harsh words accusing the Galatians of letting themselves be tricked into believing that God's love for them depends on how well they observe the laws of the Hebrew Scriptures. They have to believe in Christ Jesus just as Abraham believed in God.

Reflect: Have you experienced that faith, not compliance with the rules, leads to life? How do you explain this to others?

Pray: Pray to live trusting in the Risen Christ who loved you and gave himself for you.

Act: If you know someone more concerned with the compliance of norms and traditions than loving as Jesus loved, listen to his reasons for it and explain what Paul says.

The promise, not the law, was the gift of God

[15] Brothers and sisters, listen to this comparison. When anyone has made his will in the prescribed form, no one can annul it or add anything to it. [16] Well, now, what God promised Abraham was for *his descendant.* Scripture does not say: for the descendants, as if they were many. It means only one: *this will be for your descendant,* and this is Christ. [17] Now I say this: if God has made a testament in due form, it cannot be annulled by the law which came four hundred and thirty years later; God's promise cannot be canceled. [18] But if we now inherit for keeping the law, it is not because of the promise. Yet, that promise was God's gift to Abraham.

The law was part of God's pedagogy

¹⁹ Why then, the law? It was added because of transgressions but was only valid until the descendant would come to whom the promise had been made, and it was ordained through angels by a mediator. ²⁰ A mediator means that there are parties, and God is one.

²¹ Does the law, then, competes with the promises of God? Not at all! Only if we had been given a law capable of raising life, could righteousness be the fruit of the law. ²² But the Scriptures have declared that we are all prisoners of sin. So, the only way to receive God's promise is to believe in Jesus Christ.

We are now sons and daughters of God

²³ Before the time of faith had come, the law confined us and kept us in custody until the time in which faith would show up. ²⁴ The law then, was serving as a slave to look after us until Christ came so that we might be justified by faith. ²⁵ With the coming of faith, we no longer submit to this guidance.

²⁶ Now, in Christ Jesus, all of you are sons and daughters of God through faith. ²⁷ All of you, who were given to Christ through Baptism, have put on Christ. ²⁸ Here, there is no longer any difference between Jew or Greek, or between slave or freed, or between man and woman: but all of you are one in Christ Jesus. ²⁹ And because you belong to Christ, you are of Abraham's race and you are to inherit God's promise.

GALATIANS 3:15-29

Read: Paul points out that God promised salvation to Abraham long before religious law existed. By faith, we are all children of God, without distinction of race, condition or sex. We are all one in Christ.

Reflect: How do you react to your own failures, with despair or by trusting in Christ's mercy? What does equality mean for the Church: neither Jew nor Greek; neither slave nor free; neither man nor woman?

Pray: Pray that in your Christian community all kinds of segregation, division, discrimination, and marginalization may disappear, and may this be a testimony of the real union in Christ.

Act: Perform a gesture of fraternity with someone in your community who is in dire need of it, in order to make visible that in God we are all equal.

4 ¹But listen, as long as the heir is a child, he does not differ at all from a slave, although he is the owner of everything. ²He is subject to those who care for him and who are entrusted with his affairs until the time set by his father comes. ³In the same way, we, as children, were first subjected to the created forces that govern the world. ⁴But when the fullness of time came, God sent his Son. He came born of woman and subject to the law, ⁵in order to redeem the subjects of the law, that we might receive adoption as children of God. ⁶And because you are children, God has sent into your hearts the spirit of his Son, who cries out: Abba! that is, Father!

⁷You, yourself, are no longer a slave, but a son or daughter, and yours is the inheritance by God's grace.

⁸When you did not know God, you served those who are not gods. ⁹But now that you have known God—or rather, he has known you—how can you turn back to weak and impoverished created things? Do you want to be enslaved again? ¹⁰Will you again observe this and that day, and the new moon, and this period and that year...? ¹¹I fear I may have wasted my time with you.

GALATIANS 4:1-11

Read: The main point is that Christ is the fulfillment of the Law of Moses. God sent the spirit of Christ into our hearts so we, like Christ know God as Abba! So now the Galatians no longer need the observance of the law.

Reflect: What does it mean in your everyday life that you are a child of God? What do you do to be really a child not only by name? Do you have awareness of forming part of a single family who experience God as loving parent?

Pray: "Abba" is a word that expresses affection and intimacy. When you pray, remember that you are addressing a parent who is kind and friendly. Talk to God as a loving parent asking to be able to trust their love more fully.

Act: Talk with your loved ones about the feelings and commitments arising from your prayer with this text. Ask them for advice and help to carry out what the Holy Spirit has raised in your heart.

I still suffer for you

¹²I implore you, dearly beloved, do as I do, just as I became like you. You have not offended me in anything. ¹³Remember that it was an illness that first gave me the opportunity to announce the gospel to you. ¹⁴Although my illness was a trial to you, you did not despise or reject me, but received me as an angel of God, as Christ Jesus.

¹⁵Where is this bliss? For I can testify that you would have even plucked out your eyes to give them to me. ¹⁶But now have I become your enemy for telling you the truth?

¹⁷Those who show consideration to you are not sincere; they want to separate you from me so that you may show interest in them. ¹⁸Would that you were surrounded with sincere care at all times and not only from me when I am with you!

¹⁹My children! I still suffer the pains of childbirth until Christ is formed in you. ²⁰How I wish I could be there with you at this moment and find the right way of talking to you.

GALATIANS 4:12-20

Read: Paul reminds the Galatians of their early friendship when he first announced the freedom of Christ. How is that Paul can be disregarded by those who once accepted him as an angel. Matters of faith can create strong emotions and disagreements among friends. Why is that?

Reflect: Who helped you know the Gospel? What about them helped you believe? Is that how you have shown the Gospel to your loved ones?

Pray: Remember in your prayer those who helped you know God and give thanks to God for them. No one can earn God's love, it comes to us through the mercy of Christ who makes us all God's children, without distinction of race, condition or sex. All are one in Christ.

> **Act:** Remember some anecdotes from when you began to know the Gospel and share it with your loved ones.

The comparison of Sarah and Hagar

²¹ Tell me, you who desire to submit yourselves to the law, did you listen to it? ²² It says that Abraham had two sons, one by a slave woman, the other by the free woman, his wife. ²³ The son of the slave woman was born in the ordinary way, but the son of the free woman was born in fulfillment of God's promise.

²⁴ Here we have an allegory and the figures of two Covenants. The first is the one from Mount Sinai, represented through Hagar: her children have slavery for their lot. ²⁵ We know that Hagar was from Mount Sinai in Arabia: she stands for the present city of Jerusalem, which is in slavery with her children.

²⁶ But the Jerusalem above, who is our mother, is free. ²⁷ And Scripture says of her: *Rejoice, barren woman without children, break forth in shouts of joy, you who do not know the pains of childbirth, for many shall be the children of the forsaken mother, more than of the married woman.*

²⁸ You, dearly beloved, are children of the promise, like Isaac. ²⁹ But as at that time, the child born according to the flesh persecuted Isaac, who was born according to the spirit, so is it now. ³⁰ And what does Scripture say? *Cast out the slave woman and her son, for the son of the slave cannot share the inheritance with the son of the free woman.*

³¹ Brethren, we are not children of the slave woman, but of the free woman.

GALATIANS 4:21-31

Read: Paul resorts to Genesis. He wants the Galatians to understand that they are really free from Jewish Law. The biblical metaphor speaks about the freedom that the Gospel of Jesus offers to those who welcome it, because, like Isaac in the Biblical story, they are children of the promise, children of a free woman, not of a slave.

Reflect: Do you feel truly free? What things can enslave you?

> If everything is a gift, how can we live in the Spirit? What does Paul mean by spirit and flesh?
>
> **Pray:** Give thanks to God for the freedom offered by the Gospel. Ask for strength to overcome what enslaves you, whether the rules or your own weaknesses.
>
> **Act:** Live according to the freedom of the children of God. Don't be a slave of temporal things and aspire always to eternal salvation.

5 [1] Christ freed us to make us really free. So remain firm and do not submit again to the yoke of slavery. [2] I, Paul, say this to you: if you receive circumcision, Christ can no longer help you. [3] Once more I say to whoever receives circumcision: you are now bound to keep the whole law. [4] All you who pretend to become righteous through the observance of the law have separated yourselves from Christ and have fallen away from grace.

[5] As for us, through the Spirit and faith, we eagerly wait for the hope of righteousness. [6] In Christ Jesus it is irrelevant whether we be circumcised or not; what matters is faith working through love.

[7] You had begun your race well, who then hindered you on the way? Why did you stop obeying the truth? [8] This was not in obedience to God who calls you: [9] in fact, a little leaven is affecting the whole of you. [10] I am personally convinced that you will not go astray, but the one who confuses you, whoever he may be, shall receive punishment.

[11] I, myself, brothers, could I not preach circumcision? Then I would no longer be persecuted. But where would be the scandal of the cross? [12] Would that those who confuse would castrate themselves!

GALATIANS 5:1-12

Read: The last section of this letter contains advice, a summary of Paul's thoughts, and some practical suggestions. Jesus has freed the Galatians, in such a way that the Law of Moses which requires circumcision as a sign of commitment to God has no value for them. Now, they must respond to God's love. Paul concludes with an attack on his opponents.

> **Reflect:** Religious observance does not the place of faith working through love. Why do so many think they must earn God's love?
>
> **Pray:** In prayer call upon the Holy Spirit, grateful for the Spirit's presence in your life and the gifts given you. Ask the Spirit to help you love freely and courageously.
>
> **Act:** Be aware of your good qualities and recognize also the qualities of others. Radiate the Gospel in your life.

True freedom

¹³ You, brothers and sisters, were called to enjoy freedom; I am not speaking of that freedom which gives free rein to the desires of the flesh but of that, which makes you slaves of one another through love. ¹⁴ For the whole law is summed up in this sentence: *You shall love your neighbor as yourself.* ¹⁵ But if you bite and tear each other to pieces, be careful lest you all perish.

¹⁶ Therefore, I say to you: walk according to the Spirit and do not give way to the desires of the flesh! ¹⁷ For the desires of the flesh war against the Spirit, and the desires of the Spirit are opposed to the flesh. Both are in conflict with each other so that you cannot do everything you would like. ¹⁸ But when you are led by the Spirit you are not under the law.

¹⁹ You know what comes from the flesh: fornication, impurity and shamelessness, ²⁰ idol worship and sorcery, hatred, jealousy and violence, anger, ambition, division, factions, ²¹ and envy, drunkenness, orgies and the like. I again say to you what I have already said: those who do these things shall not inherit the kingdom of God.

²² But the fruit of the Spirit is charity, joy and peace, patience, understanding of others, kindness and fidelity, ²³ gentleness and self-control. For such things, there is no law or punishment. ²⁴ Those who belong to Christ have crucified the flesh with its vices and desires.

²⁵ If we live by the Spirit, let us live in a spiritual way. ²⁶ Let us not be conceited; let there be no rivalry or envy of one another.

> **GALATIANS 5:13-26**
> **Read:** Jesus Christ frees people from believing they must earn God's love. The Galatians should respond by loving one another

and avoiding a way of life that is opposed to Spirit of Love. Love, joy, patience and kindness rather than conceit, competition and envy should characterize their community.

Reflect: Paul contrasts living according to the flesh, by which he means a life focused only on material things, with a life motivated by the Spirit reflecting love. How are these contrasting lifestyles seen today? How does one style interfere with the other?

Pray: Ask the Spirit to help you overcome your weaknesses and to bear the fruit of love and peace. Ask for the virtues that you need in your personal life.

Act: Put into practice the fruits of patience and kindness to someone who causes you problems or you dislike for some reason.

Various counsels

6 ¹Brethren, in the event of someone falling into sin, you who are spiritual shall set him aright with the spirit of kindness. Take care; for you, too, may be tempted. ²Carry each other's burdens and so fulfill the law of Christ. ³If anyone thinks he is something when in fact he is nothing, he deceives himself. ⁴Let each one examine his own conduct and boast for himself if he wants to do so, but not before others. ⁵In this, let each one carry his own things.

⁶He who receives the teaching of the word ought to share the good things he has with the one who instructs him. ⁷Do not be fooled. God cannot be deceived. You reap what you sow. ⁸The person who sows for the benefit of his own flesh shall reap corruption and death from the flesh. He who sows in the spirit shall reap eternal life from the Spirit. ⁹Let us do good without being discouraged; in due time, we shall reap the reward of our constancy. ¹⁰So, while there is time, let us do good to all, and especially to our family in the faith.

I am crucified with Christ

¹¹See these large letters I use when I write to you in my own hand!

¹²Those who are most anxious to put on a good show in life are trying to persuade you to be circumcised. The only reason they do this is to

avoid being persecuted for the cross of Christ. ¹³Not for being circumcised do they observe the law: what interests them is the external rite. What a boast for them if they had you circumcised!

¹⁴For me, I do not wish to take pride in anything except in the cross of Christ Jesus, our Lord. Through him, the world has been crucified to me, and I to the world.

¹⁵Let us no longer speak of the circumcised and of non-Jews, but of a new creation. ¹⁶Let those who live according to this rule receive peace and mercy: they are the Israel of God! ¹⁷Let no one trouble me any longer: for my part, I bear in my body the marks of Jesus.

¹⁸May the grace of Christ Jesus our Lord be with your spirit, brothers and sisters. Amen.

GALATIANS 6:1-18

Read: Paul offers spiritual advice: correct people gently, help others with their burdens, do your own work for the good of all and don't weary of doing good. Paul says everything depends on knowing that the love of God cannot be earned through religious observance but is a gift from Christ.

Reflect: Do you usually judge your others? What motivates you to perform good works? What reward do you expect from them? How has Paul's letter to the Galatians helped you to understand your relationship with God?

Pray: Ask forgiveness for the times that you judge others without looking at your own faults. Give thanks for all the love received and ask the Holy Spirit to guide you to live with the freedom of those who believe.

Act: Be guided by the Spirit, and live with fullness as a child of God. Be faithful to the Gospel by giving testimony at all times.

The Captivity Letters

Four letters are gathered under the title of "Captivity Letters": Ephesians, Philippians, Colossians, and Philemon. It is by chance that these four letters are continuous; even if these four letters were written by Paul while in prison, they are not of the same year, nor did he send them from the same prison.

Paul was arrested many times (2 Cor 11:24; Acts 14:29; 16:23). If we speak about his being in prison for any length of time, he may have been imprisoned two times, plus another in "semi-captivity."

His first stay in prison was undoubtedly in the year 56 A.D., in Ephesus, from where he had sent to the Philippians a letter whose authenticity did not raise any doubts.

His second stay, well documented in Acts 24–26, was in Caesarea on the premises of the Roman administration. Paul stayed there for two entire years and from there, he was taken to Rome (Acts 27–28).

His third stay was in Rome. In Acts, we are told that it lasted two years after which Paul was probably acquitted (Acts 28:30). In reality, Paul enjoyed a certain freedom and he was even lodged in a private house (Acts 28:16).

With a lot of probability, Paul was executed between the years 64 and 66 A.D., during Nero's great persecution. A wrong interpretation of 2 Timothy 1:17 led some to think that Paul was again in prison in Rome before his execution.

Therefore, it was either in the years 58–60 A.D., in Caesarea, or in the years 60–62 A.D., in Rome, that Paul would have written the letters, showing him as a prisoner, to the Ephesians, Colossians, and Philemon. Many reasons suggest that these letters were written in Caesarea.

Numerous biblicists question Paul as the author of the letters to the Ephesians and even to the Colossians. There are arguments for that although the aspects of these letters in favor of their authenticity are equally numerous. As the hypotheses attributing these letters to a disciple of Paul from the following generation showed their weakness, new theories had to be created as contradictions appeared.

The letters to the Ephesians and Colossians are intimately linked and the same topics are dealt with in both letters in the same way. Therefore it is impossible that one letter be authentic and not the other. On the other hand, how could a forger convince the Church to accept these letters as written by Paul? It is clear that if the churches received these letters so early and without questioning it is because the churches of Ephesus and Colossae, necessarily well informed, would not have accepted them unless they were Paul's. Then we have the short message to Philemon that everybody accepts as Paul's; but this is inseparable from Colossians: see Colossians 4:9 and Philippians 24–26.

In some people's view, the style and content of the letters differ too much from Paul's previous letters to have been written by him. However, as they read through, they are constantly forced to recognize words and ideas that are typically Paul's. How sure are we that an author is always going to speak in the same manner and keep the same style? Who can say that Paul could not say anything new after he had written Romans and Corinthians?

It is clear that the author of the letter to the Romans is no longer the same Paul as in the first letter to the Thessalonians. In addition, after Romans, two major changes were to affect Paul. On one hand, Paul decided to leave for Rome and the West since he believed that he had completed his apostolate in Asia Minor and Greece. On the other hand, Paul was going to experience years in prison.

Under guard in Caesarea, even though he was treated humanely and well (Acts 24:23), Paul did not live like a lord and his chains impaired his apostolic activity. Paul now looked at people and institutions differently and it is here that something more than a theological revision took place: it was a spiritual change of setting. Instead of accumulating contradictions with a simplistic solution, claiming that all the captivity letters were written by a forger, we could ask ourselves what else Paul had to discover, which is precisely what emerges in these captivity letters.

Access to Fulfillment

In simple terms, we might say that, up to that time, Paul had kept the vocabulary and the images of the God of the Old Testament. God the monarch established in heaven, God the judge who welcomes all to his heaven or the one who condemns. In the commentary on Romans, we have said that *justification* primarily consists in a recreation of the human person by God. Yet, we cannot deny the juridical aspect of this justification. Whether it is a question of the relations between God and humankind, or the struggle between good and evil, Paul is always thinking within the juridical setting of the rabbis. In addition, the aggressive language is manifest. A rereading of the first letter to the Thessalonians, will show that the violence of the language corresponds to the persecutions that Paul was enduring on the part of the Jews. That violence was also in Jesus' language, a popular preacher's language that did not, in any way, diminish the mystery of God but always presented it through these images.

It was within this legalistic and Jewish setting (we dare say: biblical) that the discovery of God as Father and the experiences of the Spirit occurred, combined with Paul's creativity and interior presence. These experiences had softened up the austerity and the violence that may have been in the religion of God as king and judge and joy was prevailing in the expectation of the Lord. These new feelings, the fruits of the Spirit, continued to go hand in hand with ancient images that contained a good measure of violence. The most notorious passages are in 1 Thessalonians and also in 2 Corinthians 11:13 and Galatians 2:4.

God is Spirit. Although Paul knew it, he had not yet become fully aware of it. The day he "realized" that God is not the one "who had the right to rule over our lives" (as some put it), he understood better the way that Father looks at human beings. His encounter with the religions of Asia Minor had probably prepared Paul's new conversion. Paul did use some terms common in the region of Ephesus but changed their meaning. Was Paul thinking only of fighting them or did he discover in them a certain way of conceiving the relations of God and the universe?

Eternity is very much present in Ephesians and Colossians. In the beautiful hymn of Ephesians 1:1-14 the eternal praise of divine grace is everywhere and *predestination*, already found in Romans 8:28, took its place in the divine nature. All suggests a divine mystery liberated from rights, obligations, and laws. What appears now in Paul more prominently is a God present in everybody and everything (Eph 3:14-20).

In those years, the expectation of the Day of the Lord was running out of steam and the God of Paul was going to be situated in a radiance that the wrath of God could not reach, there where all humans could be saved (Eph 3:8 and 1 Tim 2:4). Greater than ever, Christ assumed the long history that was just beginning. Paul saw himself as being caught up in a cosmic adventure in which, despite his insignificance, he had been needed for eternal praise. Paul, a prisoner, was entering into the depth of the mystery of redemption that was lavished, from Christ, on all those who loved him, and even in his chains (Eph 4:1; Col 1:24).

LETTER TO THE
EPHESIANS

CEREZO BARREDO

Should we speak of a "letter" of Paul? It does not contain any news or personal message to a specific community. Like the letter to the Romans, it is an exposé on faith and the salvation of the world. Was it a kind of circular letter intended for the churches of the Ephesus region? Instead, should we accept testimonies according to which this letter, written as the same time as the epistle to the Colossians, was meant for the Laodiceans (Col 4:16)?

As we are told in Acts (Chaps. 24–26), Paul was a prisoner in Caesarea between the years 58–60 A.D. He thought that his apostolate in the East was over and he had been arrested as he was getting ready to leave for Rome, the capital of the empire. A few months earlier, he had written the letter to the Romans, a brilliant presentation of the work of salvation, when the news he received from Ephesus prompted Paul to elaborate a new presentation of the divine work. There were new religions springing up in the Roman province of Asia and soon they would spread to Rome. To the extent that these religions claimed to be offering everyone a way of salvation, they were challenging Christ as the sole savior of humankind.

Christians had to be given a broader vision of the hope of which they were the bearers. Where is humankind going? Is Christ the only Savior? These are questions we have to confront more insistently every day insofar as these past few years have seen a type of "mass movements" on the part of very diverse people. Those who want to dominate can only succeed if they appear to be speaking for the majority. Is there a way and hope for human beings? From his prison, Paul responds to us.

This letter to the Ephesians is parallel to the letter Paul sent to the Colossians at the same time. The same messenger took it to the two communities at the same time as the note for Philemon (Col 4:2; Phlm 2). Paul takes up again and develops God's plan that he said he had understood in a revelation. At the core of this revelation, we have Christ, the Firstborn of God and the world has been created for new Human Beings, a single family in Christ. From now on, every Christian is urged to live this call to a holy and responsible life.

Some people think that Paul is not the author of this letter. How could he have spoken so impersonally to a community where he had worked for over two years, approximately from 55 to 57? As we have said, the letter was not addressed to the Christians of Ephesus but rather to communities in the valley of the Lycus River: Hierapolis and Laodicea that Paul had not personally evangelized.

Others think that the questions raised are more suited to a time after Paul. Or when they see that, compared to Paul's previous letters, his style has been renewed, they imagine that someone else wrote those letters. However, all the theories run into enormous obstacles. When one is aware of the very low level of Christian literature immediately after the death of the apostles, it is difficult to think that a letter of such theological conviction, such doctrinal richness and so typically "Pauline" in every page, could have matured in someone other than Paul, even if that someone, Tychicus (Eph 6:21) or Timothy (Col 1:1), assisted in writing it.

LETTER TO THE
EPHESIANS

1 [1] Paul, an apostle of Christ Jesus by the will of God,
to the saints in Ephesus, to you who share the Christian faith:
[2] receive grace and peace from God our Father, and from Jesus, the Lord.

[3] Blessed be God the Father of Christ Jesus our Lord,
who, in Christ, has blessed us from heaven with every spiritual blessing.
[4] God chose us in Christ before the creation of the world,
to be holy, and without sin in his presence.

[5] From eternity, he destined us in love,
to be his adopted sons and daughters through Christ Jesus,
thus fulfilling his free and generous will.
This goal suited him:
[6] that his loving-kindness, which he granted us in his beloved,
might finally receive all glory and praise.

[7] For, in Christ, we obtain freedom sealed by his blood,
and have the forgiveness of sins.
In this, appears the greatness of his grace,
[8] which he lavished on us.
In all wisdom and understanding,
[9] God has made known to us his mysterious design,
in accordance with his loving-kindness in Christ.
[10] In him, and under him, God wanted to unite,
when the fullness of time had come,
everything in heaven and on earth.

[11] By a decree of him, who disposes all things
according to his own plan and decision,

we, the Jews, have been chosen and called,
[12] and we were awaiting the Messiah
for the praise of his glory.

[13] You, on hearing the word of truth,
the gospel that saves you,
have believed in him.
And, as promised, you were sealed with the Holy Spirit,
[14] the first pledge of what we shall receive
on the way to our deliverance as a people of God,
for the praise of his glory.

EPHESIANS 1:1-14

Read: The author addresses Christians from Ephesus. A great blessing follows pointing the result of a new life in Christ: divine filiation, forgiveness of sins, incorporation to Christ and the seal of Holy Spirit.

Reflect: Are you aware of the consequences of your Christian option in your daily life? Do you really feel like a son or a daughter of God? What does the following text suggest to you: "In Him, we have redemption through his blood, the forgiveness of our trespasses"?

Pray: Let your prayer arise from your thankfulness to God the Father, Son and Holy Spirit for all the gifts you have received through baptism.

Act: Always be conscious of your Christian vocation; try to live in a special way the generosity and solidarity that the Christian vocation demands.

God has put all things under the feet of Christ

[15] I have been told of your faith and your affection toward all the believers, [16] so I always give thanks to God, remembering you in my prayers.

[17] May the God of Christ Jesus our Lord, the Father of glory, reveal himself to you and give you a spirit of wisdom and revelation that you may know him.

[18] May he enlighten your inner vision, that you may appreciate the things we hope for since we were called by God.

May you know how great is the inheritance, the glory, God sets apart for his saints;

[19] may you understand, with what extraordinary power, he acts in favor of us who believe.

[20] He revealed his almighty power in Christ when he raised him from the dead and had him sit at his right hand in heaven, [21] far above all rule, power, authority, dominion, or any other supernatural force that could be named, not only in this world but in the world to come as well.

[22] Thus has God put all things under the feet of Christ and set him above all things as head of the church, [23] which is his body, the fullness of him who fills all in all.

EPHESIANS 1:15-23

Read: Upon knowing about the faith and love of the Ephesians, Paul does not cease to give thanks to God and remembering them in his prayers. He prays that they will get to know the Father of glory; that they value the hope to which they have been called. Jesus is the head of all things and his body now is the Church.

Reflect: Do you experience the love of God in your daily life? How? Do you share it with your people? What does it mean for you that Christ is the head of the body?

Pray: Repeat with Paul the desire to receive a Spirit of wisdom to get to a personal and real knowledge of God through the Word and prayer. Give thanks to God for the salvation He gives you in the Risen Christ.

Act: To deepen your relationship with God, spend time every day to pray with the Bible, "the Word of God."

By grace, you have been saved!

2 [1] You were dead through the faults and sins. [2] Once, you lived through them according to this world, and followed the Sovereign Ruler who reigns between heaven and earth, and who goes on working in those who resist the faith. [3] All of us belonged to them, at one time, and we

followed human greed; we obeyed the urges of our human nature and consented to its desires. By ourselves, we went straight to the judgment like the rest of humankind.

[4] But God, who is rich in mercy, revealed his immense love. [5] As we were dead through our sins, he gave us life with Christ. By grace, you have been saved! [6] And he raised us to life, with Christ, giving us a place with him in heaven.

[7] In showing us such kindness in Christ Jesus, God willed to reveal and unfold in the coming ages, the extraordinary riches of his grace. [8] By the grace of God, you have been saved through faith. This has not come from you: it is God's gift. [9] This was not the result of your works, so you are not to feel proud. [10] What we are, is God's work. He has created us in Christ Jesus for the good works he has prepared, that we should devote ourselves to them.

EPHESIANS 2:1-10

Read: Paul reminds the Ephesians that they have been saved by faith and not by their own merits. So, no one may boast; our work is to "do the good works which God prepared beforehand to be our way of life."

Reflect: As Christian, does your daily life bear witness for the gift God offers you by freeing you from sin? What are the deeds you should foment so that your life may be a channel to share with others the gift received from God?

Pray: Thank God for the free gift of a new life in Christ. Ask to live the resurrection every day.

Act: Do the actions that the Spirit inspired you to do while in prayer to realize the "task that God prepared for you" as a Christian.

Christ is our peace

[11] Remember that you were pagans, even in your flesh; and the Jews, who call themselves Circumcised (because of a surgical circumcision), called you Uncircumcised. [12] At that time, you were without Christ, you did not belong to the community of Israel; the Covenants of God and his promises were not for you; you had no hope, and were without God in

this world. [13] But now, in Christ Jesus, and by his blood, you, who were once far off, have come near.

[14] For Christ is our peace; he who has made the two people one; [15] destroying, in his own flesh, the wall—the hatred—which separated us. He abolished the law with its commands and precepts. He made peace, in uniting the two people, in him; creating out of the two, one New Man. [16] He destroyed hatred and reconciled us both to God through the cross, making the two one body.

[17] He came to proclaim peace; peace to you who were far off, peace to the Jews who were near. [18] Through him, we—the two people—approach the Father, in one Spirit.

[19] Now you are no longer strangers or guests, but fellow citizens of the holy people: you are of the household of God. You are the house, [20] whose foundations are the apostles and prophets, and whose cornerstone is Christ Jesus. [21] In him, the whole structure is joined together and rises to be a holy temple in the Lord. [22] In him, you too, are being built to become the spiritual Sanctuary of God.

EPHESIANS 2:11-22

Read: The Jews and Gentiles are now one. God has united all through Jesus in one household, that of those consecrated to God, the Church. And we are all "built together spiritually into a dwelling place for God."

Reflect: If we are all one household, one family, why are there countries, businesses, and Christian groups that because they are rich despise or abuse the poor? Can a person, a group, business or country that calls itself Christian practice violence on others? To what does the peace we received in Christ commit us to?

Pray: Pray that Christian leaders be faithful to their faith and work for the peace that Christ offers us. Ask also for yourself, to avoid the temptation of being violent with the weaker ones.

Act: Collaborate with an institution that works for peace, social justice and for the rights of the weakest ones.

God's inheritance is for all

3 [1] For this reason, I, Paul, came to be the prisoner of Christ for you, the non-Jews. [2] You may have heard of the graces God bestowed on me for your sake. [3] By a revelation he gave me the knowledge of his mysterious design, as I have explained in a few words. [4] On reading them, you will have some idea of how I understand the mystery of Christ.

[5] This mystery was not made known to past generations, but only now through revelations given to holy apostles and prophets, by the Spirit. [6] Now, the non-Jews share the inheritance; in Christ Jesus, the non-Jews are incorporated and are to enjoy the Promise.

This is the Good News, [7] of which I have become a minister by a gift of God; a grace he gave me when his power worked in me.

[8] This grace was given to me, the least, among all the holy ones: to announce to the pagan nations the immeasurable riches of Christ [9] and to make clear to all, how the mystery hidden from the beginning in God, the Creator of all things, is to be fulfilled.

[10] Even the heavenly forces and powers will now discover through the church, the wisdom of God in its manifold expression, as the plan is being fulfilled, [11] which God designed from the beginning in Christ Jesus, our Lord. [12] In him, we receive boldness and confidence to approach God.

[13] So I ask you not to be discouraged at seeing the trials I endure for you, but rather, to feel proud because of them.

EPHESIANS 3:1-13

Read: In Christ is fulfilled what man has always expected from God: universal salvation. God has blessed Paul and has chosen him to announce this news to the Gentiles, and now all can access God. Paul says his sufferings are worth it.

Reflect: Are you conscious of the meaning of Jesus in your life? Who helped you find him? Do you share this Good News with others?

Pray: Ask the help of the Spirit to understand the Word and ask for strength to be able to share it with others, especially with your own.

Act: Go to your parish and express your gratitude to those who are working there; offer your help for the work of evangelization.

¹⁴And, now, I kneel in the presence of the Father, ¹⁵from whom every family in heaven and on earth has received its name.

¹⁶May he strengthen in you the inner self, through his Spirit, according to the riches of his glory;

¹⁷may Christ dwell in your hearts, through faith;

may you be rooted and founded in love.

¹⁸All of this, so that you may understand with all the holy ones, the width, the length, the height, and the depth—in a word, ¹⁹that you may know the love of Christ that surpasses all knowledge, that you may be filled, and reach the fullness of God.

²⁰Glory to God, who shows his power in us, and can do much more than we could ask or imagine; ²¹glory to him in the Church, and in Christ Jesus, through all generations, for ever and ever. Amen.

EPHESIANS 3:14-21

Read: Paul asks for faith and love for the community of the Ephesians; he wants that they "know the love of Christ that surpasses knowledge."

Reflect: Are you aware that there is nothing bigger than the love of God? What does it mean in your life that the love of God surpasses all knowledge? How do you give glory to that love?

Pray: Give thanks for the immensely great love from God. Ask to trust in His power and pray for the needs of others.

Act: Express the generosity of the love of God by being generous with a member of your community who is in need.

We shall become the perfect creation

4 ¹Therefore, I, the prisoner of Christ, invite you to live the vocation you have received. ²Be humble, kind, patient, and bear with one another in love.

³Make every effort to keep, among you, the unity of spirit through bonds of peace. ⁴Let there be one body, and one Spirit, just as one hope is the goal of your calling by God. ⁵One Lord, one faith, one baptism; ⁶one God, the Father of all, who is above all, and works through all, and is in all.

⁷But to each of us, divine grace is given according to the measure of

Christ's gift. [8] Therefore, it is said: *When he ascended to the heights, he brought captives and gave his gifts to people.*

[9] He ascended, what does it mean, but that he had also descended to the lower parts of the world? [10] He himself, who went down, then ascended far above all the heavens to fill all things. [11] As for his gifts, to some, he gave to be apostles; to others, prophets or even evangelists, or pastors and teachers. [12] So, he prepared those who belong to him for the ministry, in order to build up the Body of Christ, [13] until we are all united in the same faith and knowledge of the Son of God. Thus, we shall become the perfect Man upon reaching maturity and sharing the fullness of Christ.

[14] Then, no longer shall we be like children, tossed about by any wave, or wind of doctrine; and deceived by the cunning of people who drag them along into error. [15] Rather, speaking the truth in love, we shall grow in every way toward him who is the head, Christ. [16] From him, comes the growth of the whole body, to which a network of joints gives order and cohesion, taking into account, and making use of, the function of each one. So, the body builds itself, in love.

EPHESIANS 4:1-16

Read: Paul preaches unity in the Church. We all form a body whose head is the Lord. Each one has a gift that allows the growth and building up in love.

Reflect: Instead of thinking about what divides us within Christianity and within the Church, think of what unites us. Is Christ the same for everybody? What is your contribution to the construction of the body of Christ?

Pray: Jesus prayed that all might be one. Pray not only for the unity of all Christians but also for understanding among the members of the Church.

Act: Promote and pray for unity in your parochial community, and for unity of the domestic church that is your family.

Put on the new self

[17] I say to you, then, and with insistence, I advise you in the Lord: do not imitate the pagans who live an aimless kind of life. [18] Their

understanding is in darkness and they remain in ignorance because of their blind conscience, very far from the life of God. [19]As a result of their corruption, they have abandoned themselves to sensuality, and have eagerly given themselves to every kind of immorality.

[20]But it is not for this that you have followed Christ. [21]For, I suppose, that you heard of him and received his teaching, which is seen in Jesus himself. [22]You must give up your former way of living, the *old self*, whose deceitful desires bring self-destruction. [23]Renew yourselves spiritually, from inside, [24]and put on the *new self*, or *self*, according to God, that is created in true righteousness and holiness.

[25]Therefore, give up lying; let all of us speak the truth to our neighbors, for we are members of one another. [26]*Be angry, but do not sin*: do not let your anger last until the end of the day, [27]lest you give the devil a foothold.

[28]Let the one who used to steal, steal no more, but busy himself, working usefully with his hands so that he may have something to share with the needy. [29]Do not let even one bad word come from your mouth, but only good words that will encourage when necessary, and be helpful to those who hear.

[30]Do not sadden the Holy Spirit of God with which you were marked. He will be your distinctive mark on the day of salvation. [31]Do away with all quarreling, rage, anger, insults and every kind of malice: [32]be good and understanding, forgiving one another as God forgave you in Christ.

EPHESIANS 4:17-32

Read: Paul offers the Ephesians a series of norms needed to be faithful to the message of Christ. Truth, peace, work, speaking well, forgiveness: these are attitudes of Christians who clothed themselves with the new self "created according to the likeness of God in true righteousness and holiness."

Reflect: Has truth become a casualty in society? Do you cut corners when dealing with the truth? How can you manifest that you are clothed with the new self? Are you friendly and compassionate with others?

Pray: Ask God to help you clothe yourself with the new self, assuming the attitudes that Jesus preached with his life.

> **Act:** Think on one of the recommendations that Paul offers the Ephesians. Try to live it in a special way this day.

Imitate God

5 [1] As most beloved children of God, strive to imitate him. [2] Follow the way of love, the example of Christ, who loved you. He gave himself up for us and became the offering and sacrificial victim, whose fragrance rises to God. [3] And since you are holy, there must not be among you, even a hint of sexual immorality or greed, or any kind of impurity: these should not be named among you. [4] So too, for scandalous words, nonsense and foolishness, which are not fitting; instead, offer thanksgiving to God.

[5] Know this: no depraved, impure, or covetous person who serves the god 'Money,' shall have part in the kingdom of Christ and of God. [6] Let no one deceive you with empty arguments for these are the sins which God is about to condemn in people who do not obey. [7] Do not associate with such people. [8] You were once darkness, but now, you are light in the Lord. Behave as children of light; [9] the fruits of light are kindness, justice, and truth, in every form.

[10] You, yourselves, search out what pleases the Lord, [11] and take no part in works of darkness that are of no benefit; expose them instead. [12] Indeed, it is a shame even to speak of what those people do in secret, [13] but as soon as it is exposed to the light, everything becomes clear; and what is unmasked becomes clear through light. [14] Therefore it is said:

"Awake, you who sleep, arise from the dead, that the light of Christ may shine on you."

[15] Pay attention to how you behave. Do not live as the unwise do, but as responsible persons. [16] Try to make good use of the present time because these days are evil. [17] So do not be foolish, but understand what the will of the Lord is.

[18] Do not get drunk: wine leads to levity, but be filled with the Holy Spirit. [19] Gather together to pray, with psalms, hymns, and spiritual songs. Sing, and celebrate the Lord in your heart, [20] giving thanks to God, the Father, in the name of Christ Jesus, our Lord, always and for everything.

EPHESIANS 5:1-20

Read: These are bad times for the Ephesians. Paul reminds them that they have been saved by Jesus and they should try to have Jesus' attitudes discerning on how to act.

Reflect: Think of one sin that needs attention in your life. What are you to do to be faithful to the Christian vocation?

Pray: Seek guidance from the Holy Spirit and an open and ready heart to avoid the sin that you know needs attention.

Act: With the help of the Holy Spirit avoid the sin needing attention by practicing the opposite virtue.

Husbands, love your wives

[21] Let all kinds of submission to one another become obedience to Christ. [22] So wives, to their husbands, as to the Lord.

[23] The husband is the head of his wife, as Christ is the head of the church, his body, of whom he is also the Savior. [24] And as the church submits to Christ, so let a wife submit in everything to her husband.

[25] As for you husbands, love your wives as Christ loved the church and gave himself up for her. [26] He washed her and made her holy by baptism in the word. [27] As he wanted a radiant church, without stain or wrinkle or any blemish, but holy and blameless, he himself had to prepare and present her to himself.

[28] In the same way, husbands should love their wives as they love their own bodies. He who loves his wife loves himself. [29] And no one has ever hated his body; he feeds and takes care of it. That is just what Christ does for the Church [30] because we are members of his body.

[31] Scripture says: *Because of this, a man shall leave his father and mother, to be united with his wife, and the two shall become one flesh.* [32] This is a very great mystery, and I refer to Christ and the Church. [33] As for you, let each one love his wife as himself, and let the wife respect her husband.

EPHESIANS 5:21-33

Read: Paul deals with a contemporary society in which the husband owned the wife and attempts to change that. He says that the husband should love his wife as himself. It is the same love Christ has for the Church, and so the Church should be obedient to Christ.

Reflect: The emphasis is on the husbands to love and care for their wives as Christ does for the Church. Is there still male chauvinism today? What is your situation? What is your attitude?

Pray: Pray for marriages that live moments of crisis because of male chauvinism; ask that the mutual and gratuitous love of spouses redeem this situation.

Act: Promote and support in your parish groups and movements that take care of the Christian formation for marriage.

Children, parents, servants, and masters

6 [1] Children, obey your parents, for this is right: [2] *Honor your father and your mother.* And this is the first commandment that has a promise: [3] *that you may be happy and enjoy a long life in the land.* [4] And you, fathers, do not make rebels of your children but educate them by correction and instruction, which the Lord may inspire.

[5] Servants, obey your masters of this world with fear and respect, with simplicity of heart, as if obeying Christ. [6] Do not serve only when you are watched, or in order to please others, but become servants of Christ who do God's will with all your heart. [7] Work willingly for the Lord and not for humans, mindful that the good each one has done, [8] whether servant or free, will be rewarded by the Lord.

[9] And you, masters, deal with your servants in the same way and do not threaten them since you know that they and you have the same Lord, who is in heaven, and he treats all fairly.

Be strong in the Lord

[10] Finally, be strong in the Lord with his energy and strength. [11] Put on the whole armor of God to be able to resist the cunning of the devil. [12] Our battle is not against human forces, but against the rulers and authorities and their dark powers that govern this world. We are struggling against the spirits and supernatural forces of evil.

[13] Therefore, put on the whole armor of God that, in the evil day, you

may resist and stand your ground, making use of all your weapons. [14]Take truth as your belt, justice as your breastplate, [15]and zeal as your shoes, to propagate the gospel of peace. [16]Always hold in your hand the shield of faith to repel the flaming arrows of the devil. [17]Finally, use the helmet of salvation and the sword of the Spirit, that is, the word of God.

[18]Pray at all times as the Spirit inspires you. Keep watch, together with sustained prayer and supplication for all the holy ones. [19]Pray also for me, so that when I speak, I may be given words to proclaim bravely the mystery of the gospel. [20]Even when in chains, I am an ambassador of God; may he give me the strength to speak, as I should.

[21]I also want you to know how I am and what I am doing. Tychicus, our beloved brother and faithful minister in the Lord, will tell you everything. [22]I am sending him precisely to give you news of us and comfort you all.

[23]May peace and love, with faith from God the Father, and from Christ Jesus the Lord, be with the brothers and sisters. [24]And may his blessing be with all who love Christ Jesus, our Lord, with undying love.

EPHESIANS 6:1-24

Read: Paul cannot change the structures of his society, but he tries to redeem them through love: owners and slaves, parents and children, they all belong and serve Christ. As Christians, we are called to fight evil by doing good.

Reflect: Can we radically change our society? Is there any kind of slavery between us? What can we do to improve this situation? Where can we get the strength to do just that?

Pray: Pray for the inspiration of the Spirit to know how to preach and live equality among all men and women, as we are all children of God.

Act: Regard the person at your side today as if this person is Jesus himself.

LETTER TO THE
PHILIPPIANS

CEREZO BARRETO

Here again a real letter from Paul, personal, full of attention and tenderness that Paul sent from prison to the community that had always been the most concerned for his well-being. More than once Paul counted on their material assistance, showing the confidence he had in them. Usually, in order to avoid any suspicion of personal interest, he preferred to earn his living while continuing his mission. In this letter, we have the famous page: "Let the same project that was in Christ Jesus be found in you."

We have just said it is a real letter from Paul. Actually, all in it does not follow, as if fragments of several letters from Paul had been combined. We shall draw attention to it as we proceed: 2:19, 21; 4:1. It may well be a question of two short letters, one where Paul wanted to give his news and to thank, the other a warning, in the same style as the letter to the Galatians.

When Paul's letters were gathered together, the most important were arranged according to length: Romans, Corinthians, Galatians. Then came those we call "captivity letters." It is there we have Philippians between Ephesians and Colossians as if the three had been sent from the same prison. Yet there is every reason to think that Philippians was not written when Paul was in Rome, about the year 60 A.D., but several years earlier, more like the year 56 A.D. Perhaps he was at that time imprisoned in Ephesus.

LETTER TO THE
PHILIPPIANS

1 ¹From Paul and Timothy, servants of Christ Jesus, to the saints in Philippi, with their bishops and deacons;

to you all in Christ Jesus:

²May grace and peace be yours from God, our Father, and Christ Jesus the Lord.

³I give thanks to my God each time I remember you, ⁴and when I pray for you, I pray with joy. ⁵I cannot forget all you shared with me in the service of the gospel, from the first day until now. ⁶Since God began such a good work in you, I am certain that he will complete it in the day of Christ Jesus.

⁷This is my hope for you, for I carry you all in my heart: whether I am in prison, or defending and confirming the gospel, you are with me and share the same grace.

⁸God knows that I love you dearly, with the love of Christ Jesus, ⁹and in my prayers, I ask that your love may lead you, each day, to a deeper knowledge and clearer discernment, ¹⁰that you may have good criteria for everything. So you may be pure of heart, and come blameless, to the day of Christ, ¹¹filled with the fruit of holiness that comes through Christ Jesus, for the glory and praise of God.

PHILIPPIANS 1:1-11

Read: From prison Paul writes to a community he loves, remembering them in prayer, grateful for their support and encouraging them to deepen their love and faith.

Reflect: Does the love Paul has for the Philippians exist in your community? Are the members ready to work for the

Gospel? How do you collaborate with the work of evangelization?

Pray: Pray for your friends and family, but also for the members
of your parish church, that they may grow stronger in love and
faith.

Act: Don't be afraid to invite someone to go to church with you.

Christ is my life

¹²I want you to know, brothers and sisters, that what has happened to
me has served to advance the gospel. ¹³Actually the whole praetorian
guard, and even those outside the palace, know that I am in chains for
Christ. ¹⁴And what is more, my condition as a prisoner has encouraged
the majority of the brothers to proclaim the word of God fearlessly.

¹⁵Some, it is true, are moved by envy and rivalry, but others preach
Christ with good intention. ¹⁶These latter are moved by love and realize
that I am here to defend the gospel. ¹⁷The former proclaim Christ to
challenge me. They do not act with pure intention but think they are
making my imprisonment more unbearable. ¹⁸But, in any case, whether
they are sincere or showing off, Christ is proclaimed and because of this
I rejoice and have no regrets.

¹⁹I know that all this will be a grace for me, because of your prayers,
and the help given by the Spirit of Christ. ²⁰I am hopeful, even certain,
that I shall not be ashamed. I feel as assured now, as before, that Christ
will be exalted through my person, whether I live or die.

²¹For to me life is Christ, and dying is even better. ²²But if I am to go
on living, I shall be able to enjoy fruitful labor. Which shall I choose? ²³So
I feel torn between the two. I desire greatly to leave this life and to be
with Christ, which will be better by far, ²⁴but it is necessary for you that
I remain in this life. ²⁵And because I am convinced of this, I know that I
will stay and remain with you for your progress and happiness in the
faith. ²⁶I will surely come to you again and give you more reason for
being proud of belonging to Christ Jesus.

Stand firm in faith

²⁷Try, then, to adjust your lives according to the gospel of Christ. May
I see it when I come to you, and if I cannot come, may I at least hear

that you stand firm in the same spirit, striving to uphold the faith of the gospel with one heart. ²⁸ Do not be afraid of your opponents. This will be a sign that they are defeated and you are saved, that is, saved by God. ²⁹ For, through Christ, you have been granted, not only to believe in Christ but also to suffer for him. ³⁰ And you now share the same struggle that you saw I had, and that I continue to have, as you know.

PHILIPPIANS 1:12-30

Read: Paul reports that he shares his faith even in prison. As long as Christ is shared he doesn't care about the motivations of those that do it. For him "life is Christ and to die is gain." He wants to be with Christ now, but he knows that his presence among the Philippians will make them grow and be joyful in faith. He encourages them to "stand side by side" in living their faith and not to be intimidated by their enemies.

Reflect: What makes it difficult to believe in God in public? What is the difference between sharing your belief and proselytizing? What does the following expression suggest to you: "live your life in a manner worthy of the gospel of Christ"?

Pray: Ask the Lord that nothing may discourage your community from preaching and living the Gospel even when it may entail some risks.

Act: How can you help your parish share faith in Jesus Christ?

Imitate the humility of Jesus

2 ¹ If I may advise you, in the name of Christ, and if you can hear it as the voice of love; if we share the same Spirit and are capable of mercy and compassion, then I beg of you, ² make me very happy: have one love, one spirit, one feeling, ³ do nothing through rivalry or vain conceit. On the contrary, let each of you gently consider the others as more important than yourselves. ⁴ Do not seek your own interest, but rather, that of others. ⁵ Your attitude should be the same as Jesus Christ had:

⁶ Though he was in the form of God,
he did not regard equality with God as something to be grasped,
⁷ but emptied himself,
taking on the nature of a servant, made in human likeness,

and, in his appearance, found as a man,
⁸ He humbled himself by being obedient to death,
death on the cross.
⁹ That is why God exalted him
and gave him the name which outshines all names,
¹⁰ so that, at the name of Jesus, all knees should bend
in heaven, on earth and among the dead,
¹¹ and all tongues proclaim that Christ Jesus is the Lord,
to the glory of God the Father.

PHILIPPIANS 2:1-11

Read: Paul wishes that the community be able to overcome any lack of unity. Jesus is the best example to follow. The community should have the same love, unselfish, having the same mind as Christ Jesus. Paul repeats a hymn that celebrates the humility and service of Jesus on the cross that illustrates that he is the Lord.

Reflect: Read each verse of the hymn and ask yourself what it might mean to you. How can you be detached from your belongings to be more generous to others?

Pray: Humility is the willingness to serve others as did Jesus, pray that you can imitate the humility of Jesus.

Act: Think of practical ways where you can be of service to your family, friends and community.

---

¹² Therefore, my dearest friends, as you always obeyed me while I was with you, even more now that I am far from you, continue working out your salvation "with fear and trembling." ¹³ It is God who makes you not only wish but also carry out what pleases him. ¹⁴ Do everything without grumbling, ¹⁵ so that without fault or blame, you will be children of God without reproach, among a crooked and perverse generation. You are a light among them, like stars in the universe ¹⁶ holding to the word of life. I shall feel proud of you on the day of Christ, on seeing that my effort and labor have not been in vain. ¹⁷ And if I am being poured out as a libation over the sacrifice, and the offering of your faith, I rejoice and continue to share your joy; ¹⁸ and you, likewise, should rejoice and share my joy.

Paul's messengers

¹⁹ The Lord Jesus lets me hope that I may soon send you Timothy, and have news of you. With this, I will feel encouraged. ²⁰ For I have no one so concerned for you as he is. ²¹ Most follow their own interest, not those of Christ Jesus. ²² But Timothy has proved himself, as you know. Like a son at the side of his father, he has been with me at the service of the gospel. ²³ Because of that, I hope to send him to you as soon as I see how things work out for me. ²⁴ Nevertheless, the Lord lets me think that I, myself, shall be coming soon.

²⁵ I judged it necessary to send back to you Epaphroditus, who worked and fought at my side, and whom you sent to help me in my great need. ²⁶ In fact, he missed you very much and was still more worried because you had heard of his sickness. ²⁷ He was, indeed, sick and almost died, but God took pity on him and on me, sparing me greater sorrow. ²⁸ And so, I am eager to send him to you so that, on seeing him, you will be glad and I will be at peace. ²⁹ Receive him, then, with joy as is fitting in the Lord. Consider highly persons like him ³⁰ who almost died for the work of Christ; he risked his life to serve me, on your behalf, when you could not help me.

PHILIPPIANS 2:12-30

Read: Paul again compliments the Philippians. God is at work in them and they must work out their salvation in a difficult world so their love shines like stars. Paul is sending Timothy and Epaphroditus and asks them to welcome them.

Reflect: "Working out your salvation 'with fear and trembling'" is a famous phrase. What does it mean to you? Do you appreciate the effort of other people who work in your parish for the good of the community? Do you ever invite them to your home?

Pray: Paul sent people to help the Philippians grow in belief in God, pray God uses you to help others in their faith.

Act: Show your gratitude and support for people who have helped you in your faith.

Do not turn back to the Jewish law

3 [1] Finally, my brothers and sisters, rejoice in the Lord.

It is not a burden for me to write again the same things, and for you, it is safer. [2] Beware of the dogs, beware of the bad workers; beware of the circumcised. [3] We are the true circumcised people since we serve according to the Spirit of God, and our confidence is in Christ Jesus, rather than on our merits.

[4] I, myself, do not lack those human qualities in which people have confidence. If some of them seem to be accredited with such qualities, how much more am I! [5] I was circumcised when eight days old. I was born of the race of Israel, of the tribe of Benjamin; I am a Hebrew, born of Hebrews. With regard to the law, I am a Pharisee, [6] and such was my zeal for the law that I persecuted the Church. As for being righteous according to the law, I was blameless.

[7] But once I found Christ, all those things that I might have considered as profit, I reckoned as a loss. [8] Still more, everything seems to me as nothing compared with the knowledge of Christ Jesus, my Lord. For his sake, I have let everything fall away, and I now consider all as garbage, if instead, I may gain Christ. [9] May I be found in him, not having a righteousness of my own that comes from the law, but with the righteousness that God gives to those who believe.

[10] May I know him and experience the power of his resurrection and share in his sufferings and become like him in his death [11] and attain, through this, God willing, the resurrection from the dead!

[12] I do not believe I have already reached the goal, nor do I consider myself perfect, but I press on till I conquer Christ Jesus, as I have already been conquered by him. [13] No, brothers and sisters, I do not claim to have claimed the prize yet. I say only this: forgetting what is behind me, I race forward and run toward the goal, [14] my eyes on the prize to which God has called us from above in Christ Jesus. [15] Let all of us who claim to be perfect have the same way of thinking, but if there is something on which you differ, God will make it clear to you. [16] Meanwhile, let us go forward from the point we have each attained.

[17] Unite in imitating me, brothers and sisters, and look at those who walk in our way of life. [18] For many live as enemies of the cross of Christ. I have said it to you many times, and now I repeat it with tears: [19] they

are heading for ruin; their belly is their god and they feel proud of what should be their shame. They only think of earthly things.

[20] For us, our citizenship is in heaven, from where we await the coming of our Savior, Jesus Christ, the Lord. [21] He will transfigure our lowly body, making it like his own body radiant in glory, through the power, which is his to submit everything to himself.

Agree with one another and be happy

4 [1] Therefore, my brothers and sisters, whom I love and long for, you, my glory and crown, be steadfast in the Lord. [2] I beg Evodia and Syntyche to agree with each other in the Lord. [3] And you, Sycygus, my true companion, I beg you to help them. Do not forget that they have labored with me in the service of the gospel, together with Clement and my other fellow-workers, whose names are written in the Book of Life.

PHILIPPIANS 3:1—4:3

Read: This may be part of a different letter that Paul writes because he has heard some have been telling the Philippians that they must first convert to Judaism to be a Christian. Through his own experience, he knows salvation comes from God through Jesus by faith and not through works.

Reflect: What does the following expression suggest to you: "Whatever gains I had, these I have come to regard as loss because of Christ my Lord." Is it possible to believe in Christ and not to live according to his Gospel? Are faith and works opposite? To what concrete deeds does your faith in Jesus commits you?

Pray: Ask the Holy Spirit to help you grow in the knowledge of Christ: love of God and of neighbor, and to be more conscious of your condition of being a "citizen of heaven," a gift received by the faith in Christ Jesus.

Act: Show your faith by serving others. Tell your people what it means for you to enjoy the condition of being a "citizen of heaven."

---

[4] Rejoice in the Lord always! I say it again: rejoice, [5] and may everyone experience your gentle and understanding heart. The Lord is near: [6] do not be anxious about anything. In everything, resort to prayer and

supplication, together with thanksgiving, and bring your requests before God. [7] Then, the peace of God, which surpasses all understanding, will keep your hearts and minds in Christ Jesus.

[8] Finally, brothers and sisters, fill your minds with whatever is truthful, holy, just, pure, lovely and noble. Be mindful of whatever deserves praise and admiration. [9] Put into practice what you have learned from me, what I passed on to you, what you heard from me or saw me doing, and the God of peace will be with you.

Paul's thankfulness

[10] I rejoice in the Lord because of your concern for me. You were indeed concerned for me before, but you had no opportunity to show it. [11] I do not say this because of being in want; I have learned to manage with what I have. [12] I know what it is to be in want and what it is to have plenty. I am trained for both: to be hungry or satisfied, to have much or little. [13] I can do all things in him who strengthens me.

[14] However, you did right in sharing my trials. [15] You Philippians, remember that in the beginning, when we first preached the gospel after I left Macedonia, you alone opened for me a debit and credit account, [16] and when I was in Thessalonica, twice you sent me what I needed.

[17] It is not your gift that I value, but rather the interest increasing in your own account. [18] Now I have enough and more than enough, with everything Epaphroditus brought me on your behalf and which I received as "fragrant offerings pleasing to God." [19] God himself will provide you with everything you need according to his riches, and show you his generosity in Christ Jesus. [20] Glory to God, our Father, for ever and ever: Amen.

[21] Greet all who believe in Christ Jesus. The brothers and sisters with me greet you. [22] All the believers here greet you, especially those from Caesar's household. [23] The grace of Christ Jesus the Lord, be with your spirit.

PHILIPPIANS 4:4-23

Read: Paul concludes by praising two outstanding women who have worked with Paul in spreading the Gospel. They should live with joy and gentleness, without anxiety, praying to God for what they need. Paul is grateful for the money they have sent him in his need and prays God will reward them.

Reflect: Does your faith in Christ make you joyous? Do you celebrate it? What does the following expression suggest to you: "I can do all things through him who strengthens me"?

Pray: Thank God for all the wonderful things especially the wonderful people in your life. Ask to be able to live either in poverty or riches with joy.

Act: Go out and celebrate life with someone you love. If your situation allows it, share also your material goods with somebody in need.

LETTER TO THE
COLOSSIANS

Toward the year 62 A.D., Paul, a prisoner in Rome, writes to the Christians of Colossae, who, without being aware of it, belittle Christ. They do not feel assured with only faith in Christ and they want to add some practices from the Old Testament. Or they try to include Christ in a board of celestial persons, or "angels" who are supposed to have the key to our destiny in hand.

Something was lacking in them and in the majority of their contemporaries. They were caught in the Roman Empire which had imposed its peace on the known world at that time, but also prevented them from living a life of their own. They fell back on the "spiritual." Secret doctrines offered to lead their "perfect ones" to a higher state and theories called "gnosis" (that is, knowledge) were drawn up on the origin of the human and the world. According to them, all comes from a cosmic soup that had been boiling for ages, with impressive celestial families of angels or "eons," male and female, who devour each other, couple and finally imprison sparks of spirit in material bodies. So people are manufactured who, after "putting on" a series of successive existences, may return to the kingdom of light.

Caught in the wind of these fine discourses, the Colossians went the way of certain Christians today who trust in their devotion to souls or who allow their life to be led by spiritualism, astrology, and horoscopes. They no longer consider Christ as the only savior since they give the priority to others or to practices that are not of the Church.

This crisis in the Church of the first century gave us this letter of Paul where he establishes the absolute supremacy of Christ. As in other letters of Paul, the letter to the Colossians mentions that Timothy is with him (1:1). Paul chose him as assistant and looked on him as "his true Son in Christ." Perhaps it was Timothy who wrote a fair part of this letter; it would explain the difference in style from the more authentic of Paul's letters while its content—exceptionally rich—is constantly faithful to the inspiration of the apostle. On this subject, see the Letter to the Ephesians which has the same themes as the one to the Colossians, but in a more developed way. In several passages of Colossians, relevant commentaries in Ephesians will be indicated.

LETTER TO THE
COLOSSIANS

1 ¹Paul, an apostle of Christ Jesus by the will of God, and Timothy our brother,

²to the saints in Colossae, our faithful brothers and sisters in Christ:

Receive grace and peace from God our Father and Christ Jesus, our Lord.

³Thanks be to God, the Father of Christ Jesus, our Lord!

We constantly pray for you, ⁴for we have known of your faith in Christ Jesus, and of your love for all the saints. Indeed, you await in hope the inheritance reserved for you in heaven, ⁵of which you have heard through the word of truth. This gospel, ⁶already present among you, is bearing fruit and growing throughout the world as it did among you from the day you accepted it and understood the gift of God in all its truth.

⁷He who taught you, Epaphras, our dear companion in the service of Christ, faithful minister of Christ on our behalf, ⁸has reminded me of the love you have for me in the Spirit. ⁹Because of this, from the day we received news of you, we have not ceased praying to God for you, that you may attain the full knowledge of his will through all the gifts of wisdom and spiritual understanding.

¹⁰May your lifestyle be worthy of the Lord and completely pleasing to him. May you bear fruit in every good work and grow in the knowledge of God.

¹¹May you become strong in everything by a sharing of the glory of God, so that you may have great endurance and persevere in joy.

¹²Constantly give thanks to the Father who has empowered us to receive our share in the inheritance of the saints in his kingdom of light. ¹³He rescued us from the power of darkness and transferred us to the kingdom of his beloved Son. ¹⁴In him, we are redeemed and forgiven.

COLOSSIANS 1:1-14

Read: The Colossian Christians are known for living lives of faith hope and love. To these virtues Paul wants to add wisdom, strength and gratitude.

Reflect: How do you evidence faith, hope and love in your life? Does one come more easily, which is more difficult?

Pray: Allow gratitude to be the heart of your prayer. Give thanks for the faith you have received. Ask that your works always manifest the love of God, and feed with prayer the hope of being one day in heaven.

Act: As you give thanks to God for a favor received, give thanks also to someone who has been generous to you. Accompany in prayer, or in person if possible, those people in your community who are having difficult times.

Christ is the beginning of everything

¹⁵ He is the image of the unseen God,
and for all creation, he is the firstborn,
¹⁶ for, in him, all things were created,
in heaven and on earth,
visible and invisible:
thrones, rulers, authorities, powers...
All was made through him and for him.
¹⁷ He is before all
and all things hold together in him.
¹⁸ And he is the head of the body that is the Church,
for he is the first, the first raised from the dead,
that he may be the first in everything,
¹⁹ for God was pleased to let fullness dwell in him.
²⁰ Through him, God willed to reconcile all things to himself,
and through him, through his blood shed on the cross,
God establishes peace
on earth as in heaven.

²¹ You, yourselves, were once estranged and opposed to God because of your evil deeds, ²² but now, God has reconciled you in the human body of his Son, through his death, so that you may be without fault, holy and

blameless before him. [23] Only stand firm upon the foundation of your faith, and be steadfast in hope. Keep in mind the gospel you have heard, which has been preached to every creature under heaven, and of which I, Paul, became a minister.

COLOSSIANS 1:15-23

Read: This passage contains probably an ancient Christian hymn. It celebrates the Christ as holding together all of creation. The fullness of God dwells within him, and he has reconciled a lost humanity to God's love, and as a result people reject evil in their lives.

Reflect: Slowly read this hymn which present the Christ as the image of God for all creation. Which of these images have meaning in your spiritual life?

Pray: Ask God the grace to be an instrument of peace and reconciliation in your family and in your community.

Act: Look around you and be amazed by the work of God. Let your actions contribute to the perfection of everything created.

---

[24] At present, I rejoice when I suffer for you; I complete, in my own flesh, what is lacking in the sufferings of Christ for the sake of his body, which is the church. [25] For I am serving the church since God entrusted to me the ministry to make the word of God fully known. [26] I mean that mysterious plan that for centuries and generations remained secret, and which God has now revealed to his holy ones.

[27] God willed to make known to them the riches, and even the glory, that his mysterious plan reserved for the pagan nations: Christ is in you, the hope for glory.

[28] This Christ, we preach. We warn and teach everyone true wisdom, aiming to make everyone perfect in Christ. [29] For this cause, I labor and struggle with the energy of Christ working powerfully in me.

Let Christ Jesus, the Lord, be your doctrine

2 [1] I want you to know how I strive for you, for those of Laodicea, and for so many who have not met me personally. [2] I pray that all may be encouraged. May you be established in love, that you may obtain all the riches of a full understanding, and know the mystery of God, Christ

himself. ³For, in him, are hidden all the treasures of wisdom and knowledge.

⁴So, let no one deceive you with persuasive arguments. ⁵Although I am far from you, my spirit is with you, and I rejoice in recalling how well-disciplined you are and how firm in the faith of Christ.

> **COLOSSIANS 1:24—2:5**
>
> **Read:** Paul presents himself as minister of the Gospel and of the Church to fulfill the plan of God: salvation is universal and is within the reach of all who accept Christ. That is why he warns the Colossians not to fall for seductive arguments that claim otherwise.
>
> **Reflect:** For Paul trust in Christ is the most valuable thing in life. It is not just an idea, it is a relationship with the God who loves us, for this he is willing to suffer. What do you commit to in your daily life? In your opinion, What part of the Christian message does the secular world reject?
>
> **Pray:** Pray to deepen your trust in Christ. Pray that your heart may be encouraged, and your faith community united in love, especially in difficult days.
>
> **Act:** Pray for all the people who minister in your parish, and give them words of encouragement from time to time.

⁶If you have accepted Christ Jesus as Lord, let him be your doctrine. ⁷Be rooted and built up in him; let faith be your principle, as you were taught, and your thanksgiving, overflowing.

⁸See that no one deceives you with philosophy or any hollow discourse; these are merely human doctrines not inspired by Christ, but by the wisdom of this world. ⁹For in him, dwells the fullness of God in bodily form. ¹⁰He is the head of all cosmic power and authority, and, in him, you have everything.

Baptized and risen

¹¹In Christ Jesus you were given a circumcision, but not by human hands, which removed completely from you the carnal body: ¹²I refer to baptism. On receiving it, you were buried with Christ; and you also rose with him for having believed in the power of God, who raised him from the dead.

[13] You were dead. You were in sin and uncircumcised at the same time. But God gave you life with Christ. He forgave all our sins. [14] He canceled the record of our debts, those regulations which accused us. He did away with all that and nailed it to the cross. [15] Victorious through the cross he stripped the rulers and authorities of their power, humbled them before the eyes of the whole world, and dragged them behind him as prisoners.

Useless doctrines

[16] So then, let no one criticize you in matters of food or drink, or about the observance of animal festivals, new moons or the Sabbath. [17] These things were only shadows of what was to come, whereas the reality is the person of Christ. [18] Do not let anyone disqualify you, insisting on humbling practices and worship of angels. In fact, they are only good to satisfy self-indulgence, [19] instead of holding firmly to the head, Christ. It is he who nourishes and gives unity to the whole body by a complex system of nerves and ligaments, making it grow according to the plan of God.

[20] If you have really died with Christ, and are rid of the principles of the world, why do you now let yourselves be taught as if you belonged to the world? [21] "Do not eat this, do not taste that, do not touch that..." [22] these are human rules and teachings referring to things that are perishable that wear out and disappear. [23] These doctrines may seem to be profound because they speak of religious observance and humility and of disregarding the body. In fact, they are useless as soon as the flesh rebels.

Seek the things that are above

3 [1] So then, if you are risen with Christ, seek the things that are above, where Christ is seated at the right hand of God. [2] Set your mind on the things that are above, not on earthly things. [3] For you have died and your life is now hidden with Christ in God. [4] When Christ, who is your life, reveals himself, you also will be revealed with him in glory.

COLOSSIANS 2:6—3:4

Read: Being a Christian is not about rules and regulations, it is living united to Christ Jesus, reconciled, forgiven and free of any superstition or idolatry. Paul exhorts: "If you have been raised with Christ, seek the things that are above, where Christ is, seated at the right hand of God."

Reflect: What does it mean for you to live one with Christ? What does "seek the things that are above" mean to you? What distracts you from your relationship with Christ?

Pray: Prayer is not magic. Praying is not pronouncing spells to control human destiny, it is trusting yourself and your concerns to God's hands; lifting up your needs and the needs of those around you to God in a spirit of trust.

Act: Prepare a special place in your room, light a candle, as a sign of the divine presence, and surrender in prayer to the will of God by repeating the following sentence: "Lord, you are my strength, my rock, and salvation."

[5] Therefore, put to death what is earthly in your life, that is, immorality, impurity, inordinate passions, wicked desires and greed, which is a way of worshiping idols. [6] These are the things that arouse the wrath of God.

[7] For a time, you followed this way and lived in such disorders. [8] Well then, reject all that: anger, evil intentions, malice; and let no abusive words be heard from your lips.

Put on the new self

[9] Do not lie to one another. You have been stripped of the old self and its way of thinking; [10] to put on the new, which is being renewed, and is to reach perfect knowledge, and the likeness of its creator. [11] There is no room for distinction between Greek or Jew, circumcised or uncircumcised, barbarian, foreigner, slave or free, but Christ is all and in all.

[12] Clothe yourselves, then, as is fitting for God's chosen people, holy and beloved of him. Put on compassion, kindness, humility, meekness, and patience [13] to bear with one another, and forgive whenever there is any occasion to do so. As the Lord has forgiven you, forgive one another. [14] Above all, clothe yourselves with love, which binds everything together in perfect harmony. [15] May the peace of Christ overflow in your hearts; for this end, you were called to be one body. And be thankful.

[16] Let the word of God dwell in you, in all its richness. Teach and

admonish one another with words of wisdom. With thankful hearts, sing to God psalms, hymns, and spontaneous praise. [17] And whatever you do or say, do it in the Name of Jesus the Lord, giving thanks to God the Father through him.

COLOSSIANS 3:5-17

Read: Paul invites the Colossians to live a new life, one that reflects the image of Christ. To do this they must put aside all selfishness, recognize the equality of all people and live so the entire community is an image of Christ.

Reflect: What does the following text tell you: "As God's chosen ones, holy and beloved, clothe yourselves with compassion, kindness, humility, meekness, and patience. Bear with one another and, if anyone has a complaint against another, forgive each other; just as the Lord has forgiven you, so you also must forgive"?

Pray: With the help of the Holy Spirit, recognize your sins and ask for forgiveness And embrace living as Christ lived so you can find happiness.

Act: Express your faith by practicing works that renew the human condition in your neighborhood: compassion, patience, forgiveness, kindness.

On obedience

[18] Wives, submit yourselves to your husbands, as you should do in the Lord. [19] Husbands, love your wives and do not get angry with them. [20] Children, obey your parents in everything because that pleases the Lord. [21] Parents, do not be too demanding of your children, lest they become discouraged.

[22] Servants, obey your masters in everything; not only while they are present to gain favor with them, but sincerely, because you fear the Lord. [23] Whatever you do, do it wholeheartedly, working for the Lord and not for humans. [24] You well know that the Lord will reward you with the inheritance. You are servants, but your Lord is Christ. [25] Every evildoer will be paid back for whatever wrong has been done, for God does not make exceptions in favor of anyone.

4 ¹ As for you, masters, give your servants what is fair and reasonable, knowing that you yourselves have a Master in heaven.

> **COLOSSIANS 3:18—4:1**
>
> **Read:** Living with Christ influences everyday life, in contrast to the prevailing social standards the relationship of husbands and wives and their children should be characterized by love not servility. Masters should even treat their slaves justly not with cruelty. But then, he adds a new shade to it: service to the Lord Jesus, Lord of everything and everyone.
>
> **Reflect:** Relationships with family, friends, workers, our community, especially the neediest, are the ways in which we serve God. Do you experience God's presence in people?
>
> **Pray:** Pray for married couples, especially those that are unhappy. Pray for parents everywhere. Pray for children who suffer abuse and human trafficking.
>
> **Act:** Be the one serving the table today but do it as if you were serving the Lord himself. At the end of the meal, share that it is in serving others that makes our life with Christ real.

Further instructions

² Be steadfast in prayer, and even spend the night praying and giving thanks. ³ Pray especially for us and our preaching: may the Lord open a door for us that we may announce the mystery of Christ. Because of this, I am in chains; ⁴ pray then, that I may be able to reveal this mystery, as I should.

⁵ Deal wisely with those who do not belong to the Church; take advantage of every opportunity. ⁶ Let your conversation be pleasing with a touch of wit. Know how to speak to everyone in the best way.

⁷ Tychicus will give news of me. He is our dear brother and, for me, a faithful assistant and fellow worker for the Lord. ⁸ I am purposely sending him to give you news of me, and to encourage you. ⁹ With him, I am sending Onesimus, our faithful and dear brother, who is one of yours. They will tell you about everything that is happening here.

¹⁰ My companion in prison, Aristarchus, greets you, as does Mark, the cousin of Barnabas, about whom you have already received instructions.

If he calls on you, receive him warmly. [11] Jesus, called Justus, also greets you. They are the only Jewish people working with me for the kingdom of God, and because of that, they have been a comfort to me.

[12] Greetings from your countryman Epaphras, a good servant of Christ Jesus. He constantly battles for you through his prayer that you be perfect and firm in whatever God asks of you. [13] I assure you that he has worked hard for you, as well as for those at Laodicea and Hierapolis.

[14] Greetings from Luke, our dear doctor and from Demas. [15] Greet the brothers and sisters of Laodicea, and don't forget Nympha and the church that gathers in her house.

[16] After reading this letter, see that it is read in the Church of the Laodiceans, and have the letter they received, read in yours. [17] And say to Archipus, "Do not forget the ministry given to you in the Lord."

[18] Greetings in my own hand, Paul. Remember, that I am in chains. Grace be with you.

COLOSSIANS 4:2-18

Read: The letter ends with Paul encouraging prayer and thanksgiving. Because he is in prison, he asks them to pray for him and he mentions many people he remembers in prayer.

Reflect: Think of all the friends you have found because of faith. What have they given you, what have you given them?

Pray: Pray for friends, living and deceased. Ask God for the grace on how to offer your friendship to everyone who approaches you.

Act: Invite your friends to your home this weekend. Share with them the Word of God and, if possible, a meal. Look for opportunities to thank people for the part they play in your life.

LETTER TO
PHILEMON

Philemon from Colossae has a slave named Onesimus: a typical name for a slave since Onesimus means "useful" (v. 11). Onesimus escapes and goes to Rome where he expects to disappear in the crowd. Accidentally, or luckily, he meets Paul whom he had known in his master's house. At this point, Paul is imprisoned in Rome, but enjoys certain privileges enabling him to go out in the company of a policeman. Onesimus is converted and baptized; then Paul makes him go back to his former master with the letter of recommendation that we read here.

Paul asks that the slave be seen as a brother, and even suggests that the slave be freed (v. 21).

We have already seen the advice Paul gives to slaves in Colossians 3:22. In those first years of the Church, obtaining God's life in Christ seemed such a tremendous privilege, providing such inner freedom, that being a slave or being free did not greatly matter (see 1 Cor 7:17).

At that time no one thought that a change of social structure was feasible: there were slaves and there would always be slaves. The Christians were few and without any influence. Thus, they were not concerned about reforming society, or about laws to eliminate slavery. Even before the time it became necessary to think about changing the laws, faith was already against treating slaves as "objects" or inferiors: because they were Christians, an increasing number of masters—in the Church—spontaneously renounced their rights and granted freedom to their slaves.

Many people think that the Christian community has nothing to say concerning their responsibilities to society. Here, on the contrary, we see how Paul involves the whole community in Philemon's problem.

LETTER TO
PHILEMON

¹ From Paul, a prisoner of Christ Jesus, and from our brother Timothy, to Philemon, our friend and fellow worker, ² to our dear sister Apphia, to Archippus, faithful companion in our soldiering, and to all the Church gathered in your house.

³ Grace and peace be with you from God, the Father, and Jesus Christ, the Lord.

⁴ I never cease to give thanks to my God when I remember you in my prayers, ⁵ for I hear of your love and faith toward the Lord and all the holy ones. ⁶ And I pray that the sharing of your faith may make known all the good that is ours in Christ. ⁷ I had great satisfaction and comfort on hearing of your charity because the hearts of the saints have been cheered by you, brother.

⁸ Because of this, although in Christ I have the freedom to command what you should do, ⁹ yet I prefer to request you, in love. The one talking is Paul, the old man, now a prisoner for Christ. ¹⁰ And my request is on behalf of Onesimus, whose father I have become while I was in prison.

¹¹ This Onesimus has not been helpful to you, but now he will be helpful, both to you and to me. ¹² In returning him to you, I am sending you my own heart. ¹³ I would have liked to keep him at my side, to serve me on your behalf while I am in prison for the gospel, ¹⁴ but I did not want to do anything without your agreement, nor impose a good deed upon you without your free consent.

¹⁵ Perhaps Onesimus has been parted from you for a while so that you may have him back forever, ¹⁶ no longer as a slave, but better than a slave, for he is a very dear brother to me, and he will be even dearer to you. ¹⁷ And so, because of our friendship, receive him as if he were I myself. ¹⁸ And if he has caused any harm, or owes you anything, charge it

to me. ¹⁹I, Paul, write this and sign it with my own hand: I will pay it... without further mention of your debt to me, which is you yourself. ²⁰So, my brother, please do me this favor for the Lord's sake. Give me this comfort in Christ.

²¹Confident of your obedience, I write to you, knowing you will do even more than I ask. ²²And one more thing, get a lodging ready for me because, thanks to all your prayers, I hope to return to you.

²³Epaphras, my fellow prisoner in Christ Jesus, sends greetings. ²⁴So do Mark, Aristarchus, Demas and Luke, my assistants.

²⁵May the grace of the Lord Christ be with you. Amen!

PHILEMON 1-25

Read: The slave Onesimus has become a Christian, and Paul makes a personal appeal to Philemon, Onesimus' master, that he may be accepted him back not as a runaway slave, but as a spiritual brother. Conversion to Christianity changes people and establishes a new relationship between them: we are all brothers and sisters since we all have the same Father: God.

Reflect: Do you feel the need to change the way you look at people and take them not for what they have or do but for what they really are? What kind of slavery do we have today that prevent a universal brotherhood? How can we eradicate it with the message of the Gospel?

Pray: Ask God to help you and your community to receive as brothers and sisters those who arrive at the faith, independently of their "enslavements."

Act: Be aware of the way you treat others, especially those who are going through some particular needs or have fewer material resources than yourself. Get close to them and talk to them with humility, respect, and generosity, knowing that before God we are all the same.

FIRST LETTER TO THE
THESSALONIANS

In the year 50 A.D., Paul arrived in Thessalonica, a major city and the capital of the province of Macedonia (see Acts 17:1). Here, after being rejected by the Jews, he addressed his preaching to the pagans and succeeded in forming a community. After barely three months, a riot caused by the Jews forced him to leave.

What is going to happen to these new Christians who have only received the basics of Christian life from Paul? Because of his concern, Paul asks Timothy to go and to strengthen this young Church. Upon his return, Timothy is optimistic and being reassured, Paul sends this letter at the beginning of the year 51 A.D. This is the oldest text of the New Testament.

We do not always find this letter very inspiring. We might say that Paul's style is still quite "green." We sense both a missionary's attachment to the converts for whom he had spared no effort, his concern about them and the remnants of Paul's early training as fanatic as it was generous.

Christian faith was going against reason in the first communities of the Greco-Roman world, just as it does in our own communities. Sexual freedom seemed just as legitimate to them as it does to our contemporaries. The resurrection of the dead and the afterlife did not readily enter into their perspectives even if, from time to time, some "mystery-prone" philosophers or some religions were trying to revive such hopes.

In Chapter 4, Paul re-asserts the biblical doctrine concerning these matters. There, we will find the clear and sound affirmation of the moral demands to form an integral part of Christ's followers: be holy, alert and be people who are waiting for something else.

We will also find the first affirmation of the resurrection of the dead expressed in apocalyptic language and images.

From its beginnings, the community is invited to live in constant prayer and to give priority to the care of its weakest members.

FIRST LETTER TO THE
THESSALONIANS

1 [1] From Paul, Sylvanus, and Timothy, to the church of Thessalonica, which is in God, the Father, and in Christ Jesus, the Lord.

May the peace and grace of God be with you.

[2] We give thanks to God at all times for you, and remember you in our prayers. [3] We constantly recall before God, our Father, the work of your faith, the labors of your love, and your endurance in waiting for Christ Jesus our Lord.

[4] We remember, brothers and sisters, the circumstances of your being called. [5] The gospel we brought you was such, not only in words. Miracles, the Holy Spirit, and plenty of everything, were given to you. You also know how we dealt with you, for your sake.

[6] In return, you became followers of us and of the Lord, when on receiving the word, you experienced the joy of the Holy Spirit in the midst of great opposition. [7] And you became a model for the faithful of Macedonia and Achaia, [8] since, from you, the word of the Lord spread to Macedonia and Achaia, and still farther. The faith you have in God has become news in so many places that we need say no more about it. [9] Others tell of how you welcomed us and turned from idols to the Lord. For you serve the living and true God, [10] and you wait for his Son from heaven, whom he raised from the dead, Jesus, who frees us from impending trial.

---

1 THESSALONIANS 1:1-10

Read: Paul praises the active faith, the labor of love and the persevering hope of the Thessalonian community. The reputation of the Thessalonians has spread far and wide and has helped in the conversion of other peoples.

> **Reflect:** What does "work of faith, labors of love, and endurance in waiting for Christ Jesus our Lord" mean to you? Does your parish community set an example for other communities? How is the faith that your parish community professes manifested in your daily life?
>
> **Pray:** Ask for the Spirit's guidance to live according to the Gospel by giving witness to what you believe.
>
> **Act:** Examine your attitudes toward others in your everyday life. Promote those that give a better witness of your faith in Jesus.

The beginning of the Church of Thessalonica

2 [1] You well know, brothers and sisters, that our visit to you was not in vain. [2] We had been ill-treated and insulted in Philippi, but trusting in our God, we dared announce to you the message of God and face fresh opposition. [3] Our warnings did not conceal any error or impure motive, nor did we deceive anyone. [4] But, as God had entrusted his gospel to us, as faithful ministers, we were anxious to please God who sees the heart rather than human beings. [5] We never pleased you with flattery, as you know, nor did we try to earn money, as God knows. [6] We did not try to make a name for ourselves among people, either with you or anybody else, although we were messengers of Christ and could have made our weight felt.

[7] On the contrary, we were gentle with you as a nursing mother who feeds and cuddles her baby. [8] And so great is our concern, that we are ready to give you, as well as the gospel, even our very lives, for you have become very dear to us.

[9] Remember our labor and toil; when we preached the gospel, we worked day and night so as not to be a burden to you. [10] You are witnesses with God that we were holy, just and blameless toward all of you who now believe. [11] We warned each of you as a father warns his children; [12] we encouraged you, and urged you, to adopt a way of life worthy of God, who calls you to share his own glory and kingdom.

[13] This is why we never cease giving thanks to God for, on receiving our message, you accepted it, not as human teaching, but as the word of God. That is what it really is, and as such, it is at work in you who believe.

[14] Brothers and sisters, you followed the example of the churches of

God in Judea, churches of Christ Jesus. For you suffered from your compatriots the same trials they suffered from the Jews, [15] who killed the Lord Jesus and the prophets, and who persecute us. They displease God and harm all people [16] when they prevent us from speaking to the pagans and trying to save them. By doing so, they are heaping up their sins, but now, judgment is coming upon them.

[17] We are for a time, deprived of your presence, but not in our heart, and we eagerly long to see you. [18] For we have wanted to visit you, and I, Paul, more than once; but Satan prevented us. [19] In fact, who but you are our hope and our joy? Who but you will be our glorious crown before Jesus, our Lord, when he returns? [20] Yes, indeed, you are our glory and our joy.

---

1 THESSALONIANS 2:1-20

Read: Paul recounts how he first came to the Thessalonians and how he ministered to them. Paul remembers how they embraced the Word of God, suffering for the Gospel just as the original churches did. He longs to see them again.

Reflect: In what way is the word of God at work in your life? How is the word of God working in your parish?

Pray: Give thanks to God for the different vocations and ministries in the Church. Ask that He continue to send "laborers for the vineyard." Pray in a special way for your parish priest and all pastoral agents of your parish; may the Lord be always for them their joy, refuge, and hope.

Act: Go to your parish and show your gratitude to all those working there, especially to the parish priest and pastoral agents.

Paul's concern

3 [1] As I could no longer bear it, I decided to go alone to Athens, [2] and send you Timothy, our brother and co-worker of God in the gospel of Christ. I wanted him to encourage you in the faith, and strengthen you, [3] so that none of you might turn back because of the trials you are now enduring. You know that such is our destiny. [4] I warned you of this when I was there: "We shall have to face persecution"; and so it was, as you have seen. [5] Therefore, I could not stand it any longer and sent

Timothy to appraise your faith and see if the Tempter had tempted you and made our work useless.

⁶ But now Timothy has just returned with good news of your faith and love. He told us that you remember us kindly, and that you long to see us as much as we long to see you. ⁷ What a consolation for us, brothers and sisters, in the midst of our troubles and trials, this faith of yours! ⁸ It is a breath of life for us when you stand firm in the Lord. ⁹ How can we thank God enough for all the joy that we feel before God because of you? ¹⁰ Day and night we beg of him to let us see you again, that we may complete the instruction of the believers.

¹¹ May God, our Father, and Jesus, our Lord, prepare the way for us to visit you. ¹² May the Lord increase more and more your love for each other and for all people, as he increases our love for you. ¹³ May he strengthen you internally, to be holy and blameless before God, our Father, on the day that Jesus, our Lord, will come with all his saints.

---

1 THESSALONIANS 3:1-13

Read: Paul sends Timothy to strengthen and encourage the community that is undergoing persecutions. Upon receiving the good news that they stand firm in the Lord, Paul rejoices and asks, "May the Lord increase, more and more your love for each other and for all people, as he increases our love for you. May he strengthen you, internally, to be holy and blameless before God, our Father, on the day that Jesus, our Lord will come with all his saints."

Reflect: Are you aware of the persecutions that the Church is suffering today? Do you feel persecuted or marginalized because of your faith in Jesus? Is faith a forbidden subject where you work or among your friends? How does you love increase from day to day? Do you feel strengthened internally?

Pray: Pray for Christians who suffer from religious persecution around the world. Pray also for those who are ridiculed for believing in Jesus.

Act: Discuss with your community about the importance of Christians supporting the missionary activity of the Church. Ask if your parish can support a church community that is suffering persecution.

A call to a life of purity and work

4 [1] For the rest, brothers and sisters, we ask you in the name of Jesus, the Lord, and we urge you to live in a way that pleases God, just as you have learned from us. This you do, but try to do still more. [2] You know the instructions we gave you on behalf of the Lord Jesus: [3] the will of God for you is to become holy and not to have unlawful sex.

[4] Let each of you behave toward his wife as a holy and respectful husband, [5] rather than being led by lust, as are pagans who do not know God. [6] In this matter, let no one offend or wrong a brother or a sister. The Lord will do justice in all these things, as we have warned and shown you. [7] God has called us to live, not in impurity, but in holiness, [8] and those who do not heed this instruction disobey, not a human, but God, himself, who gives you his Holy Spirit.

[9] Regarding mutual love, you do not need anyone to write to you, because God, himself, taught you how to love one another. [10] You already practice it with all the brothers and sisters of Macedonia, but I invite you to do more. [11] Consider how important it is to live quietly, without bothering others, to mind your own business, and work with your hands as we have charged you. [12] In obeying these rules, you will win the respect of outsiders and be dependent on no one.

Do not grieve as others do

[13] Brothers and sisters, we want you not to be mistaken about those who are already asleep, lest you grieve as do those who have no hope. [14] We believe that Jesus died and rose; it will be the same for those who have died in Jesus. God will bring them together with Jesus, and for his sake.

[15] By the same word of the Lord, we assert this: those of us who are to be alive at the Lord's coming, will not go ahead of those who are already asleep. [16] When the command by the archangel's voice is given, the Lord himself will come down from heaven, while the divine trumpet call is sounding. Then those who have died in the Lord will rise first; [17] as for us who are still alive, we will be brought along with them, in the clouds, to meet the Lord in the celestial world. And we will be with the Lord forever.

[18] So then, comfort one another with these words.

> ## 1 THESSALONIANS 4:1-18
>
> **Read:** Paul tells the community "they have been taught by God to love one another" and this love must extend to sexual and financial relationships where no one must be exploited. Since some members are dying before the second coming of Christ, Paul reassures them that they will share in the resurrection.
>
> **Reflect:** How is holiness part of your everyday life and interactions with others? How does God teach you to love others? Have you thought how you will share in the resurrection?
>
> **Pray:** Pray for an increase of everyday holiness in your life. Remember to pray for those who have died.
>
> **Act:** Live your Christian vocation fully today as if it was your last day in your life. At the end of the day, give thanks to God for all the experiences lived.

You are citizens of the light

5 ¹ You do not need anyone to write to you about the delay and the appointed time for these events. ² You know that the day of the Lord will come like a thief in the night. ³ When people feel secure and at peace, the disaster will suddenly come upon them as the birth pangs of a woman in labor, and they will not escape.

⁴ But you, beloved, are not in darkness; so that day will not surprise you like a thief. ⁵ All of you are citizens of the light and the day; we do not belong to night and darkness. ⁶ Let us not, therefore, sleep as others do, but remain alert and sober.

⁷ Those who sleep, go to sleep at night, and those who drink, get drunk at night. ⁸ Since we belong to the day, let us be sober, let us put on the breastplate of faith and love, and let the hope of salvation be our helmet. ⁹ For God has not willed us to be condemned, but to win salvation through Christ Jesus, our Lord. ¹⁰ He died for us so that we might enter into life with him, whether we are still awake or already asleep. ¹¹ Therefore, encourage one another and build up one another as you are doing now.

¹² Brothers and sisters, I want you to be thankful to those who labor among you, who lead you in the way of the Lord and also reprimand

you. [13] Esteem them highly and love them for what they are doing. Live at peace among yourselves.

[14] We urge you to warn the idle, encourage those who feel discouraged, sustain the weak, have patience with everyone. [15] See that no one repays evil for evil, but try to do good, whether among yourselves or toward others.

[16] Rejoice always, [17] pray without ceasing [18] and give thanks to God at every moment. This is the will of God, your vocation as Christians.

[19] Do not quench the Spirit, [20] do not despise the prophets' warnings. [21] Put everything to the test and hold fast to what is good. [22] Avoid evil, wherever it may be.

[23] May the God of peace make you holy and bring you to perfection. May you be completely blameless in spirit, soul, and body, till the coming of Christ Jesus, our Lord; [24] he who called you is faithful and will do it.

[25] Brothers and sisters, pray for us. [26] Greet all the brothers and sisters with a holy kiss. [27] I order you, in the name of the Lord, that this letter be read to all of them.

[28] May the grace of Christ Jesus, our Lord, be with you.

---

1 THESSALONIANS 5:1-28

Read: Before his farewell, Paul urges the Thessalonians to be confident in their calling, alert to its challenges, respectful toward one another, encouraging to the discouraged, supportive of their leaders, praying at all times and, most especially, rejoice always in the Lord.

Reflect: Do you live intensely the present moment or do you spend your life waiting always for better times? What does the following expression tell you: "God has destined us not for wrath but for obtaining salvation through our Lord Jesus Christ, who died for us, so that whether we are awake or asleep we may live with him."

Pray: Ask Jesus for the grace to be able to wait for him at all times, with joy, faith, hope, and love.

Act: Share with your people your trust in eternal life and in the definitive encounter with the Lord.

SECOND LETTER TO THE
THESSALONIANS

The First Letter to the Thessalonians taught us the importance of looking forward to the coming of Christ in Paul's preaching.

The hope of the day of Christ was a powerful incentive for the faith of the first Christians but it could also lead to an unhealthy nervousness. The church of Thessalonica appears to have suffered from a rather frequent illness among minorities and persecuted groups, namely, the expectation of the end of the world that will solve all the problems. For the time, this expectation only disturbs Christian life.

Is this letter authentic? There have been many doubts on the subject. Why was there a second letter, seemingly so close to the first? In fact, several paragraphs are almost the same as in the first letter to the Thessalonians. There is only one clear new point, in the middle of the letter and of great interest to the author, namely, the warning about the coming of the antichrist and the hour of judgment. Since this warning appears to correct the first letter in which there was an expectation of the imminent coming of the Lord, it was surmised that, in Paul's name, someone had wanted to add what Paul did not say before.

But what are these arguments worth even if we add to them some stylistic differences? What do we know about problems of communication, delays or about the way Paul dictated his letters? Some people claim that it was common to write a book under the name of a master or of someone whose ideas one wanted to interpret. This is true in the area of philosophical treatises but when we are dealing with a letter and with personal recollections, it is an entirely different situation. You will observe that in 2 Thessalonians 2:2, Paul issues a warning against letters that could be attributed to him and at the end of the letter in 3:17, he gives an example of his own handwriting. If it were the letter of an imitator, shouldn't we speak of a pure and simple lie? From the beginning, it was accepted as a letter of Paul and an inspired book. We cannot suspect the first Christians of having been overly naive and in the context of the Church of that time with so many personal contacts among the communities, it is hard to see how a forger could have succeeded in having his own work taken to be a letter of Paul.

This being the case, the letter fills a small gap in revelation as a whole. It serves to invite us not to let ourselves be impressed by rumors of revelations, tragedies and the end of the world as it has happened throughout history.

SECOND LETTER TO THE
THESSALONIANS

1 ¹From Paul, Sylvanus, and Timothy, to the church of the Thessalonians, which is in God, our Father, and in Christ Jesus, the Lord.

²May grace and peace be yours, from God, the Father, and Christ Jesus, the Lord.

³Brothers and sisters, we should give thanks to God at all times for you. It is fitting to do so, for your faith is growing and your love for one another increasing. ⁴We take pride in you among the churches of God because of your endurance, and your faith in the midst of persecution and sufferings. ⁵In this, the just judgment of God may be seen; for you must show yourselves worthy of the kingdom of God for which you are now suffering.

The judgment and the coming of Christ

⁶Indeed, it is just that God repays with affliction those who persecute you, ⁷but to you who suffer, he will grant rest with us, when the Lord Jesus will be shown in his glory, coming from heaven and surrounded by his court of angels. ⁸*Then, with flaming fire, will be punished those who do not recognize God, and do not obey the gospel of Jesus, our Lord.*

⁹They will be sent to eternal damnation, far away from the face of the Lord and his mighty glory. ¹⁰On that day, the Lord will be glorified in the midst of his saints, and reveal his wonders through those who believe in him, that is, through you who have received our testimony.

¹¹This is why we constantly pray for you; may our God make you worthy of his calling. May he, by his power, fulfill your good purposes, and your work prompted by faith. ¹²In that way, the name of Jesus, our Lord, will be glorified through you, and you through him, according to the loving plan of God and of Christ Jesus, the Lord.

2 [1] Brothers and sisters, let us speak about the coming of Christ Jesus, our Lord, and our gathering to meet him. [2] Do not be easily unsettled. Do not be alarmed by what a prophet says, or by any report, or by some letter said to be ours saying the day of the Lord is at hand.

[3] Do not let yourselves be deceived in any way. Apostasy must come first when the man of sin will appear, [4] that instrument of evil, who opposes and defiles whatever is considered divine and holy, even to the point of sitting in the temple of God and claiming to be God.

[5] Do you not remember I spoke of it when I was still with you? [6] But you also know what prevents him from appearing until his due time. [7] The mystery of sin is already at work, but the one who restrains it, at present, has to be taken away. [8] Then, the wicked one will appear, whom the Lord is to sweep away with the breath of his mouth and destroy in the splendor of his coming. [9] This lawless one will appear with the power of Satan, performing miracles and wonderful signs at the service of deception. [10] All the deceits of evil will then be used for the ruin of those who refused to love the truth and be saved. [11] This is why God will send them the power of delusion, that they may believe what is false. [12] So all those who chose wickedness, instead of believing the truth, will be condemned.

Persevere in faith

[13] But we have to give thanks for you at all times, dear brothers and

sisters in the Lord. For God chose you from the beginning to be saved through true faith and to be made holy by the Spirit. [14] To this end, he called you through the gospel we preach, for he willed you to share the glory of Christ Jesus, our Lord.

[15] Because of that, brothers and sisters, stand firm and hold to the traditions that we taught you by word or by letter. [16] May Christ Jesus, our Lord, who has loved us, and God our Father, who, in his mercy, gives us everlasting comfort and true hope, strengthen you. [17] May he encourage your hearts and make you steadfast in every good work and word.

3 [1] Finally, brothers and sisters, pray for us that the word of God may spread rapidly and be glorified everywhere, as it was with you. [2] May God guard us from wicked and evil people since not everyone has faith. [3] The Lord is faithful; he will strengthen you and keep you safe from the evil one. [4] Besides, we have, in the Lord, this confidence that you are doing, and will continue to do what we order you. [5] May the Lord direct your hearts to the love of God and to the steadfastness of Christ.

---

2 THESSALONIANS 2:1—3:5

Read: Paul admonishes the Thessalonian community not to be intimated by the fatalistic messages about the definitive coming of the Lord. He urges the Thessalonians to remain steadfast in the Good News that he preached them.

Reflect: Do you often listen to fatalistic news about the end of the world? What do you feel? Does the coming of the Lord bring joy or fear to you? What are your greatest worries?

Pray: Pray for those who live without hope or are afraid about the future. Ask the Lord for strength for you and your people so that fear and dejection will not be an obstacle to stand up for the Gospel and you may do good at all moments.

Act: Talk with your family and with your community about the final hope we Christians have: the joyful and definitive encounter with the Lord, and the need to be prepared for that.

Let everyone work

[6] We command you, beloved, to stay away from believers who are living in idleness, contrary to the traditions we passed on to you. [7] You

know how you ought to follow our example: we worked while we were with you. ⁸Day and night we labored and toiled so as not to be a burden to any of you. ⁹We had the right to act otherwise, but we wanted to give you an example.

¹⁰Besides, while we were with you, we said clearly: If anyone is not willing to work, neither should that one eat. ¹¹However, we heard that some among you live in idleness—busybodies, doing no work. ¹²In the name of Christ Jesus, our Lord, we command these people to work and earn their own living. ¹³And you, brothers and sisters, do not weary in doing what is right.

¹⁴If someone does not obey our instruction in this letter, take note and do not have anything to do with him, so that he may be ashamed.

¹⁵However, do not treat him as an enemy, but warn him as a brother.

¹⁶May the Lord of peace give you his peace at all times and in every way. May the Lord be with you all.

¹⁷I, Paul, write this greeting with my own hand. This is my signature in all my letters. This is how I write.

¹⁸May the grace of Christ Jesus our Lord be with you.

2 THESSALONIANS 3:6-18

Read: Paul advises the members of the community to be diligent and not be dependent on others. Thus, he said, "You know, how you ought to follow our example: we worked while we were with you. Day and night we labored and toiled so as not to be a burden to any of you." He also reminds them to always do what is right.

Reflect: What does the following text say to you: "If anyone is not willing to work, neither should that one eat." Can a Christian live at the expense of others? Is it easy to always do what is right? What are the challenges that you find?

Pray: Ask for peace and collaboration among the members of your community that they may always enjoy a decent work and always do what is right.

Act: Share with your people the importance for a Christian to work diligently. Do your assignments the best possible way, as a thanksgiving offering to God for the gift of work.

PASTORAL LETTERS TO
TIMOTHY and TITUS

I t is impossible to present Paul's letters to Timothy and Titus, the so-called Pastoral Letters, without dealing first with their authenticity. For over a century, many specialists have deemed it proven that they were not Paul's but that they were written after the death of the apostles Peter and Paul, under the cover of their authority, to deal with the problems of a new generation of Christians.

However, all the hypotheses attributing these letters to a disciple of Paul writing long after him also raise serious objections. We will more readily accept their authenticity if we notice that they contain many medical terms which lead us to discern the collaboration of Luke, the physician (Col 4:14). Luke was with Paul when he wrote the second letter to Timothy (4:11). On the other hand, these letters are not only meant for Paul's assistants; they could also be a type of circular letter that Paul wrote upon their request to help them to structure and to discipline the communities.

These three letters are addressed to pastors of souls, more precisely to two close collaborators of Paul and this is why, as a whole, they are called Pastoral Epistles. Like Paul, his delegates Timothy and Titus were like itinerant ministers. Although they did not enjoy the title of apostles (they were more like evangelists: 2 Tim 4:5; Acts 21:8; Eph 4:11), they had authority over the local churches and they were particularly interested in the guidelines concerning the choice and responsibilities of their ministers or pastors.

So the organization of the Church is based on two types of ministries. The first, with Timothy and Titus as examples, extends the mission of the apostles and it enjoys apostolic authority. The others remain involved with the community that presented them to exercise their responsibilities (see Acts 6:1-5 and 1 Tim 5:22). Whether they are called *episcopes* (overseers), *presbyters* (elders) or *deacons* (in charge of serving), these ministers who perform a special role for the proclamation of the word and the Eucharist, continue to belong to their families and the community.

We will have to strive to understand this complementarity, considering the evolution of the Latin Church. Within a few centuries, it unified these very different ministries within the framework of a hierarchized clergy. See the commentaries on Numbers 4:1 and Hebrews 9:1 on this topic.

The choice of the people responsible for the churches was not the only objective of these letters. They provide guidelines for the life of Christian communities as they no longer expect an imminent return of Christ and they have to learn how to persevere. They also insist on fidelity to the *tradition* of the apostles. For the Greeks, the Christian message was just as difficult to accept, as it was for the Jews, and even people of goodwill heard the message (and distorted it), just as we do, through their own way of thinking. Some wanted to do better than the apostles, to choose what fit or did not fit the perspectives of their own culture. In the end, some people were taking the liberty of teaching their own doctrine. People are quick to replace the imitation of Christ by eloquent speeches!

Therefore, the successors of the apostles had to defend the doctrine—this term comes up more than once—that they had received and Paul reminds them that the cult of the word of God goes hand in hand with the fidelity to the message received from the apostles.

FIRST LETTER TO
TIMOTHY

1 ¹From Paul, an apostle of Christ Jesus, by command of God, our Savior, and of Christ Jesus, our hope, ²to Timothy, my true son in the faith.

May God the Father, and Christ Jesus, our Lord, give you grace, mercy, and peace.

False teachers

³When I left for Macedonia, I urged you to remain in Ephesus to warn certain persons not to teach false doctrine, ⁴or to concern themselves with fables and endless genealogies. These give rise to discussions rather than promoting a better service of God through faith. ⁵The aim of our warning is love, which comes from a pure mind, a good conscience and sincere faith.

⁶Some have turned away from such motivation and have strayed into useless discussions. ⁷They claim to be teachers of the law when, in fact, they understand neither what they say nor the things they speak about.

⁸We know that the law is good, as long as it serves its purpose. ⁹The law is not for the righteous, but for the lawless, and for the wicked and sinful, for those who do not respect God, and religion, for those who kill their parents, for murderers, ¹⁰for those who indulge in unlawful sex and homosexuality, for kidnappers and exploiters, for liars and perjurers, and for all that is contrary to sound doctrine, ¹¹to the gospel of the God of glory and happiness which was entrusted to me.

¹²I give thanks to Christ Jesus, our Lord, who is my strength, who has considered me trustworthy, and appointed me to his service, ¹³although I had been a blasphemer, a persecutor, and a fanatical enemy. However, he took mercy on me because I did not know what I was doing when I

opposed the faith; ¹⁴and the grace of our Lord was more than abundant, together with faith and love that are in Christ Jesus.

¹⁵This saying is true and worthy of belief: Christ Jesus came into the world to save sinners, of whom I am the first. ¹⁶Because of that, I was forgiven; Christ Jesus wanted to display his utmost patience so that I might be an example for all who are to believe, and obtain eternal life. ¹⁷To the King of ages, the only God who lives beyond every perishable and visible creation—to him, be honor and glory forever. Amen!

¹⁸Timothy, my son, I command you to fight the good fight, fulfilling the prophetic words pronounced over you. ¹⁹Hold onto faith and a good conscience, unlike those who, ignoring conscience, have finally wrecked their faith. ²⁰Among them are Hymeneus and Alexander, whom I have delivered to Satan to be taught not to blaspheme.

---

1 TIMOTHY 1:1-20

Read: As time passes and leaders change, there is a great need to be sure that teaching remains faithful and does not become distorted. Paul speaks about the need for laws to control evil. He speaks about God's mercy toward sinners, using himself as an example.

Reflect: Are the teachings you have received about Jesus and Christian life based on the Gospel? In your opinion, what is the most important teaching of Jesus? How has God been merciful to you?

Pray: Ask the Holy Spirit to fill you with wisdom so that your heart and mind strengthens your trust in Christ Jesus and remains open to a deeper understanding of his teachings.

Act: Deepen your knowledge of Jesus and his Gospel. Commit to some spiritual reading. If possible, join a bible study.

---

2 ¹First of all, I urge that petitions, prayers, intercessions, and thanksgivings be made for everyone, ²for rulers of states and all in authority, that we may enjoy a quiet and peaceful life in godliness and respect. ³This is good and pleases God. ⁴For he wants all to be saved and come to the knowledge of truth. ⁵As there is one God, there is one mediator between God and humankind, Christ Jesus, himself human, ⁶who gave his life for the redemption of all. This is the testimony, given in its proper time, [7] and of this God has made me apostle and herald. I am not lying, I am telling the truth: He made me teacher of the nations regarding faith and truth.

[8] I want the men in every place to lift pure hands in prayer to heaven, without anger and dissension.

[9] Let women dress with simplicity and modesty, not adorned with fancy hairstyles, gold, jewels, and expensive clothes, [10] but with good works, as is fitting for women serving God. [11] Let a woman quietly receive instruction and be submissive. [12] I allow no woman to teach, or to have authority over men. Let them be quiet. [13] For Adam was created first and then Eve. [14] Adam was not deceived; it was the woman who was deceived and fell into sin. [15] But she will be saved through motherhood, provided that her life be orderly and holy, in faith and love.

---

1 TIMOTHY 2:1-15

Read: Paul urges the community that petitions, intercessions, and thanksgiving are made for everyone. The role of women in this passage is not meant to be taken literally. It reflects the limitations of his time, not to the eternal truth of the Gospel. Both men and women should pray, and their faith be expressed in everyday life.

Reflect: Do you always pray every day? Do you pray for your government officials in spite of political differences? What is it that you expect mainly from God? What do you think about the participation of women in the life of the Church? What should the Church do to protect and enhance the rights of women?

Pray: Present to the Lord all your worries and anxieties. Trust in Him; with his help, we can overcome everything. Ask the Holy Spirit to renew the hearts and minds of the members of your community so that the dignity and place of women be always respected and valued.

Act: Reserve a time for prayer every day. Invite your people to accompany you.

Regarding overseers and deacons

3 [1] If someone aspires to the overseer's ministry, he is without a doubt looking for a noble task. [2] It is necessary that the overseer (or bishop) be beyond reproach, the husband of one wife, responsible, judicious, of good manners, hospitable, and skillful in teaching. [3] He must not be addicted to wine, or quarrelsome, but gentle and peaceful, and not a lover of money, [4] but a man whose household is well managed, with obedient and well-mannered children. [5] If he cannot govern his own house, how can he lead the assembly of God?

[6] He must not be a recent convert, lest he becomes conceited and falls into the same condemnation as the devil. [7] Moreover, he must enjoy a good reputation among the outsiders, lest people speak evil about him and he falls into the snare of the devil.

[8] Deacons, likewise, must be serious and sincere, and moderate in drinking wine, not greedy for money; [9] they must keep the mystery of faith with a clear conscience. [10] Let them be first tried and, if found blameless, be accepted as deacons. [11] In the same way, the women must be conscientious, not given to gossip, but reserved and trustworthy.

[12] A deacon must be the husband of one wife, and must know how to guide his children and manage his household. [13] Those who serve well as deacons will win honorable rank, with authority to speak of Christian faith.

[14] I give you these instructions, although I hope I will see you soon. [15] If I delay, you will know how you ought to conduct yourself in the household of God, that is the Church of the living God, which is the pillar and foundation of the truth. [16] How great, indeed, is the mystery of divine blessing!

He was shown in the flesh
and sanctified by the spirit;
presented to the angels
and proclaimed to all nations.
The world believed in him:
He was taken up in glory!

4 [1] The Spirit tells us clearly that in the last days some will defect from the faith, and follow deceitful spirits and devilish doctrines, [2] led by lying hypocrites whose consciences have been branded with the stamp of infamy.

³These persons forbid marriage, and condemn the use of certain foods, which God created for those who know the truth, and which the believers receive with thanksgiving. ⁴Everything created by God is good, and all food is lawful; nothing is to be rejected, if we receive it with thanksgiving, ⁵for it is blessed with the word of God and prayer and made holy.

⁶If you explain these things to the brothers and sisters, you will prove to be a good servant of Christ Jesus, nourished by the teachings of faith and the sound doctrine that you have followed. ⁷Reject irreligious fables and old wives' tales. Train yourself in godliness. ⁸Physical training is of limited value; godliness, instead, is useful in every way, holding promise for the present life and for the life to come. ⁹Here, you have a sure doctrine you can trust. ¹⁰We toil and endure, because we trust in the living God, the Savior of all, especially of those who believe.

Advice to Timothy

¹¹Command and teach these things. ¹²Let no one reproach you on account of your youth. Be a model to the believers in the way you speak and act, in your love, your faith and purity of life. ¹³Devote yourself to reading, preaching, and teaching until I come.

¹⁴Do not neglect the spiritual gift conferred on you with prophetic words when the elders laid their hands upon you. ¹⁵Think about it, and practice it, so that your progress may be seen by all. ¹⁶Take heed of yourself and attend to your teaching. Be steadfast in doing this and you will save both yourself and your hearers.

1 TIMOTHY 3:1—4:16

Read: Paul offers practical advice to those who serve in leadership positions in the Church. Their lives should reflect the gospel.

Reflect: What is your role in your domestic Church, that is, your family? How do you show it to your people? How do you train yourself in godliness?

Pray: Ask for the help of the Holy Spirit that your life may always be a witness of service and devotion to others. Ask also that your Christian community members may always be free from

> aspiring for titles and privileges and give priority to live the Gospel of Jesus.
>
> **Act:** Go to your parish and offer your services for whatever needs they may have.

The widows in the Church

5 [1] Do not rebuke an older man; on the contrary, advise him as if he were your father. Treat the young as your brothers, [2] the elder women as mothers, and the young girls as your sisters, with great purity.

[3] Take care of widows who are really widows. [4] If a widow has children or grandchildren, they should first learn their family duties and give their parents financial help. This is correct and pleases God.

[5] A true widow is one who, on being left alone, has set her hope on God, praying day and night to God, and asking him for help. [6] On the contrary, a widow who lives for pleasure is dead even while she lives. [7] Warn them about this that they may be blameless. [8] Those who do not take care of their own, especially those of their household, have denied the faith and are worse than unbelievers.

[9] Let no one be put on the list of widows unless she is sixty years old and has been married only once. [10] She must be commended for her good works and the education of her children. Has she offered hospitality, washed the feet of the saints, helped the suffering and practiced other good deeds?

[11] Do not accept younger widows; they may have other desires than for Christ and want to marry; [12] then they deserve condemnation for breaking their first commitment. [13] Besides, they form the habit of being idle, going from house to house. And it is not just idleness! They become gossips and busybodies, saying what they should not.

[14] So I want young widows to marry and have children, to rule their household and give adversaries no grounds for criticism. [15] Some have already strayed to follow Satan. [16] If any Christian woman has widows in her family, let her assist them; in this way, the church will not be burdened and may assist those who are truly widows.

Regarding the presbyters

[17] Let the elders who preside well receive double compensation, especially

those who labor in preaching and teaching. [18]Scripture says: *Do not muzzle the ox while it threshes grain*, and: *The worker deserves his wages.*

[19]Do not accept accusations against an elder except on the evidence of two or three witnesses. [20]If he continues to sin, rebuke him in the presence of the community, as a warning to the rest.

[21]I urge you, in the presence of God and Christ Jesus and of the holy angels, to obey these rules with impartiality, without making distinctions. [22]Do not be hasty in the laying on of hands, thus becoming an accomplice in the sins of others. Keep yourself free from blame. [24]The sins of some people are plain to see, even before they are examined; the sins of others are known only later on. [25]Likewise, good deeds are conspicuous; even when they are not, they cannot remain hidden.

[23](Do not drink only water but take a little wine to help your digestion, because of your frequent illness.)

6 [1]Let those who are slaves always show respect to their masters, so that no one may speak ill of God and his teaching. [2]Those whose masters are Christians should not show less respect, under the pretext that they are members of the church. On the contrary, they must give a better service, since they are doing good works on behalf of believers and dear friends.

---

1 TIMOTHY 5:1—6:2a

Read: Paul continues to offer practical advice for service to the community (about widows, the elderly, presbyters, slaves). Underlying these advices there is a sense of justice, prudence, and compassion.

Reflect: A lot of attention is given to widows because in that day they, like many elderly who could no longer work, had no means of support. Attention to the vulnerable is important in Christian life. The comments about women reflect the prejudices of the day and should not be read literally.

Pray: Pray for yourself and for your parish that you be generous and concerned about those in need.

Act: Visit an elderly relative or neighbor and listen to their stories. Ask if your parish has a ministry to nursing homes.

Love of money

Teach and stress these things. ³Whoever teaches in some other way, not following the sound teaching of our Lord Christ Jesus, and true religious instruction, ⁴is conceited and understands nothing. This one is crazy about controversies and discussions that result in envy, insults, ⁵blows and constant arguments between people of depraved minds, and far from the truth. For them, religion is merely for financial gain.

⁶In reality, religion is a treasure, if we are content with what we have. ⁷We brought nothing into the world and we will leave it with nothing. ⁸Let us then be content with having food and clothing. ⁹Those who strive to be rich fall into temptations and traps. A lot of foolish and harmful ambitions plunge them into ruin and destruction. ¹⁰Indeed, the love of money is the root of every evil. Because of this greed, some have wandered away from the faith, bringing on themselves afflictions of every kind.

¹¹But you, man of God, shun all this. Strive to be holy and godly. Live in faith and love, with endurance and gentleness. ¹²Fight the good fight of faith and win everlasting life, to which you were called when you made the good profession of faith in the presence of so many witnesses.

¹³Now, in the presence of God, who gives life to all things, and of Jesus Christ, who expressed before Pontius Pilate the authentic profession of faith: ¹⁴preserve the message revealed to all. Keep yourself pure and blameless until the glorious coming of Christ Jesus, our Lord, ¹⁵who God will bring about at the proper time; he, the magnificent sovereign, King of kings and Lord of lords. ¹⁶To him, alone immortal, who lives in unapproachable light, and whom no one has ever seen or can see, to him be honor and power, for ever and ever. Amen!

¹⁷Command the rich of this world not to be arrogant, or to put their trust in the uncertainty of wealth. Let them, rather, trust in God who generously gives us all we need for our happiness. ¹⁸Let them do good, be rich in good deeds, and be generous; let them share with others. ¹⁹In this way, they shall heap up a sound capital for the future, and gain true life.

²⁰Timothy, guard what has been entrusted to you; avoid useless and profane words, as well as discussions arising from false knowledge. ²¹Some have lost the faith in accepting such knowledge.

The grace of God be with you all.

1 TIMOTHY 6:2b-21

Read: Finally, Paul admonishes Timothy not to fall for riches for "the love of money is the root of every evil." A man of God strives for justice, faith, and love. Thus, Paul also recommends that Timothy helps the rich people put their trust in God and not on the material things they have accumulated.

Reflect: How does love of money lead to evil today? How does it affect you? To be rich in good works, generous and ready to share is Paul's advice, in what ways is this part of your spiritual life?

Pray: Ask that God may always be in our heart so that you may be a generous and good person. Give Him thanks for all the gifts you have received.

Act: Make today a gesture of service and generosity, be it in your home or in the parish community, that it may show that you have your hope in God and not in material possessions.

SECOND LETTER TO
TIMOTHY

Read the introduction to the first letter to Timothy. While the
first letter to Timothy showed us that Paul was still free to move
about, he wrote this letter from one of his prisons. Which one?
One of Paul's remarks about the Christians who assisted him (2 Tim
1:17) seems to suggest Rome. That would be around the years 61–63
A.D., or even later, during Paul's second captivity in Rome shortly before
he was condemned to death. However, this traditional interpretation
was based on a bad translation of this passage. The themes of this letter
show that it must have been written from Caesarea where Paul was de-
tained before Governor Felix (Acts 24). The letter would have come only
a few months after the first one.

Paul speaks about his being a prisoner, a new situation that threatens
to be ongoing. Then he focuses his attention on the place of failure and
suffering within God's plan. The apparent failure of many Christian lives
after a conversion and promising beginnings and the suffering of the
apostle in chains on account of the Gospel. At times, he envisions the

worst and appears ready to sacrifice his life, as in Philippians 1:20. But at other times, he comes back to the conviction that we also read in Philippians 1:19: this captivity forms part of his mission and it will enable him to bear witness to the Gospel before the highest authorities of the Roman Empire.

Some people think Paul could not have written Chapter 3: it seems foreign to Paul's style and his concerns. We can easily compare 2 Timothy 3:1-5 with two paragraphs of Romans 1:29-32 and 3:10-19 and see that there is nothing new here. And the rest of this chapter takes up what we read in Romans 15:5 and 13. The style of this chapter might be surprising if it had been a letter meant to remain private, but this is certainly not the case. Even though he was addressing Timothy, Paul knew that the letter, not devoid of rhetoric, would be read.

Let us not forget that since leaving Miletus and even more after his arrest in the temple (Acts 21:27), Paul had turned the page. He had said goodbye to the Jewish world as well as to the Greek world that he knew and loved. He was not mistaken to foresee a rather dark future.

Timothy was the first and the most loved of Paul's assistants. Paul would like to pass on to him his own strength and apostolic conviction. Therefore, Paul reminds him that meditation and knowledge of the word of God form the foundation of a life of faith and of apostolic activity.

SECOND LETTER TO
TIMOTHY

1 ¹From Paul, an apostle of Christ Jesus, by the will of God, for the sake of his promise of eternal life in Christ Jesus, ²to my dear son Timothy.

May grace, mercy, and peace be with you from God the Father, and Christ Jesus our Lord.

God did not give us a spirit of bashfulness

³I give thanks to God, whom I serve with a clear conscience the way my ancestors did as I remember you constantly, day and night, in my prayers. ⁴I recall your tears and I long to see you that I may be filled with joy. I am reminded of your sincere faith, ⁵so like the faith of your grandmother Lois and of your mother Eunice, which I am sure you have inherited.

⁶For this reason, I invite you to fan into a flame the gift of God you received through the laying on of my hands. ⁷For God did not confer on us a spirit of fearfulness, but of strength, love, and good judgment. ⁸Do not be ashamed of testifying to our Lord, nor of seeing me in chains. On the contrary, do your share in laboring for the gospel with the strength of God. ⁹He saved us and called us—a calling which proceeds from his holiness. This did not depend on our merits but on his generosity and his own initiative. This calling, given to us in Christ Jesus before time began ¹⁰has just been manifested by the glorious appearance of Christ Jesus, our Lord, who destroyed death, and brought life and immortality to light in his gospel. ¹¹Of this message, I was made herald, apostle, and teacher.

¹²For its sake, I now suffer this trial, but I am not ashamed, for I know in whom I have believed, and I am convinced that he is capable of taking care of all I have entrusted to him, until that day.

¹³Follow the pattern of the sound doctrine, which you have heard from

me concerning faith and love in Christ Jesus. [14] Keep this precious deposit with the help of the Holy Spirit who lives within us.

[15] You must know that those from Asia have turned away from me, including Phygelus and Hermogenes. [16] May the Lord show his mercy to the household of Onesiphorus because he often comforted me and was not ashamed when he found out that I was in prison. [17] On the contrary, he showed courage, searched for me and found me. [18] May the Lord grant that he find mercy on that day. You know better than I, all the services he rendered in Ephesus.

---

2 TIMOTHY 1:1-18

Read: Paul expresses his affection and admiration for Timothy. He anticipates that Timothy, like Paul is doing now, experience hardships. His advice is "Follow the pattern of the sound doctrine which you have heard from me, concerning faith, and love in Christ Jesus. Keep this precious deposit, with the help of the Holy Spirit, who lives within us."

Reflect: Paul expresses gratitude for Timothy and his mother and grandmother. Who are the women who have strengthened your faith? When you experience hardship, how does faith help you?

Pray: Offer a prayer of thanks for those who brought you to believe and those that help you believe. As Paul said, pray for the spirit of power, love and self-discipline in times of hardship.

Act: It is good to pray for people who help you believe, but it would be really good if you could say or write a word of appreciation for them. That would strengthen them.

Labor like a good soldier of Christ

2 [1] You, my son, be strong with the grace you have in Christ Jesus. [2] Entrust to reliable people everything you have learned from me in the presence of many witnesses that they may instruct others.

[3] Labor like a good soldier of Christ Jesus. [4] No soldier gets involved in civilian trade; the soldier's aim is to please his commanding officer. [5] No athlete is crowned unless he competes according to the rules. [6] And again, the farmer who tills the land is the first to enjoy the fruits of the

harvest. [7] Think over what I am telling you; the Lord will give you understanding in everything.

[8] Remember Christ Jesus, risen from the dead, Jesus, son of David, as preached in my gospel. [9] For this gospel, I labor and even wear chains like an evildoer, but the word of God is not chained. [10] And so, I bear everything for the sake of the chosen people, that they too may obtain the salvation given to us, in Christ Jesus, and share eternal glory. [11] This statement is true:

If we have died with him, we shall also live with him;

[12] *If we endure with him, we shall reign with him;*

If we deny him, he will also deny us;

[13] *If we are unfaithful, he remains faithful for he cannot deny himself.*

Do not fight over words

[14] Remind your people of these things, and urge them in the presence of God, not to fight over words, which does no good, but only ruins those who listen. [15] Be for God, an active and proven minister, a blameless worker, correctly handling the word of truth. [16] Do not take part in useless conversations, alien to the faith. This leads to a greater impiety. [17] Such teaching spreads like gangrene: I am thinking of Hymeneus and Philetus. [18] They strayed from the truth, holding that the resurrection has already taken place; and with this, they upset the faith of some. [19] But the solid foundations laid by God are not shaken; on them, it is written: *The Lord knows those who are his, and: Let him who confesses the name of the Lord turn away from evil.*

[20] In a large house, we find, not only vessels of gold and silver, but also of wood and clay. Some are reserved for special uses, others for ordinary ones. [21] All who clean themselves of what I speak of will become a noble vessel, useful to the Lord, prepared for any holy purpose.

[22] So shun the passions of youth and seek righteousness, faith, love, and peace, together with those who call upon the Lord with a pure heart. [23] Avoid stupid and senseless discussions since such are the causes of misunderstanding. [24] God's servant must not be quarrelsome, but kind to all, always teaching, and patient with those who do not understand, [25] and gently correcting opponents; perhaps God may grant them to repent and discover the truth, [26] withdrawing them from the snare of the devil who held them captive to his own will.

---

2 TIMOTHY 2:1-26

Read: Paul uses many metaphors to encourage Timothy: a soldier, an athlete, a farmer, his own experience, the experience of Jesus, even a kitchen! He is to pursue righteousness, faith, love, peace and gentleness.

Reflect: Do any of the metaphors used strike a note with you? Paul cautions against wrangling over words, being quarrelsome, and gossiping. How do these ruin a church community?

Pray: Ask from the Lord the grace to be able to share with the members of your community the faith you have received, so that your life and the life of your family may be a living witness of the Gospel.

Act: Engage yourself in the evangelizing work in your parish. Offer personal and economic support to the works of your church community.

---

3 ¹Be quite sure that there will be difficult times in the last days. ²People will become selfish, lovers of money, boastful, conceited, gossipers, disobedient to their parents, ungrateful, impious. ³They will be unable to love and to forgive; they will be slanderers, without self-control, cruel, enemies of good, ⁴traitors, shameless, full of pride, more in love with pleasure than with God. ⁵They will keep the appearance of piety while rejecting its demands. Keep away from such people.

⁶Of the same kind are those who enter houses and captivate weak women full of sins, swayed by all kinds of passion, ⁷who are always learning, but never grasping the knowledge of the truth. ⁸These people of corrupt mind and false faith oppose the truth, just as Jannes and Jambres opposed Moses. ⁹Yet, they may not go very far, for their folly will be clear to all, as in the case of those two.

¹⁰You, instead, have closely followed my teaching, my way of life, my projects, faith, patience, love, endurance, ¹¹persecutions, and sufferings. You know what happened to me at Antioch, Iconium, and Lystra. How many trials I had to bear! Yet, the Lord rescued me from them all. ¹²All who want to serve God, in Christ Jesus, will be persecuted; ¹³while evil

persons and impostors will go from bad to worse, deceiving and being deceived.

¹⁴As for you, continue with what you have learned and what has been entrusted to you, knowing from whom you received it. ¹⁵Besides, you have known the Scriptures from childhood; they will give you the wisdom that leads to salvation through faith in Christ Jesus. ¹⁶All Scripture is inspired by God, and is useful for teaching, refuting error, for correcting and training in Christian life. ¹⁷Through Scripture, the man of God is made expert and thoroughly equipped for every good work.

Preach the word

4 ¹In the presence of God and Christ Jesus, who is to judge the living and the dead, and by the hope I have of his coming and his kingdom, I urge you ²to preach the word in season and out of season, reproving, rebuking, or advising, always with patience, and providing instruction. ³For the time is coming when people will no longer endure sound doctrine, but, following their passions, they will surround themselves with teachers to please their itching ears. ⁴And they will abandon the truth to hear fables. ⁵So be prudent, do not mind your labor, give yourself to your work as an evangelist, fulfill your ministry.

2 TIMOTHY 3:1—4:5

Read: Timothy is warned to avoid people who are lovers of themselves and of money and selfish in the way they act with others. When persecuted he should find strength in the Scripture. In good and bad times Christians must proclaim the message of Jesus Christ.

Reflect: How do you keep your faith when other Christians, especially leaders, do not live in a way that is faithful to the gospel?

Pray: Give thanks to God for the leaders and ministers of your community, especially your parish priest. Ask that he may: "Preach the word, in season and out of season...give yourself to your work as an evangelist, fulfill your ministry" (4:2-5). Ask also for yourself that, with the help of the Holy Spirit, you can actively collaborate in the life of your parish.

> **Act:** All scripture is inspired by God and is useful for teaching, correction and training in righteousness. Set aside time to read and study the Bible.

[6] As for me, I am already poured out as a libation and the moment of my departure has come. [7] I have fought the good fight, I have finished the race, I have kept the faith. [8] Now, there is laid up for me the crown of righteousness with which the Lord, the just judge, will reward me on that day, and not only me but all those who have longed for his glorious coming.

Final greetings

[9] Do your best to come to me quickly. [10] You must know that Demas has deserted me for the love of this world: he returned to Thessalonica. Crescens has gone to Galatia, and Titus to Dalmatia. [11] Only Luke remains with me. Get Mark and bring him with you, for he is a useful helper in my work. [12] I sent Tychicus to Ephesus.

[13] Bring with you the cloak I left at Troas, in Carpos' house, and also the scrolls, especially the parchments. [14] Alexander, the metalworker, has caused me great harm. The Lord will repay him for what he has done. [15] Distrust him, for he has been very much opposed to our preaching.

[16] At my first hearing in court, no one supported me; all deserted me. May the Lord not hold it against them. [17] But the Lord was at my side, giving me the strength to proclaim the word fully and let all the pagans hear it. So I was rescued from the lion's mouth. [18] The Lord will save me from all evil, bringing me to his heavenly kingdom. Glory to him for ever and ever. Amen!

[19] Greetings to Prisca and Aquila, and to the family of Onesiphorus. [20] Erastus remained in Corinth. I left Trophimus sick in Miletus.

[21] Try to come here before the winter. Eubulus, Pudens, Linus, Claudia, and all the brothers and sisters send you greetings. [22] The Lord be with your spirit.

May grace be with you all.

2 TIMOTHY 4:6-22

Read: Paul realizes his time is limited: "I have fought the good fight, I have finished the race, I have kept the faith." His hope is completely in the Lord. But he is not alone; together with him are Lucas, Eubulus, Pudens, Linus, Claudia, and all the brothers and sisters.

Reflect: Do you know people who have given up everything for the announcement of the Gospel? Does their life example help you to deepen your faith and Christian life? Do you consider yourself an active member of your community? If you were the parish priest: What would you expect from the members of the community? Do you support the pastoral activity of your parish or diocese?

Pray: Give thanks to God for all the people who give witness to the Gospel with their lives. Pray for all the ordained ministers of the Church, that the example of Paul may help them to be faithful and generous in their service.

Act: "I have fought the good fight, I have finished the race, I have kept the faith." Live so these words are your own.

LETTER TO
TITUS

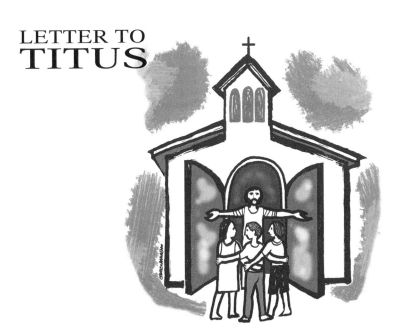

This letter appears to be the first of the Pastoral Letters: see the introduction to the first letter to Timothy.

This was early in the year 58 A.D. and shortly before, Paul had written a letter to the Christians of Rome. Paul thinks that he does not have any more work to do in the eastern part of the Roman Empire and he prepares to go to the western part of the Empire, especially Spain. In fact, God had planned things differently: in a short time, Paul would be arrested in Jerusalem and after several years of captivity in Caesarea, he would be taken to Rome to be tried before the emperor's tribunal.

Paul said goodbye to the communities of Greece and of "Asia," the province of the empire corresponding to western Turkey (Acts 20:25). It was no doubt the day before meeting with the presbyters (elders) of the Ephesus area, a meeting that took place in Miletus (Acts 20:1), that Paul wrote this letter that precisely gives special attention to pastors of the Christian communities. The other important points of the letter deal with the duties of Christians according to their situation in society, respect for their social obligations and submission to authorities. Here, Paul repeats or develops what he had presented in the second part of the letter to the Romans. This same letter inspires him a few shortcuts about God's plan that we find in 1:3-4; 2:11-14 and 3:4:7.

Paul was already thinking about his journey to Rome. He did not know that he was going to be arrested in Jerusalem and he planned to go to the capital of the empire by land after handing the collection he had brought over to the Jerusalem Christians (Rom 15:25-28). One of the stages was Nicopolis on the west coast of Greece, an area that Paul had evangelized (Rom 15:19) and where he had arranged to meet Titus who was in Crete.

LETTER TO **TITUS**

1 ¹From Paul, a servant of God, an apostle of Christ Jesus, at the service of God's chosen people, so that they may believe and reach the knowledge of truth and godliness.

²The eternal life we are waiting for was promised from the very beginning by God who never lies, ³and as the appointed time had come, he made it known through the message entrusted to me by a command of God, our Savior.

⁴Greetings to you, Titus, my true son in the faith we share. May grace and peace be with you from God the Father and Christ Jesus our Lord.

On the elders of the Church

⁵I left you in Crete because I wanted you to put right what was defective, and appoint elders in every town following my instructions. ⁶They must be blameless, married only once, whose children are believers, and not open to the charge of being immoral and rebellious. ⁷Since the overseer (or bishop) is the steward of God's House, he must be beyond reproach: not proud, hotheaded, over-fond of wine, quarrelsome, or greedy for gain.

⁸On the contrary, he must be hospitable, a lover of what is good, wise, upright, devout, and self-controlled. ⁹He must hold to the message of faith, just as it was taught, so that in his turn, he may teach sound doctrine and refute those who oppose it.

¹⁰You know that there are many rebellious minds, talkers of nonsense, deceivers, especially the party of the circumcised. ¹¹They have to be silenced when they go around disturbing whole families, teaching, for low gain, what should not be taught. ¹²A Cretan, one of their own prophets, has said, "Cretans: always liars, wicked beasts and lazy gluttons." ¹³This is true. For this reason, rebuke them sharply if you want them to have a

sound faith [14] instead of heeding Jewish fables, and practices of people who reject the truth.

[15] To the pure, everything is pure; to the corrupt and unbelieving, nothing is pure: their minds and consciences have been defiled. [16] They pretend to know God but deny him with their deeds. They are detestable, disobedient, and unfit for doing anything good.

Live as responsible persons

2 [1] Let your words strengthen sound doctrine. [2] Tell the older men to be sober, serious, wise, sound in faith, love, and perseverance.

[3] The older women, in like manner, must behave as befits holy women, not given to gossiping or drinking wine, [4] but as good counselors, able to teach younger women to love their husbands and children, [5] to be judicious and chaste, to take care of their households, to be kind, and submissive to their husbands, lest our faith be attacked.

[6] Encourage the young men to be self-controlled. [7] Set them an example by your own way of doing. Let your teaching be earnest and sincere, [8] and your preaching, beyond reproach. Then your opponents will feel ashamed and will have nothing to criticize.

[9] Teach slaves to be subject to their masters, and to give satisfaction in every respect, instead of arguing. [10] They must not steal from them, but be trustworthy. In this way, they will draw everyone to admire the doctrine of God our Savior.

[11] For the grace of God has appeared, bringing salvation to all, [12] teaching us to reject an irreligious way of life, and worldly greed, and to live in this world as responsible persons, upright and serving God, [13] while we await our blessed hope—the glorious manifestation of our great God and Savior Christ Jesus. [14] He gave himself for us, to redeem us from every evil, and to purify a people he wanted to be his own, and dedicated to what is good.

[15] Teach these things, encourage, and reprove with all authority. Let no one despise you.

TITUS 1:1—2:15

Read: Titus has been entrusted with pastoring the Christian community on Crete. Titus has to hold himself to account as well as his fellow Christians, so their lives reflect Christ.

> **Reflect:** Living the faith we believe has always been a challenge, what is most challenging for you?
>
> **Pray:** Pray for yourself, so your life witnesses Jesus Christ. Pray for the church, who has always been made up of sinners that that they may be faithful witnesses of Jesus' message in their lives.
>
> **Act:** Paul's famous words: "I have fought the good fight, I have finished the race, I have kept the faith." Live so these words are your own.

3 [1] Remind the believers to be submissive to rulers and authorities, to be obedient, and to be ready for every good work. [2] Tell them to insult no one; they must not be quarrelsome, but gentle and understanding with everyone.

[3] We ourselves were once foolish, disobedient, and misled. We were slaves of our desires, seeking pleasures of every kind. We lived in malice and envy, hateful, and hating each other. [4] But God our Savior revealed his eminent goodness and love for humankind, [5] and saved us, not because of good deeds we may have done, but for the sake of his own mercy, to the water of rebirth and renewal by the Holy Spirit [6] poured over us through Christ Jesus our Savior, [7] so that, having been justified by his grace, we should become heirs, in hope of eternal life.

[8] This is the truth. I want you to insist on these things, for those who believe in God must excel in good deeds; that is what matters and is profitable to us. [9] Avoid stupid arguments, discussions about genealogies, and quarrels about the law for they are useless and unimportant.

[10] If anyone promotes sects in the church, warn him once, and then a second time. If he still continues, break with him, [11] knowing that such a person is misled, and sinful, and stands self-condemned.

[12] When I send Artemas or Tychicus to you, try to come to me at Nicopolis, as soon as possible, for I have decided to spend the winter there. [13] Do your best to send Zenas the lawyer, and Apollos, on their way soon, and see to it that they have everything they need. [14] Our people must learn to be outstanding in good works, and to face urgent needs, instead of remaining idle and useless.

¹⁵ All who are with me send greetings. Greet those who love us in the faith.

Grace be with you all.

TITUS 3:1-15

Read: Christians have to live in the world as good citizens, avoid those things that divide the church and be focused on the mercy of God.

Reflect: Paul exhorts to be humble and obedient. How is this manifested in your life and in the life of your community? How should the new person born by the Spirit behave today?

Pray: Ask forgiveness for the times you have given witness contrary to the Gospel and ask for strength so your deeds may show the faith that you profess.

Act: Try to live today with the awareness that your faith is manifested in everything you do, including the most habitual and ordinary tasks.

LETTER TO THE
HEBREWS

"Hebrews" was the name given to the Jews who lived in Palestine, unlike the majority who had emigrated to other countries. This letter is addressed to the first Christian communities of Palestine, formed by Jews—by race—who had been persecuted and punished and whose possessions had even been confiscated, all because they had become followers of Christ. They no longer had anything in this world and they had to encourage one another with the assurance that, at the conclusion of their exile, they would find the true Home where Jesus went after his suffering. In this way they were like their Hebrew ancestors who had lived in the desert, hoping and searching for the Promised Land.

It is helpful to know that this letter is addressed to people familiar with the Old Testament: they may well have been Jewish priests who had believed in Jesus and now were going through a serious crisis. Indeed, up until then, the temple had been their whole lives, since they were priests: they would offer sacrifices and would receive part of the sacrificed animals in payment. Now, not only had they been excluded and removed from the temple by the Jews, but Christ had replaced them. For he had come as the New Temple and the perfect victim pleasing to God, as the only priest capable of putting people in touch with God.

He had relegated the temple of Jerusalem and its cult to the rank of the outmoded. He, a layman, had organized his Church, disregarding the priesthood of the "sons of Aaron," the Jewish priests. The priest, he who is the link between humans and the all-holy God, was he and he alone.

So Christ had taken their work away from them, as well as their reason for being. At times, these men who had known Jesus, the man, had their doubts: was it certain that everything had changed because of him?

To confirm their faith, this letter shows them that the Jewish religion with its imposing ceremonies in the temple of Jerusalem was but the image of something greater. The pardon of sin and the spirit of religion— the aspiration of the entire Old Testament—was to be the work of the authentic priest of all humanity, Jesus, the Son of God. There is now no other sacrifice but his, which begins on the cross and ends in glory.

Are there not many "Hebrews" in today's world? The sick who no longer have hope, the persecuted Christians, the people who do not accept the injustice and mediocrity of the society in which we live. Although many of them may not understand all the premises and biblical quotations in this letter, they will feel encouraged in the faith.

Besides, the word "priest" has become so important in the Church that it is useful to find here the biblical text which has gone deeper into the meaning of priesthood and its reorientation through the very fact of the sacrifice of Jesus.

This letter was written in Rome, perhaps in the year 66, when the war in which Jerusalem was destroyed was approaching. These were the last months of Paul's life; he was imprisoned in Rome for the second time. This letter reflects Paul's thoughts, but he did not write it. It is quite possible that the author is Apollos, mentioned in Acts 18:24-28, "a man well-versed in Scriptures" and who "proved from the Scriptures (the Old Testament) that Jesus is the Messiah."

LETTER TO THE
HEBREWS

1 ¹God has spoken in the past to our ancestors through the prophets in many different ways, although never completely; ²but, in our times, he has spoken definitively to us through his Son.

He is the one God appointed heir of all things since, through him, he unfolded the stages of the world.

³He is the radiance of God's glory and bears the stamp of God's hidden being so that his powerful word upholds the universe. And after taking away sin, he took his place at the right hand of the divine Majesty in heaven.

⁴So he is now far superior to angels, just as the name he received sets him apart from them. ⁵To what angel did God say: *You are my son, I have begotten you today?* And to what angel did he promise: *I shall be a father to him and he will be a son to me?* ⁶On sending his Firstborn into the world, God says: *Let all the angels adore him.* ⁷Whereas, about angels, we find words like these: *God sends the angels like wind, makes his servants flames of fire.* ⁸But of the Son, we read this: *Your throne, O God, will last forever and ever; a rule of justice is your rule.* ⁹*You loved righteousness and hated wickedness; therefore God, your God, has anointed you with the oil of gladness above your fellow kings.*

¹⁰And also, these words: *Lord, in the beginning, you placed the earth on its foundation and the heavens are the work of your hands.* ¹¹*They will disappear, but you remain. They all wear out like a garment;* ¹²*you will fold them like a cloak, and change them. You, on the contrary, are always the same, and your years will never end.*

¹³God never said to any of his angels: *Sit here at my right side until I put your enemies as a footstool under your feet.* ¹⁴For all these spirits are only servants, and God sends them to help those who shall be saved.

HEBREWS 1:1-14

Read: This is a sermon about the Son of God: God created the universe through the Son, the reflection of God's glory, and the universe is sustained through His powerful word. If long ago, God has spoken through the prophets, now He speaks through His Son who purified the world of sins and is seated at God's right hand. No one can be compared to the Son of God, not even the angels.

Reflect: Christ is the center of creation and redemption. What does this passage suggest for your everyday life? Can you see his creative and redeeming presence in the world? The text says that now God speaks through His Son. Do you listen to His words? What do they tell you?

Pray: Help us, Lord, to contemplate the creative and saving presence of your Son. May we be able to accept his word and to transform our lives and give you glory.

Act: Repeat interiorly today what Christ represents for you. Before going to sleep give thanks to God for what you experienced in your heart and in your relationship with others.

2 ¹ So, we must pay the closest attention to the preaching we heard, lest we drift away. ² If words, spoken through angels, became law, and all disobedience or neglect received its due reward, ³ how could we now escape, if we neglect such powerful salvation? For the Lord himself announced it first, and it was later confirmed by those who heard it. ⁴ God confirmed their testimony by signs, wonders, and miracles of every kind—especially by the gifts of the Holy Spirit that he distributed according to his will.

⁵ The angels were not given dominion over the new world of which we are speaking. ⁶ Instead, someone declared in Scripture: *What is man that you should be mindful of him, what is the son of man that you should care for him?* ⁷ *For a while, you placed him a little lower than the angels, but you crowned him with glory and honor.* ⁸ *You have given him dominion over all things.*

When it is said that God gave him dominion over all things, nothing is excluded. As it is, we do not yet see his dominion over all things. [9] But Jesus, who suffered death, and *for a little while, was placed lower than the angels*, has been *crowned with honor and glory*. For the merciful plan of God demanded that he experience death on behalf of everyone.

[10] God, from whom all come, and by whom all things exist, wanted to bring many children to glory, and he thought it fitting to make perfect through suffering, the initiator of their salvation. [11] So, he who gives and those who receive holiness are one. He, himself, is not ashamed of calling us brothers and sisters, [12] as we read: *Lord, I will proclaim your name to my brothers; I will praise you in the congregation.* [13] He also says: *I will trust in God; here I am, and the children God has given me.* [14] And because all those children share one same nature of flesh and blood, Jesus, likewise, had to share this nature. This is why his death destroyed the one holding the power of death, that is, the devil, [15] and freed those who remained in bondage all their lifetime because of the fear of death.

[16] Jesus came to take by the hand, not the angels, but the human race. [17] So, he had to be like his brothers and sisters in every respect in order to be the high priest, faithful to God and merciful to them, a priest able to ask pardon and atone for their sins. [18] Having been tested through suffering, he is able to help those who are tested.

HEBREWS 2:1-18

Read: For the first time the author mentions Jesus. Jesus is the Son of God who overcame sin by obedience to the Father's will and by his solidarity with humanity. Because Jesus is like us, God perfected humanity through him. Likened to us in every respect, Jesus became a merciful and faithful high priest for the remission of sins.

Reflect: Jesus became one of us, he knows our weaknesses. He saved us because we are important to him and he loves us. Do you trust in Jesus' redemptive love? What does this text suggest to you: "Having been tested through suffering, he is able to help those who are tested" (v. 18)?

Pray: Lord God, through the sacrifice of your Son you have redeemed us; help us to remain firm in your love.

> **Act:** Read slowly chapter 17 of the Gospel of John and compare
> that chapter with the first two chapters of Hebrews. Try that
> the testimony of your faith may help your people to share the
> gift of salvation of Jesus to others.

Christ came as the new Moses

3 [1] Therefore, holy brothers, partners in a heavenly calling, consider Jesus, the apostle and high priest of our faith.

[2] He is faithful to God, who appointed him, just as Moses was *a faithful steward over God's household*; [3] but Jesus deserves much greater honor than Moses since he who builds the house is greater than the house. [4] As every house has a builder, God is the builder of all. [5] It is said that Moses was found faithful, *as a servant of God over all his household*, and as a witness of a former revelation from God. [6] Christ came as the Son to whom the house belongs; and we are his household, provided that we stand firm in hope and courage.

[7] Listen to what the Holy Spirit says: *If only you would hear God's voice today!* [8] *Do not be stubborn, as they were in the place called Rebellion,* [9] *when your ancestors challenged me in the desert, although they had seen my deeds* [10] *for forty years. That is why I was angry with those people and said: Their hearts are always going astray and they do not understand my ways.* [11] *I was angry and made a solemn vow: They will never enter my rest.*

[12] So, brothers, be careful, lest some of you come to have an evil and unbelieving heart that falls away from the living God. [13] Encourage one another, day by day, as long as it is called today. Let no one become hardened in the deceitful way of sin. [14] We are associated with Christ, provided we hold steadfastly to our initial hope until the end.

[15] Scripture says: *If you hear God's voice, do not be stubborn as they were in the place called Rebellion.* [16] Who are those who, having heard, still rebelled? They were all those who came out of Egypt with Moses. [17] With whom was God angry for forty years? With those who sinned and whose bodies fell in the desert. [18] To whom did God swear that they would not enter into his rest? To those who had disobeyed. [19] We see, then, that unbelief prevented them from reaching their rest.

HEBREWS 3:1-19

Read: Moses was the trustworthy servant of God, as is Jesus, but on a higher level since he is the Son of God. We can place all of our trust in Jesus unlike those who rebelled against Moses as he led them in the desert.

Reflect: What does it mean for you to listen to the words of Jesus and open your heart to his words? What are the biggest difficulties you find to remain faithful to the message of Jesus?

Pray: Pray that you do not have "an evil unbelieving heart that turns away from the living God."

Act: Pray with Psalm 95. Repeat during the day the following words: "Come, let us sing to the Lord, let us make a joyful sound to the Rock of our salvation" (95:1).

---

4 ¹Therefore, let us fear while we are invited to enter the rest of God, lest any of you be left behind. ²We received the gospel exactly as they did, but hearing the message did them no good because they did not share the faith of those who did listen. ³We are now to enter this rest because we believed, as it was said: *I was angry and made a solemn vow: they will never enter my rest*—that is, the rest of God after he created the world. ⁴In another part, it was said about the seventh day: *And God rested on the seventh day from all his works.* ⁵But, now, it is said: *They will not enter my rest.* ⁶We must conclude that some will enter the rest of God and that those who first received the good did not because of their disobedience. ⁷Yet God, again, assigns a day when he says: *today*, and declares through David, many years later: *If you hear God's voice today, do not be stubborn.*

⁸So, it was not Joshua who let them enter the land of rest; otherwise, God would not have assigned another day later on. ⁹Then, some other rest, or Sabbath, is reserved for the people of God. ¹⁰For those who enter this rest of God, rest from all their works, as God rests from his work.

¹¹Let us strive then to enter the rest, and not to share the misfortune of those who disobeyed. ¹²For the word of God is living and effective, sharper than any two-edged sword. It pierces to the division of soul and spirit, of joints and marrow, and judges the intentions and thoughts of

the heart. ¹³All creation is transparent to him; everything is uncovered and laid bare to the eyes of him to whom we render an account.

Christ is our high priest

¹⁴We have a great high priest, Jesus, the Son of God, who has entered heaven. Let us then hold fast to the faith we profess. ¹⁵Our high priest is not indifferent to our weaknesses, for he was tempted in every way, just as we are, yet, without sinning. ¹⁶Let us then with confidence, approach the throne of grace. We will obtain mercy and, through his favor, help in due time.

HEBREWS 4:1-16

Read: We "enter into the rest of God" through Jesus, who is a trustworthy and merciful high priest who carries our prayers to God. Jesus' compassion for us is emphasized.

Reflect: Have you thought about the goal of your life? What is your final aim? Do you long for "the rest in God"? What does this text tell you: "We have a great high priest, Jesus, the Son of God, who has entered heaven. Let us, then, hold fast to the faith we profess. Our high priest is not indifferent to our weaknesses, for he was tempted, in every way, just as we are, yet, without sinning. Let us, then, with confidence, approach the throne of grace. We will obtain mercy and, through his favor, help in due time"?

Pray: O Lord, the strength to those who wait in you, listen to our prayers. We are frail and can do nothing without you. Help us with your grace to accept and live the message of your Son who gave his life for us.

Act: Write down a list of the worries and weaknesses that bother you at this time. Offer them to the Lord asking Him to transform them into opportunities and events of life and love, that they may manifest the saving action of God.

---

5 ¹Every high priest is taken from among mortals and appointed, to be their representative before God, to offer gifts and sacrifices for sin. ²He is able to understand the ignorant and erring, for he, himself, is subject to weakness. ³This is why he is bound to offer sacrifices for his sins, as well as for the sins of the people. ⁴Besides, one does not presume to take this dignity but takes it only when called by God, as Aaron was.

⁵Nor did Christ become high priest in taking upon himself this dignity, but it was given to him by the one who says: *You are my son, I have begotten you today.* ⁶ *And in another place: You are a priest forever, in the priestly order of Melchizedek.*

⁷Christ, in the days of his mortal life, offered his sacrifice with tears and cries. He prayed to him who could save him from death, and he was heard because of his humble submission. ⁸Although he was Son, he learned through suffering what obedience was, ⁹and, once made perfect, he became the source of eternal salvation for those who obey him. ¹⁰This is how God proclaimed him Priest in the order of Melchizedek.

HEBREWS 5:1-10

Read: The text describes, first, the characteristics of the Jewish priest: he is chosen, he does not appoint himself; he represents people to God and as a man he also offers sacrifices for himself. Then the letter mentions the suffering priesthood of Jesus: he was chosen by God to bring us to Him, and his sacrifice was forever.

Reflect: Jesus offered his own life to save us, he sacrificed for us. What sacrifices do you do for others? What does the following text tell you: "Although he was Son, he learned, through suffering, what obedience was, and, once made perfect, he became the source of eternal salvation for those who obey him" (vv. 8-9)?

Pray: Help us, Lord, to follow in your footsteps; that we may be able to show our love in the way we care for others; and that the way of Christian living may be a consolation, help, and strength for all those who suffer.

Act: Go to a hospital and, in a discrete way, try to help anybody in need. Donating blood is a good suggestion!

You should be teachers

[11] About this, we have much to say, but it is difficult to explain, for you have become dull in understanding. [12] You should be teachers by this time, but in fact, you need to be taught again the basic elements of God's teaching. You need milk, not solid food. [13] Those fed with milk are still infants: this refers to those who have not been tested in the way of righteousness. [14] Solid food is for adults who have trained themselves to distinguish good from evil.

6 [1] Therefore, let us leave the elementary teaching about Christ, and move forward to a more advanced knowledge, without laying again the foundation, that is: turning away from dead works, faith in God, [2] the teaching about baptisms and laying on of hands, the resurrection of the dead and the final judgment. [3] This is what we shall do, God permitting.

[4] In any case, it would be impossible to renew again, through penance, those who have once been enlightened and have tasted the heavenly gift, and received the Holy Spirit, [5] tasted the beauty of the word of God, and the wonders of the supernatural world. [6] If, in spite of this, they have ceased to believe and have fallen away, it is impossible to move them a second time to repentance, when they are crucifying, on their own account, the Son of God, and spurning him publicly. [7] Soil that drinks the rain falling continually on it and produces profitable grass for those who till it, receives the blessings of God, [8] but the soil that produces thorns and bushes is poor soil, and in danger of being cursed. In the end, it will be burned.

Remain firm in our hope

[9] Yet, even though we speak like this, we are more optimistic, dear friends, regarding you and your salvation. [10] God is not unjust, and will not forget everything you have done for the love of his name; you have helped, and still help, the believers. [11] We desire each of you to have, until the end, the same zeal for reaching what you have hoped for. [12] Do not grow careless but imitate those who, by their faith and determination, inherit the promise.

[13] Remember God's promise to Abraham. God wanted to confirm it with an oath, and, as no one is higher than God, [14] he swore by himself: I shall bless you and give you many descendants. [15] By just patiently waiting, Abraham obtained the promise.

¹⁶People are used to swearing by someone higher than themselves, and their oath affirms everything that could be denied. ¹⁷So God committed himself with an oath in order to convince those who were to wait for his promise, that he would never change his mind. ¹⁸Thus, we have two certainties in which it is impossible that God be proved false: promise and oath. That is enough to encourage us strongly when we leave everything to hold to the hope set before us. ¹⁹This hope is like a steadfast anchor of the soul, secure and firm, thrust beyond the curtain of the temple into the Sanctuary itself, ²⁰where Jesus has entered ahead of us—Jesus, high priest for ever in the order of Melchizedek.

HEBREWS 5:11—6:20

Read: This passage is a call to maturity and to perseverance in the faith we have received. Using the analogy of farming, believers who reject the faith are like soil that produces thorns, whereas this community, strong in work and love, are the good soil that feeds others.

Reflect: Why are you trustworthy and faithful? How do you preserve your hope in God in discouraging times?

Pray: All-powerful and eternal God, increase our faith, hope, and love that we may remain faithful to your promise and oath.

Act: Help somebody who may be downhearted or distrustful of God's love. May your company make them realize the love and care that God has for them.

Melchizedek, a figure of Christ

7 ¹Scripture says that *Melchizedek, king of Salem, a priest of the Most High God, came out to meet Abraham who returned from defeating the kings. He blessed Abraham, and Abraham gave him a tenth of everything.*

²Let us note that the name Melchizedek means king of Justice, and that king of Salem means king of Peace. ³There is no mention of a father, mother or genealogy; nothing is said about the beginning or the end of his life. In this, he is the figure of the Son of God, the priest who remains forever.

⁴See, then, how great Melchizedek was. Even Abraham gave him a tenth of the spoils! ⁵When the descendants of Levi are consecrated priests, they are commanded to collect tithes from their people, that is, from their kindred, though these also are descended from Abraham. ⁶Here, however, Melchizedek, who does not belong to the family of the Levites, is given tithes from Abraham. Still more, he blesses him, the man of God's promise. ⁷There is no doubt that he who blesses is higher than the one who is blessed. ⁸In the first case, we see that tithes are received by those who are mortals; here, instead, Melchizedek is mentioned as one who lives on.

⁹When Abraham pays the tenth, it is so to speak, the Levites, receivers of the tithes, who pay the tithe ¹⁰because, in a way, Levi was still in the body of Abraham his ancestor, when Melchizedek met him.

¹¹The institutions of the chosen people are founded upon the Levitical priesthood, but with it they could not attain what is perfect and permanent. If that were possible, why would there be a need of another priest *after the order of Melchizedek*, instead of Aaron's? ¹²If there is a change in the priesthood, the law also has to be changed. ¹³Jesus, to whom all this has a reference, was from a tribe that never served at the altar. ¹⁴All know that he belonged to the tribe of Judah that is not mentioned by Moses when he speaks of the priesthood.

¹⁵All this, however, becomes clear, if this priest, after the likeness of Melchizedek, ¹⁶has, in fact, received his mission, not on the basis of any human law, but by the power of immortal life. ¹⁷Because Scripture says: *You are a priest forever, in the priestly order of Melchizedek.* ¹⁸With this, the former disposition is removed as insufficient and useless ¹⁹(for the law did not bring anything to perfection). At the same time, a better hope is given to us: that of drawing near to God.

²⁰This change is confirmed by God's oath. When the others became priests, God did not compromise himself with an oath, ²¹but Jesus is confirmed with an oath, as it is said: *The Lord has sworn and will not change his mind: you are a priest forever.* ²²Therefore, Jesus is our assurance of a better Covenant.

²³The former priests were many, since, as mortal men, they could not remain in office. ²⁴But Jesus remains forever, and the priesthood shall not be taken from him. ²⁵Consequently, he is able to save, for all time,

those who approach God through him. He always lives to intercede on their behalf.

²⁶ It was fitting that our high priest to be holy, undefiled, set apart from sinners, and exalted above the heavens; ²⁷ a priest who does not, first, need to offer sacrifice for himself before offering for the sins of the people as high priests do. He offered himself in sacrifice, once and for all. ²⁸ And whereas, the law elected weak men as high priests, now, after the law, the word of God, with an oath, appointed the Son, made perfect forever.

HEBREWS 7:1-28

Read: The theme of priesthood is further developed. As Melchizedek is a higher form of priest than the Levites, the priesthood of Christ is higher yet, sinless, he had no need to offer a sacrifice for himself., he is the sacrificed he offered for the sins of others.

Reflect: Jesus is our high priest. What does the offering of his Body and Blood in the Eucharist mean to you? How do you unite with this offering?

Pray: Lord, may your Body and Blood shared in the Eucharist transform us into a ferment of a new life for society.

Act: Invite your people to actively participate in the Eucharist and in the life of your parish. Let this be a thanksgiving offer that you and your people make to the Lord for all the graces received.

A new Sanctuary and a new Covenant

8 ¹ The main point of what we are saying is that we have a high priest. He is seated at the right hand of the divine majesty in heaven, ² where he serves as minister of the true temple and Sanctuary, set up not by any mortal, but by the Lord.

³ A high priest is appointed to offer to God gifts and sacrifices, and Jesus also has to offer some sacrifice. ⁴ Had he remained on earth, he would not be a priest, since others offer the gifts according to the law. ⁵ In fact, the ritual celebrated by those priests is only an imitation, and

shadow of the heavenly Sanctuary. We know the word of God to Moses with regard to the construction of the holy tent. He said: *You are to make everything according to the pattern shown to you on the mountain.*

⁶ Now, however, Jesus enjoys a much higher ministry in being the mediator of a better Covenant founded on better promises. ⁷ If all had been perfect in the first Covenant, there would have been no need for another one. ⁸ Yet God sees defects when he says:

The days are coming—it is the word of the Lord—when I will draw up a new Covenant with the people of Israel and with the people of Judah.

⁹ *It will not be like the Covenant that I made with their ancestors on the day I took them by the hand and led them out of Egypt. They did not keep my Covenant, and so I myself have forsaken them, says the Lord.*

¹⁰ *But this is the Covenant that I will make with the people of Israel in the days to come: I will put my laws into their minds and write them on their hearts. I will be their God and they will be my people.*

¹¹ *None of them will have to teach one another or say to each other: Know the Lord, for they will know me from the least to the greatest.* ¹² *I will forgive their sins and no longer remember their wrongs.*

¹³ Here, we are being told of a new Covenant; which means that the first one had become obsolete, and what is obsolete and aging is soon to disappear.

HEBREWS 8:1-13

Read: The metaphor of priesthood as a way of explaining Christ Jesus reaches its main point. The first covenant gives way to a more excellent relationship with God since it is founded on better the forgiveness of sin through Christ Jesus.

Reflect: Covenants are agreements between God and His people. The original covenant had to be replaced by one written "on their hearts" and that covenant now exceeded by the sacrifice of Christ. What is your covenant with God?

Pray: All powerful God, from whom all good things come, give us the grace to know how to give witness to the New Covenant sealed by your Son, not as an external obligation, but as a Law sealed in the heart, a new way of living in this world.

> **Act:** What are the concrete consequences for you of the New Covenant inaugurated by Jesus? Make them happen in your everyday life. Participate in the Eucharist and renew your Christian commitment.

The temple in Jerusalem

9 [1] The first Covenant had rites and regulations. There was also a Sanctuary—an earthly one. [2] A first tent was prepared with the lampstand, the table and the bread of the presence; this is called the Holy Place. [3] Behind the second curtain, there is a second Sanctuary called the Most Holy Place, [4] with the gold altar for the burning of incense, and the Ark of the Covenant fully covered with gold. The ark contained a golden jar holding the manna, Aaron's rod that had sprouted leaves and the two slabs of the Covenant. [5] Above the ark, the two cherubim of glory overshadowed the Seat of Mercy. But we cannot describe it here in detail.

[6] With everything arranged as described, the priests continually enter the first room to fulfill their ministry; [7] but the high priest enters only once a year, the second one, and not without bringing the blood, which he will offer for himself and for the sins of the people. [8] By this, the Holy Spirit teaches us that the way into the inner Sanctuary is not open as long as the first tent still stands. [9] Here is a teaching, by means of figures, for the present age: the gifts and sacrifices presented to God cannot bring the people offering them to interior perfection. [10] These are no more than food, drink, and different kinds of cleansing by water; all these are human regulations, awaiting a reformation.

Jesus entered with his own blood

[11] But now, Christ has appeared as the high priest, with regard to the good things of these new times. He passed through a Sanctuary more noble and perfect, not made by hands, that is, not created. [12] He did not take with himself the blood of goats and bulls, but his own blood, when he entered, once and for all, into this Sanctuary, after obtaining definitive redemption. [13] If the sprinkling of people, defiled by sin, with the blood of goats and bulls, or with the ashes of a heifer, provides them with exterior cleanness and holiness, [14] how much more will it be with the blood

of Christ? He, moved by the eternal spirit, offered himself as an unblemished victim to God, and his blood cleanses us from dead works so that we may serve the living God.

¹⁵ So, Christ is the mediator of a new Covenant or testament. His death made atonement for the sins committed under the old testament, and the promise is handed over to all who are called to the everlasting inheritance. ¹⁶ With every testament, it is necessary to wait until its author has died. ¹⁷ For a testament infers death and has no value while the maker of it is still alive.

¹⁸ That is why the first Covenant was not ratified without blood. ¹⁹ Moses proclaimed to the assembled people all the commandments of the law; then he took the blood of bulls and goats, and mixed it with water, and with these he sprinkled the book itself, and all the people, using scarlet, wool, and hyssop, ²⁰ saying: *This is the blood of the Covenant that God commanded you.* ²¹ In the same way, he sprinkled with blood the Sanctuary and all the objects of the ritual. ²² According to the law, almost all cleansings have to be performed with blood; there is no forgiveness without the shedding of blood.

²³ It was necessary that mere copies of supernatural realities be purified, but now, these realities need better sacrifices. ²⁴ Christ did not enter some sanctuary made by hands, a copy of the true one, but heaven itself. He is now in the presence of God, on our behalf. ²⁵ He had not to offer himself many times, as the high priest does: he who may return every year because the blood is not his own. ²⁶ Otherwise, he would have suffered many times from the creation of the world. But no; he manifested himself only now, at the end of the ages, to take away sin by sacrifice, ²⁷ and as humans die only once and afterward are judged, ²⁸ in the same way Christ sacrificed himself once to take away the sins of the multitude. There will be no further question of sin when he comes again to save those waiting for him.

HEBREWS 9:1-28

Read: The metaphor switches to holy places as a place of sacrifice, where God meets humanity. From desert, to tent, to temple, and now to the person of Christ. Christ is meeting place between God and humanity and all the previous blood sacrifices have been replaced by the sacrifice of his blood, removing sin for all time.

Reflect: The purpose of this section is to emphasize that humanity is reconciled to God through Christ Jesus. What do redemption and salvation mean now? What does the following text tell you: "Christ did not enter some sanctuary made by hands, a copy of the true one, but heaven itself. He is now in the presence of God, on our behalf" (v. 24)?

Pray: Holy Spirit, help us to recognize the moments of salvation that happen in our daily lives, to give you thanks with the right witness of the faith that we profess.

Act: Share in the redemptive work of Jesus by promptly offering your help to whoever asks for it.

The old Covenant prefigures the new

10 ¹The religion of the law is only a shadow of the good things to come; it has the patterns but not the realities. So, year after year, the same sacrifices are offered without bringing the worshipers to what is the end. ²If they had been cleansed once and for all, they would no longer have felt guilt, and would have stopped offering the same sacrifices. ³But no, year after year their sacrifices witness to their sins, ⁴and never will the blood of bulls and goats take away these sins.

⁵This is why, on entering the world, Christ says: *You did not desire sacrifice and offering;* ⁶*you were not pleased with burnt offerings and sin offerings.* ⁷Then I said: "*Here I am. It was written of me in the scroll. I will do your will, O God.*"

⁸*First, he says: Sacrifice, offerings, burnt offerings and sin offerings you did not desire nor were you pleased with them—although they were required by the law.* ⁹Then he says: *Here I am to do your will.*

This is enough to nullify the first will and establish the new. ¹⁰Now, by this will of God, we are sanctified once and for all by the sacrifice of the body of Christ Jesus. ¹¹So, whereas every priest stands daily by the altar, offering repeatedly the same sacrifices that can never take away sins, ¹²Christ has offered, for all times, a single sacrifice for sins, and has taken his seat *at the right hand of God*, ¹³waiting until God *puts his enemies as a footstool under his feet.* ¹⁴By a single sacrifice, he has brought those who are sanctified to what is perfect forever.

¹⁵This also was testified by the Holy Spirit. For after having declared: ¹⁶ *This is the Covenant that I will make with them in the days to come— says the Lord—I will put my laws in their hearts and write them on their minds.* ¹⁷He says: *Their sins and evil deeds I will remember no more.* ¹⁸So, if sins are forgiven, there is no longer need of any sacrifice for sin.

HEBREWS 10:1-18

Read: The proclamation reaches its highpoint, in the sacrifice of Jesus sins have been forgiven once for all. The sacrificial work of Jesus has passed. Jesus gives his followers access to the Father. They share in his priestly consecration. God no longer remembers sins.

Reflect: "It is by God's will that have you have been sanctified" and "I will remember their sins no more." What does this tell you about God? If God forgets sin, why do people seem unable to forget sins?

Pray: "Lord you told us" This is my Body given for you, this is my blood, the blood of the new covenant" help me to trust your love for all.

Act: Go to your church and pray in front of the Blessed Sacrament. Think about the meaning of the Eucharist in your life. Practice that which the Holy Spirit inspires you to do.

Be confident in God

¹⁹So, my friends, we are assured of entering the Sanctuary, by the blood of Jesus ²⁰who opened for us this new and living way, passing through *the curtain*, that is, his body. ²¹Because we have a high priest in charge of the house of God, ²²let us approach, with a sincere heart, with full faith, interiorly cleansed from a bad conscience, and our bodies washed with pure water.

²³Let us hold fast to our hope, without wavering, because he who promised is faithful. ²⁴Let us consider how we may spur one another to love and do good works. ²⁵Do not abandon the assemblies as some of

you do, but encourage one another, all the more, since the Day is drawing near.

²⁶If we sin willfully, after receiving knowledge of the truth, there is no longer sacrifice for sin, ²⁷but only the fearful prospect of judgment and of fire, which devours the rebellious. ²⁸Anyone who disregards the law of Moses is put to death without mercy on the testimony of two or three witnesses. ²⁹What, then, do you think it will be for those who have despised the Son of God? How severely shall he be punished for having defiled the blood of the covenant by which they were sanctified, and for having insulted the spirit given to them? ³⁰For we know the one who says: *Revenge is mine, I will repay.* And also: *The Lord will judge his people.* ³¹What a dreadful thing to fall into the hands of the living God!

³²Remember the first days when you were enlightened. You had to undergo a hard struggle in the face of suffering. ³³Publicly, you were exposed to humiliations and trials, and had to share the sufferings of others who were similarly treated. ³⁴You showed solidarity with those in prison; you were dispossessed of your goods, and accepted it gladly, for you knew you were acquiring a much better and more durable possession. ³⁵Do not now throw away your confidence that will be handsomely rewarded. ³⁶Be patient in doing the will of God and the promise will be yours: ³⁷*A little, a little longer*—says Scripture—*and he who is coming will come; he will not delay.* ³⁸*My righteous one will live if he believes; but if he distrusts, I will no longer look kindly on him.*

³⁹We are not among those who withdraw and perish, but among those who believe and win personal salvation.

HEBREWS 10:19-39

Read: Through Christ we live lives of faith, hope and love with which Christians encourage each other to love and good deeds. This life should not be abandoned for sin and be lost.

Reflect: Who encourages you to "love and good deeds"? Whom do you encourage?

Pray: Loving God help me to trust your mercy and hold fast to the hope of Christ.

Act: Look for people who have lost hope and need encouragement, and strengthen their faith with yours.

Remembering the heroes of faith

11 ¹Faith is the assurance of what we hope for, being certain of what we cannot see. ²Because of their faith, our ancestors were approved.

³By faith, we understand that the stages of creation were disposed by God's word, and what is visible came from what cannot be seen.

⁴Because of Abel's faith, his offering was more acceptable than that of his brother Cain, which meant he was upright, and God himself approved his offering. Because of this faith, he cried to God, as said in Scripture, even after he died.

⁵By faith, Enoch was taken to heaven, instead of experiencing death: *he could not be found, because God had taken him.* In fact, it is said that before being taken up, he had pleased God. ⁶Yet, without faith, it is impossible to please him: no one draws near to God without first believing that he exists and that he rewards those who seek him earnestly.

⁷By faith, Noah was instructed of events which could not yet be seen, and heeding what he heard, he built a boat in which to save his family. The faith of Noah condemned the world and he reached holiness born of faith.

⁸It was by faith that Abraham, called by God, set out for a country that would be given to him as an inheritance; for he parted without knowing where he was going. ⁹By faith, he lived as a stranger in that promised land. There, he lived in tents, as did Isaac and Jacob, beneficiaries of the same promise. ¹⁰Indeed, he looked forward to that city of a solid foundation of which God is the architect and builder.

¹¹By faith, Sarah herself received power to become a mother, in spite of her advanced age, since she believed that he, who had made the promise, would be faithful. ¹²Therefore, from an almost impotent man, were born descendants as numerous as the stars of heaven, as many as the grains of sand on the seashore.

¹³Death found all these people strong in their faith. They had not received what was promised, but they had looked ahead and had rejoiced in it from afar, saying that they were *foreigners and travelers* on earth. ¹⁴Those who speak in this way prove that they are looking for their own country. ¹⁵For, if they had longed for the land they had left, it would have been easy for them to return, ¹⁶but no, they aspired to a better city, that

is, a supernatural one; so God, who prepared the city for them, is not ashamed of being called their God.

¹⁷ By faith, Abraham went to offer Isaac when God tested him. And so, he who had received the promise of God, offered his only son, ¹⁸ although God had told him: *Isaac's descendants will bear your name.* ¹⁹ Abraham reasoned that God is capable even of raising the dead, and he received back his son, which has a figurative meaning.

²⁰ By faith, also, Isaac blessed the future of Jacob and Esau. ²¹ By faith, Jacob, before he died, blessed both children of Joseph, and worshiped as he leaned on his staff. ²² By faith, Joseph, when about to die, warned the children of Israel of their exodus and gave orders about his remains.

²³ By faith, the parents of the newly-born Moses hid him for three months, for they saw the baby was very beautiful, and they did not fear the order of Pharaoh. ²⁴ By faith, Moses, already an adult, refused to be called son of Pharaoh's daughter. ²⁵ He preferred to share ill treatment with the people of God, rather than enjoy the passing pleasures of sin. ²⁶ He considered the humiliation of Christ a greater treasure than the wealth of Egypt, and he looked ahead to his reward. ²⁷ By faith, he left Egypt without fearing the king's anger, and he persevered as someone who could see the Invisible.

²⁸ By faith, Moses had the Passover celebrated, sprinkling the doors with blood so that the Destroyer would not kill their first-born sons. ²⁹ By faith, they crossed the Red Sea as if on dry land, while the Egyptians, who tried to cross it, were swallowed by the waters and drowned.

³⁰ By faith, the walls of Jericho crumbled and fell after Israel had marched round them for seven days; ³¹ by faith, also, the prostitute Rahab escaped death, which befell the unbelievers, for having welcomed the spies.

³² Do I need to say more? There is not enough time to speak of Gideon, Barak, Samson, Jephthah, David, as well as Samuel and the prophets. ³³ Through faith, they fought and conquered nations, established justice, saw the fulfillment of God's promises, shut the mouths of lions, ³⁴ quenched raging fire, escaped the sword, were healed of their sicknesses; they were weak people who were given strength to be brave in battle and repulse foreign invaders.

³⁵ Some women recovered their dead by resurrection, but there were others—persecuted and tortured believers—who, for the sake of a better

resurrection, refused to do what would have saved them. ³⁶ Others suffered chains and prison. ³⁷ They were stoned, sawn in two, killed by the sword. They fled from place to place, with no other clothing than the skins of sheep and goats, lacking everything, afflicted, ill-treated. ³⁸ These people, of whom the world was not worthy, had to wander through wastelands and mountains, and take refuge in the dens of the land.

³⁹ However, although all of them were praised because of their faith, they did not enjoy the promise, ⁴⁰ because God had us in mind, and saw beyond. And he did not want them to reach perfection, except with us.

HEBREWS 11:1-40

Read: This section of the sermon is about faith, particularly the people of faith in the bible who trusted God even though their path forward was not clear to them.

Reflect: Faith is the guarantee of what you hope for. How is your faith? Are you aware of its richness and potential? Does it help in your life? Do you trust in the saving presence and action of God in your life? Study the stories of the Old Testament for examples of faith and courage.

Pray: Slowly and with great awareness pray the Our Father.

Act: Faith has to be lived and shared with others of your parish community. Faith has to be shared with others.

Accept the correction of the Lord

12 ¹ What a cloud of innumerable witnesses surround us! So, let us be rid of every encumbrance, and especially of sin, to persevere in running the race marked out before us.

² Let us look to Jesus, the founder of our faith, who will bring it to completion. For the sake of the joy reserved for him, he endured the cross, scorning its shame, and then sat at the right of the throne of God. ³ Think of Jesus, who suffered so many contradictions from evil people, and you will not be discouraged or grow weary. ⁴ Have you already shed your blood in the struggle against sin?

⁵ Do not forget the comforting words that Wisdom addresses to you as

children: *My son, pay attention when the Lord corrects you and do not be discouraged when he punishes you.* ⁶ *For the Lord corrects those he loves and chastises everyone he accepts as a son.*

⁷ What you endure is in order to correct you. God treats you like sons, and what son is not corrected by his father? ⁸ If you were without correction, which has been received by all (as is fitting for sons), you would not be sons, but bastards. ⁹ Besides, when our parents, according to the flesh, corrected us, we respected them. How much more should we be subject to the Father of spirits to have a life? ¹⁰ Our parents corrected us as they saw fit, with a view to this very short life; but God corrects us for our own good, that we may share his holiness.

¹¹ All correction is painful at the moment, rather than pleasant; later, it brings the fruit of peace, that is holiness, to those who have been trained by it.

¹² Lift up, then, your drooping hands, and strengthen your trembling knees; ¹³ make level the ways for your feet, so that the lame may not be disabled, but healed.

Strive to be holy

¹⁴ Strive for peace with all, and strive to be holy, for without holiness no one will see the Lord.

¹⁵ See that no one falls from the grace of God, lest a *bitter plant spring up and its poison corrupt* many among you. ¹⁶ Let no one be immoral or irreligious, like Esau, who sold his birthright for a single meal. ¹⁷ You know that later when he wished to get the blessing, he was rejected, although he pleaded with tears.

¹⁸ What you have come to is nothing known to the senses: nor heat of a *blazing fire, darkness and gloom, and storms,* ¹⁹ *blasts of trumpets* or such *a voice* that the people pleaded that no further word be spoken. ²⁰ For they could not endure the order that was given: *Every human or beast reaching the mountain shall be stoned.* ²¹ The sight was so terrifying that Moses said: I tremble with fear.

²² But you came near to Mount Zion, to the City of the living God, to the heavenly Jerusalem, with its innumerable angels. You have come to the solemn feast, ²³ the assembly of the firstborn of God, whose names are written in heaven. There is God, Judge of all, with the spirits of the upright brought to perfection. ²⁴ There is Jesus, the mediator of the new

Covenant, with the sprinkled blood that cries out more effectively than Abel's.

²⁵ Be careful not to reject God when he speaks. If those who did not heed the prophet's warnings were not spared on earth, how much more shall we be punished if we do not heed the One warning us from heaven? ²⁶ His voice, then, shook the earth, but now he says: *Once more, I will shake not only the earth but also the heavens.*

²⁷ The words *once more* indicate the removal of everything that can be shaken, that is, created things, and only those that cannot be shaken will remain. ²⁸ Such is the kingdom that we receive. Let us then be grateful, and offer to God a worship pleasing to him, with reverence and awe. ²⁹ Our God is indeed a *consuming fire.*

HEBREWS 12:1-29

Read: This chapter is an exhortation to trust absolutely in Jesus. He is our inspiration and strength in difficult moments; he is our hope and our goal.

Reflect: How does suffering, your own and that of others challenge your faith? What does it mean for you to have "your eyes fixed on Jesus"?

Pray: Lord Jesus, may your cross inspire us to have absolute trust in you in difficult moments; give us the grace to confront them with serenity and patience; do not allow us to separate from you.

Act: Pray the five sorrowful mysteries of the Rosary.

Words of encouragement

13 ¹ Let mutual love continue. ² Do not neglect to offer hospitality; you know that some people have entertained angels without knowing it. ³ Remember the prisoners, as if you were with them in chains and the same for those who are suffering. Remember that you also have a body.

⁴ Marriage must be respected by all, and husband and wife, faithful to each other. God will punish the immoral and the adulterous.

⁵ Do not depend on money. Be content with having enough for today,

for God has said: *I will never forsake you or abandon you,* ⁶ and we shall confidently answer: *The Lord is my helper, I will not fear; what can man do to me?* ⁷ Remember your leaders who taught you the word of God. Consider their end, and imitate their faith. ⁸ Christ Jesus is the same today, as yesterday, and forever.

⁹ Do not be led astray by all kinds of strange teachings. Your heart will be strengthened by the grace of God rather than by foods of no use to anyone. ¹⁰ We have an altar, from which those still serving in the temple cannot eat.

¹¹ After the high priest has offered the blood in the Sanctuary for the sins of the people, the carcasses of the animals are burnt outside the camp. ¹² For this same reason, Jesus, to purify the people with his own blood, suffered his Passion outside the Holy City. ¹³ Let us, therefore, go to him outside the sacred area, sharing his shame. ¹⁴ For we have here no lasting city, and we are looking for the one to come.

¹⁵ Let us, then, continually offer, through Jesus, a sacrifice of praise to God that is the fruit of lips celebrating his name. ¹⁶ Do not neglect good works and common life, for these are sacrifices pleasing to God. ¹⁷ Obey your leaders and submit to them, for they are concerned for your souls, and are accountable for them. Let this be a joy for them, rather than a burden, which would be of no advantage for you.

¹⁸ Pray for us, for we believe our intentions are pure, and that we only want to act honorably in all things. ¹⁹ Now, I urge you all the more, to pray for me that I may be given back to you the sooner.

²⁰ May God give you peace, he who brought back from among the dead, Jesus our Lord, the Great Shepherd of the sheep, whose blood seals the eternal Covenant.

²¹ He will train you in every good work that you may do his will, for it is he who works in us what pleases him, through Jesus Christ, to whom all glory be for ever and ever. Amen!

²² Brothers, I beg you, to take these words of encouragement. For my part, I will add a few words. ²³ Know that our brother Timothy has been released. If he comes soon, I will visit you with him. ²⁴ Greetings to all your leaders and to the saints. Greetings from those in Italy.

²⁵ Grace be with you all.

HEBREWS 13:1-25

Read: The final part of the sermon is about relations between human beings. The importance of mutual love, hospitality to strangers, the sacredness of marriage and avoiding love of money are highlighted as visible signs that faith is focused on Christ Jesus, the High Priest.

Reflect: What does this last chapter of the letter to the Hebrews tell you? What does the following text tell you: "Do not neglect good works and common life for these are sacrifices pleasing to God" (v. 16)?

Pray: O God, who makes us participate in the priesthood of your Son, help us live a life caring for others and pleasing to your eyes.

Act: Help your parish efforts to support married couples, care for immigrants and build unity.

LETTER OF
JAMES

Who is this James? He is probably the "brother of the Lord," barely mentioned in the Gospel, with regard to his mother (Mk 6:3; 15:40; 16:1). And yet, he was privileged to have the risen Jesus appear to him (1 Cor 15:7). It also seems that when he is about to go underground, Peter entrusts the Church of Jerusalem to him (Acts 12:17; 15:13; 21:18). Later on, James appears to have been responsible for all the Christian communities, with a majority of Jews, that were established in Palestine, Syria, and Cilicia (see Acts 15:13-29).

Of all the apostles, James was the most attached to Jewish traditions (the opposite of Paul). Yet, although Paul harshly criticized James' associates, he seemed to have more than personal respect for James. In addressing the faithful dispersed outside Palestine, James is teaching them simple and practical things inspired by the wisdom of the Old Testament. We recognize authentic religion by the way we live and treat people around us.

We cannot fail to see that the passage where James shows that faith is nothing without works (2:14-26) contradicts, at least seemingly, Paul's declarations about justification by faith in Galatians 5 and Romans 4. However, a careful study shows that James was familiar with Paul's first letter to the Corinthians when he wrote his letter. Paul had forcefully declared that faith is nothing without love (1 Cor 13:2) and James simply approved. Without contradicting James, in Galatians and Romans, Paul emphasized that faith purifies the heart of pagans and Jews, long before we accomplish the works of love that God has prepared beforehand for us to practice (Eph 2:10).

What is evident from the many contacts between the letters of Peter, James, and Paul is that the Church was not a galaxy of dispersed communities set in their own interpretations of the faith and their attachment to a particular apostle—something we read all too often in works of the last century such as the—"Johannine circles," the "Pauline communities," the "Lukan communities," etc. The letters of the apostles traveled very fast and people received them from one end of the Mediterranean basin to the other. The Church of the apostles was a reality even when the apostles confronted one another.

Here, Christians are called the twelve tribes dispersed among the nations. In fact, the term "Diaspora," that is to say, "dispersion" was used to refer to Jews who had settled outside their homeland. In view of what we have said, James must have written his letter in the year 56 A.D., between 1 Corinthians and Galatians. In any case, we know that James was stoned to death in the year 62 A.D.

LETTER OF
JAMES

Endure trials patiently

1 ¹ James, a servant of God and of the Lord Jesus Christ, sends greetings to the twelve tribes scattered among the nations.

² Consider yourselves fortunate, my brothers and sisters, when you meet with every kind of trial, ³ for you know that the testing of your faith makes you steadfast. ⁴ Let your steadfastness become perfect with deeds, that you yourselves may be perfect and blameless, without any defect.

⁵ If any of you is lacking in wisdom, ask God, who gives to all easily and unconditionally. ⁶ But ask with faith, not doubting, for the one who doubts is like a wave driven and tossed on the sea by the wind. ⁷ Such a person should not expect anything from the Lord since the doubter has two minds ⁸ and his conduct will always be insecure.

⁹ Let the believer who is poor, boast in being uplifted, ¹⁰ and let the rich one boast in being humbled, because he will pass away like the flower of the field. ¹¹ The sun rises and its heat dries the grass; the flower withers and its beauty vanishes. So, too, will the rich person fade away even in the midst of his pursuits.

¹² Happy are those who patiently endure trials because afterward, they will receive the crown of life, which the Lord promised to those who love him. ¹³ No one, when tempted, should say, "This temptation comes from God." God is never tempted, and he can never tempt anyone. ¹⁴ Instead, each of us is lured and enticed by our own evil desire. ¹⁵ Once this desire has conceived, it gives birth to sin, and sin, when fully grown, gives birth to death.

¹⁶ Do not be deceived, my beloved. ¹⁷ Every good and perfect gift comes from above, from the Father of Light, in whom there is no change or shadow of a change. ¹⁸ By his own will, he gave us life through the word of truth, that we might be a kind of offering to him, among his creatures.

> **JAMES 1:1-18**
>
> **Read:** Written for Jewish Christians, the central theme is the public manifestation of personal commitments and their shared beliefs about God. James speaks about trials that shake faithfulness to God, blessing people who despite their difficulties remain faithful to God in their heart and action.
>
> **Reflect:** What trials in your life shake your faithfulness to God? What helps you remain faithful?
>
> **Pray:** God of faith, hope, and love: we open our hearts and minds to trust in your mercy, knowing that when we put our worries in your hands, your love sustains us.
>
> **Act:** Stay committed to doing works of mercy even when the going gets difficult.

[19] My beloved, be quick to hear but slow to speak, and slow to anger, [20] for human anger does not fulfill the justice of God. [21] So get rid of any filth, and reject the prevailing evil, and welcome the word that has been planted in you, and has the power to save you.

[22] Be doers of the word, and not just hearers, lest you deceive yourselves. [23] The hearer, who does not become a doer, is like that one who looked at himself in the mirror; [24] he looked, and then promptly forgot what he was like. [25] But those who fix their gaze on the perfect law of freedom and hold onto it, not listening and then forgetting, but acting on it, will find blessing on their deeds.

[26] Those who think they are religious but do not restrain their tongue, deceive themselves and their religion is in vain. [27] In the sight of God our Father, pure and blameless religion lies in helping the orphans and widows in their need and keeping oneself from the world's corruption.

> **JAMES 1:19-27**
>
> **Read:** The author outlines the conditions for the Word of God to be effective in those who receive it. It is not enough to just listen to it; we need live it.
>
> **Reflect:** In what ways do you hear the Word of God and make it part of you?

Pray: Help me to you Lord and trust you so much I live what I believe.

Act: Have your lifestyle mirror your faith in the God of love. Offer to help to someone in need.

Treat the rich and the poor equally

2 [1] My brothers and sisters, if you truly believe in our glorified Lord Jesus Christ, you will not discriminate between persons. [2] Suppose a person enters the synagogue where you are assembled, dressed magnificently and wearing a gold ring; at the same time, a poor person enters dressed in rags, [3] if you focus your attention on the well-dressed and say, "Come and sit in the best seat," while, to the poor one you say, "Stay standing, or else sit down at my feet," [4] have you not, in fact, made a distinction between the two? Have you not judged using a double standard?

[5] Listen, my beloved brothers and sisters, did God not choose the poor of this world to receive the riches of faith, and to inherit the kingdom, which he has promised to those who love him? [6] Yet, you despise them! Is it not the rich who are against you and drag you to court? [7] Do they not insult the holy name of Christ by which you are called?

[8] If you keep the law of the kingdom, according to Scripture: *Love your neighbor as yourself,* you do well; [9] but if you make distinctions between persons, you break the law, and are condemned by the same law. [10] For whoever keeps the whole law, but fails in one aspect, is guilty of breaking it all. [11] For he who said, "*Do not commit adultery,*" also said, "*Do not kill.*" If, then, you do not commit adultery, but you do commit murder, you have broken the law. [12] Therefore, speak and behave like people who are going to be judged by the law of freedom. [13] There will be justice without mercy for those who have not shown mercy, whereas mercy has nothing to fear of judgment.

JAMES 2:1-13

Read: That people are made in the image and likeness of God is central to Judaism, so a true believer will treat all persons equally, without distinction, loving their neighbor as themselves.

> **Reflect:** How are the preferences for the rich over the poor part of life today? How are they part of church life? What do you make of this: "For judgement will be without mercy to anyone who has shown no mercy; mercy triumphs over judgement?"
>
> **Pray:** O God, you created us in your image and likeness. Help us to see you in each of our brothers and sisters, especially in the faces of the poor.
>
> **Act:** Be aware of the prejudices you have to certain groups of people. Try to overcome them by dealing with them.

Faith is shown in action

[14] What good is it, my brothers and sisters, to profess faith without showing works? Such faith has no power to save you. [15] If a brother or sister is in need of clothes or food, [16] and one of you says, "May things go well for you; be warm and satisfied," without attending to their material needs, what good is that? [17] So it is for faith without deeds: it is totally dead.

[18] Say to whoever challenges you, "You have faith and I have good deeds; show me your faith apart from actions and I, for my part, will show you my faith in the way I act." [19] Do you believe there is one God? Well enough, but do not forget that the demons also believe, and tremble with fear!

[20] You foolish one, do you have to be convinced that faith without deeds is useless? [21] Think of our father Abraham. Was he not justified by the act of offering his son Isaac on the altar? [22] So you see, his faith was active, along with his deeds, and became perfect by what he did. [23] The word of Scripture was thus fulfilled, *Abraham believed in God so he was considered a righteous person and he was* called the friend of God.

[24] So you see, a person is justified by works, and not by faith alone. [25] Likewise, we read of Rahab the prostitute, that she was acknowledged and saved because she welcomed the spies and showed them another way to leave.

[26] So, just as the body is dead without its spirit, so faith without deeds is also dead.

JAMES 2:14-26

Read: This text highlights the importance of having faith with deeds. Faith without deeds is a dead faith. James speaks here of the works of mercy that Christians should show toward others in their community as well as the poor and needy in general. He uses the stories of Abraham and Rahab to illustrate his point.

Reflect: Faith is lived from the inside out so the way we live expresses our soul. How do the Scriptures become part of your heart?

Pray: Lord, help me love others as I love myself and to be merciful to others as you are merciful to me.

Act: Work with your parish social ministry and with some social institutions that fight for justice.

Sins of the tongue

3 [1] My brothers and sisters, don't all be teachers! You know that, as teachers, we will be judged most strictly; [2] in fact, we make mistakes like everybody else. A person who commits no offense in speech is perfect and capable of ruling the whole self. [3] We put a bit into the horse's mouth to master it and, with this, we control its whole body. [4] The same is true of ships: however big they are, driven by strong winds, they are guided by a tiny rudder. [5] In the same way, the tongue is a tiny part of the body, but it is capable of great things.

A small flame is enough to set a huge forest on fire. [6] The tongue is a similar flame; it is, in itself, a whole world of evil. It infects the whole being and sets fire to our world with the very fire of hell. [7] Wild animals, birds, reptiles, and sea creatures of every kind are, and have been ruled, by the human species. [8] Nobody, however, can control the tongue; it is an untiring whip, full of deadly poison. [9] We use it to bless God our Father, and also to curse those made in God's likeness. [10] From the same mouth come both blessing and curse.

Brothers and sisters, this should not be the case. [11] Can both fresh and saltwater gush from the same source? [12] Can a fig tree produce olives or a grapevine give figs? Neither is the sea able to give fresh water.

True wisdom

¹³ If you consider yourself wise and learned, show it by your good life, and let your actions, in all humility, be an example for others. ¹⁴ But if your heart is full of bitter jealousy and ambition, do not try to show off; that would be covering up the truth; ¹⁵ this kind of wisdom does not come from above but from the world, and it is earthly and devilish. ¹⁶ Wherever there are jealousy and ambition, you will also find discord, and all that is evil. ¹⁷ Instead, the wisdom that comes from above is pure and peace-loving. Persons with this wisdom show understanding, and listen to advice; they are full of compassion and good works; they are impartial and sincere. ¹⁸ Peacemakers who sow peace, reap a harvest of justice.

JAMES 3:1-18

Read: Not only our actions but also our words should reflect our faith. Neither destructive criticism nor gossip nor lies nor envy can contribute to making a better world.

Reflect: As actions reflect faith, so do what we say and what we write. Think about your day to day. Do you use words to build or to destroy? Do you talk too much sometimes? Do you work for peace or for discord?

Pray: May my speech praise you Lord, and reflect you in words of kindness, encouragement and peace.

Act: Avoid false or malicious words in your everyday conversations. Express your trust in others with words of encouragement, forgiveness, and respect.

Wicked ambitions

4 ¹ What causes these fights and quarrels among you? Is it not your cravings that make war within your own selves? ² When you long for something you cannot have, you kill for it, and when you do not get what you desire, you squabble and fight. The fact is, you do not have what you want because you do not pray for it. ³ You pray for something and you do not get it because you pray with the wrong motive of indulging your pleasures. ⁴ You adulterers! Don't you know that making friends with the world make you enemies of God? Therefore, whoever chooses to be the world's friend becomes God's enemy.

⁵Can you not see the point of the saying in Scripture: "The longing of the spirit he sent to dwell in us, is a jealous longing?" ⁶But God has something better to give, and Scripture also says, "*God opposes the proud but he gives his favor to the humble.*" ⁷Give in, then, to God; resist the devil and he will flee from you. ⁸Draw close to God and he will come close to you. Clean your hands, you sinners, and purify your hearts, you doubters. ⁹Recognize your distress, be miserable and weep. Turn your laughter into tears and your joy into sadness. ¹⁰Humble yourselves before the Lord and he will raise you up.

¹¹Brothers and sisters, do not criticize one another. Anyone who speaks against, or condemns another, speaks against the law and condemns the law. If, however, you condemn the law, you are no longer an observer of the law, but a judge of it. ¹²There is only one lawgiver and one judge: he who has the power to save or condemn. So you, who are you, to judge your neighbor?

JAMES 4:1-12

Read: Envy and rivalry divide human beings and separate them from God. Rather, we should befriend God, be loyal and humble and guided by the good.

Reflect: "Draw close to God and he will come close to you." Do you humbly reach out for God or do you resist trusting Him? How is the presence of God manifested in your life?

Pray: Look to me with pity, Lord, and strengthen my resolve to reject evil and to get closer to you through my brothers and sisters.

Act: Resolve to do something concrete to help you get closer to God.

---

¹³Listen now, you who speak like this, "Today or tomorrow we will go off to this city and spend a year there; we will do business and make money." ¹⁴You have no idea what tomorrow will bring. What is your life? No more than a mist, which appears for a moment and then disappears. ¹⁵Instead of this, you should say, "God willing, we will live and do this or that." ¹⁶But no! You boast of your plans: this brazen pride is wicked. ¹⁷Anyone who knows what is good and does not do it, sins.

The misfortunes of the rich

5 [1] So, now, for what concerns the rich, cry and weep for the misfortunes that are coming upon you. [2] Your riches are rotting, and your clothes eaten up by the moths. [3] Your silver and gold have rusted and their rust grows into a witness against you. It will consume your flesh like fire, for having piled up riches in these last days.

[4] You deceived the workers who harvested your fields, but now, their wages cry out to the heavens. The reapers' complaints have reached the ears of the Lord of hosts. [5] You lived in luxury and pleasure in this world, thus fattening yourselves for the day of slaughter. [6] You have easily condemned and killed the innocent since they offered no resistance.

Look forward to the Lord's coming

[7] Be patient, then, beloved, until the coming of the Lord. See how the sower waits for the precious fruits of the earth, looking forward patiently to the autumn and spring rains. [8] You, also, be patient and do not lose heart, because the Lord's coming is near.

[9] Beloved, do not fight among yourselves and you will not be judged. See, the judge is already at the door. [10] Take for yourselves, as an example of patience, the suffering of the prophets who spoke in the Lord's name. [11] See how those who were patient are called blessed. You have heard of the patience of Job and know how the Lord dealt with him in the end. *For the Lord is merciful and shows compassion.*

[12] Above all, my beloved, do not swear either by heaven or by earth, or make a habit of swearing. Let your *yes* be yes and your *no* be no, lest you become liable to judgment.

The sick

[13] Are any among you discouraged? They should pray. Are any of you happy? They should sing songs to God. [14] If anyone is sick, let him call on the elders of the Church. They shall pray for him, anointing him with oil in the name of the Lord. [15] The prayer said in faith will save the sick person; the Lord will raise him up and if he has committed any sins, he will be forgiven.

[16] There will be healing if you confess your sins to one another, and pray for each other. The prayer of the upright man has great power, provided he perseveres. [17] Elijah was a human being like ourselves, and

when he prayed earnestly for it not to rain, no rain fell for three and a half years. [18] Then he prayed again: the sky yielded rain and the earth produced its fruit.

[19] Brothers, if any one of you strays far away from the truth and another person brings him back to it, [20] be sure of this: he who brings back a sinner from the wrong way will save his soul from death and *win forgiveness for many sins.*

JAMES 4:13—5:20

Read: The relationship between the wealthy and the poor must be one of justice and generosity. The heart is the locus of the spirit and fattened hearts are unresponsive to the needs of others. A righteous person does not resist God, speaks with God's prophetic voice, believes through trials, and cares for others when sick and in need of forgiveness.

Reflect: Our closeness to God is mirrored in relationships with others. What do your actions reveal to you about your relationship with God?

Pray: Ask the Lord for the grace to be generous, to assist the poor, help the sick and recognize your own sins in order to lead others.

Act: Make a gesture for the kingdom of God: be generous to those in need, visit a sick or comfort a person who is sad.

FIRST LETTER OF
PETER

We know almost nothing about the life of the apostle Peter after the Council of Jerusalem in the year 49 A.D. (see Acts 15). What was his situation in Jerusalem after his miraculous deliverance the night before his execution (Acts 12)? It was in the year 44 A.D. The death of Herod Agrippa, a few months later, did not prevent the high priests from wanting Paul's death. When did he leave for the Greek world? What contacts did he have with the communities that Paul established? We do know that, in Corinth, a party laid claim on him and apparently knew him (1 Cor 1:12). When did he get to Rome? This letter is helpful in finding an answer.

This is an important letter not only because of what it says but also because it gives us a glimpse of the Church of the apostles. It has many points of contact with the letters of James and Paul, especially the epistle to the Romans. Faith was not made up of beliefs evolving according to the feelings of diverse communities. The testimonies about Jesus, his person and his Gospel, were not left to anonymous writers ready to alter them according to the needs of the moment. There was a solid and coordinated preaching of the apostles based on untouchable information that was already called Tradition or Doctrine. Prophets, who were used to giving a Christian interpretation of the Old Testament, were gradually creating a Christian language and since they were itinerant, this language had to agree with the testimony of the apostles.

Peter tells us that his letter, handwritten by Silas or Silvanus, Paul's former companion (5:12), is addressed to the communities of the different Roman provinces located in today's Turkey. Did Peter know them personally? He refers to a persecution threatening them or, at least, to the hostile attitude of the authorities, and he encourages them by showing them the example of Christ. We do not have to imagine a widespread and official persecution as the one that occurred under Domitian at the time of Revelation or under Trajan in the year 110 A.D. Instead, it was a matter of nuisances and slander on the part of unbelievers before the courts. An analysis of the themes and the terminology seems to show that Peter's letter precedes Paul's letters to the Ephesians and Colossians, therefore, before the year 60 A.D. It would be very difficult to deny that it was known by the author of the letter to the Hebrews, written before the year 66 A.D. The occasion for writing it may have been Paul's arrest in Jerusalem in the year 58 A.D., an event that impacted the provinces of Asia where the Jews were influential.

In looking for the originality of this letter, we should emphasize the following three points:

– From 1:3 to 3:7, everything draws its inspiration from the baptismal ceremony, hymns and the homily on the meaning of baptism and the type of life that the newly baptized will lead.

– The letter praises the new people of the baptized, living stones of the real temple and priests of God for spiritual worship.

– On many occasions, Peter invites us to meditate on Christ's passion: his sacrifice is still present at the heart of God's people and persecution is part of their vocation.

An ancient tradition assures us that Peter was killed during Nero's persecution and that he was buried on the property of Vatican hill. Recent excavations have enabled us to find a tomb containing bones and bearing different inscriptions. It is almost certainly the tomb of the apostle Peter, the first stone of the Church.

FIRST LETTER OF
PETER

1 ¹From Peter, an apostle of Jesus Christ, to all those living as aliens in the Dispersion, in Pontus, Galatia, Cappadocia, Asia and Bithynia, ²to those whom God the Father has called according to his plan, and made holy by the Spirit to obey Jesus Christ, and be purified by his blood: may grace and peace increase among you.

You have been saved

³Let us praise God, the Father of our Lord Jesus Christ, for his great mercy. In raising Jesus Christ from the dead, he has given us new life, and living hope. ⁴The inheritance that does not corrupt, nor goes bad, nor passes away, was reserved for you in heaven, ⁵since God's power shall keep you faithful until salvation is revealed in the last days.

⁶There is cause for joy, then, even though you may, for a time, have to suffer many trials. ⁷Thus will your faith be tested like gold in a furnace. Gold, however, passes away, but faith, worth so much more, will bring you, in the end, praise, glory, and honor when Jesus Christ appears.

⁸You have not yet seen him, and yet you love him; even without seeing him, you believe in him, and experience a heavenly joy beyond all words, ⁹for you are reaching the goal of your faith: the salvation of your souls.

¹⁰This was the salvation for which the prophets, so eagerly looked when in days past, foretold the favor of God with regard to you. ¹¹But they could only investigate when the Spirit of Christ present within them, pointed out the time and the circumstances of this—the sufferings of Christ, and the glories which would follow.

¹²It was revealed to them that they were working, not for themselves, but for you. Thus, in these days, after the Holy Spirit has been sent from heaven, the gospel preachers have taught you these mysteries, which even the angels long to see.

> **1 PETER 1:1-12**
>
> **Read:** Peter is writing to an audience who were once pagans but now are Christians. The challenge is to maintain the integrity of their Christian lives in a world that does not share their values.
>
> **Reflect:** Think of a big challenge that tested your faith. How did you live those moments? Has that situation helped you deepen the faith? What does this mean to you: "the salvation obtained through Jesus Christ"?
>
> **Pray:** Ask God to strengthen your faith, that trials may increase your hope. Ask, too, to be a prophetic voice in difficulties.
>
> **Act:** Convey optimism to your people; share with them the joy and Christian hope you experience in life.

Be holy

[13] So, then, let your spirit be ready. Be alert, with confident trust, in the grace you will receive when Jesus Christ appears. [14] Like obedient children, do not return to your former life, given over to ignorance and passions. [15] Imitate the one who called you. As he is holy, so you, too, be holy in all your conduct [16] since Scripture says: *Be holy for I am holy.*

[17] You call upon a Father who makes no distinction between persons, but judges according to each one's deeds; take seriously, then, these years which you spend in a strange land. [18] Remember that you were freed from the useless way of life of your ancestors, not with gold and silver, [19] but with the precious blood of the Lamb without spot or blemish. [20] God, who has known Christ before the world began, revealed him to you in the last days. [21] Through him, you have faith in God who raised him from the dead and glorified him in order that you might put all your faith and hope in God.

[22] In obeying the truth, you have gained interior purification, from which comes sincere mutual love. Love one another then, with all your heart, [23] since you are born again, not from mortal beings, but with enduring life, through the word of God who lives and remains forever. [24] It is written: *All flesh is grass and its glory like the flowers of the field. The grass withers and the flower falls,* [25] *but the word of the Lord endures forever.* This word is the gospel, which has been brought to you.

> ## 1 PETER 1:13-25
>
> **Read:** Now baptized, they must grow in holiness, trusting God, loving one another and confident of the resurrection. They must live together trusting in God.
>
> **Reflect:** What does this sentence mean to you: "Be holy for I am holy"? What are the consequences in your everyday life? Is your community a holy community? What are the biggest difficulties a Christian has to overcome to live a holy life?
>
> **Pray:** Pray to God that the love you have for others be a visible sign of the love that He has for all of humanity.
>
> **Act:** Share how important it is for a Christian to live a holy life.

Christis the cornerstone

2 ¹ So, give up all evil and deceit, hypocrisy, envy, and every kind of gossip. ² Like newborn children, seek eagerly for the pure milk of the word that will help you grow and reach salvation. ³ *Did you not taste the goodness of the Lord?* ⁴ He is the living stone rejected by people but chosen by God and precious to him; set yourselves close to him, ⁵ so that you, too, become living stones built into a spiritual temple, a holy community of priests, offering spiritual sacrifices that please God through Jesus Christ. ⁶ Scripture says: *See, I lay in Zion, a chosen and precious cornerstone; whoever believes in him will not be disappointed.*

⁷ This means honor for you who believed, but for unbelievers, also *the stone which the builders rejected has become the cornerstone* ⁸ and it is *a stone to stumble over, a rock which lays people low.* They stumble over it, in rejecting the word, but the plan of God is fulfilled in this.

⁹ You are a *chosen race, a community of priest-kings, a consecrated nation, a people God has made his own, to proclaim his wonders*, for he called you from your darkness to his own wonderful light. ¹⁰ At one stage, you were *no people*, but now you are *God's people*, you had not received *his mercy*, but now you *have been given mercy*.

> **1 PETER 2:1-10**
>
> **Read:** Faced with hostility Christians grow closer to Christ. The world throws them away as unwanted stones, but they are precious in God's eyes and Christ will build them into a holy place where God dwells.
>
> **Reflect:** Peter tells the Christians they are "precious in God's sight" and that they are "offering spiritual sacrifices though Christ." How is this reflected in your life? In the life of your parish?
>
> **Pray:** Ask the Lord to transform the members of your community into "living stones"; that the way you live may help in the improvement and growth of the life of the Church.
>
> **Act:** Commit yourself with your community to make some specific action to improve the life of the church, be it at the parish or the diocese. Do not be afraid to be recognized as Christian before others.

Live a blameless life

¹¹ Beloved, while you are strangers and exiles, I urge you not to indulge in selfish passions that wage war on the soul. ¹² Live a blameless life among the pagans; so, when they accuse you falsely of any wrong, they may see your good works and give glory to God on the day he comes to them.

¹³ For the Lord's sake, respect all human authority: the king as the chief authority, ¹⁴ the governors, as sent by him to punish evildoers, and to encourage those who do good. ¹⁵ And God wants you to do good, so that you may silence those fools who ignorantly criticize you. ¹⁶ Behave as free people, but do not speak of freedom as a license for vice; you are free men, and God's servants. ¹⁷ Reverence each person, love your brothers and sisters, fear God and show respect to the emperor.

¹⁸ Servants must respect their masters, not only those who are good and understanding but also those who are difficult. ¹⁹ For there is merit in putting up with unprovoked suffering for the sake of God. ²⁰ What merit would there be in taking a beating when you have done wrong? But if you endure punishment when you have done well, that is a grace before God.

²¹This is your calling: remember Christ, who suffered for you, leaving you an example, so that you may follow in his way. ²²*He did no wrong and there was no deceit in his mouth.* ²³He did not return insult for insult, and when suffering, he did not curse but put himself in the hands of God who judges justly. ²⁴He went to the cross, bearing our sins in his own body on the cross, so that we might die to sin and live an upright life. *For, by his wounds, you have been healed.* ²⁵You were like *stray sheep*, but you have come back to the Shepherd and Guardian of your souls.

---

1 PETER 2:11-25

Read: In a world that regards them as aliens because of their faith, they must take special care that their lives reflect Christ, even those who are slaves with unjust masters. Their example in suffering is Christ.

Reflect: Can Christians be identified by the way they live? How does this sentence influence your life: "Christ suffered for you, leaving you an example so that you follow in his steps"?

Pray: Ask God the grace to love others as Christ loved us. Pray for Christians who have civil responsibilities, that the law of love be visible in their decisions.

Act: Join any public initiative that may help you meet the commandment of love and solidarity in your society.

Duties of husbands and wives

3 ¹In the same way, wives must be submissive to their husbands. If any of them resists the word, they will be won over without words by the conduct of their wives. ²It will be enough for them to see your responsible and blameless conduct.

³Do not be taken up with outward appearances: hairstyles, gold necklaces, and clothes. ⁴There is something more permanent that shines from within a person: a gentle and peaceful disposition. This is really precious in God's eyes. ⁵This was the way the holy women of the past dressed. They put their trust in God, and were obedient to their husbands; ⁶namely, Sarah, who had such respect for Abraham that she called him her lord. You are her children if you do what is right and are not afraid.

⁷Husbands, in your turn, be sensible in your life together. Be considerate, realizing that the woman is of a more frail disposition and that you both share in the gift of life. This will prevent anything from coming in the way of your prayer.

---

1 PETER 3:1-7

Read: Christians reflect Christ in their families, even when married to someone who is not a Christian. As with the Pauline letters, the theme of the living a Christian life within the family has value, where the specific advice reflects the patriarchal and sexist thinking of those days and is not appropriate now.

Reflect: How do you live your faith in your family environment? If you are married, how do you face the challenges of married life? Do you trust the love of God that heals and redeems everything?

Pray: Raise your family up in prayer to the Lord. May Christ be the sustenance, strength and consolation for your family.

Act: Invite the members of your family to have a moment of prayer at home, where they can express their concerns, desires, and thanksgiving. If you are married, invite your spouse to read and reflect on some biblical passages (1 Cor 13, for example) together, and later on renew your marriage vows.

---

⁸Finally, you should all be of one mind: share each other's troubles with mutual affection, be compassionate and humble. ⁹Do not repay evil for evil, or answer one insult with another. Give a blessing instead, since this is what you have been called to do, and so you will receive the blessing. ¹⁰*For if you seek life and want to see happiness, keep your tongue from evil and your mouth from speaking deceit.* ¹¹*Turn away from evil and do good; seek peace and pursue it.* ¹²Because *the Lord's eyes are turned to the just and his ears listen to their appeal. But the Lord frowns on evildoers.*

Do not fear or be disturbed

¹³Who can harm you if you devote yourselves to doing good? ¹⁴If you suffer for the sake of righteousness, happy are you. *Do not fear what they fear or be disturbed as they are,* ¹⁵but *bless the Lord* Christ in your

hearts. Always have an answer ready when you are called upon to account for your hope, but give it simply and with respect. [16]Keep your conscience clear so that those who slander you may be put to shame by your upright Christian living. [17]Better to suffer for doing good, if it is God's will, than for doing wrong.

Endure sufferings as Christ did

[18]Remember how Christ died, once and for all, for our sins. He, the just one, died for the unjust, in order to lead us to God. In the body he was put to death, in the spirit he was raised to life, [19]and it was then that he went to preach to the imprisoned spirits. [20]They were the generation who did not believe, when God, in his great patience, delayed punishing the world while Noah was building the ark, in which a small group of eight persons escaped through the water. [21]That was a type of the baptism that now saves you; this baptism is not a matter of physical cleansing, but of asking God to reconcile us through the resurrection of Christ Jesus. [22]He has ascended to heaven, and is at the right hand of God, having subjected the angels, Dominions and Powers.

1 PETER 3:8-22

Read: As with the family so with the Church community, they should have "sympathy for one another, a tender heart and a gentle mind." The example in suffering is Jesus Christ, Jesus Christ is their example. Just as God was with Noah, so God is with them in baptism.

Reflect: This passage shows how baptism is to change the lives of Christians. What lines in this reading do you take to heart?

Pray: Thank God for the new life received at Baptism and for each new member who receives it in your community. Ask for strength, courage, and conviction so that Christians may give good witness of their faith.

Act: Pledge to live with sympathy for others, with a tender heart and a gentle mind.

4 ¹Given that Christ suffered in his human life, arm yourselves with this certainty: the one who suffers in his body has broken with sin, ²so as to spend the rest of his life following the will of God, and not human passions.

³You have given enough time, in the past, to living as the pagans do: a life of excess, evil passions, drunkenness, orgies and worship of idols. ⁴They now find it strange that you are no longer swept along with them in this ruinous flood, and then abuse you for it. ⁵But they will be accountable to the one who is ready to judge the living and the dead. ⁶The gospel has been preached to many who are now dead. As humans, they received a deadly sentence, but through the spirit, they shall live for God.

⁷The end of all things is near; keep your minds calm and sober, for prayer. ⁸Above all, let your love for one another be sincere, for love covers a multitude of sins. ⁹Welcome one another into your houses without complaining. ¹⁰Serve one another with the gifts each of you received, thus becoming good managers of the varied graces of God. ¹¹If you speak, deliver the word of God; if you have a special ministry, let it be seen as God's power, so that, in everything, God may be glorified in Jesus Christ. To him belong glory and power forever and ever. Amen.

---

1 PETER 4:1-11

Read: Christians should expect that when they change their lives to live the will of God others will not understand them. Love, hospitality and mutual service define the Christian community. If they suffer for their faith, they are sharing Christ's sufferings, and like Christ trust themselves to their faithful Creator.

Reflect: How do you live a Christian life? What's the difference between the lives of Christians and those who are not Christians? Have you ever felt marginalized by the faith you profess? What do you think of "love covers a multitude of sins"?

Pray: Give thanks to God for the gifts in your life. Ask for a generous spirit to always put it at the service of the community and of anyone in need.

Act: "Serve one another with whatever gift each of you has received," says Peter. Identify your gifts and put them at the service of others.

Be glad to share in the sufferings of Christ

[12] My dear people, do not be surprised at the testing by fire, which is taking place among you, as though something strange were happening to you. [13] Instead, you should be glad to share in the sufferings of Christ because, on the day his glory is revealed, you will also fully rejoice. [14] You are fortunate if you are insulted because of the name of Christ, for the Spirit of glory rests on you. [15] I suppose that none of you should suffer for being a murderer, a thief, a criminal or an informer; [16] but if anyone suffers on account of being a Christian, do not consider it a disgrace; rather, let this name bring glory to God.

[17] The time of judgment has come, and it begins with God's household. If it's beginning so affects us, what will be the end of those who refuse to believe in the gospel? [18] *If the just one is barely saved, what will happen to the sinner and unbeliever?* [19] So then, if you suffer according to God's will, entrust yourself to the faithful creator, and continue to do good.

---

1 PETER 4:12-19

Read: Christians model their life after Christ, suffer as Christ suffered, and like Jesus, trust themselves into the hands of the Creator.

Reflect: Even in our days, there are Christians who are persecuted. Is it easy to live the Christian hope today? From your personal situation, do you endure with confidence and faith the difficulties of being Christian?

Ask: Pray for persecuted Christians. Pray also for those who suffer ridicule or rejection. Pray for everyone's strength and Jesus' constant presence in our lives.

Act: If you know anyone being persecuted, mocked, or discriminated against, offer your support and assistance in whatever way you can help.

Further admonitions

5 [1] I now address myself to those elders among you; I, too, am an elder, and a witness to the sufferings of Christ, hoping to share the glory that is to be revealed. [2] Shepherd the flock which God has entrusted to you, guarding it, not out of obligation, but willingly, for God's sake; not as one looking for a reward, but with a generous heart; [3] do not lord it over those in your care, rather be an example to your flock. [4] Then, when the Chief Shepherd appears, you will be given a crown of unfading glory.

[5] In the same way, let the younger ones among you respect the authority of the elders. All of you must clothe yourselves with humility in your dealings with one another because *God opposes the proud but gives his grace to the humble.*

[6] Bow down, then, before the power of God, so that he will raise you up at the appointed time. [7] Place all your worries on him, since he takes care of you.

[8] Be sober and alert, because your enemy the devil prowls about like a roaring lion seeking someone to devour. [9] Stand your ground, firm in your faith, knowing that our brothers and sisters, scattered throughout the world, are confronting similar sufferings. [10] God, the giver of all grace, has called you to share in Christ's eternal glory, and after you have suffered a little, he will bring you to perfection: he will confirm, strengthen and establish you forever. [11] Glory be to him forever and ever. Amen.

[12] I have had these few lines of encouragement written to you by Silvanus, our brother, whom I know to be trustworthy. For I wanted to remind you of the kindness of God really present in all this. Hold on to it.

[13] Greetings from the community in Babylon, gathered by God, and from my son, Mark.

[14] Greet one another with a friendly embrace. Peace to you all who are in Christ.

---

1 PETER 5:1-14

Read: Peter addresses first the community "elders," that is, the leaders and those responsible for the community. He asks them to take care of the flock as God wants. Then he asks the young people for understanding with their leaders. Finally, he urged the community to have a life sober and firm, according to God's will.

Reflect: "Restore, support, strengthen, establish" are the verbs Peter urges on the leaders of the Christian community. How are these verbs active in your parish?

Pray: Give thanks to God for the universal Church. Ask for all vocations, and in particular, for those who are devoted to the service of the community. Ask also for the members of your parish, that they give good witness of Christian life.

Act: Decide when and how you will seek to practice the virtue of humility.

SECOND LETTER OF
PETER

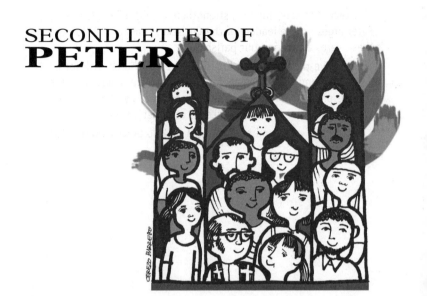

A ccording to the prevailing opinion today, it is a later book, probably written around the year 100 A.D. So it is presented as the second letter of Peter and it does its best to convince us. If it is not by Peter, that would not prevent it from being the word of God even if, at times, it expresses thoughts that seem strange on Peter's lips.

Those who deny its authenticity lean, at times, on the idea that the letter duplicates many passages from the letter of Jude, a text surely written after the death of Peter and Paul (Jd 17-18). In fact, as the early Church used to say, it seems more natural to think that Jude took up the predictions already mentioned in Peter's second letter (3:3-4). Therefore, we cannot invoke this argument to deny its authenticity.

Its three chapters refer to three concerns of the Church of the time, when the generation of those formed by the apostles appeared before the Church had set the main thrust of its organization. The author wants:

– to preserve the faith just as the witnesses of Jesus taught it;

– to fight against false teachers who distort the faith and also lead to immorality;

– to explain through God's patience why Christ had not yet returned.

SECOND LETTER OF
PETER

1 ¹Symeon Peter, a servant and apostle of Jesus Christ, to those who have been sanctified by our God and Savior Jesus Christ, and have received a faith as precious as ours:

²may grace and peace abound in you through the knowledge of God and of Jesus, our Lord.

We share in the divine nature

³His divine power has given us everything we need for life and piety. First, the knowledge of the One who called us through his own glory and Might, by which we were given the most extraordinary and precious promises. ⁴Through them, you share in the divine nature, after repelling the corruption and evil desires of this world.

⁵So strive with the greatest determination, and increase your faith with goodness, goodness with knowledge, ⁶knowledge with moderation, moderation with constancy, constancy with piety, ⁷piety with mutual affection, mutual affection with charity. ⁸If all these riches are in you, so as to abound in you, you will not be idle and useless; you will, rather, be rooted in the knowledge of Jesus Christ, our Lord. ⁹Whoever is not aware of this, is blind and shortsighted, and is forgetful of the cleansing of former sins.

¹⁰Therefore, brothers and sisters, strive more and more to respond to the call of God who chose you. If you do so, you will never stumble. ¹¹Moreover, you will be generously granted entry to the eternal kingdom of our Lord and Savior Jesus Christ.

¹²So, I shall always remind you of these things, though you know them, and remain firm in the truth that you have. ¹³It seems fitting that as long as I live in the tent of this body, I refresh your memory of them, ¹⁴knowing that my tent may soon be folded up, as our Lord Jesus Christ

has shown me. [15] I will, nonetheless, endeavor to see, that after my departure you will be constantly reminded of all this.

---

2 PETER 1:1-15

Read: This section and indeed the entire letter is a plea for Christians to "participate in the divine nature. "This is there vocation and their life flows from it.

Reflect: What are your thoughts about the call to participate in the divine nature? What do you think of when you read this?

Pray: Christ Jesus, stay close to me, help live as you live, lead me to the kingdom of God.

Act: Think of a specific virtue you need to cultivate and make a conscious effort to integrate it into your daily life.

The foundation of faith

[16] Indeed, what we taught you about the power, and the return of Christ Jesus our Lord, was not drawn from myths or formulated theories. We, ourselves, were eyewitnesses of his majesty [17] when he received glory and honor from God the Father, when, from the magnificent glory, this most extraordinary word came upon him: "This is my beloved Son, this is my Chosen One." [18] We, ourselves, heard this voice from heaven when we were with him on the holy mountain.

[19] Therefore, we believe most firmly in the message of the prophets, which you should consider rightly as a lamp shining in a dark place until the break of day when the Morning Star shines in your hearts.

[20] Know this well: no prophecy of Scripture can be handed over to private interpretation, [21] since no prophecy comes from human decision, for it was men of God, moved by the Holy Spirit, who spoke.

---

2 PETER 1:16-21

Read: The teaching they received comes directly from Christ and is the authentic teaching, the lamp that shines in the darkness.

Reflect: The Transfiguration passage expresses Jesus as God's chosen one. Do you also feel chosen by God? When you think of your life, of your faith in God the Father, how do you feel about him?

Pray: Surrender yourself to the love of God, like a child in the arms of his mother. Feel protected, loved and safe. Give thanks for this love.

Act: Take concrete action to provide protection or security to someone in need.

False teachers

2 [1] Just as there have been false prophets in the midst of the people of Israel, so will there be false teachers among you. They will introduce harmful sects and, by denying the Master who saved them, they will bring upon themselves sudden perdition. [2] Many, nonetheless, will imitate their vices and, because of them, the way of truth will be discredited. [3] They will take advantage of you with deceitful words for the sake of money. But the judgment made upon them long ago is not idle, and the destruction awaiting them is not asleep.

[4] In fact, God did not pardon the angels who sinned, but cast them into hell, confining them in the dark pits, keeping them there until the day of judgment. [5] Neither did he pardon the ancient world when he unleashed the waters of the flood upon the world of wicked people, but protected only Noah, the preacher of righteousness, along with seven others. [6] God also condemned the cities of Sodom and Gomorrah, reducing them to ashes, to serve as a warning to the wicked in the future. [7] But he saved Lot, a good man, deeply afflicted by the unbridled conduct of those vicious people. [8] For Lot, a righteous man, who lived in their midst, suffered day after day in the goodness of his heart, as he saw and heard of their crimes.

[9] So, then, the Lord knows how to free from trial those who serve him and keep the wicked for punishment on the day of judgment.

[10] He will do this, especially for certain people who follow the baser desires of their nature and despise the Lord's majesty. Proud and daring they are, not afraid of insulting fallen spirits, [11] while the angels who are superior to them in strength and power, do not permit themselves any injurious accusation in the presence of the Lord.

¹²Those people are like irrational animals, born to be caught and killed; after they have slandered what they cannot understand, they will end like animals ¹³and they will suffer the repayment of their wickedness.

They delight in giving themselves to depravity, even in the daytime; they are deceiving you, even when they are sharing your table. ¹⁴With their eyes always looking for adultery, they do not tire of sinning and seducing weak souls. They are full of greed—an accursed people.

¹⁵They abandoned the right way and followed Balaam, son of Beor, who was attached to what he gained from his wrongdoing. ¹⁶But he was rebuked for his sin: his she-ass began to speak with a human voice, stopping the prophet in his madness. ¹⁷These people are like waterless springs, clouds driven by a storm which move swiftly into the blackest darkness.

¹⁸With their boastful and empty discourses, they encourage the lust and impure desire of those who have just freed themselves from the common errors.

¹⁹They promise freedom, when they, themselves, are slaves of corruption: for people are slaves to whatever dominates them. ²⁰Indeed, after being freed from worldly vices through the knowledge of the Lord and Savior Jesus Christ, they returned to those vices and surrendered to them; and their present state has become worse than the first. ²¹It would have been better for them not to know the way of holiness than, knowing it, to turn away from the sacred doctrine that they had been taught. ²²In their case, these proverbs are relevant: "The dog turns back to its own vomit," and: "Hardly the pig has been washed, it wallows back in the mud."

2 PETER 2:1-22

Read: Teachers who mislead the Christian community are condemned in the strongest possible terms.

Reflect: The Church seems to have always had divisions between authentic and false teachers. Can you see this in your parish, in the universal church?

Pray: Ask God for the grace to remain faithful to the faith you have received and that you may be able to give valid testimony of Jesus, way, truth, and life for humanity.

> **Act:** Invite your loved ones to deepen their knowledge of the faith they have received, and to witness it in everyday life.

Why is the second coming of Christ delayed?

3 ¹ Dearly beloved, this is the second letter I write to you. In both of them, I have intended to remind you of sound doctrine. ² Do not forget the words of the holy prophets, and the teaching of our Lord and Savior, as you heard it through his apostles.

³ Remember, first of all, that in the last days, scoffers will appear, their mockery serving their evil desires. ⁴ And they will say, "What has become of his promised coming? Since our fathers in faith died, everything still goes on as it was from the beginning of the world." ⁵ Indeed, they deliberately ignore that, in the beginning, the heavens existed first, and earth appeared from the water, taking its form by the word of God. ⁶ By the same word of God, this world perished in the Flood. ⁷ Likewise, the word of God maintains the present heavens and earth until their destruction by fire; they are kept for the day of judgment when the godless will be destroyed. ⁸ Do not forget, beloved, that with the Lord, one day is like a thousand years, and a thousand years are like one day. ⁹ The Lord does not delay in fulfilling his promise, though some speak of delay; rather, he gives you time, because he does not want anyone to perish, but that all may come to conversion. ¹⁰ The Day of the Lord is to come like a thief. Then the heavens will dissolve with a great noise; the elements will melt away by fire, and the earth, with all that is on it, will be burned up.

¹¹ Since all things are to vanish, how holy and religious your way of life must be, ¹² as you wait for the day of God and long for its coming, when the heavens will dissolve in fire and the elements melt away in the heat. ¹³ We wait for a new heaven and a new earth, in which justice reigns according to God's promise.

¹⁴ Therefore, beloved, as you wait in expectation of this, strive that God may find you rooted in peace, without blemish or fault.

¹⁵ And consider that God's patience is for our salvation, as our beloved brother, Paul, wrote to you with the wisdom given him. ¹⁶ He speaks of these things in all his letters. There are, however, some points in them that are difficult to understand, which people who are ignorant

and immature in their faith, twist, as they do with the rest of the Scriptures, to their own destruction.

¹⁷So then, dearly beloved, as you have been warned, be careful, lest those people who have gone astray deceive you, in turn, and drag you along, making you stumble, and finally fall away. ¹⁸Grow in the grace and knowledge of our Lord and Savior Jesus Christ: to him be glory, now, and to the day of eternity. Amen.

---

2 PETER 3:1-18

Read: The delay of the second coming of Jesus concerns the believers and is being mocked by nonbelievers. The response of the author to this situation is that God does not measure time as we do. If there is a delay, it is "because he does not want anyone to perish, but that all may come to conversion."

Reflect: Do you expect a better world? Do you think that by the end of time love will conquer hate and death? What can we Christians do so that hope would not fail over the years?

Pray: Ask for wisdom, patience, and faith so that all Christians may know how to wait and rely on God's salvation, and that we will be prepared for the final encounter with the Lord.

Act: Encourage in your family and your community conversations about the ultimate hope that we Christians have: the rejoicing and final encounter with the Lord. Talk about the need to be prepared for that.

LETTERS OF
JOHN

INTRODUCTION TO THE FIRST LETTER OF JOHN

This first letter of John, inseparable from his Gospel, reminds us that the Christian way is nothing less than a divinization: our own.

From all time, the Christian ideal has seemed too pale or too narrow for many people. Without directly criticizing the values of Christianity and its benefits to humanity, they saw it as limiting people. We think of all those, like Marx, who affirmed that a real human liberation involves a struggle against faith. We think of those who today rely on science to widen the possibilities of life. We again think of all those who, shunning western activism, seek in oriental wisdom a way to the Absolute which they have failed to see in Christian faith.

Even for Christians, the sentimental religion springing from enthusiasm for Jesus, the good Master teaching universal love, often hides an ignorance of the ambitions of faith. For in Jesus it is God himself we want to reach, we are seekers of truth and we want to merge into this truth from which we have come.

John affirms in this first letter: If you have the Son of God you have total truth, you are on the way to authentic love and you are in communion with God himself.

However, perhaps, we are deceiving ourselves when we pretend to be in Christ. This is why John specifies the criteria, the conditions enabling us to verify if we are truly walking in the light and living in Love:

– In Christ we recognize God himself; yet we must always remember to interiorize his actions, his mission, his way of being human.

– We believe we have been reborn from God: that does not mean that we are above his commandments, nor that we should neglect daily efforts to be worthy of him.

– Faith has renewed our knowledge of God. What matters most is to understand his love and, for that, there is no better teaching than that of the cross.

This letter of John seeks to settle many doubts and confusion concerning Christian faith. It was written when "Gnosticism" or knowledge was beginning. Gnosticism involved an elaborate system that included many elements, already present in the so-called Asian religious, namely, from the Roman province of Asia, today's Turkey. Paul had already encountered them some thirty years before (see Captivity Letters: Ephesians, Philippians, Colossians, and Philemon; Paul wrote these letters while in prison) and now John was noticing the expansion of Gnosticism.

The Gospel of John had freed from all ambiguity the faith in Christ, Son of God, and divine person, born from God and having returned to God. But Gnostics were always ready to grasp onto beliefs they ran across to recast them into their endless tales. Gnostics tried to integrate the person of Jesus into their intellectual dialectics, their conflicts of angels and spiritual powers. According to Gnostics, Jesus did come from God although he was only a spirit. He only had a human appearance and he did not die for us. Redemption continues to be a process through which divine sparks come out of matter and what matters to them is to know the secrets of these celestial conflicts. Gnostics claimed to be spiritual and yet, while they condemned marriage, they did not see anything wrong with sexual freedom.

Therefore, it was necessary to reaffirm that Jesus was fully human; he was the Christ who had come in the flesh. Several times, the letter will refer to the sacrifice and to the blood of Jesus.

Some people think that this letter sought to correct some improper interpretations that could be given of John's Gospel. It must have been written around the years 95–100 A.D.

FIRST LETTER OF
JOHN

1 ¹This is what has been from the beginning, and what we have heard and have seen with our own eyes, what we have looked at and touched with our hands, I mean the *Word* who is Life....

²The *Life* made *itself* known. We have seen Eternal Life and we bear witness, and we are telling you of it. It was with the Father and made himself known to us.

³So, we tell you what we have seen and heard that you may be in fellowship with us, and us with the Father and with his Son, Jesus Christ.

⁴And we write this that our joy may be complete.

---

1 JOHN 1:1-4

Read: The relationship between Jesus and his disciples comes from personal experience. Jesus Christ is not an idea but a reality. The apostles are his witnesses and announce him to those who have not yet heard, seen or touched him that they may also believe in him and enjoy the salvation that he brings.

Reflect: Why do you believe in Jesus? What is the foundation of your faith? From whom did you receive it? How do you give witness that Jesus is "the word of life"?

Pray: Pray for the gift of insight to see through the eyes of faith and to recognize the divine presence in ordinary daily life.

Act: Share your experience of God with other believers.

Walk in the light

⁵We heard his message from him, and announce it to you: God is light and there is no darkness in him.

⁶If we say we are in fellowship with him while we walk in darkness, we lie, instead of being in the truth. ⁷But if we walk in the light, as he is in the light, we are in fellowship with one another; and the blood of Jesus, the Son of God, purifies us from all sin.

⁸If we say, "We have no sin," we deceive ourselves and the truth is not in us. ⁹If we confess our sins, he who is faithful and just will forgive us our sins and cleanse us from all wickedness.

¹⁰If we say that we do not sin, we make God a liar, his word is not in us.

Fulfill the commandment of love

2¹My little children, I write to you that you may not sin. But if anyone sins, we have an intercessor with the Father, Jesus Christ, the Just One. ²He is the sacrificial victim for our sins and the sins of the whole world.

³How can we know that we know him? If we fulfill his commands.

⁴If you say, "I know him," but do not fulfill his commands, you are a liar and the truth is not in you. ⁵But if you keep his word, God's love is made complete in you. This is how we know that we are in him:

⁶he who claims to live in him, must live as he lived.

---

1 JOHN 1:5—2:6

Read: God is light and truth, sin is darkness and lies. If a Christian sins, he or she should trust in the loving mercy of God and ask for forgiveness, since Jesus "offered himself in sacrifice so that our sins may be forgiven."

Reflect: Have you personally experienced that "God is light" in your moments of darkness? Do you trust in God's forgiveness? Do you illumine your daily life with the Word of God and with his Gospel? Are you light for others?

Pray: Give thanks to God for all the times God has to illumine your life and ask to live always in His light: in His love and in loving your neighbors. Ask also for all those men and women who are going through moments of "darkness," that Christian witness may reflect divine light.

Act: Refuse to live in darkness. Trust in God's love and ask

> forgiveness for your sins. When forgiven, share the gift of reconciliation with others, especially with those whom you have offended.

[7] My dear friends, I am not writing you a new commandment, but reminding you of an old one, one you had from the beginning. This old commandment is the word you have heard.

[8] But, in a way, I give it as a new commandment that is true in him and in you, because the darkness is passing away, and the true light already shines.

[9] If you claim to be in the light but hate your brother, you are still in darkness.

[10] If you love your brothers and sisters, you remain in the light, and nothing in you will make you fall. [11] But if you hate your brother, you are in the dark, and walk in darkness without knowing where you go, for the darkness has blinded you.

[12] My dear children, I write this to you: you have already received the forgiveness of your sins through the name of Jesus. [13] Fathers, I write this to you: you know him who is from the beginning. Young men, I write this to you: you have overcome the evil one. My dear children, I write to you because you already know the Father.

[14] Fathers, I write to you, because you know him who is from the beginning. Young men, I write to you because you are strong, and the word of God lives in you who have, indeed, overcome the evil one.

[15] Do not love the world, or what is in it. If anyone loves the world, the love of the Father is not in him.

[16] For everything in the world—
the craving of the flesh,
the greed of eyes
and people boasting of their superiority—
all this belongs to the world, not to the Father.

[17] The world passes away with all its craving, but those who do the will of God remain for ever.

> **1 JOHN 2:7-17**
>
> **Read:** To live in light is to live in love. Our goal for loving God is our constantly keeping His word, which is to love others. The life of Jesus is the model of life for all Christians.
>
> **Reflect:** How closely do people associate the love of God with the love of others? Do people even try to love God, or is the love of material things stronger?
>
> **Pray:** Pray for God's assistance in helping you to overcome any difficulty you are having with relationships at this time of your life. Ask for the grace to live in the love that Jesus, God's Son, taught us.
>
> **Act:** Perform simple actions that will show in your relationship with others that you "walk in the light" and not "in darkness."

Reject the antichrist

[18] My dear children, it is the last hour. You were told that an antichrist would come; but several antichrists have already come, by which we know that it is now the last hour.

[19] They went out from us, though they did not really belong to us. Had they belonged to us, they would have remained with us. So it became clear, that not all of us were really ours.

[20] But you have the anointing from the Holy One so that all of you have true wisdom.

[21] I write to you, not because you lack knowledge of the truth, but because you already know it, and lies have nothing in common with the truth. [22] Who is the liar?

The one who denies that Jesus is the Christ.

This is an antichrist who denies both the Father and the Son. [23] The one who denies the Son is without the Father, and those who acknowledge the Son also have the Father.

[24] Let what you heard from the beginning remain in you. If what you heard from the beginning remains in you, you too will remain in the Son and in the Father. [25] And this is the promise he, himself, gave us: eternal life.

[26] I write this to you thinking of those who try to lead you astray.

²⁷You received from him an anointing, and it remains in you, so you do not need someone to teach you. His anointing teaches you all things. It speaks the truth and does not lie to you; so remain in him, and keep what he has taught you.

²⁸And now, my children, live in him, so that when he appears in his glory, we may be confident and not ashamed before him when he comes.

²⁹You know that he is the Just One: know, then, that anyone living justly is born of God.

---

1 JOHN 2:18-29

Read: Once again the Christian community is divided by different factions. The "antichrist" faction looks after their own benefit instead of the community.

Reflect: What does it mean for you to "abide in God"? In what ways does God "abide" in you? Can a person be a Christian without being a part of the Church?

Pray: Ask for the grace to always be united with God and His Son through the Holy Spirit. Pray that your parish that its everyday life will live according to the teachings of the Gospel.

Act: Decide what you need to do to abide in God in your everyday life and as a member of your parish.

---

3 ¹See what singular love the Father has for us: we are called children of God, and we really are. This is why the world does not know us because it did not know him.

²Beloved, we are God's children, and what we shall be has not yet been shown. Yet, when he appears in his glory, we know that we shall be like him, for then, we shall see him as he is. ³All who have such hope try to be pure as he is pure.

⁴Anyone who commits a sin acts as an enemy of the law of God; any sin acts wickedly because all sin is wickedness. ⁵You know that he came to take away our sins and that there is no sin in him. ⁶Whoever remains in him has no sin, whoever sins has not seen or known him.

⁷My little children, do not be led astray; those who do what is right are upright, just as Jesus Christ is upright. ⁸But those who sin belong to the devil, for the devil sins from the beginning.

This is why the Son of God was shown to us, he was to undo the works of the devil.

⁹Those born of God do not sin, for the seed of God remains in them; they cannot sin because they are born of God.

¹⁰What is the way to recognize the children of God, and those of the devil? The one who does not do what is right is not of God; so, too, the one who does not love his brother or sister.

---

1 JOHN 3:1-10

Read: The Father's love makes us his children who will continually grow in love by doing good and rejecting evil.

Reflect: Are you aware of being a child of God? What are its implications for you? Do you recognize others as your brothers and sisters since they are also children of God? What does the following expression tell you: "The one who does not do what is right is not of God; so, too, the one who does not love his brother or sister"?

Pray: Ask for the grace to live as a child of God, doing good and avoiding evil. Ask also that the Christian community may be a witness to the universal fellowship willed by God in its day-to-day living.

Act: Express the love of God to the people near you with gestures that will make them feel loved, special persons, sons, and daughters of God.

---

¹¹For this is the message taught to you from the beginning: we must love one another. ¹²Do not imitate Cain, who killed his brother, for he belonged to the Evil One. Why did he kill him? Because he, himself, did evil, and his brother did good.

¹³So, be not surprised, brothers, if the world hates us; ¹⁴we love our brothers and sisters, and with this, we know that we have passed from death to life. The one who does not love remains in death.

¹⁵The one who hates his brother is a murderer, and, as you know, eternal life does not remain in the murderer.

¹⁶This is how we have known what love is: he gave his life for us. We, too, ought to give our life for our brothers and sisters.

¹⁷ If anyone enjoys the riches of this world but closes his heart when he sees his brother or sister in need, how will the love of God remain in him? ¹⁸ My dear children, let us love, not only with words and with our lips, but in truth and in deed.

¹⁹ Then, we shall know that we are of the truth, and we may calm our conscience in his presence. ²⁰ Every time it reproaches us, let us say: God is greater than our conscience, and he knows everything.

²¹ When our conscience does not condemn us, dear friends, we may have complete confidence in God. ²² Then, whatever we ask, we shall receive, since we keep his commands and do what pleases him.

²³ His command is that we believe in the name of his Son Jesus Christ and that we love one another as he has commanded us.

²⁴ Whoever keeps his commands remains in God and God in him. It is by the Spirit God has given us that we know he lives in us.

---

1 JOHN 3:11-24

Read: The central message of the Gospel is mutual love. This love is the sign that identifies Christians. Love begets life, hatred death. Jesus gave his life for us and sent us his Spirit, the same one who impels us to live as Jesus lived.

Reflect: What does the following text suggest to you: "Let us love, not only in words and with our lips, but in truth and in deed"? How can we give our life for others nowadays?

Pray: Preaching as an old man, St. John would repeat again and again, "Love one another." Repeat these words as a mantra, a prayer.

Act: Share what God inspired you in this moment of reflection. Express your faith by loving others not only in words but also with concrete deeds.

Do not trust every inspiration

4 ¹ My beloved, do not trust every inspiration. Test the spirits to see whether they come from God because many false prophets are now in the world.

² How will you recognize the Spirit of God? Any spirit, recognizing Jesus as the Christ who has taken our flesh, is of God. ³ But any spirit

that does not recognize Jesus is not from God, it is the spirit of the antichrist. You have heard of his coming, and even now, he is in the world.

[4] You, my dear children, are of God, and you have already overcome these people because the one who is in you is more powerful than he who is in the world.

[5] They are of the world and the world inspires them, and those of the world listen to them.

[6] We are of God, and those who know God, listen to us, but those who are not of God, ignore us. This is how we know the spirit of truth and the spirit of falsehood as well.

God-Love is the source of love

[7] My dear friends, let us love one another, for love comes from God. Everyone who loves is born of God and knows God.

[8] Those who do not love have not known God, for God is love.

[9] How did the love of God appear among us? God sent his only Son into this world, that we might have life through him.

[10] This is love: not that we loved God, but that he first loved us and sent his Son as an atoning sacrifice for our sins.

[11] Dear friends, if such has been the love of God, we, too, must love one another.

[12] No one has ever seen God, but if we love one another, God lives in us, and his love comes to its perfection in us.

[13] How may we know that we live in God and he in us? Because God has given us his Spirit.

[14] We ourselves have seen and declare that the Father sent his Son to save the world. [15] Those who confess that Jesus is the Son of God, God remains in them and they in God.

[16] We have known the love of God and have believed in it. God is love. The one who lives in love, lives in God and God in him.

[17] When do we know that we have reached a perfect love? When, in this world, we are like him in everything, and expect, with confidence, the Day of Judgment.

[18] There is no fear in love. Perfect love drives away fear, for fear has to do with punishment; those who fear do not know perfect love.

[19] So, let us love one another since he loved us first.

[20] If you say, "I love God," while you hate your brother or sister, you

are a liar. How can you love God whom you do not see, if you do not love your brother whom you see? [21] We received from him this commandment: let those who love God also love their brothers.

---

1 JOHN 4:1-21

Read: The summit of Christian life is love because God is love. And out of love, God sent us His Son. And out of love, His Son died on the cross for us. And because of love, His Spirit is with us. Christians live in God by sharing their love with the world.

Then it is our task as Christians to show this love in the world with mutual love and loving everybody.

Reflect: Have you experienced the love of God in your life? How? Do you think that you love God? How is it manifested? What does the following expression suggest to you: "If you say, 'I love God,' while you hate your brother or sister, you are a liar. How can you love God, whom you do not see if you do not love your brother, whom you see"?

Pray: Ask God the grace to love others with the same passion as how God loves us. Give Him thanks for His loving presence in your life.

Act: Show in your dealing with others the love that God has for you. Try to see in the face of others the face of God who loves you.

Faith comes from God

5 [1] All those who believe that Jesus is the Anointed are born of God; whoever loves the Father loves the Son. [2] How may we know that we love the children of God? If we love God and fulfill his commands,

[3] for God's love requires us to keep his commands. In fact, his commandments are not a burden

[4] because all those born of God overcome the world. And the victory, which overcomes the world, is our faith. [5] Who has overcome the world? The one who believes that Jesus is the Son of God.

[6] Jesus Christ was acknowledged through water, but also through blood.

Not only water but water and blood.

And the Spirit, too, witnesses to him, for the Spirit is truth.

⁷ There are, then, three testimonies:

⁸ the Spirit, the water and the blood, and these three witnesses agree.

⁹ If we accept human testimony, with greater reason must we accept that of God given in favor of his Son. ¹⁰ If you believe in the Son of God you have God's testimony in you.

But those who do not believe make God a liar, since they do not believe his words when he witnesses to his Son.

¹¹ What has God said? That he has granted us eternal life, and this life is in his Son. ¹² The one who has the Son has life; those who do not have the Son of God do not have life.

---

1 JOHN 5:1-12

Read: God's love for humanity is shown by His Son, Jesus Christ. As Christians, we should give witness of this.

Reflect: What does it mean for you personally to say Jesus Christ is the Son of God? What are the implications for your life?

Pray: Give thanks to God for His Son sent to the world and for the faith that you have received. Ask for strength and courage to be a witness of this truth.

Act: Describe the contents of your faith. In what you believe and why. Share your reflection with others and encourage them to witness to the love of God in the world.

Keep yourselves from idols

¹³ I write you, then, all these things, that you may know that you have eternal life, all you who believe in the name of the Son of God.

¹⁴ Through him, we are fully confident that whatever we ask according to his will, he will grant us. ¹⁵ If we know that he hears us whenever we ask, we know that we already have what we asked of him.

¹⁶ If you see your brother committing sin, a sin which does not lead to death, pray for him, and God will give life to your brother. I speak, of course, of the sin which does not lead to death. There is also a sin that leads to death; I do not speak of praying about this. ¹⁷ Every kind of wrongdoing is sin, but not all sin leads to death.

¹⁸ We know that those born of God do not sin, but the one who was born of God protects them, and the evil one does not touch them.

¹⁹ We know that we belong to God, while the whole world lies in evil.

²⁰ We know that the Son of God has come and has given us power to know the truth. We are in him who is true, his Son Jesus Christ. He is the true God and eternal life.

²¹ My dear children, keep yourselves from idols.

1 JOHN 5:13-21

Read: This section repeats the main themes of the letter and concludes by encouraging Christians to help and support each other in believing in Jesus. This support requires a communal effort.

Reflect: Do you trust in God's goodness? How do you show this trust? In your opinion, nowadays, how do people show their trust? Is Christian witnessing an alternative to this situation?

Pray: Ask from God what you really need, knowing that you are talking to a God who loves you and whom you can completely trust.

Act: As much as possible, share what gives security in your life: accepting people in your home; inviting to your table friends or relatives who may be going through some difficulties.

SECOND LETTER OF
JOHN

Chosen Lady: this is the way John greets the community of an unknown city. The Church is chosen and holy, just as the people
in it are the chosen and holy ones of God.

John invites the people to have a steadfast and emphatic attitude toward those who do not accept the faith of the apostles. At the same
time, he reminds them of the fundamental law for Christians: love.

To remain zealously faithful to the truth is to love Christ who entrusted
this truth to us. We need the whole truth and not only what is most
pleasing to people today.

¹I, the elder, to the chosen Lady and her children, whom I love sincerely—and with me, all who know the truth—²because of this same
truth which is, and will be, in us forever.

³Grace, mercy, and peace be with you, in the name of God the Father,
and of his Son, Christ Jesus, in truth and love.

⁴I rejoiced greatly on meeting some of your children who live in accordance with the truth, according to the command we have received
from the Father. ⁵And now, I ask you, Lady—I write to you not a new

commandment, but that which we had from the beginning—I ask you: *let us love one another.*

⁶This is love: to walk according to his commandments. And this is the commandment: that you walk in love, as you have learned from the beginning.

⁷Many deceivers have gone out into the world, people who do not acknowledge that Jesus is the Christ, who came in the flesh. They are impostors and antichrists. ⁸Take care of yourselves that you do not lose the fruit of your labors, but receive a perfect reward. ⁹Everyone who goes beyond, and does not remain within the teaching of Christ, does not have God. The one who remains in the teaching has both the Father and the Son. ¹⁰If anyone comes to you and does not bring this teaching, do not receive him into your houses, or even greet him. ¹¹Even in greeting him, you would become an accomplice in his wicked deeds.

¹²I have many things to write to you, but I prefer not to use paper and ink. I hope to meet you and speak to you personally, that our joy may be full.

¹³The children of your chosen sister greet you.

2 JOHN 1-13

Read: This letter calls the community to the grace, mercy and truth that come from God. The image suggested by the words "chosen Lady" seems to reflect a united Christian community as if they were all brothers and sisters.

Reflect: Love is the commandment we must walk in. How do you walk in love? What role does Jesus have in your walk of love?

Pray: Instead of considering the negative aspects of evaluating our lives, offer a prayer of rejoicing for those who live and walk following the commandments of God's love.

Act: Determine to walk in a path of love you have avoided because of fear of what it may cost you.

THIRD LETTER OF JOHN

To the Christians who knew him, the apostle John was not "Saint John," but a man. For a certain Diotrephes, to whom John gave the responsibility of a community that we do not know, John was a bothersome old man. To better dominate his church, Diotrephes was cutting off the relationship.

John, however, in his three letters, as in the Gospel, speaks of the "communion" which must exist among Christians. Any church or group must remain open to others, maintaining constant contact with them. Paul also insists on this responsibility: to welcome in their homes all Christians coming from other places in order to strengthen the bonds of the common faith.

¹ I, the elder, to my dear friend Gaius, whom I love sincerely.

² Dear friend, may everything go well with you and may you enjoy health of body and soul. ³ I greatly rejoiced with the friends who arrived and testified to your faithfulness to the truth, namely, how you walk in the truth. ⁴ Nothing gives me greater joy than to know that my children live in the truth.

⁵ Beloved, you do well to care for the brothers and sisters as you do. I mean those coming from other places. ⁶ They spoke of your charity before the assembled Church. It will be well to provide them with what they

need to continue their journey, as if you did it for God. [7] In reality, they have set out on the road for his name without accepting anything from the pagans. [8] We should receive such persons, making ourselves their cooperators in the work of the truth.

[9] I have written these words to the Church. But Diotrephes, who is anxious to preside over it, does not acknowledge our authority. [10] So when I come, I will not cease reproaching his manner of acting, since he discredited us with words of evil intent. And not content with that, he does not receive the friends, and even restrains those who want to receive them, and expels them from the Church.

[11] Dear friend, do not imitate evil, but only the good. Whoever does good is of God. Whoever does evil does not know God. [12] Now, about Demetrius: everyone praises him, even the truth itself. We, too, praise him, and you know that our testimony is true. [13] I have many things to tell you, but I do not want to do it in writing. [14] I hope to see you soon, and we will talk face to face.

[15] Peace be with you. Your friends greet you. Greet the friends for me, each one by name.

---

3 JOHN 1-15

Read: Scholars believe that this is a reply to a letter Gaius wrote to John, that letter is lost. But it appears to have concerned a misuse of authority by Diotrephes who seems to be creating some divisions and problems in the community.

Reflect: Two references are made to friendship: first, what you do faithfully for friends, do for strangers; and secondly, "he even refuses to welcome his friends." In what way is friendship part of your faith?

Pray: Ask for understanding and patience in dealing with someone like Diotrephes, who seems to like to dominate the group and who does not know how to work well with others.

Act: This letter concludes with a particular instruction to greet others, each one by name. Take the necessary time and make an effort to know the name of a person who is now a casual acquaintance or whose name you do not know. From now on, greet that person by name.

LETTER OF
JUDE

The Holy Spirit may have wanted to leave us the Letter of Jude so that we could appreciate the Gospels and other writings of the apostles better. We would have to be familiar with the literature of those days to know how complicated and incredible religious books were, both the books of the Jews and of the non-Jews. In comparison, the Gospels and Paul seem to belong to this century.

This letter, which is attributed to the apostle Jude Thaddeus, was written, in fact, about the end of the first century. It denounces the false teachers like those mentioned in the letters to Timothy and Titus.

Nevertheless, the comparisons and the examples which are used come from the Jewish books of the time. The Church had not yet defined which books were inspired by God and were part of the Scriptures. Besides the Old Testament, Christians used the religious literature of the Jews (for example, the Book of Enoch, the Testament of the Twelve Patriarchs, and the Assumption of Moses). So there are many legends concerning ancient times which we find in this letter. In this literary form, which seems rather antiquated to us, there is a strong call to preserve the integral faith of the apostles, which at the time was a serious concern of the Church. Therefore, a few years later, the author of the second Peter copied part of this letter.

LETTER OF
JUDE

¹ Jude, a servant of Jesus Christ, and a brother of James, to those called to the faith, beloved by God the Father, and kept in Christ Jesus.

² May mercy, peace and love abound in you. ³ Most beloved, I had wanted to write to you about the salvation we all share, but now I feel I must urge you to fight for the faith God has given, once for all, to the saints.

⁴ Some individuals have slipped into your midst, godless people who were, long ago, marked down for condemnation. They make use of the grace of our God as a license for immorality and deny our only Master and Lord Jesus Christ.

JUDE 1:1-4

Read: The letter begins by encouraging the Christian community to be faithful and not to be misled by people who, with the excuse of being in God's grace, live a disorderly life.

Reflect: Do you live in accordance with the faith that you profess? What are the concrete implications in your everyday life? What does it mean for you "to fight for the faith"?

Pray: Pray that mercy, peace and love be yours in abundance.

Act: Reflect on the times you have not been faithful to the faith you profess. Why did you do it? What difficulties did you have? What consequences did it have in your life? Ask forgiveness for that, be it through the sacrament of reconciliation or expressing your sorrow to those you have offended.

---

⁵ Although you may be aware of it, I wish to remind you that the Lord saved his people from the land of Egypt, but later delivered to death

those who did not believe. [6] He did the same with the angels who did not keep their rank but abandoned their dwelling places. God enclosed them in eternal prisons, in the pit of darkness, until the great day of judgment. [7] Sodom and Gomorrah, and the surrounding cities that prostituted themselves and were lured into unnatural unions are also a warning of the punishment of eternal fire. [8] In spite of all this, these people now do the same: in their ravings, they debase their bodies, scorn the celestial authorities, blaspheme against the angels.

[9] When the archangel Michael fought against the devil and disputed about the body of Moses, he did not dare insult him, but simply said, "May the Lord rebuke you!" [10] Not so these people, they insult and scorn what they cannot understand; what they know by instinct, like animals, they use for their corruption. [11] Woe to them! They follow the footsteps of Cain, and like Balaam, go astray because of money: they will finally perish like the rebellious Korah. [12] When you celebrate your love-meals, they spoil everything, coming only for the food, and shamelessly seeing to their own needs. They are like clouds carried along by the wind, which never bring rain, like trees without fruit at the end of autumn, twice dead when uprooted. [13] The scum of their vices is splashed like foam on the rough waves of the sea; they are like shooting stars, which the thick darkness engulfs for ever. [14] The patriarch Enoch, the seventh after Adam, said these words about them: The Lord comes with thousands of angels [15] to judge everyone and call the wicked to account for all the evil deeds they committed; he will punish all the injurious words, the impious sinners uttered against him. [16] All these are discontented, who curse their lot and follow their passions. Their mouth is full of arrogant words, and they flatter people for their own interest.

[17] But, most beloved, remember what the apostles of Christ Jesus our Lord announced to you. [18] They said to you, "At the end of time, there will be scoffers, led by their desires, which are those of godless people." [19] Actually, these people are those who cause divisions, they are worldly people, and do not have the Holy Spirit.

[20] But, dearly beloved, build your life on the foundation of your most holy faith, praying in the Holy Spirit. [21] Remain firm in the love of God, welcoming the mercy of Jesus Christ our Lord, which leads to eternal life.

[22] Try to convince those who doubt; [23] others you will save, snatching

them from condemnation. Treat the others with compassion, but also with prudence, shunning even the clothes that touched their body.

²⁴To the one God, who is able to keep you from all sin and bring you, happy and without blemish before his own glory, ²⁵to the one God who saves us through Jesus Christ our Lord, to him be glory, honor, might, and power, from past ages, now and forever. Amen.

JUDE 1:5-25

Read: Jude uses a variety of stories to show that God has weeded out evil doers among the angels, Cain who killed Abel, people in the time of Abraham and Moses, God will weed out those evil doers from their midst. The community should remain faithful to the teachings of the Lord as announced by the apostles. Its witness is a life built "on the foundation of your most holy faith."

Reflect: Some of the most colorful insults and curses are found in this section. God is not neutral in the face of evil. God wants the community to be built up in the Holy Spirit. Is your community living according to the faith they profess? Are prayer and mutual service encouraged in your community? What do you do to deepen and to propagate your faith?

Pray: Ask forgiveness from the Lord for the times you have not been faithful to his teachings and commandments, especially the commandment of love. Ask also for the grace of solidarity that your community may also live in love.

Act: Begin to pray to the Holy Spirit that you keep yourself in the love of God.

REVELATION

John the Evangelist, brother of James the Martyr (Acts 12), was deported to Patmos Island because of his faith. From there he sent us this "Revelation." Skies opened, angels and tragedies, corruption of the well-to-do and the blood of martyrs: God's judgment goes down the centuries. God's glory has come near and only a curtain divides us. Everything is brought to an end in the heavenly city.

Why does *Revelation* have the reputation of being a mysterious book, hard to understand and why, for many people, does it have a terrifying meaning? Can it be because there, many seek secret figures and messages which might be adapted to current events as if John had announced them in detail?

If we want to avoid misunderstanding the images and the style of the Revelation of John we should first know that "revelations," or "apocalypses," were a popular form of literature at the time of Jesus. There was an Apocalypse of Isaiah, one of Moses, and many others. It was a way of interpreting contemporary events wrapped up in formidable images, with visions and angels. The author of the book attributed it to a known prophet of the past, but only related events that were already known, trying to draw conclusions and showing what God wanted to achieve.

The style and the images of Revelation (Apocalypse) bewilder many people to the extent that today the term is mostly used to refer to world-wide tragedies. We are going to give the needed explanations, but from the beginning, we have to understand that John was answering the questions that his Christian contemporaries were asking, and questions that we are still asking ourselves today. Why didn't the Savior bring justice and peace to the world and why do we see so much evil and suffering?

John answers that if centuries follow after Christ's coming, this is not so that we may enjoy heaven on earth but rather because this world is at stake in the conflict between good and evil. John probably wrote at the time of Emperor Domitian, namely, the start of the great Church persecutions in the Roman Empire. John is going to say, again and again, that being Christian means being faithful and if need be, being a martyr.

Understanding the importance of this conflict in today's history is much more useful than searching the Book of Revelation for secret messages that would surely enable us to expect extraordinary events and, perhaps, to have the chance to survive. We will better understand this Revelation if we interpret the visions, numbers, and symbols according to the rules of apocalyptic literature. Then we shall see that the Revelation of Jesus Christ is neither difficult nor terrifying but full of joy and hope.

The risen Christ is the center of history; the world is the place of the struggle between the Church, headed by Christ, and Satan's forces; Christians are called to give their witness with courage.

In this book we can see seven series, each with seven elements, in four major parts:

– the seven messages to the churches, Chapters 1–3;
– the fulfillment of the Old Testament, Chapters 4–11;
– the Church facing the Roman Empire, Chapters 12–19;
– the last days and the heavenly Jerusalem, Chapters 20–22.

We have attributed the Book of Revelation to John the Evangelist. In fact, there were many doubts on this point during the first two centuries. The western Church, differently from that in the East, did not see it as the work of John the Evangelist and while today's criticism does not raise major difficulties, it does raise many doubts. It is interesting to notice that the image of the Sacrificed Lamb, a central theme of the book, is found throughout the entire book. This theme, along with the same quotation from the prophet Zechariah (Rev 1:7), bears the personal mark of John in his Gospel (Jn 19:31-37).

REVELATION

1 ¹ *The Revelation of Jesus Christ.*

God gave it to him to let his servants know what is soon to take place.
He sent his angel to make it known to his servant, John,
²who reports everything he saw, for this is the word of God and the declaration of Jesus Christ.

³Happy is the one who reads aloud these prophetic words,
and happy those who hear them, and treasure everything written here,
for the time is near.

⁴From John to the seven churches of Asia:
receive grace and peace from him who is, who was, and who is to come,
and from the seven spirits of God, which are before his throne,

⁵and from Jesus Christ, the faithful witness, the firstborn of the dead,
the ruler of the kings of the earth.

To him who loves us, and has washed away our sins with his own blood, ⁶making us a kingdom and priests for God his Father,

to him be the glory and power, for ever and ever. Amen.

⁷*See, he comes with the clouds*, and everyone will see him, even *those who pierced him*; on his account, *all the nations of the earth will beat their breast.* Yes. It will be so.

⁸"I am the *Alpha* and the *Omega*," says the Lord God, "*the one who is, and who was, and who is to come: the Master of the universe.*"

REVELATION 1:1-8

Read: The Book of Revelation is not about the future, it is about the presence of God with us in every trial; we are never alone. It is a song of hope for Christians: "Happy those who hear them, and treasure everything written here, for the time is near."

Reflect: Are you aware of God's presence in your life? Is the Word of God a source of joy for you? Are you optimistic toward the future knowing that your life leads to God?

Pray: Place your life in God's hands and ask for the strength to be faithful to the faith you profess.

Act: Look back at your life and see how Jesus has been present in it. Plan your life in such a way that Jesus will occupy a relevant place.

[9]I, John, your brother, who shares with you, in Jesus, the sufferings, the kingdom, and the patient endurance, was on the island of Patmos, because of the word of God and witnessing to Jesus. [10]On the Lord's day, the spirit took possession of me and I heard a voice behind me, which sounded like a trumpet, [11]"Write down all that you see in a book, and send it to the seven churches; of Ephesus, Smyrna, Pergamum, Thyatira, Sardis, Philadelphia and Laodicea."

[12]I turned to see who was speaking to me; behind me were seven golden lampstands [13]and, in the middle of these, I saw someone like a *son of man* dressed in a long robe tied with a golden girdle.

[14]*His head and his hair are white as wool*, or as snow, and his eyes are like flames of fire. [15]His feet are like burnished bronze when it has been refined in a furnace. His voice is like the roaring of the waves.

[16]I saw seven stars in his right hand, and a sharp, double-edged sword coming out of his mouth; his face shone like the sun in all its brilliance.

[17]Seeing him, I fell at his feet like one dead; but he touched me with his right hand and said, "Do not be afraid. It is I, the First and the Last. [18]I am the living one; I was dead; and now I am alive, for ever and ever; and mine are the keys of death and the netherworld. [19]Now write what you have seen, both what is and what is yet to come. [20]Know the secret of the seven stars you saw in my right hand, and the seven golden lampstands: the seven stars are the angels of the seven churches, and the seven lampstands are the seven churches.

REVELATION 1:9-20

Read: Writing to all the churches, John describes Christ using the words of the Book of Daniel. His point is Christ is always with them.

Reflect: The Risen Lord was present and active in the Church of that time. Are you aware of the presence of the Lord in today's Church? How do you think is this manifested?

Pray: Ask the Lord the grace to profoundly feel his presence in today's Church. Ask also that your life be an inspiration and a manifestation of his real and active presence in the world.

Act: Trust in the Lord's presence in the midst of the Church in spite of the scandals and mistakes of her members.

The seven messages to the churches

2 ¹ Write this to the angel of the church in Ephesus, "Thus says the one who holds the seven stars in his right hand, and who walks among the seven golden lampstands:

² I know your works, your difficulties, and your patient suffering. I know you cannot tolerate evildoers, but have tested those who call themselves apostles, and have proved them to be liars. ³ You have persevered, and have suffered for my name without losing heart.

⁴ Nevertheless, I have this complaint against you: you have lost your first love. ⁵ Remember from where you have fallen, and repent, and do what you used to do before. If not, I will come to you and remove your lampstand from its place; this I will do unless you repent. ⁶ Yet, it is in your favor that you hate the doings of the Nicolaitans, which I also hate.

⁷ Let anyone who has ears listen to what the Spirit says to the churches: To the victor, I will give to eat of the tree of life, which is in God's paradise."

REVELATION 2:1-7

Read: Revelation has a pattern: start with Christ, a short list of good and bad points about the local church, what they must do, and the promise of the Lord to strengthen them to do it.

Reflect: Being a Christian is not just about doing good, it is based on a love for Christ. Do you feel that love, have you ever?

Pray: Ask that Jesus may renew your faith; that he may bring you to a passion for his person, his life and his message. Ask: "Show me your face, O Lord."

Act: Make a re-examination of life at night and see if your faith is growing stale or boring. Know where Jesus is present, where you could and could not recognize him.

[8] Write this to the angel of the church in Smyrna, "Thus says the first and the last, he who was dead, and returned to life:

[9] I know your trials and your poverty: you are rich, indeed. I know how you are slandered by those who pretend to be Jews but are not, for they are, in fact, the synagogue of Satan. [10] Do not be afraid of what will happen to you. The devil will throw some of you into prison, to test you, and there will be ten days of trials. Remain faithful, even to death, and I will give you the crown of life.

[11] Let anyone who has ears listen to what the Spirit says to the churches: The victor has nothing to fear from the second death."

REVELATION 2:8-11

Read: The Church of Smyrna will be persecuted for her fidelity to Jesus. Listening to the Spirit they will be faithful in the face of death and be with Christ forever. In spite of that, Jesus asks her to be faithful until death and thus conquer life eternal.

Reflect: How does the contemporary world make it difficult for you to be a Christian? There are places in this reading where anti-Semitic feeling creeps in: "synagogue of Satan." Do you see Christians as intolerant of others?

Pray: Ask God for strength to remain firm and faithful in times of difficulties, fortitude to confront sufferings, and Faith to realize Jesus is always at your side.

Act: Think of a particular situation when you have not been faithful to the message of Jesus. Resolve to act differently in similar circumstances in the future: following the way Jesus taught us.

¹²Write this to the angel of the church in Pergamum, "Thus says the one who has the sharp, double-edged sword:

¹³I know where you live, where Satan's throne is, but you cling firmly to my name; you have not renounced me, not even in the days when Antipas, my faithful witness, was killed; in your place where Satan lives.

¹⁴Nevertheless, I have a few complaints against you: Some among you hold the teaching of Balaam, who taught Balak how to make the Israelites stumble by eating food sacrificed to idols and committing adultery. ¹⁵Also among you, some follow the teaching of the Nicolaitans. ¹⁶Therefore, repent; if not, I will come to you soon to attack these people with the sword of my mouth.

¹⁷Let anyone who has ears listen to what the Spirit says to the churches: To the victor, I will give the hidden manna. And I will also give a white stone with a new name written on it, which no one knows, except the one who receives it."

REVELATION 2:12-17

Read: The speaker is Jesus who knows they are being persecuted (Satan's throne). Struggling to remain faithful, their behavior is negatively affected by local customs and beliefs. The faithful are fed by God as Israel in the desert.

Reflect: Do you live in the midst of a social, economic and political environment that is far from the Word of God and the doctrine of the Church? How are we to show our fidelity to Jesus in these circumstances?

Pray: Ask God for wisdom to stay faithful to the Gospel when peer pressure and public opinion try to lead you elsewhere.

Act: Identify specific instances of Church teaching at odds with current lifestyle. How do you articulate what you believe? Try to form and inform yourself regarding those issues.

---

¹⁸Write this to the angel of the church in Thyatira, "Thus says the Son of God, whose eyes are like flames of fire, and whose feet are like burnished bronze. ¹⁹I know your works: your love, faith, service, patient endurance; and your later works, greater than the first.

²⁰Nevertheless, I have a complaint against you: you tolerate your

Jezebel, this woman who calls herself a prophetess; and is deceiving my servants; she teaches them prostitution, and the eating of food sacrificed to idols. ²¹I have given her time to repent, but she is unwilling to leave her prostitution. ²²So I am going to throw her onto a bed, and inflict severe trials on her partners in adultery, unless they repent of their evil. ²³I will strike her children dead, and all the churches will know that I am he who probes the heart and mind; I will give each of you what your conduct deserves.

²⁴Listen to me, now, the rest of you in Thyatira. You do not hold with this teaching and have not learned 'the secrets,' as they are called, which are in fact, those of Satan. So I have no cause to reproach you, ²⁵only, hold on to what you have, until I come. ²⁶To the victor who keeps to my ways to the end, *I will give power over the nations*, ²⁷*to rule them with an iron rod, and shatter them like earthen pots*; he will be like me, who received this power from my Father. ²⁸Moreover, I will give him the Morning Star.

²⁹Let anyone who has ears listen to what the Spirit says to the churches."

REVELATION 2:18-29

Read: The early days of Christianity were made difficult by public persecutions and internal fights about what Christian life should be. The basic theme is repeated: the good and bad works of the community, the changes that are needed, and the promise of Christ's presence in the Spirit.

Reflect: How do conflicts outside and inside the Church affect our faith? How is Christ present to you when this happens? "Morning Star" refers to fresh beginnings, the new day promised by Christ to those working through difficult times. Have you experienced this?

Pray: Ask the Lord for wisdom to discern what really comes from Christ and what is contrary to the Gospel.

Act: External and external conflict is part of the life of the Church and can confuse your heart. Find that private place where the Spirit speaks to you for clarity.

3 ¹Write this to the angel of the church in Sardis, "Thus says he who holds the seven spirits of God and the seven stars:

I know your worth: you think you live, but you are dead. ²Wake up, and strengthen that which is not already dead. For I have found your works to be imperfect in the sight of my God. ³Remember what you were taught; keep it, and change your ways. If you do not repent, I will come upon you like a thief, at an hour you least expect.

⁴Yet, there are some left in Sardis who have not soiled their robes; these will come with me, dressed in white, since they deserve it. ⁵The victor will be dressed in white, and I will never erase his name from the book of life; instead, I will acknowledge it before my Father and his angels.

⁶Let anyone who has ears listen to what the Spirit says to the churches."

REVELATION 3:1-6

Read: All the churches experience trouble, this time Sardis, whose faith looks alive and awake but has grown tired and flat. They are encouraged to wake up and walk with Christ who will bring them mercy and eternal life.

Reflect: Think of a time when your faith life went flat. How did you wake up your heart and walk with the Lord?

Pray: Give thanks to God for the gift of His Word and ask for strength and resolution to live according to its teaching.

Act: Read the Word of God every day and look for something to refresh your life. Instead of doing the same old thing, challenge your faith with something new.

---

⁷Write this to the angel of the church in Philadelphia, "Thus says he who is holy and true, who holds the key of David; if he opens, nobody shuts, and if he shuts, nobody opens.

⁸I know your worth; I have opened a door before you, which nobody can close, because you have kept my word, and not renounced me in spite of your lack of power. ⁹I am giving you some of the synagogues of Satan, who call themselves Jews, but they are only liars. I will make them fall at your feet, and recognize that I have loved you.

¹⁰Because you have kept my words with patient endurance, I, for my part, will keep you safe in the hour of trial that is coming upon the whole world, to test the people of the earth. ¹¹I am coming soon; hold fast to what you have, lest anyone take your crown.

¹²I will make the victor into a column, in the Sanctuary of my God where he will stay forever. I will write on him the name of my God, and the name of the city of my God, the new Jerusalem, which comes down from my God in heaven, and my own new name. ¹³Let anyone who has ears listen to what the Spirit says to the churches."

REVELATION 3:7-13

Read: The Christ has set up an open door through which he passes to be near the persecuted Church in Philadelphia, so others know Christ loves them. "Conquering" means martyrdom, and when this happens Christ will bring them to God.

Reflect: How would you describe your faith community: weak but faithful to the Word or distant and self-reliant? Do you feel God's presence in your community? When you die do you believe Christ will bring you God?

Pray: Give thanks to God for your community and ask that it may remain faithful to the Gospel in spite of difficulties.

Act: How does your church support people who are struggling with life, with faith? Find a way to participate in these efforts.

---

¹⁴Write this to the angel of the church in Laodicea, "Thus says the Amen, the faithful and true witness, the beginning of God's creation:

¹⁵I know your works: you are neither cold nor hot. Would that you were cold or hot! ¹⁶You are lukewarm, neither hot nor cold; so I will spit you out of my mouth. ¹⁷You think you are rich and have piled up so much that you need nothing, but you do not realize that you are wretched, and to be pitied; poor, blind, and naked.

¹⁸I advise you to buy from me gold that has been tested by fire, so that you may be rich, and white clothes to wear, so that your nakedness may not shame you; and ointment for your eyes, that you may see. ¹⁹I reprimand and correct all those I love. Be earnest, and change your ways.

20 Look, I stand at the door and knock. If you hear my call and open the door, I will come in to you and have supper with you, and you with me. 21 I will let the victor sit with me, on my throne, just as I was victorious, and took my place with my Father on his throne. 22 Let anyone who has ears listen to what the Spirit says to the churches."

REVELATION 3:14-22

Read: Laodicea was pathetically self-complacent and had become lukewarm with the Gospel. But God wants her to return and be faithful, thus, He reproaches her and gives her another chance.

Reflect: Are you trapped in routine and comfort? How do you live your Christian witness? What does the following text suggest to you: "I stand at the door and knock. If you hear my call and open the door, I will come into you and have supper with you, and you with me"?

Pray: Ask God the grace to be fervent in your faith; that it may not become lukewarm because of comfort or lack of problems. When Christ knocks at your door, listen and allow the Spirit to enter your life.

Act: Make an examination of conscience focusing on the things and people you used to care about but have not done much for lately.

A LOOK AT THE PAST: CHRIST AND ISRAEL

The throne in heaven

4 1 After this, I looked up to the wall of the sky and saw an open door. The voice, which I had first heard speaking to me like a trumpet, said, "Come up here and I will show you what will come in the future."

2 Immediately, I was seized by the spirit. There, in heaven, was a throne, and one sitting on it. 3 He who sat there looked like jasper and carnelian, and, round the throne was a rainbow, resembling an emerald.

4 In a circle, around the throne, are twenty-four thrones, and seated on these are twenty-four elders, dressed in white clothes with golden crowns on their heads. 5 Flashes of lightning come forth from the throne, with

voices and thunderclaps. Seven flaming torches burn before the throne; these are the seven spirits of God.

⁶Before the throne, there is a platform, transparent like crystal. Around and beside the throne, stand four living creatures, full of eyes, both in front and behind. ⁷The first living creature is like a lion, the second, like a bull; the third has the face of a man, and the fourth looks like a flying eagle. ⁸Each of the four living creatures has six wings, full of eyes, all around as well as within; day and night, they sing without ceasing,

Holy, holy, holy is the Lord God,
master of the universe,
who was, and is, and is to come.

⁹Whenever the living creatures give glory, honor, and thanks to the one on the throne, he who lives for ever and ever, ¹⁰the twenty-four elders fall down before him and worship the one who lives for ever and ever. They lay their crowns in front of the throne and say,

¹¹ *Our Lord and God, worthy are you*
to receive glory, honor, and power!
For you have created all things;
by your will, they came to be and were made.

REVELATION 4:1-11

Read: Worship of God is prominent in the imagery of this chapter which is borrowed from the prophets. God cannot be completely described even by the most precious elements, but is worshiped.

Reflect: In the middle of all their problems the Churches are asked to focus their attention on God. They don't escape their troubles by worshiping God but find the strength to deal with them because they worship God.

Pray: Proclaim the greatness of God who cares for you as part of Creation.

Act: Write a one sentence prayer that focuses your attention on the love of the Creator and use it in times of struggle.

The coming of the Lamb

5 [1] Then, I saw in the right hand of him who was seated on the throne, a scroll written on both sides, sealed with seven seals. [2] A mighty angel exclaimed in a loud voice, "Who is worthy to open this and break the seals?"

[3] But no one in heaven or on earth, or in the netherworld, was found able to open the book and read it. [4] I wept much when I saw that no one was found worthy to open the book and read it. [5] Then one of the elders said to me, "Do not weep. Look, the lion of the tribe of Judah, the shoot of David, has conquered; he will open the book of the seven seals."

[6] And I saw next to the throne, with its four living creatures, and the twenty-four elders, a Lamb, standing, although it had been slain. I saw him with seven horns and seven eyes, which are the seven spirits of God sent out to all the earth.

[7] The Lamb moved forward and took the book from the right hand of him who was seated on the throne. [8] When he took it, the four living creatures and the twenty-four elders bowed before the Lamb. They all held in their hands, harps, and golden cups full of incense, which are the prayers of the holy ones.

[9] This is the new song they sang:

You are worthy to take the book
and open its seals,
for you were slain,
and by your blood, you purchased for God,
people of every race, language, and nation;
[10] *and you made them a kingdom, and priests for our God,*
and they shall reign over the land.

[11] I went on looking; I heard the noise of a multitude of angels, gathered around the throne, the living creatures and the elders, numbering millions of millions, [12] crying out with a loud voice:

Worthy is the Lamb who was slain, to receive
power and riches, wisdom and strength,
honor, glory, and praise.

[13] Then, I heard the voice of the whole universe, heaven, earth, sea, and the place of the dead; every creature cried out:

To him who sits upon the throne, and to the Lamb,
be praise, honor, glory, and power, for ever and ever.

¹⁴ And the four living creatures said, Amen, while the elders bowed down and worshiped.

REVELATION 5:1-14

Read: A sealed parchment contains God's meaning and will for the world. Only Christ Jesus, the Lamb who sacrificed himself for the world, can open it. As they worshiped the Creator, so do people now worship Christ the Lamb.

Reflect: Do you recognize in Jesus the fullness and realization of the saving plan of the Father? What does the following expression suggest to you: "To him who sits upon the throne, and to the Lamb, be praise, honor, glory, and power, for ever and ever"?

Pray: Give thanks to God for Jesus' presence in your life and in history and ask for his guidance to follow in his steps.

Act: Praise God by inviting your people to pray the Rosary. Afterward, share with them what Jesus means in your life.

The seven seals

6 ¹ I saw the Lamb opening the first of the seven seals, and I heard one of the four living creatures cry out, with a voice like thunder, "Come and see!"

² A white horse appeared, and its rider had a bow. He was crowned, and he went out as a conqueror, and he will conquer.

³ When he opened the second seal, I heard the second living creature cry out, "Come!" ⁴ Then, another horse, the color of fire, came out. Its rider was ordered to take peace away from the earth, that people might kill one another; so he was given a great sword.

⁵ When he opened the third seal, I heard the third creature cry out, "Come!" This time, it was a black horse, and its rider held a balance in his hand. ⁶ Then, from the midst of the four living creatures, a voice was heard: "A measure of wheat for a piece of silver, and three measures of barley for a piece, as well! Do not spoil the oil or the wine."

⁷ When he opened the fourth seal, I heard a cry from the fourth living creature, "Come!" ⁸ A greenish horse appeared, its rider was called

Death, and *the Netherworld* rode behind him. He was allowed to utterly destroy, by sword, famine, pestilence and wild beasts, a fourth of the inhabitants of the earth.

REVELATION 6:1-8

Read: The Lamb opens the first four seals. Fear, want, hunger, pestilence, and beasts appear. It is the description of the destructive power of humanity.

Reflect: Are you scared about the future of humanity? How is it possible that with such an abundance of food production we have more hungry people now than 50 years ago? Do you trust in God's power? How does God show Himself in these circumstances?

Pray: Ask God to increase your faith and confidence to live with serenity and committed to the wellbeing of humanity. Ask the Lamb to help you open the seals of your own life.

Act: Do something concrete to make out of this a better world: share your table with your friends, visit prisoners, and take care of the earth.

---

[9] When he opened the fifth seal, I saw, under the altar, the spirits of those who proclaimed the word of God and were slain for its sake. [10] They began to cry aloud, "Holy and righteous Lord, how long will it be before you render justice, and avenge our blood on the inhabitants of the earth?" [11] Then each one of them was given a white garment, and they were told to wait a little while, until the number of their brothers and sisters, and fellow servants who would be killed, as they had been, would be completed.

REVELATION 6:9-11

Read: The Lamb opens the fifth seal and the martyrs of the faith appear. They are alongside God who has embraced them, not forgotten them.

Reflect: Do you know anyone who, because of being a Christian, is suffering ridicule, marginalization or persecution? How can we express our solidarity with them?

Pray: Give thanks to God for the witnesses of a strong faith that are present in the Church, and ask also for help that you can endure difficulties and thus be on the side of God.

Act: Look for a biography, or a martyr's witness, from the old or recent times. Look at your life and see how you can imitate those examples.

[12]And my vision continued. When the Lamb opened the sixth seal, there was a violent earthquake. The sun became black as a mourning dress, and the whole moon turned blood-red, [13]and the stars in the sky fell to the earth, like dry figs falling from a fig tree shaken by a hurricane. [14]The sky was folded up like rolled parchment; there was no mountain or continent that was not removed from its place. [15]The kings of the earth and their ministers, the generals, the rich and the powerful, and all the people, slaves, as well as free persons, hid in caves, or among rocks, on the mountains, [16]saying, "Fall on us, mountains and rocks, and hide us, for we are afraid of him who sits on the throne, and of the wrath of the Lamb. [17]The great day of his wrath has come, and who can endure it?"

REVELATION 6:12-17

Read: With the opening of the sixth seal, the world as we know it is being dismantled. This is especially true for the leading powers. (In the following chapters we learn it will be replaced by a new world from God.)

Reflect: Sometimes things need to change altogether to make room for God. What about change frightens you? The kings and generals have to be replaced for change to happen, how do you understand this?

Pray: Ask for serenity and trust when confronted with the dangers and disaster of our time. Place your life in God's hands and be faithful to the commandment of love.

Act: Show in your life God's goodness: love others, forgive, share your food, welcome the marginalized, be generous with those who approach you.

144,000 from Israel and the great crowd from every nation

7 [1] After this, there were four angels standing at the four corners of the earth, holding back the four winds, to prevent their blowing against the earth, the sea, and the trees. [2] I saw another angel ascending from the sunrise, carrying the seal of the living God, and he cried out with a loud voice to the four angels empowered to harm the earth and the sea, [3] "Do not harm the earth or the sea or the trees, until we have sealed the servants of our God upon their foreheads."

[4] Then, I heard the number of those marked with the seal: a hundred and forty-four thousand from all the tribes of the people of Israel:

[5] from the tribe of Judah, twelve thousand were sealed;
from the tribe of Reuben, twelve thousand;
from the tribe of Gad, twelve thousand;
[6] from the tribe of Asher, twelve thousand;
from the tribe of Naphtali, twelve thousand;
from the tribe of Manasseh, twelve thousand;
[7] from the tribe of Simeon, twelve thousand;
from the tribe of Levi, twelve thousand;
from the tribe of Issachar, twelve thousand;
[8] from the tribe of Zebulun, twelve thousand;
from the tribe of Joseph, twelve thousand;
from the tribe of Benjamin, twelve thousand.

REVELATION 7:1-8

Read: The winds moving over the waters created the world and they will destroy it so it can be reformed. God takes care of his own, marking them with a seal. The number 144,000 is a perfect one (12 x 12 x 1000). It is the number of the chosen people of the new Israel, much more numerous than the former twelve tribes of Israel.

Reflect: God does not just care for individuals, they are cared for as a people, a new Israel. Do you feel that you belong to a community loved by God?

Pray: Give thanks to God for knowing Him, for having Him present in your life, and ask for an increase in faith and help for sharing that with others.

> **Act:** Knowing that you have been chosen by God (one of the 144,000 sealed), share this Good News by the way you live your everyday life: forgiving, helping, welcoming, showing that Jesus continues to be present today.

⁹After this, I saw a great crowd, impossible to count, from every nation, race, people and tongue, standing before the throne and the Lamb, clothed in white, with palm branches in their hands, ¹⁰and they cried out with a loud voice, "Who saves, but our God, who sits on the throne, and the Lamb?"

¹¹All the angels were around the throne, the elders and the four living creatures; they then bowed before the throne with their faces to the ground, to worship God. ¹²They said,

Amen. Praise, glory, wisdom, thanks, honor, power and strength to our God forever and ever. Amen!

¹³At that moment, one of the elders spoke up and said to me, "Who are these people clothed in white, and where did they come from?" ¹⁴I answered, "Sir, it is you who know this."

The elder replied, "They are those who have come out of the great persecution; they have washed and made their clothes white in the blood of the Lamb.

¹⁵This is why they stand before the throne of God,

and serve him, day and night, in his Sanctuary.

He, who sits on the throne, will spread his tent over them.

¹⁶Never again will they suffer hunger or thirst,

or be burned by the sun, or any scorching wind.

¹⁷For the Lamb, near the throne, will be their Shepherd,

and he will bring them to springs of life-giving water,

and God will wipe away their tears."

REVELATION 7:9-17

Read: The martyrs of the faith are "a great crowd, impossible to count, from every nation, race, people, and tongue." This scene is reminiscent of the worship service the Feast of Booths, a worship service that rejects idolatry, praises God for the gifts of water and life, and asks God's protection from hunger, thirst and sorrow. The prayers are answered.

Reflect: When you face trouble, do you pray for an awareness of God's presence with you? Are ordeals likely to lead you to trust or abandon God?

Pray: Ask God to increase your trust in Him and in the fullness of life that He promises. Ask also that persecuted Christians may be helped and sustained by the prayers and solidarity of the universal Church.

Act: Give witness of hope in the fullness and happiness of life that Jesus offers. Share with a member of your community the reflection that the Holy Spirit inspires you today.

8 [1] When the Lamb opened the seventh seal, there was silence in heaven for about half an hour. [2] Then, I looked at the seven angels standing before God, who were given seven trumpets.

[3] Another angel came, and stood before the altar of incense, with a golden censer. He was given much incense to be offered, with the prayers of all the holy ones, on the golden altar before the throne; [4] and the cloud of incense rose with the prayers of the holy ones, from the hands of the angel to the presence of God. [5] Then, the angel took the censer, and filled it with burning coals from the altar, and threw them on the earth: and there came thunder, lightning and earthquakes.

REVELATION 8:1-5

Read: The Lamb opens the seventh seal. It is a solemn moment. Seven trumpets are given to the seven angels who are in the presence of God. The prayer of all the saints goes up to God together with the perfume of the incensory carried by another angel.

Reflect: These verses are like a slow beginning of a worship service, deliberately slow clearing our minds for God. Prayers don't control God; in prayer we wait for God. How do you experience waiting for God?

Pray: Ask for God's grace to recognize His manifestations in your daily life, and the grace to honor and praise Him; and to follow His commandments.

Act: Pray without words, just trying to be present to the presence of God.

The seven trumpets

[6] The seven angels with the seven trumpets prepared to sound them. [7] When the first angel blew his trumpet, there came hail and fire mixed with blood, which fell on the earth. And a third of the earth was burned up with a third of the trees and the green grass.

[8] When the second angel blew his trumpet, something like a great mountain was thrown into the sea, and a third of the sea was turned into blood. [9] At once, a third of the living creatures in the sea died, and a third of the ships perished.

[10] When the third angel sounded his trumpet, a great star fell from heaven like a ball of fire, on a third of the rivers and springs. [11] The star is called *Wormwood*, and a third of the waters were turned into wormwood, and many people died because of the water, which had turned bitter.

[12] The fourth angel blew his trumpet, and a third of the sun, the moon, and the stars were affected. Daylight decreased one third, and the light at night as well.

[13] And my vision continued: I noticed an eagle flying through the highest heaven and crying with a loud voice, "Woe, woe, woe to the inhabitants of the land when the last three angels sound their trumpets."

9 [1] And the fifth angel blew his trumpet. I, then, saw a star fall from heaven to earth. The star was given the key to the depths of the abyss. [2] He opened the abyss and a cloud of smoke rose as if from a great furnace, which darkened the sun and the air.

[3] Locusts came from this smoke and spread throughout the earth. They were given the same harmful power as the scorpions of the earth. [4] Then they were told not to harm the meadows, the green grass or the trees, but only the people who do not bear the seal of God upon their foreheads. [5] They were not to kill them, but only torture them for five months. This pain is like the sting of scorpions. [6] In those days, people will look for death, but will not find it; they will long to die, but death

will elude them. ⁷These locusts look like horses equipped for battle; they wear golden crowns on their heads, and their faces are like those of human beings. ⁸Their hair is like women's hair, and their teeth, like lion's teeth; ⁹their chests are like iron breastplates; and the noise of their wings, like the roar of an army of chariots and horses rushing for battle.

¹⁰Their tails are like those of scorpions and have stings; the power they have to torture people for five months is in their tails. ¹¹These locusts have a king who is the angel of the abyss, whose name in Hebrew is Abaddon, or Apollyon in Greek (Destruction).

REVELATION 8:6—9:11

Read: The sound of the first six trumpets is heard calling attention to the analogy to the plagues sent to Egypt to soften the hard heart of Pharaoh. These represent the urgent call that God makes to us for conversion. Time is running out; we should always be ready for the encounter with the Lord.

Reflect: Trumpets are sounded to get attention; how does God get your attention? Do you pay attention to God only when bad things happen?

Pray: Ask for God's forgiveness for the mistakes of humanity and also of your own. Ask for the grace of conversion and that each day, men and women may work to transform this world close to His will.

Act: Do not panic for today's catastrophes. Rather work with your people and with your parish community to help those who are being affected.

---

¹²The first woe has passed. Two others are to come.

¹³The sixth angel blew his trumpet. Then, I heard a voice calling from the corners of the golden altar before God. ¹⁴It said to the sixth angel who had just sounded the trumpet, "Release the four angels chained at the banks of the great river Euphrates."

¹⁵And the four angels were released, who had been waiting for this year, this month, this day and this hour, ready to utterly destroy a third of humankind. ¹⁶The number of soldiers on horses was two hundred million; this is the number I heard.

¹⁷In my vision, I saw those horses and their riders: they wore breast-plates the color of fire, hyacinth, and sulfur. The heads of the horses look like lions' heads; and fire, smoke, and sulfur come out of their mouths.

¹⁸Then, a third of humankind was killed by these three plagues: fire, smoke and sulfur, which the horses released through their mouths, ¹⁹for the power of the horses was both in their mouths and in their tails. Their tails, in fact, look like serpents, and their heads are able to inflict injury as well.

²⁰However, the rest of humankind who were not killed by these plagues did not renounce their way of life: they went on worshiping the demons, keeping those idols of gold, silver, bronze, stone, and wood that cannot see, hear or walk. ²¹No, they did not repent of their crimes, or their sorcery, or their sexual immorality or their theft.

What has been proclaimed by the prophets is fulfilled

10 ¹Then, I saw another mighty angel coming down from heaven, wrapped in a cloud. A rainbow was around his head; his face was like the sun, and his legs, like pillars of fire. ²I could see a small book open in his hand. He stood with his right foot planted on the sea and his left on the land, ³and called in a loud voice like the roaring of a lion. ⁴Then, the seven thunders sounded their own message.

I was about to write what the seven thunders had sounded, when a voice from heaven said to me, "Keep the words of the seven thunders secret and do not write them down."

⁵And the angel I saw standing on the sea and land, raised his right hand to heaven, ⁶swearing by him who lives for ever and ever, and who created the heavens, the earth, the sea and everything in them.

He said, "There is no more delay; ⁷as soon as the trumpet call of the seventh angel is heard, the mysterious plan of God will be fulfilled, ac-cording to the good news he proclaimed through his servants, the prophets."

⁸And the voice I had heard from heaven spoke again, saying to me, "Go near the angel who stands on the sea and on the land, and take the small book open in his hand." ⁹So, I approached the angel and asked him for the small book; he said to me, "Take it and eat; although it be sweet as honey in your mouth, it will be bitter to your stomach."

¹⁰I took the small book from the hand of the angel and ate it. It was

sweet as honey in my mouth, but when I had eaten it, it turned bitter in my stomach. ¹¹Then I was told, "You must again proclaim God's words about many peoples, nations, tongues, and kings."

REVELATION 9:12—10:11

Read: The process of breaking open the final scroll which reveals God's will is compared with the seven days of Creation. The message that must be preached is God is acting now as God has acted in the past.

Reflect: God entrusts His Word to those who will share it with others. Have you made the Word of God your own? Is your life a witness to that? Is it Good News for others?

Pray: Ask from God the grace to be faithful and strong in giving witness to His Word; that it may be Good News for others.

Act: Give yourself time for prayer and biblical formation, at the personal and the communitarian level. Talk to your people about the importance to share the Word of God with others.

The two witnesses

11 ¹Then I was given a staff, like a measuring stick, and I was told, "Go and measure the temple of God and the altar, and count those who worship there. ²Do not bother to measure the outer courtyard, for this has been given to the pagans who will trample over the holy city for forty-two months. ³Meanwhile, I will entrust my word to my two witnesses, who will proclaim it for one thousand two hundred and sixty days, dressed in sackcloth."

⁴These are *the two olive trees, and the two lamps, which are before the Lord of the earth.* ⁵If anyone intends to harm them, fire will come out of their mouths to devour their enemies: this is how whoever intends to harm them will perish. ⁶They have the power to close the sky and hold back the rain during the time of their prophetic mission; they also have the power to change water into blood and punish the earth with a thousand plagues, any time they wish.

⁷But when my witnesses have fulfilled their mission, the beast that comes up from the abyss will make war upon them and will conquer and kill them. ⁸Their dead bodies will lie in the square of the great city,

which the believers figuratively call Sodom, or Egypt, where their Lord was crucified. ⁹And their dead bodies will be exposed for three days and a half to people of all tribes, races, languages, and nations, who will be ordered not to have them buried.

¹⁰Then, the inhabitants of the earth will rejoice, congratulate one another, and exchange gifts among themselves because these two prophets were a torment to them.

¹¹But after those three and a half days, a spirit of life, coming from God, entered them. They then stood up, and those who looked at them were seized with great fear. ¹²A loud voice from heaven called them, "Come up here." So they went up to heaven, in the midst of the clouds, in the sight of their enemies.

¹³At that moment, there was a violent earthquake, which destroyed a tenth of the city and claimed seven thousand victims. The rest were overcome with fear and acknowledged the God of heaven.

¹⁴The second woe has passed. The third is coming soon.

REVELATION 11:1-14

Read: The temple represents the Christian community. It is the place where God dwells and where He receives worship from His faithful. The Christian community are also God's witnesses to the entire world. These are going to be killed by the evil that comes from the world, but they will rise like Jesus and will have eternal life.

Reflect: Those who are inside the temple, in the Church, are saved. But does that guarantee us to stay in the Church as authentic followers of Jesus? Are you prepared to give witness to your faith until the last consequences? Do you believe in eternal life? What are the implications in your daily life?

Pray: Ask for God's forgiveness for the times you were not faithful to the commandment of love. Ask also for strength and valor to be always His witness, even in the midst of difficulties.

Act: What are the most important messages you want to say with your life? How are you delivering your message?

¹⁵ The seventh angel blew his trumpet; then, loud voices resounded in heaven: "The world has now become the kingdom of our God and of his Christ. He will reign for ever and ever."

¹⁶ The twenty-four elders, who sit on their thrones before God, bowed down to worship God, ¹⁷ saying,

We thank you, Lord God,
Master of the universe,
who are and who were,
for you have begun your reign,
making use of your invincible power.
¹⁸ The nations raged
but your wrath has come,
the time to judge the dead
and reward your servants the prophets,
the saints and those who honor your Name—
whether great or small—
and destroy those who destroy the earth.

¹⁹ Then, the Sanctuary of God in the heavens was opened, and the Ark of the Covenant of God could be seen inside the Sanctuary. There were flashes of lightning, peals of thunder, an earthquake, and a violent hailstorm.

REVELATION 11:15-19

Read: Finally, the last trumpet sounds. Strong voices announce the coming of the kingship of God. The time for judgment has arrived: "the time to judge the dead and reward your servants the prophets, the saints and those who honor your Name—whether great or small—and destroy those who destroy the earth."

Reflect: What reaction does the divine judgment give you? Do you trust in God's mercy? Do you hope in the final triumph of good over evil? How does it show in your everyday life?

Pray: Pray God's grace sustains you in times of trouble and give you the energy to build the kingdom of God.

Act: Show your hope in the final triumph of good over evil by performing the works of mercy that the Gospel presents to Christians (read Mt 25:31-46).

TOWARD THE FUTURE: THE WORLD AND THE CHURCH

The woman and the dragon

12 ¹A great sign appeared in heaven: a woman, clothed with the sun, with the moon under her feet, and a crown of twelve stars on her head. ²She was pregnant, and cried out in pain, looking to her time of delivery.

³Then, another sign appeared: a huge red dragon, with seven heads and ten horns, and wearing seven crowns on its heads. ⁴It had just swept along a third of the stars of heaven with its tail, throwing them down to the earth.

The dragon stood in front of the woman who was about to give birth so that it might devour the child as soon as it was born. ⁵She gave birth to a male child, the one who is to rule all the nations with an iron scepter; then, her child was seized and taken up to God, and to his throne, ⁶while the woman fled to the desert where God had prepared a place for her; there, she would be looked after for one thousand two hundred and sixty days.

REVELATION 12:1-6

Read: The final conflict is between the work of God, represented by the woman who has been interpreted as either Mary, or the Church, or both, and the dragon—the forces of evil thought to be the Romans.

Reflect: Mary and the Church have been recognized by tradition as "our mothers." Do you feel like a son/daughter of Mary and the Church? Do you think that the way you live gives testimony to the teachings of Jesus? Where do you see evil today?

Pray: Give thanks to God for the incarnation of His Son, for the faith and companionship of Mary, for the Church that gathers us as a mother. Ask God for the grace to respond to God like what Mary, our mother, did.

Act: Read John 19:25-27. Contemplate Mary with Jesus on the cross. Contemplate also her presence in your life and the life of the Church. Promote the Marian devotion in your family.

⁷War broke out in heaven, with Michael and his angels battling with the dragon. The dragon fought back with his angels, ⁸but they were defeated and lost their place in heaven. ⁹The great dragon, the ancient serpent, known as the devil, or Satan, seducer of the whole world, was thrown out. He was hurled down to earth, together with his angels.

¹⁰Then, I heard a loud voice from heaven:

Now has salvation come,
with the power and the kingdom of our God,
and the rule of his anointed.
For our brothers' accuser has been cast out,
who accused them night and day, before God.
¹¹ They conquered him by the blood of the Lamb,
and by the word of their testimony,
for they gave up their lives, going to death.
¹² Rejoice, therefore, O you heavens,
and you who dwell in them;
but woe to you, earth and sea,
for the devil has come to you in anger,
knowing that he has but a little time.

¹³When the dragon saw that he had been thrown down to earth, he pursued the woman who had given birth to the male child. ¹⁴Then the woman was given the two wings of the great eagle so that she might fly into the desert, where she would be looked after for three and a half years. ¹⁵The serpent poured water out of his mouth after the woman to carry her away in the flood, ¹⁶but the earth came to her rescue: it opened its mouth and swallowed the flood, which the dragon had poured from its mouth. ¹⁷Then the dragon was furious with the woman and went off to wage war on the rest of her children, those who keep God's commandments and bear witness to Jesus. ¹⁸And he stood on the seashore.

REVELATION 12:7-18

Read: Evil, represented by the dragon, is not as strong as God. The dragon is defeated by the Lamb and continues to "make war on the rest of her children, those who keep the commandments of God and the testimony of Jesus."

Reflect: How do you think of the conflict between good and evil? In what ways does evil continues to make war on those who follow Christ? How does evil make war on you?

Pray: Ask for the Risen Lord's protection for the whole Church that she may be a good witness of the Good News she announces: the final victory of good over evil.

Act: Evil drains people's hope. Do an act of goodness that gives encouragement to someone who has lost hope.

The beast and the false prophet

13 [1] Then, I saw a beast rising out of the sea, with ten horns and seven heads, with ten crowns on its horns. On each head was a title challenging God. [2] The beast I saw looked like a leopard, with paws like a bear and a mouth like a lion. The dragon passed on his power, his throne and his great authority to the beast.

[3] One of its heads seemed to be fatally wounded, but this wound healed. The whole earth wondered and they followed the beast. [4] People prostrated themselves before the dragon who had given such authority to the beast, and they prostrated themselves before the beast saying, "Who is like the beast? Who can oppose it?"

[5] The beast was given speech, and it spoke boastful and blasphemous words against God; it was allowed to wield its power for forty-two months. [6] It spoke blasphemies against God, his name and his Sanctuary, that is, those who already dwell in heaven.

[7] It was allowed to make war on the saints and to conquer them. It was given authority over people, of every tribe, language, and nation; [8] this is why all the inhabitants of the earth will worship before it, those whose names have not been written in the book of life of the slain Lamb since the foundation of the world.

[9] Let anyone who has ears to hear, listen: [10] *If your lot is the prison, to prison you will go; if your lot is to be killed by the sword, by the sword will you be slain.* This is, for the holy ones, the time of endurance and faith.

[11] Then, I saw another beast rise out of the earth with two horns like the Lamb but speaking like the dragon. [12] This second beast is totally at

the service of the first one and enjoys its authority. So, it makes the world, and its inhabitants, worship the first beast, whose mortal wound has been healed. [13] It works great wonders, even making fire descend from heaven to earth in the sight of all.

[14] Through these great wonders, which it is able to do on behalf of the beast, it deceives the inhabitants of the earth, persuading them to make a statue of the beast, which, although wounded by the sword, is still alive. [15] It has been allowed to give a spirit to this statue; the statue of the beast speaks, and those who refuse to worship it are killed. [16] So, this second beast makes everyone—great and small, rich and poor, free and enslaved—be branded on the right hand, or on the forehead, [17] and no one can buy or sell, unless he has been branded with the name of the beast, or with the number of its name.

[18] Let us see who is wise! If you are clever, you can interpret the number of the Beast; it is 666 and it is the name of a certain person.

REVELATION 13:1-18

Read: The poetic images of dragons and beasts are drawn from the Hebrew Scriptures. When written they referred to the Roman Empire, perhaps Nero, perhaps the imperial Roman cult that everyone had to worship. The passage talks about what is happening right then rather than predicting the future.

Reflect: What does contemporary evil look like? Are people persecuted for their religious beliefs particularly vulnerable? Who else do you see evil attacking?

Pray: Ask God for the grace not to give up when confronting temptations of power, riches and fame. May your life always be praised to the only true God.

Act: Review your life and identify the circumstances when you were swayed by the cult of the false gods of power, wealth, and prestige. Renew your Christian commitment and in the future, in similar circumstances, remember that the only God that deserves adoration is the God of Jesus.

144,000 on Mount Zion

14 ¹I was given another vision:

The Lamb was standing on Mount Zion, surrounded by one hundred and forty-four thousand people, who had his name and his Father's name written on their foreheads. ²A sound reverberated in heaven like the sound of the roaring of the waves, or deafening thunder; it was like a chorus of singers, accompanied by their harps.

³They sing a new song before the throne, in the presence of the four living creatures and the elders, a song which no one can learn, except the hundred and forty-four thousand who have been taken from the earth. ⁴They are those who were not defiled with women, but were chaste; these are given to follow the Lamb wherever he goes. They are the first taken from humankind who are already of God and the Lamb. ⁵No deceit has been found in them; they are faultless.

REVELATION 14:1-5

Read: Good triumphs over evil, John's vision presenting all the saints brought close to God by Jesus—the Lamb. They are those who remained faithful, uncontaminated, and trustworthy, those who lived as Jesus lived.

Reflect: The phrase "uncontaminated by women" is problematic and harkens back to concepts of ritual purity. It should not be taken literally and reflects cultural bias against women.

Pray: In your small ways, ask Jesus to help you to be holy in your daily life, to live at all times as Jesus lived.

Act: Help someone struggling to live in communion with Christ. Invite someone to come to Church with you.

---

⁶Then, I saw another angel flying high in the sky, sent to proclaim the definitive good news to the inhabitants of the earth, to every nation, race, language, and people. ⁷He cried out with a loud voice, "Give God glory and honor, for the hour of his judgment has come. Worship him, who made the heavens, the earth, the sea, and all the waters."

⁸Another angel followed him, crying out, "Fallen is Babylon the great, fallen the prostitute who has made all the nations drunk with her unleashed prostitution!"

⁹A third angel then followed, shouting aloud, "If anyone worships the beast, or its image, or has his forehead or hand branded, ¹⁰he will also drink the wine of God's anger, which has been prepared undiluted in the cup of his fury: he will be tortured by fire and brimstone in the presence of the holy angels and the Lamb."

¹¹The smoke of their torment goes up for ever and ever; for there is no rest, day or night, for those who worshiped the beast and its image, and for those who were branded with the mark of its name.

¹²This is the time for patient endurance among the holy ones, for those who keep the commandments of God and faith in Jesus. ¹³I heard someone from heaven say, "Write this: Happy from now on are the dead who have died in the Lord. The Spirit says: Let them rest from their labors; their good deeds go with them."

¹⁴Then, I had this vision. I saw a white cloud, and the one sitting on it like a *son of man*, wearing a golden crown on his head and a sharp sickle in his hand. ¹⁵An angel came out of the Sanctuary calling loudly to the one sitting on the cloud, "Put in your sickle and reap, for harvest time has come, and the harvest of the earth is ripe." ¹⁶He, who was sitting on the cloud, swung his sickle at the earth and reaped the harvest.

¹⁷Then, another angel, who also had a sharp sickle, came out of the heavenly Sanctuary. ¹⁸Still, another angel, the one who has charge of the altar fire, emerged and shouted to the first who held the sharp sickle, "Swing your sharp sickle, and reap the bunches of the vine of the earth, for they are fully ripe." ¹⁹So, the angel swung his sickle and gathered in the vintage, throwing all the grapes into the great winepress of the anger of God. ²⁰The grapes were trodden outside the city, and blood flowed from the wine press to the height of the horses' bridles, and over an area of sixteen hundred furlongs.

REVELATION 14:6-20

Read: These angels will reap the grapes of wrath that the enemies of God will drink at the last judgment.

Reflect: Could you name the false gods of today? How do you live your fidelity to Jesus' message in your everyday life?

Pray: Ask the Spirit for fortitude and fear of God to be faithful to Jesus' message and to build his kingdom already now among us.

> **Act:** Make a gesture or a concrete deed today that shows the presence of the kingdom in the world. Share with your group what the Spirit inspired you in your reflection.

15 ¹Then, I saw another great and marvelous sign in the heavens: seven angels brought seven plagues, which are the last, for, with these, the wrath of God will end. ²There was a sea of crystal mingled with fire, and the conquerors of the beast, of its name and the mark of its name, stood by it.

They had been given the celestial harps, ³and they sang the song of Moses, the servant of God, and the song of the Lamb:

Great and marvelous are your works,
O Lord,
God and Master of the universe.
Justice and truth guide your steps,
O King of the nations.
⁴Lord, who will not give honor and glory to your name?
For you alone are holy.
All the nations will come and bow before you,
for they have now seen your judgments.

The seven cups

⁵Then, the Sanctuary of the Tent of Divine Declarations was opened, ⁶and the seven angels, bringing the seven plagues, came out of the Sanctuary clothed in pure and bright linen, with their waists girded with golden belts. ⁷One of the four living creatures gave the seven angels seven golden cups, full of the wrath of God who lives for ever and ever. ⁸Then the Sanctuary was filled with smoke that wraps God's glory and power so that no one could enter until the seven plagues of the seven angels were completed.

REVELATION 15:1-8

Read: The last seven plagues are announced in heaven. There "the conquerors of the beast, of its name and the mark of its name" sing praise to God. From inside the celestial temple come seven angels carrying seven plagues with the wrath of God.

Reflect: This judgment scene is to reassure us that God is greater than evil, an important message when it seemed there was no end to the Roman Empire. In the light of evil present today, what reassures you that God is stronger?

Pray: Pray that God increase your faith and hope that you have the strength and optimism to follow Christ.

Act: Talk to your people about the importance for Christians to be prepared for the final encounter with the Lord. God is love and we shall be judged by the love we had given to others (read Mt 25:31-46).

16 [1] I heard a loud voice calling from the Sanctuary to the seven angels, "Go and empty on the earth the seven cups of the wrath of God."

[2] The first angel went to empty his cup on the earth, and malignant and painful sores appeared on the people who bore the mark of the beast and had bowed before its image. [3] The second angel emptied his cup into the sea, which turned into blood like that of the dead, and every living thing in the sea died.

[4] The third angel emptied his cup into the rivers and springs that turned into blood. [5] And I heard the angel of the waters say, "You, who are and who were, O Holy One, you are just in punishing them in this way; [6] since they have shed the blood of your holy ones and the prophets, you have made them drink blood; they rightly deserved it." [7] I heard another cry from the altar, "Yes, Lord and God, Master of the universe, your judgments are true and just."

[8] The fourth angel poured out his cup on the sun, and its heat began to scorch people. [9] They were severely burned and began to insult God, who has power over those plagues, instead of acknowledging him.

[10] The fifth angel emptied his cup on the throne of the beast, and suddenly his kingdom was in darkness, and the people bit their tongues in agony. [11] They insulted the Most High God for their pain and wounds, but they did not repent.

[12] The sixth angel poured out his cup on the great river Euphrates;

then, its water was dried up, leaving a free passageway for the kings of the east. [13]I saw coming from the mouths of the monster, the beast and the false prophet, three unclean spirits, which looked like frogs. [14]They are, in fact, spirits of demons that perform marvelous things, and go to the kings of the whole world to gather them for battle on the great day of God, the master of the universe.

[15]"Beware! I come like a thief; happy is the one who stays awake, and does not take off his clothes; so he will not have to go naked, and his whole body be exposed for all to see."

[16]Then, they assembled them at the place called Armageddon in Hebrew (or the Hills of Megiddo).

[17]The seventh angel emptied his cup into the air. Then, a voice came forth from the throne, and was heard outside the Sanctuary saying, "It is done." [18]And there were flashes of lightning, peals of thunder and a violent earthquake. No, never has there been an earthquake, so violent, since people existed on earth. [19]The great city was split into three while the cities of the nations collapsed. For the time had come for Babylon the Great to be remembered before God, and to be given the cup of the foaming wine of his anger.

[20]Then, the continents withdrew and the mountain ranges hid. [21]Great hailstones from heaven, as heavy as stones, dropped on the people, and the people insulted God, because of this disastrous hailstorm, for it was truly a terrible plague.

REVELATION 16:1-21

Read: There have been seven letters, seals, trumpet calls, visions and now the outpouring of God's wrath. The imagery is drawn from the Old Testament and applied to contemporary manifestations of evil forces attacking God's beloved. The seven plagues reach the earth, gradually destroying everything on earth. Babylon, the sin city, is destroyed.

Reflect: How do you understand God's judgment of evil? What sources of evil anger you?

Pray: Loving God, forgive me a sinner.

Act: Make an examination of conscience and ask for God's forgiveness for the times you were not able to listen to his voice inviting you to conversion.

The judgment of Babylon

17 [1] Then, one of the seven angels of the seven cups came to me, and said, "Now, I will show you the judgment of the sovereign prostitute who dwells on the great waters. [2] She, it is, who let the kings of the earth sin with her; and with the wine of her lewdness, the inhabitants of the earth have become drunk."

[3] The angel brought me to the desert: it was a new vision. There, a woman was seated on a red beast. The beast, which had seven heads and ten horns, covered itself with titles, and statements that offend God. [4] The woman was clothed in purple and scarlet, with ornaments of gold, precious stones, and pearls. She held in her hands a golden cup full of loathsome idolatry and impure prostitution. [5] Her name could be read on her forehead, written in a mysterious way: *Babylon the Great, mother of prostitutes and of the loathsome idols of the whole world.* [6] And I saw that the woman was drunk with the blood of the holy ones and the martyrs of Jesus.

What I saw greatly surprised me, [7] but the angel said to me, "Why are you surprised? I will reveal to you the secret of this woman, and of the beast with seven heads and ten horns that she mounts. [8] The beast you saw has been, though, it, is not. It will come up from the abyss and then go to perdition. What a surprise for the inhabitants of the earth, whose names are not written in the book of life, from the creation of the world! They will marvel on discovering that the beast who has been, is not, and passes away.

[9] Let us see if you guess: the seven heads are seven hills on which the woman sits. And they are also seven kings, [10] five of which have already fallen, one is in power, and the seventh has not yet come, but will remain only a short while. [11] The beast that has been but, is not, can be considered as the eighth, though it takes place among the seven; and it goes to perdition.

[12] The ten horns are ten kings, who have not yet received power, but will have authority, for an hour, with the beast. [13] They all have, only one aim, and they place their authority and power at the service of the beast. [14] They will fight against the Lamb, but the Lamb will conquer them, for he is Lord of lords and King of kings; and with him will be his followers, who have been called, and chosen, and are faithful.

¹⁵ The angel went on, "Those waters you saw, on which the prostitute is seated, are peoples, multitudes, and nations of every language. ¹⁶ The ten horns, and the beast itself, will plan evil against the prostitute. They will destroy her, and leave her naked; they will eat her flesh and set her on fire. ¹⁷ God makes use of them to carry out his plan, so he has inspired them with their common purpose, and they will place their power at the service of the beast until the words of God are fulfilled. A last word: ¹⁸ the woman you saw, is the great city which reigns over the kings of the whole world."

REVELATION 17:1-18

Read: John speaks enigmatically of the political power of the time: Rome and its rulers. Their struggle against the Lamb is futile because the Lamb will destroy them. He is the lord of lords and king of kings.

Reflect: Do you trust in the total power of Jesus? Do you trust that love is mightier than hatred? How do you picture the coming of the kingdom of God in the world?

Pray: Ask God the grace to trust in His power, His love and His justice. May the Holy Spirit help you to wait for the irruption of the kingship of God by putting into practice the commandment of love He left us.

Act: In the difficult moments of your everyday life, keep trusting in the presence and company of the Lord. Repeat interiorly the following invocation: "Lord Jesus, Lord of lords, king of kings."

---

18 ¹ After this, I saw another angel coming down from heaven. So great was his authority that the whole earth was lit up with his glory. ² In a strong voice he cried out:

"Fallen is Babylon the great! Fallen!
She has become a haunt of demons,
a lodge for every unclean spirit,
a nest for any filthy and disgusting bird.
³ She has made all nations drunk
with the wine of her lewdness,

fornicated with kings of the earth,
and glutted the world's merchants
with her wantonness and wealth."
[4] Then, I heard another voice from heaven:
"Depart from her, my people,
lest you share in her evil,
and so share in her punishments;
[5] for her sins are piled up to heaven,
and God keeps count of her crimes.
[6] Give back to her as she has given,
pay her twice for what she has done.
Let her drink a double portion
of what she made others do.
[7] Give her as much torment and grief
as the wantonness she enjoyed herself.
For she said to herself,
'I sit as queen, I am not a widow,
never will I go into mourning!'
[8] And so, suddenly, her plagues will come—
death, mourning, and famine.
She will be consumed by fire,
for mighty is the Lord, the judge,
who has passed sentence on her."

[9] The kings who shared her luxury, and committed adultery with her, will see the smoke as she burns, and they will weep and lament. [10] They will, nevertheless, keep their distance, terrified at her punishment, and exclaim:

"Alas, alas! Great city that you are,
O Babylon, seat of power!
Your doom has come in a single hour!"

[11] The merchants of the world will mourn over her, for they will lose a market for their goods—[12] their cargoes of gold and silver, precious stones and pearls, fine linen and purple garments, silk and scarlet cloth, fragrant wood, ivory pieces and expensive furniture, bronze, iron and marble, [13] cinnamon and spices, perfume, myrrh and frankincense, wine and olive oil, fine flour and grain, cattle and sheep, horses and carriages, slaves and human lives. [14] They will say:

"Gone is the fruit you longed for.

Gone are your luxury and splendor.

Never will you recover them, never!"

¹⁵ The merchants who dealt in these goods, who grew rich from business with the city, will stand at a safe distance for fear of her punishment. Weeping and mourning, ¹⁶ they will cry out:

"Woe, woe to the great city,

to the linen and purple and scarlet you wore,

to your gold and pearls, your finery,

¹⁷ your great wealth, destroyed in an hour!"

Every captain and navigator, every sailor and seafarer, will stand afar, ¹⁸ crying out, on seeing the smoke going up as the city burns to the ground. "What city could have compared with this one?" ¹⁹ They will pour dust on their heads and cry out in mourning:

"Alas, alas, great city,

where all who had ships at sea

grew rich through her trade!

In an hour, she has been devastated."

²⁰ *Rejoice over her, O heavens!*

Rejoice, prophets, saints, and apostles!

God has rendered justice to you.

²¹ A powerful angel picked up a boulder, the size of a large millstone, and threw it into the sea, saying:

"With such violence will Babylon, the great city, be thrown down, never again to be seen.

²² Never again will tunes of harpists, minstrels, trumpeters, and flutists be heard in you. Never again will an artisan of any trade be found in you. Never again will the noise of the mill be heard.

²³ Never again will the light of a lamp shine in you. The voice of bridegroom and bride will never again be heard in you.

Because your traders were the world's great, and you led the nations astray by your magic spell. ²⁴ In this city was found blood of prophets and saints—yes, the blood of all who have been slain on the earth."

Songs in heaven

19 ¹ After this, I heard what sounded like the loud singing of a great assembly in heaven:

Alleluia! Salvation, glory and might belong to our God,
² *for his judgments are true and just.*

He has condemned the great harlot who corrupted the world with her adultery.

He has avenged his servants' blood, shed by her hand, in harlotry.
³ *Once more, they sang: Alleluia! The smoke from her goes up for ever and ever!*

⁴ The twenty-four elders and the four living creatures fell down and worshiped God seated on the throne. And they cried: *Amen! Alleluia!*

REVELATION 18:1—19:4

Read: Babylon falls, the great sinful city: idolatrous, unjust, and lustful. Its followers cry its fall. On the contrary, the martyrs and saints rejoice because the power of God will now reign in its place.

Reflect: Does your community have inequalities and injustices? What can Christians do to change this situation?

Pray: Ask from God the grace to be always able to act according to justice; may your community give witness to the divine will.

Act: Identify in your community a situation of inequality or injustice that could be eliminated. Discern with the community how to carry that out.

---

⁵ A voice came from the throne: "Praise our God, all you, his servants, all you who revere him, both small and great!"

⁶ Then, I heard what sounded like a great crowd, like the roaring of the waves, like peals of thunder, answering:

Alleluia! The Lord now reigns,
our Lord, the Master of the universe!
⁷ *Let us rejoice and be glad*
and give him glory!
This is the time to celebrate the wedding of the Lamb,
his bride has made herself ready.
⁸ *Fine linen, bright and clean,*
is given her to wear.

This linen stands for the good works of the holy ones.

⁹Then, the angel told me, "Write: Happy are those invited to the wedding of the Lamb." And he went on, "These are true words of God."

¹⁰As I fell down at his feet, to worship him, he said to me, "Beware, I am but a servant, like you and your brothers, who utter the testimonies of Jesus (these testimonies of Jesus are proclaimed through the spirit of the prophets). Worship God alone."

REVELATION 19:5-10

Read: This heavenly worship celebrates God's victory over evil, and is attended by all who stand with God, those who accepted Jesus' invitation to the wedding feast.

Reflect: The Lamb and his Church are inseparable. Can one be a Christian without belonging to the Church? How are Christians to respond when those in the Church do evil? What does it mean to say the Church is a place for sinners?

Pray: Ask that the Church may always show the merciful love she receives from Jesus.

Act: Be an active member of your parish and, in spite of her faults, contemplate in her the ever-living presence of Jesus.

The triumph of the word of God

¹¹Then, I saw heaven opened, and a white horse appeared. Its rider is the *Faithful and True*; he judges, and wages just wars. ¹²His eyes are flames of fire; he wears many crowns, and written on him is his own name, which no one can understand, except himself. ¹³He is clothed in a cloak drenched in blood. His name is the Word of God.

¹⁴The armies of heaven, clothed in pure white linen, follow him on white horses. ¹⁵A sharp sword comes out of his mouth. With it, he will strike the nations, for he must *rule them with an iron rod*. He treads the winepress of the burning wrath of God, the Master of the universe. ¹⁶This is why this title is written on his cloak and on his thigh: King of kings and Lord of lords.

¹⁷I also saw an angel standing in the sun. He cried out with a loud voice to all the birds of the air, "Come here, to the great feast of God. ¹⁸Come and eat the flesh of kings, of generals and of the mighty; come

and devour the soldier and his horse, flesh of all, both free and slaves, both small and great."

¹⁹Then, I saw the beast with the kings of the earth and their armies, gathered together to fight against him who rides on the horse, and his army. ²⁰But the beast was captured, with the false prophet who served it and performed signs by which he deceived those who had received the mark of the beast and worshiped its statue. The two were thrown, alive, into the fiery lake of burning sulfur, and all ²¹the rest were killed by the sword, which comes from the mouth of the rider who mounts the horse. And all the birds were fed with their flesh.

REVELATION 19:11-21

Read: A horse rider appears. He is Jesus himself; his name is the Word of God. With it, he will overcome evil and its followers.

Reflect: The sword of Jesus does not hurt by force but through the Word of God. Do Christians use the Word of God to overcome evil? Is the Word of God a source of inspiration for your Christian life?

Pray: Ask the Holy Spirit for the inspiration to always use wise and saintly words to overcome the evil that surrounds us.

Act: May your word always be a witness to the Word of God that welcomes, heals, and liberates.

The thousand years

20 ¹Then, an angel came down from heaven, holding in his hand the key to the Abyss and a huge chain. ²He seized the monster, the ancient serpent, namely Satan or the devil, and chained him for a thousand years. ³He threw him into the abyss, and closed its gate with the key, then secured it with locks, that he might not deceive the nations in the future until the thousand years have passed. Then he will be released for a little while.

⁴There were thrones, and seated on them were those with the power to judge. I then saw the spirits of those who had been beheaded for having held the teachings of Jesus, and on account of the word of God. I saw all those who had refused to worship the beast, or its image, or receive its mark on the forehead, or on the hand. They returned to life and

reigned with the Messiah for a thousand years. This is the first resurrection. [5] The rest of the dead will not return to life before the end of the thousand years.

[6] Happy and holy is the one who shares in the first resurrection, for the second death has no power over them; they will be priests of God, and of his Messiah, and reign with him a thousand years.

[7] At the end of these thousand years, Satan will be released from his prison; [8] then, he will set out to deceive the nations of the four corners of the world, namely Gog and Magog, and gather them for war. What an army, so numerous, like the sand of the seashore! [9] They invaded the land and surrounded the camp of the holy ones, the most beloved city, but fire came down from heaven and devoured them.

[10] Then, the devil, the seducer, was thrown into the lake of fire and sulfur, where the beast and the false prophet already were. Their torment will last day and night, for ever and ever.

REVELATION 20:1-10

Read: Now, a period of a thousand years begins with the dragon captive; the martyrs reign together with Jesus. And we can once more imagine a world without evil.

Reflect: The poetry is drawn from Ezekiel 38, and requires a careful reading to appreciate what is being said. The thousand years cannot be understood literally. The point is that evil is not inevitable, but that empowered by Christ, we can defeat it. Is it possible to think of a world without evil? How is evil to be combatted?

Pray: Ask God for the grace to overcome evil daily in your personal struggles. May the Holy Spirit be your shield and strength in difficult moments.

Act: Next time that evil threatens to conquer your life, overcome it by doing good, trusting in the power of Jesus, Lord of lords and king of kings.

The last judgment

[11] After that, I saw a great and splendid throne and the one seated upon it. At once, heaven and earth disappeared, leaving no trace. [12] I saw the

dead, both great and small, standing before the throne, while books were opened. Another book, the book of life, was also opened. Then the dead were judged according to the records of these books, that is, each one according to his works.

¹³The sea gave up the dead it had kept, as did death and the netherworld so that all might be judged according to their works. ¹⁴Then death and the netherworld were thrown into the lake of fire. This lake of fire is the second death. ¹⁵All who were not recorded in the book of life were thrown into the lake of fire.

REVELATION 20:11-15

Read: In a last judgment scene, a book with the deeds of all are judged against that found in the "book of life" that comes from God.

Reflect: What have you written so far in your "book of life"? How are you writing this book?

Pray: Place your life in God's hands. Ask that He always be at your side, that He may guide your hand so you can write your life with words of love, goodness, and truth.

Act: Read Matthew 25:31-46 and see what concrete actions you are asked to do in this earthly life to have life forever.

The new heaven and the new earth

21 ¹Then, I saw a new heaven and a new earth. The first heaven and the first earth had passed away and no longer was there any sea. ²I saw the new Jerusalem, the holy city, coming down from God out of heaven, adorned as a bride prepared for her husband. ³A loud voice came from the throne, "*Here is the dwelling of God among mortals: He will pitch his tent among them, and they will be his people*; he will be God-with-them.

⁴He will *wipe every tear from their eyes*. There shall be no more death or mourning, crying out or pain, for the world that was has passed away." ⁵The One seated on the throne said, "See, I make all things new."

And then, he said to me, "Write these words, because they are sure and true."

⁶And he said to me: "It is already done! I am the Alpha and the

Omega, the Beginning and the End. I, myself, will give the thirsty to drink without cost from the fountain of living water. ⁷Thus, the winner will be rewarded: *For him, I shall be God and he will be my son.*

⁸As for cowards, traitors, depraved, murderers, adulterers, sorcerers, and idolaters—all those who live in falsehood, their place is the lake of burning sulfur. This is the second death."

REVELATION 21:1-8

Read: John speaks about a new heavens and new earth, he does not mean heaven, but rather this world transformed by the love made known by Jesus Christ. Renewal, not chaos, is the divine plan.

Reflect: God will live among people and will console them. Do we enjoy already God's presence among us? Can we feel consoled by Him? How can you come to see Christ as the Alpha and Omega, the beginning and end of your life?

Pray: Do not ask from God to be free of all the pain you may suffer in this life, but that He may always be at your side giving you joy.

Act: Approach the joy of God together with your community. Celebrate a communitarian penitential act or the sacrament of the unction of the sick, for the consolation of the older people, those who are sick or physically challenged.

The new Jerusalem

⁹Then, one of the seven angels came to me, one of those with the seven bowls full of the seven last plagues. And he said, "Come, I am going to show you the bride, the wife of the Lamb." ¹⁰He took me up in a spiritual vision, to a very high mountain, and he showed me the holy city Jerusalem, coming down out of heaven, from God. It shines with the glory of God ¹¹like a precious jewel, with the color of crystal-clear jasper.

¹²Its wall, large and high, has twelve gates; stationed at them are twelve angels. Over the gates are written the names of the twelve tribes of the sons of Israel. ¹³Three gates face the east; three gates face the north; three gates face the south and three, face the west. ¹⁴The city

wall stands on twelve foundation stones, on which are written the names
of the twelve apostles of the Lamb.

[15] The angel who was speaking to me had a golden measuring rod to
measure the city, its gates, and its wall. [16] The city is laid out like a
square: its length is the same as its breadth. He measured it with his rod
and it was twelve thousand furlongs; its length, breadth, and height are
equal. [17] Then he measured the wall: it was a hundred and forty-four cu-
bits high. The angel used an ordinary measure.

[18] The wall is made of jasper, and the city of pure gold, crystal-clear.
[19] The foundations of the wall are adorned with every kind of precious
jewel: the first is jasper, the second sapphire, the third turquoise, the
fourth emerald, [20] the fifth agate, the sixth ruby, the seventh chrysolite,
the eighth beryl, the ninth topaz, the tenth chrysoprase, the eleventh hyacinth, and the twelfth amethyst. [21] The twelve gates are twelve pearls,
each gate made of a single pearl, and the square of the city is paved
with gold, as pure as transparent crystal.

[22] I saw no temple in the city, for the Lord God, Master of the universe,
and the Lamb, are themselves its temple. [23] The city has no need of the
light of the sun or the moon since God's glory is its light and the Lamb
is its lamp.

[24] *The nations will walk in its light, and the kings of the earth will
bring their treasures to it.* [25] *Its gates will not be closed at sunset, for there
will be no night there.* [26] It is there that the wealth, and the most precious
things of the nations, will be brought. [27] *Nothing unclean will enter it,* or
anyone who does what is evil and false, but only those whose names
are written in the Lamb's book of life.

22 [1] Then, he showed me the river of life, clear as crystal, gushing
from the throne of God and of the Lamb. [2] In the middle of the
city, on both sides of the river, are the trees of life, producing fruit twelve
times, once each month, the leaves of which are for healing the nations.

[3] No longer will there be a curse; the throne of God and of the Lamb
will be in the city, and God's servants will live in his presence. [4] They will
see his face, and his name will be on their foreheads. [5] There will be no
more night. They will not need the light of lamp, or sun, for God, himself,
will be their light, and they will reign forever.

REVELATION 21:9—22:5

Read: The imagery comes from Ezekiel and Isaiah's understanding of the temple as the meeting place between God and humankind. An angel shows the glory of the bride who is united with God: it is heaven, a splendorous and perfect world illumined by the glory of God, where everything is holy.

Reflect: The intimacy between God and the people is described as marriage. Would you use intimate language to describe your relationship with God?

Pray: Jesus Christ, Risen Lord, be close to me.

Act: See if there are sharing groups in your parish with whom you can grow in faith.

I am coming soon

⁶ Then, the angel said to me, "These words are sure and true; the Lord God, who inspires the prophets, has sent his angel to show his servants what must happen soon."

⁷ "I am coming soon! Happy are those who keep the prophetic words of this book."

⁸ I, John, saw and heard all this. When I had seen and heard them, I fell at the feet of the angel who had shown me everything, to worship him. ⁹ But he said, "No, I am a fellow servant like you and your brothers, the prophets, and those who heed the words of this book. It is God you must worship."

¹⁰ He, then, said to me, "Do not keep secret the prophetic words of this book, because the time is near. ¹¹ Let the sinner continue to sin, and the defiled remain in his defilement; let the righteous continue to do what is right, and he who is holy grow holier."

¹² "I am coming soon, bringing with me the recompense I will pay to each one according to his deeds. ¹³ I am the Alpha and the Omega, the First and the Last, the Beginning and the End."

¹⁴ Happy are those who wash their robes, for they will have free access to the tree of life and enter the city through the gates. ¹⁵ Outside are the dogs, sorcerers, the immoral, murderers, idolaters, and all who take pleasure in falsehood!

[16] "I, Jesus, sent my angel, to make known to you these revelations concerning the churches. I am the shoot and offspring of David, the radiant morning star."

[17] The Spirit and the Bride say, "Come!" Whoever hears, let him say, "Come!" Whoever thirsts, let him approach, and whoever desires, let him freely take the water of life. [18] As for me, I warn everyone who hears the prophetic words of this book: If anyone adds anything to them, God will pile on him, the plagues described in this book. [19] And if anyone takes away words from this book of prophecy, God will take from him his share in the tree of life, and the holy city described in this book.

[20] He who has declared all this says, "Yes, I am coming soon."
Amen! Come, Lord Jesus.

[21] May the grace of the Lord Jesus be with you all!

REVELATION 22:6-21

Read: The Book of Revelation closes as it opened, with the announcement that what was revealed is the Word of God, reaching us through Jesus. Those who follow him will obtain glorification.

Reflect: The Book of Revelation is not a book of doom but a song of Christian hope: at the end of time good will conquer evil. Do you also expect that? How? What does the following expression suggest to you: "Come, Lord Jesus"? Are you prepared for the final encounter with the Lord?

Pray: Ask the Holy Spirit to enlighten you to understand His Word, strength to carry it out and the eternal joy that, through your faith and good deeds, will allow you to be always with God.

Act: Promote in your parish community biblical courses, so that no one will be alarmed with fundamentalist readings. If possible reserve each day a special time for praying with the Bible.

BIBLICAL READINGS IN THE MASS

With the help of this perpetual liturgical calendar you will be able to use your Bible as a missal.

The Sunday Readings are in three cycles: A, B, and C. Sundays also have three readings: the first reading is from the Old Testament, the second is ordinarily from one of the Epistles or Letters of the New Testament. In the three-year cycle almost all the Letters are read. The third reading is the Gospel. There is an "Evangelist of the Year"—Matthew is read on cycle A, Mark on cycle B, and Luke on cycle C. The Gospel of John comes at various times in each liturgical year: on Advent and Lent Sundays and in some readings of cycle B year.

Weekly Masses have two readings: the first from the Old or New Testament and the Gospel. The first reading during ordinary weeks of the year (see the chart below) is arranged in a two-year cycle. Series I is for the odd years (2021, 2023, 2025, etc.) and series II is for even years (2020, 2022, 2024, etc.).

The readings for weekdays are arranged semi-continuously or thematically depending on the presence of a theme for a particular season.

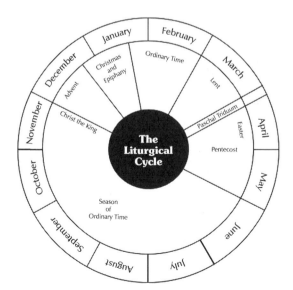

Table of Movable Liturgical Days

| Year | Cycle | First Sunday Advent | Ash Wednes-day | Easter Sunday | Pentecost Sunday | Ordinary Weeks of the Year | | | |
| | | | | | | Before Lent | | After Pentecost | |
						Until	Week	From	Week
2020	A	Dec 1 '19	Feb 26	April 12	May 31	Feb 25	7	June 1	9
2021	B	Nov 29 '20	Feb 17	April 4	May 23	Feb 16	6	May 24	8
2022	C	Nov 28 '21	Mar 2	April 17	June 5	Mar 1	8	June 6	10
2023	A	Nov 27 '22	Feb 22	April 9	May 28	Feb 21	7	May 29	8
2024	B	Dec 3 '23	Feb 14	Mar 31	May 19	Feb 13	5	May 20	7
2025	C	Dec 1 '24	Mar 5	April 20	June 8	Mar 4	8	June 9	10
2026	A	Nov 30 '25	Feb 18	April 5	May 24	Feb 17	6	May 25	8
2027	B	Nov 29 '26	Feb 10	Mar 28	May 16	Feb 9	5	May 17	7
2028	C	Nov 28 '27	Mar 1	April 16	June 4	Feb 29	8	June 5	9
2029	A	Dec 3 '28	Feb 14	April 1	May 20	Feb 13	6	May 21	7
2030	B	Dec 2 '29	Mar 6	April 21	June 9	Mar 5	8	June 10	10
2031	C	Dec 1 '30	Feb 26	April 13	June 1	Feb 25	7	June 2	9

READINGS FOR ADVENT AND CHRISTMAS

	Date		1st Reading	2nd Reading	Gospel
ADVENT TIME	1st SUNDAY of Advent		A. Is 2:1-5	Rom 13:11-14	Mt 24:37-44
			B. Is 63:16-17,19;64:2-7	1Cor 1:3-9	Mk 13:33-37
			C. Jer 33:14-16	1Thes 3:12—4:2	Lk 21:25-28,34-36
	1st Week of Advent	M	Is 2:1-5 (Cycle A: Is 4:2-6)		Mt 8:5-11
		TU	Is 11:1-10		Lk 10:21-24
		W	Is 25:6-10		Mt 15:29-37
		T	Is 26:1-6		Mt 7:21,24-27
		F	Is 29:17-24		Mt 9:27-31
		S	Is 30:19-21,23-26		Mt 9:35—10: 8
	2nd SUNDAY of Advent		A. Is 11:1-10	Rom 15:4-9	Mt 3:1-12
			B. Is 40:1-5,9-11	2P 3:8-14	Mk 1:1-8
			C. Bar 5:1-9	Phil 1:4-6,8-11	Lk 3:1-6
	2nd Week of Advent	M	Is 35:1-10		Lk 5:17-26
		TU	Is 40:1-11		Mt 18:12-14
		W	Is 40:25-31		Mt 11:28-30
		T	Is 41:13-20		Mt 11:11-15
		F	Is 48:17-19		Mt 11:16-19
		S	Sir 48:1-4,9-11		Mt 17:10-13
	3rd SUNDAY of Advent		A. Is 35: 1-6,10	James 5:7-10	Mt 11:2-11
			B. Is 61:1-2,10-11	1Thes 5:16-24	Jn 1:6-8,19-28
			C. Zep 3:14-18	Phil 4:4-7	Lk 3:10-18
	3rd Week of Advent	M	Num 24:2-7,15-17		Mt 21:23-27
		TU	Zep 3:1-2,9-13		Mt 21:28-32
		W	Is 45:6-8,18,21-25		Lk 7:18-23
		T	Is 54:1-10		Lk 7:24-30
		F	Is 56:1-3,6-8		Jn 5:33-36

From December 17 to January 7 the weekday readings are as follows:

		17	Gen 49:2,8-10		Mt 1:1-17
		18	Jer 23:5-8		Mt 1:18-24
		19	Jdg 13:2-7,24-25		Lk 1:5-25
		20	Is 7:10-14		Lk 1:26-38
		21	Song 2:8-14 or Zep 3:14-18		Lk 1:39-45
	4th SUNDAY		A. Is 7:10-14	Rom 1:1-7	Mt 1:18-24
	of Advent		B. 2S 7:1-5,8-11,16	Rom 16:25-27	Lk 1:26-38
			C. Mic 5:1-4	Heb 10:5-10	Lk 1:39-45
		22	1S 1:24-28		Lk 1:46-56
		23	Mal 3:1-4,23-24		Lk 1:57-66
		24	2S 7:1-5,8-11,16		Lk 1:67-79
CHRISTMAS	Midnight		Is 9:1-6	Tit 2:11-14	Lk 2:1-14
	Dawn		Is 62:11-12	Tit 3:4-7	Lk 2;15-20
Stephen, 1st Martyr		26	Acts 6:8-10;7:54-59		Mt 10:17-22
John, Apostle & Evang.		27	1Jn 1:1-4		Jn 20:2-8
Holy Innocents		28	1Jn 5—2:2		Mt 2:13-18
5th Day Octave		29	1Jn 2:3-11		Lk 2:22-35
6th Day Octave		30	1Jn 2:12-17		Lk 2:36-40
Holy Family (Sunday after			Sir 3:2-6,12-14	Col 3:12-21	A. Mt 2:13-15,19-23
Christmas or Dec. 30 if					B. Lk 2:22-40
Christmas falls on Sunday)					C. Lk 2:41-52
7th Day Octave Christmas		31	1Jn 2:18-21		Jn 1:1-18
Mary, Mother of God		1	Num 6:22-27	Gal 4:4-7	Lk 2:16-21
If before Epiphany		2	1Jn 2:22-28		Jn 1:19-28
If before Epiphany		3	1Jn 2:29—3:6		Jn 1:29-34
If before Epiphany		4	1Jn 3:7-10		Jn 1:35-42
If before Epiphany		5	1Jn 3:11-21		Jn 1:43-51
If before Epiphany		6	1Jn 5:5-13		Mk 1:7-11
If before Epiphany		7	1 Jn 5:14-21		Jn 2:1-12
EPIPHANY SUNDAY			Is 60:1-6	Eph 3:2-3,5-6	Mt 2:1-12
After Epiphany		M	1Jn 3:22—4:6		Mt 4:12-17,23-25
After Epiphany		TU	1Jn 4:7-10		Mk 6:34-44
After Epiphany		W	1Jn 4:11-18		Mk 6:45-52
After Epiphany		T	1Jn 4:19—5:4		Lk 4:14-22
After Epiphany		F	1Jn 5:5-13		Lk 5:12-16
After Epiphany		S	1Jn 5:14-21		Jn 3:22-30
BAPTISM OF THE LORD SUNDAY					

From the Baptism of the Lord (Sunday after Epiphany) to Ash Wednesday runs the first part of Ordinary Time. This can be four to nine weeks according to the date of Easter, which varies every year.

Year	Baptism of the Lord	Until Ash Wednesday	Year	Baptism of the Lord	Until Ash Wednesday
2020	January 12	February 25	2026	January 11	February 17
2021	January 10	February 16	2027	January 10	February 9
2022	January 9	March 1	2028	January 9	February 29
2023	January 8	February 21	2029	January 14	February 13
2024	January 14	February 13	2030	January 13	March 5
2025	January 12	March 4	2031	January 12	February 25

READINGS FOR LENT AND EASTER

	Date		1st Reading	2nd Reading	Gospel
	ASH WEDNESDAY		Joel 2:12-18	2Cor 5:20—6:2	Mt 6:1-6,16-18
		T	Dt 30:15-20		Lk 9:22-25
		F	Is 58:1-9		Mt 9:14-15
		S	Is 58:9-14		Lk 5:27-32
	1st SUNDAY of Lent		A: Gen 2:7-9; 3:1-7 B: Gen 9:8-15 C: Dt 26:4-10	Rom 5:12-19 1P 3:18-22 Rom 10:8-13	Mt 4:1-11 Mk 1:12-15 Lk 4:1-13
	1st Week of Lent	M	Lev 19:1-2,11-18		Mt 25:31-46
		TU	Is 55:10-11		Mt 6:7-15
		W	Jonah 3:1-10		Lk 11:29-32
		T	Es C, 12,14-16,23-25		Mt 7:7-12
		F	Ezk 18:21-28		Mt 5:20-26
		S	Dt 26:16-19		Mt 5:43-48
	2nd SUNDAY of Lent		A. Gen 12:1-4 B. Gen 22:1-2,9,10-18 C. Gen 15:5-12,17-18	2Tim 1:8-10 Rom 8:31-34 Phil 3:17—4:1	Mt 17:1-9 Mk 9:2-10 Lk 9:28-36
LENT TIME	2nd Week of Lent	M	Dn 9:4-10		Lk 6:36-38
		TU	Is 1:10,16-20		Mt 23:1-12
		W	Jer 18:18-20		Mt 20:17-28
		T	Jer 17:5-10		Lk 16:19-31
		F	Gen 37:3-4,12-13,17-28		Mt 21:33-43,45-46
		S	Mic 7:14-15,18-20		Lk 15:1-3,11-32
	3rd SUNDAY of Lent		A. Ex 17:3-7 B. Ex 20:1-17 C. Ex 3:1-8,13-15	Rom 5:1-2,5-8 1Cor 1:22-25 1Cor 10:1-6,10-12	Jn 4:5-42 Jn 2:13-25 Lk 13:1-9
	3rd Week of Lent	M	2Kgs 5:1-15		Lk 4:24-30
		TU	Dn 3:25,34-43		Mt 18:21-35
		W	Dt 4:1,5-9		Mt 5:17-19
		T	Jer 7:23-28		Lk 11:14-23
		F	Hos 14:2-10		Mk 12:28-34
		S	Hos 6:1-6		Lk 18:9-14
	4th SUNDAY of Lent		A. 1S 16:1,6-7,10-13 B. 2Chr 36:14-17,19-23 C. Jos 5:9,10-12	Eph 5:8-14 Eph 2:4-10 2Cor 5:17-21	Jn 9:1-41 Jn 3:14-21 Lk 15:1-3,11-32
LENT TIME	4th Week of Lent	M	Is 65:17-21		Jn 4:43-54
		TU	Ezk 47:1-12		Jn 5:1-3,5-16
		W	Is 49:8-15		Jn 5:17-30
		T	Ex 32:7-14		Jn 5:31-47
		F	Wis 2:1,12-22		Jn 7:1-2,10,25-30
		S	Jer 11:18-20		Jn 7:40-53
	5th SUNDAY of Lent		A. Ezk 37:12-14 B. Jer 31:31-34 C. Is 43:16-21	Rom 8:8-11 Heb 5:7-9 Phil 3:8-14	Jn 11:1-45 Jn 12:20-33 Jn 8:1-11
	5th Week of Lent	M	Dn 13:41-62		Jn 8:1-11 C. Jn 8:12-20
		TU	Num 21:4-9		Jn 8:21-30
		W	Dn 3:14-20,91-92,95		Jn 8:31-42
		T	Gen 17:3-9		Jn 8:51-59
		F	Jer 20:10-13		Jn 10:31-42
		S	Ezk 37:21-28		Jn 11:45-57
	PALM SUNDAY		Is 50:4-7	Phil 2:6-11	A. Mt 26:14—27:66 B. Mk 14:1—15:47 C. Lk 22:14—23:56
		M	Is 42:1-7		Jn 12:1-11
		TU	Is 49:1-6		Jn 13:21-33,36-38
		W	Is 50:4-9		Mt 26:14-25
	Holy Thursday		Ex 12:1-8,11-14	1Cor 11:23-26	Jn 13:1-15
	Good Friday		Is 52:13—53:12	Heb 4:14-16;5:7-9	Jn 18:1—19:42

	Easter Vigil	Gen 1:1—2:2	Ex 14:15—15:1		A. Mt 28:1-10 B. Mk 16:1-8 C. Lk 24:1-12
	EASTER SUNDAY	Acts 10:34,37-43	Col 3:1-4		Jn 20:1-9
	1st Week of Easter	M	Acts 2:14,22-32		Mt 28:8-15
		TU	Acts 2:36-41		Jn 20:11-18
		W	Acts 3:1-10		Lk 24:13-35
		T	Acts 3:11-26		Lk 24:35-48
		F	Acts 4:1-12		Jn 21:1-14
		S	Acts 4:13-21		Mk 16:9-15
	2nd SUNDAY of Easter	A. Acts 2:42-47	1P 1:3-9		Jn 20:19-31
		B. Acts 4:32-35	1Jn 5:1-6		Jn 20:19-31
		C. Acts 5:12-16	Rev 1:9-13,17-19		Jn 20:19-31
	2nd Week of Easter	M	Acts 4:23-31		Jn 3:1-8
		TU	Acts 4:32-37		Jn 3:7-15
		W	Acts 5:17-26		Jn 3:16-21
		T	Acts 5:27-33		Jn 3:31-36
		F	Acts 5:34-42		Jn 6:1-15
		S	Acts 6:1-7		Jn 6:16-21
EASTER TIME	**3rd SUNDAY** of Easter	A. Acts 2:14,22-28	1P 1:17-21		Lk 24:13-35
		B. Acts 3:13-15,17-19	1Jn 2:1-5		Lk 24:35-48
		C. Acts 5:27-32,40-41	Rev 5:11-14		Jn 21:1-19
	3rd Week of Easter	M	Acts 6:8-15		Jn 6:22-29
		TU	Acts 7:51—8:1		Jn 6:30-35
		W	Acts 8:1-8		Jn 6:35-40
		T	Acts 8:26-40		Jn 6:44-51
		F	Acts 9:1-20		Jn 6:52-59
		S	Acts 9:31-42		Jn 6:60-69
	4th SUNDAY of Easter	A. Acts 2:14,36-41	1P 2:20-25		Jn 10:1-10
		B. Acts 4:8-12	1Jn 3:1-2		Jn 10:11-18
		C. Acts 13:14,43-52	Rev 7:9,14-17		Jn 10:27-30
	4th Week of Easter	M	Acts 11:1-18		A. Jn 10:11-18 B.&C. Jn 10:1-10
		TU	Acts 11:19-26		Jn 10:22-30
		W	Acts 12:24—13:5		Jn 12:44-50
		T	Acts 13:13-25		Jn 13:16-20
		F	Acts 13:26-33		Jn 14:1-6
EASTER TIME		S	Acts 13:44-52		Jn 14:7-14
	5th SUNDAY of Easter	A. Acts 6:1-7	1P 2:4-9		Jn 14:1-12
		B. Acts 9:26-31	1Jn 3:18-24		Jn 15:1-8
		C. Acts 14:21-27	Rev 21:1-5		Jn 13:31-33,34-35
	5th Week of Easter	M	Acts 14:5-18		Jn 14:21-26
		TU	Acts 14:19-28		Jn 14:27-31
		W	Acts 15:1-6		Jn 15:1-8
		T	Acts 15:7-21		Jn 15:9-11
		F	Acts 15:22-31		Jn 15:12-17
		S	Acts 16:1-10		Jn 15:18-21
	6th SUNDAY of Easter	A. Acts 8:5-8,14-17	1P 3:15-18		Jn 14:15-21
		B. Acts 10:25-26,34-48	1Jn 4:7-10		Jn 15:9-17
		C. Acts 15:1-2,22-29	Rev 21:10-14,22-23		Jn 14:23-29
	6th Week of Easter	M	Acts 16:11-15		Jn 15:26—16:4
		TU	Acts 16:22-34		Jn 16:5-11
		W	Acts 17:15,22—18:1		Jn 16:12-15
		T	Acts 18:1-8		Jn 16:16-20
		F	Acts 18:9-18		Jn 16:20-23
		S	Acts 18:23-28		Jn 16:23-28
	ASCENSION SUNDAY	Acts 1:1-11	A. Eph 1:17-23		Mt 28:16-20
			B. Eph 4:1-13		Mk 16:15-20
			C. Heb 9:24-28; 10:19-23		Lk 24:46-53
	7th Week	M	Acts 19:1-8		Jn 16:29-33
		TU	Acts 20:17-27		Jn 17:1-11
		W	Acts 20:28-38		Jn 17:11-19

	of Easter	T	Acts 22:30; 23:6-11		Jn 17:20-26
		F	Acts 25:13-21		Jn 21:15-19
		S	Acts 28:16-20,30-31		Jn 21:20-25
	PENTECOST SUNDAY		Acts 2:1-11	A. 1Cor 12:3-7, 12-13 B. Gal 5:16-25 C. Rom 8:8-17	Jn 20:19-23 Jn 15:26—16:15 Jn 14:15-26
	TRINITY SUNDAY		A. Ex 34:4-6,8-9 B. Dt 4:32-34,39-40 C. Pro 8:22-31	2Cor 13:11-13 Rom 8:14-17 Rom 5:1-5	Jn 3:16-18 Mt 28:16-20 Jn 16:12-15
	BODY & BLOOD OF CHRIST		A. Dt 8:2-3,14-16 B. Ex 24:3-8 C. Gen 14:18-20	1Cor 10:16-17 Heb 9:11-15 1Cor 11:23-26	Jn 6:51-58 Mk 14:12-16,22-26 Lk 9:11-17

FIRST PART OF ORDINARY TIME

In Ordinary Time, weekdays are distributed on a cycle of two years, year I and year II, which are in fact odd and even years. The year 2021 is I, and 2022 is II.

Sundays, instead, are distributed on a cycle of three years: year A, year B, and year C. Years 2020, 2023, 2026, etc., are A.

	Date		1st Reading	2nd Reading	Gospel
	BAPTISM OF THE LORD		Is 42:1-7 Is 55:1-11 Is 40:1-5,9-11	Acts 10:34-38 1Jn 5:1-9 Tit 2:11-14; 3:4-7	A. Mt 3:13-17 B. Mk 1:7-11 C. Lk 3:15-16,21-22
	1st week	M	I Heb 1:1-6	II 1S 1:1-8	Mk 1:14-20
		TU	I Heb 2:5-12	II 1S 1:9-20	Mk 1:21-28
		W	I Heb 2:14-18	II 1S 3:1-10,19-20	Mk 1:29-39
		T	I Heb 3:7-14	II 1S 4:1-11	Mk 1:40-45
		F	I Heb 4:1-5,11	II 1S 8:4-7,10-22	Mk 2:1-12
		S	I Heb 4:12-16	II 1S 9:1-4,17-19; 10:1	Mk 2:13-17
	2nd SUNDAY Ordinary Time		A. Is 49:3,5-6 B. 1S 3:3-10,19 C. Is 62:1-5	1Cor 1:1-3 1Cor 6:13-15,17-20 1Cor 12:4-11	Jn 1:29-34 Jn 1:35-42 Jn 2:1-12
ORDINARY TIME	2nd week	M	I Heb 5:1-10	II 1S 15:16-23	Mk 2:18-22
		TU	I Heb 6:10-20	II 1S 16:1-13	Mk 2:23-28
		W	I Heb 7:1-3,15-17	II 1S 17:32-33,37,50-51	Mk 3:1-6
		T	I Heb 7:25—8:6	II 1S 18:6-9; 19:1-7	Mk 3:7-12
		F	I Heb 8:6-13	II 1S 24:3-21	Mk 3:13-19
		S	I Heb 9:2-3,11-14	II 2S 1:1-4,11-12,19,23-27	Mk 3:20-21
	3rd SUNDAY Ordinary Time		A. Is 8:23—9:3 B. Jon 3:1-5, 10 C. Ne 8:2-4,5-6,8-10	1Cor 1:10-13,17 1Cor 7:29-31 1Cor 12:12-30	Mt 4:12-23 Mk 1:14-20 Lk 1:1-4; 4:14-21
	3rd week	M	I Heb 9:15,24-28	II 2S 5:1-7,10	Mk 3:22-30
		TU	I Heb 10:1-10	II 2S 6:12-15,17-19	Mk 3:31-35
		W	I Heb 10:11-18	II 2S 7:4-17	Mk 4:1-20
		T	I Heb 10:19-25	II 2S 7:18-19,24-29	Mk 4:21-25
		F	I Heb 10:32-39	II 2S 11:1-4,5-10,13-17	Mk 4:26-34
		S	I Heb 11:1-2,8-19	II 2S 12:1-7,10-17	Mk 4:35-41

Year	4th Sunday Ordinary
2020	February 2 (Presentation)
2021	January 31
2022	January 30
2023	February 5

Year	4th Sunday Ordinary
2024	February 4
2025	February 2 (Presentation)
2026	February 1
2027	January 31

Year	4th Sunday Ordinary
2028	January 30
2029	January 28
2030	February 3
2031	February 2 (Presentation)

ORDINARY TIME	**4th SUNDAY** Ordinary Time		A. Zep 2:3; 3:12-13	1Cor 1:26-31	Mt 5:1-12
			B. Dt 18:15-20	1Cor 7:32-35	Mk 1:21-28
			C. Jer 1:4-5,17-19	1Cor 12:31—13:13	Lk 4:21-30
	4th week	M	I Heb 11:32-40	II 2S 15:13-14,30;16:5-13	Mk 5:1-20
		TU	I Heb 12:1-4	II 2S 18:9—19:3	Mk 5:21-43
		W	I Heb 12:4-7,11-15	II 2S 24:2,9-17	Mk 6:1-6
		T	I Heb 12:18-19,21-24	II 1K 2:1-4,10-12	Mk 6:7-13
		F	I Heb 13:1-8	II Sir 47:2-11	Mk 6:14-29
		S	I Heb 13:15-17,20-21	II 1K 3:4-13	Mk 6:30-34
	5th SUNDAY Ordinary Time		A. Is 58:7-10	1Cor 2:1-5	Mt 5:13-16
			B. Job 7:1-4,6-7	1Cor 9:16-23	Mk 1:29-39
			C. Is 6:1-2,3-8	1Cor 15:1-11	Lk 5:1-11
	5th week	M	I Gen 1:1-19	II 1K 8:1-7,9-13	Mk 6:53-56
		TU	I Gen 1:20—2:4	II 1K 8:22-23,27-30	Mk 7:1-13
		W	I Gen 2:5-9,15-17	II 1K 10:1-10	Mk 7:14-23
		T	I Gen 2:18-25	II 1K 11:4-13	Mk 7:24-30
		F	I Gen 3:1-8	II 1K 11:29-32; 12:19	Mk 7:31-37
		S	I Gen 3:9-24	II 1K 12:26-32;13:33-34	Mk 8:1-10

Remember that this first part of Ordinary Time ends with Ash Wednesday. Some years it will still be in the 5th week; other years it will be in the 9th week. Either way, Lent begins with Ash Wednesday.

ORDINARY TIME	**6TH SUNDAY** Ordinary Time		A. Sir 15:15-20	1Cor 2:6-10	Mt 5:17-37
			B. Lev13:1-2,44-46	1Cor 10:31—11:1	Mk 1:40-45
			C. Jer 17:5-8	1Cor 15:12,16-20	Lk 6:17,20-26
	6th week	M	I Gen 4:1-15,25	II James 1:1-11	Mk 8:11-13
		TU	I Gen 6:5-8; 7:1-5,10	II James 1:12-18	Mk 8:14-21
		W	I Gen 8:6-13,20-22	II James 1:19-27	Mk 8:22-26
		T	I Gen 9:1-13	II James 2:1-9	Mk 8:27-33
		F	I Gen 11:1-9	II James 2:14-24,26	Mk 8:34—9:1
		S	I Heb 11:1-7	II James 3:1-10	Mk 9:2-13
	7th SUNDAY Ordinary Time		A. Lev 19:1-2,17-18	1Cor 3:16-23	Mt 5:38-48
			B. Is 43:18-19,21-22,24-25	2Cor 1:18-22	Mk 2:1-12
			C. 1S 26:2,7-9,12-13,22-23	1Cor 15:45-49	Lk 6:27-38
	7th week	M	I Sir 1:1-10	II James 3:13-18	Mk 9:14-29
		TU	I Sir 2:1-11	II James 4:1-10	Mk 9:30-37
		W	I Sir 4:11-19	II James 4:13-17	Mk 9:38-40
		T	I Sir 5:1-8	II James 5:1-6	Mk 9:41-50
		F	I Sir 6:5-17	II James 5:9-12	Mk 10:1-12
		S	I Sir 17:1-15	II James 5:13-20	Mk 10:13-16
	8th SUNDAY Ordinary Time		A. Is 49:14-15	1Cor 4:1-5	Mt 6:24-34
			B. Hos 2:16-17,21-22	2Cor 3:1-6	Mk 2:18-22
			C. Sir 27:4-7	1Cor 15:54-58	Lk 6:39-45
	8th week	M	I Sir 17:19-27	II 1P1:3-9	Mk 10:17-27
		TU	I Sir 35:1-12	II 1P 1:10-16	Mk 10:28-31
		W	I Sir 36:1,5-6,10-17	II 1P 1:18-25	Mk 10:32-45
		T	I Sir 42:15-25	II 1P 2:2-5,9-12	Mk 10:46-52
		F	I Sir: 44:1,9-13	II 1P 4:7-13	Mk 11:11-26
		S	I Sir 51:12-20	II Jd 17,20-25	Mk 11:27-33

SECOND PART OF ORDINARY TIME

This second part of Ordinary Time begins with Pentecost and ends with the 1st Sunday of Advent. Depending on the date of Easter, this second part can begin earlier or later. When it begins with the 7th or 8th week, you find these weeks at the end of the first part of Ordinary Time before Lent.

2nd part of Ordinary time begins with:

Year	Date	week number
2020	June 1	9th week
2021	May 24	8th week
2022	June 6	10th week
2023	May 29	8th week
2024	May 20	7th week
2025	June 9	10th week

2nd part of Ordinary time begins with:

Year	Date	week number
2026	May 25	8th week
2027	May 17	7th week
2028	June 5	9th week
2029	May 21	7th week
2030	June 10	10th week
2031	June 2	9th week

	Date		1st Reading	2nd Reading	Gospel
ORDINARY TIME	**9th SUNDAY** Ordinary Time		A. Dt 11:18,26-28	Rom 3:21-25,28	Mt 7:21-27
			B. Dt 5:12-15	2Cor 4:6-11	Mk 2:23—3:6
			C. 1K 8:41-43	Gal 1:1-2,6-10	Lk 7:1-10
	9th week	M	I Tb 1:1,2; 2:1-9	II 2P 1:2-7	Mk 12:1-12
		TU	I Tb 2:9-14	II 2P 3:12-15,17-18	Mk 12:13-17
		W	I Tb 3:1-11,16	II 2Tim 1:1-3,6-12	Mk 12:18-27
		T	I Tb 6:11; 7:1,9-14; 8:4-7	II 2Tim 2:8-15	Mk 12:28-34
		F	I Tb 11:5-15	II 2Tim 3:10-17	Mk 12:35-37
		S	I Tb 12:1,5-15,20	II 2Tim 4:1-8	Mk 12:38-44
	10th SUNDAY Ordinary Time		A. Hos 6:3-6	Rom 4:18-25	Mt 9:9-13
			B. Gen 3:9-15	2Cor 4:13—5:1	Mk 3:20-35
			C. 1K 17:17-24	Gal 1:11-19	Lk 7:11-17
	10th week	M	I 2Cor 1:1-7	II 1K 17:1-7	Mt 5:1-12
		TU	I 2Cor 1:18-22	II 1K 17:7-16	Mt 5:13-16
		W	I 2Cor 3:4-11	II 1K 18:20-39	Mt 5:17-19
		T	I 2Cor 3:15—4:1,3-6	II 1K 18:41-46	Mt 5:20-26
		F	I 2Cor 4:7-15	II 1K 19:9,11-16	Mt 5:27-32
		S	I 2Cor 5:14-21	II 1K 19:19-21	Mt 5:33-37
	11th SUNDAY Ordinary Time		A. Ex 19:2-6	Rom 5:6-11	Mt 9:36—10:8
			B. Ezk 17:22-24	2Cor 5:6-10	Mk 4:26-34
			C. 2S 12:7-10,13	Gal 2:16,19-21	Lk 7:36—8:3
	11th week	M	I 2Cor 6:1-10	II 1K 21:1-16	Mt 5:38-42
		TU	I 2Cor 8:1-9	II 1K 21:17-29	Mt 5:43-48
		W	I 2Cor 9:6-11	II 2K 2:1,6-14	Mt 6:1-6
		T	I 2Cor 11:1-11	II Sir 48:1-14	Mt 6:7-15
		F	I 2Cor 11:18,21-30	II 2K 11:1-4,9-18,20	Mt 6:19-23
		S	I 2Cor 12:1-10	II 2Chr 24:17-25	Mt 6:24-34
	12th SUNDAY Ordinary Time		A. Jer 20:10-13	Rom 5:12-15	Mt 10:26-33
			B. Job 38:1,8-11	2Cor 5:14-17	Mk 4:35-41
			C. Zec 12:10-11	Gal 3:26-29	Lk 9:18-24
	12th week	M	I Gen 12:1-9	II 2K 17:5-8,13-15,18	Mt 7:1-5
		TU	I Gen 13:2,5-18	II 2K 19:9-11,14-21,31-36	Mt 7:6,12-14
		W	I Gen 15:1-12,17-18	II 2K 22:8-13; 23:1-3	Mt 7:15-20
		T	I Gen 16:1-12,15-16	II 2K 24:8-17	Mt 7:21-29
		F	I Gen 17:1,9-10,15-22	II 2K 25:1-12	Mt 8:1-4
		S	I Gen 18:1-15	II Lm 2:2,10-14,18-19	Mt 8:5-17
	13TH SUNDAY Ordinary Time		A. 2K 4:8-11,14-16	Rom 6:3-4,8-11	Mt 10:37-42
			B. Wis 1:13-15; 2:23-24	2Cor 8:7,9,13-15	Mk 5:21-43
			C. 1K 19:16-21	Gal 5:1,13-18	Lk 9:51-62
	13th week	M	I Gen 18:16-33	II Am 2:6-10,13-16	Mt 8:18-22
		TU	I Gen 19:15-29	II Am 3:1-8; 4:11-12	Mt 8:23-27
		W	I Gen 21:5,8-20	II Am 5:14-15,21-24	Mt 8:28-34

		T	I	Gen 22:1-19	II Am 7:10-17	Mt 9:1-8
		F	I	Gen 23:1-4,19;24:1-8,62-67	II Am 8:4-6,9-12	Mt 9:9-13
		S	I	Gen 27:1-5,15-29	II Am 9:11-15	Mt 9:14-17

If you are lost with week numbers, look at these hints. Depending on the year, you find the 14th, the 18th, and the 22nd Sunday on the following dates:

Year	14th	18th	22nd
2020	July 5	August 2	August 30
2021	July 4	August 1	August 29
2022	July 3	July 31	August 28
2023	July 9	August 6	September 3
2024	July 7	August 4	September 1
2025	July 6	August 3	August 31

Year	14th	18th	22nd
2026	July 5	August 2	August 30
2027	July 4	August 1	August 29
2028	July 9	August 6	September 3
2029	July 8	August 5	September 2
2030	July 7	August 4	September 1
2031	July 6	August 3	August 31

ORDINARY TIME	**14th SUNDAY** Ordinary Time			A. Zec 9:9-10	Rom 8:9,11-13	Mt 11:25-30
				B. Ezk 2:2-5	2Cor 12:7-10	Mk 6:1-6
				C. Is 66:10-14	Gal 6:14-18	Lk 10:1-12,17-20
	14th week	M	I	Gen 28:10-22	II Hos 2:16,17-18,21-22	Mt 9:18-26
		TU	I	Gen 32:23-33	II Hos 8:4-7,11-13	Mt 9:32-38
		W	I	Gen 41:55-57; 42:5-7,17-24	II Hos 10:1-3,7-8,12	Mt 10:1-7
		T	I	Gen 44:18-21,23-29; 45:1-5	II Hos 11:1,3-4,8-9	Mt 10:7-15
		F	I	Gen 46:1-7,28-30	II Hos 14:2-10	Mt 10:16-23
		S	I	Gen 49:29-33; 50:15-24	II Is 6:1-8	Mt 10:24-33
	15th SUNDAY Ordinary Time			A. Is 55:10-11	Rom 8:18-23	Mt 13:1-23
				B. Am 7:12-15	Eph 1:3-14	Mk 6:7-13
				C. Dt 30:10-14	Col 1:15-20	Lk 10:25-37
	15th week	M	I	Ex 1:8-14,22	II Is 1:10-17	Mt 10:34—11:1
		TU	I	Ex 2:1-15	II Is 7:1-9	Mt 11:20-24
		W	I	Ex 3:1-6,9-12	II Is 10:5-7,13-16	Mt 11:25-27
		T	I	Ex 3:13-20	II Is 26:7-9,12,16-19	Mt 11:28-30
		F	I	Ex 11:10—12:14	II Is 38:1-6,21-22,7-8	Mt 12:1-8
		S	I	Ex 12:37-42	II Mic 2:1-5	Mt 12:14-21
	16th SUNDAY Ordinary Time			A. Wis 12:13,16-19	Rom 8:26-27	Mt 13:24-43
				B. Jer 23:1-6	Eph 2:13-18	Mk 6:30-34
				C. Gen 18:1-10	Col 1:24-28	Lk 10:38-42
	16th week	M	I	Ex 14:5-18	II Mic 6:1-4,6-8	Mt 12:38-42
		TU	I	Ex 14:21—15:1	II Mic 7:14-15,18-20	Mt 12:46-50
		W	I	Ex 16:1-5,9-15	II Jer 1:1,4-10	Mt 13:1-9
		T	I	Ex 19:1-2,9-11,16-20	II Jer 2:1-3,7-8,12-13	Mt 13:10-17
		F	I	Ex 20:1-17	II Jer 3:14-17	Mt 13:18-23
		S	I	Ex 24:3-8	II Jer 7:1-11	Mt 13:24-30
	17th SUNDAY Ordinary Time			A. 1K 3:5,7-12	Rom 8:28-30	Mt 13:44-52
				B. 2K 4:42-44	Eph 4:1-6	Jn 6:1-15
				C. Gen 18:20-32	Col 2:12-14	Lk 11:1-13
	17th week	M	I	Ex 32:15-24,30-34	II Jer 13:1-11	Mt 13:31-35
		TU	I	Ex 33:7-11; 34:5-9,28	II Jer 14:17-22	Mt 13:36-43
		W	I	Ex 34:29-35	II Jer 15:10,16-21	Mt 13:44-46
		T	I	Ex 40:16-21,34-38	II Jer 18:1-6	Mt 13:47-53
		F	I	Lev 23:1,4-11,15-16,27,34-37	II Jer 26:1-9	Mt 13:54-58
		S	I	Lev 25:1,8-17	II Jer 26:11-16,24	Mt 14:1-12
	18th SUNDAY Ordinary Time			A. Is 55:1-3	Rom 8:35,37-39	Mt 14:13-21
				B. Ex 16:2-4,12-15	Eph 4:17,20-24	Jn 6:24-35
				C. Ecl 1:2; 2:21-23	Col 3:1-5,9-11	Lk 12:13-21
	18th week	M	I	Num 11:4-15	II Jer 28:1-17	Mt 14:13-21 Year A: Mt 14:22-36
		TU	I	Num 12:1-13	II Jer 30:1-2,12-15,18-22	Mt 14:22-36 Year A: Mt 15:1-2,10-14
		W	I	Num 13:1-2,25; 14:1,26-29,34-35	II Jer 31:1-7	Mt 15:21-28
		T	I	Num 20:1-13	II Jer 31:31-34	Mt 16:13-23

		Day	First Reading (I)	Second Reading (II)	Gospel
		F	Dt 4:32-40	Nh 2:1,3; 3:1-3,6-7	Mt 16:24-28
		S	Dt 6:4-13	Hb 1:12—2:4	Mt 17:14-20
	19th SUNDAY Ordinary Time		A. 1K 19:9,11-13	Rom 9:1-5	Mt 14:22-33
			B. 1K 19:4-8	Eph 4:30—5:2	Jn 6:41-51
			C. Wis 18:6-9	Heb 11:1-2,8-19	Lk 12:32-48
	19th week	M	Dt 10:12-22	Ezk 1:2-5,24-28	Mt 17:22-27
		TU	Dt 31:1-8	Ezk 2:8—3:4	Mt 18:1-5,10,12-14
		W	Dt 34:1-12	Ezk 9:1-7; 10:18-22	Mt 18:15-20
		T	Jos 3:7-10,11,13-17	Ezk 12:1-12	Mt 18:21—19:1
		F	Jos 24:1-13	Ezk 16:1-15,60,63	Mt 19:3-12
		S	Jos 24:14-29	Ezk 18:1,10-13,30-32	Mt 19:13-15
	20th SUNDAY Ordinary Time		A. Is 56:1,6-7	Rom 11:13-15,29-32	Mt 15:21-28
			B. Pro 9:1-6	Eph 5:15-20	Jn 6:51-58
			C. Jer 38:4-6,8-10	Heb 12:1-4	Lk 12:49-53
	20th week	M	Jdg 2:11-19	Ezk 24:15-24	Mt 19:16-22
		TU	Jdg 6:11-24	Ezk 28:1-10	Mt 19:23-30
		W	Jdg 9:6-15	Ezk 34:1-11	Mt 20:1-16
		T	Jdg 11:29-39	Ezk 36:23-28	Mt 22:1-14
ORDINARY TIME		F	Ru 1:1,3-6,14-16,22	Ezk 37:1-14	Mt 22:34-40
		S	Ru 2:1-3,8-11;4: 13-17	Ezk 43:1-7	Mt 23:1-12
	21st SUNDAY Ordinary Time		A. Is 22:15,19-23	Rom 11:33-36	Mt 16:13-20
			B. Jos 24:1-2,15-17,18	Eph 5:21-32	Jn 6:60-69
			C. Is 66:18-21	Heb 12:5-7,11-13	Lk 13:22-30
	21st week	M	1Thes 1:2-5,8-10	2Thes 1:1-5,11-12	Mt 23:13-22
		TU	1Thes 2:1-8	2Thes 2:1-3,14-16	Mt 23:23-26
		W	1Thes 2:9-13	2Thes 3:6-10,16-18	Mt 23:27-32
		T	1Thes 3:7-13	1Cor 1:1-9	Mt 24:42-51
		F	1Thes 4:1-8	1Cor 1:17-25	Mt 25:1-13
		S	1Thes 4:9-12	1Cor 1:26-31	Mt 25:14-30
	22nd SUNDAY Ordinary Time		A. Jer 20:7-9	Rom 12:1-2	Mt 16:21-27
			B. Dt 4:1-2,6-8	James 1:17-18,21-22,27	Mk 7:1-8,14-15,21-23
			C. Sir 3:17-18,20,28-29	Heb 12:18-19,22-24	Lk 14:1,7-14
	22nd week	M	1Thes 4:13-18	1Cor 2:1-5	Lk 4:16-30
		TU	1Thes 5:1-6,9-11	1Cor 2:10-16	Lk 4:31-37
		W	Col 1:1-8	1Cor 3:1-9	Lk 4:38-44
		T	Col 1:9-14	1Cor 3:18-23	Lk 5:1-11
		F	Col 1:15-20	1Cor 4:1-5	Lk 5:33-39
ORDINARY TIME		S	Col 1:21-23	1Cor 4:6-15	Lk 6:1-5
	23rd SUNDAY Ordinary Time		A. Ezk 33:7-9	Rom 13:8-10	Mt 18:15-20
			B. Is 35:4-7	James 2:1-5	Mk 7:31-37
			C. Wis 9:13-18	Phlm 9-10,12-17	Lk 14:25-33
	23rd week	M	Col 1:24—2:3	1Cor 5:1-8	Lk 6:6-11
		TU	Col 2:6-15	1Cor 6:1-11	Lk 6:12-19
		W	Col 3:1-11	1Cor 7:25-31	Lk 6:20-26
		T	Col 3:12-17	1Cor 8:1-7,11-13	Lk 6:27-38
		F	1Tim 1:1-2,12-14	1Cor 9:16-19,22-27	Lk 6:39-42
		S	1Tim 1:15-17	1Cor 10:14-22	Lk 6:43-49
	24th SUNDAY Ordinary Time		A. Sir 27:30—28:7	Rom 14:7-9	Mt 18:21-35
			B. Is 50:5-9	James 2:14-18	Mk 8:27-35
			C. Ex 32:7-11,13-14	1Tim 1:12-17	Lk 15:1-32 or 15:1-10
	24th week	M	1Tim 2:1-8	1Cor 11:17-26,33	Lk 7:1-10
		TU	1Tim 3:1-13	1Cor 12:12-14,27-31	Lk 7:11-17
		W	1Tim 3:14-16	1Cor 12:31—13:13	Lk 7:31-35
		T	1Tim 4:12-16	1Cor 15:1-11	Lk 7:36-50
		F	1Tim 6:2-12	1Cor 15:12-20	Lk 8:1-3
		S	1Tim 6:13-16	1Cor 15:35-37,42-49	Lk 8:4-15
	25th SUNDAY Ordinary Time		A. Is 55:6-9	Phil 1:20-24,27	Mt 20:1-16
			B. Wis 2:17-20	James 3:16—4:3	Mk 9:30-37
			C. Am 8:4-7	1Tim 2:1-8	Lk 16:1-13
	25th week	M	Ezra 1:1-6	Pro 3:27-34	Lk 8:16-18
		TU	Ezra 6:7-8,12,14-20	Pro 21:1-6,10-13	Lk 8:19-21
		W	Ezra 9:5-9	Pro 30:5-9	Lk 9:1-6

		T	I	Hg 1:1-8	II Ecl 1:2-11	Lk 9:7-9
		F	I	Hg 1:15—2:9	II Ecl 3:1-11	Lk 9:18-22
		S	I	Zec 2:5-9,14-15	II Ecl 11:9—12:8	Lk 9:43-45

If you are lost with week numbers, look at these hints. Depending on the year, you find the 26th, the 30th, and the 34th Sunday on the following dates:

Year	26th	30th	34th
2020	September 27	October 25	November 22
2021	September 26	October 24	November 21
2022	September 25	October 23	November 20
2023	October 1	October 29	November 26
2024	September 29	October 27	November 24
2025	September 28	October 26	November 23

Year	26th	30th	34th
2026	September 27	October 25	November 22
2027	September 26	October 24	November 21
2028	October 1	October 29	November 26
2029	September 30	October 28	November 25
2030	September 29	October 27	November 24
2031	September 28	October 26	November 23

ORDINARY TIME	**26th SUNDAY** Ordinary Time			A. Ezk 18:25-28 B. Num 11:25-29 C. Am 6:1,4-7	Phil 2:1-11 James 5:1-6 1Tim 6:11-16	Mt 21:28-32 Mk 9:38-43,45,47-48 Lk 16:19-31
	26th week	M	I	Zec 8:1-8	II Job 1:6-22	Lk 9:46-50
		TU	I	Zec 8:20-23	II Job 3:1-3,11-17,20-23	Lk 9:51-56
		W	I	Ne 2:1-8	II Job 9:1-12,14-16	Lk 9:57-62
		T	I	Ne 8:1-4,5-6,7-12	II Job 19:21-27	Lk 10:1-12
		F	I	Bar 1:15-22	II Job 38:1,12-21; 40:3-5	Lk 10:13-16
		S	I	Bar 4:5-12,27-29	II Job 42:1-3,5-6,12-16	Lk 10:17-24
	27th SUNDAY Ordinary Time			A. Is 5:1-7 B. Gen 2:18-24 C. Hb 1:2-3; 2:2-4	Phil 4:6-9 Heb 2:9-11 2Tim 1:6-8,13-14	Mt 21:33-43 Mk 10:2-16 Lk 17:5-10
	27th week	M	I	Jon 1:1—2:1,11	II Gal 1:6-12	Lk 10:25-37
		TU	I	Jon 3:1-10	II Gal 1:13-24	Lk 10:38-42
		W	I	Jon 4:1-11	II Gal 2:1-2,7-14	Lk 11:1-4
		T	I	Mal 3:13-20	II Gal 3:1-5	Lk 11:5-13
		F	I	Jl 1:13-15; 2:1-2	II Gal 3:7-14	Lk 11:15-26
		S	I	Jl 4:12-21	II Gal 3:22-29	Lk 11:27-28
	28th SUNDAY Ordinary Time			A. Is 25:6-10 B. Wis 7:7-11 C. 2K 5:14-17	Phil 4:12-14,19-20 Heb 4:12-13 2Tim 2:8-13	Mt 22:1-14 Mk 10:17-30 Lk 17:11-19
	28th week	M	I	Rom 1:1-7	II Gal 4:22-24,26-27,31—5:1	Lk 11:29-32
		TU	I	Rom 1:16-25	II Gal 5:1-6	Lk 11:37-41
		W	I	Rom 2:1-11	II Gal 5:18-25	Lk 11:42-46
		T	I	Rom 3:21-29	II Eph 1:1-10	Lk 11:47-54
		F	I	Rom 4:1-8	II Eph 1:11-14	Lk 12:1-7
		S	I	Rom 4:13,16-18	II Eph 1:15-23	Lk 12:8-12
	29th SUNDAY Ordinary Time			A. Is 45:1,4-6 B. Is 53:10-11 C. Ex 17:8-13	1Thes 1:1-5 Heb 4:14-16 2Tim 3:14—4:2	Mt 22:15-21 Mk 10:35-45 Lk 18:1-8
	29th week	M	I	Rom 4:20-25	II Eph 2:1-10	Lk 12:13-21
		TU	I	Rom 5;12,15,17-19,20-21	II Eph 2:12-22	Lk 12:35-38
		W	I	Rom 6:12-18	II Eph 3:2-12	Lk 12:39-48
		T	I	Rom 6:19-23	II Eph 3:14-21	Lk 12:49-53
		F	I	Rom 7:18-25	II Eph 4:1-6	Lk 12:54-59
		S	I	Rom 8;1-11	II Eph 4:7-16	Lk 13:1-9
	30th SUNDAY Ordinary Time			A. Ex 22:20-26 B. Jer 31:7-9 C. Sir 35:12-14,16-18	1Thes 1:5-10 Heb 5:1-6 2Tim 4:6-8,16-18	Mt 22:34-40 Mk 10:46-52 Lk 18:9-14
	30th week	M	I	Rom 8:12-17	II Eph 4:32—5:8	Lk 13:10-17
		TU	I	Rom 8:18-25	II Eph 5:21-33	Lk 13:18-21
		W	I	Rom 8:26-30	II Eph 6:1-9	Lk 13:22-30
		T	I	Rom 8:31-39	II Eph 6:10-20	Lk 13:31-35
		F	I	Rom 9:1-5	II Phil 1:1-11	Lk 14:1-6
		S	I	Rom 11:1-2,11-12,25-29	II Phil 1:18-26	Lk 14:1,7-11

			A	B	C
ORDINARY TIME	**31st SUNDAY** Ordinary Time		A. Mal 1:14—2:2,8-10	1Thes 2:7-9,13	Mt 23:1-12
			B. Dt 6:2-6	Heb 7:23-28	Mk 12:28-34
			C. Wis 11:22—12:1	2Thes 1:11—2:2	Lk 19:1-10
	31st week	M	I Rom 11:29-36	II Phil 2:1-4	Lk 14:12-14
		TU	I Rom 12:5-16	II Phil 2:5-11	Lk 14:15-24
		W	I Rom 13:8-10	II Phil 2:12-18	Lk 14:25-33
		T	I Rom 14:7-12	II Phil 3:3-8	Lk 15:1-10
		F	I Rom 15:14-21	II Phil 3:17—4:1	Lk 16:1-8
		S	I Rom 16:3-9,16,22-27	II Phil 4:10-19	Lk 16:9-15
	32nd SUNDAY Ordinary Time		A. Wis 6:12-16	1Thes 4:13-17	Mt 25:1-13
			B. 1K 17:10-16	Heb 9:24-28	Mk 12:38-44
			C. 2Mac 7:1-2,9-14	2Thes 2:16—3:5	Lk 20:27-38
	32nd week	M	I Wis 1:1-7	II Tit 1:1-9	Lk 17:1-6
		TU	I Wis 2:23—3:9	II Tit 2:1-8,11-14	Lk 17:7-10
		W	I Wis 6:2-11	II Tit 3:1-7	Lk 17:11-19
		T	I Wis 7:22—8:1	II Phlm 7-20	Lk 17:20-25
		F	I Wis 13:1-9	II 2Jn 4-9	Lk 17:26-37
		S	I Wis 18:14-16; 19:6-9	II 3Jn 5-8	Lk 18:1-8
	33rd SUNDAY Ordinary Time		A. Pro 31:10-20,19-31	1Thes 5:1-6	Mt 25:14-30
			B. Dn 12:1-3	Heb 10:11-14,18	Mk 13:24-32
			C. Mal 3:19-20	2Thes 3:7-12	Lk 21:5-19
	33rd week	M	I 1Mac 1:10-15,41-43,54-57,62-63	II Rev 1:1-4; 2:1-5	Lk 18:35-43
		TU	I 2Mac 6:18-31	II Rev 3:1-6,14-22	Lk 19:1-10
		W	I 2Mac 7:1,20-31	II Rev 4:1-11	Lk 19:11-28
		T	I 1Mac 2:15-29	II Rev 5:1-10	Lk 19:41-44
		F	I 1Mac 4:36-37,52-59	II Rev 10:8-11	Lk 19: 45-48
		S	I 1Mac 6:1-13	II Rev 11:4-12	Lk 20:27-40
	CHRIST THE KING		A. Ezk 34:11-12,15-17	1Cor 15:20-26,28	Mt 25:31-46
			B. Dn 7:13-14	Rev 1:5-8	Jn 18:33-37
			C. 2S 5:1-3	Col 1:12-20	Lk 23:35-43
	34th week	M	I Dn 1:1-6,8-20	II Rev 14:1-3,4-5	Lk 21:1-4
		TU	I Dn 2:31-45	II Rev 14:14-19	Lk 21:5-11
		W	I Dn 5:1-6,13-14,16-17,23-28	II Rev 15:1-4	Lk 21:12-19
		T	I Dn 6:12-28	II Rev 18:1-2,11-23; 19:1-3,9	Lk 21:20-28
		F	I Dn 7:2-14	II Rev 20:1-4,11—21:2	Lk 21:29-33
		S	I Dn 7:15-27	II Rev 22:1-7	Lk 21:24-36
	1st SUNDAY of Advent